# Police Misconduct

legal remedies

Fourth Edition

**John Harrison** is a solicitor and partner practicing in London. He is a former law centre worker and was deputy director of law and administration of an inner London borough. He wrote the first edition of *Police Misconduct: Legal Remedies* while at Paddington Law Centre. Between 1995 and 1996 he was Visiting Scholar and Harkness Fellow at Harvard Law School and senior consultant at the Consensus Building Institute, Cambridge, Mass. He writes and lectures widely.

**Stephen Cragg** is a barrister at Doughty Street Chambers in London specialising in civil actions against the police and public law in social welfare and human rights areas. Prior to being called to the Bar in 1996, Stephen was a solicitor at the Public Law Project and Hackney Community Law Centre. He is an experienced trainer and lecturer, consultant editor for the *UK Human Rights Reports* (Jordans), an editor of *Community Care Law Reports* and a regular contributor to *Legal Action*. He writes a weekly column for *The Times* on new legislation and case law of interest to public sector employees. Stephen Cragg has been vice-chair of the Law Centres Federation (1993–1994); Fellow in Public Law Essex University (1997–1999); and a member of the Civil Justice Council (1998–2000).

**Heather Williams** is a barrister at Doughty Street Chambers in London specialising in civil liberties and in particular actions against the police and discrimination law. She has been involved in leading cases concerning actions against the police and assists clients with applications to the Home Office for compensation for miscarriages of justice. Heather regularly undertakes related work, such as professional negligence actions arising out of litigation against the police and judicial review applications. She regularly writes and lectures on civil actions and discrimination law. She was a contributing author to Making Rights Real (Using the Human Rights Act to Challenge Racism and Race Discrimination) and is an active member of the Police Lawyers Actions Group. She is ranked in the 2004–2005 Chambers and Partners Directory as the joint number 1 leading junior for police actions and for human rights work.

The Legal Action Group is a national, independent charity which campaigns for equal access to justice for all members of society. Legal Action Group:
- provides support to the practice of lawyers and advisers
- inspires developments in that practice
- campaigns for improvements in the law and the administration of justice
- stimulates debate on how services should be delivered.

# Police Misconduct

legal remedies

FOURTH EDITION

by John Harrison, Stephen Cragg
and Heather Williams

*with Sadiq Khan*

Legal Action Group
2005

This edition published in Great Britain 2005
by LAG Education and Service Trust Limited
242 Pentonville Road, London N1 9UN
www.lag.org.uk

1st edition 1987: © John Harrison
2nd edition 1991: © John Harrison and Stephen Cragg
3rd edition 1995: © John Harrison and Stephen Cragg

© John Harrison, Stephen Cragg and Heather Williams

British Library Cataloguing in Publication Data
a CIP catalogue record for this book is available from the British Library.

Crown copyright material is produced with the permission of the Controller of HMSO and the Queen's Printer for Scotland.

ISBN-10  0 905099 91 5
ISBN-13  978 0 905099 91 5

Typeset and printed by Hobbs the Printers, Totton, Hampshire

# Preface

It is the peculiar paradox of police misconduct cases that it is the very agents of the state who are notionally charged with the task of upholding law and order that are the alleged perpetrators of illegality and disorder. Almost uniquely among the numerous types of cases that come before the courts the complainant is in practice not only denied the protection of the agency that in other circumstances would impartially investigate and prosecute the wrongdoer but typically finds him- or herself ranged against one of the most powerful institutions in the land which can seem bent upon discrediting their version of events and vindicating its own officers. Against this background these cases can be especially challenging. Little wonder then that taking a stand against unlawful or abusive conduct by the police can seem lonely and frightening to the individual complainant.

Lawyers and advisers in this area can provide important support in community struggles for social, economic and political change, and for those groups and individuals who are singled out for police harassment. For complainants who are prepared to confront misconduct there can be significant dividends. Civil actions can provide compensation for groups and individuals who have been the direct victims of police illegality. But complaints and litigation can also expose misconduct to wider public scrutiny and serve to bring practices and patterns of police behaviour to the attention of those who would otherwise never hear of it. Action by complainants can also serve a wider purpose of holding the police to account and vindicating the rule of law. By demonstrating that members of the public are ready to exercise their rights, and that a body of lawyers and advisers have the expertise and ability to pursue those rights, it is possible to exert a powerful influence in curbing misconduct in the future if it can be demonstrated that the legal limits to police powers cannot be breached with impunity.

In this book we aim to explain the procedures and tactics of the two major routes to remedying police misconduct: police complaints and civil actions in the courts. Police complaints and disciplinary procedures are tightly controlled by a statutory framework of primary legislation, regulations and guidance. Civil actions against the police have highly individual rules and procedures due to the nature of the torts involved, the availability of exemplary and aggravated damages and, of course, the possibility of trial by jury. As well as describing the advantages, we have attempted to indicate the pitfalls of the two procedures and how best to avoid them.

Since the last edition of this book in 1995 the legal background to the field of police misconduct has been transformed. Among the more significant developments, the Human Rights Act 1998 has made Convention Rights deriving from the European Convention on Human Rights directly enforceable in the domestic courts. The effects of this are capable of reaching into almost every aspect of the law and practice of police misconduct and are still only beginning to be felt. In the previous year the landmark case of *Thompson v Commissioner of Police of the Metropolis* clarified the law on damages and removed much of the uncertainty inherent in leaving questions of quantum to juries in civil action cases. The 1999 Macpherson report on the Stephen Lawrence Inquiry contributed to the Police Reform Act 2002 which established the Independent Police Complaints Commission. The Act revolutionises the system of police complaints and for the first time allows for the investigation of the most serious complaints to be taken out of the hands of the police themselves and undertaken instead by genuinely independent investigators. The Macpherson report also led to changes to the race relations legislation in 2000 and 2003 – broadening the scope for actions for racial discrimination by the police. The Police Act 1997 and the Regulation of Investigatory Powers Act 2000 nominally regulate but greatly broaden the scope for covert policing and surveillance. Constitutional changes to the organisation of the police have centralised the policing of terrorist and organised crime and consolidated the grip of the Home Secretary on police functions at both the national and local level. All this is set against a background of seemingly ever widening police powers justified by public concerns ranging from the threat of terrorist attacks to anti-social behaviour.

In addition, we have outlined other remedies which might be appropriate in cases of police misconduct. The whole work has been greatly expanded. The basic structure of the book follows the format of earlier editions starting with a consideration of the crucial decision of whether to sue or to complain, the first steps that need to be considered in all cases, a detailed description of the complaints and disciplinary systems, the civil causes of action, the practice and procedure of suing and the other remedies available in particular cases.

However new chapters have been added to incorporate additional material and to present the more detailed analysis of all the major causes of action in a more structured and useable way. We have aimed to provide practitioners with a thorough explanation of the most important legal remedies and to equip the reader with all the essentials for advising on the full range of procedures, strategies and tactics available.

## Acknowledgements

Many people contributed to this book. Some, particularly those who have brought civil actions and complaints against the police, cannot be identified; our debt to them is none the less for that. Others encouraged us with ideas, suggestions and practical help, without which this book would be immeasurably poorer. The authors must particularly thank Sadiq Khan for his valuable contribution and insights into the practical issues facing solicitors in this area and for the benefit of his outstanding experience of race discrimination claims. We also acknowledge our thanks to Nogah Ofer, Tony Murphy, Phillippa Kaufmann, Andrew Nicol QC, Henrietta Hill, John Wadham, Peter Mahy, Paddy O'Connor QC and Richard Hemmings.

The views expressed in this work are those of the authors and not of any organisations with which they may be associated.

The law is stated as at 13 March 2005 but in some places it has been possible to include later developments.

John Harrison
Stephen Cragg
Heather Williams

March 2005

# Contents

# Table of cases

# Table of statutes

# Table of statutory instruments

# Abbreviations

| | |
|---|---|
| AA | Appropriate authority |
| ACPO | Association of Chief Police Officers |
| AEAC | Atomic Energy Authority Constabulary |
| Appeals Rules | Police Appeals Tribunals Rules 1999 |
| BTP | British Transport Police |
| CAD | Computer aided despatch |
| CFA | Conditional fee agreement |
| CJPAA 2001 | Criminal Justice and Police Act 2001 |
| Complaints Regs | Police (Complaints and Misconduct) Regulations 2004 |
| Conduct Regs | Police (Conduct) Regulations 2004 |
| CPR | Civil Procedure Rules |
| CPS | Crown Prosecution Service |
| DDA 1995 | Disability Discrimination Act 1995 |
| DPA 1998 | Data Protection Act 1998 |
| DPP | Director of Public Prosecutions |
| ECHR | European Convention on Human Rights |
| ECRC | Enhanced Criminal Record Certificate |
| ECtHR | European Court of Human Rights |
| Efficiency Regs | Police (Efficiency) Regulations 1999 |
| FCDMG | Funding Code Decision Making Guidance |
| FME | Forensic Medical Examiner |
| FOIA 2000 | Freedom of Information Act 2000 |
| GP | General practitioner |
| The guidance | Guidance on Police Unsatisfactory Performance, Complaints and Misconduct Procedures |
| ICCPR | International Covenant on Civil and Political Rights |
| IO | Investigation officer |
| IPCC | Independent Police Complaints Commission |
| LSC | Legal Services Commission |
| MoD | Ministry of Defence |
| NCIS | National Criminal Intelligence Service |
| NCS | National Crime Squad |
| PACE | Police and Criminal Evidence Act 1984 |
| PCA | Police Complaints Authority |
| PD | Practice direction |
| PI Protocol | Pre-Action Protocol for Personal Injury Claims |
| RIPA 2000 | Regulation of Investigatory Powers Act 2000 |
| RRA 1976 | Race Relations Act 1976 |
| RR(A)A 2000 | Race Relations (Amendment) Act 2000 |

| | |
|---|---|
| RRA(A) R 2003 | Race Relations Act 1976 (Amendment) Regulations 2003 |
| SCU | Special Cases Unit |
| SDA1975 | Sex Discrimination Act 1975 |
| UKAEA | United Kingdom Atomic Energy Authority |

# Introduction

# Introduction

1.1   This book aims to guide lawyers and advisers through the law, practice and procedure of the remedies available to meet abuses of police powers. The remedies that may be open to the victim of police misconduct are sometimes inadequate, illogical and contradictory and advisers will need to select the correct remedy, or mixture of remedies, to meet the objectives of the client and the particular circumstances of each case. This is one of the most difficult areas of law in which to advise. The police have wide-ranging powers to protect the public from crime and most of the time exercise these powers lawfully. When the powers are abused, all too often it is a very vulnerable person who is the victim. And there are still concerns that minority groups, and in particular ethnic minority groups, are on the receiving end of police misconduct in a disproportionate number of cases.

1.2   The two main remedies considered in this book and which most directly address alleged misconduct are a complaint through the statutory police complaints system (overseen since April 2004 by the Independent Police Complaints Commission (IPCC)) and/or a civil claim for damages. A complaint can lead to disciplinary action or even a criminal prosecution against the officers responsible for the misconduct. A civil action against the police can only lead to an award of damages. They can be (and often are) pursued simultaneously. There will be occasions when these remedies are not the most appropriate, however, and other remedies will need to be considered in these circumstances.

1.3   For example, where there has been a death in custody, representation at the inquest for the family of the deceased may be the most important issue. If the police are implementing policies and practices unlawfully, an application for judicial review may be the most appropriate remedy. And if a miscarriage of justice is revealed where police misconduct is responsible, the schemes for compensating victims of the miscarriage of justice may provide the best route for action. All these options are covered in this book.

1.4   Lawyers and advisers need to be aware that clients may have a number of objectives in seeking to challenge police misconduct. The task of the lawyer is to use the battery of remedies available singly or in combination to achieve the client's objective. Often a client will seek damages and the lawyer will pursue a civil claim to obtain these. However, in many cases clients are motivated by wider concerns: to seek symbolic justice for the wrong done, to clear their name and restore their reputation, to establish a point of principle, to see an officer personally held to account or punished, or to seek an apology and admission that the client's rights were abused.

1.5 In these circumstances a civil action may (or may not) still be the best route, possibly used in combination with the complaints procedure or, much more rarely, a private prosecution. But the lawyer needs to keep the client's objective clearly in mind: it may be felt that even a substantial award against a chief constable will miss the mark if it is made in an out-of-court settlement, when the client was really seeking public vindication and to hold the individual officer to account. Having said this, of course, it must be recognised that any significant offer of settlement is an indication of the concerns the police have about the strength of their case and provides some, albeit indirect, acknowledgement of the wrong committed against the claimant.

1.6 Similarly, broader concerns may emerge from the specific wrong committed against a client and it may be appropriate to use the legal process to challenge a widespread police practice or to challenge a conventional interpretation of the law. Here the usual notions of 'success' in the sense of winning the case in court may be of less importance if the case grapples with the wider issue involved and provides some clarity in the law while perhaps stimulating wider debate.[1] The remedies described in chapter 17, in particular judicial review, may be more suited to such a task. Similarly a private prosecution may, in very particular circumstances, be appropriate.

1.7 However, the majority of cases that involve legal action concern an incident involving an individual and, at most, a small group of police officers which may give rise to a complaint that there has been abuse of power, and/or civil proceedings for, say, assault, false imprisonment and malicious prosecution as a result of a fabricated version of events by the police, and possibly the loss of or damage to goods.

1.8 In the past the availability of the two routes for pursuing a grievance, suing for damages and making a complaint, posed a difficult dilemma for victims of police misconduct and their advisers. On the one hand, the civil procedure system allowed claimants to keep their cards close to their chest and not to reveal their case until the civil action came to trial. On the other, the police complaints system meant making full

---

1 For example, *R (S) v Chief Constable of South Yorkshire* [2004] 1 WLR 2196, concerning the refusal of the police to destroy the DNA samples of those acquitted of criminal offences, sought clarity on the compatibility of recent changes to the Police and Criminal Evidence Act 1984 with the European Convention on Human Rights, and stimulated debate as to the justice of retention and use of such samples in these cases.

statements to police officers at an early stage of the complaint which would then be available to the police lawyers defending the civil claim. This led to the controversial tactic of making a complaint but declining to co-operate with its investigation, either until the civil case had been disposed of or until an undertaking was received from the police that nothing revealed by the complaints investigation would be used in the civil case. As such an undertaking would be routinely refused, the complaints investigation would in practice be stalled. Further, until the case of *R v Chief Constable of West Midlands ex p Wiley*,[2] the fruits of any complaints procedure (for example, statements taken by the police, reports obtained and transcripts of interviews with the police officers complained about) would not be disclosed by the police to the claimant in a civil action.

1.9     Things have changed to an extent. After *Wiley*, the fruits of the police complaints investigation (described above) are routinely disclosed in civil actions. In any event, it is now likely that the investigation report will be disclosed at the end of the investigation (see para 4.164). In civil actions, the emphasis, following the Woolf reforms, is much more on both sides revealing the respective version of events of their witnesses well before any trial.

1.10    Most incidents of police misconduct, however, do not result in a civil action. The figures available for 2002–2003 show that in that period there were 15,248 complaints cases involving 23,113 individual complaints received by the police.[3] A significantly smaller number of civil actions is brought every year. There are no national figures but, for example, the Metropolitan Police Service received 146 civil claims in 2002–2003 (with 423 further claims threatened),[4] whereas it received 4,277 complaints in the same period.[5]

1.11    Generally, suing is only suitable in the more serious cases, both because the causes of action only concern serious abuses and because the cost of a case will not usually be justified if damages are expected to be low. A complaint, however, may be appropriate in both minor cases, such as rudeness, and also in really serious cases, since what starts as a complaint may develop into a disciplinary matter and even a criminal prosecution.

2   [1995] 1 AC 274, HL.
3   *Police Complaints and Discipline* 2003–2004, Home Office Statistical Bulletin 04/04.
4   Metropolitan Police Service and Metropolitan Police Authority Joint Annual Report 2003–2004.
5   *Police Complaints and Discipline* 2003–2004, Home Office Statistical Bulletin 04/04.

# The decision to sue

1.12    There are powerful reasons to bring a civil action. Compensation can be awarded and the amount awarded may be considerable – sums of several thousands of pounds are now common in serious cases. There are no national figures available but in 2003–2004 the Metropolitan Police paid out well over £2 million (as it had also done the year before) in 166 cases (including settled cases and those that went to trial).[6] Furthermore, a civil action keeps the case in the control of the complainant. He or she can say who should be interviewed as witnesses, what evidence should be produced, which officers must answer the allegations and how the case should be conducted. In addition, if a civil action goes to court, the police must answer for their conduct in public and, if a matter of principle (such as a common police practice) is at stake, this will be brought to public attention.

1.13    If it is a possibility, then, many advisers will be keen to explore this route. This involves looking both at the question of whether there has been a technical breach of the civil law and at more practical issues, such as the real chances of success and the availability of public funding to pursue a case. The most important civil wrongs (torts) are:

- assault and battery if someone is injured, hurt or searched;
- false imprisonment if someone is stopped, detained or arrested;
- malicious prosecution if someone is prosecuted when the police do not believe in the charges brought;
- negligence, for example, where in certain circumstances damage is caused by careless policing to victims or suspects of crime or towards those in police custody;
- trespass if the police enter premises without a warrant or other legal authority;
- seizure of goods if the police take property without excuse or fail to return it;
- damage to goods if property is damaged, for example, when entering or searching a house.

1.14    These grounds are explained in more detail in chapters 7, 8 and 9. In addition, an action for discrimination might be available (this might be sex, race or disability discrimination), and a case for damages where the police action has been incompatible with the rights in the European Convention of Human Rights (now listed in Human Rights Act 1998

6    Metropolitan Police Service and Metropolitan Police Authority Joint Annual Report 2003–2004.

Sch 1)(see chapter 10). In a case, for example, where a person's home was searched without lawful authority; he or she is arrested without there being reasonable grounds to suspect him or her of an offence; assaulted and subjected to racist abuse; and then prosecuted on a fabricated version of events provided by the police, many of these torts may be applicable.

1.15    A civil action which goes to trial and where a claimant is successful in convincing a judge and jury of his or her case and that there should be a substantial award of damages, can provide vindication and compensation for the claimant, and embarrassment and a very public punishment for the police. However, there are many difficulties in bringing a civil action against the police and it is important to warn a client of these.

1.16    First, it is accepted practice that police officers complete their note-books together very shortly after an incident. Any subsequent statement will be based on the notebook entry and the officers may be allowed to refer to their notebooks when giving evidence. A claimant may not provide his or her account to an adviser or solicitor until days, weeks or even months after the incident and there is a risk that the account will be inaccurate as a result. Clearly, this risk will be increased if the claimant had been drinking or under the influence of drugs at the time of the incident.

1.17    Second, if the case goes to court, often the police officers will typ-ically come across very well, being experienced at giving evidence in court, and will often support their colleagues' version of events. A claimant may find it hard to convince a judge that his or her version is correct, especially if he or she has no witnesses, or especially if he or she has previous convictions for dishonesty which may be raised in cross-examination.

1.18    Third, obtaining (and keeping) public funding for a case may be difficult unless substantial damages can be expected. A civil action against the police can be expensive, especially if there is a jury trial at the end of the case. The case of *Thompson v Commissioner of Police of the Metropolis*[7] gives guidance on levels of damages, and in many cases aggravated or exemplary damages will need to be awarded if a case is to be worth enough to attract public funding (see further chapter 14).

1.19    Fourth, many police forces have become very sophisticated in deal-ing with actions against them. For example, the Metropolitan Police have a civil actions investigation unit which makes decisions about cases brought against the force, with targets set to be reached for

---

7   [1998] QB 498.

success in civil trials. Early decisions are often made as to whether to offer settlement and at what level. Although this can sometimes mean that a claimant obtains swift compensation for the misconduct, it may also mean that a publicly funded client anxious for his or her 'day in court' will be denied this because his or her advisers will need to inform the Legal Services Commission if a reasonable offer of settlement has been made.

1.20    Fifth, whether the claimant is successful at trial or in obtaining a settlement of the case, it is still very rare for the individual police officers involved to be investigated or punished solely as a result of the civil action. If this is the client's main motivation, he or she should be advised at the start of the case that statistically this is unlikely to happen.

1.21    Last, the civil action process, if it goes to trial, may take years. A claimant needs to know that he or she may have a long fight before the case is resolved, and that any witnesses for the claimant will need to be kept 'on board' for a lengthy period of time. A claimant who is half-hearted or unenthusiastic about pursuing a civil action may be best not pursuing this route.

## The decision to complain

1.22    Perhaps the greatest attraction of making a complaint is that the procedure is fairly straightforward, it is completely free and it entails comparatively little effort compared with the civil action. Once the complaint has been made, the business of proving what happened is in the hands of others – albeit usually other police officers. The system is described in chapter 5.

1.23    Another advantage is the range of behaviour that can form the subject of a complaint. Any breach of the Police Discipline Code (set out in chapter 6) or the PACE Codes of Practice[8] will be a good ground for complaint. The range of misconduct is thus very wide and includes rudeness, racism, corruption, planting evidence, violence, mistreating prisoners, conducting coercive interviews and many other abuses of the rights of individuals. The potential grounds for a complaint are therefore much wider than the narrow and technical civil wrongs for which a case for damages may be brought.

1.24    Since April 2004 the police complaints system has been overseen by the IPCC.[9] Compared with the previous system under the Police

8    Made under Police and Criminal Evidence Act 1984 s66.
9    Pursuant to Police Reform Act 2002.

Complaints Authority (PCA),[10] the current system is much more transparent, more information has to be shared with the complainant and the complainant should feel much more involved in the process than previously. There is scope also for the most serious complaints to be investigated by the IPCC itself, rather than by local police officers, and for the IPCC to manage the investigation of a complaint.

1.25    However, as under the PCA, the vast majority of complaints will be investigated by police officers, thus continuing to bring into question the independence of the system, although now there is a right of appeal about the outcome to the IPCC at the end of the process.

1.26    About a third of all complaints are not investigated at all, but are subject to what is now called local resolution. Once a complaint has been recorded, if it concerns relatively minor circumstances the police can agree a procedure with the complainant whereby a solution to the concerns raised can be achieved without formal investigation and without the officer having anything noted in his or her records. While this is a sensible and often speedy procedure, there are fears that many complainants are channelled into local resolution in order to avoid the expense and inconvenience of a formal investigation.

1.27    There are a number of limitations to the complaints procedure. While the standard of proof for disciplinary matters was changed in 1999 from the criminal standard to the civil standard, there are fears that in practice this has not significantly affected the number of complaints that are upheld.

1.28    Next, there is no compensation payable if a complaint is substantiated. Indeed, the complaints system itself is not designed to reach a conclusion that a complaint is 'upheld'. Instead, the outcome of the process is a decision made by the Crown Prosecution Service as to whether criminal proceedings should be brought against an officer as a result of the matters raised by a complainant, or a decision by the police or the IPCC as to whether disciplinary proceedings should be brought against an officer.

1.29    As indicated above, the IPCC has taken over a system where few complaints are substantiated. For example, of 7,262 complaints which required investigation under the PCA system (that is, the more serious allegations) in the year to March 2003, only 941 were substantiated (less than 13 per cent).[11] This is after all the withdrawn or informally resolved complaints have been removed from the figures. Many com-

---

10  Pursuant to Police Act 1996.

11  *Police Complaints and Discipline* 2003–2004, Home Office Statistical Bulletin 04/04.

mentators find it hard to believe that all of the 87 per cent of complaints rejected were fabricated or mistaken. The suspicion is that many examples of serious police misconduct continue to go unpunished. Only nine complaints of racially discriminatory behaviour were substantiated in 2002–2003, while 617 complaints about this type of behaviour were received in the same period. Criminal proceedings resulted from 16 substantiated complaints in 2002–2003 and disciplinary proceedings were brought as a result of 88 substantiated complaints.[12]

1.30    At the time of writing, no figures have been produced about the numbers of substantiated complaints under the IPCC system. But given the large number of similarities between the old system and the new, and the fact that the vast majority of complaints will continue to be investigated by the same police investigating officers as before, the signs are not necessarily hopeful.

1.31    One area of uncertainty appears to have been resolved in the new system. Under the PCA system there was nothing in the statutory framework which meant that there would be an investigation under the complaints system of allegations of misconduct raised in civil actions. Thus, advisers or lawyers had to decide with their clients whether or not to make a complaint as well as commencing a civil action. Many advisers pointed to the low success rate figures and clients would often decline to make a complaint. The new system now specifically states that the police must consider whether to treat matters raised in a civil claim as 'conduct matters', which means that in appropriate cases they will be investigated by the police or the IPCC in much the same way as if a formal complaint had been made (see chapter 5).

12  ibid.

# First steps

2.1    This chapter focuses on the initial steps and lines of inquiry that an adviser should consider when first instructed by someone who wishes to make a complaint to the Independent Police Complaints Commission (IPCC) and/or who wishes to bring a civil action against the police.

2.2    At the first meeting, it is useful for the adviser to prepare a draft statement containing the complainant's instructions. Often, there will already be a proof of evidence that was used in the criminal trial, or the complainant may have made his or her own notes or given a statement to the IPCC in relation to the complaint. All these are useful sources for checking the accuracy of this statement and for refreshing the complainant's memory. In addition to the statement, it is also important for other evidence to be gathered as soon as possible. The main routes to obtaining such evidence are described below. Advisers should also be aware of the possibility of using the Data Protection Act 1998 and/or the Freedom of Information Act 2000 to obtain information or documentation from the police or other relevant bodies (this is covered in detail at paras 10.27–10.52).

## Identification

2.3    A civil action may be brought against an identifiable police officer or (more usually) against the chief officer of the individual officer concerned, since the chief officer is usually responsible for the torts of his or her officers.[1] However, it should be noted that this is not always the case.[2]

2.4    A complaint is usually made against a specific officer. In the case of an unidentified officer, the complaint must still be investigated, but provisions which relate to notifying the officer complained about are not applied and decisions do not need to be made about criminal or disciplinary proceedings. If the officer is identified during the investigation then the full requirements of the complaints process can be applied.[3]

---

1  Police Act 1996 s88(1).
2  *Makanjuola v Commissioner of Police for the Metropolis* [1992] 3 All ER 617. For a fuller discussion of the vicarious liability of chief officers of police see para 11.107 onwards.
3  Police (Complaints and Misconduct) Regulations 2004 SI No 643, reg 22.

2.5      In a civil action, while it is ideal to identify a specific officer, it is not essential. Advisers should try and demonstrate to the relevant force:

- that the incident occurred;
- that a police officer or police officers were involved;
- that those officers were acting under the control of the chief officer.

Even where it is not possible to ascertain the name or identification number of the individual officer concerned, if the complainant is able to provide a good physical description and/or the time and place of the incident, this may be sufficient to enable the police to use their own records to identify the officer involved in the incident.

2.6      It may be possible to identify the police officer concerned from official police records which the complainant should be entitled to see at an early stage. These are set out in detail at paras 2.47–2.58 below. It is very unusual for the police not to complete a custody record for an arrested person at the police station, particularly following the introduction of CCTV into most custody areas. However, it remains much easier for police officers to avoid completing records of stop and searches. The requirement to give individuals who are stopped and searched a copy of the search record is discussed below.

2.7      In the case of *Wilson v Commissioner of Police of the Metropolis*,[4] the claimant was unable to identify any of the individual police officers who, he alleged, assaulted him during disturbances in Trafalgar Square. The defendant was also unable to identify the actual officer involved in the assault, which was captured on CCTV footage. However, as the officer was clearly a Metropolitan police officer, it was held that the Commissioner of Police of the Metropolis was vicariously liable for the assault and battery of Mr Wilson.

2.8      If an incident occurs during a demonstration there are other ways of seeking to identify the officers. Sympathetic magazines should be approached to carry a 'witness appeal'. Through making inquiries other witnesses may be identified. Consideration should also be given to whether there may be video evidence either from participants in the demonstration, from the police, or from CCTV cameras located on the streets. There is a short time limit for obtaining CCTV footage. Most local authorities record over footage, thereby destroying it, within

4  [2002] EWCA Civ 434.

30 days after the date of recording unless a specific request has been made to preserve the footage. CCTV cameras are installed in many town centres and surrounding areas.

## Evidence gathering

2.9 The quality and quantity of evidence gathered may impact directly upon:

- Whether a complaint, or an aspect of a complaint, is substantiated. For example, a complaint of assault is unlikely to succeed in the absence of medical evidence corroborating injury (although the investigators of the complaint may well arrange for such evidence to be obtained).
- Whether a civil action is successful, in whole or in part, and in particular whether a claim is compromised before trial and produces a good settlement figure for the claimant.

## Client

2.10 In most cases the complainant will be the starting point for evidence gathering, although there may be cases where the complainant is unconscious or where there has been a death in custody, where this is not the case. In the latter instances it will be necessary to look to other sources of evidence (see para 2.47 onwards below).

2.11 In the overall majority of cases the complainant will be able to make a significant and valuable contribution to the evidence gathering process. However, he or she may not necessarily be able to identify or understand all the important aspects of the case, therefore careful questioning at an early stage is vitally important, as the complainant may be able to identify numerous avenues for further investigation.

2.12 The complainant's instructions should be obtained on every aspect of the material incident, from its inception to its conclusion. The credibility of the account given should be assessed and any apparently problematic areas explored. Consideration will need to be given to any aspects that might affect the accuracy of the complainant's recollection, for example whether and to what extent he or she might have been affected by alcohol or drugs at the relevant time.

2.13 The initial proof of evidence should not be restricted to a narrative of the incident with the police, but should look to explore other issues as well. Evidence in relation to previous convictions, cautions or warnings at the police station, previous complaints to the Police Complaints Authority or Independent Police Complaints Commission, any mental health or other relevant health problems, and witness details will also be highly relevant. Such information will impact directly upon the risk assessment of the case and may determine the view taken on settlement. If the complainant has previous convictions and/or mental health problems, these are facts that the police may well be aware of and will almost certainly seek to exploit, with a view to damaging his or her credibility.

2.14    Evidence in relation to the impact the incident has had on the complainant is also highly relevant. There may be evidence from the complainant (supported by medical records), that he or she has suffered, or may have suffered, minor, moderate or serious psychiatric injury as a direct result of the incident. Symptoms such as nightmares, flashbacks, sleeplessness, pronounced anxiety and/or depression may provide an indication of this.[5] The adviser will need to request and consider the full details of any treatment. Previous psychiatric illness may persuade the adviser to pursue a claim for psychiatric injury (if for example there has been exacerbation in the complainant's condition) or to avoid such a claim if it may present difficulties with causation and/or credibility.

2.15    Details of previous convictions can be obtained from the police if the complainant cannot provide an accurate record. If the police will not provide them voluntarily, a Data Protection Act inquiry form can be collected from any police station and completed by the complainant. There is a fee of £10.00 payable when submitting the application.[6]

## Medical evidence

2.16    The value of medical evidence varies enormously. It can be used to corroborate or to undermine an assault or its extent. It is therefore important to the complaint/claim that the victim sees a doctor as soon as is practicable after the incident. If possible, he or she should see more than one doctor, as doctors often do not record all injuries

---

5   See Diagnostic and Statistical Manual of Mental Disorders (DSM-IV-TR) (4th ed) which sets out the criteria for Post-Traumatic Stress Disorder and other forms of psychiatric illness.

6   The right of access to personal data under the Data Protection Act 1998 is discussed in more detail in chapter paras 10.39–10.40.

and sometimes have a tendency to focus on the most serious injuries. The complainant should go to hospital and then to his or her general practitioner (GP). Any injury should be noted on a detained person's custody record (the requirements in relation to keeping such records are summarised at paras 2.51–2.52). Code C issued under the Police and Criminal Evidence Act 1984 (PACE)[7] provides that a custody officer must carry out a risk assessment of the detained person's condition. If the complainant made a complaint at a police station, sometimes the police will have arranged for photographs to have been taken of any visible injuries.

2.17 It is important that all of the relevant clinical medical documents are gathered before a decision is taken to obtain expert opinion. In this way the adviser can ensure that the most suitable or advantageous expert is approached for his or her opinion. It is also important as the existing medical information will assist the expert to give an accurate opinion of the nature and causes of the injury.

## Forensic Medical Examiner

2.18 The complainant may have seen the Forensic Medical Examiner (commonly known as the FME or 'police doctor') while detained at the police station. If so, the FME would have made an entry in the medical register and/or the custody record.

2.19 The medical register is usually maintained as a separate book and kept in the police station. However, one copy of the medical register entry is appended to the custody record and will usually be served as part of the custody record. If it is not provided as part of the custody record, a further request should be made to the Criminal Justice Unit at the police station concerned, or to the custody suite. Alternatively, a request can be made in accordance with Data Protection Act 1998 s7: see paras 10.39–10.40.

2.20 Additionally, many FMEs make a separate clinical record that they take with them from the police station. The police should not have access to this separate clinical note without the client's authority. A request for these separate clinical notes should be made directly to the FME. His or her name should appear in the custody record (although it sometimes does not in practice) and in the medical register form. The FME can usually be traced through the police or by searching the medical register or by making a direct inquiry to the General Medical Council.

7 Code C, paras 3.6–3.10.

## GP and Hospital Accident & Emergency Department

2.21    Whether or not the complainant saw the FME, if he or she is alleging assault by the police it is important that the complainant sees his or her own GP and/or attends the Accident & Emergency Department of the local hospital.

2.22    The complainant should ask a doctor to record all of his or her injuries and record how the complainant says they were caused, as a report may later be requested based on the notes taken at the time.

## Expert opinion

2.23    In some cases it may be necessary to obtain an expert opinion from a consultant on causation and/or the nature and extent of the injury. In relation to physical injuries, a consultant's report is commonly sought if the injury sustained is more serious than one that resolves within a few weeks of the incident.

2.24    If the first opinion is unhelpful, consideration may need to be given to obtaining a second opinion from a different consultant. However, advisers should proceed with caution. In such a situation in a civil action, the costs of the first opinion will not be recoverable from the police. Further, if acting for a claimant who is publicly funded then the cost of the first opinion will be recouped from any damages recovered by way of the statutory charge. Prior authority should be obtained from the Legal Services Commission before seeking any expert's report. If no request for prior authority has been made, there is a risk that the cost of the report will not be allowed subsequently.

2.25    If there is a possibility that a complainant sustained psychiatric injury, a report from a consultant psychiatrist should be considered. Evidence of possible psychiatric injury will be apparent if the complainant reports symptoms such as nightmares, sleeplessness, panic attacks at the sight of police, flashbacks and/or low self-esteem following the incident.

2.26    It is important when contemplating approaching a consultant for an expert opinion in relation to a proposed civil action, that the claimant understands that he or she may later need to:

- attend a medical examination with the expert(s) instructed by the police;
- disclose all relevant medical records to that expert. In the case of psychiatric injury in particular, this may entail disclosure of all of the claimant's medical records, as discussed below.

The claimant will need to consider carefully whether he or she wishes to pursue a claim for psychiatric injury if there are matters in the medical records that he or she would rather keep from the public domain, such as serious sexually transmitted diseases, child abuse, etc.

## Disclosure of medical records in civil actions

2.27 A claimant in a civil action is obliged, by virtue of the Civil Procedure Rules (CPR) Part 31 concerning disclosure, to make a reasonable search for documents that may assist the claimant's case, adversely affect the claimant's case or support the opponent's case. The obligation extends no further than making a reasonable search. What is reasonable will vary from case to case bearing in mind the importance of the document to the issues to be determined.[8]

2.28 If the claim is for physical injury then in most instances the claimant need only search for medical records that relate to that injury and/or to previous and subsequent injuries of a similar nature to the same part of the body. For example, if a claimant alleged that rough handling during arrest had caused a back strain, records of any previous or subsequent back injuries would be of potential relevance. Where the claim for physical injuries is confined to minor injuries such as bruising or grazing, which resolved within a matter of days or weeks, records of previous or subsequent injuries are unlikely to be relevant at all.

2.29 If a claim is to be brought for psychiatric damage, the obligation to search for documents is much wider. Consideration needs to be given to approaching the GP for the complete clinical records/medical history. Consideration also needs to be given to approaching any Accident & Emergency hospital department(s) that have been attended and hospital(s) in relation to admissions, whether psychiatric or simply in respect of physical ailments. Counselling notes may also be relevant. These may be with a counsellor organised by a GP or through social services. Each case turns on its own facts but the adviser should be able to demonstrate that he or she has the documents themselves or has considered the various avenues of inquiry and has concluded that they are not relevant. The issue here is whether the police action caused the claimant psychological damage or whether there are other possible candidates for such damage which may be revealed by the medical records.

---

8 Disclosure in general is dealt with in detail in chapter 12.

2.30    Likewise, where a claim is to be made for loss of earnings as a result of the claimant's inability to work due to the injury sustained, broad disclosure of medical records is likely to be required, so that the claimant can show there was no other factor affecting his or her capabilities at the time.

2.31    Article 8 of the European Convention on Human Rights provides a complainant with a right to privacy. In the context of disclosure obligations in civil litigation, this right has to be balanced against the right to a fair trial contained in article 6 of the Convention. Accordingly, a claimant may be able to resist the disclosure of private material, including medical records, where they are not relevant to the issues in the case and so are not required by a defendant for the fair disposal of the claim.

## Identifying an expert

2.32    When trying to identify an expert, it is best to research an expert's background before instructing him or her. Often it will be possible to obtain a recommendation for an expert from other solicitors. Some solicitors take care to avoid instructing experts who undertake police work routinely or have a close association with others that do. Objections may also be taken by the client if an expert routinely acts for the police. However, if a jointly instructed expert is contemplated, the police may object to an expert who only does claimant work.

## Instructions of experts in relation to civil actions

2.33    Instructions and enclosures sent to an expert are liable to be disclosed to the police in the course of civil proceedings if they come within the ambit of standard disclosure. CPR 31.14 provides that a party may inspect a document mentioned in an expert's report that has not already been disclosed in the proceedings. However, CPR 35.10(4) provides that while instructions to an expert are not privileged, a court will not order disclosure of any specific document unless it is satisfied that there are reasonable grounds for considering that the statement of instructions contained in the report is inaccurate or incomplete. Accordingly, advisers should ask the expert instructed to state clearly his or her instructions in the report so as to take advantage of CPR 35.10(4). The courts have interpreted the concept of 'instructions' widely in this context.[9] This means that earlier drafts of the claimant's

---

9    *Lucas v Barking, Havering and Redbridge NHS Trust* [2003] 4 All ER 720, CA.

or other witnesses' statements provide to the expert may come within the protection afforded to the expert's instructions.

2.34     The adviser will need to consider carefully which documents should be enclosed to the expert with the instructions. Guidance is set out below:

- Ensure that all relevant medical records are sent. If the expert only sees some of the medical records, he or she may be disadvantaged when later entering into discussions with the defence expert and/or giving evidence at trial.
- All medical reports should be sent to the expert. In the situation where a psychiatrist is being instructed it would perhaps be advisable to obtain comprehensive medical reports in relation to physical injuries and other losses/damage before instructing the psychiatrist. The psychiatrist may want to see such evidence before preparing the report.
- Photographs of the injuries, where available, should be included.
- Any CCTV footage of the incident where the injuries were sustained should be provided to the expert.
- Witness statements should be sent. (If the statements are still in draft form at this stage, they may be protected from disclosure to the defendant, as discussed at para 2.33 above.)
- Police documents should be provided, if these have been obtained. Custody records and/or documents containing the officers' accounts of the material events may assist the expert.
- The Particulars of Claim and the Defence, if available at this stage, should be included.

## Checking the expert's report

2.35     Once a report is completed it should be checked carefully to ensure that it:

- sets out the facts correctly and in a balanced manner;
- highlights the medical notes upon which the conclusion has been reached;
- addresses and counters any negatives from the medical notes;
- deals effectively with issues of causation and prognosis;
- complies with the CPR.[10]

---

10 CPR 35.10.

## Single/joint experts in civil actions

2.36   The modern approach of the courts is to favour the parties using one jointly instructed expert in relation to a disputed issue in a civil claim.[11] This is dealt with in more detail in chapter 12. However, in practice, in claims against the police, the courts will generally accept that a claimant has acted reasonably in instructing his or her own expert in relation to psychiatric injury or in relation to a substantial physical injury before issuing proceedings, particularly where it is necessary to obtain this information before getting sufficient Legal Services Commission funding to write a letter of claim. On the other hand, when more minor physical injuries are involved, the court would usually expect a jointly instructed expert to be used, or at least to see evidence that the claimant tried to secure this.

2.37       In practice in a civil action against the police, a claimant will often see his or her own expert before issue and an expert on behalf of the police after issue (once the pleadings have been served and directions have been made).

## Attending the claimant's own expert

2.38   Where physical injuries are involved, the expert will usually want to see the claimant, unless all symptoms have already resolved. Even in those circumstances, it will be useful for the expert to see the claimant if any complaint is made about residual effects, such as scarring. Where a claim for psychiatric injury is contemplated it is always necessary for the claimant to see the expert. The expert will need to discuss with the claimant how the incident has impacted upon him or her.

## Attending the expert instructed by the police

2.39   Sometimes claimants can be very anxious about meeting, or refuse to see, a police expert. The expert instructed by the defendant can on occasion be viewed as too closely linked to the police. The claimant may need to be reminded that a civil claim may be halted in whole or in part if he or she fails to attend an appointment with a police expert.[12]

2.40       When the claimant attends a medical examination in relation to physical injuries, it is important that he or she is able to articulate the

---

11   *Daniels v Walker* [2000] 1 WLR 1382; *Peet v Mid-Kent Health Care Trust* [2002] 3 All ER 688.
12   *Edmeades v Thames Board Mills* [1969] 2 All ER 127, CA.

manner in which the injury was sustained. It is also important that the account given by the claimant remains consistent with previous accounts he or she has given to other doctors (FME, GP or hospital). Refreshing their memory from their witness statement prior to the appointment with the expert is advisable, as the police will latch onto any such inconsistencies and seek to deploy them to damage the claimant's credibility. Similarly, it is important that before the claimant attends an examination in relation to psychiatric injury, he or she is aware of the relevant contents of his or her medical records.

2.41    If the claimant is particularly anxious about attending a medical examination or if he or she suffers from a disability it would be advisable for the claimant to be accompanied. They do have the right to be accompanied to the appointment, but it has been held not to be unreasonable for an expert conducting an examination to refuse to allow the companion to be present during the examination.[13] (In such cases the accompanying friend would need to stay in the waiting room.)

2.42    The claimant is entitled to insist upon the police paying reasonable travel costs for attending an appointment with a police expert (in advance if necessary), or upon production of receipts.

## Service of medical reports in civil actions

2.43    The claimant's medical reports will usually be disclosed before the start of proceedings. It is good practice to serve medical reports with the letter of claim (for the contents of the letter of claim see para 11.83). This should improve the chances of early settlement. The police may ask for inspection of the claimant's medical records. Care should be exercised before deciding to reject any request for medical records. However, only those medical records that are relevant to the claim should be disclosed, as discussed above at paras 2.27–2.31.

# Photographs

2.44    The importance of photographs to record injuries to a claimant and/or damage to his or her property should not be underestimated. Where possible, a professional photographer should be used, as the injuries will be shown much more clearly in such photographs and also records will be available to avoid any disputes as to when the pictures were

---

13   *Whitehead v Avon CC* (1996) 29 BMLR 152, (1995) *Times* 3 May.

taken. If a professional photographer is not used then care should be taken to ensure that the photographs are of the best quality possible.

2.45    In relation to a civil action, the photographs would be disclosed to the defendant as part of the standard disclosure process, once the action is in progress. (Disclosure is discussed in chapter 12.) However, where the pictures provide strong support for the claim, it may well be helpful to serve them on the defendant with the letter of claim (see para 11.83), to prompt consideration of an early settlement.

2.46    If photographs are not agreed they must be proved as genuine. Ordinarily a statement from the taker of the photograph is enough. The police solicitors are unlikely to object to photographs, unless they genuinely believe that there has been some improper interference. The negatives and prints should be kept sealed until they are needed at trial, preferably with the claimant's solicitor.

## Collecting evidence from the police and other official sources

2.47    Some information held by the police is available as a right, if requested within the prescribed period. Other information will only be made available by the defendant in response to a letter of claim or at the disclosure stage of a civil action.[14] The information available as of right is listed below. Other records commonly held by the police are then identified, so that advisers can consider which documents to request (usually when a letter of claim is sent) and also so that the adequacy of disclosure given by the defendant can be reviewed. Advisers should also consider whether relevant information might be held by other bodies such as the Crown Prosecution Service (CPS) and the criminal courts, when a complaint and/or a civil action are contemplated. In all cases it is important to request that the information is preserved (where there is no immediate right to disclosure). This should be done as soon as it becomes clear that a particular body may have relevant documents or material. If the third party is unwilling to disclose the documents/material, an application for third party disclosure may be feasible once the claim has commenced.[15]

---

14   See chapters 11 and 12, respectively.
15   CPR 31.17.

## Police records available on request

2.48 Advisers will wish to consider obtaining copies of the following at an early stage of their inquiries:

- stop and search records;
- custody records;
- returned search warrants;
- records of property seized.

These are dealt with in turn below.

2.49 These records may be helpful in supporting a complaint or a civil action. They may assist advisers to evaluate whether the proposed claim or complaint has merit, for example whether there were grounds for a particular stop and search. They may also assist in clarifying issues, for example, by establishing the identity or role of a particular officer or by establishing a chronology of events. They may also highlight discrepancies in the police version of events.

### Stop and search records

2.50 PACE requires a police officer to make a record of a stop and search in writing unless it is not practical to do so. The record must include information such as the suspect's name, the object of the search, the grounds of the search, the date, time and place when the search was made, whether anything was found and what injury or damage resulted from the search, and the name of the officer making the search.[16] The record must be provided on request, if sought within 12 months of the date of the search.[17]

### Custody records

2.51 A separate custody record must be opened as soon as is practicable for each person brought to a police station. A custody officer is responsible for the accuracy and completion of the record and for ensuring that the record or a copy of it accompanies any prisoner who is transferred to another police station. All entries made in the custody record must be timed and signed by the person making the entry.[18]

---

16 PACE s3(1)–(6) and Code A, para 4. From 1 April 2005 the police will also be obliged to make equivalent records where they require a person to stop and account for themselves, even if no search is conducted: Code A, paras 4.11–4.20.

17 PACE s3(7) and (9).

18 Code C, paras 2.1A–2.3.

2.52    A person detained or his or her solicitor is entitled to a copy of the custody record as soon as is practicable after the detained person has been released or taken to court. This entitlement lasts for 12 months.[19] The information contained in the custody record includes:

- times of detention;
- grounds for detention;
- any comment a detained person made in response to being told the reason(s) for detention;
- whether the detained person has been given a written notice of his or her rights to have somebody informed of his or her detention and his or her right to independent free legal advice (and whether he or she signed to acknowledge receipt of the same);
- a record of property taken (signed by the detainee) by the police;
- the reason why a police officer retained an article found on the detainee;
- a record of all the detainee's requests to have someone informed, letters and messages sent, calls made or visits received, including reasons for any that were refused;
- a record of meals and replacement clothes offered;
- a record of complaints about treatment;
- a record of medical examinations, medical directions to the police and any medicines found on or needed by the detainee;
- a record of all times that the detainee was not in the custody of the custody officer and the reasons (for example because he or she was being interviewed);
- the reasons for any refusal to deliver the detainee out of custody;
- a record of any interpreter called to the station;
- a record of any postponement in undertaking a prescribed review of detention, the outcome of reviews of detention and the grounds upon which any further detention was authorised;
- a record of any charges brought and anything which a detainee said when charged;
- a record of any strip search and/or intimate body search, including reasons/results and, when an intimate search has been conducted, which parts of the body were searched, who carried out the search and who else was present;

---

19  Code C, para 2.4A.

- a record of fingerprints taken without consent and reasons for taking them;
- a record of non-intimate samples taken from the detainee.

2.53    Requests for the custody record should be made directly to the Criminal Justice Unit at the police station concerned. If there is difficulty in obtaining the custody record from the police station a request should be made to the senior officer at that police station and/or to the legal department for the police force concerned.

2.54    Often if the complainant has been interviewed on tape while in police custody, he or she will have been served with a Notice of Entitlement to a copy of the tape. When requesting the custody record a request should be made for a copy of the interview tape. Often the complainant's account in interview is likely to provide his or her best recollection of the incident and will be important in terms of establishing the chronology of events, identifying police officers and clarifying particular issues.

### Returned search warrants

2.55    PACE empowers magistrates to issue search warrants for evidence of serious arrestable offences (see the discussion at para 9.13). PACE also lays down the procedure for applying for a warrant and for carrying out the search.[20]

2.56    Once a warrant has been executed (or if it has not been executed within the time authorised for its execution) it is returned to the Clerk to the Justices or the appropriate officer of the court, depending on where the warrant was issued. The warrant is then retained for 12 months from its return. If during the period for which a warrant is to be retained the occupier of the premises to which it relates wants to inspect the warrant, he or she shall be allowed to do so.[21]

### Records of property seized

2.57    Police officers can seize and retain certain items discovered during a search; the extent of these powers is considered in chapter 9. PACE provides that a police officer who makes a seizure should provide the occupier of the premises or the controller of the item with a record of anything seized 'within a reasonable time' from the making of a request.[22]

---

20   PACE ss15 and 16; see para 9.13.
21   PACE s16(12).
22   PACE s20(1) and (2).

## Other police records

2.58    Like any large bureaucracy, the police keep an enormous quantity of official records. These cover everything from lost dogs to deaths in police custody. The volume of all this paperwork means that much of it has to be destroyed after a period of time. Each force has a police manual. The police manual will identify when documents should be destroyed. The periods vary from force to force. Most documents should be retained for six years, but some can be destroyed earlier. If documents have been destroyed before the expiry of the usual period for retention, issues will arise as to why this has occurred and as to whether intentional concealment was involved.

2.59    It is not possible to prepare a comprehensive list of police records. Police records are often changed and the nature and description of various forms are different from one police force to another. However, the main kinds of police records to look out for are listed below.

2.60    If these documents have not been disclosed to the claimant during the criminal prosecution, they are unlikely to be obtainable until pre-action disclosure or disclosure itself, during the course of civil proceedings.[23]

### Previous convictions

2.61    The police can provide a printout. Alternatively a Data Protection Act request should be made (see paras 10.39–10.40).

### Search register[24]

2.62    A search register must be kept at every sub-divisional police station. After any search of premises, the officer in charge of the search must make a record that includes:

- the address of the premises searched;
- the date, time and duration of the search;
- the authority under which the search was made (a copy of the warrant or consent must be attached to the record or kept in an identified place);
- the names of the officers who carried out the search;
- the names, if known, of anyone on the premises searched;
- a list of all articles seized or a note of where such a list is kept and the reasons for seizure if they were not covered by the warrant;

23  See chapters 11 and 12 respectively.
24  Code B, paras 8 and 9.

- whether any force was used and the reason for it being used;
- details of any damage caused and the circumstances.

2.63   If premises were searched under a warrant, the warrant must be endorsed to show:

- whether the articles listed in the warrant were found;
- whether any articles not listed were seized;
- the date and time of the search;
- the name of the officers who carried out the search;
- whether a copy was handed to the occupier or left at the premises and if so where.

2.64   Search warrants whether executed or not must be returned by the police to the magistrates' clerk or court officer. The occupier of any premises to which a warrant relates can inspect the returned warrant within 12 months of its return, as described at paras 2.55–2.56 above.

## Written and tape recorded records of interviews[25]

2.65   An accurate record must be kept of any interview with anyone suspected of an offence, whether or not the interview takes place at a police station. The record must state:

- the place of the interview;
- the time it began and ended;
- the time the record was made (if not the same);
- any breaks in the interview;
- the names of those present.

A record of this must be made on the forms provided for this purpose or in the officer's notebook. At the end of the taped interview, the police officer must make a note in his notebook of:

- the fact that the interview has taken place and has been tape recorded;
- the time, duration and date of the interview;
- the identification number of the master tape.[26]

2.66   When criminal proceedings follow an arrest, the tape recording of an interview and any written record of the interview must be prepared by the police in accordance with national guidelines issued by the

25   Code C, paras 11 and 12.
26   Code E, para 5.1.

Home Office and the seal of the master tape may only be broken in restricted circumstances.

2.67    Where no criminal proceedings are brought the tape must be kept securely, and the chief officer of the police must establish arrangements (including the interviewee or his representative being present) before breaking the seal.

## Photographs

2.68    Photographs of the detained person are normally taken after charge. Copies should be obtained when it is likely that they will show relevant evidence of injury and/or general appearance.

## Fingerprints/DNA

2.69    These should be requested where a prosecution was purportedly brought on the basis of fingerprint/DNA evidence and it appears likely that the claimant will want to challenge this evidence (or the collection of it) during the course of the civil proceedings. Similarly, any documents in relation to the comparison of fingerprints/DNA should also be sought where relevant.

## Identification parade records

2.70    Records of any identification parade should be completed by the identification officer responsible for the parade.

2.71    If a parade cannot be held for any reason, that reason must be reported, including any refusals to participate. The names of every person present at the parade or group identification which are known to the police must be recorded.[27] Recording obligations also apply where video identifications are conducted.[28]

## Notebooks

2.72    CID officers have only one notebook. Uniformed officers have four notebooks.

- **Arrest Report/Incident Report Book (IRB):** The incident report book will contain details of the date and time the record was made and details of any witness at the scene of the incident and/or present when the notebook was completed. This will

27    Code D, paras 3.25–3.27 and Annex B, paras 23–28.
28    Code D, Annex A, paras 17 and 18.

also include details of arrests and other incidents such as those involving mentally disordered persons, civil disputes, dog fights, fires, meetings, processions and strikes, prostitute cautions, injury on duty and racial discrimination. The contents will have been typed up into the form of a formal statement (pursuant to Criminal Justice Act 1967 s9), if part of the prosecution evidence in relation to criminal proceedings.

- **Notebook**: This notebook records details of other matters such as property lost and found, absences from duty and request for police attendance at a scene.
- **Accident Report Book**: This notebook records accidents other than those involving damage only, where there is no allegation of a criminal offence.
- **Process Report Book**: This includes details of traffic and other offences where a person will be summonsed rather than charged.

## Police station records

2.73   These include the following:

- **Duty state books**: These record every officer working from a particular station on any given day at any given time. They show details of the officers on duty, where they are on duty and the time at which they came off duty, refreshments taken and overtime. On occasion together with Computer Aided Despatch (CAD) message printouts (see below) these may help identify officers who were involved in the particular incident.
- **Parade books**: Parades at the beginning of each shift are no longer the formal occasion they used to be and not all officers attend. The parade book contains routine information such as current demonstrations and football matches and may include the collator's report summarising recent crime, criminal intelligence and general police gossip. There should also be records of which police officers were posted to a particular car or carrier and records of which officers have attended a particular incident.
- **Messages**: Message pads are kept in a communications room at the station. Mainly they record messages by telephone from the public. A message is recorded on a pad in a standard form together with details of the person assigned to deal with it and the results. It may also be recorded on computer. If there is no

result by the end of the shift, it must be passed to the next police shift.

All messages must be signed by the station officer in the course of their shift and by the duty officer.

In the case of all 999 calls in the Metropolitan Police area, these are taken by central command and control. Details of the call are typed directly into the command and control computer. The computer holds up-to-date information on the whereabouts of all police vehicles. The officer taking the 999 call can dispatch the nearest available vehicle to deal with the call. The computer can provide a printout of the details of the call and the action taken on it.

Radio messages are often recorded on CAD records and a printout should be requested, together with any other records of radio messages.

- **Current office records**: A variant of record books which are kept on the counter of each station. Common examples are:
  - missing persons;
  - minor meetings and notes of parades;
  - doctors booked;
  - firearm certificates issued;
  - firearms found;
  - property, lost and found;
  - log of radio message recordings (CAD records);
  - officers' messages;
  - production of driving documents;
  - verbal warning to motorists.
- **Crime reports**: The police should complete a crime report on a standard computer form for every crime reported. It records details of:
  - the offence, victims, witnesses, suspects, comments made by the officer in charge of the investigation or officers who have undertaken a task in relation to the investigation;
  - any statements taken;
  - any arrests made;
  - any charges brought;
  - the outcome.

Offences investigated by the CID are kept in the 'Major Crime Book'. Records of petty thefts, car thefts and criminal damage and assaults of the kind dealt with by uniformed officers are kept in 'The Crime Book'. Records of burglaries are kept in a separate 'Burglaries Book'.

*Book 116 procedure*

2.74 These records contain details relevant to the breathalyser test procedure carried out at the police station.

*Drugs*

2.75 Laboratory submissions and results records will exist for any substance submitted for analysis.

*CCTV*

2.76 CCTV recording of custody areas is now commonplace for most forces.

## Documentation from the criminal courts

2.77 Findings made or evidence given in a criminal trial may make it impossible or unrealistic for the police to defend a claim in whole or in part or may impact upon the credibility of the officers involved in the action or complaint. Consideration should therefore be given to obtaining records of evidence if the complainant was prosecuted and acquitted at trial.

2.78 Examples of documents that it may be worth obtaining are:

- **In relation to trials in the magistrates' court**: the court clerk's notes of the evidence. Notes of preliminary hearings should also be requested if any issues arise, for example the basis upon which bail was denied. If the court is not prepared to disclose the notes until a civil action has been commenced, the preservation of the notes should be requested in the meantime. In order to prove the outcome of proceedings, it may also be necessary to obtain a copy of the memorandum of register entry, which details the result of the case. The notes of evidence and the entry from the register are usually provided either free of charge or for a modest fee of up to £10.00 to anyone who is on income support or who is publicly funded.
- **In relation to trials in the Crown Court**: the proceedings are recorded and a verbatim transcript of evidence can be obtained from the agencies. These can be very costly. It is sensible to get an estimate. If the complainant is publicly funded, prior authority from the Legal Services Commission to incur this expenditure is advisable. The transcripts obtained should be

limited to what is essential. Where possible the cost of the tran-script should be shared with the defendant. Usually, the claimant would wish to confine the transcript to the evidence given by those who are likely to be significant witnesses in the civil action. If the outcome of the proceedings is in dispute, or any ruling made by the trial judge is in issue, transcripts of these parts of the trial may be desirable.

2.79   The notes or transcript of evidence may be vital to a complaint or civil action since:

- the police may have made damaging admissions during evidence;
- there may be major inconsistencies between the testimony given by police officers in the criminal courts and the account they now seek to advance;
- details of the claimant's own evidence may be in dispute and this is the best way to resolve such issues. Further, the claimant will probably benefit from refreshing his or her memory from the transcript of their evidence in any event;
- comments made by a judge in respect of the police conduct or the behaviour of any other witness (including the client), may be influential. For example, a chief officer of police may be inclined to settle a civil claim promptly if the officers involved in the incident were the subject of judicial criticism;
- the court may have made legal rulings and/or findings of fact that make the police's position unsustainable. Equally, such rulings and findings may make it clear that it will be difficult to prove the necessary element of malice for a malicious prose-cution claim (for example if the judge considered that the police acted in good faith but misunderstood their legal powers).

2.80   Where there is a gap in the magistrates' court clerk's notes and there is a dispute in relation to what was said at trial, consideration should be given to relying upon the notes of the claimant's solicitor or counsel or the CPS representatives' notes of evidence. It is good practice for lawyers to take notes during a hearing, though many find it difficult to write while they are speaking. Occasionally these notes are destroyed but barristers are becoming better at keeping a record of trials they have done and tend to hold onto the records for several years. They will also record details of conversations with pros-ecution counsel and in particular offers that are made (for example, of a bind over). Sometimes the lawyer's notes will assist in identifying those sections of the court transcript that are most relevant to the complaint and/or civil claim.

## Credibility of witnesses

2.81 In criminal cases the police/CPS cannot usually advance evidence of previous convictions. This is not so in civil cases against the police where evidence of spent convictions is often admissible[29] and the claimant, defendant and witnesses can all be cross-examined on previous convictions which go to their credit: see paras 13.14–13.17.

2.82 It is good practice to obtain details of previous convictions for all individuals likely to give evidence at trial, and to seek clarification of this from the police at an early stage.

2.83 It is also important to note that police officers can be cross-examined on previous disciplinary findings, where they have been found guilty of wrongdoing. Invariably there is difficulty is accessing such information and the police will not ordinarily disclose it voluntarily. There are organisations, however, such as the Defendant Information Service,[30] who have records of officers who have been the subject of allegations of police misconduct. Consideration should also be given to contacting other specialist claimants' solicitors to see if they have information that may assist the civil action in relation to the officers involved. Police officers may also be cross-examined on discredited evidence given in previous criminal trials and/or in previous civil cases: as discussed at paras 13.5–13.16.

## Documentation relating to police complaints

2.84 If a complaint has been informally resolved (for complaints made before 1 April 2004) or resolved locally (for those made after that date), a record of the informal resolution/local resolution should be requested. A complainant is entitled to a copy of the informal resolution notice and has a right to appeal against the procedure adopted for the local resolution (see chapter 4).

29 *Thomas v Commissioner of Police for the Metropolis* [1997] 1 All ER 747, see para 13.14 below.

30 Defendant Information Service, PO Box 7459, London N16 8WS: dis@km551818.demon.co.uk.

2.85    If the complaint has been made prior to the solicitor's involvement or the solicitor was not present when the complaint was made by the client, a copy of the complaint should be requested from the police. During the complaint investigation much documentation will be generated. As well as appraising the complainant of the progress of the complaint, this documentation will be of potential relevance to the civil claim. Disclosure of documentation as part of the complaints process is dealt with in more detail in chapter 4. However, in summary, documents that are commonly sought and disclosed after a complaint has been completed and in contemplation of or during civil proceedings include:

- statements from witnesses and officers;
- those officers who are the subject of the complaint will normally be interviewed on tape under caution. A copy of the tape of their interview should be requested together with the typed summary;
- the notices which inform an officer under investigation that a complaint has been made and a brief summary of the allegation, and the outcome of the investigation;
- the IPCC will write to the chief officer of the relevant force notifying him of the outcome of the investigation. On occasion separate letters are sent to the chief officer highlighting any additional concerns the IPCC have in relation to the officers' conduct or aspects of the force's policies;

Disclosure of the investigating officer's report is discussed at paras. 12.119–12.123.

## Civilian witnesses

2.86    Potential witnesses should be identified as soon as possible. Each potential witness should be approached at the earliest opportunity. If the complainant intends to make a complaint, consideration should be given as to whether the witness should produce his or her own statement or whether he or she will simply be interviewed by the police force's investigating officer.

2.87    Both the complainant and any witness should be alive to the fact that statements drafted by the investigating officer may be phrased in such a way as to compromise a complaint and/or a civil claim for damages. The investigating officer may not necessarily focus upon the interests of the complainant and may feel some allegiance to the chief constable and/or the officer(s) under investigation. The maker of the statement should be satisfied with the content and language used in the statement and should not sign it if he or she has concerns.

2.88    If a civil action is contemplated, advisers should obtain statements from potential witnesses before memories fade. However, the draft statement may need to be revisited and perfected as further material documentation becomes available.

# CHAPTER 3

# The constitutional and organisational position of the police

## 3.60    Independent police forces

# Introduction

3.1     The accountability of the police, both legally and politically, to the citizens they serve, is complicated and frequently incoherent. Control over the police is exercised by a variety of different bodies with a patchwork of roles and responsibilities that can seem bewildering. Nevertheless it is important to understand the constitutional position of the police and the organisational framework of police institutions so that claimants seeking remedies for police misconduct can direct their efforts where they are most likely to achieve success.

3.2     This chapter sets out a brief explanation of the office of constable, the position of civilians within the police service, a description of the main institutions that exercise control over the police (police authorities, chief officers of police and the Home Secretary and the main national police bodies: the National Criminal Intelligence Service and the National Crime Squad), and it ends with a description of the so-called 'independent' police forces such as the Ministry of Defence Police and the British Transport Police.

# The office of constable

## Status of constable

3.3     The office of constable, which is quite distinct from the rank of constable, is an ancient one deriving from the common law and pre-dates the creation of modern police forces by centuries. All members of a police force[1] irrespective of their rank will hold the office of constable.[1a]

3.4     Centuries ago each parish was required to elect a parish constable. However the office was unpopular and many parishes failed to make appointments. From the middle of the seventeenth century the local justices of the peace had power to appoint a constable if elections were not held, but even then practice varied around the country and many areas effectively had no constable at all. Where constables did exist it was customary for them to be sworn into office by justices of the

---

1   That is, a force maintained by a police authority: Police Act 1996 s101(1). For other police bodies see para 4.33.

1a   Neither the Commissioner of the Metropolitan Police nor assistant commissioners hold the office of constable, nor are they members of the metropolitan police: Metropolitan Police Act 1829 s1 as amended; Metropolitan Police Act 1856 s2 as amended.

peace. By reason of this oath, and because of the relationship with the local justices, constables were recognised as officers of the Crown.[2]

## Attestation

3.5    Every member of a police force maintained for a police area and every special constable appointed for a police area must on appointment be attested as a constable by making a declaration in the prescribed form.[3] It is the act of attestation that confers the status of constable.[4]

3.6    The modern form of attestation is:

> I ......... of ......... do solemnly and sincerely declare and affirm that I will well and truly serve the Queen in the office of constable, with fairness, integrity, diligence and impartiality, upholding fundamental human rights and according equal respect to all people; and that I will, to the best of my power, cause the peace to be kept and preserved and prevent all offences against people and property; and that while I continue to hold the said office I will, to the best of my skill and knowledge, discharge all the duties thereof faithfully according to law.[5]

## Original authority

3.7    The powers of a constable acting as a police officer, whether conferred by common law or statute, are exercised by virtue of the office of constable and cannot be exercised on the responsibility of any other person. A constable therefore exercises an original authority, not a delegated authority,[6] except when acting in execution of a lawfully issued warrant. A constable cannot therefore be ordered to exercise his powers in a particular manner by the Crown or by a local police authority. Nor can a constable rely upon a claim that he was simply obeying the orders of a superior officer as a defence to a civil, disciplinary or criminal charge of wrongdoing. Neither a superior officer, nor even the courts, can order a constable to exercise a power which can only be lawfully done if the constable himself forms a suspicion on reasonable grounds.[7]

3.8    However this doctrine sits uncomfortably with the reality that police forces are disciplined and hierarchical organisations in which orders

---

2  *Mackalley's Case* (1611) 9 Co Rep 65b at 68b.

3  Police Act 1996 s29.

4  *Sheikh v Chief Constable of Greater Manchester Police* [1990] 1 QB 637, CA.

5  Police Reform Act 2002 s83.

6  *Enever v R* (1906) 3 CLR 969, 977, Aust HC.

7  *R v Chief Constable of Devon and Cornwall ex p CEGB* [1982] QB 458.

must be obeyed. The police Code of Conduct partly seeks to reconcile these conflicting principles by providing that:

> The police service is a disciplined body. Unless there is good and sufficient cause to do otherwise, officers must obey all lawful orders and abide by the provisions of legislation applicable to the police. Officers should support their colleagues in the execution of their lawful duties, and oppose any improper behaviour, reporting it where appropriate.[8]

## Liability for wrongful acts

3.9    Although a member of a police force holds a public office and is sometimes said to be a 'public servant' or a 'servant of the Crown' this does not mean that a member of the police force is an employee of the Crown.[9] Nor is a member of a police force an employee, or the agent, of the local police authority.[10] Consequently at common law the police authority cannot be held vicariously liable for the wrongful acts of a police officer. As it was plainly undesirable – both for the police and for potential claimants – that there should be no form of vicarious liability for police misconduct, parliament has provided that the chief officer shall be liable in respect of any unlawful conduct of constables under his direction and control in the performance or purported performance of their functions in the same manner in which an employer is liable in respect of any unlawful conduct of his employees in the course of their employment.[11] Given that the constable exercises his powers on his own authority and does not require authorisation from his superior officers, it follows that a chief officer can be vicariously liable for the actions of an off-duty officer, at least where it is apparent that the officer is a constable because, for example, he identifies himself as such to the complainant and is improperly using a marked police vehicle at the time.[12]

3.10    The significance of the statutory liability of chief officers in the tactical conduct of civil actions against the police is described at para 11.107.

---

8   Police (Conduct) Regs 2004 SI No 645, Sch 1, para 6.
9   *Att-Gen for New South Wales v Perpetual Trustee Co Ltd* [1955] AC 457.
10   *Fisher v Oldham Corporation* [1930] 2 KB 364; *Farah v Metropolitan Police Commissioner* [1998] QB 65.
11   Police Act 1996 s88(1) as amended.
12   *Weir v Bettison (Chief Constable of Merseyside Police)* [2003] ICR 708.

## Duties of constables

3.11    There is no single and comprehensive statement of all the duties of constables. The duties derive from common law and have been formulated in a number of ways in various leading cases[13] including *Rice v Connelly*[14] in which it was said that 'it is part of the obligations and duties of a police constable to take all steps which appear to him to be necessary for keeping the peace, for preventing crime or for protecting property from criminal injury. There is no exhaustive definition of the powers and obligations of the police but they are at least these and they would further include the duty to detect crime and to bring offenders to justice.'

3.12    These general principles are augmented by the Police (Conduct) Regulations 2004[15] which state in a note to Schedule 1:

> The primary duties of those who hold the office of constable are the protection of life and property, the preservation of the Queen's peace, and the prevention and detection of criminal offences.

3.13    However there are limits to these broadly stated duties. Chief officers have 'the widest possible discretion' in their choice of the methods by which they discharge their duties to keep the peace and enforce the law.[16] The courts have taken the view that it is for the chief officer and individual members of a police force to weigh up the competing demands upon their limited resources in deciding how and when to exercise their duties. Provided they act even-handedly and not in a discriminatory manner the courts will be reluctant to second guess their judgments (see paras 17.67, 10.63 and 15.1).

## Jurisdiction of constables

3.14    A member of a police force has all the powers and privileges of a constable throughout England and Wales and the adjacent UK waters.[17] A constable of a police force in England and Wales may also have powers of arrest without a warrant (and related powers) in Scotland and

---

13    See, for example *Glasbrook Brothers v Glamorgan CC* [1925] AC 270;
      *R v Commissioner of Police for the Metropolis ex p Blackburn* [1968] 2 QB 118;
      *R v Chief Constable of the North Wales Police ex p Evans* [1982] 1 WLR 1155.
14    [1966] 2 QB 414.
15    SI No 645.
16    *R v Commissioner of Police for the Metropolis ex p Blackburn* [1968] 2 QB 118.
17    Police Act 1996 s30(1). For the position of special constables and members of the British Transport Police see paras 3.15–3.19 and 3.60–3.61 below.

Northern Ireland if he has reasonable grounds for suspecting that the person has committed or attempted to commit an offence in England or Wales.[18]

## Special constables

3.15 Special constables typically serve as a part-time reserve for regular police forces. They will often be called upon to assist in the policing of large public events and demonstrations or to help in major investigations. A special constable has all the powers and privileges of a constable in the police area for which he or she is appointed and in any police area which is contiguous to his or her own area, and where the boundary of this area includes the coast, in the adjacent UK waters.[19]

3.16 A special constable who is required to serve under a collaboration agreement or mutual aid agreement has all the powers and privileges of a constable in any police area in which special constables for that area have jurisdiction, that is, the area itself and its contiguous police areas.[20]

3.17 Special constables are appointed by the chief officer for the area and are under the direction and control of, and subject to dismissal by, the chief officer.[21] Every special constable appointed for a police area must on appointment be attested as a constable by making a declaration in the prescribed form.[22] As with the regular members of a police force it is the act of attestation which confers the status of constable.

3.18 Special constables are personally liable for their unlawful conduct in the civil courts in the same way as regular members of a police force. Equally chief officers can be statutorily vicariously liable for their unlawful conduct. The main difference between special constables and regular members of a police force in the context of misconduct cases lies in the extent of their geographical jurisdiction. A person who is a special constable and who purports to act as a police officer outside an area in which he or she has jurisdiction is in the same position as an ordinary member of the public.

---

18 Criminal Justice and Public Order Act 1994 ss136–140.
19 Police Act 1996 s30(2). Special constables of the City of London police force, in addition to their powers in the City, also have powers in both the Metropolitan Police area and in police areas contiguous to the Metropolitan Police area: s30(3).
20 Police Act 1996, s30(4).
21 Police Act 1996, s27.
22 Police Act 1996, s29.

3.19    For complaints and disciplinary measures against special constables see paras 4.29 and 5.50.

## Cadets

3.20    A police cadet is not a constable or a member of a police force but is treated as being a person undergoing training with a view to becoming a member of a police force.[23] Police cadets may be dismissed by their chief officer after being afforded the opportunity of a personal interview. For the civil liability of police cadets see para 11.123.

## Civilian employees

3.21    There has been a significant move in recent years towards the 'civilianisation' of functions formerly carried out by police officers. There are over 40,000 civilian staff carrying out a range of duties, including those of control room staff, front desk staff, scene of crime officers and the handling and transportation of prisoners.

3.22    Civilian staff necessarily do not hold the office of constable. However civilian staff employed by police authorities (including traffic wardens)[24] are under the direction and control of the chief officer of police, but the employing police authority nevertheless remains vicariously liable for their wrongful acts. An action may therefore be brought against either the individual or the police authority, although it will usually be preferable to proceed only against the authority.

3.23    A chief officer can designate four categories of civilian employee as persons who, although not constables, nevertheless can exercise certain powers normally exercised by a constable. The categories are:

- community support officer;
- investigating officer;
- detention officer;
- escort officer.[25]

---

23   Police Act 1996, s28.
24   Road Traffic Regulation Act 1984 s95.
25   Police Reform Act 2002 s38. Home Office Circular 67/2002, *Guidance on Powers for Designated Civilian Investigating, Detention and Escort Officers*, 6 December 2002.

The powers of each category of civilian officer are specific to that category and none has all the powers of a constable. Nevertheless the powers are extensive.[26] A person may be designated to more than one category. Traffic wardens may also be designated, for example, as community support officers.[27]

3.24 Since 1 April 2004 complaints against civilian employees, as persons under the direction and control of the chief officer, have come within the police complaints system (for actions after that date) – see para 4.29.

3.25 For the purpose of determining liability for unlawful conduct of a civilian employee of a police authority, conduct in reliance or purported reliance on a designation is taken to be conduct in the course of the person's employment. In the case of a tort the police authority is treated a joint tortfeasor.[28]

## Contracted-out staff

3.26 A chief officer can designate the civilian employee of a private sector contractor as either a detention officer or an escort officer.[29] Such a person will have the powers and duties conferred or imposed by the designation but these cannot exceed the powers and duties of a detention or escort officer directly employed by the police authority.[30] The Home Secretary can make regulations for the handling of complaints against detention or escort officers employed by such contractors.[31]

3.27 For the purpose of determining liability for unlawful conduct of an employee of a contractor, conduct in reliance or purported reliance on a designation is taken to be conduct in the course of the person's employment. In the case of a tort the contractor is treated a joint tortfeasor.[32]

---

26  Police Reform Act 2002 Sch 4.
27  Home Office Circular 65/2002, November 2002. But see Road Traffic Regulation Act 1984 s95(5).
28  Police Reform Act 2002 s42(7). Similar arrangements exist for persons designated by the NCIS and the NCS: s42(8).
29  Police Reform Act 2002, s39.
30  Police Reform Act 2002, s39(6).
31  Police Reform Act 2002, s39(9). Home Office Circular 67/2002, note 25 above, paras 38 and 39.
32  Police Reform Act 2002, s42(9).

## Community safety accreditation schemes

3.28    Community safety accreditation schemes were introduced by the Police Reform Act 2002 to contribute to community safety and security, and (in co-operation with the police) to combat crime and disorder, public nuisance and other forms of anti-social behaviour. They are a means by which chief officers can accredit or 'quality assure' the employees of bodies such as a local authority, housing association, licensed private security firm, NHS trust, organisations responsible for railway security or vehicle inspection, charities or employers of stewards in sports stadiums.[33] However the employee of *any* body approved by the chief officer can be accredited, including civilian employees of police authorities such as community support officers, investigating officers, detention officers or escort officers.

3.29    Accredited members of a scheme can be given limited powers usually exercised by the police such as the power to issue fixed penalty notices and to confiscate alcohol and tobacco in certain circumstances.[34]

3.30    Chief officers must ensure that the employers have established and maintained satisfactory arrangements for handling complaints relating to the carrying out by accredited persons of the functions for the purposes of which powers are conferred.[35] For the purpose of determining liability for unlawful conduct of a non-police authority employee, conduct in reliance or purported reliance on an accreditation is taken to be conduct in the course of the person's employment. In the case of a tort the employer is treated as a joint tortfeasor.[36] Similar arrangements exist for employees of police authorities (see para 3.25).

## Civilians and misconduct in a public office

3.31    Civilian staff employed by police authorities (in common with police officers), as people who are paid out of public funds for discharging a public duty in an office of trust, can be convicted of the common law offence of misconduct in a public office (see para 5.117).[37] It would be anomalous if detention officers or escort officers employed by a private contractor could escape liability in circumstances where an officer employed directly by a police authority would be guilty of an offence. The better view is that all detention and escort officers discharge a

33    Police Reform Act 2002, ss40 and 41.
34    Police Reform Act 2002, Sch 5.
35    Police Reform Act 2002, s40(9).
36    Police Reform Act 2002, s42(10).
37    *R v Bowden* [1996] 1 WLR 98; *R v Bembridge* (1783) 3 Doug 327.

public duty in an office of trust and that the contractual arrangements that lie behind such an office cannot provide any protection for civilian officers who are employed by a contractor.

# Police organisation

## Police authorities

3.32    There are 43 police authorities in England and Wales. In the 41 police areas outside London the police authority is made up of 17 members of whom nine are members of the relevant local authority council, three are magistrates and five are appointed 'independent members'.[37a]

3.33    In London the Metropolitan Police Authority, a functional body of the Greater London Authority, is the police authority for the metropolitan police area.[38] It consists of 23 members, 12 of whom are appointed by the Mayor of London, seven of whom are 'independent members' and four of whom are magistrates.[39] Until July 2000 the Home Secretary had been the police authority for the metropolitan police area. The Common Council of the City of London is the police authority for the City of London Police.[40]

3.34    The general function of a police authority is to secure the maintenance of an efficient and effective police force for its area.[41] Although police authorities must issue three-year strategy plans, annual policing objectives and annual policing plans, their functions are in reality largely administrative. At common law they do not have power to direct a chief officer or any other member of a police force how to exercise a power (such as a power of arrest or search) that arises from the officer's individual discretion as a constable.[42] Under the police authority's mandatory code of conduct a member must 'not do anything which compromises or which is likely to compromise the impartiality of a police officer or those who work for, or on behalf of, the authority'.[43]

---

37a The government has announced plans for greater local authority representation on police authorities: *Building Communities, Beating Crime: A better police service for the 21st century*, November 2004, Cm 6360.

38  Police Act 1996 s5B as amended.

39  Police Act 1996, s5C and Schs 2A and 3 as amended.

40  Police Act 1996, s101(1).

41  Police Act 1996, s6. For the anomalous arrangements concerning the City of London police authority see *Halsbury's Laws*, Vol 36(1) Police, para 315.

42  *Fisher v Oldham* [1930] 2 KB 364; *Att-Gen for New South Wales v Perpetual Trustee Co Ltd* [1955] AC 457.

43  Police Authorities (Model Code of Conduct) Order 2001 SI No 3578, Sch para 2(c).

In discharging the functions they do have police authorities must have regard to:

- any objectives determined by the Home Secretary;
- any objectives determined by the authority;
- any performance targets determined by the authority;
- any local policing plan issued by the authority.[44]

However the authority's objectives and performance targets must comply with objectives and performance targets set by the Home Secretary.[45]

3.35    Even where a police authority's decisions could be said to have related to securing the maintenance of an efficient and effective police force they have soon discovered the limits of their powers. During the miners' strike in the mid-1980s, for example, South Yorkshire Police Authority, dissatisfied with the operational methods of their chief constable, attempted to limit his spending powers to £2,000 without the approval of the chair of the authority. However the decision to impose the spending limit was reversed in the face of threatened legal action by the Attorney-General. Later in the same strike the authority attempted to dispose of all of the force's police horses and half of its police dogs on the grounds that it need to save £1.6 million given its heavy expenditure on policing the strike. The authority withdrew the decision in the face of threatened legal action by the Home Secretary.[46]

3.36    The issuing of a circular by the Home Secretary allowing chief officers to draw on a central store of plastic baton rounds and CS gas even in the face of a refusal of a police authority to allow expenditure on such items has been held to be a lawful exercise of the royal prerogative.[47]

3.37    Where HM Inspectorate of Constabulary issues an adverse report on a force's efficiency or effectiveness, the Home Secretary can issue

---

44  Police Act 1996 s6. The authority must also have regard to any code on police authority functions issued by the Home Secretary.

45  Police Act 1996, ss6, 37 and 38.

46  A Brown, *Police Governance in England and Wales*, Cavendish, 1998.

47  *R v SSHD ex p Northumbria Police Authority* [1988] 2 WLR 590. The CA also held that the provision of such supplies from a central store was the maintenance of an 'organisation' under the now repealed Police Act 1964 s41 (see Police Act 1996 s57 which now permits provision and maintenance of 'organisations, facilities and services').

directions requiring the authority to take remedial measures. This can include directions as to the minimum amount of the authority's budget.[48] Thus police authorities have little autonomy and are effectively under the influence of the Home Secretary in virtually all significant respects.

3.38    Police authorities have a duty to keep themselves informed about complaints and misconduct matters in their areas and to provide all such assistance as the Independent Police Complaints Commission and its staff may reasonably require for the purposes of or in connection with their investigations.[49]

## Chief officers

3.39    The Commissioners of the Metropolitan Police and the City of London Police and the chief constables of the other 41 police forces in England and Wales[50] are collectively called chief officers or chief officers of police.[51] The direction and control of their respective forces is vested by statute in the Commissioner of the Metropolitan Police and the 41 chief constables.[52]

3.40    In discharging his or her functions every chief constable and the Commissioner of the Metropolitan Police must have regard to the local policing plan issued by his or her police authority.[53]

3.41    The Commissioners of the Metropolitan Police and the City of London Police have certain functions in addition to those of chief constables, for example concerning the routes to be followed by public processions, etc.[54]

3.42    The complaints and disciplinary procedures relevant to chief officers and other senior officers are explained at para 4.32.

---

48  Police Act 1996 ss40 and 41.
49  Police Reform Act 2002 s15.
50  That is, those listed in Police Act 1996, Sch 1.
51  Police Reform Act 2002, s101(1).
52  Police Reform Act 2002, ss9A and 10. The Commissioner of the City of London Police appears to have direction and control of the City of London Police although without explicit statutory authority. However, s88(1) applies to all chief officers including the Commissioner of the City of London Police and constables under his direction and control.
53  Police Reform Act 2002, s10(2).
54  Metropolitan Police Act 1839 s52 as amended; City of London Police Act 1839 s22 as amended.

## Home Secretary

3.43   The Home Secretary[55] must exercise his powers under the Police Act 1996 in such manner and to such extent as appears to him best calculated to promote the efficiency and effectiveness of the police.[56]

3.44   Each year the Home Secretary must prepare and lay before parliament a National Policing Plan setting out the strategic policing priorities generally for the next three years. The Plan also sets objectives and performance indicators for police authorities.[57]

3.45   The Home Secretary has extensive powers to make regulations concerning the government, administration and conditions of service of police forces including regulations with respect to the conduct, efficiency and effectiveness of members of police forces, the maintenance of discipline, the suspension from a police force and from the office of constable.[58] Among numerous other powers he also has control over the annual police grant, grants for capital expenditure and in respect of national security.[59]

3.46   The Home Secretary can require a police authority to call upon a chief officer, in the interests of efficiency or effectiveness, to retire or resign.[60] He can also require the police authority to suspend the chief officer in certain circumstances where he considers it necessary for the maintenance of public confidence in the force in question.[61] This must be decided by reference to public confidence at large, that is, nationally, rather than the confidence of the public in the police area in question.[62]

---

55   Most modern statutes refer simply to the 'Secretary of State' meaning one of Her Majesty's Principal Secretaries of State: Interpretation Act 1978 s5, Sch 1. Responsibility for police matters is discharged by the Secretary of State for the Home Department, referred to in this book as the Home Secretary.

56   Police Act 1996 s36(1).

57   Police Act 1996, s36A.

58   Police Act 1996, s50(1) and (2).

59   Police Act 1996, ss46, 47 and 48.

60   Police Act 1996, s42 as amended by Police Reform Act 2002 s33. He can also require the Metropolitan Police Authority (MPA) to call upon the Commissioner or Deputy Commissioner to retire or resign on the same basis.

61   Police Act 1996, ss9E and 11 as amended by Police Reform Act 2002 s32. A national protocol concerning the exercise of the Home Secretary's powers has been agreed.

62   *R (Secretary of State for the Home Department) v Humberside Police Authority and Westwood* [2004] EWHC 1642 (Admin).

## National Criminal Intelligence Service

3.47    The National Criminal Intelligence Service (NCIS) provides criminal intelligence in the field of serious and organised crime. NCIS is maintained by the NCIS Service Authority but its objectives are set by the Home Secretary.[63] It is headed by a Director General who holds the rank of chief constable.[64] NCIS is set to be abolished and to become part of the Serious Organised Crime Agency (SOCA), see para 3.58 below.

3.48    Other members of NCIS are either police members of NCIS or other persons appointed to be members of NCIS as employees of the NCIS Service Authority.[65] Police members of NCIS have all the powers and privileges of a constable throughout England and Wales.[66]

3.49    The Director General of NCIS is liable in respect of any unlawful conduct of constables under his direction and control in the performance or purported performance of their functions in the same manner in which an employer is liable in respect of any unlawful conduct of his or her employees in the course of their employment.[67]

3.50    The Director General may designate a civilian employee of the service authority as an investigating officer.[68] For the purpose of determining liability for the unlawful conduct of employees of the service authority, conduct by such an employee in reliance or purported reliance on such a designation shall be taken to be conduct in the course of his or her employment. In the case of a tort the service authority is treated a joint tortfeasor.[69] The service authority can pay costs and damages, etc, for unlawful conduct of its police and civilian members.[70]

3.51    The complaints and disciplinary procedures relevant to police and civilian members of NCIS are explained at paras 4.30 and 4.33.

---

63  NCIS (Secretary of State's Objectives) Order 1999 SI No 822.
64  Police Act 1997 s6(7). As to whether he holds the office of constable see ss5 and 5A as amended.
65  Police Act 1996, s9(1) .
66  Police Act 1996, s9(4) and 6(6). For the powers of senior police members of NCIS to interfere with property and wireless telegraphy and to authorise intrusive surveillance see Police Act 1997 ss93 and 94(3).
67  Police Act 1996, s42(1) as amended.
68  Police Reform Act 2002 s38(3).
69  Police Reform Act 1996, s42(8).
70  Police Act 1997 s42(4) and (5). For the position of a member of an international joint investigation team formed under the leadership of NCIS who is neither a police nor a civilian member of NCIS see Police Act 1997 s42(5A), (5B) and (5C)

## National Crime Squad

3.52    The function of the National Crime Squad (NCS) is to prevent and detect serious crime which is of relevance to more than one police area in England and Wales.[71] It may also:

- act in support of a force in the prevention and detection of serious crime (if a chief officer so requests);
- act in support of NCIS if the Director General of NCIS so requests;
- institute criminal proceedings;
- co-operate with other police forces in the United Kingdom in the prevention and detection of serious crime;
- act in support of other law enforcement agencies in the prevention and detection of crime.

3.53    NCS is maintained by the NCS Service Authority. The authority sets its objectives but these must be consistent with any objectives set by the Home Secretary.[72] It is headed by a Director General who holds the office of constable and the rank of chief constable.[73] NCIS is set to be abolished and become part of the Serious organised Crime Agency (SOCA), see para 3.58 below.

3.54    Other members of NCS are either police members of NCS or other persons appointed to be members of NCS as employees of the NCS Service Authority.[74] Police members of NCS have all the powers and privileges of a constable throughout England and Wales.[75]

3.55    The Director General of NCS is liable in respect of any unlawful conduct of constables under his direction and control in the performance or purported performance of their functions in the same manner in which an employer is liable in respect of any unlawful conduct of his or her employees in the course of their employment.[76]

3.56    The Director General may designate a civilian employee of the service authority as an investigating officer.[77] For the purpose of determining liability for unlawful conduct of a civilian employee of NCS, conduct in reliance or purported reliance on such a designation is

---

71   Police Act 1997, s 48(2).
72   Police Act 1997, ss49 and 71.
73   Police Act 1997, s52 as amended.
74   Police Act 1997, s55.
75   Police Act 1997, s52(6) and 55(4) .
76   Police Act 1997, s86.
77   Police Reform Act 2002 s42(4).

taken to be conduct in the course of the person's employment. In the case of a tort the service authority is treated as a joint tortfeasor.[78] The service authority can pay costs and damages, etc, for unlawful conduct of its police and civilian members.[79]

3.57 The complaints and disciplinary procedures relevant to police and civilian members of NCS are explained at paras 4.30 and 4.33.

## Serious Organised Crime Agency

3.58 The government has announced plans to create a Serious Organised Crime Agency (SOCA) by amalgamating the National Crime Squad, the National Criminal Intelligence Service, elements of HM Customs and Excise and the organised immigration crime section of the Home Office.[79a]

## Independent Police Complaints Commission

3.59 The Independent Police Complaints Commission (IPCC) is responsible for overseeing the police complaints system and related matters. It is responsible for maintaining suitable arrangements for the handling of complaints and for recording disciplinary matters and criminal offences committed by police officers. It has powers under certain circumstances to investigate complaints itself. It has responsibilities not only for the 43 police forces maintained by police authorities for their areas but also for NCIS, NCS and the so-called independent police forces (see below). Its functions are described in chapter 4.

# Independent police forces

3.60 Apart from the 43 police forces maintained by the police authorities for those areas, the NCS and the NCIS, a number of organisations have powers to maintain bodies of constables. The most important are the British Transport Police, the Ministry of Defence Police and the Atomic Energy Authority Constabulary. For other bodies of constables see para 4.35.

78 Police Reform Act 2002, s 42(8).

79 Police Act 1997 s86(4) and (5). For the position of a member of an international joint investigation team formed under the leadership of NCS who is neither a police nor a civilian member of NCIS see Police Act 1997 s86(6)

79a *One Step Ahead: A 21st century strategy to defeat organised crime*, March 2004, Cm 6167; Serious Organised Crime and Police Bill.

## British Transport Police

3.61   Since 1 July 2004 the British Transport Police (BTP) has been maintained by the British Transport Police Authority.[80] Their function is to police the railways, specifically the railways of England and Wales, Scotland, the London Underground system, the Docklands Light Railway, the Midland Metro Tram System and the Croydon Tramlink. The BTP has its own chief constable, deputy chief constable and assistant chief constable.[81] The British Transport Police Authority appoints and employs constables of the force,[82] and consequently may be sued in vicarious liability for the wrongful acts of its constables.[83] The chief constable can appoint special constables and cadets.[84] As special constables are not employees of the British Transport Police Authority, and the Authority therefore cannot be vicariously liable, the chief constable is made vicariously liable for their wrongful acts.[85]

3.62   A constable of the BTP has all the powers and privileges of a constable on track, network, in a station, in a light maintenance depot, on other land used for purposes of or in relation to a railway, on other land in which a person who provides railway services has a freehold or leasehold interest and throughout Great Britain for a purpose connected to a railway or to anything occurring on or in relation to a railway.[86]

## Ministry of Defence police

3.63   The Ministry of Defence (MoD) police force (which is quite separate and distinct from the military police) has a wide variety of responsibilities covering UK military, naval and air force installations, dockyards and ordnance companies. The police force was put on a statutory basis in 1987[87] and consists of special constables who are nevertheless under the

---

80   Railways and Transport Safety Act 2003 s20.
81   Railways and Transport Safety Act 2003, ss21, 22 and 23.
82   Railways and Transport Safety Act 2003, s24.
83   Personal communication, Chief Executive and Clerk BTPA to John Harrison, 28 July 2004.
84   Railways and Transport Safety Act 2003 ss25 and 26.
85   Railways and Transport Safety Act 2003, s25(5).
86   Railways and Transport Safety Act 2003, s31. Policing of the Channel Tunnel system is the responsibility of the Kent Constabulary, see *Halsbury's Laws*, Vol 36(1). For harbour constables and civil aviation and airport constables see Halsbury's Laws, Vol 36(1), paras 308 and 309 respectively.
87   Ministry of Defence Police Act 1987 s(1).

direction and control of its chief constable.[88] Members of the MoD police are civil servants in the employment of the Crown; any civil proceedings may be brought against the individual officer or the Ministry of Defence.[89] For the complaints procedures of the MoD police see para 4.34.

## Atomic Energy Authority Constabulary

3.64    The United Kingdom Atomic Energy Authority (UKAEA) maintains the Atomic Energy Authority Constabulary (AEAC). The AEAC has a chief constable who is responsible for the operational control, recruitment, supervision and general efficiency of the constabulary; however he has no special statutory status. All members of the AEAC (including the chief constable) are sworn in as special constables[90] on the nomination of the UKAEA and are employees of the UKAEA. A non-statutory police authority for the UKAEA was established in 1995.[91]

88  Ministry of Defence Police Act 1987, s1(3).

89  Crown Proceedings Act 1947 s2(1).

90  Special Constables Act 1923 s3; Atomic Energy Authority Act 1954 Sch 3; Ministry of Defence Police Act 1987 s7. Although they are nominally only special constables, members of the AEAC have exceptional statutory powers to carry firearms which give them a legal status similar to members of the armed services: Atomic Energy Authority (Special Constables) Act 1976 s1. For the powers and jurisdiction of AEA constables see Anti-terrorism, Crime and Security Act 2001 s76.

91  For the civil liability of AEA constables see *Halsbury's Laws*, Vol 36(1) Fourth Edition Reissue paras 301 and 305.

# CHAPTER 4

# Police complaints

# Introduction

4.1 This chapter is a guide to the police complaints system introduced by the Police Reform Act 2002 on 1 April 2004. It starts with general sections explaining the background to the Act and the constitution and general powers of the new Independent Police Complaints Commission (IPCC) which will run the new system, having taken over from the Police Complaints Authority (PCA). The chapter then provides a detailed description of the working of the new system, making reference to the Act, regulations, policy papers, case law and guidance issued by the IPCC. The chapter describes:

- How and where to make a complaint
- What and who can be complained about
- Recording the complaint
- Local resolution
- The various methods of formal investigation
- The investigation of 'conduct' matters
- Disclosure of information to the complainant and others
- Withdrawn and discontinued complaints, and those that do not require investigation
- What happens after the investigation including rights to appeal

The situation where complaints are upheld and disciplinary proceedings invoked is described in chapter 7. At time of writing, draft guidance 'Making the Police Complaints System Work Better' is being finalised by the IPCC under its statutory powers (see para 4.14) and is likely to be published in June 2005. The guidance is mainly couched in general terms but reference is made to it where helpful in the text. It can be found in the IPCC website (see note 1 below).

# Background

4.2 The IPCC took over as the body dealing with complaints against the police from the PCA on 1 April 2004, having been created by the Police Reform Act 2002.

4.3 The new regime was introduced after a lengthy period spent considering possible reforms. The two main criticisms of the PCA had long been (a) that all police complaints had to be investigated by police officers as there was no provision for independent investigation; and (b) that the system provided for very limited disclosure to complainants and others of information gleaned as a result of the complaints investigation (this especially referred to the disclosure of the investigating officer's report which was covered by 'class' public interest immunity). Both these criticisms were raised in the Home Affairs Committee report into police complaints and discipline in 1997 and the Stephen Lawrence Inquiry report in 1999.[1]

4.4   The government issued a consultation paper in May 2000 entitled *Complaints against the Police: A Consultation Document.*[2] This paper was based on a KPMG study commissioned by the Home Office on *Feasibility of an Independent System for Investigating Complaints against the Police*[3] and a study by Liberty on *An Independent Police Complaints Commission.*[4] The paper sought views on various aspects of the police complaints system including independent investigation and the openness of the system, together with the recording of complaints and police discipline.

4.5   In response to the consultation exercise, in December 2000 the government issued a framework document entitled *Complaints against the Police: Framework for a New System.*[5] This document set out the emerging framework for the new complaints procedures, explained how this framework was developed, and eventually led to the statutory provisions described below. The explanatory note to the 2002 Act describes the overall direction of the reforms.

18. The IPCC will have referred to it all serious cases falling into specified categories, whether or not a complaint has been made. It will have its own powers of investigation and will have a body of independent investigators at its disposal. It will also have the power to manage or to supervise police investigations of complaints. The IPCC will have the power to call in any case to investigate, to manage or to supervise.

19. Chief officers of police will have to co-operate with IPCC investigations. They will have a legal obligation to provide the IPCC with access to documentation or other material, allow the IPCC to copy such documentation, and allow the IPCC access to police premises.

20. Access to the complaints system will be increased. Persons other than the victim will be able to make a complaint against the police. Furthermore, complainants will be able to make their complaints via a third party or through independent organisations. Complainants will also have a right of appeal to the IPCC against the refusal by the appropriate authority to record a complaint.

1   Both available on the IPCC website: www.ipcc.gov.uk.
2   Available on the Home Office website: www.homeoffice.gov.uk.
3   ISBN 1-84082-453-0.
4   Available through Liberty's website: http://liberty-human-rights.org.uk.
5   Available at www.homeoffice.gov.uk.

21. Subject to a test relating to any risk that harm may be caused by disclosure of the information, complainants will be provided with an account of how the complaint investigation has been conducted, a summary of the evidence and an explanation of why the conclusions to an investigation were reached. A complainant will have a right of appeal to the IPCC if they feel that the written account does not provide a satisfactory explanation of the investigation. In certain circumstances, information may be disclosed to persons other than the complainant but they will not have a right of appeal.

22. These provisions are intended to provide a more robust system for dealing with complaints against the police and to increase public confidence in the complaints system as a whole.

# Structure and functions of the IPCC

## Structure

4.6    The IPCC is a body set up by Police Reform Act 2002 Part 2. The IPCC replaces the PCA. It consists of a chairman formally appointed by the Queen (who is, therefore, not an appointee of the Home Secretary) and 'not less' than ten other Commissioners appointed by the Home Secretary. All must be independent of the police.

4.7    The chairman and members of the Commission can be appointed for up to five years, and such period can be renewed.[6] The extension of the appointment period from three years for the PCA is intended to increase the independence of the chairman and the commissioners from the Home Secretary. There are very limited provisions for removing the chairman or other members of the Commission from office.[7] The IPCC can have up to two deputy chairmen, has a chief executive, and can appoint staff (including staff on secondment from the police).[8]

4.8    The IPCC has the power to set up regional offices and has offices in Manchester, the Midlands, Cardiff and London.

## The functions

4.9    The IPCC's functions are exercised in relation to three matters:

(a) the handling of complaints made about the conduct of 'people serving with the police' (see para 4.29 for definition);
(b) recording other matters where there may have been misconduct

---

6   Police Reform Act 2002 Sch 2 paras 1(3) and 2(4).
7   Police Reform Act 2002 Sch 2 paras 1(5) and 2(6).
8   Police Reform Act 2002 Sch 2 paras 3, 5 and 6

justifying criminal or disciplinary proceedings (known as 'conduct matters');

(c) the manner in which complaints or conduct matters are dealt with by the police and police authorities.[9]

4.10 The IPCC has to ensure that suitable arrangements under Police Reform Act 2002 Part 2 are maintained by itself, police authorities and chief officers in relation to these functions. The arrangements must be conducive to and facilitate the reporting of misconduct.[10] The arrangements must be kept under review, be efficient and effective, 'manifest an appropriate degree of independence' and ensure that public confidence is established and maintained in the arrangements.[11]

4.11 The IPCC has a proactive role in recommending changes to the arrangements, and also advising on 'police practice in relation to other matters' arising from its work as it feels necessary or desirable. The IPCC can do anything which facilitates, or is conducive or incidental to, its functions. However, it has no functions in relation to any aspect of a complaint or conduct matter which relates to the direction and control of a police force by a chief officer or his delegate.[12]

4.12 The IPCC has a number of formal reporting functions. In addition to the requirement to produce annual reports, the IPCC must also report to the Home Secretary, when requested, on the exercise of its general functions.[13] The IPCC can also submit other reports on exceptional or grave matters which it feels should be drawn to the Home Secretary's attention, and can produce reports containing advice and recommendations in relation to police practice.[14]

4.13 The IPCC has the power to require that information from police forces is provided for the purposes of fulfilling its functions[15] and to impose time limits within which the information must be provided. The IPCC can also require a police force to allow it access to premises and to documents and other things on the premises to examine the efficiency and effectiveness of the police force's arrangements for handling complaints,[16] and for the purposes of any investigation the IPCC is supervising, managing or carrying out itself.

9 Police Reform Act 2002 s10(2).
10 Police Reform Act 2002 s 10(4)(b).
11 Police Reform Act 2002 s10(1).
12 Police Reform Act 2002 s10(8) (see para 4.38 on the issue of 'direction and control').
13 Police Reform Act 2002 s11(2).
14 Police Reform Act 2002 s11(3) and (4).
15 Police Reform Act 2002 s17.
16 Police Reform Act 2002 s18.

4.14    The IPCC must keep a register of all the information provided to it by the police in relation to the complaints procedure and can publish or disclose all of this information for the purposes of learning lessons, raising public awareness and improving the system, so long as the rules restricting certain types of disclosure (see para 4.168) are complied with.[17]

4.15    The operational advice note issued by the IPCC to police forces about its guardianship policy[18] recommends at para 3.9.3 that:

> Regular two or three day inspections should be carried out in each force every eighteen months to two years, with the possibility of targeted inspections to support themed projects reflecting regional or national priorities in the interim.

4.16    The Home Secretary has issued orders allowing the IPCC to engage in 'directed and intrusive surveillance' and the use of informers for the purposes of carrying out its functions.[19] The powers are similar to those enjoyed by the police themselves.[20]

4.17    The IPCC also has a role in issuing guidance to police authorities, chief officers and other officers about the complaints system, how it should be run, and the detection and deterrence of misconduct.[21] This was previously the job of the Home Secretary. Every person to whom the guidance relates must 'have regard' to it in carrying out their functions. The IPCC must consult with police authorities, chief officers, and others 'as it sees fit' on any proposed guidance and the guidance must be approved by the Home Secretary. The Home Secretary also retains the power to make regulations on a wide range of police complaints matters.[22]

4.18    These more general and proactive roles of the IPCC, over and above its responsibilities in individual complaints, are said to constitute a guardianship role. This is described in the operational advice note on guardianship of the police complaints system as having four components:

- monitoring, review and inspection of police force complaints systems;
- promoting confidence in the complaints system as a whole;

17  Police (Complaints and Misconduct) Regulations 2004 SI No 643 (hereinafter Complaints Regs) reg 25.
18  See www.ipcc.gov.uk/guardianship0402.pdf.
19  Police Reform Act 2002 s19.
20  IPCC (Investigatory Powers) Order 2004 SI No 815.
21  Police Reform Act 2002 s22.
22  Police Reforms Act 2002, s23.

- ensuring the accessibility of the complaints system;
- drawing and promoting the lessons of the IPCC'S role.

4.19 Thus the IPCC is expected to have a proactive responsibility for the development of the system for recording and investigating complaints and conduct matters. The IPCC has a clear mandate to raise standards, increase consistency and performance where necessary within the complaints system, and be able to make recommendations on wider areas of police practice from its work.

4.20 Clearly, complainants and their advisers can have a role in drawing matters to the IPCC's attention and urging the organisation to concentrate on specific failings of the system which have been identified either locally or nationally, for example the way lawful police policies and practices are deployed, stop and search, use of firearms, police pursuits, community policing, etc. The IPCC is in a strong position to make credible contributions to these areas and to encourage improvements where possible to discourage misconduct and complaints arising from these areas of policing. The IPCC may also become more active in on-going legal proceedings such as police-related judicial reviews or inquests into deaths in custody. For example, the IPCC was represented at the inquest into the death of Harry Stanley (who was shot by police officers) in October 2004.

## Transitional arrangements

4.21 Any new complaint about a police officer made after 1 April 2004 will be investigated under the new system, whether the conduct complained about happened before that date or not. However, for civilian staff (who were not previously included in the police complaints system) only complaints received about conduct after 1 April 2004 will be entertained. The IPCC does not have the power to re-open any complaints which have been completed by the PCA before that date. However, the IPCC will take over the PCA's role in all uncompleted complaints cases, applying the old law to these matters.[23]

## Making a complaint

4.22 The procedure for making a complaint about the conduct of a police officer is simple and informal. A complaint is best made in writing, but may be made orally. However, the rules about who can make a

---

23 IPCC (Transitional Provisions) Order 2004 SI No 671.

complaint and what about are more complicated. The explanatory notes to the Police Reform Act 2002 say that:

> The intention is that any conduct of a person serving with the police which has an adverse effect on a member of the public or is sufficiently serious to bring the police into disrepute, whether the subject of a complaint or not, should be dealt with effectively and efficiently in order that public confidence in the police can be maintained.

## Who can make a complaint?

4.23    There are detailed rules as to who can make a complaint. They fall into three main groups, but all must be 'members of the public' which excludes a police officer on duty, or anybody under the control of the same chief officer as the officer complained about.[24] The three groups who can complain about the conduct of a person serving with the police are members of the public who claim to be:

- victims (persons in relation to whom the conduct took place); or
- witnesses to the conduct; or
- adversely affected by the conduct.[25]

4.24    In all these categories someone can act on behalf of the complainant if they have been given the written authority to do so.[26] In addition the IPCC can designate other organisations through which complaints may be made. These organisations can pass complaints on to the police without the written consent of the complainant.[27] At the time of writing no groups have been designated, although the IPCC has issued an 'Information Package for Complaints Access Points'[28] which indicates that such organisations will include Citizens Advice Bureaux, faith groups and advice centres.

### Victims

4.25    The statutory provisions do not define this group of complainants further than to say that their complaint must be that the conduct complained about happened to them. This will include the vast majority of complaints from people who have been on the receiving end of police misconduct.

24  Police Reform Act 2002 s29(4).
25  Police Reform Act 2002, s12(1)(a)–(c).
26  Police Reform Act 2002, s12(1)(d) and (6)(b).
27  Police Reform Act 2002, s12(6)(a).
28  See www.ipcc.gov.uk./gateway-org-guidance.pdf

### Witnesses

4.26 To make a complaint as a witness a person must have acquired knowledge of the misconduct in a manner which would enable him or her to be a witness in criminal proceedings. Alternatively, the person must have in his or her possession anything which would constitute admissible evidence of the misconduct. Thus, eye witnesses are, of course, included but are not the only witnesses. Someone who has evidence such as a videotape would also be able to make a complaint.

### Those adversely affected

4.27 A person is adversely affected by conduct if he or she:

- suffers any form of loss or damage, distress or inconvenience;
- is put in danger; or
- is otherwise put at risk of being adversely affected.[29]

4.28 A person can only claim to have been adversely affected if he or she saw or heard the conduct complained about or its effects, or if the person already knew the person to whom the conduct occurred.[30] Thus a person who simply saw the conduct on television would not be able to make a complaint about police misconduct unless he or she knew the victim already.

## Who can be complained about?

4.29 Under the IPCC system, a complaint can be made against 'a person serving with the police'. This is further defined as:

- a member of a police force;
- an employee of a police authority who is under the control of the chief officer;
- a special constable under the control of the chief officer.[31]

### Civilian employees

4.30 As mentioned above, civilian employees of the police are now brought within the police complaints system. The role of police staff interfacing with the public is increasing with the introduction of police

---

29 Police Reform Act 2002 s29(5).
30 Police Reform Act 2002, s12(3)(4).
31 Police Reform Act 2002, s12(7). There will be slightly different disciplinary procedures for special constables (see chapter 5).

community support officers, designated escort and detention officers
(both employed by the police authority and in some cases employed by
a private contract provider), designated investigators, staff dealing
with telephone queries and front desk duties, etc. These people are
often a point of contact for the public with the police service.

4.31　　Although civilian employees and contracted staff (for the latter,
only those who are detention officers or escort officers)[32] will be subject
to the complaints procedure, the police discipline procedures do not
apply to them.[33] However, the relevant thematic paper from the Home
Office states:[34]

> In the interests of fairness, we would expect that sanctions taken against
> police staff (and thus referred to in contracts) be similar to those that are
> taken against police officers so that there is proportionality in disciplinary
> arrangements for police staff and police officers.

## Senior officers

4.32　The new system of complaints includes complaints against senior
officers (as did the previous system). A senior officer is defined as an
officer holding a rank above that of chief superintendent.[35] The only real
difference between the investigation of complaints against these
officers and other officers is that it is generally the police authority
rather than the chief officer of the police force who has the responsibilities under the legislation,[36] and this should be borne in mind when
consulting the description of the IPCC system set out below.

## Other police forces

4.33　The provisions of the complaints regime apply primarily to the 43
police forces in England and Wales. However, there are provisions to
ensure that the National Crime Squad (NCS) and the National
Criminal Intelligence Service (NCIS) are brought under the auspices
of the IPCC.[37]

4.34　　In addition, there are around 30 other specialist police forces that
operate within England and Wales, which will not automatically come
within the new complaints system (see chapter 3). These include

---

32　Complaints Regs reg 28.
33　Complaints Regs reg 30.
34　*Police Staff*, thematic paper No 8, July 2003.
35　Police Reform Act 2002 s29(1).
36　See Police Reform Act 2002, s29(1) for the definition of 'appropriate authority'.
37　Police Reform Act 2002, s25 and Complaints Regs reg 29.

various park constabularies and ports police and Ministry of Defence Police and the British Transport Police. The IPCC is empowered to agree with these forces a complaints system corresponding or similar to the system enacted for other police forces.[38] Regulations covering the Ministry of Defence Police and the British Transport Police have been made.[39]

4.35    Where there is no agreement in place between a given force and the IPCC, the Home Secretary can direct that an agreement be reached.[40] Once an agreement has been established it cannot be terminated or amended without the permission of the Home Secretary.

**List of non-Home Office forces in England and Wales**

| Force | Lead department |
|---|---|
| British Transport Police | Department for Transport |
| Ministry of Defence Police | Ministry of Defence |
| UK Atomic Energy Authority Constabulary | Department of Trade and Industry |
| Royal Parks Constabulary | Department for Culture, Media and Sport |
| Ports Police Forces | Department for Transport |
| Port of Liverpool Police | Department for Transport |
| Port of Bristol Police | Department for Transport |
| London Port of Tilbury Police | Department for Transport |
| Port of Dover Police | Department for Transport |
| Port of Felixstowe Police | Department for Transport |
| Port of Falmouth Police | Department for Transport |
| Tees and Hartlepool Port Authority Harbour Police | Department for Transport |
| London Borough Park Constabularies | Local authority control |
| Wandsworth Parks Constabulary | Local authority control |
| Royal Borough of Kensington and Chelsea Parks Police | Local authority control |
| Newham Parks Constabulary | Local authority control |
| Hammersmith and Fulham Parks | Local authority control |
| Sutton Parks | Local authority control |

38   Police Reform Act 2002, s26.
39   IPCC (Forces Maintained Otherwise than by Police Authorities) Order 2004 SI No 672.
40   Police Reform Act 2002 s26(2).

**List of non-Home Office forces in England and Wales** *continued*

| Force | Lead department |
|-------|-----------------|
| Finsbury Park Patrol (Haringey) | Local authority control |
| Hillingdon Parks | Local authority control |
| Barking and Dagenham | Local authority control |
| Royal Botanic Gardens Constabulary | Department for Culture, Media and Sport |
| Mersey Tunnels Police | Department for Transport |
| Epping Forest Keepers | Corporation of London |
| Hampstead Heath Park Constabulary | Corporation of London |
| Cambridge University Police | Local Authority Control |
| London Central Markets Constabulary | Local Authority Control |
| Liverpool Market Constabulary | Local Authority Control |
| Brighton Parks Police | Local Authority Control |
| Birmingham Parks Police | Local Authority Control |

*IPCC staff*

4.36   It is not unusual for complainants to be dissatisfied with the actions of an investigating officer. In these circumstances, it is possible to make a complaint about that officer in the normal way. However, the IPCC is able to investigate complaints and conduct matters itself, using its own staff. These staff will hold police powers for the purposes of conducting an investigation on behalf of the Commission, but are not subject to the police complaints system.

4.37   Thus, a complaints system has been introduced which covers both administrative staff and police officers.[41] These provisions require that serious complaints (as defined by the IPCC) are investigated by the IPCC and the complainant is kept informed of the progress and outcome of the report. Less serious complaints are dealt with internally.

## What cannot be complained about?

4.38   It has been stated above that for a complaint to come within the complaints procedure it must be about 'conduct' of a person serving with the police. It cannot be about the direction and control of a police force by the chief officer or the acting chief officer. The Home Secretary has

---

41   Police Reform Act 2002, s27 and IPCC (Staff Conduct) Regulations 2004 SI No 660.

power to issue to chief officers and police authorities guidance about how to deal with such complaints, but none has been issued to date.[42] Sometimes it can be difficult to tell whether the complaint is about 'direction and control'. For example, police officers who arrive late on a scene, might have done so because they were lazy, or because the force simply does not have enough officers. If it is not immediately clear which it is then the complaint should be initially recorded and dealt with until such time as the matter is clarified.

4.39    However, when the PCA oversaw the system it made a clear distinction between the tactical execution of plans or tactical control of detachments on the ground by subordinate officers, and strategic and central command of an entire force by a chief officer. It is hoped that the IPCC will adopt the same approach although the draft guidance does not do so. Tactical decisions by officers of any rank can properly be the subject of a complaint. So, for example, a decision to take a very large number of officers to conduct a search of a small house, where no violent resistance is expected and which seems calculated to strike terror into the occupants, will not be treated as relating to the 'direction or control' of a police force. Complaints that junior officers have acted improperly on the instructions or with the authority of more senior officers should be made against both the junior officers and the senior officers concerned. Criticisms of strategic decisions by a chief officer will not be recorded as a complaint and should be made instead to the police authority.

4.40    Just because a complaint is hopeless does not mean that it should not be recorded and dealt with according to the rules which includes provisions for seeking dispensation from investigating a complaint (para 4.137). Neither should the fact that the complaint is couched in general terms (with no specific part of the Code of Conduct referred to) prevent the complaint being recorded. Chief officers under the PCA system were advised that where a complaint is couched in general terms and the subsequent investigation reveals a number of breaches of discipline, all such breaches arising directly from the incident and affecting the well-being of the complainant should be treated as separate items of complaint. Any other ancillary matters and breaches of discipline arising from the incident which did not affect the complainant need not be recorded.

42  Police Reform Act 2002, s14.

## Where and how to make a complaint

4.41   One of the criticisms of the PCA system was that complaints could only be made to the police, and it was the job of the police to record and accept complaints. In the past, there have been cases of systematic failure to record complaints. In 1993 HM Inspectorate of Constabulary reported that officers in Area 8 of the Metropolitan Police district were breaching the Police and Criminal Evidence Act 1984 by treating serious complaints as if they simply related to policy questions: 'Most should have been dealt with at least by informal resolution, but many, in other forces, would have led to a full investigation'. If the police persist in refusing to record a complaint, they could be compelled to do so by an application for judicial review.

4.42   The IPCC system still places the responsibility of recording complaints on the various police forces. The Home Office view is that a centralised system would lead to delay and confusion and 'also diminish police ownership of complaints which in the main relate to matters that are best responded to at a local management level'.[43]

4.43   The IPCC website contains leaflets in a number of different languages about how to make a complaint and how to appeal decisions. As mentioned above (para 4.24), the IPCC intends to designate appropriate community groups and advice centres to be 'complaints access points' through which complaints can be channelled, recognising that not everyone is comfortable with making a complaint at a police station.

4.44   The legislation itself envisages complaints being made to three different places: the IPCC, a police authority, or the chief officer.

4.45   In cases where the complaint is not against a senior officer (over the rank of chief superintendent)[44] then the chief officer (in practice through a more junior officer acting on his behalf) must record the complaint if he is chief officer of the officer complained about. If he or she is not or the complaint is about a senior officer then the chief officer must notify the complainant as to where the complaint should be sent.[45] Complaints against senior officers should be sent to the officer's police authority and the police authority must record such complaints.

4.46   If a complaint is sent to the police authority rather than the chief officer (in the case of junior officers), or to the wrong police authority (in the case of senior officers) then the police authority must inform the complainant of the correct person to send the complaint to.[46]

43   Thematic paper No 10, August 2003.
44   Police Reform Act 2002 s29(1).
45   Police Reform Act 2002 Sch 3 para 2(3), (5) and (6).
46   Police Reform Act 2002 Sch 3 para 2(2), (5) and (6).

4.47    If a complaint is sent straight to the IPCC then the IPCC must ask the complainant if it can be sent on to the chief officer or the police authority.[47] The IPCC can only pass on the complaint if the complainant consents. However, if the complainant does not consent but the IPCC decides it is in the public interest that the matter is recorded by the chief officer or the police authority, the IPCC can refer the complaint on to be dealt with as a recordable conduct matter (see para 4.142). Thus, in the rare situation where a complainant complains to the IPCC but does not want the complaint passed on to the police, there is a mechanism for this happening anyway, against his or her wishes.[48]

4.48    In practice, then, the ways in which complainants make their complaints are unlikely to change from the PCA system (until the IPCC designates 'complaints access points' – see para 4.43 above). Other than for senior officers where the police authority is the correct place to send a complaint, the most sensible thing to do is to make the complaint in writing and address it to the Chief Constable or, in London, to the Commissioner of Police.

4.49    However, the likelihood is that many people will make complaints orally to their local police station. If an oral complaint is made, the usual practice is for an inspector to be called to record it. Brief details at least will be recorded. Even with the best will in the world, this is likely to be less satisfactory than a statement made in the complainant's own words or with the help of a sympathetic adviser. Furthermore, there is evidence that complainants who attempt to make oral complaints are often discouraged with assurances or excuses (or simply being made to wait for long periods of time to see an inspector) and their complaints are not recorded.

4.50    Complaints should be made as soon as possible after the event while recollections are still fresh in the mind. Furthermore, the police have the power to apply to dispense with any investigation if it is more than 12 months after the conduct complained about (see para 4.176).

## Records

4.51    Chief officers and police authorities must keep records of all complaints and purported complaints made to them, every conduct matter (see para 4.142) recorded and every exercise of a power or duty made during the complaints process.[49]

---

47  Police Reform Act 2002 Sch 3 para 2(1).
48  Police Reform Act 2002 Sch 3 para 2(4).
49  Complaints Regs reg 24.

## Appeals

4.52   As an additional safeguard there is a right to appeal to the IPCC in relation to decisions to record complaints. The explanatory notes to the 2002 Act state:

> Under the provisions of the [Police Act 1996], failure or refusal to record a complaint was a major source of concern for complainants and for observers and there was no redress. The new system places a duty on a chief officer or a police authority, as the case may be, to advise the complainant of the reasons for not recording the complaint and of his right to appeal to the Commission against that decision.[50]

4.53   In any situation where the police authority or the chief officer has declined or failed to notify or record the whole or part of the complaint, then the complainant must be told of this and the grounds for it, and informed of the right to appeal the decision.[51] The appeal must be brought within 28 days of the notification to the complainant of the failure.[52] Presumably this is an open-ended time period where the chief officer has failed to make a determination at all.

4.54   Any appeal must be in writing and contain the details of the complaint, when it was made, the grounds for the appeal and the date the complainant was informed of the subject matter of the appeal.[53] To assist with appeals the IPCC has produced leaflets and forms for complainants.[54]

4.55   The IPCC has to decide if the complaint should have been recorded or notified and, if it finds in the complainant's favour, can give such directions to the chief officer or the police authority as it thinks fit. A decision must be reached on the appeal 'as soon as practicable'.[55] All parties including the complainant must be informed of the decision and any directions given.[56]

---

50   Explanatory notes, para 70.
51   Police Reform Act 2002 Sch 3 para 3(3).
52   Complaints Regs reg 8(1).
53   Complaints Regs reg 8(2).
54   See www.ipcc.gov.uk/index/making-complaint/appeal.htm.
55   Complaints Regs reg 8.
56   Police Reform Act 2002 Sch 3 para 2(6).

## Copies of complaints

4.56 The police are under a duty to supply a copy of the record made of a complaint to the complainant and to the officer complained about.[57] This could include the letter in which the complaint was made or the record made of an oral complaint.

4.57 It is worth bearing in mind that the police have the power to anonymise the record disclosed to the officer, and this should be pointed out in the initial complaint if it will be relevant.[58] The police also have the power not to provide a copy of the complaint if it may prejudice criminal investigations or proceedings or if it is otherwise in the public interest not to do so.[59] It would be rare that this will be appropriate as the complainant will know the content of his or her complaint in any event.

## Initial procedure

4.58 When a complaint is made, the police are under a duty to take any steps that are appropriate for the purposes of the complaints system to obtain or preserve evidence relating to the conduct forming the subject of the complaint as soon as practicable. The duty is on-going throughout the investigation.[60]

4.59 This might involve such things as preserving documentary records, conducting searches, taking photographs and seeking medical examinations of the parties to an assault; both the complainant and the police officer(s). Medical examinations can be carried out only by consent. If an examination by a police doctor is carried out, the complainant should be warned not to discuss the circumstances of the injury with the doctor. Complainants should also arrange for an examination by an independent doctor as soon as possible. This is often achieved by a visit to a GP or to the local casualty department.

4.60 If the complainant is aware of any evidence that ought to be obtained or preserved, this should be specified in the letter of complaint, even if it has been mentioned orally. Failure by the police to obtain or preserve evidence may itself justify a further complaint.

---

57 Complaints Regs reg 14.
58 Complaints Regs reg 14(2).
59 Complaints Regs reg 14(3).
60 Police Reform Act 2002 Sch 3 para 1.

# Local resolution[61]

4.61    A feature of the PCA system was the procedure for 'informal resolution' whereby 30–40 per cent of complaints were dealt with without the need for a formal investigation. Many complaints systems in other areas have an informal part to the procedure. The intention is almost always that less serious complaints can be dealt with quickly and simply and not involve disproportionately expensive investigations. This clearly can have advantages for complainants and the police. However, in the past there has been a perceived danger that the police attempt to funnel more complaints than they should through the informal procedure in order to save time and money.

4.62    Under the IPCC system, the principles of the PCA informal resolution system are retained, but renamed 'local resolution'. Local resolution is only appropriate for the less serious complaints. It allows the complainant, if he or she chooses, to see whether the complaint can be resolved to his or her satisfaction without a formal investigation. It usually involves a minimal element of investigation with an attempt at conciliation.

4.63    On receiving a complaint the chief officer must decide whether it is suitable for local resolution (see para 4.67 below). If it is, the police must seek to resolve it locally, that is, they must ask if the complainant will agree to local resolution. This is solely a matter for the complainant; the police cannot insist on it.

4.64    The appointed officer's task is to achieve a position in which the complainant is satisfied that his or her complaint has been dealt with in an appropriate manner. It is also important to remember that the complainant is agreeing only to attempt a local resolution. If, having made the *attempt*, the complaint has not been resolved, the complainant can still insist on a formal investigation. There is also now a right of appeal against the procedure adopted during the local resolution stage.

4.65    The Home Office thematic paper number 7 produced in July 2003 explains the current intentions behind the local resolution process.

> It may take different forms but in simple terms amounts to gaining the complainant's consent to resolve a complaint outside of an investigation and instead seek to resolve it through dialogue. It might entail a member of the police service meeting with the complainant to establish the nature

---

61    The key provisions relating to local resolution are to be found in the Police Reform Act 2002 Sch 3 paras 6, 8 and 9, and in the Complaints Regs regs 4 and 9.

of their concerns and meeting with the officer complained against. An attempt is then made to address the complainant's concerns through an explanation, some form of apology or procedural changes. No disciplinary sanctions can be brought against an officer as a result of informal resolution.

It is hoped that local resolution will cover various mechanisms such as mediation or a restorative conference, in addition to the mechanism currently referred to as informal resolution. This change received wide support during the consultation.

4.66    Although local resolution will in practice be a major part of the regime, it is thought that more detail will be contained in guidance to be issued by the IPCC.

## Complaints that qualify for local resolution

4.67    Once a complaint has been recorded by the chief officer then, subject to some important exceptions, the chief officer must decide whether a complaint is suitable for local resolution.[62] The exceptions are:

- cases where the complaint must be referred to the IPCC;[63]
- cases where the IPCC has referred a complaint back to the chief officer;[64]
- cases where the IPCC is currently considering what form of investigation is appropriate for a complaint.[65]

4.68    Complainants should be given a clear explanation of what local resolution will involve before they give their consent. In addition, the complainant must be informed of his or her right to appeal at the end of the local resolution procedure[66] (see para 4.83). The complainant should be aware that once consent has been given it cannot be withdrawn once the informal resolution procedure has begun.[67]

4.69    If the complainant is serious about pursuing a formal complaint, it is important that he or she is forewarned that the police may try to persuade him or her to agree to local resolution or withdrawal. The police may use various tactics, from assurances that the officer has learned a salutary lesson to pointing out that the chances of success are

---

62  Police Reform Act 2002 Sch 3 para 6(1) and (2).
63  Police Reform Act 2002 Sch 3 para 4.
64  Police Reform Act 2002 Sch 3 para 5.
65  Police Reform Act 2002 Sch 3 para 15.
66  Police Reform Act 2002 Sch 3 para 6(6).
67  Police Reform Act 2002 Sch 3 para 6(7).

very slim. They may also say that the officer is young and that a complaint will blight his or her future career or conversely that he or she is nearing retirement and that a complaint will jeopardise his or her pension. Complainants are also frequently, and misleadingly, 'warned' that a formal investigation will mean that they and their witnesses will have to take a day off work in order to attend a disciplinary hearing, despite the tiny number of cases that result in such hearings. If the investigating officer attempts this tactic, it is worth pointing out that if the police honestly believe that the case is sufficiently serious to merit a disciplinary hearing they should encourage the complainant to pursue the matter and not attempt to discourage him or her. Conversely, if they honestly believe the complaint is insufficiently serious to warrant formal investigations, it is underhand to suggest that a disciplinary hearing is likely.

4.70    Even where a complaint does not fall within one of the exceptions to local resolution and the complainant consents, the chief officer may only decide that the complaint is suitable for local resolution in certain circumstances as follows:

- the chief officer is satisfied that the complaint even if proved would not justify bringing criminal or disciplinary proceedings; or
- the IPCC has approved the use of local resolution for this particular complaint.

4.71    This latter provision refers to the power of the chief officer in any case to apply to the IPCC for such approval. The IPCC can only grant approval in one of two circumstances. The first is where, even if proved, the IPCC is satisfied the complaint would not lead to criminal proceedings or serious penalties in disciplinary proceedings (dismissal, requirement to resign, demotion or a fine).[68] The second is where it would be not be practicable for such criminal or disciplinary proceedings to be brought with any likelihood of success even if the complaint were thoroughly investigated. [69]

4.72    Thus, in effect, the local resolution procedure can be extended to include matters which would not have fallen within the PCA informal resolution regime, namely cases which might attract minor disciplinary penalties and cases where there is little prospect of a successful criminal or disciplinary outcome even if the complaint is fully investigated.

68  Police Reform Act 2002 Sch 3 para 6(4)(a).
69  Police Reform Act 2002 Sch 3 para 6(4)(b).

# The procedure

4.73    Detailed regulations or guidance as to the procedure to be followed for local resolution have not been produced. The Home Secretary has a number of regulation-making powers which have not been exercised. These include the power to make regulations setting out different descriptions of procedures available during local resolution.[70] In fact the complaint regulations say that the procedures to be available are 'any procedures which are approved' by the IPCC.[71] Detailed guidance can be expected but 'operational guidance notes' have been available on the website since February 2004. The thematic paper issued by the Home Office gives some indication as to what might be approved by the IPCC.

- *Management resolution*: a member of the police will meet the complainant to establish the nature of the allegation, meet with the officer concerned to obtain his or her account of the incident, and attempt to resolve the issue through dialogue with both sides. This is similar to how informal resolution is currently used.
- *Restorative conference*: where there is commitment from both parties they are brought together. This may allow for the member of the force to give an explanation of his or her actions, view, or an apology in a 'no consequence' environment.
- *Mediation*: similar to management resolution, but with an independent mediator from or approved by the IPCC.
- Any other procedures the IPCC designs or endorses.

4.74    The operational advice note issued by the IPCC on 'Local Handling of Complaints'[72] adds little of substance to this approach and is mired in much management-speak about the process being value-driven and person-centred, etc. It does not contain any examples of the kind of procedures that might be adopted in local resolution. However, it does emphasise the importance of the complainant properly understanding and agreeing to the process to be adopted. It also indicates that in all but exceptional cases the IPCC would expect the local resolution process to be completed within 28 days.

---

70  Police Reform Act 2002, Sch 3 para 8(2)(a).
71  Complaints Regs reg 4(1).
72  See www.ipcc.gov.uk/local-resolution1702.pdf.

4.75    The police can appoint a person serving with the police and under the control of the chief officer to secure the local resolution of the complaint,[73] presumably using one of the methods approved by the IPCC. Persons from outside the police can be involved (for example, trained mediators) so long as the appointed person, so defined, co-ordinates the local resolution procedure for that particular complaint.

4.76    If it seems to the appointed person that the complaint has already been satisfactorily dealt with by the time it comes to his or her notice then, subject to the complainant having the opportunity to make representations, the complaint can be treated as locally resolved. This may happen, for example, if the officer has already apologised to the complainant. The requirement to seek the representations of the complainant gives the complainant the opportunity to make it clear that he or she wishes to pursue the complaint, if that is the case.

4.77    The appointed person must, as part of the process, provide the complainant and the officer or civilian employee complained about an opportunity to comment on the complaint as soon as practicable.[74] This might not always include the making of statements by the parties but, where it does, those statements cannot be used in subsequent criminal, civil or disciplinary proceedings.[75] This is intended to encourage all parties to discuss the incident as freely as possible, without the fear that what they say will be used against them in a subsequent hearing. However, a statement is not inadmissible if it consists of or includes an admission which is not subject to local resolution.[76] Thus if an officer during the local resolution of a trivial matter makes an admission about a serious matter which would justify criminal or disciplinary proceedings, the serious matter is admissible in subsequent proceedings. The opportunity to comment could also be provided through a meeting with the complainant or by an oral account.

4.78    Often what a complainant wants is for the officer to apologise for the misconduct complained about. Officers are usually reluctant to do so, feeling it will reflect badly on them and their careers. The appointed person cannot apologise on behalf of the officer unless the officer has admitted the conduct complained about and has agreed to the apology.[77] One formulation that is sometimes used is an apology to the complainant that they have felt the need to complain. This, of course, is not

74  Complaints Regs reg 4(3).
75  Police Reform Act 2002 Sch 3 para 8(3).
76  Police Reform Act 2002 Sch 3 para 8(3).
77  Complaints Regs reg 4(4).

an admission that any officer has done anything wrong and should not be accepted as resolving the complaint. If the officer refuses to make any comment at all about the complaint, then the appointed person must make a written record of this.[78]

4.79 There will clearly be cases where, although local resolution has been commenced, it is not possible to complete it, either, for example, because the complainant is not content to accept any solution put forward, or because the officer refused to accept that he or she was in the wrong. The appointed person may be frustrated by this especially if time and effort have been put into the case, and it may put pressure on the complainant to accept an unsatisfactory resolution of the complaint. One of the reasons for this might be that no person involved in an attempt to resolve a complaint locally can be involved or assist in formally investigating a complaint.[79]

4.80 If attempts have been made to resolve the complaint locally and it appears to the police that this has not been possible, or where it appears to the police that the complaint is not suitable for local investigation, the police must formally investigate the complaint.[80]

4.81 Additionally, if the IPCC decides that the complaint should be referred to it or the complaint is otherwise referred then the local resolution must come to an end. This may happen if the conduct complained about turns out to be much more serious than initially thought, or where the complaint becomes part of a wider investigation carried out by the IPCC.

4.82 Whether or not the local resolution is successful, a record must be made of the outcome of the procedure and the complainant and the officer complained about have three months thereafter to apply for a copy of the record.[81] It does not appear that there is any duty on the appointed person to inform the complainant of this right. The copy of the record must be provided by the police within 14 days.[82]

## Appeals

4.83 A new aspect of the local resolution procedure is the right for the complainant to appeal against the conduct of the local resolution.[83]

78 Complaints Regs reg 4(5).
79 Police Reform Act 2002 Sch 3 para 8(5).
80 Police Reform Act 2002 Sch 3 para 8(4).
81 Police Reform Act 2002 Sch 3 para 8(2)(c) and Complaints Regs, reg 4(6).
82 Complaints Regs reg 4(7).
83 Police Reform Act 2002 Sch 3 para 9(1).

4.84    However, there is only an appeal against contravention of procedural requirements relating to local resolution.[84] This means that if the appointed officer has failed to follow the procedure set out in the Act or the Regulations then the complainant can appeal. Thus, for example, a failure to make a record of the outcome of the procedure could be appealed against. It may also be possible to appeal if the appointed officer fails to follow the procedure as laid down by the IPCC for the particular complaint. There is probably little point in having an appeal against the failure of local resolution to find a satisfactory outcome to the complaint as the complainant has the right to move on to the formal investigation stage in any event. The point of the appeal is that the complainant, having agreed to a certain procedure for local resolution, should have the right to enforce that procedure.

4.85    The operational guidance on appeals[85] recognises that this is an extremely limited form of appeal against procedure, and is concerned about the need to manage expectations of complainants whose real concern is to appeal against the outcome of the local resolution.

4.86    The appeal is to the IPCC and must be brought within 14 days of the complainant being notified of the outcome of the local resolution,[86] although the IPCC has discretion to extend this time limit and all others set out in the appeal process where on the special circumstances of the case it is satisfied that it is just to do so.[87] The appeal must be made in writing and contain details and date of the complaint, the grounds of appeal and the date the complainant was informed of the outcome of the local resolution.[88] It is likely that an explanatory leaflet and a standard form will be produced by the IPCC. The IPCC must give the police and the officer complained about the chance to make representations on the appeal.[89] The IPCC can also request further information from the police.[90]

4.87    The IPCC must decide whether there has been a breach of the local resolution procedural requirements as soon as practicable.[91] The Home Office describes the matters the IPCC should consider as follows:[92]

84  Police Reform Act 2002 Sch 3 para 9(2).
85  See www.ipcc.gov.uk.
86  Complaints Regs reg 9(1).
87  Complaints Regs reg 9(9).
88  Police Reform Act 2002 Sch 3 para 9(2).
89  Police Reform Act 2002 Sch 3 para 9(3) and Complaints Regs reg 9(4) and (5).
90  Complaints Regs reg 9(3)(c).
91  Police Reform Act 2002 Sch 3 para 9(4) and Complaints Regs reg 9(6).
92  Thematic paper on local resolution (2003) p9.

- how the process was applied and whether or not it was in accordance with the procedure originally set out by, or recognised as sound by, the IPCC;
- whether the complainant was provided with information on that procedure when consenting to its use;
- whether the procedure consented to by the complainant was in fact followed;
- all factors which may have had an effect on the conduct of the process, as notified by the appropriate authority and the complainant.

4.88　When it has determined the appeal the IPCC must inform the chief officer, the complainant and the officer complained about of the outcome with reasons within three days if it allows the appeal and within five days if it does not.[93] Where the appeal is allowed the IPCC also has the power to provide the police with directions as to the future handling of the complaint, and these must be complied with.[94] Such directions might include ordering that there should be a formal investigation (and whether this should be independent, managed, supervised, or carried out solely by the police), for example, or another attempt at local resolution. The complainant and the officer complained about must be informed of any directions within five days of their making.[95]

## The interview

4.89　The interview is the key event in the complaints process. It is often the only opportunity the complainant will have to get his or her version of events over to a sometimes sceptical or hostile investigating officer or appointed person (depending on whether the complaint is being formally investigated or locally resolved). It is also the time when the complainant may come under the greatest pressure to withdraw the complaint or accept informal resolution. Many complainants expect the interview to be a neutral investigation of the facts, only to find that they are subjected to forceful interrogation at which they feel everything they say is challenged or disbelieved. It is therefore crucial to make sure the complainant is well prepared for the interview.

93　Complaints Regs reg 9(7).
94　Police Reform Act 2002 Sch 3 para 9(5).
95　Complaints Regs reg 9(8).

4.90      It is wise for a friend or adviser to be present at the interview and to help the complainant prepare for it in advance. The complainant and the friend or adviser should discuss beforehand whether the former is prepared to accept local resolution. If the complainant wants a formal investigation, the friend or adviser should be clear about this so that he or she can provide support if the police appear to be exerting contrary pressure.

4.91      Many complainants feel uncomfortable if the interview is held at a police station, possibly the very scene of the incident they are complaining about. Equally they may be reluctant to allow the police into their home. Interviews can therefore be arranged on neutral territory such as a citizens advice bureau or a solicitor's office where the complainant may feel more confident and relaxed.

4.92      Strictly, a complainant does not have to agree to be interviewed about the complaint, but, not surprisingly, if he or she refuses, the chances of having the complaint upheld are reduced and will depend on whether there is other compelling evidence. It is possible that the complaint would be dispensed with on the ground that it would not be reasonably practicable to investigate it; see para 4.180.

## Interview checklist

4.93      If the complainant agrees to an interview, the adviser who is going to be present should run through the following points in advance. In particular, the adviser should discuss beforehand what, if anything, the complainant is prepared to agree with the police.

- The adviser should be aware of all the relevant facts. A written statement about the incident should be prepared in advance so that this can be used as an aide-memoire in the interview. If the complainant is represented by a solicitor the statement should be prepared in a form that satisfies Criminal Justice Act 1967 s9. A properly prepared section 9 statement can be handed to the police at the start of the interview and will save time as the interview can then be confined to questions that clarify the complainant's allegations. The complainant will also have greater control of the interview and can be confident that no mistakes will be made about the order of events, who was present at the incident, the dates and times of incidents and any other points that might otherwise be forgotten or confused. However, if there is any possibility of a civil action being brought an interview should take place, if at all, only with a solicitor present or at least after legal advice has been obtained. In this event such a statement should be drafted by the solicitor acting in the civil action.

- Understandably, the appointed person or investigating officer will want to know exactly what the complaint is about, especially if this has not been spelt out clearly when the complaint was initially made. The investigation will be seeking to ascertain whether there has been a breach of the Police Discipline Code, and it is useful for an adviser to consult the Code (see chapter 5) to see what breaches are being alleged by the complainant.

- Before the interview begins, agree with the police that they will supply the complainant at the end of the interview with a copy of any statement and of any notes they make. Although the IPCC is committed to disclosure of as much information as possible, this may not always be reflected in the practice of individual investigating officers. Even where a civil action is brought there can be difficulties, both legal and practical, in obtaining copies. If the police do not agree to supply a copy, the complainant can either insist the interview takes place sufficiently slowly to allow the adviser to make a full record, or call off the interview and refer the matter to the IPCC.

- Start the interview by asking whether the investigating officer has already interviewed the offending officers. If the original complaint contained sufficient detail to identify the officers it is probable that they will already have been interviewed and that their version of events may have gained credibility in the eyes of the investigating officer. The complainant may then effectively have to disprove the officers' explanation.

- The role of the adviser is to intervene if the police try to press the complainant to make an admission or if they become overbearing or oppressive.

- The adviser should discuss beforehand whether the complainant is prepared to accept local resolution or to withdraw the complaint. The complainant should be made aware in advance of the kinds of tactics the police may use to persuade him or her to reconsider; see para 4.69.

- If the questioning becomes aggressive or new facts emerge, the adviser should call for an adjournment to discuss the matter in private.

• At the end of the interview, press the investigating officer to provide a timetable as to the progress of the complaint. There are duties to provide information to the complainant in any event (see para 4.158).

## Formal investigations

4.94    The explanatory notes to the Police Reform Act 2002 state:

> One of the general functions of the [IPCC] is to secure public confidence in the arrangements for handling complaints (and other conduct matters) ... In order to achieve this, there needs to be provision to enable complaints about serious misconduct or which attract high public interest or which involve exceptional circumstances to go to the [IPCC] for determination as to how they should be handled.[96]

### Complaints that do not need to be referred to the IPCC

4.95    If a complaint is not one which must be or has been referred to the IPCC (see para 4.97 below) and is not suitable for local resolution (or the complainant has not consented to local resolution) (see para 4.63) then the complaint stays with the police and is not referred to the IPCC. The police must make arrangements to have the complaint investigated on their own behalf.[97]

4.96    In practice, therefore, many police complaints will be investigated by the police with no input at all from the IPCC unless and until there is an appeal at the end of the process (see para 4.226). In cases where there is no duty on the police to refer the case to the IPCC, advisers will want to consider whether to attempt to persuade the police to use their discretion to refer a case in any event (see para 4.109).[98]

### When will a case be referred to the IPCC?

4.97    There are two categories of complaints which will be referred to the IPCC, for the IPCC to decide on the kind of investigation appropriate. The first is complaints that have to be referred to the IPCC ('mandatory referrals'). The second is where the police exercise their discretion to refer a case ('discretionary referrals').

96  Explanatory notes, para 71.
97  Police Reform Act 2002 Sch 3 para 6(3).
98  Police Reform Act 2002 Sch 3 para 4(2) and (3).

## Mandatory referrals

4.98 The police must refer a complaint to the IPCC:

(a) where the complaint alleges conduct which has led to serious injury or death;[99]

(b) where the conduct comes within a description set out in regulations;[100]

(c) where the IPCC decides to call in the complaint.[101]

4.99 Serious injury for the purposes of category (a) is defined as 'a fracture, a deep cut, a deep laceration or an injury causing damage to an internal organ or the impairment of any bodily function'.[102] Clearly there is some room for interpretation here as to what is a 'deep' cut or laceration and what amounts to 'damage' or 'impairment'. If the police appear to be adopting a restrictive interpretation it may well be worthwhile re-questing the IPCC to call in the case in an event (see para 4.108).

4.100 The list of conduct, complaints about which must be referred under category (b) is as follows:[103]

(i) a serious assault, as defined in guidance issued by the Commission;

(ii) a serious sexual offence, as defined in guidance issued by the Commission;

(iii) serious corruption, as defined in guidance issued by the Commission;

(iv) a criminal offence or behaviour which is liable to lead to a disciplinary sanction and which in either case was aggravated by discriminatory behaviour on the grounds of a person's race, sex, religion, or other status identified in guidance by the Commission;

(v) a serious arrestable offence, within the meaning of section 116 of the Police and Criminal Evidence Act 1984 [which contains a list of such offences].

4.101 At the time of writing the IPCC has introduced an 'operating advice note' on mandatory referrals[104] which is referred to in appendix B of the draft guidance. The draft guidance states that where there is doubt

---

99 Police Reform Act 2002 Sch 3 para 4(1)(a).
100 Police Reform Act 2002 Sch 3 para 4(1)(b).
101 Police Reform Act 2002 Sch 3 para 4(1)(c).
102 Police Reform Act 2002 s29(1).
103 Complaints Regs reg 2(2)(a).
104 See www.ipcc.gov.uk/mandatory-referrals.pdf.

whether a complaint falls within the mandatory criteria the IPCC expects the force to refer. The guidance provides definitions of some of the important terms.

## Serious assault

4.102   Serious assault is to be construed in accordance with the charging guidelines agreed between the Crown Prosecution Service and the Association of Chief Police Officers. Thus any injury caused by an assault which is more than would be required for a charge of actual bodily harm, amounts to a serious assault, and must be referred to the IPCC. The charging guidelines are annexed to the operating advice note. Those injuries which are normally prosecuted as actual bodily harm include breaking or losing a tooth, temporary unconsciousness, multiple bruising, displaced broken nose, minor fractures, minor cuts and some psychiatric injuries.

## Serious sexual offences

4.103   These are defined as including triable by indictment only offences under the various Sexual Offences Acts, and other sexual offences where magistrates are likely to refuse jurisdiction.

## Serious corruption

4.104   This is defined as including attempts to pervert the course of justice; receiving benefits, payments and favours likely to be tried in the Crown Court; corrupt 'controller/handler/informer' relationships; providing confidential information for payment, etc, in certain circumstances; supplying drugs or firearms. Attempts or conspiracies to commit these offences are included.

## Behaviour aggravated by discrimination

4.105   In addition to the definitions provided in the regulations, discrimination on the basis of the following is included: age, sexual orientation, disability.

4.106   In addition, any complaint that arises out of the same incident as a mandatory referral complaint, must also be referred to the IPCC.[105] Thus, if the complaints are that an officer swore at a person and then broke his or her leg, both complaints must be referred to the IPCC.

105   Complaints Regs reg 2(2)(b).

4.107    For the purposes of category (c) (see para 4.98), no indication has been given at the time of writing as to which complaints will be called in by the IPCC which do not fall within the above categories. The explanatory notes to the Act suggest that the IPCC will exercise this power 'because it may have particular concerns about the conduct complained of'.[106] It will be open to a complainant to make a case to the IPCC that they should require a particular complaint to be referred.

4.108    A case can be called in by the IPCC even where it has previously considered the complaint and even if it is already being investigated 'by any person'.[107] The purpose of this is to allow a late referral where concerns arise after an investigation has started.

### Discretionary referrals

4.109    The chief officer has a discretion to refer a complaint to the IPCC if it does not fall within one of the mandatory categories above[108] by reason of (a) the gravity of the subject matter of the complaint; or (b) any exceptional circumstances. The explanatory notes to the Act suggest examples such as 'high incidence of a particular conduct attracting complaints or a particular sensitivity'.[109]
The draft guidance lists examples such as:

- 'near misses' where someone nearly died or was seriously injured;
- an allegation that serious arrestable offence has been committed;
- discharge of firearms and Tasers;
- allegations of domestic violence by a member of the police service.

Thus, complaints about the local exercise of stop and search powers against particular groups in the community might come within these examples.

4.110    Even where a chief officer does not exercise these powers to refer, his or her police authority can, for the same reasons, refer the case to the IPCC.[110]

4.111    The discretion to refer a case to the IPCC can be exercised even after an investigation has begun.[111]

---

106  Explanatory notes, para 72.
107  Police Reform Act 2002 Sch 3 para 4(5).
108  Police Reform Act 2002 Sch 3 para 4(2).
109  Explanatory notes, para 72.
110  Police Reform Act 2002 Sch 3 para 4(3).
111  Police Reform Act 2002 Sch 3 para 4(5).

## Time limits for referral

4.112　A complaint about one of the matters for which referral is mandatory must be referred to the IPCC by the end of the day following the day when it became clear that the complaint should be referred.[112] If the IPCC calls in a complaint then it must be referred by the end of the day following the day the IPCC gave the police notice.[113] The IPCC can determine how it wants to be notified of a referral.[114] The operating advice note indicates that this is a matter for the police, but oral referral must be followed up by some form of written confirmation within 24 hours. The advice note also contains a list of the information the IPCC would like to be provided with when cases are referred which is now included in appendix C of the draft guidance.[115]

# The form of a formal investigation

4.113　When a complaint or recordable conduct matter (see para 4.142) is referred to the IPCC or is called in, the IPCC must decide first whether it is necessary to investigate the complaint[116] and if so what form of investigation should take place.[117]

4.114　　In deciding the form of the investigation the IPCC must take into account the seriousness of the case and the public interest.[118] It will be open to a complainant to make representations to the IPCC as to which method of investigation is appropriate. There are four possible forms of investigation for the IPCC to consider.[119]

(a) investigation by the police themselves;
(b) investigation by the police under supervision of the Commission;
(c) investigation by the police under management of the Commission;
(d) investigation by the Commission itself.

At the time of writing the draft guidance says that:

- an investigation by the IPCC will take place in the cases of greatest public concern;

112　Complaints Regs reg 2(3).
113　Complaints Regs reg 2(3).
114　Complaints Regs reg 2(3) and (4).
115　Operating advice note, para 6.
116　Police Reform Act 2002 Sch 3 para 5.
117　Police Reform Act 2002 Sch 3 para 15(1).
118　Police Reform Act 2002 Sch 3 para 15(2).
119　Police Reform Act 2002 Sch 3 para 15(4).

- managed investigations will take place in cases of great public concern which do not require an independent investigation;
- supervised and local investigation will account for the remainder of the cases.

4.115 In its first year the IPCC expects to investigate 30 cases itself, and to manage about 70 more. About 650 cases will be supervised by the IPCC.[120] The IPCC is empowered to change its mind as to the method of investigation if it thinks another method has become more appropriate,[121] for instance if there is a change of circumstances or further information comes to light. If the IPCC decides that a complaint investigation should 'downgraded' from a managed or supervised investigation then it must normally inform the complainant, the police and the person complained about and provide reasons for its decision.[122] Both the police and the IPCC can decide to split or combine investigations if this would be more efficient, effective, or in the public interest.[123]

4.116 The differences between the four kinds of investigation are reflected not so much in the content of the investigation itself but in the arrangements for appointing and overseeing the person to investigate the complaint, known as the investigating officer (IO). Where the investigating officer is a police officer then regulations apply to the nature of the person appointed. The IO must be independent of the officer investigated.[124] If the officer complained about is a senior officer then the IO must be from a different force (other than in the metropolitan police force).[125]

4.117 For other officers, the IO must be at least the rank of the officer complained about and in any event at least the rank of sergeant. If the officer being investigated is a superintendent or chief superintendent then the IO must be at least an assistant chief constable (or, in the metropolitan and City of London forces, of at least the rank of commander).[126]

---

120  See the Deputy Chairman's presentation, 11 March 2004, at www.ipcc.gov.uk.
121  Police Reform Act 2002 Sch 3 para 15(5).
122  Complaints Regs reg 20.
123 Complaint Regs reg 19.
124  Complaint Regs reg 18(1)(b)(c).
125  Complaint Regs reg 18(1)(d).
126  Complaint Regs reg 18.

## Police investigations

4.118   If the complaint is to be investigated by the police (either because it has not initially been referred to the IPCC or because the IPCC so decides) then the chief officer must appoint 'a person serving with the police' (either from the chief officer's force or another force) or a member of the NCIS or the NCS as the IO.[127]

## Supervised investigations

4.119   If the IPCC is to supervise the investigation of the complaint (for example, if an element of independence is seen as desirable) then the chief officer must likewise appoint a person serving with the police (or the NCIS or the NCS) as the IO, but subject to the IPCC's power of approval.[128]

4.120   As mentioned above, if the IPCC supervises the investigation, it can require the chief officer to obtain its approval of his or her choice of investigating officer. If the investigating officer has already been appointed and the IPCC is dissatisfied with the appointment, it can require the chief officer to select another officer who meets its approval. In many cases, the IPCC's interest in the appointment will not go beyond the broad question of whether the officer should come from a different division of the force, or from outside the force.

4.121   In some cases, complainants often prefer to have their cases investigated by an officer from another force. If this is the case and the seriousness of the complaint warrants it, it is a good idea to ensure that the complaint receives wide publicity and to make it clear to the IPCC that an investigation by an insider will not enjoy public confidence.

4.122   The IPCC will leave the day-to-day management of the complaint to the IO, but is empowered to impose any reasonable requirements as appear to be necessary for the conduct of the investigation.[129] This might cover directions, for example, to interview particular witnesses or to carry out searches or forensic tests.

4.123   This power is subject to two conditions. First, if it appears that criminal proceedings are possible the IPCC can only impose conditions relating to obtaining or preserving evidence of a criminal offence with the consent of the Director of Public Prosecutions (DPP).[130] This is

127   Police Reform Act 2002 Sch 3 para 16.
128   Police Reform Act 2002 Sch 3 para 17.
129   Complaints Regs reg 6(1).
130   Complaints Regs reg 6(2).

presumably because the DPP is primarily responsible for the investigation of criminal offences. Second, if the condition imposed will affect the resources to be spent on the complaint (for example, the obtaining of independent expert reports or a direction to release extra officers to assist the investigating officer) then the IPCC must consult first with the chief officer.[131]

4.124 In supervised cases, responsibility for the supervision is delegated to an individual member of the IPCC. The degree of involvement of that member will depend on the nature of the case, but the member will at least confer with the investigating officer at the outset, to ensure that steps have been taken to preserve evidence and to identify all possible witnesses and suspects. There will also be discussion and agreement on the plan of investigation and the general lines of inquiry. Usually supervision is conducted by telephone and letter, and perhaps will include a meeting with the investigating officer. The member may attend when complainants, witnesses and even the officers about whom the complaint has been made are being interviewed and asked to make statements.[132]

4.125 The latest figures available for 2002/03 show that the PCA accepted 447 complaint cases for supervision and also supervised 133 voluntary referrals of serious incidents.[133]

4.126 One of the major reasons for the lack of public confidence in the police complaints system has been the impression that investigating officers do not always pursue their inquiries into police misconduct as rigorously and as conscientiously as they would if they were investigating an offence by a member of the public. There has been criticism in the past that, in a significant minority of cases, investigations have not been as thorough as might have been expected and that more thorough cross-examination and tracing of witnesses might have resulted in better evidence to substantiate the complaint.

4.127 While it remains the case that, under the IPCC, police wrongdoing will still usually be investigated by other police officers, each supervised investigation, and to an even greater extent, each managed investigation will be individually scrutinised by a named member of the IPCC. In supervised cases and in cases where the police investigate with no input from the IPCC, there will be a right of appeal to the IPCC (see para 4.226)

---

131 Complaints Regs reg 6(3).
132 *R v PCA ex p Thompson* [1990] COD 205, DC.
133 See www.ipcc.gov.uk.

4.128    The individual member of the IPCC who is responsible for supervising or managing the case should be available by telephone to discuss the investigation with complainants or their representatives. Complainants and their representatives should consider taking advantage of this opportunity and in serious cases should consider arranging a meeting between themselves, the IPCC member and the investigating officer in order to discuss the progress and direction of the investigation.

4.129    Of course, the overwhelming majority of cases will not be scrutinised by the IPCC. So, where it seems that the police are, for example, failing to interview a particular witness, the complainant should inform the IPCC, inviting it to supervise or manage the investigation and to issue directions ordering the police to conduct the interview.

## Managed investigation

4.130    If the IPCC is to manage an investigation then the IPCC (as in supervised cases, see para 4.119) has power of approval of the person appointed as IO, but the IO is then under the Commission's 'direction and control'.[134]

4.131    The explanatory notes to the Act have this to say about managed investigations:

> This is a new concept which is similar to the supervised investigation but will be used in more serious or more sensitive cases which require a greater degree of independence. This independence will come from the strategy and direction provided in an investigation by the [IPCC] and the managerial control it will exercise on a day-to-day basis. The [IPCC] will be responsible for the investigation but the investigation itself will be carried out by the appointed investigating officer.[135]

4.132    It could be said that the difference between supervised and managed complaints has the potential to be very small indeed if the responsible member of the IPCC has a caseload which makes hands-on management difficult. The appointment of senior IPCC investigators to manage the complaint, as intended by the IPCC, may go some way to deal with this potential problem. One additional reason for encouraging the IPCC to manage rather than to supervise an investigation is the enhanced role the IPCC has in the disciplinary stages of the process (see chapter 5) if it manages a complaint investigation.

134   Police Reform Act 2002 Sch 3, para 18.
135   Explanatory notes, para 107.

## IPCC investigation

4.133  If the IPCC is to investigate the complaint itself then it designates a staff member to be the IO. The IPCC has recruited staff specifically to be investigators. If such staff do not already have the powers of a constable then these are bestowed upon them for the purposes of carrying out the investigation.[136]

4.134  An investigation by the IPCC is a totally new concept which has come about mainly because of recommendations (in recent years) of the Home Affairs Committee report of 1997–98, and the Stephen Lawrence Inquiry[137] Both recommendations for independent investigations reflect the long-standing demands from many sectors of the community and from the police service itself. However, independent investigations will be used only for the most serious complaints or conduct matters (such as those involving deaths in custody) and those of the highest public interest (the use of force by police at the pro-hunting demonstration in September 2004 is an example). Realistically, at least at first, only a handful of complaints will be investigation in this way.

## Unidentified officers and officers who leave the force

4.135  Two issues have been a source of embarrassment for the police complaints system. The first is when it is not possible to identify the officer whose misconduct has been complained of. This is especially frustrating when it is known that one of a group of officers is the alleged culprit, but none of the officers will provide information to identify that officer.

4.136  The second is officers who are allowed to retire while a complaint is on-going, thus making it impossible to proceed with disciplinary action against the officer.

4.137  In the case of the unidentified officer, the complaint must still be investigated, but provisions which relate to notifying the person complained about are not applied and decisions do not need to be made about criminal or disciplinary proceedings. If the officer is identified

---

136  Police Reform Act 2002 Sch 3 para 19.
137  See especially recommendation 58 of the Macpherson report (Cm 4262–I, TSO, 1999).

during the investigation then the full requirements of the complaints process can be applied.[138] If it is known that the complaint is about a member of a group of officers (and the other members must know who the culprit is) then there should be nothing to stop the IPCC investigating complaints against all members of the group for neglect of duty for failing to identify the guilty officer.[139]

4.138    In relation to an officer 'who ceases to be a person serving with the police since the time of the conduct' the complaint is investigated as usual, with consideration of criminal proceedings, but no decisions about disciplinary proceedings will be made.[140]

## Criminal and disciplinary proceedings pending the complaints investigation

4.139    Decisions about criminal and disciplinary proceedings will be made as a result of the outcome of the complaint. Therefore, such proceedings are usually prohibited pending the delivery of the investigation report.[141] However, the DPP has the power to bring criminal proceedings despite the usual rule, if there are exceptional circumstances or it is undesirable to delay bringing proceedings. This is most often the case where there are specific time limits for bringing proceedings, for example, for some driving offences.[142]

## Investigation where there is no complaint

4.140    There are cases where there has been misconduct by police officers, but there has been no complaint made to be investigated. The IPCC system ensures that these matters are considered by the police and the IPCC, and in certain cases ensures that the matters are investigated in any event.

4.141    In addition, the regime ensures that civil claims against the police are examined for possible misconduct by particular officers. Complaints which are withdrawn can also continue to be investigated by the police and the IPCC in certain cases.

138  Complaints Regs reg 22.
139  This was the policy of the PCA: see Annual Report 1987, para 2.15, and the third edition of this book, p94.
140  Complaints Regs reg 21.
141  Police Reform Act 2002 Sch 3 para 20(1).
142  ibid, Sch 3 para 20(3).

# Conduct matters

4.142 A 'conduct matter' is defined in the Act as being a matter which has not been the subject of a complaint but where there is an indication that a 'person serving with the police'[143] may have committed a criminal offence or behaved in a way which would justify the bringing of disciplinary proceedings.[144] It includes complaints of such conduct made to the IPCC by a complainant, where the complainant declines to give permission to the IPCC to pass the complaint on to the police.[145]

4.143    In certain situations, where a conduct matter comes to the attention of the police then it must be recorded[146] and is defined as a 'recordable conduct matter'. These situations are where:[147]

- it appears that the conduct has lead to death or serious injury[148] of a person;
- a member of the public has been adversely affected by it;
- it is in the category of cases where there would a mandatory referral to the IPCC if a complaint had been made;[149]
- there is grave or exceptional conduct which make it appropriate to record the matter;[150]
- the conduct matter has arisen in an actual or potential civil claim.[151]

4.144 In practice most of the serious cases involving deaths and serious injuries will start as a result of the referral of conduct matters rather than as complaints. This is because in these cases referrals will be made within hours of the incident by the police to the IPCC, sometimes before interested persons have even been told about it. The IPCC has an emergency telephone number which has been given to all police forces. It also has a rota of staff and commissioners for out of office hours to make decisions quickly and where necessary to attend a scene at any time.

143   Police Reform Act 2002 s12(7) for definition.
144   Police Reform Act 2002 s12(2).
145   Police Reform Act 2002 Sch 3 para 2(4).
146   Police Reform Act 2002 Sch 3 para 11.
147   Police Reform Act 2002 Sch 3 para 11(3).
148   Meaning a fracture, a deep cut, a deep laceration or an injury causing damage to an internal organ or the impairment of any bodily function: Police Reform Act 2002, s29.
149   Complaints Regs reg 5(1)(a)-(e).
150   Complaints Regs reg 5(1)(f).
151   Police Reform Act 2002 Sch 3 para 10.

4.145    Once a case has been referred and the IPCC has agreed to investigate, there may be little incentive for a potential complainant to make a complaint. However if the IPCC decides to supervise a conduct case and there is no complaint then the potential complainant will not have any appeal rights at the end of the investigation (see para 4.226). In most cases of this type, therefore, the potential complainant should be advised to make a complaint to enable him or her to have appeal rights at the end of the process. This is specifically included in the draft guidance.

4.146    The IPCC has the power to direct the police to record a matter which appears to it to be a recordable conduct matter which has not been recorded by the police.[152]

4.147    Once it has been decided to record a recordable conduct matter, there is a continuing duty to obtain and preserve evidence.[153]

4.148    Any recordable conduct matter must be referred to the IPCC if it falls within the same categories defined for the mandatory referral of complaints (see para 4.98)[154] within similar time limits as those imposed for referral of complaints (see para 4.112).[155]

4.149    There is a discretion to refer a recordable conduct matter to the IPCC on grounds of gravity or exceptional circumstances.[156] This can be exercised by the police authority even if the chief officer decides not to do so.[157]

4.150    Once a recordable conduct matter has been referred to the IPCC, then the IPCC must decide whether the matter needs to be investigated. If it decides not to investigate, the case is sent back to the police.[158]

4.151    If the police are not under a duty to refer a recordable conduct matter to the IPCC, or decide not to exercise their discretion to refer, or the IPCC has sent a matter back to the police, then there is a power for the police to deal with the matter in any way they may determine.[159] In many cases, of course, this will mean that nothing further is done, but if the police decide to take further management action or otherwise to review the action of officers, this will be open to them.

152    Police Reform Act 2002 Sch 3 para 11(5).
153    Police Reform Act 2002 Sch 3 para 12.
154    Police Reform Act 2002 Sch 3 para 13(1).
155    Complaints Regs reg 5(3).
156    Police Reform Act 2002 Sch 3 para 13(2) & (3).
157    Police Reform Act 2002 Sch 3 para 13(3).
158    Police Reform Act 2002 Sch 3 para 14.
159    Police Reform Act 2002 Sch 3 paras 10(4) and 11(3).

4.152    The Home Office states that the intention, so far as conduct matters arising in civil claims are concerned, is that 'all civil cases will be reviewed by forces at their outset and at their outcome to consider any criminal and disciplinary issues'.[160] Thus, officers are subject to possible disciplinary action whether the allegation appears in a complaint or a civil action. The Home Office view is that possible disciplinary investigation and action should be considered as soon as the conduct is notified at the start of the claim. It recognises that there may be difficulties if the claimant in the civil action decides not to co-operate with the complaints process until after the civil action has been completed.[161]

The IPCC draft guidance says that each force needs to have arrangements for identifying when civil claims give rise to conduct matters and these arrangements should be readily available to lawyers who act for claimants.

4.153    There is probably no right or wrong answer as to whether the claimant in a civil action should co-operate with an investigation triggered through the 'recordable conduct matter' mechanism. In some cases, a finding of misconduct will lead to a rapid settlement of the civil action. In others, it may be thought so unlikely that the investigation of the matter will lead to disciplinary action (for whatever reason) that the claimant decides not to co-operate with the investigation and to concentrate on the civil action.

## Disclosure

4.154    This issue is so central to the proper working of the complaints process that it is dealt with here in a section of its own rather than referring to it in piecemeal fashion throughout the text. Disclosure is the information provided by the investigation to the complainant at various stages of the process. It includes information disclosed during the investigation and information disclosed at the end of the investigation. In particular, as explained below, there has long been a feeling that for the public and the complainant to have any confidence in the complaints process, at least the investigators officer's report should be disclosed at the end of the complaint.

4.155    The consultation exercise carried out by the Home Office in 2000 confirmed that a lack of disclosure and openness is a major factor in

---

160   Home Office thematic paper No 2, May 2003.
161   Home Office thermatic paper No 2, May 2003.

the low public confidence in the complaints system. The requirements of the Human Rights Act 1998 add further weight to the need for openness in the process (especially where complaints involve arguable breaches of articles 2 and 3 of the European Convention on Human Rights (ECHR), and there is a duty to conduct an effective official investigation which includes the involvement of the complainant as one of its requisite factors.[162]

4.156    Under the PCA system there was a statutory presumption against disclosure[163] which the PCA often said left it feeling frustrated. However, the new IPCC system reverses that presumption in favour of disclosure to the complainant. The draft guidance states that 'the IPCC believes that making the police complaints system as open and transparent as possible would help to increase public confidence that complaints are handled fairly.'

4.157    The Police Reform Act 2002[164] requires that the IPCC or the appropriate authority (AA) must keep the complainant informed of certain decisions and actions if and when they happen throughout the process. These are as follows:[165]

- that an allegation has been brought to the AA's attention (notification) (IPCC or AA);
- that a matter is to be dealt with other than as a statutory complaint (AA);
- that a matter is not going to be recorded, why it is not going to be recorded and the complainant's right of appeal (AA);
- the outcome of a determination by the IPCC on a complainant's appeal against non-recording (IPCC);
- that a complaint has been referred to the IPCC (AA);
- that the IPCC has deemed that a complaint does not require investigation and has referred it back to the appropriate authority (IPCC);
- that an application to dispense with a complaint has been made (AA);
- the outcome of the dispensation application (IPCC);

---

162  See R (*Amin*) v SSHD [2004] 1 AC 653 and R (*Green*) v PCA [2004] 1 WLR 725.
163  Police Act 1996 s80.
164  Police Reform Act 2002 s20 and Sch 3.
165  The brackets show whether it is the responsibility of the IPCC or the AA (the chief officer unless the complaint is about a senior officer in which case it will be the police authority) to provide the relevant information. Where the brackets show the IPCC or the AA it will usually depend on the mode of investigation – independent, managed, supervised or local (see para 4.113).

- the outcome of an appeal made by a complainant against local resolution (IPCC);
- the progress of any investigation (IPCC or AA);
- the discontinuation of any investigation (IPCC);
- any provisional findings of the person carrying out the investigation (IPCC or AA);
- whether the investigation report has been finalised and submitted to the appropriate authority or IPCC (IPCC or AA);
- the findings of the investigation report (IPCC or AA);
- if criminal proceedings have been brought (IPCC or AA);
- whether the IPCC/AA has made recommendations/directions to the appropriate authority about action that should be taken (IPCC or AA);
- the complainant's right of appeal (AA);
- the IPCC's determination on a complainant's appeal (IPCC);
- whether there will be any disciplinary action (IPCC or AA);
- the outcome of any action taken as a result of the report (IPCC or AA).

## The rights to disclosure

### During the investigation

4.158    There is a duty on the IPCC and/or the police (depending on the type of investigation) to provide the complainant with information about the investigation 'to keep him properly informed', effectively limited to information about the progress of the investigation,[166] any provisional findings of the investigator,[167] and the decisions made subsequent to the investigation.[168]

4.159    The first notification of progress must be made within four weeks of the start of the investigation, and then at four-weekly intervals.[169] It is for the police (or the IPCC if it is conducting the investigation itself) to decide how frequently provisional findings should be provided in order to keep the complainant properly informed.[170] The implication here is that provisional findings can be disclosed as the investigation progresses.

---

166   Police Reform Act 2002 s20(4)(a).
167   Police Reform Act 2002, s20(4)(b).
168   Police Reform Act 2002, s20(4)(c)–(e).
169   Complaints Regs reg 11(1)(a) and (2)(a).
170   Complaints Regs reg 11(1)(b) and (2)(b).

4.160    The Home Office thematic paper on disclosure explains what complainants should expect under the IPCC system during the investigation:

> ... the complainant could be given or sent a full written explanation of how the investigation will be handled, outlining the process for disclosure of information and the appeal process which will cover the following aspects. The explanation would cover:
>
> (a) methodology of the investigation
> (b) periodic progress reports
> (c) addressing initial or emerging concerns
> (d) opportunities for face-to-face meetings

The paper goes on to consider that:

> Forces and the IPCC can also consider whether disclosure of other documents such as witness statements, other material evidence, cctv footage is required to keep people properly informed.

4.161    However, this last passage needs to be considered in the light of the restrictions set out below, and the comments of the House of Lords in *R (Green) v PCA*[171] about the undesirability of disclosing witness statements to complainants before decisions about criminal and disciplinary proceedings have been made. In this case a man who claimed that a police officer had run him over twice trying to kill him, asked the PCA to disclose to him witness statements gathered during the investigation to enable him to comment upon them prior to the conclusion of the investigation. It was claimed that the entitlement to see the documents was supported by ECHR articles 2 and 3 which required a complainant to be involved in investigations as part of the effective official investigation into complaints raising potential breaches of these articles. The House of Lords found, among other things, that the risk of contamination of evidence in criminal and disciplinary proceedings (for example, the complainant tailoring his or her evidence after having access to other witnesses' statements) would usually be too great to allow such disclosure. The IPCC's draft guidance suggests that disclosure prior to disciplinary hearings is much more likely than before criminal proceedings for a number of reasons including the professional nature of the adjudicators and the public interest.

4.162    Further, in *R v Roberts*,[172] the Court of Appeal indicated that disclosing video evidence after a witness had made an initial statement was

171    [2004] 1 WLR 725.
172    [1998] Crim LR 682.

a desirable practice, and complainants should expect to have such evidence disclosed during the investigation after an initial statement has been taken from the complainant.

### After the investigation

4.163 A complainant must also be informed, once the investigation has been completed, when the final report will be submitted and when the complainant will receive notification of the findings.[173] In carrying out these duties the IPCC and the police must consider whether a meeting with the complainant is appropriate and, if so, provide a written record of the meeting.[174]

4.164 There is a further duty imposed on the IPCC or the police to disclose to the complainant the 'findings' of the investigation report.[175] The police or the IPCC are empowered to discharge this last duty by disclosing a copy of the investigation report itself.[176] These provisions reverse the effect of the case of *Taylor v Anderton*[177] where 'class' public interest immunity was said to apply to investigating officers' reports, which effectively prevented their disclosure in all but the most exceptional cases.

4.165 This bar on the disclosure of the IO's report has been a source of much criticism in the past. The House of Commons Home Affairs Select Committee *Report on Police Disciplinary and Complaints Procedures* (16 December 1997) recommended that 'investigating officers' reports should be subject to disclosure on the same basis as other documents relating to the complaint'.[178] The Stephen Lawrence Inquiry Report (24 February 1999) recommended that:

> Investigating officers' reports resulting from police complaints should not attract public interests immunity as a class. They should be disclosed to complainants, subject only to a 'substantial harm' test for withholding disclosure.[179]

4.166 In support of this recommendation, the Report explained:

> 46.35 ... We consider that to make such reports available to complainants would be a helpful short-term step in building public confidence in the

---

173   Complaints Regs reg 11(3).
174   Complaints Regs reg 11(4) and (5).
175   Police Reform Act 2002 Sch 3 paras 23(10) & 24(8).
176   Police Reform Act 2002, Sch 3 paras 23(12) or 24(10).
177   [1995] 1 WLR 447.
178   Para 172 and recommendation 38 (HC 258–I, TSO, 1997).
179   Recommendation 10 (CM 4262–I, TSO, 1999).

complaints system, and would be in accord with the principle of ensuring the greatest degree of openness and accountability.

4.167    The IPCC's view as expressed in the draft guidance is that the general presumption should be that the IO's report should be disclosed in cases where the 'harm test' (see para 4.168) is satisfied.[180] There may be a number of police forces, however, wedded to the idea of restricting access to the report. It must be likely that this will be an issue upon which there will be litigation from the police forces reluctant to follow the guidance. The view of the IPCC is that any decision not to disclose part or all of an IO's report must be recorded with reasons, and of course such a decision by the police may be subject to an appeal to the IPCC (see para 4.227).

## The restrictions

4.168    The Home Secretary can make regulations for exceptions to the various duties to disclose information during the complaints process.[181] The power to make regulations is limited to the purpose of:

(a) preventing the premature or inappropriate disclosure of information that is relevant to, or may be used in, any actual or prospective criminal proceedings;

(b) preventing the disclosure of information in any circumstances in which it has been determined in accordance with the regulations that its non-disclosure:

(i)   is in the interests of national security;

(ii)  is for the purposes of the prevention or detection of crime, or the apprehension or prosecution of offenders;

(iii) is required on proportionality grounds; or

(iv)  is otherwise necessary in the public interest.

'Proportionality grounds' essentially refers to an adverse effect which would be disproportionate to the benefits arising from disclosure.

4.169    The regulations set out the exception to the full extent allowed by the Act,[182] to be exercised where in the opinion of the IPCC or the police it is 'necessary'. However, the IPCC and the police cannot conclude that a restriction on disclosure is 'necessary' unless there is a real risk that disclosure of the information will cause a significant adverse effect.[183]

180   See disclosure consultation paper at www.ipcc.gov.uk.

181   Police Reform Act 2002 s20(6).

182   Complaints Regs reg 12.

183   Complaints Regs reg 12(2).

4.170 The IPCC and the police must consider whether non-disclosure is justified in specific cases,[184] namely (i) information relevant to actual or prospective disciplinary proceedings; (ii) where disclosure of that information may lead to the contamination of the evidence of witnesses during disciplinary hearings; (iii) where third party health or safety may be prejudiced; and (iv) where the information 'constitutes criminal intelligence'.

## Disclosure to other parties

4.171 Certain interested parties have the right to be kept informed about the progress or the outcome of a complaint or conduct matter investigation.[185] The groups concerned are:

- a relative (spouse, partner, parent or adult child)[186] of a person who, it is alleged, has died from misconduct;
- a relative of a person who, it is alleged, has suffered serious injury as a result of misconduct and who is incapable of making a complaint;
- someone who themselves was seriously injured as a result of the misconduct;
- anyone else who the IPCC or the police decide has a sufficient interest to be kept informed.

4.172 Thus, the police and the IPCC have wide powers to ensure that relatives, victims and others (who may include friends, community organisations, MPs, etc) are kept fully informed about an investigation. The same considerations about openness and limited restrictions on disclosure as discussed above apply in relation to interested persons also. In all cases the person to whom it is proposed to disclose information must consent. Interested parties do not have the rights of appeal granted to complainants.

# Complaints which cannot or need not be investigated

4.173 The issue of the police not investigating complaints is a very sensitive one. Some complainants have certainly been pressurised into

---

184 Complaints Regs reg 12(3).
185 Police Reform Act 2002 s21.
186 Complaints Regs reg 13.

agreeing to withdraw a complaint, and the police are sometimes perceived as being in a hurry to apply to dispense with an investigation. There are now four situations in which the police may not have to begin or continue a complaint investigation, and each has its own procedure. The situation is complicated by the introduction of 'conduct matters' in the IPCC system (see para 4.142). Thus, even if a complainant wishes to withdraw a complaint, for example, or the police have grounds to dispense with an investigation, the IPCC will have the power to say that the investigation must continue as a 'conduct matter' rather than as a complaint.

4.174   The four situations dealt within this section are as follows:

- applications to the IPCC for permission to dispense with an investigation;
- discontinuing a complaints investigation after it has begun;
- dealing with complaints where the complainant fails to co-operate after a sub judice postponement;
- withdrawn complaints.

## Applications for dispensation

4.175   The police can apply to the IPCC for permission 'to handle the complaint in any manner' they think fit, rather than by investigating the complaint.[187] In effect, a successful application gives the police the right to dispense with an investigation. If the investigation has already begun then an application for discontinuance (see para 4.190) should be considered. The complainant must be informed by the police that such an application is being made.[188] This gives the complainant the opportunity to make representations to the IPCC as to why it should not grant permission to dispense with investigation (whether or not the requirements set out below are met). The draft guidance states that the IPCC will invite the complainant to provide their views within seven days.

4.176       The circumstances in which an application will be appropriate are as follows:[189]

(a) more than 12 months have elapsed between the incident, or the latest incident, giving rise to the complaint and the making of the complaint and either that no good reason for the delay has

---

187   Police Reform Act 2002 Sch 3 para 7(1).
188   Police Reform Act 2002 Sch 3 para 7(2).
189   Complaints Regs reg 3(2).

been shown or that injustice would be likely to be caused by the delay;

(b) the matter is already the subject of a complaint;

(c) the complaint discloses neither the name and address of the complainant nor that of any other interested person and it is not reasonably practicable to ascertain such a name or address;

(d) the complaint is vexatious, oppressive or otherwise an abuse of the procedures for dealing with complaints;

(e) the complaint is repetitious; or

(f) it is not reasonably practicable to complete the investigation of the complaint or any other procedures under Schedule 3 to the 2002 Act.[190]

4.177　There are further definitions as to what constitutes a repetitious complaint and the situations in which it is not reasonably practicable to complete an investigation of a complaint.

## Repetitious complaints

4.178　The following summarises the list of cases which can be considered as repetitious for the purposes of the police applying to dispense with an investigation:[191]

- the complaint is substantially the same as a previous complaint; and
- there are no fresh allegations which 'significantly affect the conduct complained about'; and
- no fresh evidence is tendered in support of it.

4.179　In addition, the previous complaint must have reached some kind of conclusion either by local resolution, a formal decision as to what action to take by the police, or because it has been withdrawn, or because investigation of the complaint had formally been dispensed with.[192]

## Not reasonably practicable to complete an investigation

4.180　This can be a ground for applying to the IPCC for dispensation by the police when it is not possible to contact the complainant or his or her representative, and/or the complainant has failed to give a statement or provide other reasonable assistance to the IO.[193]

---

190　Which sets out the detail of the complaints system.
191　Complaints Regs reg 3(3).
192　Complaints Regs reg 3(3).
193　Complaints Regs reg 3(4).

4.181    Sometimes complainants are reluctant to provide statements or assistance prior to the exchange of witness statements in a civil action relating to the officer's conduct. This may be a reason for persuading the IPCC not to grant the police's request. There will also be complaints where evidence other than that of the complainant will be more important and a statement from the complainant is not essential for completing an investigation (for example, if the complainant was knocked unconscious and did not see the source of the blow). In these cases the application for dispensation may not be granted.

4.182    There are also many cases where the complainant attempts to attach conditions to co-operation, such as relying on a statement prepared by a solicitor, refusing a face to face meeting with the police or only agreeing to a meeting at, say, a solicitor's office. The IPCC's emphasis in its current consultation document is that reasonable conditions should not lead to a dispensation application[194] and an explanation should be given to the police as to why any conditions are seen as unreasonable.

4.183    The lapse of time since the incident which led to the complaint can also justify an application for dispensation on the basis that it is not reasonably practicable to complete a satisfactory investigation. Thus, in some cases if essential evidence has been destroyed or lost before the investigation has begun, there may simply be no point in investigating the complaint.[195]

### Procedure

4.184    In practice the police have to send certain documentation to the IPCC with the application for a dispensation. This includes a copy of the complaint, the reasons for making the application and any other relevant material. If it is said that the complaint is repetitious then the previous complaint and a record of its outcome must be sent.[196]

4.185    If the complainant has had special difficulties affecting his or her ability to respond to requests for co-operation from the police (literacy, language, age, etc) then the police should notify the IPCC of these.

4.186    The police must also inform the complainant that an application for dispensation has been made.

---

194    Dispensations consultation, para 4.1.5.
195    Complaints Regs 3(4)(b)(ii).
196    Complaint Regs reg 3(6) and see appendix D of the draft guidance.

## The IPCC

4.187 The IPCC can call for further information from the police before making the decision to dispense with investigation of a complaint.[197] The draft guidance states that the IPCC will consider the attempts made to contact the complainant and any practical help required by the complainant before deciding whether to grant the request for dispensation. As only one application for dispensation can be made,[198] it may well be the case that the IPCC will consult with the police if they are 'minded' to refuse the application. The IPCC will also consider asking the complainant or interested parties for any views on the matter.[199]

4.188    The IPCC says it will ask the police force not to withdraw the regulation 9 notices served on the officer(s) complained about (see chapter 5) until it has confirmed that dispensation has been granted.[200] If a complaint is dispensed with because a previous complaint on the same matter has already been considered, the IPCC can direct that the new complainant should be provided with information from the previous complaint.

4.189    Both the police and the complainant should be informed of the result of the application. There is no right of appeal but judicial review of the decision can be considered (see para 17.67). It appears that the IPCC will have the power to revoke the dispensation and direct that the investigation continues if, for example, a complainant decided subsequently to co-operate with an investigation.[201] The High Court stated that officers complained about would not be prejudiced if this happened as there was a general interest in complaints being properly investigated.

## Discontinuation

4.190 Once an investigation has begun, circumstances may arise that mean it is impracticable for it to continue. Thus the IPCC has the power to order discontinuance of an investigation (whether on an application from the police or on its own motion) in certain cases, whether it is the police or the IPCC carrying out the investigation.[202]

---

197  Complaints Regs reg 3(7).
198  Police Reform Act 2002 Sch 3 para 7(7).
199  Dispensation consultation, para 4.5.2.
200  Dispensation consultation, para 3.4.
201  R (*Wilkinson*) v *Police Complaints Authority* [2004] EWHC 678.
202  Police Reform Act 2002 Sch 3 para 21(1).

4.191    The circumstances in which an investigation can be discontinued are any complaint or conduct matter:[205]

> (a) in which the complainant refuses to co-operate to the extent that the IPCC considers that it is not reasonably practicable to continue the investigation;
>
> (b) which the complainant has agreed may be subjected to local resolution;
>
> (c) which the [IPCC] considers is vexatious, oppressive or otherwise an abuse of the procedures for dealing with complaints or conduct matters;
>
> (d) which is repetitious, as defined in regulation 3(3) [see para 4.178]; or
>
> (e) which the [IPCC] otherwise considers is such as to make it not reasonably practicable to proceed with the investigation.

4.192    If the police apply to the IPCC to discontinue an investigation this must be done in writing and be accompanied by a copy of the complaint, a memorandum detailing the steps taken in the investigation so far and the reasons for discontinuing the application.[206] The police must send a copy of the application to the complainant on the day it is sent to the IPCC;[207] and must send the IPCC any further information requested.[208] If the police have not applied for discontinuance, the IPCC is not permitted to order it without consulting first with the police.[209]

4.193    As with the dispensation procedures, it would be good practice to seek the views of the police and the complainant before taking a final decision on discontinuance. If the IPCC decided to order discontinuance, then the police, the complainant and interested parties for the purposes of Police Reform Act 2002 s21 (see para 4.171) must be informed.

4.194    The IPCC can give directions to the police to bring the investigation to a close where it has ordered discontinuance.[210] The police can be directed to produce an investigation report (presumably rejecting the complaint) and take subsequent steps; close the complaint; subject the complaint to local resolution; or otherwise deal with the complaint

---

205   Complaints Regs reg 7(2).
206   Complaints Regs reg 7(4).
207   Complaints Regs reg 7(5).
208   Complaints Regs reg 7(5).
209   Complaints Regs reg 7(6).
210   Police Reform Act 2002 Sch 3 para 21(4).

as they think fit.[211] The IPCC has similar powers if it has been investigating the complaint itself.[212]

## Resumption of investigation after criminal proceedings

4.195 It has long been felt by the police that many complaints are falsely brought or are 'tactical'. This is often said to be the case where there are criminal charges against the complainant arising out of the same incident. Certainly, complainants may be discouraged from continuing with a complaint if they have been convicted themselves. It can often be the case that a complainant has run out of energy and determination to pursue a complaint once the criminal proceedings have come to an end, whatever the outcome. The IPCC system now puts the onus on the complainant to signal an intention to continue with a complaint once criminal proceedings have finished.

4.196 The background to this provision is as follows. A complaint investigation is often initially suspended if there are linked criminal proceedings against a complainant, and if, in the view of the IPCC or the police, the proceedings would be prejudiced.[213] For example, a complainant would have to provide the police with a statement setting out his or her version of events if an investigation continued, and the complainant may be able to argue that this would breach the sub judice rule in relation to the pending criminal case.

4.197 The IPCC can direct that, despite the potential prejudice to criminal proceedings, the investigation should continue if it is in the public interest[214] (although it must consult with the police before making such a direction)[215]. Thus, it may be that there is little dispute as to the facts and the complainant is happy to give a statement, and the public interest in having complaints speedily resolved might outweigh any potential prejudice to the criminal trial.

4.198 In cases where the complaint investigation is suspended and, after the resolution of criminal proceedings, the complainant has not indicated that he or she wants the investigation to be restarted, certain steps must be taken by the police or the IPCC.[216] Essentially, the views of the complainant must be sought. If these cannot be ascertained

---

211 Complaints Regs reg 7(7).
212 Complaints Regs reg 7(9).
213 Complaints Regs reg 16(1) & (2).
214 Complaints Regs reg 16(3).
215 Complaints Regs reg 16(4).
216 Complaints Regs reg 17(1).

and he or she does not respond within 21 days to a letter, or if the complainant does not want to continue with the complaint, then the IPCC or the police (whichever has been investigating the complaint) must decide whether it is in the public interest to treat the complaint as a 'recordable conduct matter' (see para 4.142).[217]

4.199    If it is decided to treat the complaint as a recordable conduct matter then it will be investigated (if possible) in the usual way. If it cannot, then the complaint will not continue.[218] Thus, in effect, if the police have been investigating a complaint in these circumstances, they are entitled to dispense with an investigation without applying to the IPCC and with no right of appeal. The Home Office view is that the IPCC will be able to ensure that the power is not being abused through its guardianship functions (see para 4.18).[219]

4.200    The officer complained about must be told the decision unless it would prejudice criminal or disciplinary proceedings, or be against the public interest.[220]

## Withdrawn complaints

4.201    The provisions about withdrawal of complaints contain a number of safeguards against abuse by the police, and offer the possibility that the complaint will continue to be investigated in any event and against the complainant's wishes.

4.202    A number of things happen when the complainant or his or her representative notifies the police or the IPCC that the complainant wishes to withdraw the complaint.

- First, the police or the IPCC must record the withdrawal, and if the withdrawal is sent to the IPCC then it must be copied to the police.[221]
- Second, if the police receive a withdrawal of a complaint which was 'referred' to the IPCC (and was not referred back) (see para 4.97), or if the complainant has an outstanding appeal, or where a complaint was initially made to the IPCC (who passed it on to the police), then the police must inform the IPCC that it has recorded the withdrawal. Otherwise, it does not need to do so.[222]

217    Complaints Regs reg 17(3) and (4).
218    Complaints Regs reg 17(5) and (6).
219    Home Office thematic paper on dispensations, August 2003.
220    Complaints Regs reg 17(7) and (8).
221    Complaints Regs reg 15(2).
222    Complaints Regs reg 15(3).

- Third, in cases which have been formally referred to the IPCC (and not referred back) the IPCC must decide whether it is in the public interest to treat the complaint as a 'recordable conduct matter', and if so then the investigation process continues to be applied.[223]
- Fourth, in all other cases where withdrawal has been notified the police must also make a decision whether to continue the investigation in the 'public interest'. However, if the police have been investigating the complaint on their own behalf and it is subject to an appeal, the IPCC has the power to direct that the an investigation should continue in the public interest even where the police have decided not to do so.[224]

4.203 There are sometimes difficulties if the complainant indicates orally that he or she does not wish to continue with a complaint. In these circumstances, the police must write to the complainant to ascertain his or her views. A 'nil response' after 21 days will be treated as a formal written withdrawal.[225] As this puts the onus on the complainant, advisers should be vigilant in ensuring that casual or ambiguous oral remarks are not misinterpreted by the police in such a way as to abuse the system.

4.204 The officer or civilian complained about must be kept informed of all the decisions taken as part of this process, unless criminal or disciplinary proceedings would be prejudiced or unless it would be contrary to the public interest to do so.[226]

# PCA and IPCC approaches to particular complaints' issues

4.205 In the third edition of this work, various reports of the PCA were summarised. These set out the views of the PCA on such issues as restraint techniques, handcuff application, police dogs, high speed pursuits, forcible entry techniques and demonstrations. There is no certainty that these policies will be adopted by the IPCC and most of them are no longer easily available, and so are not repeated here.[227] However, some PCA reports are still made available on the IPCC website and they are mentioned below.

223 Complaints Regs reg 15(5).
224 Complaints Regs reg 15 (4), (7) and (8).
225 Complaints Regs reg 15(9) and (10).
226 Complaints Regs reg 15(11) and (12).
227 See the third edition of this book, chapter 3.

## The role of alcohol in police-related deaths (March 2004)

4.206　This report, based on original research, suggested that vulnerable people, particularly those with gross alcohol intoxication, are not cared for adequately in police custody and that, when medical crises occur, police officers do not have the support, resources, skills or training to provide the emergency interventions required.

## A new report on stop and search complaints (24 March 2004)

4.207　This report studies complaints made in 2001–02 about stop and search matters, and considers the ethnicity of complainants and the outcomes of the complaints made.

## Investigating allegations of racially discriminatory behaviour (August 2003)

4.208　This document presents the PCA guidelines on investigating allegations of racially discriminatory behaviour, and offers practical help to police officers investigating such alleged behaviour. For complainants' advisers it is an especially useful document for ensuring that the investigating officer has followed the correct procedures for investigating such complaints.

## Safer restraint (June 2003)

4.209　This is a conference report on reducing the risks of restraint deaths. It also provides a list of the conference's strong recommendations both for preventing restraint-related deaths and for investigating such incidents when they do occur, 'in a way that is open, accountable and transparent and takes into account the feelings, responses and needs of the friends and families of the victims'.

## Alcoholic consumption and deaths in custody (February 2003)

4.210　A PCA research report entitled 'Sleeping it off' which looks at standards of supervision from custody officers and forensic medical examiners in eight custody suites and criticises levels of training and action taken.

## Firearms report 2003 (January 2003)

4.211 This report contains a review by the PCA of shootings by police in England and Wales 1998–2001, and concludes:

> There are a number of management, policy, tactical and training issues for the police forces and ACPO to address ... There would appear to be significant problems with command and management of some of the incidents, and there were several incidents where the methods employed would suggest a lack of strategic thinking or planning by both experienced firearms officers and by their commanders. Similarly, the use of proactive methods designed to generate an expeditious and timely conclusion may result in an increased risk of weapon discharges that forces may have to consider in the light of human rights legislation.

## Fatal pursuit (June 2002)

4.212 This report was commissioned because of the increasing numbers of fatal incidents arising from pursuit and other high-speed driving referred to the PCA. It stated:

> The key conclusion from the study is that the police continue to engage in too many pursuits/follows that endanger public safety and that the most effective way to reduce this is by increasing management control on the evolution of pursuits and reducing officer discretion about both initiating and continuing with pursuits. Forces may need to consider whether officers who pursue without control room permission, or who fail to adequately communicate risk, or who fail to pull over when instructed to call off a chase by the control room, should be at risk of being disciplined as a result.

## CS gas – increasing public safety (March 2000)

4.213 This report examines the use of CS gas by police officers and complaints about its use, and makes recommendations for training and research for the future.

# After the investigation

## The investigating officer's report

4.214 An investigation report must be completed by the investigating officer (IO) at the end of the investigation. The IPCC has produced consultation on the format of the report in an attempt to produce some uniformity between police forces and between IOs as to what should be in the report. It is likely that the report will be disclosed, at some point (see para 4.167) to complainants in most cases. This is one of the biggest changes between the IPCC and the PCA, as under the PCA 'class' public interest immunity applied to the IO's report, and it was almost never disclosed to the complainant (see para 4.164).

4.215    Once the report has been completed, if the complaint has been investigated by the police with no formal involvement from the IPCC then a copy of the report must be sent to the chief officer.[228] If the case has been supervised or managed by the IPCC, a copy of the report must be sent to the IPCC and the police.[229] If the IPCC is investigating the complaint its IO will submit the report to the IPCC[230] and the IPCC must also ensure that a copy of the report has been sent to the police.[231]

## Considering the report

4.216    At this stage consideration must be given to criminal and/or disciplinary proceedings which should be taken against the officer based on the IO's report.

4.217    The first stage is whether to refer the case to the Director of Public Prosecutions (DPP). In police-investigated and supervised cases this is the responsibility of the chief officer. For managed and IPCC-investigated cases the responsibility is that of the IPCC.

4.218    The IPCC/chief officer must consider whether the report indicates that a criminal offence *may* have been committed by the officer. If they do so consider, the case must be referred to the DPP with a copy of the report.[232] The DPP must notify the IPCC/chief officer of any action it is then proposed to take.[233] The IPCC/chief officer must inform the complainant and other interested persons if criminal prosecution against the officer will take place.[234] It does not seem that there is any duty on the IPCC or the police to inform a complainant either that the case will not be referred to the DPP, or that the DPP has decided not to take action, although the complainant should ask for this

228   Police Reform Act 2002 Sch 3 para 22(1).
229   Police Reform Act 2002 Sch 3 para 22(2).
230   Police Reform Act 2002 Sch 3 para 22(4).
231   Police Reform Act 2002 Sch 3 para 23(2).
232   Police Reform Act 2002 Sch 3 paras 23(2) and 24(2).
233   Police Reform Act 2002 Sch 3 para 23(3) and 24(3).
234   Police Reform Act 2002 Sch 3 paras 23(4) and (5), 24(4) and (5).

information to be provided. In practice, the DPP will write to inform the complainant if no action was to be taken against an officer.

4.219 Once all criminal proceedings have been completed or (more commonly) where the DPP decides not to prosecute an officer, or the IPCC/chief officer decides not to refer the case to the DPP in the first place, then the chief officer has to decide what further action to take.

4.220 In managed and IPCC-investigated cases, the IPCC must refer the case back to the chief officer for this decision to be taken.[235]

4.221 At this stage the procedure is different depending whether the complaint is managed/IPCC-investigated or supervised/police investigated.

4.222 In managed and IPCC-investigated cases, once the chief officer has decided whether disciplinary (or other) action is going to be taken, the IPCC must be informed of this decision along with reasons if it is decided not to bring disciplinary action against an officer.[236] The IPCC then has to decide whether the proposed (in)action is appropriate. If the IPCC decides that it is not then, effectively, the IPCC has the power to override the decision of the chief officer.

4.223 This is done by the IPCC exercising its power to recommend to the chief officer that disciplinary proceedings are brought or modified (to include other charges) against an officer. If the chief officer does not agree with the IPCC, then the IPCC has the power to direct that proceedings are brought, and to set out further directions to the chief officer. The IPCC's reasons for this must be presented to the chief officer in writing. The chief officer must comply with any directions given by the IPCC and keep the IPCC informed of any action taken.[237] The IPCC must keep the complainant and other interested parties informed of the various stages of this process.[238]

4.224 There is no right of appeal for the complainant against any of the decisions made in this process. However, upon deciding whether to make a recommendation to the chief officer the IPCC must also send a notification to the complainant and interested parties setting out the findings of the IO report and whether the chief officer has been recommended to take any action. The disclosure provisions detailed above (see para 4.154) apply to this notification. The IPCC is entitled to disclose the IO's report in fulfilling the duty to notify the

235  Police Reform Act 2002 Sch 3 para 23(6).
236  Police Reform Act 2002 Sch3 para 23(7).
237  Police Reform Act 2002 Sch 3 para 27.
238  Police Reform Act 2002 Sch 3 para 28.

complainant of the findings of the report (see para 4.164).[239] There is no right of appeal against the findings of the report, the information disclosed, or the steps it is proposed to take where the complaint has been investigated by the IPCC or managed by it.

4.225    There is a different process for police-investigated complaints. Once the possibility of criminal proceedings has been dealt with, the chief officer must decide what further action to take against the officer complained about, but then only has a duty to inform the complainant and other interested persons (not the IPCC) of the decision made.[240] The notification sent to the complainant must include the findings of the report, what action the chief officer is proposing to take and, importantly, the complainant's right to appeal. The chief officer is specifically empowered to disclose the IO's report as a means of informing the complainant of the findings of the report.[241] The process of disclosure is governed by the rules set out in Police Reform Act 2002 s20 and regulations.

## Appeals in police investigated and supervised cases

4.226    The lack of involvement of the IPCC in the decision-making process in 'local investigation' cases (under the PCA system a 'certificate of satisfaction' had to be issued at the end of the investigation), is rectified by the detailed right of appeal to the IPCC for the complainant at the end of the process. The IPCC's operational advice note has the following to say about the process:[242]

> As a replacement for the current PCA review, this right of appeal carries both strengths and weaknesses. The strength will be to underline police accountability for their own investigations and disciplinary proposals, and to give the police the opportunity to resolve the complaint at a local level by satisfying a complainant that the investigation has been thorough and that the outcome is fair. It also underlines the independence of the IPCC in carrying out a review. The weakness will be to raise complainant expectations, which may not be fulfilled.

---

239   Police Reform Act 2002 Sch 3 para 23(9)–(11).
240   Police Reform Act 2002 Sch 3 para 24(7).
241   Police Reform Act 2002 Sch 3 para 24(10).
242   The Appeal Functions of the IPCC, para 20.

4.227  There are three rights of appeal to the IPCC:[243]

- the complainant has not been provided with adequate information (by the police) about the findings of the investigation or disciplinary proposals;
- against the (police) findings of the investigation;
- against the (police) proposal to take action in respect of the complaint.

4.228  There is no threshold to be met before an appeal must be considered by the IPCC: mere dissatisfaction with the outcome from the police investigation will qualify as grounds for appeal, and the IPCC has no power to refuse to consider an appeal that is made within time, although it may decide not to uphold it.

4.229  Any appeal must be lodged within 28 days of the complainant being sent a notification of the determination made by the police as to what action to take on the basis of the IO's report[244] (although there is discretion to extend time where there are special circumstances). The appeal must be in writing and there is a standard form and guidance notes available on the IPCC website. The IPCC can accept an appeal which does not contain the information required on the form.[245]

4.230  Upon receipt of an appeal the IPCC can request information from the police about the decision-making process, and can require the police to provide it with a copy of the IO report.[246] It can seek information from any other person where necessary to dispose of the appeal.[247]

4.231  It appears that any appeal to the IPCC (about information, findings or action) will lead to the IPCC having to decide on all of the following:[248]

- whether the information provided is adequate;
- whether the findings of the investigation need to reconsidered; and
- whether the action proposed by the police is adequate.

4.232  If the information provided is, in the view of the IPCC, inadequate, then it can order the police to make further disclosure, subject to the

243  Police Reform Act 2002 Sch 3 para 25(2).
244  Complaints Regs reg 10.
245  Police Reform Act 2002 reg 10(4).
246  Police Reform Act 2002 Sch 3 para 25(3) and (4).
247  Complaints Regs reg 10(3).
248  Police Reform Act 2002 Sch 3 para 25(5).

disclosure provisions considered above.[249] As the policy of the IPCC is that the IO's report should normally be disclosed (see para 4.164), the police can expect a direction to disclose it if they have not done so already unless the 'harm' test is satisfied. In some circumstances it may also be appropriate to disclose some or all of the documentation upon which the IO's report is based.

4.233    If the IPCC decide that the findings of the report need to be reconsidered they can review the findings themselves or order a re-investigation of a complaint.[250] If the IPCC decides to review the findings itself it can, as a result of the review, either uphold the findings (in whole or in part) or give directions to the police as it sees fit for:

- the police carrying out their own review;
- providing information to the complainant;
- generally as to the handling of the matter.[251]

4.234    If the IPCC decides to direct a re-investigation of a complaint then the form of the re-investigation must be decided by the IPCC (see para 4.113 for the various options).

4.235    In relation to the action proposed by the police as a result of the complaint (for example, disciplinary proceedings) the IPCC can consider whether to make recommendations (and thereafter directions) to the police about this as a result of the appeal.[252] Generally, the IPCC must keep the chief officer, the complainant and the officer complained about informed of its determinations.[253]

## When are complaints upheld?

4.236    It is a peculiar aspect of the system (carried over from the PCA) that there is no provision in the IPCC scheme for a decision to be made whether to 'uphold' a complaint or not. Rather the system is organised to make decisions at various stages as to whether an officer should face criminal or disciplinary proceedings (the latter based on the Code of Conduct – see chapter 6).

4.237    As described above, the complainant will be notified if his or her complaint leads to criminal or disciplinary action taken by the CPS

249  Police Reform Act 2002 Sch 3 para 25(6) and (7).
250  Police Reform Act 2002 Sch 3 para 25(8).
251  Police Reform Act 2002 Sch 3 para 26(1).
252  Police Reform Act 2002 Sch 3 paras 25(9) and 27.
253  Police Reform Act 2002 Sch 3 paras 25(10)–(12) and 28.

or the police. If the police decline to take disciplinary action then it falls to the IPCC to decide whether to recommend disciplinary action or not. There are no statutory provisions to provide guidance as to how this discretion should be exercised by the IPCC. The approach adopted by the IPCC is similar to that adopted by the CPS in deciding whether to prosecute. In the case of the IPCC the decision is based on a judgment as to whether there are reasonable prospects that a tribunal would find the allegations against an officer proved on the relevant standard of proof, that is, on the balance of probabilities.

4.238    This would seem, on the face of it, to be a fairly low standard to reach. However, the approach taken by the PCA reflected the maxim followed in civil cases that the cogency of evidence required to satisfy the civil standard of proof was greater where the outcome of the complaint had serious consequences for the officer complained about. Sometimes the standard applied is described as requiring a high degree of probability before a serious allegation can be proved, in some cases coming so close to the criminal standard that any difference is hard to find. It is submitted that this is the wrong approach – the only test is whether the 'more probable than not' test has been reached. Explaining how this concept should work in *R v Secretary of State for the Home Department ex p Rehman*[254] Lord Hoffman said:

> It would need more cogent evidence to satisfy one that the creature seen walking in Regent's Park was more likely than not to have been a lioness than to be satisfied to the same standard of probability that it was an Alsatian. On this basis, cogent evidence is generally required to satisfy a civil tribunal that a person has been fraudulent or behaved in some other reprehensible manner. But the question is always whether the tribunal thinks it more probable than not.

4.239    However, there is nothing in the legislation which requires the IPCC to take the approach discussed in para 4.327 and so long as a decision to recommend or direct disciplinary proceedings is not perverse then it will be lawful.

---

254  [2003] 1 AC 153 194.

# CHAPTER 5

# Discipline procedures and criminal prosecutions

# Discipline procedures and criminal prosecutions

5.1     Disciplinary or criminal proceedings can arise whether or not a complaint is made by a member of the public. However, if a complaint is upheld, the police may take disciplinary proceedings against the officer or, if a criminal offence has been committed, the Director of Public Prosecution (DPP) may decide that a prosecution should be brought. In either case the complainant has a very limited role to play and members of the public have often complained that they are not provided with sufficient information about how the case is progressing. This chapter explains the various procedures involved when disciplinary and/or criminal proceedings are considered, together with the review and appeal processes. It also describes how, in exceptional cases, to bring a private prosecution.

## Police discipline

5.2     In 2002–2003 disciplinary and misconduct allegations were proved against 1,529 officers. As a result 115 officers were dismissed or required to resign. Nearly three quarters of those officers sanctioned for misconduct received written warnings.[1] In 202 discipline cases that arose from complaints in 2002–2003 at least one misconduct allegation was found proved.[2]

5.3     As well as statutory provisions referred to in this chapter, there is guidance issued by the Home Office entitled 'Guidance on Police Unsatisfactory Performance, Complaints and Misconduct Procedures' ('the guidance').[3] Those responsible for discipline procedures must take its provisions into account when discharging their functions. The guidance says that its provisions 'should not be departed from without good reason'.[4] A failure to have regard to the guidance during disciplinary proceedings can be raised during a review or an appeal (see para 5.90), and an explanation can be sought as to why this has

---

1   Police Complaints and Discipline 2002–2003, Home Office research bulletin 04/04.

2   Police Complaints and Discipline 2002–2003.

3   The guidance is issued pursuant to Police Act 1996 ss83 and 87 and is available at www.policereform.gov.uk. The version on the Home Office website at the time of writing is dated January 2003 and does not take into account the most recent changes to the system.

4   Guidance, Introduction. This is likely to be the approach taken by the court as well: see *R v Islington LBC ex p Rixon* [1997] ELR 66.

happened. The weight to be given to such a departure from the guidance will depend on the circumstances of the case, but any departure should not be detrimental to the correct outcome of the case against an officer.[5]

5.4    The police disciplinary system is, in theory, distinct from the complaints procedure. In practice, however, if a disciplinary matter arises as a result of a complaint, the one runs into the other almost imperceptibly. Most disciplinary matters do not arise from complaints; it is much more common for them to arise as the result of internal management by the police themselves. This may, in part, explain why the existing system often seems ill-suited to dealing with complaints from members of the public. Since the last edition of this book it has been sought to introduce major changes in the ethos behind disciplining police officers. These were summarised in a Home Office research report as follows:

- a reduction in the standard of proof at disciplinary hearings from 'beyond reasonable doubt' to the 'balance of probabilities';
- the introduction of tribunal panels to preside over proceedings;
- new fast-track procedures for cases with clear evidence of serious misconduct;
- a code of conduct setting out standards of behaviour expected from police officers;
- written warnings for dealing with less serious incidents of police misconduct; and
- separate procedures for dealing with poor performance outside the disciplinary process.[6]

5.5    However, the same report found that there was a widespread view within the police that the new procedures had had little impact in practical terms, and that the number of investigations and hearings leading to findings against officers had also not changed significantly. However, the research did find that the use of written warnings had increased substantially, and that they were seen as a useful compromise between words of advice to an officer and formal disciplinary proceedings.[7]

---

5  Guidance, Introduction.
6  Paul Quinton, *An evaluation of the new police misconduct procedures*, Home Office online report 10/03.
7  *An evaluation of the police misconduct procedures* pp ii-iii.

## The initial decision

5.6 Once an allegation of poor performance or misconduct is raised against an officer then a decision must be made how it should be dealt with. Where the allegation is raised as a result of a complaint then the procedure in chapter 4 must be followed, however serious the matter raised. The nature of the complaint may well determine whether the matter is subject to local resolution or formal investigation. Less serious complaints which are upheld may not be referred for formal disciplinary proceedings, but may result in the kinds of outcome more appropriate to poor performance procedures such as words of advice or further training.

5.7 This part of the chapter deals mainly with the disciplinary procedures once the initial decision has been made to deal with the case as a misconduct matter, or once the complaints procedure has led to the referral of a case for disciplinary proceedings. A short description of the unsatisfactory performance procedures is also included (see paras 5.104–5.110).

5.8 For there to be misconduct there must be a failure to meet the standard set out in the code of conduct. The current code of conduct is a statutory code and consists of the following:[8]

**Honesty and integrity**
1. It is of paramount importance that the public has faith in the honesty and integrity of police officers. Officers should therefore be open and truthful in their dealings; avoid being improperly beholden to any person or institution; and discharge their duties with integrity.

**Fairness and impartiality**
2. Police officers have a particular responsibility to act with fairness and impartiality in all their dealings with the public and their colleagues.

**Politeness and tolerance**
3. Officers should treat members of the public and colleagues with courtesy and respect, avoiding abusive or deriding attitudes or behaviour. In particular, officers must avoid: favouritism of an individual or group; all forms of harassment, victimisation or unreasonable discrimination; and overbearing conduct to a colleague, particularly to one junior in rank or service.

**Use of force and abuse of authority**
4. Officers must never knowingly use more force than is reasonable, nor should they abuse their authority.

---

8 Police (Conduct) Regulations 2004 SI No 645 (hereafter Conduct Regs) Sch 1.

### Performance of duties

5. Officers should be conscientious and diligent in the performance of their duties. Officers should attend work promptly when rostered for duty. If absent through sickness or injury, they should avoid activities likely to retard their return to duty.

### Lawful orders

6. The police service is a disciplined body. Unless there is good and sufficient cause to do otherwise, officers must obey all lawful orders and abide by the provisions of Police Regulations. Officers should support their colleagues in the execution of their lawful duties, and oppose any improper behaviour, reporting it where appropriate.

### Confidentiality

7. Information which comes into the possession of the police should be treated as confidential. It should not be used for personal benefit and nor should it be divulged to other parties except in the proper course of police duty. Similarly, officers should respect, as confidential, information about force policy and operations unless authorised to disclose it in the course of their duties.

### Criminal offences

8. Officers must report any proceedings for a criminal offence taken against them. Conviction of a criminal offence or the administration of a caution may of itself result in further action being taken.

### Property

9. Officers must exercise reasonable care to prevent loss or damage to property (excluding their own personal property but including police property).

### Sobriety

10. Whilst on duty officers must be sober. Officers should not consume alcohol when on duty unless specifically authorised to do so or it becomes necessary for the proper discharge of police duty.

### Appearance

11. Unless on duties which dictate otherwise, officers should always be well turned out, clean and tidy whilst on duty in uniform or in plain clothes.

### General conduct

12. Whether on or off duty, police officers should not behave in a way which is likely to bring discredit upon the police service.

5.9    The code has explanatory notes which include the following:

> This Code sets out the principles which guide police officers' conduct ... [I]t is important to note that any breach of the principles in this Code may result in action being taken by the organisation, which, in serious cases, could involve dismissal.

Police behaviour, whether on or off duty, affects public confidence in the police service ... Accordingly, any allegation of conduct which could, if proved, bring or be likely to bring discredit to the police service should be investigated in order to establish whether formal disciplinary action is appropriate ...

5.10 However, simply because there is a potential breach of the code of conduct does not necessarily mean, in a non-complaint matter, that there will be an investigation with a view to a misconduct hearing. The guidance makes it clear that a judgment must be made by line management officers as to whether the allegations are minor enough to be inquired into locally and dealt with by management approaches such as words of advice, training or further guidance.[9] It is also possible that a written warning could be given if the officer admits the conduct alleged (but formal proceedings will be instituted if an officer had two written warnings already).

5.11 While this approach is sensible for less serious breaches of the code, such as lateness for duty, it can be seen that the police have a wide area of discretion in non-complaint cases not to proceed by way of the formal misconduct proceedings.

5.12 The exercise of the discretion is made more complex given the wording of the new code of conduct, which has moved away from a description of specific offences as was previously the case and towards an expression of ethical standards. Research indicates that formulating charges within the code of conduct can be a tricky task for complaints and discipline departments who sometimes see the code as 'vague' or 'wishy-washy'.[10]

5.13 The guidance states that where it has been decided that a misconduct case needs to be investigated formally, responsibility for the investigation will normally be assumed by the complaints and discipline department of the force.[11] This department will also be in charge of complaints investigations carried out by the police themselves.

## Suspension

5.14 A chief officer (or the police authority in the case of senior officers) has power to suspend an officer if it appears that he or she might have committed a disciplinary or criminal offence.[12] However, the power to suspend an officer can only be exercised if the investigation would

9 Guidance paras 3.10–3.15.
10 *An evaluation of the new police misconduct procedures*, Home Office online report 10/03 p21.
11 Guidance para 3.16.
12 Conduct Regs reg 4(1).

otherwise be prejudiced or if the public interest (having regard to the nature of the matter being investigated) requires suspension.[13] The guidance suggests that the public interest test will only be met if the allegation is serious enough to warrant criminal proceedings or serious sanctions in disciplinary proceedings.[14] In *Coughlan v Chief Constable of Greater Manchester Police*[14a] it was held that it was unlawful for the police not to have regard to the guidance on this issue before lifting an officer's suspension. It is also suggested that suspension in serious cases can be used to prevent an officer retiring or resigning from the service before a disciplinary hearing takes place.[15] In 2002–2003, 30 officers resigned or retired while suspended before charges were preferred.[16]

5.15　　Senior officers have the added protection that the Independent Police Complaints Commission (IPCC) must generally approve their suspension[17] (although there is provision for immediate suspension in urgent cases).[18] The power to suspend (and to continue the suspension) exists, in effect, until such time as the disciplinary process comes to an end (or, in the case of senior officers, the IPCC decides otherwise).[19] An officer required to resign at the end of the disciplinary process, who has been suspended already, remains suspended during his or her notice period.[20]

5.16　　Officers are suspended with pay unless in custody or if their whereabouts are unknown.[21] It is not necessarily unlawful to prevent a suspended officer from attending Police Federation meetings in appropriate circumstances.[22]

## Fast track procedures

5.17　In almost all cases, the usual procedures set out below in this chapter will apply to police misconduct proceedings. However, in a small number of cases, and only exceptionally, it will be appropriate to use the

---

13　Conduct Regs reg 4(2).

14　Guidance para 3.18.

14a [2004] EWHC 2801 Admin

15　Guidance para 3.18.

16　Police Complaints and Discipline 2002–2003. Home Office research bulletin 04/04.

17　Conduct Regs reg 4(3) and (4).

18　Conduct Regs reg 5.

19　Conduct Regs reg 4(5) and (6).

20　Conduct Regs reg 4(7).

21　Guidance para 3.19.

22　*R v Chief Constable of North Wales ex p Hughes* [1991] ICR 180, CA (pre-Human Rights Act 1998).

fast track procedures.[23] They are designed to deal with cases of gross misconduct where an officer has been caught 'red-handed' committing a serious crime, either as a single incident (for instance, a serious assault) or, more likely, after a long-running inquiry which uncovers serious apparent wrongdoing by a police officer (for instance, corruption). Such cases are described as 'special cases'.

5.18      Each of the following criteria must be met for the fast track procedure to be applied.[24]

- The alleged breach of the code of conduct must be serious, criminal in nature such that, if the officer concerned was convicted, a period of imprisonment would be likely to result; and
- if proved, the conduct would be likely to attract a sanction of dismissal; and
- the evidence is sufficient without further evidence (such as oral witness testimony) to establish a breach of the code of conduct on the balance of probabilities; and
- it is in the public interest for the officer to be removed from the service as quickly as possible.

5.19   The effect of fast track procedures is to deal swiftly with an officer in advance of any criminal proceedings which may be brought in due course, and would normally expect to result in an officer's dismissal from the force. From the decision to put the case onto fast track, the guidance states that it is expected that the procedure will be completed within six weeks. In short, the usual misconduct proceedings are modified to allow this to happen.[25]

5.20      The misconduct 'hearing' is heard by the officer's chief officer[26] with a right of review by another chief officer[27] and, in due course, a right of appeal to a Police Appeals Tribunal (see para 5.98). Unlike standard track cases, there is no oral witness testimony at first hearings of fast track cases. Instead, there will be the initial written record of the report, allegation or complaint accompanied by supporting evidence which might typically be written statements, supported by photographs, video or audio tapes, computer records and documentary evidence such as bank statements. However, any appeal to a Police Appeals Tribunal, as in other cases, affords full rights to call witnesses.

---

23  See Conduct Regs reg 45 and Sch 2 for procedures, and Appendix to chapter 3 of the guidance.
24  Conduct Regs Sch 2 para 1.
25  Conduct Regs Sch 2.
26  Conduct Regs Sch 2 para 6.
27  Conduct Regs Sch 2 para 21.

5.21    Where a matter which meets the criteria for fast track has arisen from a complaint by a member of the public, the complainant will have the right to attend the fast track hearing. However, since the officer concerned will not be giving evidence, the complainant will have no right or opportunity to put questions to the officer concerned. This will need to be explained carefully to the complainant in advance of the hearing.

5.22    A case may be transferred from standard track to fast track, or from fast track to standard track, but on only one occasion either way. A decision to fast track may be made at any stage during an inquiry into a report, allegation or complaint. In some cases this will be simultaneous with a decision to lay a criminal charge and pass the file to the Crown Prosecution Service (CPS) for consideration of prosecution. In others, particularly during a long-running surveillance operation, the point may be reached where the criteria for fast track are met and it would clearly be right to invoke the procedure and lay a criminal charge, but those carrying out the investigation need to continue to gather evidence before submitting a file to the CPS.[28]

## Medical retirement

5.23    Every year a small but significant number of officers escape disciplinary action by retiring on medical grounds before the investigation has run its course. The Police Complaints Authority (PCA) reported:

> In a number of high-profile cases prior to the Authority being able to announce disciplinary proceedings we have been faced by a considerable volume of both early retirements and medical retirements which have removed officers from the scope of discipline ... The announcement in major cases of an exodus from the service, some leaving under privileged conditions, continues to damage the image of a service which should be seeking to ensure publicly either an acquittal or a penalty in discipline cases. Justice should not be seen to be denied. Yet the appearance for some is one of evasion.[29]

5.24    The PCA said it was particularly concerned about cases where officers have been judged unfit for further service but where there are no grounds for believing that they are unfit to face a disciplinary hearing.[30] However, if a chief officer decides that an officer could or should take medical retirement, it has been held that that decision

28  Guidance, Appendix to chapter 3.
29  PCA Annual Report 1992, p9.
30  PCA Annual Report 1993, p34.

takes effect immediately and cannot thereafter be postponed pending possible disciplinary proceedings.[31]

5.25    The issue was addressed by the Home Affairs Committee who drew attention to possible abuse by officers facing disciplinary proceedings.[32] However, the most recent research indicates that the new discipline procedures have not reduced the problem and that 'about half of those interviewed [in police complaints and discipline departments] stated that the procedural reforms had not restricted the ability of officers to avoid disciplinary action through sickness absence or ill-health retirement'.[33]

## Investigation

5.26    Where a complaint, report or allegation is received by a chief officer which indicates that an officer may have breached the code of conduct then he or she can appoint a supervising officer to supervise the investigation of the matter.[34] As described above, this will usually happen when it has been decided that a formal investigation must be carried out and the case has been referred to the complaints and discipline department of the force (para 5.13).

5.27    This does not apply if the IPCC is involved in investigating, managing or supervising a complaint or conduct matter investigation.[35]

5.28    A supervising officer must be at least the rank of superintendent, at least one rank higher than the officer to be investigated but in the same force, and not be an 'interested party' to the matter.[36]

5.29    There are detailed provisions as to who can be appointed by the supervising officer to investigate the case where the case is not being investigated as a formal complaint or conduct matter (see para 5.28 for the situation where it is). In summary the rules are as follows:

(a) the investigating officer (IO) should usually be in the same force as the investigated officer (although an IO can be requested from another force);

(b) the IO must be at least the rank of inspector, and at least the same rank as the officer investigated (but if the investigated

---

31  *R v Chief Constable of Northumbria Police ex p Charlton* (1994) *Times* 6 May.
32  Home Affairs Committee report 1998.
33  Paul Quinton, *An evaluation of the new misconduct procedures*, Home Office online report 10/03, p17.
34  Conduct Regs reg 7(1).
35  Conduct Regs reg 7(2).
36  Conduct Regs reg 7(3).

officer is a superintendent or chief superintendent then at least
of the rank of assistant chief constable or commander);

(c) IOs for cases involving senior officers will be appointed by the
police authority;

(d) IOs for cases involving senior officers shall not be the chief
officer of the force or serving in the same division of the senior
officer concerned.[37]

5.30   So far as an IO from another force is concerned, the guidance states that
matters such as the seriousness of the allegations, the seniority of
the officer concerned, the need to bring greater independence to the
investigation, and the level of publicity or public concern are all matters which should be taken into account. It is suggested that cases
alleging widespread malpractice or where a particular incident has
led to serious public concern may be especially appropriate for
investigation by an officer from another force with no recent contact
with the force in question.[38]

## Written notice to accused officer and subsequent statements

5.31   As soon as is practicable, the IO must notify the officer who is subject
to investigation of the report, allegation or complaint.[39] The written
notice, known as a 'regulation 9 notice', must inform the officer of a
number of matters:

(a) that there is to be an investigation;

(b) the nature of the complaint, report or allegation;

(c) that he or she is not obliged to say anything concerning the
matter, but 'that it may harm his defence if he does not mention
in writing or orally when questioned something which he later
relies on' in any subsequent disciplinary proceedings;[40]

(d) he or she may, if he or she so desires, make a written or oral
statement (such a statement may be used in any subsequent
disciplinary proceedings);

(e) of the right to seek advice from his or her staff association
(the Police Federation for most officers);

37  Conduct Regs reg 8.
38  Guidance, Annex A.
39  Conduct Regs reg 9.
40  Conduct Regs reg 9(a). This, together with Police Reform Act 2002 s36, brings
into force Criminal Justice and Public Order Act 1994 s34, in introducing a new
caution in line with criminal proceedings.

(f) that he or she has the right to be accompanied by another police officer to any meeting, interview or hearing.

5.32 It should be noted that the duty to give notice to the officer is subject to a proviso that any investigation of the matter should not be prejudiced by giving of notice.[41] Thus, it is possible for the IO to delay the giving of notice, and the guidance confirms this approach stating that any decision not to inform the officer should be kept under regular scrutiny.[42] The guidance notes that the IO may be called upon to justify any delay which the officer investigated claims has been prejudicial to him or her.[43]

5.33 Of course, if the allegation also amounts to a criminal offence, this will be investigated in the usual way, and there will be no obligation to give notice to the officer if this would impede the investigation.

5.34 Although an inference can be drawn if an officer raises a matter at a subsequent hearing which he or she could have raised when given the opportunity to give an account when served with a notice or interviewed as part of the investigation, the officer still has the right not to answer questions about the incident. Some officers do exercise this right. In the last edition of this book we hoped that reforms would mean that a refusal to give a full and accurate account of an incident should be capable of raising an inference casting doubt on the officer's conduct and fitness for service. However, this has not happened. In explanation the Home Office has said, somewhat unsatisfactorily that:

> The officer's duty to obey lawful orders and the power of management has to be balanced with a person's right not to incriminate themselves. It is not a question of allowing officers to say nothing but allowing them their right to choose to say nothing.[44]

5.35 The usual practice is that an officer who is being investigated will be interviewed by the IO under caution. The guidance states that the object is twofold: first, to provide the officer concerned with an opportunity to give his or her account of the matter, and second, to enable the officer to offer any explanatory detail which might serve to explain or defend the matter. The officer may not be compelled to answer any question put to him or her, and the interview should be tape recorded.[45]

41 Conduct Regs reg 9.
42 Guidance para 3.21.
43 Guidance Annex B.
44 Home Office thematic paper No 12, *Disciplinary arrangements for officers*, August 2003.
45 Guidance para 3.24.

The complaint or other matter under consideration will be put to the officer as a series of questions. It is usual for the investigated officer to be able to refer to his or her notebook of events during the interview. Complainants often see transcripts of these interviews if a civil action is subsequently brought against the police arising out of the same facts as the complaint. Although some interviews are clearly rigorously carried out by IOs, there is, in other interviews, an impression that the IO is simply going through the motions.

5.36    At any time during the investigation, if the IO thinks that the conditions are likely to apply for the 'special cases' procedure to be followed (see para 5.17) (essentially the procedure when an officer is caught red-handed having committed serious misconduct), then he or she must submit a statement to this effect and a written report on the investigation so far to the supervising officer (or in the case of senior officers, to the police authority). A decision must then be made whether to invoke the special cases procedure.[46]

## Action after investigation

5.37    Once the investigation has been completed, a number of 'safeguards', intended to ensure that the possibility of disciplinary or criminal proceedings is properly considered, come into play.

5.38    The IO must submit his or her report when it is completed:

(a) to the police authority for senior officers;
(b) to the supervising officer in other cases; or
(c) to the IPCC if it has been managing or supervising the investigation (in which case there is no supervising officer).[47]

The contents and form of the IO report are subject to guidance from the IPCC (see chapter 4).

5.39    In most cases the supervising officer (or police authority in the case of senior officers) has a discretion as to whether to refer the case for a hearing upon receipt of the IO's report.[48] However, in some circumstances referring the case for a hearing is mandatory if it is considered that the report reveals that the officer's conduct has fallen below the standards set out in the code of conduct. This is the case if the officer concerned has previously received two written warnings, and

---

46   Conduct Regs regs 10(2) and 11.
47   Conduct Regs reg 11.
48   Conduct Regs reg 11(1).

accepts in the present case that his or her conduct has not met the standard in the code of conduct.[49] Referral for a hearing is also mandatory where there has been a direction from the IPCC (see chapter 4), and where there is a duty to take action or to ensure that disciplinary proceedings are undertaken.[50]

5.40    In other cases a decision has to be made whether to refer the case for a formal misconduct hearing. The guidance sets out the matters that should be considered:[51]

> In deciding whether a hearing is required, it will be necessary to consider the seriousness of the possible failure to meet standards and whether there is any evidence that it arose, for example, through inadequate training or knowledge. Where an officer has declined to answer questions when being interviewed this in itself should not be considered as evidence of a possible failure to meet standards: the evidence available will need to be considered to be sufficient, in its own right, before a decision is taken to hold a formal hearing. Similarly, any misleading statement contained in a response by an officer to the notification of investigation, or in any written or oral statement made earlier, should not in itself normally be considered as evidence of a failure to meet standards. However, where such a misleading statement is of greater seriousness than the original conduct in question (for example, if it is intended as a means of falsely implicating another officer) it would be reasonable to take account of it in reaching any decisions regarding the officer's conduct.

5.41    Following consideration of the investigation report, it might be decided that a formal hearing was not required but that it would be more appropriate for the matter to be dealt with by the officer's line management, for example, by way of words of advice. There might also be cases, where the officer admitted the failure to meet the standards set out in the code of conduct, in which it would be appropriate for a written warning to be given to the officer. The guidance states that in a complaints case, the agreement of the PCA (now IPCC, of course) should be reached before an approach is made to the officer about accepting a written warning.[52]

5.42    If it is decided not to refer the case to a hearing then the officer concerned must be informed as soon as possible and the case will not

---

49   Conduct Regs reg 11(2)(b). Written warnings can only be administered if the officer accepts the allegations, a system criticised by the PCA in its 2002–2003 annual report at p19.

50   Conduct Regs reg 11(2)(a) and Police Reform Act 2002 Sch 3 para 27(2)(a).

51   Guidance para 3.31.

52   Guidance Annex C.

be referred to on the officer's person record.[53] A case may be withdrawn at any time before the hearing takes place.[54]

## The disciplinary decision and criminal proceedings

5.43  Disciplinary proceedings will usually be deferred pending any criminal proceedings unless there are exceptional circumstances,[55] and the criminal proceedings should not, in any event, be prejudiced by any disciplinary action.

5.44  Prior to 1999, an officer who had been convicted or acquitted of a criminal offence could not be charged with an offence against discipline which was in substance the same as the criminal offence (the so-called rule against double jeopardy).[56] However, the relevant provision was repealed from 1 April 1999[57] and the double jeopardy rule no longer exists in relation to disciplinary proceedings brought subsequent to criminal proceedings. That there is no common law rule of double jeopardy other than between courts of competent jurisdiction was confirmed in the case of *R (Redgrave) v Metropolitan Police Commissioner.*[58] However, this does not mean that where an officer has been acquitted of an offence, this is irrelevant to whether disciplinary charges should be laid against that officer. Simon Brown LJ specifically commended to disciplinary boards generally the following paragraph included in the 1999 Home Office Guidance on Police Unsatisfactory Performance, Complaints and Misconduct Procedures:[59]

> Where criminal proceedings have taken place for an offence arising out of the matter under investigation and those proceedings have resulted in the acquittal of an officer, that determination will be relevant to a decision on whether to discipline an officer: (a) where the conduct under investigation is in substance the same as the criminal charge so determined, and where the alleged failure is so serious and the likely sanction serious such that it would be reasonable to look for proof to a high degree of probability ... it will normally be unfair to institute disciplinary proceedings; or (b) where the conduct under investigation is not in substance the same as the criminal charge so determined, it may

---

53  Conduct Regs reg 11(3) and (7).
54  Conduct Regs reg 12.
55  Conduct Regs reg 6, and guidance, para 3.30.
56  Police and Criminal Evidence Act 1984 s104.
57  Police and Magistrates' Courts Act 1994 s93 and Sch 9 part I.
58  [2003] 1 WLR 1136.
59  Guidance para 3.32.

nevertheless be unfair to proceed where a matter essential to the proof of the misconduct was in issue in criminal proceedings and had been resolved in the officer's favour.

5.45 Thus, whether in fact the repeal of the double jeopardy rule will make much difference in practice must be open to question. Indeed, the final annual report of the PCA found that the Home Office guidance 'tended to undermine' parliamentary intention in repealing the double jeopardy rule and that no further disciplinary action had been taken in the 23 cases in 2002–2003 where an officer had been acquitted of criminal offences. The PCA concluded:

> We predict that police officers whose professionalism clearly needs to be judged by their employer against the code of conduct will continue to avoid such accountability whilst the presumption against disciplinary action remains so strongly reinforced by Home Office guidance.[60]

5.46 Where there are outstanding criminal proceedings against a complainant or other people involved in the complaint, then the usual practice is to wait until those proceedings are completed before investigating the complaint. However:

> There will be rare and exceptional occasions when the investigation into possible misconduct is taken forward while criminal proceedings are in progress. Where the investigation brings to light any material which is likely to assist a complainant or any other person in defending criminal proceedings, or which suggests that such proceedings are unsafe or ill-founded, the relevant material should immediately be drawn to the attention of the CPS (headquarters).[61]

5.47 In one case it was strongly suggested by the court that in such circumstances a representative of the CPS should attend the proceedings where the police officers complained about are to be witnesses in a future criminal case against the complainant, in order to gauge the strength of the evidence. It was suggested that any subsequent trial of the complainant might not be fair if this was not done.[62]

5.48 Disciplinary proceedings cannot be dismissed on the grounds that a complaint has only been made as a collateral attack on a criminal conviction of the complainant. Thus, where a complainant alleges that officers made false statements to secure his or her conviction, those statements can form the subject of disciplinary proceedings even though the complainant's criminal conviction still stands.

60 PCA Annual Report 2002–2003, pp16–17.
61 Guidance para 3.35.
62 *R (Melia) v Merseyside Police* [2003] EWHC 1121 Admin.

## Probationers

5.49   Quite apart from the discipline procedures, a chief officer can discharge a probationer constable at any time if he or she considers that the probationer is not fitted, physically or mentally, to perform the duties of his or her office, or that he or she is not likely to become an efficient or well-conducted constable. However, this procedure should not be used as an alternative means of dismissing a probationer where disciplinary proceedings should properly be brought. It is an unlawful breach of the duty of fairness to discharge a probationer without the opportunity of a hearing where the allegations against him or her would support disciplinary proceedings.[63]

## Special constables

5.50   As under the complaints procedure (see chapter 4), special constables are now dealt with as if they are regular police officers and the disciplinary procedures apply to them accordingly.[64] Any differences in the application of the procedures to special constables are referred to in the text.

## Police officers acting in a group

5.51   There are sometimes allegations that a complainant has suffered misconduct, such as assault, at the hands of one or more of a group of officers, but that the complainant is unable to identify the actual member or members of the group. This was previously thought to be an insurmountable obstacle to successful disciplinary proceedings. However, the PCA concluded that provided there was strong evidence of the complainant having been assaulted by someone and strong evidence of the presence of the group during the assault, there were two practicable courses of action, first to charge the entire group jointly with assault, or second, to choose other appropriate headings from the code of conduct to address the failures of officers to prevent the assault or to fail to report it.[65] It is submitted that this is the approach that should still be taken by the IPCC when guidance is issued.

---

63   *Chief Constable of North Wales Police v Evans* [1982] 1 WLR 1155, HL; *R v Chief Constable of West Midlands Police ex p Carroll* (1994) 7 Admin LR 45, CA.

64   Conduct Regs reg 3(2).

65   PCA Annual Report 1987, para 2.15.

5.52      If the case concerns a senior officer who admits that his conduct did not meet that set by the code of conduct then the police authority has a degree of discretion how to proceed. It can proceed to impose a sanction as described below (see para 5.87) or otherwise in its discretion. It can decide not to take any action, or it can decide to refer the case for a hearing in any event.

5.53      If the senior officer does not accept that his or her conduct was deficient then, if the police authority does not agree, the case must be referred for a hearing, unless the authority is satisfied that, even if proved, the alleged conduct would not justify one of the sanctions set out below. If this is the case then the authority can use its discretion as to how to deal with the case. Presumably, this means that the senior officer could still receive an admonishment or advice about his or her conduct. [66]

## Delay

5.54   A Joint Statement of Intent on delays was agreed by the PCA, the CPS and the Association of Chief Police Officers (ACPO) in 1992. The target within which disciplinary hearings should be arranged is four months from the decision to bring proceedings, and in all cases within six months, unless the circumstances are wholly exceptional. The statement provides that while 'every effort will be made to meet the accused officer's wishes, a hearing will not be unreasonably delayed because of the inability of a particular friend or counsel to attend'.

5.55   The most recent research states that early data from the new system shows that 'the average timescale between the regulation notice being served and the conclusion of the hearing fell from 301 days under the old discipline procedures to 190 days under the new misconduct procedures'. However, the same research reports that complaints and discipline staff 'were negative about the impact of the new misconduct procedures on reducing delays in the system'. [67]

5.56   A delay in holding a hearing can result in an application being made that because of the passage of time it would be an abuse of process and contrary to natural justice for the officer to face disciplinary proceedings. A chief officer's refusal to discontinue proceedings on the grounds of prejudicial delay can be quashed by judicial review. [68]

---

66  Conduct Regs reg 13.
67  Paul Quinton, *An evaluation of the new police misconduct procedures*, Home Office online report 10/03 p16.
68  *R v Chief Constable of Merseyside Police ex p Merrill* [1989] 1 WLR 1077, CA.

It has even been held, exceptionally, that judicial review may be available to quash a decision to find disciplinary charges proved against officers after a two-year delay in serving what is now a reg 9 notice (see para 5.31), even though the officers had exercised their statutory right of appeal.[69] However, other than in exceptional circumstances, the courts ought not to exercise their discretion to grant judicial review until the statutory appeals process has been exhausted. Since the issue is one of delay, to entertain applications for judicial review in advance of the appeals process is simply to delay further the hearing of the case. A disciplinary tribunal should make its own decisions on matters such as delay, and any review of such a decision should generally be made through the appeal process.[70]

5.57　　A chief officer will not be liable in damages for an unreasonable delay (for example, in respect of loss of overtime payments or damage to reputation), either in negligence, breach of statutory duty or misfeasance in a public office.[71]

## Procedure

5.58　　For all officers, once a decision has been made to refer a case for a hearing then the officer must be notified within 14 days of this decision and of the conduct alleged not to meet the code of conduct and the paragraph number(s) relevant to the case. Senior officers must be informed by an independent solicitor. At least 21 days before the hearing the officer must be served with all the relevant documents in the case against him or her.[72] It is only if a case has been referred for a hearing that one of the sanctions set out below (para 5.87) can be imposed on an officer.[73] Other measures such as words of advice do not carry this requirement.

5.59　　All officers must be given at least 21 days' notice of the hearing. However, the hearing may be heard within the 21-day period if the officer is serving a prison sentence or has received a suspended sentence, or elects not to be legally represented.[74]

---

69　*R v Chief Constable of Merseyside Police ex p Calveley* [1986] QB 424.

70　*R v Police Complaints Authority ex p Wells* [1991] COD 95.

71　*Calveley v Chief Constable of Merseyside* [1989] AC 1228, HL.

72　Conduct Regs reg 14.

73　Conduct Regs reg 15.

74　Conduct Regs reg 16.

5.60     The officer so served is invited, within 14 days, to state whether the alleged conduct is admitted and provide details of witnesses to be called. The attendance of police officers at the hearing as witnesses can be enforced.[75]

5.61     If an officer, other than a senior officer, accepts the allegations made against him or her then a summary of the facts will be prepared and served on the officer (about which the officer concerned has the chance to make representations).[76]

5.62     So far as the officers conducting the hearing are concerned, they are provided with the notice of hearing and, if the officer admits the offence, the prepared summary of facts and the officer's response.[77] It does not seem that they have the statutory right to see any other documentation, although they must have access to the important factual documents as well in practice.

## Misconduct hearings

### Who hears the case?

5.63     Disciplinary hearings are heard by three persons appointed by the chief constable for a particular force. Where a disciplinary tribunal hearing arises from a complaint or conduct matter (see chapter 4) the following rules apply for officers who have been complained about who are not senior officers:[78]

- the presiding officer must be at least the rank of assistant chief constable (or at least a commander, in the metropolitan and City of London forces);
- a second officer on the tribunal must be at least the rank of superintendent (unless the officer complained about is a superintendent or chief superintendent in which case the second officer must be at least an assistant chief constable or commander) and a member of the same force as the officer complained about;
- the third member must be appointed from a list of candidates maintained by the police authority concerned.

75   Conduct Regs reg 18.
76   Conduct Regs reg 21.
77   Conduct Regs reg 22
78   Conduct Regs reg 19.

5.64    As to this last point, there appear to be no provisions to prevent the persons on the list of candidates being serving or retired police officers. Conversely, there is nothing to prevent them being ordinary members of the public. In fact the Association of Police Authorities has drawn up guidance for police authorities on appointing people to the list. While recognising the breadth of the discretion for membership, the guidance makes it clear that serving and retired officers should not be on the list. The guidance advocates advertising vacancies on the list and aiming for a diverse range of members so long as the necessary skills and experience needed to sit on the panel are present.[79]

5.65    If the disciplinary hearing concerns a senior officer (that is, one over the rank of chief superintendent)[80] then the hearing is conducted by a person chosen by the police authority from a list maintained by the Lord Chancellor, assisted on police matters by an assessor who is, or has, been a chief constable of a different force to the senior officer complained about (to be appointed by the police authority with the approval of the tribunal, and subject to a number of other conditions).[81]

## Who presents the case?

5.66    Under the previous regime, in any case where the chief officer initially decided not to bring a disciplinary charge and had done so only because the PCA had recommended or directed that he or she do so, the charge had to be heard by a tribunal, usually consisting of the chief officer and two members of the PCA. This rule has now been repealed (the PCA having said it was uncomfortable with its dual role of prosecutor and judge) and in the same circumstances the IPCC now has the power to present the case against the officer complained about, either itself or through a solicitor or counsel if it has directed that proceedings should be brought.[82] This power deals with a further complaint sometimes made by the PCA that some cases are not presented with the force and clarity that it would have expected.

5.67    In other cases, the supervising officer must appoint a member of the police force to present the case, but has the power to instruct an

---

79  'Guidance to police authorities on the establishment of lists of independent people to sit on misconduct panels' December 2003. See Association of Police Authorities website for contact details: www.apa.police.uk.

80  See Police Reform Act 2002 s29.

81  Conduct Regs reg 20.

82  Conduct Regs reg 25.

83  Conduct Regs reg 23.

independent solicitor or counsel if the officer is legally represented.[83] The case must be presented by an independent solicitor if the officer complained about is a senior officer.[84]

## Legal representation for officers

5.68    The officer complained about has the right to elect to have legal representation at the tribunal if the supervising officer is of the view that the tribunal should have available to it the sanctions of dismissal, requirement to resign or reduction in rank, and the officer complained about must be given notice of this right when given notice that the case is to be referred to a tribunal.[85] If the officer is a senior officer he or she must be given similar notice by the police authority if dismissal or requirement to resign may be an option.[86]

5.69    Police Federation funds are available for legal representation (or from ACPO for officers over the rank of superintendent), but officers are not given the opportunity of representation automatically, and it is for the supervising officer to decide whether to offer the opportunity to be legally represented. If the officer responsible for formulating the charge underestimates the seriousness of the case, whether blamelessly or otherwise, and does not allow the accused the opportunity of legal representation, the tribunal would be prevented from imposing any punishment more serious than a reduction in pay. To deal with this potential problem, the presiding officer has the power to remit the case for another hearing if it appears that it would be appropriate to have available the more serious penalties if the officer is found guilty, to give the officer the opportunity to obtain legal representation.[87]

5.70    If the officer complained about does not give notice that he or she wishes to be legally represented then he or she can only be represented by a member of the same police force.[88] This restriction does not apply to senior officers who can be legally represented whether or not notice has been given.[89]

## Hearing in private or public?

5.71    The general rule is that the hearing will be in private, with rights for certain persons (see below) to attend. As a result the process gives the

84   Conduct Regs reg 24.
85   Conduct Regs reg 17.
86   Conduct Regs reg. 17
87   Conduct Regs reg 33.
88   Police Act 1996 s84(3).
89   Conduct Regs reg 24(3).

appearance of being shrouded in mystery, which detracts from the credibility of the system. Partly as a result of this, the regulations now include circumstances in which the case will be heard, wholly or in part, in public. Thus, where the case arises from a complaint or conduct matter, and the IPCC has investigated the matter itself, the IPCC then has power to direct that all or part of the hearing will be in public because of the gravity of the matter or other exceptional circumstances, where it would be in the public interest to do so. The IPCC must consult with most of the parties involved before making this decision.[90]

5.72    There is no reason why complainants and those advising them should not seek to persuade the IPCC to exercise this power, although the width of the discretion given to the IPCC would make it difficult for any refusal to be challenged by way of judicial review (see chapter 17).

## Attendance of the officer complained about

5.73    The procedure is designed to ensure that the hearing can go ahead even if the officer complained about is not present. Thus, although the officer will be ordered to attend the hearing, if he or she fails to attend then the hearing can proceed and be concluded in his or her absence.[91] There is power to adjourn if the officer informs the tribunal in advance of ill-health or other unavoidable reason for absence, but equally the tribunal is empowered to dispense with any procedure which requires the officer's presence.[92]

## Attendance of complainant, 'interested persons' and others

5.74    If a disciplinary hearing arises from a complaint or conduct matter, the complainant and/or interested persons (see chapter 4 and Police Reform Act 2002 s21(5) for definition) are allowed to attend the hearing 'up to and including the point at which the hearing decides whether the conduct of the officer concerned' met the code of conduct (see para 5.8).[93] However, if the complainant or interested person is to be a witness then he or she cannot attend the hearing before giving evidence.

---

90  Conduct Regs reg 30(5).
91  Conduct Regs reg 28.
92  Conduct Regs reg 28
93  Conduct Regs reg 29(1).

It does not appear that there is any provision for the complainant or interested person to stay to hear what punishment (if any) is given to the officer if his or her conduct did not meet the code of conduct.

5.75    The complainant or interested person can be accompanied by up to three persons at the hearing.[94] The regulations do not appear to limit who these persons may be. The previous regulations allowed a 'friend or relative' to accompany the complainant (at the discretion of the presiding officer).[95] The regulations also allowed a solicitor to attend, subject to the consent of all the parties.[96] In one case, it was found that a solicitor who had been refused permission to attend under the latter provision, could not then claim to be the complainant's 'friend' under the former.[97] There now seems to be nothing prohibiting a solicitor accompanying a complainant, although of course he or she will not be able to represent the complainant.

5.76    If the accused officer gives evidence, the complainant or interested person may, after any cross-examination, put his or her own questions (so long as they could have been properly put by the presenting officer) either through the presiding officer or, at that officer's discretion, directly.[98] In effect, this gives the complainant a valuable opportunity to cross-examine the accused officer about the incident and to draw out any inconsistencies in the officer's evidence. It is, therefore, helpful to make a detailed note of the evidence presented to the hearing as a reminder of the points which are open to challenge. Effective cross-examination of the accused may have a real influence on the final decision. However, there is no point in cross-examining an officer if the presenting officer has already done the job satisfactorily.

5.77    Members of the IPCC are entitled to attend the hearing in cases involving complaints or conduct matters. The officer complained about can be accompanied by a fellow officer and his or her spouse/partner at the tribunal's discretion. Witnesses can also be accompanied by a friend at the tribunal's discretion.[99]

5.78    The tribunal can impose conditions relating to the attendance of any person permitted to attend. The complainant should be careful not to intervene or interrupt without the permission of the officer conducting the hearing. If he or she (or anyone else permitted to attend)

94  Conduct Regs reg 29(3).
95  Police (Conduct) Regulations 1999 SI No 730, reg 25.
96  Police (Conduct) Regulations 1999 reg 26.
97  *R (Melia) v Merseyside Police* [2003] EWHC 1121 Admin.
98  Conduct Regs reg 29(5).
99  Conduct Regs reg 30(2)–(4).

behaves in a disorderly or abusive manner or otherwise misconducts him/herself, he or she can be excluded from the rest of the hearing.[100]

5.79    In addition, the tribunal can exclude people otherwise entitled or allowed to attend, including the complainant, from part of the hearing if a witness may give evidence which in the public interest should not be disclosed to the public. This, might apply to information about informers or undercover operations, for example.[101]

## Procedure at the hearing

5.80    The people who may be present during some or all of the hearing, if it is not held in public, are described above. They will include the tribunal members (or the presiding officer and assessor in the case of senior officers), the officer complained about, a presenting officer, witnesses, the complainant, lawyers and representatives, and people accompanying the officer, the complainant and the witnesses.

5.81    The tribunal is largely able to determine its own procedure. Its job is to review the facts and decide whether there has been a failure to meet the standard set out in the code of conduct. Any legal issues should be resolved at the start of the hearing.[102] In practice, if the officer contests the charges, the presenting officer or lawyer will call his or her witnesses first of all, who will be examined in chief and then cross-examined; and then the accused officer will call his or her witnesses. Both sides will make closing submissions to the tribunal. It is up to the tribunal to decide whether evidence is admissible and what questions can be asked.[103] New documents not served on the accused officer can only be adduced in evidence if that officer consents.[104]

5.82    If the officer admits the charges then the tribunal may dispose with the need to call witnesses as to the facts.[105] The complainant should be permitted to attend to hear the presenting officer outline the case and for the tribunal to make its formal finding.

5.83    The purpose of the hearing is to decide whether the officer has breached the code of conduct. A decision that there has been a breach of the standards in the code of conduct can only be reached where the

100   Conduct Regs reg 30(7).
101   Conduct Regs reg 31.
102   Guidance para 3.58.
103   Guidance Annex F.
104   Conduct Regs reg 32.
105   Guidance para 3.61.

officer complained about admits the misconduct alleged, or where the presenting officer proves on the balance of probabilities that there has been a failure to meet that standard.

5.84 Until 1999 the case had to be proved on the criminal standard of proof, namely beyond reasonable doubt. The PCA and the Royal Commission on Criminal Justice both recommended that the criminal standard of proof for discipline cases was too high and was bringing the discipline system into disrepute. Although this has now been replaced by the civil standard of proof, there is authority for the proposition that the more serious the allegations made, the more cogent the evidence needs to be to satisfy the civil standard. However, it is noted that this cannot mean that, in effect, the criminal standard is reintroduced by the back door: the case still only needs to be proved on the balance of probabilities (see chapter 4).

5.85 When considering the evidence of the accused officer, the tribunal is entitled to draw inferences from any matter which is raised in the officer's defence, which could have been (but was not) raised by the officer when he made a statement upon being served with the reg 9 notice (see para 5.31) or in response to questioning from the IO.[106]

## Where there has been a breach of the code of conduct

5.86 If the tribunal concludes that the standards in the code of conduct have not been met then it must decide whether to impose a sanction on the officer, and if so, what.[107] For senior officers, the tribunal has an advisory role only and provides to the police authority its opinion as to what sanction should be imposed.[108]

5.87 For officers other than senior officers, if a charge is found proved, the tribunal may impose one of the following sanctions:[109]

- dismissal from the force;
- a requirement that he or she resign from the force;
- reduction in rank;
- a fine;
- a reprimand;
- a caution;
- in the case of a special constable only, suspension for a period of up to three months.

106  Conduct Regs reg 27(4) and (5).
107  Conduct Regs reg 27(7).
108  Conduct Regs reg 27(8).
109  Conduct Regs reg 35.

5.88    For senior officers, the police authority can either dismiss the case, record the breach of the code of conduct (if there has been one), or decide to impose one of the sanctions listed above (other than a reduction in rank or a caution).[110]

5.89    In 2002–2003, 44 officers were dismissed and 71 officers were required to resign; 18 received a reduction in rank; 169 were fined; 58 were reprimanded; 42 were cautioned and seven received no sanction even though a misconduct allegation was proved. 1,120 received a written warning (only possible where a misconduct charge is admitted).[111]

## Chief constable's review

5.90    An officer (other than a senior officer) has a right to request a review of any misconduct hearing where a sanction has been imposed or where there has simply been a finding of misconduct without the imposition of a sanction.[112] The review is carried out by the chief constable (or in some cases by another senior officer).[113]

5.91    The chief constable has the power to confirm or overturn the outcome and/or the sanction imposed by the tribunal and can impose a different (but not more serious) sanction.[114]

5.92    Although the guidance states that the review provides the chief constable with an opportunity to take quick action to rectify clear errors and inconsistencies in process or determination by the earlier hearing,[115] there is no formal restriction in the regulations for these purposes.

5.93    The review can take place in the absence of the officer requesting it, but he or she has the right to insist on a personal hearing where he or she can be represented.[116]

5.94    The chief constable will have the grounds for requesting the review, and an account of the tribunal's decision from the presiding officer. Although the review is not meant to be a rehearing, the chief constable can ask questions of the officer and has the power to invite any other person to attend the hearing.[117] Presumably, this could include key witnesses and could include the complainant.

110    Conduct Regs reg 35(2) and (3).
111    Police and Complaints and Discipline 2002–2003, Home Office research bulletin 04/04
112    Conduct Regs reg 40.
113    Conduct Regs reg 43.
114    Conduct Regs reg 42(2).
115    Guidance para 4.2.
116    Conduct Regs reg 41.
117    Guidance paras 4.8–4.9.

5.95 Other than this possibility, the review procedure is one upon which a complainant will have little influence. There appears to be no provision for the complainant to be told that the review procedure has been invoked or of its outcome. The chief constable has the power simply to reverse the findings of the tribunal without having had the benefit of hearing the evidence. Even if the original hearing has been held in public (see para 5.71 above), the review will take place behind closed doors.

5.96 The IPCC role is equally limited. Even if the original proceedings were brought at the IPCC's direction, it does not have to be consulted about the chief constable's decision on review, although it does have to be notified of the decision and be provided with a written copy of reasons.[118] The only possible remedy for the complainant or the IPCC if they disagree with the decision on review is an application for judicial review. The chief constable must keep a record of proceedings and findings.[119]

5.97 Where the review decision is that an officer is dismissed, required to resign or reduced in rank, he or she must be informed of the right to appeal to a Police Appeals Tribunal.[120] Unless the officer has been through the review procedure or if a lesser sanction has been imposed, there is no right to appeal.

## Police Appeals Tribunal

5.98 An officer has the right to appeal in circumstances as described above. The appeal is to a Police Appeals Tribunal arranged by the local police authority. The tribunal is set up by statute and consists of three members, including a legally qualified chairperson from a list kept by the Lord Chancellor. For senior officers there must also be an Inspector of Constabulary or ex-Metropolitan Commissioner and a member of another police authority. For other officers a member of their police authority, a former or current chief officer (other than from the force in question) and a retired officer of appropriate rank must be appointed.[121]

5.99 There are procedural rules which set out time limits for the various stages before a hearing.[122] These provide for exchange of documents and

---

118 Conduct Regs reg 42(5).
119 Conduct Regs reg 44.
120 Conduct Regs reg 42(4).
121 Police Act 1996 Sch 6.
122 Police Appeals Tribunals Rules 1999 SI No 818 (hereafter Appeals Rules).

grounds between the appellant officer and the respondent force.[123]
The hearing is essentially a rehearing of the evidence with similar
rules to the original disciplinary hearing. Thus from a complainant's
point of view the following factors are important:

(a) he or she must be provided with 28 days' notice of the hearing
(although there is no requirement to be notified or to attend if
the appeal is against sanction only);[124]

(b) the hearing will be in private, although the tribunal has a discretion to allow any person to attend the hearing (this could,
in theory, include a solicitor present on behalf of the complainant, or a member of the IPCC);[125]

(c) the complainant does not appear to have any rights to receive any
other information (for example, the grounds of appeal and any
response from the police force);

(d) the complainant is only permitted to be present for the
examination and cross-examination of witnesses and not for
any other aspect of the hearing (for example, during the giving
of antecedents, mitigation or at the announcement of the result
of the appeal);[126]

(e) in any event, the complainant (and any person permitted to
attend with him or her) is not allowed to attend before the
complainant has given evidence;[127]

(f) the right for the complainant to have someone accompany him
or her to the hearing is subject to the discretion of the tribunal
'on account of the age of the complainant, or otherwise';[128]

(g) the tribunal can require the complainant and any other member
of the public to withdraw if evidence is given by a witness which
it is not in the public interest to be disclosed to a member of
the public;[129]

(h) the complainant can put proper questions in cross-examination through the chair, and at the discretion of the chair can
put questions him or herself;[130]

123   Appeals Rules r6.
124   Appeals Rules r12(2).
125   Appeals Rules r9.
126   Appeals Rules r12(3).
127   Appeals Rules r12(3).
128   Appeals Rules r12(3).
129   Appeals Rules rr9 and 12(3).
130   Appeals Rules r12(3).

(i) the complainant must be told the outcome of the appeal by the police authority,[131] whether or not he or she attended the hearing, including whether there was a variation of the sanction imposed.[132]

5.100    Thus the complainant has somewhat fewer rights at the appeal tribunal than at the original hearing, and there is clearly an argument that the appeal rules need to be brought into line with the tribunal rules.

5.101    Although the statutory rules do not set out the basis upon which an appeal should be considered by the tribunal, the guidance states that the role of the tribunal is to decide whether the original decisions on conduct and sanction reached were reasonable on the material available. If the appeal is allowed on sanction alone, a lesser sanction can be imposed.[133]

5.102    The tribunal must keep a verbatim record of the evidence given,[134] and prepare a written copy of its determination with reasons which will be provided to the police authority, the Home Secretary (in the case of senior officers), the officer, and the police force[135] (but not the IPCC or the complainant, even in cases originating from a complaint).

5.103    There is no further appeal from the tribunal, although the officer, the IPCC and the complainant may all have standing to apply for judicial review of the decisions reached.

## Unsatisfactory performance

5.104    Before 1999 there were no formal procedures for dealing with police inefficiency and unsatisfactory performance which fell short of misconduct. This was resolved by the Police (Efficiency) Regulations 1999[136] which set out the procedure by which inefficiency and unsatisfactory performance could be dealt with. The regulations do not apply to senior officers or probationers.

5.105    The guidance explains the purpose of the procedures as follows:

> 1.3. The purpose of these procedures is to enable line managers and officers to discuss in an objective and systematic way any perceived failures to meet performance standards. In this way it is intended that any such

---

131  Appeals Rules r13(4).
132  Guidance para 5.27.
133  Guidance para 5.24.
134  Appeals Rules r10.
135  Appeals Rules r13.
136  SI No 732 (hereafter Efficiency Regs).

failures and appropriate remedial action can be identified and imple-
mented early enough to avoid the need for formal action.

5.106    The guidance explains the relationship between the complaints process
and the unsatisfactory performance procedures:

> 1.5. It is also possible that managers may be alerted to poor work per-
> formance on the part of one of their officers as a result of information
> from a member of the public. The information from the member of the
> public may be in the form of a formal complaint. Where it is, it must be
> dealt with in accordance with the established procedures for the handling
> of complaints.

5.107    However, the guidance goes on to note that a single complaint about
unsatisfactory performance may be insufficient to trigger the procedures as they are designed more for dealing with poor work patterns
rather than isolated incidents.[138]

5.108    The guidance also sets out the relationship between the unsatisfactory performance procedures and the misconduct procedures as
follows.

> 1.57. The misconduct and unsatisfactory performance procedures are sep-
> arate but complementary. They should ensure that both poor conduct and
> poor performance on the part of police officers are dealt with effectively,
> having regard to the public interest, the interests of the police service and
> the interests of individual officers.

> 1.58. During the course of misconduct enquiries it may emerge that all or
> part of the matter in question relates more to issues of poor performance
> than poor conduct on the officer concerned's part. In such circumstances
> it may be appropriate for the case, or at least that aspect of it relating to per-
> formance, to be dealt with by the officer's line management. In many
> cases, this will probably take the form of advice and/or further training
> being provided to the officer. However, if the misconduct enquiries have
> disclosed further evidence of a pattern of poor performance by the officer
> concerned, it may be appropriate to institute or, if the officer is already
> subject to the procedures, continue the formal unsatisfactory perform-
> ance procedures at whatever stage is applicable to the officer concerned.

5.109    The unsatisfactory performance procedures are designed only to be
invoked when normal line management approaches have not worked
and the officer has failed to avail him or herself of an opportunity to
improve performance. When the informal process does not work the
regulations require a series of two formal interviews between the
officer and line management aimed at improving performance.[139]

138   Guidance para 1.7.
139   Efficiency Regs regs 4–11, and Guidance, paras 1.17–1.33.

The results of these interviews are recorded. The first interview will be with the officer's immediate superior; the second interview will involve the personnel department, possibly leading to a written warning. However, if there is no improvement in the officer's performance then a formal unsatisfactory performance hearing can be held.[140] This is normally in private and before a panel of three senior police officers.[141]

5.110    If the panel decides that there has been unsatisfactory performance, an officer can be given a formal warning to improve; can be reduced in rank with a formal warning; or required to resign.[142] The officer has the right to seek a review by the chief constable[143] and if required to resign or reduced in rank then has the option of an appeal to the Police Appeals Tribunal[144] (see para 5.98).

## Disclosure of police disciplinary records and allegations in criminal trials

5.111    There has been uncertainty whether police disciplinary records and notice of suspensions and pending complaints investigations should properly be disclosed where this might assist the defence in a criminal trial, and whether any information disclosed can be deployed at trial.

5.112    Where a prosecution witness is of bad character, there is a general duty on the prosecution at common law to disclose that fact and any material upon which the defence could cross-examine the witness as to his or her character. In 1991, *R v Edwards*[145] extended this to require the disclosure of certain police discipline records. In a criminal case in which a police officer's credibility is in issue it is permissible to cross-examine the officer about any criminal or disciplinary charges proved against him or her in respect of other matters, as they may cast doubt on his or her credibility. Where there is a right to cross-examine there is a corresponding duty upon the prosecuting authorities to volunteer disclosure to the defence.

5.113    The disclosure of any convictions and disciplinary findings against the police officers in a case to the defendant was confirmed in the case of *R v Guney*.[146] The Court of Appeal widened the ambit of the material to be disclosed to include transcripts of Court of Appeal decisions

---

140   Efficiency Regs reg 12.
141   Efficiency Regs reg 14, and Guidance, paras 1.34–1.47.
142   Efficiency Regs reg 17.
143   Efficiency Regs regs 19–21.
144   Efficiency Regs reg 21(4).
145   [1991] 1 WLR 207.
146   (1998) 27 February, CA, unreported.

where convictions had been quashed on the express basis of misconduct or lack of veracity of identified police officers, and transcripts where a trial judge had stopped a trial on that basis. The court thought that material should be disclosed as of right and then any arguments as to whether the information could be deployed at trial could take place.

5.114   The Court of Appeal also explored the limits to cross-examination of police officers on matters of credibility. The court confirmed that cross-examination on disciplinary charges of which the officer had been found guilty would be permitted. However:

> Cross-examination of police officers on the basis of unresolved criminal charges or complaints to the Police Complaints Authority is not permitted. Accordingly the fact that an allegation has been made does not provide a secure foundation for cross-examination. The same reasoning applies ... once the complaint has been heard and dismissed or the witness has been acquitted of the criminal charge.

5.115   At the time of writing the Crown Prosecution Service (CPS) legal advice disclosed on its website simply states that guidance is being agreed between ACPO and the CPS and that the principle is that:

> The CPS is under a duty to disclose to the defence information about police officers who are witnesses that might undermine the prosecution case or that might reasonably assist a defence. It does not matter whether the officers are called as witnesses, their statements are read to the court or their statements are unused material.

## Criminal proceedings against the police

5.116   Like any other citizen, a police officer may be prosecuted at the instigation of either the CPS or a private prosecutor. Provided a constable acts within his or her powers in, for example, making an arrest, conducting a stop and search, entering or searching premises or seizing evidence, he or she may well have a complete defence to a criminal charge arising out of that act. However, if a constable acts beyond his or her powers, he or she should, in theory, be as answerable to the criminal law as a private citizen in the same position. In practice, however, the decision to bring a prosecution against a police officer will often not be as straightforward as the decision to bring a prosecution against a member of the public in similar circumstances, and, although the policy of the CPS is to treat all cases the same, this can weight the decision in favour of the officer.

5.117    In these circumstances the right of an individual to bring a private prosecution is an important constitutional guarantee of the fundamental principle that no one is above the law. It is beyond the scope of this work to consider all the offences that might come within the ambit of criminal police misconduct. However they will include various types of assault, perverting the course of justice, indecent assault (for example, arising out of intimate body searches), criminal damage (for example, caused in the course of a search), obtaining unauthorised access to computer material, perjury, corruption and false imprisonment. In one exceptional case, *R v Dytham*,[147] a police officer was convicted of the offence of 'misconduct of an officer of justice' after he stood by without intervening and watched a group of men kick another man to death.

5.118    This section considers, first, prosecutions brought by the CPS following a complaint or disciplinary investigation and, second, private prosecutions brought by members of the public.

## Investigating officers' reports and the DPP

5.119    The question of criminal proceedings is usually considered at the end of the investigation of a complaint but before any disciplinary proceedings are brought (see chapter 4). If the chief officer considers that the report indicates that a criminal offence may have been committed, and that the officer ought to be charged, he or she must send a copy of the report to the Director of Public Prosecutions (DPP) (see chapter 4).

5.120    However, the CPS may well become involved earlier in more serious cases. There is a CPS and IPCC protocol designed to improve the effectiveness of investigations into deaths in police custody and other major incidents.[148] The protocol also covers investigations such as fatal shootings, serious assaults, perverting the course of justice, corruption, racially discriminatory behaviour and cases involving organised crime or drug trafficking.

5.121    In the best interests of the investigation, the IPCC is encouraged to liaise with the CPS at the earliest opportunity at the start of an investigation, so that a CPS lawyer can be allocated. The IPCC is also encouraged to consult the CPS for advice at any stage.

---

147    [1979] 3 All ER 641.
148    Protocol between the CPS and the IPCC available at www.ipcc.gov.uk

## Action by the DPP

5.122   The decision to prosecute a police officer lies with the DPP. Two tests are applied. First, is there sufficient evidence to justify a prosecution? Second, would it be in the public interest for a prosecution to be brought? The DPP will deal with the questions in turn, only asking the second question if satisfied as to the first.

5.123   The Code for Crown Prosecutors is issued by the DPP under Prosecution of Offences Act 1985 s10. It sets out the basic principles Crown Prosecutors should follow when they make case decisions. It is a public document, and although it is written for members of the CPS, it is widely used by others to understand the way in which Crown Prosecutors make decisions.[149]

5.124   There are general principles which must be followed. Thus, for example:

> 2.2 Crown Prosecutors must be fair, independent and objective. They must not let any personal views about ethnic or national origin, sex, religious beliefs, political views or the sexual orientation of the suspect, victim or witness influence their decisions. They must not be affected by improper or undue pressure from any source.[150]

5.125   In relation to the evidential test the code explains as follows:

> 5.2 Crown Prosecutors must be satisfied that there is enough evidence to provide a 'realistic prospect of conviction' against each defendant on each charge. They must consider what the defence case may be, and how that is likely to affect the prosecution case.
>
> 5.3 A realistic prospect of conviction is an objective test. It means that a jury or bench of magistrates, or a judge hearing a case alone properly directed in accordance with the law, is more likely than not to convict the defendant of the charge alleged ...

5.126   In relation to the public interest test (if the evidential test is satisfied) the code says:

> 5.7 The public interest must be considered in each case where there is enough evidence to provide a realistic prospect of conviction. A prosecution will usually take place unless there are public interest factors tending against prosecution which clearly outweigh those tending in favour. Although there may be public interest factors against prosecution in a particular case, often the prosecution should go ahead and those factors should be put to the court for consideration when sentence is being passed.

149   See www.cps.gov.uk/victimswitnesses/code.html.
150   Code, para 2.2.

5.127   The code includes a long non-exhaustive list of public interest factors in favour and against prosecution, but none of these specifically refers to a situation where a police officer is the alleged perpetrator of an offence, nor where a member of the public is the victim of an alleged crime by a police officer.

## The DPP's decision

5.128   The DPP will inform the complainant whether or not the police officer complained about will be prosecuted. The complainant will usually be told either that the evidence is insufficient to justify criminal proceedings (that is, that the case fails the '51 per cent rule') or that criminal proceedings are not necessary in the public interest.

5.129      This decision of the DPP is susceptible to judicial review but the power to intervene will only be exercised 'sparingly'[151] because the decision is often one of judgment which will be impossible to stigmatise as 'wrong' even if it is disagreed with. However, at the same time the court is reluctant to set the standard of review too high, recognising that judicial review is the only remedy open to a citizen. In practice, judicial review will only be possible if the decision of the DPP is clearly perverse or if established policy has not been followed.[152] However, there may also be circumstances, for example after an inquest verdict indicating unlawful killing by a police officer, where a decision not to prosecute will also require the DPP to provide sufficient reasons to allow the decision to be understood.[153]

## Delay and abuse of process

5.130   The general rule for offences tried on indictment is that time never runs against the Crown. The same rule is applied to offences triable either way which are heard in the magistrates' court. For other cases tried in the magistrates' court the general rule is that the information must be laid within six months of the commission of the offence. However many statutes contain individual limitation periods specific to particular offences.

5.131      In a very limited range of circumstances a prosecution may be stayed because a delay in starting the case or bringing it to trial amounts

---

151   *R v DPP ex p Manning* [2001] QB 330.
152   *R v DPP ex p C* (1999) 7 Admin LR 385.
153   *R v DPP ex p Manning* [2001] QB 330. See also *R v DPP ex p Treadaway* (1997) *Times* 31 October.

to an abuse of process.[154] Once a case has been commenced, under European Convention on Human Rights article 6 an accused person has the right for the case to be determined within a reasonable time.[155] Where the prosecution has not been responsible for the delay then a stay is even less likely to be granted. In cases where the reason for the delay has been the failure of the victim to report the crime then the usual position is that the reasons for the delay will be explored in the trial and may, for example, go to the credibility of the victim, rather than a stay to be granted.[156]

## Private prosecutions

5.132    The right of a private citizen to bring a prosecution is a useful and effective safeguard against 'improper inaction' by the prosecuting authority.[157] The right of individuals to bring private prosecutions (with certain exceptions) was included under the Prosecution of Offences Act 1985. When the potential defendants are police officers and the authority responsible for investigating offences is a police force, the potential for improper inaction becomes obvious and the right of the citizen to bring a prosecution takes on the character of a constitutional guarantee. In the notorious 'rhino whip case', for example, a Sheffield solicitor prosecuted two officers in order to expose the fact that they were systematically beating confessions out of suspects and that senior officers were turning a blind eye to wholesale abuses.[158]

5.133    Nevertheless, there are formidable obstacles to bringing a private prosecution, including the risk of the prosecution being taken over by the DPP and discontinued, the need for official consent in some cases, the expense of bringing the case (legal aid is not available) and the difficulty in obtaining evidence sufficient to meet the criminal standard of proof. For most victims of police misconduct the possibility of bringing a private prosecution will not be a viable alternative to bringing a civil action for damages. Indeed it should not be viewed as an alternative at all, as the purposes of the two procedures are so different: the former being to punish the wrongdoer, the other to compensate the victim. A private prosecution will usually only be an option

154    See *Att-Gen's Ref (No 1 of 1990)* [1992] QB 630 for principles.
155    See *Porter v Magill* [2002] 2 AC 357 for principles.
156    See *R v Jenkins* [1998] Crim LR 411 for an exceptional case where a stay was granted (28 years since alleged offences committed when victims were infants).
157    *R v Bow Street Stipendiary Magistrate ex p South Coast Shipping Co Ltd* [1993] QB 645.
158    Sheffield Police Appeal Enquiry, Cmnd 2176, HMSO, 1963.

if some wider purpose is sought, such as to demonstrate the failure of the police in investigating the incident or the failure of the DPP to bring a prosecution, to prevent the police committing contempt of court,[159] challenge a prosecutor's interpretation of the law[160] or to expose a pattern of malpractice or a desire to see justice done and to vindicate the rule of law.

5.134    If it is proposed to run both a prosecution and a civil action based on the same incident, a number of tactical issues will arise. Limitation periods for both the civil action and the prosecution will need to be observed. Evidence of a criminal conviction can be pleaded in a civil case, but a successful civil judgment is obviously not probative of criminal guilt. Exemplary damages could be reduced to nil if a criminal court has previously imposed a punishment (see chapter 14); on the other hand, a sentence (and any compensation order) may presumably be reduced if exemplary damages had already been awarded against an individual officer subsequently convicted (although, of course, exemplary damages are usually sought against the chief officer).

5.135    If the DPP is initially reluctant to prosecute, a successful civil action can serve to demonstrate that witnesses will come up to proof, and may thus prompt the DPP to change his mind.

## The right to prosecute

5.136    As a general principle any citizen can bring a prosecution. This right is preserved by Prosecution of Offences Act 1985 s6, which, in the context of police misconduct, for all practical purposes does not restrict the right to bring a private prosecution.

5.137    The DPP has a duty to institute and have the conduct of criminal proceedings in any case where it appears to him or her that:

(a) the importance or difficulty of the case makes it appropriate that proceeding should be instituted by him or her; or
(b) it is otherwise appropriate for proceedings to be instituted by him or her.[161]

5.138    However, this does not oblige the DPP to take over the conduct of such cases, nor is there any implied limitation in the Act so as to preclude more than one prosecution arising out of the same incident, as

159   For Example, where the police seek to prevent a criminal defendant identifying alibi witnesses: *Connolly v Dale* (1995) 13 July, DC.
160   *R v Lemon* [1979] AC 617.
161   Prosecution of Offenders Act 1985 s3(2)(b).

where, for example, the DPP has already brought a minor charge and the private prosecutor seeks to bring a more serious charge.[162] It may, however, be an abuse of process to allow a private prosecutor to continue with a summons where the CPS has dropped a case in exchange for a defendant agreeing to be bound over to keep the peace.[163]

5.139    The choice of the charge that is to be preferred is generally in the discretion of the private prosecutor, not the magistrate.[164] In one case of a private prosecution of a police officer for malicious wounding, contrary to Offences Against the Person Act 1861 s20, the prosecutor wanted the case to be heard in the Crown Court and told the defendant that unless he agreed to elect for trial on indictment, leave would be sought to issue a summons charging an offence under section 18, which could only be heard in the Crown Court. The defendant's application for judicial review of the justices' decision to grant the second summons (in respect of the section 18 charge) was dismissed. The fact that the prosecutor wished to add or substitute new charges, to ensure that the case was tried either summarily or on indictment, was not a ground for refusing the issue of a summons, provided that the issue of the summons was a proper course on the facts.[165]

5.140    The issuing of a summons is, of course, a judicial act, not an automatic formality. Where the question has already been considered by the CPS, it has been held that the magistrate is entitled to have regard to the likelihood of the DPP taking over the prosecution in deciding whether to issue a summons on the information of a private prosecutor.[166] However, it is submitted that this gives insufficient weight to the principle that private prosecutions are 'a useful constitutional safeguard against inertia or partiality on the part of authority',[167] and poses the risk that magistrates may usurp the functions of the DPP.

5.141    A summons should not be refused on the grounds that a private prosecutor has a civil remedy.[168] Nor should a private prosecution be

---

162  *R v Bow Street Stipendiary Magistrate ex p South Coast Shipping Co Ltd* [1993] QB 645; for exceptions in drink driving cases, see *R v Moxon-Tritsch* [1988] Crim LR 46 and *R v Forest of Dean JJ ex p Farley* [1990] RTR 228.

163  *R v Grays JJ ex p Low* [1990] QB 54; see also *R v Croydon JJ ex p Dean* (1994) 98 Cr App R 76, DC.

164  *R v Nuneaton JJ ex p Parker* (1954) 118 JP 524.

165  *R v Redbridge JJ ex p Whitehouse* (1992) 94 Cr App R 332.

166  *R v Tower Bridge Metropolitan Stipendiary Magistrate ex p Chaudhury* [1994] QB 340, DC.

167  *Gouriet v Union of Post Office Workers* [1978] AC 435, [1977] 3 WLR 300 at 310, per Lord Wilberforce.

168  *R v Bennett and Bond ex p Bennett* (1908) 72 JP 362, 52 SJ 583, 24 TLR 681.

adjourned pending the outcome of civil proceedings concerning the same facts.[169]

## Procedure

5.142   Prosecutions by the police can be commenced by laying an information before a magistrate or magistrates' clerk, either orally or in writing, or by the defendant being charged at a police station. There is some uncertainty as to whether a private prosecution can be commenced by way of a charge[170] but for all practical purposes a private prosecutor should be advised to proceed only by way of a written information. An arrest warrant may also be sought; however, careful consideration should be given as to whether this is necessary or tactically appropriate in the circumstances of the case.

## Official consent

5.143   Some offences require official consent, either from the Attorney-General or from the DPP, before a prosecution can be brought.[171] For example the consent of the Attorney-General is necessary in order to bring a prosecution for bribery or corruption[172] and the consent of the DPP is a prerequisite of a prosecution for the offence of making an unauthorised disclosure of a spent conviction.[173] It is the duty of the person issuing the summons to ensure that consent has been obtained. There is a presumption that this has been done. Any objection that a necessary consent has not been obtained should be made before the prosecution case is closed, whereupon the burden passes to the prosecution to prove that the proceedings are properly authorised.[174]

5.144   Official consent is unlikely to be forthcoming if, on the same evidence, the DPP has already refused to prosecute.

---

169   *R v Evans* (1890) 62 LT 570, 54 JP 471, 6 LRT 248, 17 Cox CC 81, DC.

170   *R v Ealing JJ ex p Dixon* [1990] 2 QB 91 (disapproved in *R v Stafford JJ ex p Customs and Excise Commissioners* [1990] 3 WLR 656); cf *R v Croydon JJ ex p Holmberg* [1992] Crim LR 892; see *Blackstone's Criminal Practice* 2005, p1040 for a fuller discussion.

171   See Prosecution of Offences Act 1985 s25.

172   Prevention of Corruption Act 1906 s2(1).

173   Rehabilitation of Offenders Act 1974 s9(3).

174   *Price v Humphries* (1958) 122 JP 423; *R v Waller* [1910] 1 KB 364.

## Discontinuance of proceedings

5.145　The DPP has wide powers to take over the conduct of a private prosecution, even where he or she is under no duty to do so, at any stage. The policy of the DPP is set out on the CPS website and reads as follows:

> A private prosecutor or a defendant might ask the CPS to take over a private prosecution; or a justice's clerk might refer a private prosecution to the CPS, or the CPS might learn of a private prosecution in some other way. The CPS will take over and discontinue a private prosecution when:
>
> - There is so little evidence that there is no case to answer; or
> - The prosecution falls far below the public interest test in the Code for Crown Prosecutors; or
> - The prosecution is likely to damage the interests of justice.
>
> The CPS will take over and continue a prosecution when the case in an important or difficult one that merits a public prosecution.
>
> We would take over the case and prosecute only if the case passes the two tests in the Code, ie, there is sufficient evidence and a prosecution is in the public interest.
>
> If it seems that the case should be taken over, the CPS will call for the papers. This means asking the private prosecutor to pass evidence and documents to the CPS so that the CPS can decide whether to take over. It also includes asking the police for any evidence or information they have.
>
> Sometimes the papers will not contain enough evidence or information for The CPS to be able to decide whether or not to take over the prosecution. If this happens, The CPS will, if it seems that further investigation is necessary, ask the police to investigate.
>
> If the CPS takes over a private prosecution, it will review the case in accordance with the tests contained in the Code for Crown Prosecutors (published on The CPS website at www.cps.gov.uk). If the case passes both tests, The CPS will continue with the private prosecution.

5.146　Thus, if the DPP decides not to prosecute a police officer because the 'reasonable prospect of conviction' test in the Code for Crown Prosecutors is not met, this does not mean that a private prosecution for the same offence will necessarily be taken over and discontinued. This will only happen if there is 'clearly no case to answer'; a much higher hurdle to cross. This was exactly the position in *R v DPP ex p Duckenfield*,[175] where the Court of Appeal upheld the DPP's decision not to

175　[2000] 1 WLR 55.

take over a private prosecution in these circumstances. The case involved a private prosecution against senior police officers involved in the Hillsborough disaster of 1989.

5.147    If it is too late to discontinue the proceedings, the DPP may offer no evidence, or in the Crown Court, the Attorney-General may enter a nolle prosequi[175a] to bring the case to an end at any stage. The decision of the Attorney-General cannot be reviewed by the courts.[176]

## Expense

5.148    The cost of bringing the prosecution will usually fall on the prosecutor. If the offences charged are tried in the Crown Court, both solicitor and counsel will in practice usually have to be engaged. While the Crown Court has a discretion to allow a private prosecutor to appear in person, this is only likely to be exercised occasionally. If the offences are to be tried in the magistrates' court, a prosecutor may appear in person, although this would rarely be advisable against police defendants. If the offences are triable either way, the prosecutor will not know in advance whether the defendants will opt for Crown Court trial, and this is will make for uncertainty about the likely expense of the proceedings. In addition, there will often be unforeseen costs in investigating the incident and collecting evidence. Public funding is not available to commence a private prosecution.

5.149    If the defendant is acquitted, the prosecutor can expect to be ordered to pay the defendant's costs as well as his or her own. A successful private prosecutor can expect to be awarded costs out of central funds unless there is good reason for not doing so, for instance, where proceedings have been instituted or continued without good cause; but the award may not cover the full cost of the prosecution.[177]

5.150    It appears the police officers prosecuted can have their costs paid by their police authority (if not ordered to be paid by the prosecutor).[178]

---

175a  Literally, "not to wish to prosecute".

176   *R v Comptroller-General of Patents, Designs and Trade Marks* [1899] 1 QB 909; *Gouriet v Union of Post Office Workers* [1978] AC 435 at 487; *Turner v DPP* (1978) 68 Cr App R 70 at 76; *R v Solicitor-General ex p Taylor* (1995) *Times* 14 August.

177   Practice Direction (Costs in Criminal Proceedings) (1991) 93 Cr App R 89 para 3.1.

178   *R v DPP ex p Duckenfield* [2000] 1 WLR 55, CA.

## Professional ethics

5.151   Lawyers who usually undertake civil actions against the police or criminal defence work but who are unused to conducting private prosecutions will need to make some mental readjustments to their new role as a prosecutor. Their duty is no longer to win their client's case, but rather to present the case fairly and allow the court to decide. Indeed their client will not be a party to the case: prosecutions are brought on behalf of the Crown. The lawyer's first duty as a prosecutor is no longer to the client, but to the wider public interest; having commenced a prosecution, the lawyer must act as an officer of the court and must be ready to distance him or herself from instructions from the client that are at variance with this public duty. Thus, for example, the duty of disclosure must be scrupulously observed. It is also prudent to review the DPP's guidance (Code for Crown Prosecutors) and professional guidance from the Law Society and the Bar Council.

# Intentional torts to the person

6.1    This chapter examines civil claims that can arise out of interference with the person. The main focus is upon claims for false imprisonment and for assault and battery. The former relates to wrongful arrest and/or detention. The latter concerns the use, or threat, of force. In both instances the elements necessary to establish a claim are described and the defences that the police may raise are considered. The chapter then goes on to deal more briefly with three other causes of action that may arise out of threatening or other physically intrusive behaviour: harassment (under the Protection from Harassment Act 1997 and at common law); intentional infliction of nervous shock; and intimidation. Compensation is addressed in chapter 14.

## False imprisonment

6.2    The right to freedom of movement without fear of arbitrary arrest or detention is a fundamental civil liberty. In the civil law it is protected in part by the right to sue for false imprisonment, which can arise if the police, directly and intentionally, confine a person without lawful excuse. False imprisonment most commonly occurs when the police make an arrest which is not legally justified. This may explain why it is sometimes, inaccurately, called false or wrongful arrest: there is no such tort in English law and the 'wrongful arrest' is usually just the act at the start of a period of false imprisonment.

6.3    There are two elements which together constitute false imprisonment:

- the detention; and
- the lack of a lawful authority for the detention.

6.4    The burden of proof is on the claimant to prove that the detention has occurred, but on the police to prove that they had a lawful excuse or authority for the detention. In most cases, the authority that the police are most likely to rely upon is that they were carrying out a lawful arrest. Accordingly, the nature and type of detention is explained first below, and the types of defence the police can raise to show that they had a lawful authority are considered subsequently.

6.5    The right to liberty is also reflected in European Convention on Human Rights (ECHR) article 5. In general terms the courts, both before and after the commencement of the Human Rights Act 1998, have sought to ensure that domestic case law and statutory provisions set out in the Police and Criminal Evidence Act 1984 (PACE) reach the same conclusions where liberty of the person is concerned as are required by article 5.

6.6      Article 5 sets out first the right to liberty and the security of the person, and the limited (and exhaustive) cases in which this can be compromised where prescribed by law, and then sets out a number of procedural protections for those who have been detained. The most relevant parts of article 5 for the purposes of a discussion of false imprisonment and the police are as follows:

### Article 5 – Right to liberty and security

1. Everyone has the right to liberty and security of person. No one shall be deprived of his liberty save in the following cases and in accordance with a procedure prescribed by law:

    (a) the lawful detention of a person after conviction by a competent court;

    (b) the lawful arrest or detention of a person for non-compliance with the lawful order of a court or in order to secure the fulfilment of any obligation prescribed by law;

    (c) the lawful arrest or detention of a person effected for the purpose of bringing him before the competent legal authority on reasonable suspicion of having committed an offence or when it is reasonably considered necessary to prevent his committing an offence or fleeing after having done so;

6.7      There are procedural requirements included in article 5 which are also reflected in domestic case law and statutory provisions. Article 5(2) and (3) read:

2. Everyone who is arrested shall be informed promptly, in a language which he understands, of the reasons for his arrest and of any charge against him.

3. Everyone arrested or detained in accordance with the provisions of paragraph 1(c) of this article shall be brought promptly before a judge or other officer authorised by law to exercise judicial power and shall be entitled to trial within a reasonable time or to release pending trial. Release may be conditioned by guarantees to appear for trial.

6.8      Article 5 concludes by providing rights for a person to have the lawfulness of his or her detention speedily determined by a court.[1] The criminal justice system, judicial review and habeas corpus applications generally allow this to happen. There is also provision for an enforceable right to compensation where there has been a breach of article 5,[2] which is generally complied with by the right to sue for false imprisonment in the civil courts.

---

1   ECHR art 5(4).
2   ECHR art 5(5).

6.9      Where article 5 impacts on the law of false imprisonment it is referred to at para 6.13 below.

## Detention

6.10    Detention of a person may occur in many common situations: in the course of a stop and search in the street; during questioning, whether at the police station or anywhere else; or on arrest. The place of detention is irrelevant but the restraint must be total. A person may, for example, be held in prison,[3] in a car,[4] in his or her own home,[5] or in the street;[6] provided that he or she is restrained within an area set by the police, all these amount to detention. A person is imprisoned even if he or she is moved from one place to another, for instance to a police station from the place of arrest. The means used for detention need not be physical; a threat of force can be used, and an assertion of authority by a police officer, such as saying, 'You're under arrest', is enough. There is no need to show that the person was touched by the officer,[7] nor is there any need to resist arrest. In fact, use of a person's wish to avoid embarrassment to make them submit to arrest can amount to restraint.[8] However, a person placed on an unlocked mental health ward, sedated and monitored, and lacking capacity to consent to his presence there was held not to be detained because he was free to leave and unrestrained by barriers from doing so.[9]

### The duration of the detention

6.11    In theory, there is no minimum period of confinement for a claim for false imprisonment to succeed.[10] In practice, the duration is important, as a long period will usually justify a larger sum of damages

3   *Cobbett v Grey* (1849) 4 Exch 729.
4   *Burton v Davies* [1953] QSR 26 (Queensland).
5   *Warner v Riddiford* (1858) 4 CB(NS) 180.
6   Termes de la Ley c1520; see *Merring v Grahame-White Aviation Co* (1920) 122 LT 44.
7   *Warner v Riddiford* (1858) 4 CB(NS) 180; *Chinn v Morris* (1826) 2 C & P 361; *Grainger v Hill* (1838) 4 Bing NC 200; *Wood v Lane* (1834) 6 C & P 774.
8   *Conn v David Spencer* (1930) 1 DLR 805.
9   *R v Bournewood Community and Mental Health NHS Trust ex p L* [1998] 3 WLR 107 (although note the dissent of Lord Steyn who found that any notion that the claimant was free to leave was a 'fairy tale'). Indeed, the ECtHR found that the patient was detained for the purposes of article 5: *HL v UK* (2004) 7 CCLR 498.
10  *Brooks v Commissioner of Police of the Metropolis* [2002] EWCA Civ 407; and see *Clerk & Lindsell on Torts* (18th edn, Sweet & Maxwell, 2000) para 13–19.

if the detention is unlawful (see chapter 14). However, being confined for even a short period can be serious. For example, a person wrongly arrested in a public place in circumstances that attracted a lot of attention, even if released after a few minutes, might suffer more embarrassment, distress and damage to his or her reputation than if he or she were arrested at home but kept for several hours. In one case, the Court of Appeal ordered a retrial of a case in which a judge implied that a 30-minute false imprisonment was a 'technical' false imprisonment.[11] In another case, a person held at gun-point for two minutes was held to have been detained in the context of a claim for false imprisonment.[12]

6.12    In addition, an assault and battery can constitute false imprisonment if the person is restrained during its occurrence. This may be of importance as it may well give rise to a right to a jury trial not usually available in an assault and battery case (see chapter 7).[13]

## Article 5

6.13    The European Court of Human Rights (ECHR) adopts a very similar approach to domestic law when deciding whether a person has been deprived of his or her liberty. It draws a distinction for the purposes of article 5(1) between 'deprivation' and 'restriction' of liberty, to be decided according to the individual and concrete circumstances of the case. The degree or intensity of the restriction must be examined.[14] Examples of the relevant factors are:

- the extent of the denial or loss of liberty;
- its duration;
- the degree of compulsion behind the restriction in the sense of the immediacy of any use of force, and/or the existence of penal sanctions;
- its characterisation in municipal law;
- its manner of implementation.

6.14    There are a number of relevant examples of findings of 'deprivation of liberty' despite there being a degree of freedom of movement left to the citizen which possibly may not have had a similar outcome in a domestic court deciding whether a person had been detained at

---

11    *Kay v James* (1989) 21 April, unreported.
12    *Parry v Sharples* (1991) 17 July, CA, LexisNexis.
13    *Foley v Commissioner of Police of the Metropolis* (1989) 14 December, unreported.
14    See *Guzzardi v Italy* (1981) 3 EHRR 333 at [92]–[93].

common law. In *Guzzardi v Italy*,[15] a suspected mafioso was required to reside within 2.5 square kilometres of a Mediterranean island. His confinement, in all the circumstances, engaged article 5(1). Similarly, in *Amuur v France*[16] there was a breach of article 5(1) where a person was restricted to the international transit area of an airport, and an attached hotel.

6.15    In *R (Laporte) v Chief Constable of Gloucestershire*,[17] the police purported to use their powers under Criminal Justice and Public Order Act 1994 s60 to stop a coach of demonstrators and to force it to return to London. The court held that this detention went far beyond anything that could be justified to prevent a breach of the peace. The Divisional Court said that this constituted a breach of ECHR article 5(1) whereas the Court of Appeal was content to hold that the detention was unlawful in domestic law.

## Knowledge of detention

6.16    It is now clear that someone can bring an action for false imprisonment even though he or she did not know that he or she was being detained unlawfully, or he or she was not harmed by the detention.[18] Thus an unconscious person could be falsely imprisoned. However, in cases where there is no knowledge and no harm caused, a person 'can normally expect to recover no more than nominal damages'.[19] However, a person who is aware of his or her detention, but not that it is unlawful, will be entitled to more than nominal damages.[20]

## Voluntary attendance at police station

6.17    Under PACE, someone who attends a police station voluntarily for the purpose of assisting with an investigation, without having been arrested, is entitled to leave at will, unless he or she is then placed under arrest.[21] There is no requirement on the police to tell a person who is attending voluntarily that he or she is free to leave, but the Act does make it clear that if a police officer decides to arrest a person,

---

15    (1981) 3 EHRR 333 at [91]–[95].

16    (1996) 22 EHRR 533 at [42]–[49].

17    [2004] 2 All ER 874 (Divisional Court) and [2005] 1 All ER 473 (Court of Appeal).

18    *Murray v Ministry of Defence* [1988] 2 All ER 521, HL, approving the dictum of Atkin LJ in *Merring v Grahame-White Aviation Co* (1920) 122 LT 44 at 53-54.

19    *Murray v Ministry of Defence*, at 529 per Lord Griffiths.

20    *Roberts v Chief Constable of Cheshire* [1999] 2 All ER 326; *R v Governor of HMP Brockhill ex p Evans* [1997] 2 WLR 236.

21    PACE s29.

he or she must be informed immediately.[22] A failure to do so will make
the detention thereafter unlawful.

6.18    An example of where voluntary attendance would become unlawful can be seen in the following situation. A person agrees to go
to a police station voluntarily to answer some questions. The officer
questioning leaves the interview room to check on something that has
been said, locking the door in the process so that the person cannot
leave. As there has been no proper arrest the confinement is unlawful
and the confined person can sue for false imprisonment. Alternatively,
after a period of questioning the person decides that enough is enough
and decides to leave. An officer stops the person and says, 'You can't go;
you're helping us with our inquiries'. Again, in the absence of a proper
arrest, the person could sue for false imprisonment.

6.19    Conversely, a person who is prepared to co-operate by, for example,
voluntarily attending at the police station may have an action for false
imprisonment if the police decide, unnecessarily or in bad faith,
to exercise their discretion to arrest the person.[23]

## Deterioration in conditions of detention

6.20    When a prisoner has been lawfully committed to custody, a deterio-
ration in the conditions of detention will not give rise to a claim for false
imprisonment. In two Court of Appeal cases, the court had, first,
refused to strike out an action for false imprisonment by a convicted
prisoner held overnight in a strip cell[24] and, second, suggested that an
action for false imprisonment might be possible if the conditions of
detention became unbearable.[25] However, when these cases were
further appealed, the House of Lords ruled that there is no such thing
as a person's 'residual liberty' which can be taken away when he or
she is otherwise lawfully held in prison.[26] Therefore, if conditions
deteriorate, there can be no further deprivation of liberty which could
constitute the tort of false imprisonment. The House of Lords went on
to say that, if conditions of an otherwise lawful detention are truly
intolerable, the law ought to be capable of providing a remedy directly
relating to those conditions, without characterising the detention itself
as unlawful. Lord Bridge said that this remedy is already provided by

22    PACE s29. Compare *R v Lemsatef* [1977] 2 All ER 835 and Code C para 3.15.
23    See, eg, *Paul v Chief Constable of Humberside* [2004] EWCA Civ 308 Compare
      *Al-Fayed v Metropolitian Police Commissioner* [2004] EWCA Civ 1579.
24    *Weldon v Home Office* [1990] 3 All ER 672, CA.
25    *R v Deputy Governor of Parkhurst Prison ex p Hague* [1990] 3 All ER 687, CA.
26    *R v Deputy Governor of Parkhurst Prison ex p Hague* [1991] 3 WLR 340, HL.

the law, as a person in lawful detention is owed a duty of care by those holding him or her in custody and could sue in negligence if there was a breach of this duty (see chapter 8). An action might also lie in assault and battery and/or misfeasance in public office,[27] and for breach of ECHR article 3 and/or 8.[28]

6.21    If a person is held unlawfully in intolerable conditions, or in conditions which breach the PACE Code of Practice on the treatment of prisoners (Code C) then this may sound in increased compensatory or exemplary damages (see chapter 14).

## Who is liable: police or informant?

6.22    If an informant, say a shopkeeper, calls a police officer who then makes an arrest and the arrest amounts to false imprisonment. Who is liable? The police officer or the shopkeeper? The normal test is, who was 'active in promoting and causing' the detention?[29]

6.23    In *Davidson v Chief Constable of North Wales*[30] the Court of Appeal considered the question in relation to store detectives who had provided information to the police leading to an arrest and whether they could thus be said to be the 'instigator, promoter and active inciter of the arrest and imprisonment'. On the facts of that case the court found that there was no evidence that the store detective's actions went beyond the giving of information to the police officers for them to take such action as they thought fit, and that therefore it did not amount to a direction or direct request that the police should act by arresting the suspect.

6.24    If the informant signs a charge sheet at the police station, that in itself is not evidence that he or she was active in promoting and causing the confinement.[31] If the charge sheet also states that the informant 'did give him charge', it may be evidence that the informant was active in promoting and causing the confinement.[32] However, if a police officer refuses to make an arrest unless the informant accepts responsibility for charging the person, it is the informant who is liable for false imprisonment.[33]

27  See *Racz v Home Office* [1994] 2 WLR 23.
28  *Munjaz v Mersey Care NHS Trust* (2004) QB 395; and see *R (P) v SSHD* [2003] EWHC 1963 (Admin).
29  *Aitken v Bedwell* (1827) Mood & M 68; see also *Ansell v Thomas* [1974] Crim LR 31, CA.
30  [1994] 2 All ER 597.
31  *Sewell v National Telephone Co* [1907] 1 KB 557, CA.
32  *Clubb v Wimpey & Co* [1936] 1 All ER 69; the point was not decided by the Court of Appeal when ordering a new trial: [1936] 3 All ER 148.
33  *Hopkins v Crowe* (1836) 4 Ad & E 774; *Austin v Dowling* (1870) LR 5 CP 534.

6.26    The position is different if the informant merely identifies a person when asked to do so by a police officer.[36] Thus, if someone were picked out from an identification parade, he or she would not have a claim for false imprisonment against the person who identified him or her.

6.27    A store detective or a private security guard has no special powers of arrest other than the general 'citizen's arrest' power, which can be exercised only where an arrestable offence has in fact been committed.[37] Whether or not there were reasonable grounds to suspect that an offence had been committed by the person arrested, if that person succeeds in showing that no offence was committed, then the arrest will have been unlawful.[38]

### Excessive force and false imprisonment

6.28    The use of undue force in effecting an arrest (whether under a warrant or not) or using other powers to detain someone, will not make the arrest unlawful if the arrest was otherwise justified in law,[39] although the use of excessive force may amount to assault.

### Lawful detention becoming unlawful

6.29    As described below (para 6.68), a perfectly lawful detention may become unlawful (and therefore constitute false imprisonment) if a person is detained for an excessive amount of time or if statutory reviews of detention are not undertaken. Advisers should carefully check official documentation such as the custody record to ensure that the police have justified not only the initial decision to arrest and detain, but also the entire length of the detention thereafter.

### Detention after court proceedings

6.30    As a general principle, if someone is held after a court has ordered his or her confinement, there is no claim against the police for false imprisonment. Thus, any case against the police for false imprisonment will come to an end once the magistrates have decided to remand a person in custody. However, if there is a claim for malicious prosecution (see para 7.2) then damages can be claimed for any period spent in custody on remand.

---

36  *Gosden v Elphick* (1849) 4 Exch 445.
37  PACE s24(4), (5).
38  See, eg, *R v Self* [1992] 3 All ER 476, CA.
39  *Simpson v Chief Constable of South Yorkshire* (1991) *Times* 7 March.

## Defences to false imprisonment

6.31    If it is established that the police have detained a person, the general principle is that the police have a defence to any claim then brought for false imprisonment if they can show that they had a lawful excuse or authority for their action. The burden of proof thus lies with the police. The police must prove that the detention was lawful minute by minute and hour by hour.[40]

6.32    The most common defences open to the police are that they were (a) carrying out a lawful arrest or stop and search; (b) that they were detaining a person at a police station in accordance with PACE; or (c) that they were lawfully acting on a warrant issued by a court. It is beyond the scope of this work to deal with every power that the police have to detain someone, but some of the most common that arise in civil actions against the police are described here.

### Stop and search

6.33    The police have no power to stop or detain a person simply to question him or her. If an officer detains a person who walks away after refusing to answer questions then it is likely this will amount to false imprisonment if the detention is based on nothing more than this.[41] However, the police have various powers to carry out a stop and search of a person without a warrant and to detain the person for the purposes of the search. Two of the most commonly used powers are as follows:

- PACE s1: a police officer can search any person or vehicle for stolen or prohibited[42] articles, and detain the person or vehicle to carry out that search, where there are reasonable grounds for suspecting that such items will be found.
- Misuse of Drugs Act 1971 s23(2): a police officer may stop and search a person if there are reasonable grounds to suspect that the person is in possession of a controlled drug and the officer can detain the person for the purpose of searching him or her. This power to detain includes taking a person to a place where the search can properly be carried out.

---

40    *Mercer v Chief Constable of Lancashire* [1991] 1 WLR 367 at 373 per Lord Donaldson MR.
41    *Samuels v Commissioner of Police of the Metropolis* (1999) 3 March, unreported.
42    Including offensive weapons, and tools used for burglary and theft: PACE s1(7).

6.34 Guidance on what can amount to reasonable grounds to suspect for the purposes of carrying out a search is included in PACE Code of Practice A at para 2.2:[43]

> Reasonable grounds for suspicion depend on the circumstances in each case. There must be an objective basis for that suspicion based on facts, information, and/or intelligence which are relevant to the likelihood of finding an article of a certain kind ... Reasonable suspicion can never be supported on the basis of personal factors alone without reliable supporting intelligence or information or some specific behaviour by the person concerned. For example, a person's race, age, appearance, or the fact that the person is known to have a previous conviction, cannot be used alone or in combination with each other as the reason for searching that person. Reasonable suspicion cannot be based on generalisations or stereotypical images of certain groups or categories of people as more likely to be involved in criminal activity.

6.35 There are also controversial powers to stop and search a person where there are no reasonable grounds to suspect that the person is in possession of the prohibited items referred to above. Criminal Justice and Public Order Act 1994 s60 gives an inspector or above the power to authorise the stop and search of persons and vehicles within a locality where he or she has a reasonable belief that serious violent incidents may take place within that locality and he or she believes it is expedient to make the authorisation to prevent their occurrence. The power also exists where there is reasonable belief that there are persons in the area carrying offensive weapons without good reason. The authorisation is for up to 24 hours. Any constable then has the power to stop any pedestrian and search him or her for dangerous instruments or offensive weapons. Such a search can take place whether or not there are reasonable grounds for suspecting a person of carrying such weapons or articles.

6.36 These powers to stop, search and detain are subject to the procedural provisions of PACE being carried out. Thus a uniformed officer must tell the person it is proposed to search his or her name and police station, the object of the proposed search, the grounds and the suspect's right to a record of the search.[44] It is likely that failure to comply with these rules will make the search and detention unlawful.[45]

---

43 'Reasonable grounds to suspect' are also described in relation to arrest powers – see para 6.44.

44 PACE s2.

45 *Osman v DPP* [1999] COD 446.

The officer must make a record of the search with prescribed information included such as the object of the search and the ground.[46] Failure to provide this information does not make the search and detention unlawful.[47]

6.37    The power to detain a person to carry out the search is for such period as is reasonably practicable for the search to take place either at the place where the person is stopped or nearby.[48] This could include, presumably, taking a person to a nearby police station to carry out the search. Certainly it is commonplace for police officers needing to carry out a strip-search or intimate search of a person suspected of being in possession of drugs to take the person to be searched to a police station for this to take place. There is a specific requirement in PACE that a person to be searched should not be made to remove more than outer clothing in public.[49]

6.38    In addition, PACE s117 (which allows a police officer to use reasonable force in carrying out functions under the Act) extends to detaining a person to allow a search under the Act to be effected.[50] In *Parry v Sharples* police officers detained a man at gun-point without giving any reasons while his house was searched under the authority of a warrant, but the Court of Appeal said that the 'controlling or restraining', which amounted to a wrongful arrest, was otherwise justified under PACE s117, which allows a police officer to use reasonable force in carrying out his or her duties under the Act. In *DDP v Meaden*,[51] the court confirmed that restricting the occupants of a house to one room while a lawful search was underway was also justified under PACE s117.

6.39    It is arguable that stop and search powers where a person is detained, for however short a period of time, do not comply with ECHR article 5(1). It could be said that the detention comes within article 5(1)(b) and that the detention is necessary 'in order to secure the

---

46   PACE s3.
47   *Basher v DPP* [1993] COD 372.
48   PACE s2(8).
49   PACE s2(9).
50   (1991) 17 July, CA, unreported.
51   [2004] 1 WLR 945.

fulfilment of any obligation prescribed by law', but this has been held to apply only to a pre-existing positive duty under the law.[52]

6.40 However, it is submitted that the better answer might be that the 'reasonable suspicion' prescribed by PACE s1 is consistent with the test in article 5(1)(c) that detention is 'reasonably considered necessary to prevent his committing an offence', because the officer must have reasonable grounds for suspecting that he will find stolen or prohibited articles. This necessarily involves the officer reasonably suspecting that the suspect is then and there committing a criminal offence, such as handling stolen goods or possession of an offensive weapon. Of course, by article 5(3) 'everyone arrested or detained in accordance with the provisions of paragraph 1(c) ... shall be brought promptly before a judge'. However, simply because a person is released after preliminary inquiries does not a constitute a breach of article 5(3).[53]

6.41 A third approach is that adopted in the case of *R (Laporte) v Chief Constable of Gloucestershire*.[54] In that case the Divisional Court found that a transitory detention to prevent a breach of the peace would not constitute a breach of the article 5 right not to be deprived of liberty. Presumably, it would be argued that a detention of a few minutes to carry out a search would likewise be a 'transitory' detention which would not engage article 5.

6.42 That the detention for a stop and search is compatible with article 5 will not necessarily apply (other than the last point made above) where the stop and search is carried out pursuant to Criminal Justice and Public Order Act 1994 s60 as 'reasonable suspicion' is not a legal requirement for such a stop and search.

### Arrest without warrant

6.43 There are many powers to arrest a person without a warrant. The following is a list of the powers which frequently arise in civil action cases against the police:

---

52  *R (Laporte) v Chief Constable of Gloucestershire* [2004] 2 All ER 874 at [45] (but see judgment of Court of Appeal [2005] 1 All ER 473 which does not deal with the article 5 point); and see *Engels v Netherlands (No 1)* (1976) EHRR 647 at [69]. The general obligation upon all citizens to obey the law cannot be invoked as founding the article 5(1)(b) exception: see *Lawless v Ireland (No 3)* (1961) 1 EHRR 15.

53  *Ergadoz v Turkey* (1997) 21 October, ECtHR, unreported.

54  [2004] 2 All ER 874 at [46]–[47].

- The police have reasonable grounds for suspecting that an arrestable offence[55] has been, or is about to be, committed; and they have reasonable grounds for suspecting the person arrested to be guilty of the offence, or for suspecting the person is about to commit the offence.[56]
- There are many offences which do not come within the definition of arrestable offence which, confusingly, carry their own power of arrest. Examples include the power to arrest without warrant anyone whose conduct is reasonably suspected as likely to cause harassment, alarm or distress (following a warning to stop such conduct);[57] and the power to arrest a person who is drunk and disorderly.[58]
- In relation to non-arrestable offences, then the police can still arrest a person if they have reasonable grounds for suspecting that the offence has been committed, attempted or is in the process of being committed or attempted, and reasonable grounds for suspecting that the person arrested has done any of these acts; and either the service of a summons is impracticable or inappropriate because any of the general arrest conditions are satisfied.[59] The general arrest conditions relate to failure of the suspected person to provide a satisfactory name or address, or the need to protect others or the person arrested or property, or prevent an unlawful obstruction of the highway.[60]
- The police may arrest without warrant a person committing a breach of the peace;[61] a person who, it is reasonably apprehended,

---

55  Arrestable offence is defined by PACE s24(1). It includes offences for which there is a power to imprison for five years or more. It also includes offences listed in PACE Sch 1A which do not fit this qualification, including assaulting a police officer in the execution of his or her duty. For a list of arrestable offences (over 100) see further Cape and Luqmani, *Defending Suspects at Police Stations*, (4th edn, LAG, 2003).

56  PACE s24(6) and (7).

57  Public Order Act 1986 s5.

58  Criminal Justice Act 1967 s91(1).

59  PACE s25(1) and (2).

60  PACE s25(3).

61  In the leading case of *R v Howell* [1982] QB 416 at 427, Watkins LJ stated that a breach of the peace is committed '...whenever harm is actually done or is likely to be done to a person or in is presence to his property; or a person is in fear of being harmed through an assault, an affray, a riot, unlawful assembly or other disturbance'. See also *Porter v Commissioner of Police of the Metropolis* (1999) 20 October, unreported (arrest for breach of the peace where claimant resisted removal from shop premises).

will imminently commit a breach of the peace;[62] or a person who, having committed a breach, is reasonably expected to be about to renew it.[63] In *McGrogan*,[64] the Court of Appeal noted that the common law power to arrest had been given a 'clean bill of health' by the European Court of Human Rights in the case of *Steel v UK*[65] and noted the need, under the breach of the peace power, to comply with the requirement under article 5(1)(c) to bring a lawfully detained person before a court at the earliest opportunity.[66]

## Reasonable grounds to suspect

6.44   For both arrestable and non-arrestable offences the test of 'reasonable grounds to suspect' a person of committing an offence is of crucial importance. It must be established by the police for an arrest and detention to be lawful. It is very often claimed by claimants (and becomes a pivotal issue at trial) that such reasonable grounds to suspect were lacking. Not surprisingly, there is a significant body of caselaw on the issue.

6.45   A mere suspicion, in the sense of a hunch, would not be sufficient to justify an arrest, but the present law on 'reasonable grounds' for that suspicion shows that the standard the police have to meet is not a high one.

62  A police officer must 'honestly believe on reasonable grounds' that a breach of the peace is imminent for an arrest before the breach takes place to be lawful: *Lewis v Chief Constable of Greater Manchester* (1991) *Independent* 23 October. Where the behaviour of a person is provocative but lawful, the power to arrest must only be exercised in the clearest of circumstances that violence was imminent: *Foulkes v Chief Constable of Merseyside* [1998] 3 All ER 705; and see also *Maguire v Chief Constable of Cumbria* [2001] EWCA Civ 619.

63  The breach of the peace (actual or imminent) can occur in private or in public: *McConnell v Chief Constable of Greater Manchester* [1990] 1 WLR 364. If in private it is not necessary that persons outside the property are affected, although this could be a highly relevant factor: *McQuade v Chief Constable of Humberside* [2002] 1 WLR 1347.

64  *Chief Constable of Cleveland v McGrogan* [2002] 1 FLR 707.

65  (1998) 28 EHRR 603.

66  See also *R (Laporte) v Chief Constable of Gloucestershire* [2004] 2 All ER 874 where the Divisional Court found that a transitory detention to prevent an imminent breach of the peace would not engage the right to liberty under article 5, provided a person was quickly released once the danger of the breach of the peace had gone. How long a transitory detention could last was not defined, but the 2.5 hours in that case 'went far beyond anything which could conceivably constitute transitory detention': at [47] per May LJ. See, though the judgment of the Court of Appeal at [2005] 1 All ER 473 which did not deal with the article 5 point.

6.46    Suspicion itself (whether or not based on reasonable grounds) is a state of conjecture or surmise where proof is lacking[67] and is something much less than knowledge of guilt. In the often cited case of *Hussein v Chong Fook Kam*[68] Lord Devlin said:

> Suspicion in its ordinary meaning is a state of conjecture or surmise where proof is lacking: 'I suspect but I cannot prove'. Suspicion arises at or near the starting point of an investigation of which the obtaining of prima facie proof is the end.

6.47    Something more, though, is required to show that the suspicion is based on reasonable grounds. Whether the suspicion is reasonable is an objective test based on what a reasonable person who knew the law and was told the facts of the case would believe at the material time.[69] However, in general terms it is important to note that where the police have ostensibly reliable information concerning a crime from a third party then, in the vast majority of circumstances, this will constitute reasonable grounds to suspect a person of a crime.[70]

6.48    If the suspect provides an explanation when challenged then the police should take this into account in deciding whether their initial suspicion can be maintained or remains based on reasonable grounds.[71]

6.49    In *O'Hara v Chief Constable of the Royal Ulster Constabulary*,[72] the House of Lords considered the situation where an officer arrests a person on the basis of information he or she obtains at a police briefing. It was held that an officer could not simply be instructed to carry out an arrest as a result of such a briefing. However, so long as the officer has information from the briefing which gives him or her suspicion of guilt which is reasonably held, then an arrest will be lawful. In practice, this approach is applied not only where there are formal briefings but in any situation where one police officer arrests a person on the basis of information received from another. The European Court of Human Rights approved the approach in *O'Hara* and found that it complied with the requirements of article 5(1).[73]

---

67    *Holtham v Commissioner of Police of the Metropolis* (1987) *Times* 28 November, CA.

68    [1970] AC 942 at 948.

69    *Bull v Chief Constable of Sussex* (1995) 159 LGR 893.

70    *Jones v Chief Constable of Bedfordshire* (1999) 30 July, unreported.

71    *Banjo v Chief Constable of Greater Manchester* (1997) 24 June, unreported; *Mabey v Chief Constable of Hampshire* (1995) 29 June, CA, unreported.

72    [1997] AC 286.

73    *O'Hara v UK* (2002) 34 EHRR 32.

6.50    However, the suspicion of a police officer could not be reasonably held if, for example, the briefing made it clear that sources were unreliable or non-existent. And if the briefing officer has told the arresting officer that there is reliable information when there is not, the chief constable may become vicariously liable for false imprisonment on the basis that the first officer has wrongly procured the arrest.[74]

6.51    If the arresting officer's information comes from an entry on the police national computer then it may only be sufficient to found reasonable suspicion if there is such urgency so as to make further inquiry impractical.[75] Presumably the police will claim this is often the case if they receive the information during a stop and search of a person on the street or in a vehicle.

6.52    However, in *James v Chief Constable of South Wales Police*,[76] the Court of Appeal warned that, while it was not the law that reasonable suspicion could not be based solely upon information received from an informant, 'such information should be treated with considerable reserve, and any police officer should hesitate before regarding it, without more, as a basis for reasonable suspicion'.

6.53    If suspicion falls on more than one person in circumstances where only one person could have committed that crime (for example, where the police suspect that one member of a group is responsible but cannot identify which) then it may be appropriate to arrest all the suspects until evidence is available to establish whether the suspicion is well-founded by interview.[77] However, the police should clearly take whatever steps they can to exclude any members of the group if possible.

6.54    In *Castorina v Chief Constable of Surrey*[78] (a case often cited in civil actions against the police), police investigated a burglary from a company which appeared to have been committed by someone with inside information. The managing director informed the police that the only person with a grudge against the company was an ex-employee. She was arrested and held for nearly four hours before being released without charge. Her claim for false imprisonment failed, because the police successfully argued to the Court of Appeal that, on this

---

74  *Clarke v Chief Constable of North Wales* (2000) 5 April, unreported at [23].
75  *Hough v Chief Constable of Staffordshire* (2001) *Times* 14 February.
76  (1991) *Daily Telegraph* 3 May, CA per Lord Donaldson MR.
77  *Clarke v Chief Constable of North Wales* (2000) 5 April, unreported; *Cumming v Chief Constable of Northumbria* (2004) *Times* 2 January.
78  (1988) 138 NLJ Rep 180, CA. See also the more recent discussion in *Al-Fayed v Metropolitan Police Commissioner* [2004] EWCA Civ 1579.

information, they had reasonable cause to suspect that she had committed the burglary and, in these circumstances, it was unnecessary for them to make further inquiries before arresting her.

6.55 Lord Woolf in *Castorina* identified the three questions to be answered in a case where it is alleged there has been an unlawful arrest and the question is whether the exercise of the power of arrest without warrant was lawful:

(1) Did the arresting officer suspect that the person who was arrested was guilty of the offence? (The answer to this question depends entirely on the findings of fact as to the officer's state of mind.)

(2) Assuming the officer had the necessary suspicion, was there reasonable cause for that suspicion? (This is a purely objective requirement to be determined by the judge on the facts alone.)

(3) (If the answer to the two previous questions is in the affirmative, then the officer has a discretion which entitles him to make an arrest.) Has that discretion been exercised in accordance with the principles laid down by Lord Greene MR in *Associated Provincial Picture Houses Ltd v Wednesbury Corporation* [1948] 1 KB 223?

6.56 The question of actual suspicion (see question 1 in *Castorina* above) is a matter to be left to the jury at trial. However, there must be some 'cogent evidence' upon which the jury could conclude that such suspicion was lacking before the judge can leave this matter to them.[79] However, recently the Court of Appeal indicated that such evidence can be circumstantial in nature and that a claimant may only be called upon to provide slight evidence of a lack of honest belief or an ulterior motive.[80] This question is most relevant in cases where it is alleged by a claimant that the police have falsified their version of events (for example that the claimant had assaulted a police officer before the claimant was arrested). If the claimant's version of events that this is not true is accepted then it must follow that the police officer had no honestly held suspicion that the claimant had carried out the offence of assault.

6.57 The question of what amounts to 'reasonable grounds' is a question of law which must be decided by the judge, not the jury.[81] The jury's role is to resolve any conflicting evidence as to what

---

79 *Dallison v Cafferty* [1965] 1 QB 348.

80 *Paul v Chief Constable of Humberside* [2004] EWCA Civ 308 at [44] citing *Gibbs v Rea* [1998] AC 786.

81 *Lister v Perryman* (1870) LR 4 HL 521; *McArdle v Egan* [1933] All ER Rep 611.

happened. It is important that the judge leaves any factual issues to the jury.[82] The same approach is applied where the court has to decide whether an arresting officer had 'a reasonable belief' that a breach of the peace is likely to occur.[83]

6.58    As indicated in Lord Woolf's third question in *Castorina*, police officers have a discretion whether to exercise their powers of arrest or not, even where there are reasonable grounds to suspect a person. So even where the police have satisfied the condition precedent for arrest, it is open to the claimant to show that the power to arrest was exercised, in a public law sense (see para 17.67), unreasonably[84] and therefore unlawfully. The power to arrest must be exercised in good faith to be lawful. The court will evaluate the exercise of the discretion in the same way as it evaluates the exercise of any public law discretion, but will bear in mind the important right to liberty, protected by ECHR article 5 , which is at stake.[85] This might be relevant for example where there were straightforward inquiries that the police might have carried out to ascertain whether the suspicion held about a person was reasonably held or not. For example, if a suspect says that he has a till receipt in the next room which will show he was in a shop at the time the offence was committed, then it might be unreasonable to arrest him without first providing an opportunity for the person to present that till receipt.

6.59    The burden of proof to show that the arrest was unreasonable is on the claimant and, as in all cases where public law unreasonableness has to be proved, the hurdle to cross is a high one. There are few successful cases, but in one case where an arresting officer had reasonable grounds to suspect that the person arrested was guilty of an arrestable offence but also knew that the arrested person's victim had accepted an apology and was not pressing charges, the court held it would be possible for the claimant to argue that, as there was no prospect at all of him being prosecuted, the arrest was unlawful.[86] If the police had an ulterior motive for the arrest (that is, the arrest was carried out in bad faith) such as, in one case, an intention to prevent the claimant taking

---

82    See *Balchin v Chief Constable of Hampshire* (2001) *Times* 4 May for a case where the trial judge was found to have usurped the jury's fact-finding function.

83    *Kelly v Chief Constable of Hampshire* (1993) *Independent* 25 March, CA (see further Chapter 13 on the respective roles of judge and jury).

84    *Holgate Mohammed v Duke* [1984] AC 437; and *Associated Provincial Picture Houses v Wednesbury Corporation* [1948] 1 KB 223.

85    *Cumming v Chief Constable of Northumbria* [2003] EWCA Civ 1844 at [44].

86    *Plange v Chief Constable of South Humberside* (1992) *Times* 23 March.

part in civil proceedings, then the arrest may be unreasonable.[87] In *Paul v Chief Constable of Humberside*[88] the Court of Appeal held that questions of fact regarding the police motives should have been left to the jury in a trial where it was argued that the decisions of the police were vitiated by the ulterior motive of distracting public attention from their own improper conduct.

6.60    So far as the justification for detention on grounds of reasonable suspicion in article 5(1)(c) is concerned, the Strasbourg test is very similar to the domestic test:

> Having a 'reasonable suspicion' presupposes the existence of facts or information which would satisfy an objective observer that the person concerned may have committed the offence in question.[89]

6.61    In *O'Hara v United Kingdom*[90] the European Court of Human Rights made a number of other observations. The court emphasised that the 'reasonableness' of the suspicion on which an arrest must be based forms an essential part of the safeguard against arbitrary arrest and detention laid down in article ECHR 5(1)(c). The court also commented that the standard imposed by article 5(1)(c) does not presuppose that the police have sufficient evidence to bring charges at the time of arrest.

> The object of questioning during detention under sub-paragraph (c) of Article 5.1 is to further the criminal investigation by way of confirming or dispelling the concrete suspicion grounding the arrest. Thus facts which raise a suspicion need not be of the same level as those necessary to justify a conviction, or even the bringing of a charge which comes at the next stage of the process of criminal investigation.[91]

6.62    As regards 'terrorist crime' and proving reasonable suspicion, the court said:[92]

> ... the police may be called upon, in the interests of public safety, to arrest a suspected terrorist on the basis of information which is reliable but which cannot be disclosed to the suspect or produced in court, without jeopardising the informant. However, though Contracting States cannot be

---

87    *Matin v Commissioner of Police of the Metropolis* (2001) 21 June, unreported, where the judge refused for this reason to strike out a false imprisonment claim.

88    (2004) 17 March, unreported.

89    *Fox, Campbell and Hartley v United Kingdom* (1981) 13 EHRR 157.

90    (2002) 34 EHRR 32.

91    (2002) 34 EHRR 32 at [36].

92    (2002) 34 EHRR 32 at [35].

required to establish the reasonableness of the suspicion grounding the arrest of a suspected terrorist by disclosing confidential sources of information, the Court has held that the exigencies of dealing with terrorist crime cannot justify stretching the notion of 'reasonableness' to the point where the safeguard secured by Article 5.1(c) is impaired. Even in those circumstances, the respondent Government have to furnish at least some facts or information capable of satisfying the Court that the arrested person was reasonably suspected of having committed the alleged offence.

## Information to be provided upon arrest

6.63    Even if an arrest or stop and search can be justified by the police, a claim for false imprisonment may still succeed if it can be shown that legal requirements at the time of arrest have not been complied with. The requirement that most often arises in civil actions is the necessity for the police to inform a person upon arrest of the fact and of the grounds for the arrest, either at the time of the arrest or as soon as practicable afterwards. If the police fail to do either of these things, the arrest is unlawful.[93] The Court of Appeal[94] has held that the best statement of the principles involved are to be found in the decision of the European Court of Human Rights in *Fox v United Kingdom.*[95] The court was considering, not PACE s28(3), but ECHR article 5(2), which provides as follows: 'Everyone who is arrested shall be informed promptly, in a language which he understands, of the reasons for his arrest and of any charge against him'. The court said:

> Paragraph 2 of Article 5 contains the elementary safeguard that any person arrested should know why he is being deprived of his liberty. This provision is an integral part of the scheme of protection afforded by Article 5: by virtue of paragraph (2) any person arrested must be told, in simple, non-technical language that he can understand, the essential legal and factual grounds for his arrest, so as to be able, if he sees fit, to apply to a court to challenge its lawfulness in accordance with paragraph (4) ... Whilst this information must be conveyed 'promptly' (in French: *'dans le plus court délai'*), it need not be related in its entirety by the arresting officer at the very moment of the arrest. Whether the content and promptness of the information conveyed were sufficient is to be assessed in each case according to its special features.[96]

---

93   PACE s28(1) and (3). The provisions enact the common law requirements as set out in *Christie v Leachinsky* [1947] AC 573.

94   *Taylor v Chief Constable of Thames Valley* [2004] 3 All ER 503.

95   (1991) 13 EHRR 157.

96   (1991) 13 EHRR 157 at [40].

6.64    Thus, it may not be necessary to specify a particular crime or to use precise and technical language if, by using commonplace language, it is clear to the suspect what type of offence he was being arrested for, so that he has an opportunity to volunteer information which would avoid the arrest.[97] For example, in *Clarke v Chief Constable of North Wales*, Sedley LJ said:

> Although no constable ever admits to saying 'You're nicked for handling this gear' or 'I'm having you for twoc-ing this motor', either will do and, I have no doubt, frequently does.[98]

6.65    Whether sufficient information has been provided will include a consideration of the particular suspect (for example, if the suspect is a minor).[99] If the police have specific information about the alleged offence (such as when and where it occurred) it may be unlawful for this information not to be relayed to the arrested person at the time of the arrest.[100] However, in *Clarke* the majority found that the police did not have to specify which class of controlled drugs a person was being arrested for, even though there is no power to arrest for Class C drugs (although see the judgment of Sedley LJ for doubts about this approach). The police cannot argue that the reason for the arrest is obvious.[101] In *Edwards v DPP*,[102] a case where the officer failed to state one of the general arrest conditions in addition to the non-arrestable offence for which a person was being arrested (see para 6.43), the Divisional Court said that it:

> ... had sympathy for police officers in difficult circumstances but it had to be borne in mind that giving the correct information as to the reason for an arrest was a matter of the utmost constitutional significance in a case where a reason can be and is given at the time of the arrest.

---

97    *Abbassy v Commissioner of Police of the Metropolis* [1990] 1 WLR 385, CA; and see *Christie v Leachinsky* [1947] AC 573; *Ghafar v Chief Constable of West Midlands* (2000) 12 May, unreported; *Clarke v Chief Constable of North Wales* (2000) 5 April, unreported.

98    (2000) 5 April, unreported at [36].

99    *Taylor v Chief Constable of Thames Valley* [2004] 3 All ER 503.

100    *Wilson v Chief Constable of Lancashire* [2001] 2 WLR 302; but see *Taylor v Chief Constable of Thames Valley* [2004] 3 All ER 503 where the Court of Appeal overturned the trial judge's finding that reference to throwing stones should have been made when arresting a person for public order offences at a demonstration.

101    PACE s28(3) and (4).

102    [1993] COD 378.

6.66 It is not necessary for the arresting officer to provide the reasons him or herself, so long as these are provided by another officer.[103] It is lawful for the police to arrest a person and not provide him or her with the necessary information if it is not reasonably practicable to do so (for instance, if the person is struggling violently). The police still have a duty to inform the person that he or she is under arrest and the ground for the arrest as soon as it becomes practicable:[104] the arrest and detention will be lawful up to the time when it would have been practicable to have informed the person.[105]

6.67 Where it would have been practicable to inform a person of the reason for his or her arrest, but this was not done until some time later, the arrest and the detention will be unlawful until those reasons are given.[106] In practice, this will usually happen when a person is taken before the custody officer at the police station and the circumstances of his or her arrest are recounted by the arresting officer in the presence of the person arrested and recorded on the custody record.

### False imprisonment and detention after arrest

6.68 Even if the arrest was based on lawful grounds and the procedural requirements have been complied with, the detention of a person can become unlawful if the police do not comply with the detailed rules set out in PACE. The custody officer at a police station is not under a duty to determine whether the initial arrest was lawfully made.[107] However the custody officer does have a duty to determine whether there is sufficient evidence to justify a charge against a suspect as soon as practicable after the suspect has arrived at the station.[108] If there is not sufficient evidence at this point, then the further detention of the suspect should only be authorised if there are 'reasonable grounds for believing that his detention without charge is necessary to secure or preserve evidence relating to an offence for which he is under arrest or to obtain evidence by questioning him'.[109]

6.69 If this 'necessity principle' is not met, then it seems that a suspect should be released at once and, if appropriate, be given a date to return

---

103 *Dhesi v Chief Constable of West Midlands* (2000) *Times* 9 May.
104 PACE s28(1) and (3).
105 *DPP v Hawkins* [1988] 1 WLR 1166, DC.
106 *Lewis v Chief Constable of South Wales* [1991] 1 All ER 206, CA.
107 *Clarke v Chief Constable of North Wales* (2000) 5 April, unreported.
108 PACE s37(1) and (10).
109 PACE s37(2) and (3).

to the station. In practice, however, custody officers almost automatically authorise detention without taking the principle into consideration and without recording on the custody record what were the 'reasonable grounds' that made the detention 'necessary'.[110] However, it should be noted that the Court of Appeal has held that the necessity principle is met unless the decision of the custody officer to authorise detention is so unreasonable that no custody sergeant could have reached that conclusion.[111] If this is right it waters down considerably an important safeguard for the detained person.

6.70    If the detention is not necessary, this failure by custody officers can make the 'authorised' detention unlawful. Sedley LJ provided a practical explanation of the test in relation to when it will be lawful to detain a person for questioning:

> To detain a person for questioning in the hope that something incriminating will come out is clearly illegal. To detain someone until she has been questioned about an offence which she is suspected on reasonable grounds of having committed is, by contrast, lawful so long as the suspicion has not meanwhile been dispelled and the questioning is not unnecessarily delayed.[112]

6.71    The police may be liable for false imprisonment if other provisions of PACE are not complied with during detention. For instance, PACE requires that the detention should be reviewed at periodic intervals, and consideration given whether continued detention is necessary using a similar test to that applied when the original detention is authorised.[113] If the review is not properly carried out, then the detention from the time of the review will become unlawful. This is the case even if the police can argue that if the review had been carried out, further detention would have been authorised.[114]

6.72    If, during a person's detention, it becomes clear that the reasonable grounds for suspecting them of an offence which justified the initial arrest have disappeared, then the grounds for continued detention

---

110 McKenzie et al, 'Helping the police with their enquiries: the necessity principle and voluntary attendance at the police station' [1990] Crim LR 22, and Mackenzie, 'Detention in a police station and false imprisonment' (1992) 142 NLJ 534.

111 *Wilding v Chief Constable of Lancashire* (1995) 22 May, CA, unreported.

112 *Clarke v Chief Constable of North Wales* (2000) 5 April, unreported at [43].

113 PACE s40.

114 See PACE s40(3)(a) and *Roberts v Chief Constable of Cheshire* [1999] 2 All ER 326.

also disappear and a custody officer must release the person immediately.[115] For example, if the suspected package found on a person turns out not to be an illegal drug then a person must be released. However, if a number of people are arrested for the same offence, it may be reasonable to detain them all until all have been interviewed about the offence.[116] If a person is arrested for both an arrestable offence and an offence for which there is no power of arrest, then if the grounds for detention for the arrestable offence have disappeared, it will be unlawful (unless the general arrest conditions apply (see para 6.43)) to continue to detain the person for the offence with no power of arrest attached (a summons can be issued instead). If there is unreasonable delay[117] in investigating the case for which a person has been arrested, for example delay in carrying out an interview, this delay may lead to a claim for a period of false imprisonment.[118]

6.73    In addition, if the police fail to follow the provisions enabling them to detain someone in excess of the statutory time limits (generally 24 hours in the first instance),[119] the detention becomes unlawful. Even after the granting of a warrant of extended detention, the regime of reviews should be continued to make the detention lawful. The powers of a custody officer should normally be performed by an officer designated for that purpose, but it seems as though the courts will not strictly enforce this provision and other officers will be able to exercise the powers in his or her place.[121]

6.74    Unless a person is released from police custody after being charged, the detention will be unlawful unless one or more of the limited grounds exist for keeping a person at the police station.[122]

6.75    Where a person is detained after arrest for breach of the peace, continued detention at the police station of the person is justified (for the purpose of bringing the person before a magistrates' court to obtain

---

115    PACE s34(2). See *Youssef v Home Office* (2004) 9 August, unreported, for an example in the immigration detention context.

116    *Clarke v Chief Constable of North Wales* (2000) 5 April, unreported.

117    *Wilding v Chief Constable of Lancashire* (1995) CA Transcript 574.

118    *Taylor v Chief Constable of Thames Valley* [2004] 3 All ER 503 where the Court of Appeal referred to the 'relevant principles' relating to expedition set out in paras 1.1 and 1.1A of Code C of the PACE Codes of Practice.

119    PACE ss34 and 41–43.

121    PACE, s31(6) and see *Vince v Chief Constable of Dorset* [1992] 3 All ER, 98, QBD.

122    PACE s38; and see *Paul v Chief Constable of Humberside* [2004] EWCA Civ 308 at [53]–[59] for discussion of this area by the Court of Appeal.

a bind-over) where there is a reasonably held apprehension that the breach of the peace will be renewed within a short time but otherwise a person should be released.[123] Arrest and detention to bring before a court for a breach of the peace is a common law power and PACE does not apply.[124] However, the Court of Appeal has commented that it is 'good practice' for the police to treat any person detained for breach of the peace as if PACE applied to the detention, as there is a need to review the detention regularly to ascertain if it remains justified.[125]

## Arrest under warrant

6.76    If a person is arrested under a warrant, he or she has no claim against the police officer who acts in obedience to the warrant.[126] Thus, it will be a complete defence to a claim for false imprisonment that a court has issued the warrant and that the police have executed it by taking the person into custody. However, the police would not be protected if they did not, in fact, comply with the warrant, for example by arresting someone who was not named in the warrant,[127] or if the warrant was not signed or sealed.

6.77    In *Ward v Commissioner of Police of the Metropolis*[128] a warrant issued to the police by a magistrate under the Mental Health Act 1983 included a condition as to which doctors should be present when the warrant was executed. The condition was not complied with, and even though there was no statutory provision to impose such a condition, the Court of Appeal held that the warrant had been unlawfully executed. The court held that in deciding the important question of the lawfulness of the execution of the warrant, ECHR article 5 must be borne in mind.

6.78    Problems may arise if the warrant does not use the correct form of words. While it has been held that an officer is protected in obeying a warrant that was 'invalid or unlawful' because it did not contain the form of words required,[129] it is doubtful whether he or she would

123   *Chief Constable of Cleveland v McGrogan* [2002] 1 FLR 707.
124   *Williamson v Chief Constable of West Midlands* [2004] 1 WLR 14.
125   *Chief Constable of Cleveland v McGrogan* [2002] 1 FLR 707 at [44]; *Williamson v Chief Constable of West Midlands* [2004] 1 WLR 14 at [23].
126   Constables Protection Act 1750 s6.
127   *Hoye v Bush* (1840) 1 Man & G 775.
128   [2003] EWCA Civ 1152.
129   *Horsfield v Brown* [1932] 1 KB 355 at 369.

be protected by a warrant that had a more substantial defect, such as the omission of the cause of arrest or the address at which it should be executed (if this is required by statute).[130]

6.79    If an officer is executing a warrant to arrest a person for an offence, the warrant does not need to be in the officer's possession at the time of the arrest but should be shown to the arrested person as soon as practicable on demand.[131]

## Remedies

6.80    In theory there are three legal remedies for false imprisonment:

- self-help, that is escape;
- habeas corpus;
- damages.

### Escape

6.81    In practice the dangers, both physical and legal, of attempting to escape from unlawful custody mean it should not be regarded as a 'remedy' at all. Its practical importance is rather as a defence if charged with a criminal offence, say, assault with intent to resist arrest.[132]

### Habeas corpus and judicial review

6.82    Habeas corpus is an emergency remedy. It can be used to bring a false imprisonment to an end but is suitable only where there is no legal basis for the detention.[133] It is often used in conjunction with an application for judicial review challenging the lawfulness on public law grounds of a detention. Public funding can be obtained to apply to the High Court, and the urgency procedure can be used to secure an urgent hearing. In some cases, where for example a detention at a police station is clearly unlawful, a telephone application to a judge for an injunction to order the release of the person may be possible. Such applications are unusual given the amount of time a person will usually be detained at a police station. The usual remedy is to sue for damages after the event.

---

130  See *Ward v Commissioner of Police of the Metropolis* [2003] EWCA Civ 1152 for discussion of the lawfulness of a 'sloppily drafted' warrant.

131  Magistrates' Courts Act 1980 s125.

132  Offences Against the Person Act 1861 s38, as amended.

133  *R v Holmes ex p Sherman* [1981] 2 All ER 612.

*Damages*

6.83    Damages for false imprisonment are discussed at para 14.51.

# Assault and battery

6.84    Assault and battery are two of the torts which constitute trespass to the person. False imprisonment is the third. Clerk and Lindsell define the principles on which the torts are based and explain the differences between them as follows:

> Interference, however slight, with a person's elementary civil right to security of the person, and self-determination in relation to his own body, constitutes trespass to the person ... A battery is committed when there is an actual infliction of an unlawful physical contact with the claimant, and assault where the claimant is caused to apprehend the immediate infliction of such a contact.[134]

## Battery

### Definition

6.85    The fundamental principle of the tort of battery is that everybody's person is inviolate and even the slightest touching of another person may amount to a battery. The effect is 'that everyone is protected not only against physical injury but against any form of physical molestation'.[135] It is not necessary that the claimant suffers pain or physical injury as a result. Thus cutting hair,[136] taking fingerprints[137] and taking hold of the plaintiff's arm by a police officer in order to administer a caution[138] can all amount to battery, just as much as rough handling during an arrest or a deliberate attack. A battery usually involves direct physical contact being made with the claimant, either by the assailant's body or by something under his direct control. In the case of police officers common examples of the latter are the use of a baton, CS gas spray or a police dog.

6.86    Unless the police are exercising a power of arrest or another specific power (see para 6.98), they have no greater rights than members of the public and therefore any physical contact by a police officer

---

134   *Clerk & Lindsell on Torts* (18th edn, Sweet & Maxwell, 2000) para 13-01.
135   See *Collins v Wilcock* [1984] 1 WLR 1172 at 1177 per Robert Goff LJ.
136   *Forde v Skinner* (1830) 4 C & P 239.
137   *Dumbell v Roberts* [1944] 1 All ER 326.
138   *Collins v Wilcock* [1984] 1 WLR 1172.

with another person may be unlawful as a battery. They may, of course, raise the same defences to the battery that members of the public can raise.

## Intent

6.87 The physical contact must be intentional or reckless for it to amount to a battery. The conduct is intentional if the claimant shows that the police deliberately used some physical force against him or her. There does not need to be any intention to cause the claimant injury or damage through the physical contact. Nor does the extent of the claimant's injuries have to be foreseen.[139] Thus, the police may be liable for unintended, serious injuries resulting from a relatively minor but deliberate act of force.[140] Although for many years it had been argued that there must be an element of 'hostility' in the intentional contact for there to be a battery,[141] it now seems clear that any conduct exceeding ordinary acceptable boundaries will suffice.[142] A battery will also be established if the force is applied recklessly, in the sense that the officer foresaw the risk of harm to the claimant but nonetheless proceeded to act and caused such harm.[143] If the act was not undertaken intentionally or recklessly, there cannot be a battery, but there may still be a claim in negligence.[144] The distinction is illustrated by the cases involving injuries caused to claimants by police dogs. If the dog is instructed by his police handler to attack the claimant and does so, the officer has committed a battery (subject to the defences discussed below). Whereas if the dog bites the claimant without the handler intending or specifically anticipating this, the only available claim would be in negligence.[145]

139 In contrast to the position in a negligence claim: see chapter 8.
140 See, eg, *Wilson v Commissioner of Police of the Metropolis* [2002] EWCA Civ 434 where the claimant sustained serious head injuries, for which the defendant was liable, as a result of an officer deliberately barging him to the ground.
141 *Cole v Turner* (1704) Holt KB 108; *Wilson v Pringle* [1986] 2 All ER 440.
142 *Wainwright v Home Office* [2003] 4 All ER 969 at [9], approving *Collins v Wilcock* [1984] 1 WLR 1172 on this point. See also para 6.91.
143 *Haystead v Chief Constable of Derbyshire* [2000] 3 All ER 890, CA.
144 There was a tort of negligent trespass to the person but it is generally thought to be effectively obsolete: see, eg, *Clerk & Lindsell on Torts* (18th edn, Sweet & Maxwell, 2000) paras 13-03 and 13-04; John Murphy, *Street on Torts* (11th edn, Lexis Nexis Butterworths) 2003 pp25–27.
145 See *Pollard v Chief Constable of West Yorkshire* (1998) 28 April, CA, unreported; *Coles v Chief Constable of South Yorkshire* (1998) 12 October, CA, unreported; although Clayton and& Tomlinson argue for a broader approach to battery in this context, see *Civil Actions Against the Police* (3rd ed, Thomson Sweet & Maxwell, 2004) para 4-010.

6.88       If a police officer intends to commit a battery against one person but mistakenly strikes a second, then a battery has been committed against the second person. In one case a soldier shot a rioter while in fact aiming for another. It was no defence to battery that he shot the 'wrong' person in those circumstances.[146] Similarly, where a blow aimed at a mother caused her to drop her child, the assailant was guilty of a battery to the child.[147]

## Defences to battery

6.89       The main issues that arise in practice are whether the claimant consented to the force employed and whether that force was a legitimate use of police powers and/or within the doctrine of self-defence.

### Consent

6.90       There is a general principle of law that, if a person consents to something that would otherwise be an infringement of his or her rights, he or she cannot later complain about it. Thus, if the police search someone in circumstances that are otherwise illegal, but with that person's permission, then he or she cannot subsequently bring an action for battery. Although it is convenient to consider consent as a form of defence, authority indicates the claimant must prove an absence of consent as part of establishing his or her claim.[148]

6.91       In relation to the tort of battery there is an initial presumption that the claimant consents to such contact as is 'generally acceptable in everyday life'.[149] This was illustrated in the case of *Collins v Wilcock* thus:

> ... nobody can complain of the jostling which is inevitable from his presence in, for example a supermarket, an underground station or a busy street ... Among such forms of conduct, long held to be acceptable, is touching a person for the purpose of engaging his attention, though of course using no greater degree of physical contact than is reasonably necessary in the circumstances for that purpose.[150]

6.92       In that case it was held that a claimant who had been grabbed by the arm by a police officer could not be said to have consented to such

146   *Livingston v Ministry of Defence* [1984] 15 NIJB, CA.
147   *Haystead v Chief Constable of Derbyshire* [2000] 3 All ER 890, CA.
148   *Freeman v Home Office (No 2)* [1984] QB 524, CA. Although *Clerk & Lindsell on Torts* (18th edn, Sweet & Maxwell, 2000) consider that lack of consent should be treated as a defence, see para 3-58.
149   *Collins v Wilcock* [1984] 1 WLR 1172 at 1177.
150   [1984] 1 WLR 1172 at 1177.

contact, but in the case of *Donnelly v Jackman*[151] it was held that an officer who had tapped a person twice on the shoulder to question him about an offence had not exceeded the bounds of acceptable conduct and had not therefore committed a battery. The court in *Collins* felt that *Donnelly* was 'an extreme case',[152] as the touching was very slight and the claimant's reaction very violent. Thus, it is submitted that in the vast majority of cases where a police officer, not exercising arrest or other powers, makes physical contact with a member of the public, a battery will have been committed.

6.93     A number of police powers under PACE can be exercised only with the consent of the suspect and/or the authority of an officer of at least the rank of inspector. Consent to the taking of an intimate sample, for example a swab from the anus or vagina, is required[153] so that, if refused, force cannot be used to take the sample. Although consent in writing is required for the taking of a non-intimate sample,[154] such as a nail-clipping or a sample of saliva from the mouth,[155] in contrast to intimate samples, reasonable force to take the sample may be used in certain circumstances where authorised by an inspector (or more senior officer).[156] However, the person must generally be in police detention or in custody under a court order.[157] Similarly, consent to fingerprinting must be in writing[158] if it is given at a police station but, again, there are circumstances where fingerprints can be taken without consent, if authority is given by an officer of at least the rank of inspector.[159] Those detained at a police station may be photographed either with their consent or in circumstances where consent is withheld or it is not practicable to seek to obtain it.[160]

6.94     'Consent' in this context means the consent of the person if aged 17 or over, the consent of the person and the parent or guardian if between the ages of 14 to 16 and the consent of the parent or guardian alone if under the age of 14.[161] If consent is not given by the correct person,

---

151  [1970] 1 WLR 562.
152  [1984] 1 WLR 1172 at 1179.
153  PACE s62(1), save for a urine sample to test for class A drugs after charge: s62B.
154  PACE s63(2).
155  PACE s65(1).
156  PACE s63(3) and (4).
157  PACE ss63(3) and 118(2), unless s63(3A), (3B) or (3C) applies.
158  PACE s61(2).
159  PACE s61(3) and (6).
160  PACE s64A.
161  PACE s65.

it is presumably invalid and a claim for battery should succeed, unless of course the procedures for taking samples or fingerprints without consent have been properly followed.

6.95   A claimant may also be faced with the argument that he or she consented to the conduct complained of in instances where he or she appeared to agree to or participate in the events at the time, for example a claimant who removes his or her clothes during a strip search.

6.96   Special problems may arise if a person appears to consent to the relevant bodily contact, but subsequently denies that the consent was freely given. There is a general principle that:

> ... a man cannot be said to be truly 'willing' unless he is in a position to choose freely, and freedom of choice predicates, not only full knowledge of the circumstances on which the exercise of choice is conditional, so that he may be able to choose wisely, but the absence of any feeling of constraint so that nothing shall interfere with the freedom of his will.[162]

6.97   Thus, a situation might arise where a person is arrested and told at the police station to sign a form to consent to the taking of intimate body samples and threatened that if he or she refuses he or she will be kept there until they do sign. If he or she eventually signs and the samples are taken, then the 'consent' would be invalid because it was obtained under duress and the person could sue for battery. However, while it is clear that an abuse of authority may negate apparent consent,[163] the mere fact that consent was obtained by a show of authority appears to be insufficient. In *Wainwright v Home Office*[164] the Court of Appeal held that consent to strip searching an inmate's visitors, obtained by prison officers indicating that the visit would not go ahead unless the searches were undertaken, was not vitiated by duress. The decision also illustrates another important principle, namely that consent can only be raised against the claimant where he or she consented to the nature and the degree of force that was actually used. In *Wainwright* the defendants could not rely upon the claimants' consent because the searches had been conducted in breach of procedures, whereas the consent had been to searches carried out in the prescribed manner. Additionally, if the police obtain consent by fraudulently representing that they had powers to, for example, take samples in situations where they did not, an action for battery will lie.[165]

---

162   *Bowater v Rowley Regis Corp* [1944] KB 476 at 479.

163   See *Freeman v Home Office (No 2)* [1984] QB 524.

164   [2003] 3 All ER 943. The case went to the House of Lords on other grounds: [2003] 4 All ER 969.

165   See, eg, the discussion in *Clerk & Lindsell on Torts* (18th edn, Sweet & Maxwell, 2000) paras 13-08-13-11.

## Police acting within their powers

6.98 The police have wide powers to make arrests, to stop and search people, to conduct searches, including intimate searches, to take fingerprints and intimate and non-intimate samples, including samples of body tissues and fluids. Where the police have a power under PACE and the power can be exercised without consent, the police may use reasonable force, if necessary, to exercise the power.[166] Two questions will therefore arise:

- did the police act within their powers? and
- where the use of force is permitted in exercising those powers, was the force used reasonable and necessary?

6.99 If the police have acted outside their powers it is unnecessary to consider the second issue as all force used will be tortious. Thus, hand-cuffing or other restraint of a suspect during an unlawful arrest will be a battery.[167]

6.100 The police have a wide range of powers; considerations of space prohibit all those powers being detailed here, though reference will be made to the more common instances. The police have a number of powers to stop and search people.[168] They also have statutory powers to take samples and fingerprints.[169] The police also have statutory powers of arrest.[170] If the police fail to comply with the provisions of the relevant Act when purporting to exercise these powers, they may lay themselves open to an action for battery and assault. The police (and members of the public) also have a power under the Criminal Law Act 1967 to use such force as is reasonable in the circumstances to prevent crime.[171] In addition to statutory powers, the police have common law powers of arrest, most notably where a breach of the peace is, or reasonably appears about to be, committed.[172]

6.101 Police powers relating to a suspect's detention in custody under PACE are further circumscribed by the provisions of Code C of the

---

166 PACE s117.
167 As will force used during an unlawful stop and search: eg, *Samuels v Commissioner of Police of the Metropolis* (1999) 3 March, CA, unreported.
168 See, eg, the powers under PACE ss1, 32, 54 and 55; Misuse of Drugs Act 1972 s23; Criminal Justice and Public Order Act 1994 s60; and Terrorism Act 2000 s44.
169 PACE ss61–63C.
170 See the discussion on false imprisonment at paras 6.2 onwards.
171 Section 3.
172 See *R v Howell* [1982] QB 416.

Codes of Practice issued under s67 of the Act. However, the Act states that a failure on the part of a police officer to comply with a provision of the Code will not of itself render him or her liable to civil (or criminal) proceedings.[173] Thus, a breach of the Code may not lead to a successful civil action in the way that breach of the statutory requirements for the exercise of the power would. For example, an intimate search of body orifices can only be carried out by someone of the same sex,[174] unless the person carrying out the search is a doctor or a nurse. Thus, if a policeman carried out an intimate search of a woman, the search would be unlawful and the woman would have an action for assault and battery. However, Code C provides that nobody of the opposite sex, except a doctor or a nurse, should be present during intimate searches. It is unlikely that breach of this provision would give rise to a civil claim. The only possibility would be to argue, whilst the effect of s67(10) is that a breach of the Code does not of itself amount to a tort; where a tort, such as battery, has been committed unless the action was justified, the police cannot establish the defence of acting within their powers where the Code has not been complied with. This contention has not been directly considered by the courts. Where liability is established for a battery, for example in relation to an unlawful body search, breaches of the Code can certainly be relied upon as features that aggravate the appropriate level of damages.[175]

6.102    Strip searches frequently give rise to difficult legal problems. There are two main issues that require consideration in each instance.[176] First, whether the search was conducted within the terms of the officers' powers. For example, strip searches of detainees at police stations are permitted if the custody officer thinks it necessary in order to remove an article that the detainee would not be allowed to keep and reasons are given (if practicable) and recorded.[177] Second, if the search was not so conducted, whether an assault or battery or any other tortious conduct has been committed. If officers touch the claimant during the course of the search, for example in examining genitals, a battery is established. But in many instances the person being searched removes his or her own clothes and no question of a battery arises. In *Wainwright v Home Office*[178] the House of Lords

---

173   PACE s67(10).
174   PACE s55(7).
175   Aggravated damages in general are discussed in chapter 14.
176   In addition to the issue of consent – see para 6.97.
177   PACE s54 and Code C, Annex A, paras 9–12.
178   [2003] 4 All ER 969.

rejected an argument that the circumstances fell within a new tort of invasion of privacy, saying that it was for parliament, not the courts, to create such a tort if it was required. They also rejected the argument that the circumstances fell within the principle in *Wilkinson v Downton*.[179] The events in *Wainwright* occurred before the Human Rights Act 1998 came into force. A strip search conducted on or after 2 October 2000 may give rise to a freestanding claim under ECHR article 3 and 8.[180] However, in *Wainwright* doubt was expressed that a monetary remedy could be obtained in respect of distress for a breach of article 8 where the improper conduct of the strip search was careless, rather than deliberate.[181] In *Wainwright* it was not argued that the strip searches constituted assaults; this contention would be possible where a claimant establishes that he or she reasonably apprehended force by the officers, if he or she did not remove clothes as instructed.

## Where the use of force is permitted, is it reasonable?

6.103 If the police rely upon their powers under PACE, they may use reasonable force, where necessary.[182] Thus, a defence to this effect may be defeated if the claimant can show, for example, that he or she would have performed the relevant act voluntarily, making the use of force superfluous.[183]

6.104 The issue of whether the force used was reasonable, commonly arises in relation to the exercise of powers under PACE and under the Criminal Law Act 1967 s3 and in respect of common law powers for suppressing breaches of the peace.[184] If some force is justified, then whether the police used more than reasonable force must be judged objectively on the facts. This generally involves a consideration of whether the officers had lesser measures at their disposal that would have sufficed in the circumstances, for example assessing whether an attempt should have been made to handcuff a suspect, before striking him or her with a baton or spraying CS gas. In *Sturley v Commissioner of Police of the Metropolis*[185] a middle-aged woman arrested after a minor traffic offence was restrained by means of a hammer-lock and bar,

179  [1897] 2 QB 57. That principle is discussed subsequently at para 6.128 onwards.
180  See para 6.128 onwards.
181  [2003] 4 All ER 969 at [51] per Lord Hoffmann in particular.
182  PACE s117, above.
183  See *Swales v Cox* [1981] 1 All ER 1115.
184  See para 6.100 above.
185  (1984) *Times* 27 June.

that is holding her arm behind her back and twisting the wrist. Her wrist was twisted so forcefully that the bone was fractured and it was held that, as two officers were present, the degree of force used to restrain someone of the claimant's age was unreasonable and she succeeded in a claim for assault and battery. It has also been held to be unreasonable (on the facts of the case) to restrain a convicted prisoner for 24 hours in a body belt. Damages were awarded for assault.[186] In *Glowacki v Long and Chief Constable of Lancashire*[187] a battery was established where an officer went beyond using approved holds in bringing the claimant to the ground. However, even extreme force will be justified in some circumstances. In *Carey v Commissioner of Police of the Metropolis*[188] it was held that the shooting by police of two men believed to be carrying out an armed robbery, and believed to be attacking the officers, was justified. Clerk and Lindsell state that:

> The degree of force reasonable must be judged in the light of the circumstances apparent to the arrestor and he will not be found to have used unreasonable force because of a defect in the planning of the arrest or crime prevention which with hindsight can be seen to render the amount of force unnecessary.[189]

6.105　In attempting to establish whether the degree of force used was reasonable, the claimant's solicitor should seek access to police manuals (where they are disclosable) on practice and procedure. These are in existence, for example, in the areas of the use of firearms, road craft, self-defence and restraint, the training of police dogs, the use of CS gas sprays and public order.[190]

## Self-defence

6.106　The police (like members of the public) have a good defence to a claim for assault or battery if they can show that they were acting only in self-defence against an attack or attempted attack made on them. However, the amount of force an officer can use in self-defence must be reasonable. In one old case the principle was discussed thus: 'hitting a man

---

186　*Rodrigues v Home Office* February 1989 *Legal Action* 14.
187　(1998) 18 June, CA, unreported.
188　(1989) unreported, but cited in Clayton & Tomlinson, *Civil Actions Against the Police* (3rd edn, Thomson Sweet & Maxwell, 2004) para 4-081.
189　*Clerk & Lindsell on Torts* (18th edn, Sweet & Maxwell, 2004) para 13-41.
190　The website of the Association of Chief Police Officers is also a useful source of policies and guidance provided to Forces on a wide range of policing topics – see www.acpo.police.uk.

a little blow with a little stick on the shoulder is not a reason for him to draw a sword and cut and hew the other'.[191]

6.107 The stress or 'unexpected anguish' of the moment will be taken into account in deciding whether the amount of force used is reasonable,[192] as may the fact that an officer acted instinctively under pressure.[193] The law recognises that it is not always realistic to apply a consideration of all the theoretical options to a stressful situation and cases have deprecated 'using jeweller's scales to measure reasonable force'.[194]

## The European Convention on Human Rights

6.108 Freestanding claims pursuant to ECHR article 3 may arise in circumstances where officers use excessive force.[195] Article 3 provides that: 'No one shall be subjected to torture or to inhuman or degrading treatment or punishment'.

6.109 Unlike the common law claim for battery, article 3 confers an absolute protection, so that if the force used is sufficiently severe to come within these parameters, the officers involved will not be able to try and justify its use. Equally, because of the unqualified nature of the protection afforded, the threshold for conduct coming within article 3 has been set at a relatively high level by the case law of the European Court of Human Rights. Treatment in police custody has been found to come within article 3 where the acts complained of went beyond officers' powers and aroused in the applicant feelings of fear, anguish and inferiority and were capable of humiliating him or her and breaking his or her physical or moral resistance and/or caused the applicant serious injury and suffering.[196] 'Torture' is confined to the most serious of cases, in particular those where force was used deliberately to encourage the applicant to make a confession.[197] Routine handcuffing of detainees, even in public, is unlikely to amount to inhuman or degrading treatment.[198] However, handcuffing of an elderly prisoner to a hospital bed,

---

191 *Cockroft v Smith* (1705) 2 Salk 642.
192 *Palmer v R* (1971) 55 Cr App R 223.
193 For a recent example of lawful self-defence where a civilian caused serious injuries when responding instantly under pressure of attack see *Cross v Kirby* [2000] 18 February, CA, unreported.
194 *Reed v Wastie* [1972] Crim LR 221.
195 For claims under the Human Rights Act 1998 see chapter 10.
196 See *Selmouni v France* (2000) 29 EHRR 403; *Rehbock v Slovenia* (2000) ECHR 29462/95.
197 *Selmouni v France,* (2000) 29 EHRR 403.
198 *Raminen v Finland* (1997) 26 EHRR 563.

while he awaited an operation, did amount to an infringement of article 3.[199] A number of cases have considered the extent to which strip searches will amount to a violation of article 3.[200] The effect of article 3 caselaw upon the burden of proof in a claim for battery or assault is considered below (see para 6.113).

6.110    Intrusive police methods may give rise to freestanding claims under ECHR article 8. The concept of a 'private life' protected by this article includes physical integrity.[201] Thus, for example, searches (particularly intimate or strip searches), the taking of bodily samples, fingerprinting and photographing could all raise article 8 issues.[202] However, conduct falling within article 8(1) is lawful if it can be justified by reference to the criteria set out in article 8(2).

6.111    If the use of force by officers leads to the death of the victim, a freestanding claim under ECHR article 2 may arise. This provides that deprivation of life by force used to effect an arrest or defend a person from violence is only justified where it is 'absolutely necessary'.[203]

## The burden and standard of proof

6.112    It has sometimes been argued that a higher standard of proof should apply in cases of severe wrongdoing, such as serious assaults by public officers. However, in *Rehman v Secretary of State for the Home Department*[204] Lord Hoffman confirmed that the civil standard of proof always means showing that the allegation is more likely than not to have happened and that no higher degree of probability was required in civil cases. However, he also observed that some things are inherently more likely than others, thus the more out of the ordinary the allegation, the more cogent the evidence that will be needed to establish it. For example, in a police context, it would usually be easier to prove that a claimant was subject to undue roughness on arrest, than it would be to prove that an officer sexually assaulted him or her.

6.113    In *Sheppard v Secretary of State for the Home Department*[205] the Court of Appeal considered the effect in domestic law of cases decided by

199  *Henaf v France* (2003) 27 November, ECtHR, unreported.
200  See in particular *Yankov v Bulgaria* (2003) 12 BHRC 266; *Iwanczuk v Poland* [2001] ECHR 25196/94; *Valasinas v Lithuania* (2001) 15 BHRC 592.
201  *X and Y v Netherlands* (1986) 8 EHRR 235.
202  See paras 10.13 and 10.212 on privacy and on claims under the Human Rights Act 1998.
203  See, eg, *McCann v UK* (1996) 21 EHRR 97. Article 2 is dealt with in more detail at paras 10.177–10.182.
204  [2002] 1 All ER 122 at [55].
205  [2002] EWCA Civ 1921.

the European Court of Human Rights under ECHR article 3, indicating that where a detainee sustained injuries while in police custody, there was an onus on the police to account for how they were sustained.[206] The Court of Appeal held that the effect of these authorities was not to shift the legal burden of proving the unlawful battery from the claimant to the defendant; rather they were a recognition of the evidential reality that if the defendant was unable to explain convincingly how the injuries occurred, the claimant would usually succeed in discharging the burden of proof.

## The claimant's behaviour

6.114    In certain circumstances the wrongful actions of the claimant at the time when he or she was subjected to force will preclude a successful action for battery or assault. In other circumstances the claimant's actions will not prevent liability from being established, but may impact negatively upon the level of damages awarded. These will be dealt with in turn.

6.115    Where a claimant has been convicted of a criminal offence, a doctrine called the rule against collateral challenge precludes him or her from bringing a claim in the civil courts which effectively disputes the soundness of that conviction.[207] The reasoning behind this doctrine is to encourage convictions to be challenged directly by appeals within the criminal justice system seeking to have the conviction quashed, rather than by an indirect attack on the soundness of the conviction in a civil action. Also the courts are concerned to prevent inconsistent decisions on the same issues arising between the criminal courts and the civil courts. However, the principle is only applied where the fact of the conviction necessarily precludes the case that the claimant seeks to raise in the civil claim. In *Simpson v Chief Constable of South Yorkshire*[208] the Court of Appeal refused to strike out a claim for battery against the police on the ground that the claimant had been convicted of crimes of violence in respect of the same incident, since the convictions did not, on the facts of the case, preclude the proposition that the claimant had also been assaulted by the police as he alleged.

---

206   See cases such as *Ribitsch v Austria* (1995) 21 EHRR 573; *Aksoy v Turkey* (1996) 23 EHRR 553 and *Rehbock v Slovenia* (2000) ECHR 29462/95.
207   *Hunter v Chief Constable of West Midlands* [1982] AC 529, HL; *Arthur JS Hall & Co v Simons* [2000] 3 All ER 673, HL.
208   (1991) *Independent* 14 March, CA.

6.116     The doctrine known as 'ex turpi causa non oritur actio' is a rule of policy that the courts will not assist a person who founds his or her claim upon an immoral or illegal act. This does not prevent a claimant from bringing a damages claim simply because he or she was engaged in criminal activity at the time when he or she was injured; successful claims against the police for injuries sustained by excessive force used during a lawful arrest are commonplace.[209] A distinction is drawn between a situation where the criminal activity of the claimant is incidental to the tort of the defendant and circumstances where the defendant's act which has given rise to the civil claim is inextricably linked with the claimant's criminal activity.[210] The distinction is illustrated by two recent claims for battery. In *Revill v Newberry*,[211] where the defendant discharged a shotgun at the claimant burglar who had shown no intention of violence towards him, it was held that the ex turpi causa doctrine did not apply as the act of violence was not an integral part of or a necessary consequence of the burglary. In contrast, in *Cross v Kirby* the doctrine was applied to disallow the claim where the claimant was hit on the head with a baseball bat that he had been using to attack the defendant. For ex turpi causa to apply, the claimant's wrongdoing must be sufficiently serious for the defendant's response to be considered an integral part of it, but, other than in that limited sense, no account is taken of the proportionality of the defendant's response to the claimant's misconduct.[212]

6.117     If the claimant's conduct does not preclude a successful claim, the defendant may still argue that to some extent he or she provoked the battery and thus the overall award of compensation should be reduced. There is current uncertainty as to whether the defendant to an intentional tort, such as assault or battery, can rely upon contributory negligence pursuant to Law Reform (Contributory Negligence) Act 1945 s1(1). *Murphy v Cullane*[213] indicated that contributory negligence could be raised to reduce a claimant's damages in response to an assault or battery claim. However, in *Standard Chartered Bank v Pakistan National Shipping Corp (No 2)*[214] Lord Roger suggested that this

209   See, eg, *Glowacki v Long and Chief Constable of Lancashire* (1998) 18 June, CA, unreported.

210   *Cross v Kirby* [2000] 18 February, CA, unreported; *Vellino v Chief Constable of Greater Manchester* [2002] 3 All ER 78.

211   [1996] QB 567, CA.

212   As is well illustrated by *Cross v Kirby* [2000] 18 February, CA, unreported.

213   [1977] QB 94, CA.

214   [2003] 1 All ER 173 at [42]–[45].

approach may not be sound. In any event, the extent to which the claimant's misconduct caused or contributed to the defendant's wrong-doing can be taken into account in relation to an award of aggravated and/or exemplary damages.[215]

### Prior prosecution

6.118 Battery constitutes a crime as well as a civil wrong. Usually it is no defence to a civil action for the defendant to show that he or she has already been prosecuted in the criminal courts for the same incident. An acquittal on a criminal charge does not usually prevent a subsequent civil action for the same misconduct as a different standard of proof applies. However, if a person brings a private prosecution for a criminal offence of assault or battery and the defendant is convicted and pays the appropriate fine or serves any term of imprisonment imposed or the magistrates hearing the case make out a certificate stating that the case was dismissed because the assault was not proved, was justi-fied or was so trifling as not to merit any punishment, then that person is released from all further or other proceedings, whether civil or criminal, based on the same facts.[216] In *Wong v Parkside Health NHS Trust*[217] the Court of Appeal emphasised that the release covers all further proceedings which rely on the same allegation; it is not limited to those where the cause of action pleaded is assault or battery, nor where the claimant is the same person as the one who brought the prosecution. The court did not consider the position of the alleged assailant's employer (the case based on vicarious liability having been adjourned). Thus it is not clear whether this ruling casts doubt on *Dyer v Munday*[218] which suggests that although the individual officer may be released from a subsequent civil action, a civil action against the chief officer of police may still be possible.

## Assault

6.119 To show that there has been an assault the claimant must prove that there has been an act by the defendant which causes the claimant reasonably to apprehend an immediate intention by the defendant to

---

215 *Thompson & Hsu v Commissioner of Police of the Metropolis* [1997] 2 All ER 762, CA – see chapter 14.

216 Offences Against the Person Act 1861 ss44–45.

217 [2003] 1 All ER 932.

218 [1894–99] 2 All ER 1022.

commit a battery.[219] Thus, there can be an assault without there in fact being a battery. However, a mere threat of violence is not enough to constitute an assault unless there is also the means to carry out the threat.[220] A person who with fists raised runs at another and would have hit that other if he or she had not been stopped will probably have committed an assault.[221] However, large numbers of people shouting abuse at others on a bus whom they cannot reach do not commit an assault if they have no means of carrying out their threat.[222] There is no need to show that the officer actually intended to use force, provided the claimant had a reasonable basis for believing this at the time: *Chief Constable of Thames Valley Police v Hepburn*.[223] In *Hepburn* the claimant was assaulted in circumstances where an officer who had no lawful basis to stop him leaving premises held out his baton as he tried to exit. The principles that govern defences to battery by the police, as described above, also apply to the tort of assault.

## Other causes of action

### Harassment

6.120   A person may complain that they have experienced irritating or upsetting treatment at the hands of the police that involves no physical contact, or threat of physical contact and no detention or prosecution. In those circumstances the conventional torts of assault, battery, false imprisonment and malicious prosecution will not apply. The complaint might relate, for example, to use of abusive language by officers. Alternatively, it might be suggested that offices are 'making their presence felt', such as following the complainant's vehicle, because he or she has made a previous complaint that they have taken exception to. Where it can be shown that officers are abusing their powers in bad faith, a claim in misfeasance may well lie.[224] A further cause of action to consider is provided for by the Protection from Harassment

---

219   See *Clerk & Lindsell on Torts* (18th edn, Sweet & Maxwell, 2000) para 13-13.
220   *Stephens v Myers* (1830) 4 C & P 349.
221   *Stephens v Myers* (1830) 4 C & P 349.
222   *Thomas v National Union of Mineworkers (South Wales Area)* [1986] Ch 20. Nonetheless, in certain circumstances mere use of words can amount to an assault: *R v Ireland & Bristow* [1998] AC 147.
223   [2002] EWCA Civ 1841.
224   See para 7.39 onwards on misfeasance.

Act 1997.[225] The Act was brought in predominantly to provide criminal and civil liabilities for stalking. However, as the courts have acknowledged, the language of the statute covers a much wider scope of activity.[226]

6.121 Section 1 of the 1997 Act provides:

(1) A person must not pursue a course of conduct –

(a) which amounts to harassment of another; and
(b) which he knows or ought to know amounts to harassment of the other.

(2) For the purposes of this section, the person whose course of conduct is in question ought to know that it amounts to harassment of another if a reasonable person in possession of the same information, would think the course of conduct amounted to harassment of the other.

6.122 'Harassment' is not defined in the Act, although it states that references to harassing a person 'include alarming the person or causing the person distress'.[227] In *Thomas v News Group Newspapers Limited*[228] the Court of Appeal said that this provision is dealing with the effect of the behaviour, but does not explain the types of conduct that produce that effect; many activities may foreseeably generate alarm or cause a person distress that could not possibly be described as harassment. The Court of Appeal said that 'harassment' was a word that was generally understood and described conduct targeted at an individual which was calculated to produce the consequences described in Protection from Harassment Act 1997 s7 and which was oppressive and unreasonable. The Act does make clear that 'conduct' includes speech.[229] As well as showing that the behaviour complained of amounted to harassment, the claimant will need to show that the defendant knew or ought to have known that it amounted to harassment. As will be seen from the wording of section 1 of the Act quoted above, the test of whether the harasser should have perceived his or her conduct in that way is an objective, rather than a subjective, one.[230] Thus, the claimant

225 The Act came into force on 16 June 1997.
226 For example, the publication of arguably racist press articles concerning the claimant in *Thomas v News Group Newspapers Ltd* [2002] EMLR 4, CA.
227 Protection from Harassment Act 1997 s7(2).
228 Protection from Harassment Act 1997 s7(2).
229 Protection from Harassment Act 1997 s7(4).
230 As confirmed in *R v Colohan* (2001) 2 FLR 757, CA.

need not show that the harasser appreciated the nature of his or her behaviour.[231]

6.123　The claimant also has to show that there was a 'course of conduct'. This must involve conduct on at least two occasions.[232] Whether two or more incidents amount to a course of conduct is based on an evaluation of all the circumstances, and will depend upon the degree of linking features, the number of incidents and the time gap between them.[233] Thus a claim under the Act could not be brought for a one-off incident of abusive or other unpleasant behaviour.

6.124　A civil claim for damages and/or an injunction may be brought in relation to conduct that amounts to harassment as defined by the Act.[234] Damages may be awarded for, among other things, anxiety caused by the harassment and for any financial losses resulting from it.[235] Thus, importantly, if the statutory ingredients of the unlawful conduct are shown, a claim may be brought for compensation even if the claimant has suffered no psychiatric loss or other 'damage' in the conventional sense. In this respect the Act may provide a useful remedy to a claimant who has suffered consequential distress but no ill health, since in these circumstances he or she cannot sue in negligence nor, probably, in misfeasance.[236]

6.125　However, the Act also provides that the person sued will have a defence if he or she can show that the course of conduct was pursued:

- for the purpose of preventing or detecting crime;
- under any enactment or rule of law or to comply with any requirement imposed by any person under any enactment; or
- was reasonable in the particular circumstances.[237]

6.126　In police cases harassment claims are usually resisted on the basis of the first and third of these defences. Note, that the first limb is not subject to a qualification that the conduct was reasonable. Thus any conduct aimed at preventing or detecting crime would arguably come within the defence even if its effect was oppressive and excessive from the claimant's perspective. The courts have yet to consider in detail

---

231　A greater degree of awareness is required for a claim in misfeasance, as discussed at paras 7.42–7.44 and 7.46.

232　Protection from Harassment Act 1997 s7(3).

233　*Lau v DPP* [2000] FLR 719, DC.

234　Protection from Harassment Act 1997 s3(1). The Act also provides for criminal liabilities in ss 2 and 4.

235　Protection from Harassment Act 1997 s3(2).

236　See paras 7.45 and 8.85.

237　Protection from Harassment Act 1997 s1(3).

the scope of this limb of the defence. However, the wide wording suggests that a claimant would only succeed if he or she could show that police powers were exercised in bad faith and or the behaviour complained of was by its nature beyond any concept of preventing or detecting crime, such as officers using gratuitous abuse.

6.127 The courts have discouraged the suggestion that any common law tort of harassment exists, which goes beyond the scope of the leg- islation.[238] As Lord Hoffman commented in *Wainwright v Home Office:*[239]

> The requirement of a course of conduct [in the Protection from Harassment Act 1997] shows that Parliament was conscious that it might not be in the public interest to allow the law to be set in motion for one boorish incident. It may be that any development of the common law should show similar caution.

## Intentionally causing nervous shock

6.128 In *Wainwright v The Home Office* the House of Lords considered the scope of an old line of authority, frequently quoted as the basis of a tort of intentional infliction of injury in the absence of any actual or threatened physical contact. Where liability has stemmed from this concept, it has usually been in circumstances where the defendant has said something to the claimant that has caused him or her psychiatric harm.

6.129 In the first authority in this area, *Wilkinson v Downton,*[240] the claimant was falsely informed as a practical joke that her husband has been badly injured in a road accident. This produced a violent shock in her, causing her serious and permanent physical consequences, at one time threatening her reason and entailing weeks of suffering. It was plain that the defendant had not wanted to harm the claimant; he had simply desired to play a rather unpleasant 'joke' upon her. However, the trial judge, Wright J, reasoned that as such a statement would produce grave effects in all but an exceptional person, the defen- dant must be taken to have intended to produce those effects in the claimant. Accordingly, such an intention would be imputed to him and his conduct regarded as calculated to cause harm to the claimant. *Wilkinson v Downton* was followed in *Janvier v Sweeny*[241] where a man

---

238  *Hunter v Canary Wharf Ltd* [1997] AC 655 HL; *Wong v Parkside Health NHS Trust* [2003] 3 All ER 932, CA.

239  [2003] 3 All ER 943.

240  [1897] 2 QB 57.

241  [1918–19] All ER Rep 1056, CA.

called at the claimant's house and falsely told her he was a detective
from Scotland Yard and that she was wanted for corresponding with a
German spy. In consequence the woman suffered a severe nervous
shock and a long period of illness. She was able to recover damages for
the psychiatric harm she underwent as a result of the deliberately false
statement made to her. These cases were taken as authority for the
proposition that where the defendant's conduct was calculated to cause
the claimant harm and such harm resulted, a claim could be sustained.[242] However, the Court of Appeal decided that the doctrine was
not broad enough to encompass a situation where a claimant had suffered anxiety and distress as a result of unpleasant behaviour towards
her by work colleagues, where she had not suffered psychiatric harm
in consequence.[243]

6.130    The House of Lords reviewed this line of authority in *Wainwright v
Home Office*.[244] The trial judge in that case had applied and extended the
doctrine to permit recovery by a mother and son who visited a
relative in a prison and were strip searched in circumstances that
breached the Prison Rules. The trial judge had decided that the doctrine could extend to circumstances where the officers had said something – that is, the instruction to remove clothes – which had then
caused the son to do something to himself – that is, take his clothes off
– which had in turn caused him psychiatric injury. The judge also found
that the doctrine could extend to the claim of the mother who had suffered distress, but no psychiatric injury. The House of Lords disagreed.
Lord Hoffman[245] emphasised that there was no finding in this case that
the officers had intended to cause harm – on the contrary the trial judge
had found they acted in good faith throughout. He dismissed the notion
that a *Wilkinson v Downton* tort was necessary where psychiatric harm was
suffered, as if the defendant was at fault in causing this, liability in negligence could in any event now result.[246] Where the claimant suffered distress, short of psychiatric harm, Lord Hoffman considered – without
having finally to decide the question – that if common law liability
resulted it should only do so where the wrongdoer intended to cause
distress in the strictest sense of the word, that is, where he or she wanted

242    *Wong v Parkside Health NHS Trust* [2003] 3 All ER 932, CA.

243    [2003] 3 All ER 932, CA.

244    [2003] 4 All ER 969.

245    Who gave the leading speech with which the other members of the Judicial
Committee agreed.

246    Prior to *Dulieu v White & Sons* [1901] 2 KB 669, DC psychiatric harm could not
be recovered in negligence.

to bring about that result. He emphasised that the form of imputed intention relied upon in *Wilkinson v Downton* would not be sufficient to establish liability for consequences short of actual ill-health. However, he doubted whether liability for consequences short of psychiatric harm would arise at all outside of the circumstances prescribed by the Protection from Harassment Act 1997.

6.131    Thus, in the light of the observations made in *Wainwright*, it seems unlikely that a court would decide there was a common law tort of intentionally inducing anxiety or distress, even where this was the perpetrator's desired result.[247] It may be that a *Wilkinson v Downton* form of liability does still have a relevance where psychiatric harm is intentionally inflicted and that, contrary to Lord Hoffman's suggestion, negligence does not provide an adequate alternative in all circumstances. Establishing a duty of care is not always straightforward in negligence and awards of aggravated and exemplary damages, which commonly flow from intentional wrongdoing, are rare in negligence claims. Thus if, for example, out of spite and intending to cause harm, a police officer falsely told a friend or relative that a loved one had been arrested/charged/convicted of a serious offence and psychiatric harm was sustained, a common law claim for intentional infliction of injury should be considered.

## Intimidation

6.132    The tort of intimidation involves the wrongdoer using an unlawful threat successfully to compel another to act (or refrain from acting) in a particular manner, if the claimant is thereby occasioned harm.[248] The threat can be made either to the claimant directly or to a third party. The threat may be unlawful because it amounts to a criminal act, a tort, a breach of contract or, probably, a breach of an equitable obligation (such as one of confidentiality).[249] The tort of intimidation will not be made out, however, if the alleged wrongdoer simply threatens something he or she is entitled to do. The threat must be coercive in the sense that it causes the recipient to act in a way that he or she would not otherwise have done. If the recipient stoutly refuses to be swayed by the threat, there is no claim in intimidation. Additionally, it must be shown

247    See Clayton & Tomlinson *Civil Actions Against the Police* (3rd edn, Thomson Sweet & Maxwell, 2004) para 4-068 for a summary of other jurisdictions where the intentional infliction of distress constitutes a recoverable tort.

248    *News Group Newspapers Ltd v SOGAT '82 (No 2)* [1987] ICR 181.

249    *Dixon v Dixon* [1904] 1 Ch 161; *Rookes v Barnard* [1964] AC 1129, HL.

that the wrongdoer intended to cause harm to the claimant.[250]
Circumstances where the threat was made directly to the claimant
could now be covered by the Protection from Harassment Act 1997 if
there was a 'course of conduct', as discussed at paras 6.121–6.123.
However, this might not be the case if the claimant suffered as a result
of a threat made to a third party.

6.133    The tort of intimidation has been applied in cases where employers
have mistreated domestic servants.[251] It is rarely used in police cases.
However, in circumstances where, for example, police officers used
threats to induce a confession, such as suggesting that they would
ensure that social services took the suspect's children into care, a claim
in intimidation might be appropriate.[252]

---

250    *News Group Newspapers Ltd v SOGAT '82 (No 2)* [1987] ICR 181.
251    See, eg, *Goodwin v Uzoigwe* (1992) *Times* 18 June.
252    Particularly if there was other available evidence that the claimant committed
the criminal act, so that a claim in malicious prosecution would be unlikely to
succeed.

# CHAPTER 7

# Abuse of power

7.1   This chapter focuses upon three common law civil wrongs that provide a remedy for deliberate misuse of power. The chapter initially looks at the tort of malicious prosecution, discussing the elements that need to be established for a successful claim. The closely analogous action for malicious process is then considered. This covers misuse of the criminal courts other than by a prosecution, such as by applications for warrants. Lastly the chapter focuses on the emerging, broader tort of misfeasance in a public office. The inter-relationship between malicious prosecution and misfeasance is also closely examined. Compensation for these torts is dealt with in chapter 14. The separate remedy of obtaining compensation from the Home Office for wrongful conviction is discussed in chapter 17.

## Malicious prosecution

7.2   It is a tort maliciously and without reasonable and probable cause to initiate criminal proceedings against another person, which terminate in favour of that other and which result in damage to reputation, person, freedom or property.

7.3   The right to sue for malicious prosecution is intended to protect people from unwarranted accusations being brought against them in the criminal courts. Facing false charges may lead a person to suffer detention in custody, financial damage, loss of standing in his or her community, anxiety and/or even psychiatric injury. However, the courts also recognise the importance of people, in particular the police, not feeling inhibited in using the legal process to prosecute crime and consider that collateral litigation following the resolution of criminal proceedings should be closely controlled. In framing the ingredients of the common law tort of malicious prosecution, the courts have had to weigh up these competing considerations. As Fleming says:

> The tort of malicious prosecution is dominated by the problem of balancing two countervailing interests of high social importance: safeguarding the individual from being harassed by unjustifiable litigation and encouraging citizens to aid in law enforcement.[1]

7.4   As we shall see in more detail below, the balance has been struck by the courts requiring claimants to go so far as to prove (among other

---

1   Fleming, *The Law of Torts* (9th edn, LBC Information Services, 1998), p673. See this text for a fuller discussion of the competing public interests.

things) bad faith on the part of those responsible for the prosecution. A prosecution brought for a proper purpose will never be a malicious prosecution, even if based on slender evidence. Thus, although thousands of people are acquitted of the offences of which they were accused every year, only a relatively small proportion of those people will have a viable claim for malicious prosecution. The collective effect of the criteria that the claimant must prove to establish a claim in malicious prosecution has led one commentator to observe that 'the action for malicious prosecution is held on a tighter rein than any other in the law of torts'[2] and a number have called for reform in this area.[3]

7.5     To succeed in a claim for malicious prosecution against the police, it must be shown that damage has been suffered because:

- the police prosecuted; and
- the criminal case was concluded in the accused's favour; and
- reasonable and probable cause were absent in the bringing of the prosecution; and
- the police acted maliciously.

These elements are described in more detail in turn below.

7.6     Malicious prosecution claims are particularly useful where the claimant alleges that the prosecution case against him was based on evidence concocted by the police. It is much more difficult to establish a malicious prosecution claim where the prosecution evidence was substantially based upon accounts given by independent third parties, even if that evidence was discredited during the criminal proceedings. If a claimant wishes to allege police fabrication of evidence in circumstances where the prosecution was also based on significant incriminating evidence from other sources, a claim of misfeasance in a public office may be a more viable option, if the fabrication can be established, than an action for malicious prosecution.[4]

7.7     A malicious prosecution claim usually entitles the parties to choose trial by judge and jury, unless any of the prescribed exceptions apply.[5] The six-year limitation period for commencing a claim runs from the date when the criminal proceedings terminated in the claimant's

---

2   Fleming, *The Law of Torts* (9th edn, LBC Information Services, 1998).
3   See eg Clayton and Tomlinson, *Civil Actions Against the Police* (3rd ed, Thomson Sweet & Maxwell, 2004) para 8-006.
4   See paras 7.50–7.51 looking at the inter-relationship between the two torts.
5   See Supreme Court Act 1981 s69 and County Court Act 1984 s66, discussed in more detail at paras 12.78–12.90.

favour.[6] If the claimant's conviction was quashed on appeal, this may be some considerable time after the misconduct took place.

7.8 It is uncertain, on the current state of the caselaw, whether a defence to liability can be established by proving on a balance of probabilities that the claimant did in fact commit the offence in question. It is suggested that the better view is that technically this affects quantum rather than liability.[7] However, if the police have strong evidence that he or she did in fact carry out the relevant crime, the claimant's credibility as a witness may well be too damaged to enable the elements of the tort to be established.

## Necessary elements

### Damage

7.9 Unlike some other types of police misconduct (primarily assault, battery and false imprisonment), it is necessary to show that damage has been suffered by the claimant for the action to succeed. In practice this requirement is sometimes overlooked, but historically only three types of damage fulfilled this criterion in a malicious prosecution claim, namely: loss of reputation, the risk of loss of 'life, limb or liberty;' and financial loss.[8] Loss of reputation is shown if the charge was 'necessarily and naturally' defamatory, that is to say, it was one that lowered the claimant in the estimation of right-thinking members of society generally.[9] Accordingly, an alleged failure to pay a tram fair met this test as it involved an imputation of dishonesty.[10] On the other hand, an allegation of pulling a communication cord on a train without sufficient cause did not convey a sufficiently discreditable reflection on the claimant.[11] It will always depend upon the degree of moral stigma attached to the particular offence. For example some motoring offences, such as drink driving or driving while disqualified carry with them a strong element of this stigma, whereas other motoring offences, such as driving with a bald tyre or a defective

---

6 *Dunlop v HM Customs & Excise* (1998) 12 March, CA. Limitation is discussed in more detail at paras 11.69–11.71.

7 See *Clerk & Lindsell on Torts* (18th edn, Sweet & Maxwell, 2000) para 16-35 and Clayton and Tomlinson *Civil Actions Against the Police* (3rd edn, Thomson Sweet & Maxwell, 2004) para 8-075.

8 *Savile v Roberts* (1698) 1 Ld Raym 374, 378.

9 *Wiffen v Bailey & Romford UDC* [1915] 1 KB 600, CA.

10 *Rayson v S London Tramways Co* [1893] 2 QB 304.

11 *Berry v British Transport Commission* [1962] 1 QB 306, CA.

light, would be unlikely to qualify. In respect of loss of liberty, it is enough if the offence for which the claimant is prosecuted is one punishable by imprisonment;[12] there need not be actual loss of liberty. Legal costs incurred in defending oneself against a malicious prosecution constitute sufficient damage to qualify as financial loss, even where the court grants an allowance towards those costs.[13] It is sufficient for a claimant to prove that one of these three elements resulted from the prosecution. If 'damage' in this sense is proved and the other elements necessary for liability are established, the claimant can then recover for all the consequences of the prosecution at the stage when compensation is assessed. Thus, distress and anxiety caused by the prosecution will be taken into account when the level of damages is determined (see chapter 14). It has not been decided whether the requirement to show 'damage' could be satisfied by the claimant having suffered psychiatric injury; arguably this could come within the concept of risk of injury to limb. However in practice, if psychiatric injury has resulted from the prosecution, it is likely that the charge involved damage to reputation and/or risk of imprisonment and so the criterion would be satisfied in any event.

## Police prosecution

7.10 The claimant needs to show both that he or she was prosecuted and that the person who he or she alleges brought the proceedings maliciously should be treated as a 'prosecutor'.

7.11 A prosecution consists of 'setting a judicial officer in motion'.[14] Thus the first of these ingredients will only raise a potential difficulty if an allegation is withdrawn at a very early stage, before the claimant is actually brought before a criminal court at all. However, it has been held that laying an information before a magistrate is sufficient in itself to amount to a prosecution for these purposes. Most criminal proceedings commence with a charge. Clayton and Tomlinson submit that a prosecution will have begun if the claimant has been charged,[15] as this is the point from which damage to the claimant may result. On this basis an action in malicious prosecution would lie even if the charge was then withdrawn before the case ever came before the court.

---

12  *Wiffen v Bailey & Romford UDC* [1915] 1 KB 600, CA.
13  *Berry v British Transport Commission* [1962] 1 QB 306, CA.
14  *Sewell v National Telephone Co* [1907] 1 KB 557, CA.
15  Clayton and Tomlinson *Civil Actions Against the Police*, para 8-024.

7.12    The prosecutor who is sued must be a person who was 'actively instrumental' in putting the law in motion.[16] There has been no recent appellate case law which has considered the meaning of this phrase. It seems relatively clear that for the purposes of this tort, a prosecution may have a number of different 'prosecutors'. Under Prosecution of Offenders Act 1985 s3(2) the Crown Prosecution Service (CPS) takes responsibility for the conduct of the prosecution following charge or summons by the police. Thus the CPS could be a prosecutor for the purposes of a malicious prosecution action (in the relatively unlikely event that there was evidence that the CPS had acted in bad faith). In addition, police officers who provide material evidence in support of the prosecution would also appear to be 'actively instrumental' in the charge being brought or summons being issued. In the majority of malicious prosecution claims where it is alleged that officers fabricated evidence against the claimant, it is accepted by the defendant that those officers were prosecutors for the purposes of the tort.[17] Less commonly, defendants argue that the only police officer who should be regarded as the prosecutor for these purposes is the officer who determined there was sufficient evidence to charge (usually the custody sergeant on duty at the time; although more senior officers will be involved if the offences are serious). It is suggested that this line of argument does not accord with the 'actively instrumental' test which is broad enough to include any officer whose account formed a significant part of the pros-ecution case. Furthermore, such a narrow view of who is the prosecutor does not accord with the division of labour in modern policing and would severely emasculate the tort, as in many instances the officer determining whether there is sufficient evidence to charge would be unaware of any concoction in the officers' accounts.

7.13    Where the evidence that forms the prosecution case comes from civilian witnesses it may be more difficult to argue that the police were prosecutors for the purposes of the tort and/or that there was any lack of belief in the case or malice on their part. (Unless it is contended that officers had improperly induced such witnesses to provide evidence against the accused in circumstances where the officers knew such accounts were likely to be unreliable.) In limited situations it is possible to establish that a member of the public who made a false complaint to the police is him or herself a prosecutor and so potentially

---

16  *Danby v Beardsley* (1880) 43 LT 603.
17  In cases before the Court of Appeal this approach has not been questioned, eg, *Isaac v Chief Constable of the West Midlands Police* [2001] EWCA Civ 1405.

liable in a malicious prosecution claim instead of the police. The House of Lords considered this issue in *Martin v Watson*.[18] They decided that a civilian reporting an alleged offence to the police could be a prosecutor if he or she falsely and maliciously gave information to the police, making clear that he or she is prepared to be a witness for the prosecution and where the facts of the offence are such that they are exclusively within the complainant's own knowledge, making it virtually impossible for the police to make an independent judgment on whether or not to proceed with the prosecution. The test was satisfied on the facts of *Martin v Watson* where the defendant had made a deliberately false complaint to the police that the claimant had exposed himself to her and there were no other witnesses to the incident. In contrast, the test was not satisfied in *Mahon v Rahn (No 2)*[19] where the Serious Fraud Office had considered information supplied by the defendants and also had obtained information from other sources before forming an independent judgment on whether to prosecute.

7.14    A defendant may be liable not only for initiating, but also for adopting or continuing proceedings if he or she is actively instrumental in this process and, having acquired positive knowledge indicating the accused's innocence, nonetheless perseveres.[20] Thus, for example, if police officers came to learn of information that indicated the person charged was in fact innocent, but they deliberately suppressed the material, rather than passing it on to the CPS, liability might result.

### The criminal case must end in favour of the person suing

7.15    The criminal prosecution must have ended in favour of the person suing for malicious prosecution.[21] This can be achieved by a verdict of acquittal, by the conviction being quashed on appeal,[22] by an acquittal on a technicality, such as an error in the indictment,[23] or by the discontinuance of proceedings.[24]

---

18  [1996] AC 74, HL.
19  [2000] 1 WLR 2150, CA.
20  See *Tims v John Lewis & Co Ltd* [1951] 2 KB 459, CA (reversed on another point by the House of Lords: *John Lewis & Co Ltd v Tims* [1952] AC 676).
21  *Parker v Langley* (1713) 10 Mod 145 and 209.
22  *Herniman v Smith* [1938] AC 305, HL; *Berry v British Transport Commission* [1961] 3 All ER 65, CA.
23  *Jones v Gwynn* (1712) 10 Mod 148, 214; *Wicks v Fentham* (1791) 4 Term Rep 247.
24  *Watkins v Lee* (1839) 5 M & W 270.

7.16    A claim can still succeed even if there was a conviction for a less serious offence than the one for which a person is charged.[25] Where a trial concludes in a person being acquitted of some offences but convicted of others, there may be claims for malicious prosecution in relation to those offences on which there has been an acquittal.[26] If offences are ordered to 'lie on the file' after the defendant has pleaded guilty to other offences, it is likely that this will be treated as an 'adjournment' of the proceedings rather than a termination, favourable or otherwise. If proceedings have been stayed because they have been held to be an abuse of process (for instance, because of the length of time it has taken to bring the prosecution), then the 'stay' would probably be regarded as a termination in favour of the claimant, given that those reasons usually advanced for the imposition of this requirement in the tort of malicious prosecution, would not be applicable in the circumstances. The most commonly stated reasons for the rule requiring a favourable termination of the prosecution are that the rule exists to prevent individuals challenging the correctness of a subsisting judgment by a criminal court in collateral civil proceedings and that it exists to preclude civil actions where the criminal proceedings have shown that there was sufficient evidence to support a prosecution.[27]

7.17    Special problems arise if someone is bound over to keep the peace and to be of good behaviour. If he or she is bound over after the hearing of a 'complaint',[28] the case does not end in his or her favour and he or she cannot sue.[29] More commonly, however, bind-overs are agreed to by the defence before the case is heard, in exchange for the prosecution offering no evidence on the charge before the court. In *Hourihane v Metropolitan Police Commissioner*[30] the police applied to strike out a claim for malicious prosecution where the claimant had agreed to a bind-over, the CPS had offered no evidence, and the charges (of disorderly behaviour) were duly dismissed. The Court of Appeal

---

25  *Boaler v Holder* (1887) 51 JP 277.

26  *Reed v Taylor* (1812) 4 Taunt 616; *Leibo v Buckman Ltd* [1952] 2 All ER 1057, CA, provided 'damage' in the sense discussed above results from the offences that terminated in the claimant's favour.

27  See, eg, Fleming *The law of Torts* (9th edn, LBC Information Services, 1998) p678.

28  Under Magistrates' Courts Act 1980 s115.

29  *Everett v Ribbands* [1952] 1 All ER 823, CA; see also *Bynoe v Bank of England* [1900–03] All ER Rep 65. If the complaint is rejected and thus the opportunity to sue arises, strictly speaking the action lies in malicious process, as discussed below.

30  (1994) *Times* 27 December, CA.

held that it was impossible to draw any inference that proceedings had terminated adversely to a defendant from the mere statement that he or she was bound over to keep the peace. The court said there might be many reasons why a defendant would prefer to agree to be bound over rather than run the risk of conviction. As the issue in the civil proceedings was whether the charges were brought maliciously and without reasonable and probable cause, the existence of a record showing that, following dismissal of the charges, the claimant was bound over, could not be a good ground for striking out the claim. However, in practice it is likely that the credibility of the claim for malicious prosecution would be adversely affected unless the claimant can convincingly explain why he or she accepted a bind-over in the circumstances.

7.18     If there is a subsisting conviction, a claim for malicious prosecution cannot succeed, even if there is no further right of appeal and even if it can be proved that the conviction was obtained by fraud.[31]

### The prosecution must lack reasonable and probable cause

7.19     Reasonable and probable cause has been defined as:

> ... an honest belief in the guilt of the accused based upon a full conviction, founded on reasonable grounds, of the existence of a state of circumstances which, assuming them to be true, would reasonably lead any ordinary prudent and cautious man, placed in the position of the accuser, to the conclusion that the person charged was probably guilty of the crime imputed.[32]

7.20     This definition has been approved and followed in subsequent cases. In *Glinski v McIver*[33] the House of Lords held that a claimant has to prove one of two things in order to establish that there was a lack of reasonable and probable cause, namely:

- the prosecutor did not believe in the guilt of the claimant; or
- a person of ordinary prudence and caution would not conclude in the light of the facts honestly believed at the time that the claimant was probably guilty of the relevant offence.

---

31  *Basebe v Matthews* (1867) LR 2 CP 684. Although where a dishonest abuse of authority can be shown a claim might arise in misfeasance, as discussed at para 7.50.

32  *Hicks v Faulkner* (1878) 8 QBD 167, 171.

33  [1962] AC 726.

7.21    The first element involves a subjective evaluation of the state of the prosecutor's mind at the time of the prosecution. The second element entails an objective assessment of whether there was a sufficient basis for the prosecution on the information known at the time. Thus there must be actual belief and reasonable belief in the probable guilt of a person for there to be reasonable and probable cause to prosecute. The two elements will be considered in turn.

### Belief in the claimant's guilt

7.22    In a trial by judge and jury, this is an issue to be evaluated by the jury, provided there is some evidence to support the claimant's contention that police officers lacked an honest belief in his or her guilt.[34] If the criminal prosecution is based on the accounts of officers as eye-witnesses to the alleged crime involving the claimant (for example where he or she is charged with assaulting an officer or obstructing the officer in the execution of his or her duty), the legal position is relatively straightforward. If the claimant gives a conflicting account of events and contends that the officers fabricated their statements in support of the criminal prosecution, the jury simply has to determine which party is giving the truthful version. If the jury finds that the officers produced a concocted account of events, it must follow that they lacked an honest belief in the claimant's guilt. The strength of the claimant's case in such circumstances is likely to depend upon factors such as the credibility of his or her own account, whether he or she has witnesses to the events in question, whether there are discrepancies between the officers' accounts and/or inconsistencies with contemporaneous documentation and/or inconsistencies with other known facts such as injuries.

7.23    The position is more complicated if the evidence in support of the prosecution comes from a number of sources, including non-police sources, and the relevant police officers did not witness the alleged offence. If the central evidence against the claimant comes from civilian witnesses or from expert forensic analysis, in many circumstances it will be difficult to establish that officers did not honestly believe in the prosecution. However, it is important to bear in mind that it is insufficient for officers to believe in the claimant's guilt in a general sense; they must believe in the charge brought and in the case that is

---

34  *Herniman v Smith* [1938] AC 305, HL; *Dallison v Caffery* [1965] QB 348. For further detail see the discussion of the respective roles of judge and jury at paras 13.31–13.34 and 13.39–13.40.

put forward against the claimant.[35] Thus, to take an example, police may genuinely believe that X is a drugs supplier on the basis of circumstantial evidence concerning his lifestyle and associates, but if they were to plant drugs at X's address and then prosecute on the basis of the discovery of those drugs, they would not honestly believe in their case. Situations in which police officers dishonestly create evidence to support the prosecution of someone who they believe has committed crime is sometimes referred to as 'noble cause corruption'. Whether there is any nobility in such actions is debatable. In any event, it is submitted that such conduct may amount to a lack of honest belief in the case put forward and thus a lack of reasonable and probable cause, for the purposes of the claim in malicious prosecution (provided, of course, the claimant can prove the officers' alleged misconduct). Nonetheless, the current state of the caselaw does not make clear what proportion of the prosecution evidence must be discredited by the claimant as dishonest concoction in order to show that officers lacked an honest belief in their case. Thus, if in the previous example, police officers genuinely found drugs at X's address but fabricated incriminating admissions purportedly from X to bolster the prosecution, would the subjective element of lack of reasonable and probable cause have been established? It is submitted that the answer should be in the affirmative, as officers could not have believed a central element of their case. Equally, the same conclusion should apply if officers were shown to have obtained significant witness accounts by intimidation or inducements and then, knowing the circumstances in which they had been obtained rendered them suspect, dishonestly suppressed those circumstances and put forward the same as reliable evidence.[36] Whether the claimant can show a lack of honest belief by proving that part of the evidence was obtained by officers dishonestly or improperly, is likely to depend upon the significance of that evidence to the overall prosecution case.

7.24    A further aspect to consider is how a claimant raises sufficient evidence of bad faith for the case to be left to the jury on this issue, in circumstances where he or she cannot deny the officers account from first-hand knowledge. Mere suspicion that officers concocted evidence or bullied witnesses will not suffice, but a process of inference may be relied upon where there are (for example) substantial inconsistencies

---

35  See the speeches of Viscount Simmonds, Lord Radcliffe, Lord Denning and Lord Devlin in *Glinski v McIver* [1962] AC 726.

36  A potential claim in misfeasance could also arise in these circumstances if the officers' conduct amounted to a dishonest abuse of their authority.

with contemporaneous records or inexplicable changes in accounts given.[37] A very good example of this enquiry in to the officer's state of mind is the decision of the Court of Appeal in *Paul v Chief Constable of Humberside Police.*[38] The court decided that the trial judge had erred in withdrawing claims in false imprisonment and malicious prosecution from the jury, as there was sufficient material on the particular facts to enable inferences to be drawn that the officers were not acting in good faith, in that they had arrested and charged the claimant to deflect attention from their own potential culpability in relation to the death of Christopher Alder in police custody, rather than out of a considered assessment of the evidence. Less commonly, there may be direct evidence available, for example from witnesses themselves that they were threatened or intimidated by officers into falsely incriminating the claimant, or evidence from what officers themselves said at the time, for example telling a claimant 'we know you didn't do it, but we're going to nick you anyway'. However, it is impermissible to rely simply on the objectively weak nature of the prosecution case and contend from this that officers could not have honestly believed in the claimant's guilt.[39] However, it is arguable that the weakness of the case is one circumstance that should be considered, along with all others, when assessing whether inferences as to a lack of honest belief can be drawn.[40]

7.25    It is well established that a lack of honest belief in the case cannot be inferred simply from proof that officers had an ulterior motive for the prosecution.[41] Thus, if officers prosecute Y because she brought a previous complaint against one of their colleagues, but the case was supported by sufficient, genuine evidence indicating that Y was probably guilty, she would not have a viable claim in malicious prosecution. Similarly, if there is evidence that a white man and a black man are both guilty of a crime, but out of racism the police prosecute only the black man, a claim in malicious prosecution would not be made out.[42] This is not to say that the same facts cannot be used to support both a finding of malice and a finding of lack of reasonable and probable cause,

---

37  See the speech of Lord Denning in *Glinski v McIver* [1962] AC 726.
38  [2004] EWCA Civ 308.
39  *Glinski v McIver* [1962] AC 726. See, eg, the speech of Lord Radcliffe.
40  See Clayton and Tomlinson *Civil Actions Against the Police* (3rd edn, Thomson Sweet & Maxwell, 2004) para 8-042.
41  *Glinski v McIver* [1962] AC 726; *Matin v Commissioner of Police fof the Metropolis* [2002] EWCA Civ 907.
42  Although an action under the Race Relations Act 1976 (as amended) may arise, see chapter 10.

if those facts point to officers lacking honest belief in the evidence put forward, for instance where evidence is fabricated. In the relatively unusual event that the defendant fails to offer any explanation for the basis of the prosecution in circumstances that appear to call for one, the omission can be treated as evidence of a lack of reasonable and probable cause.[43] Sometimes a defendant will seek to defend a contention of lack of honest belief on the basis that the prosecution was approved by the CPS and/or counsel and so, it is said, officers were simply following advice. However, this will not avail the defendant if officers withheld information or the decision was based on evidence that the officers knew to be concocted or otherwise substantially flawed.[44]

## Objective lack of evidence supporting the prosecution

7.26    Even if the prosecutor honestly believed in the case put forward against the claimant, there will be a lack of reasonable and probable cause for the proceedings if the evidence was too weak to properly support a case. If the judge is sitting with a jury, the jury first decides any disputed facts that bear on this issue, for example, as to what information was known to the prosecutor at the time or as to the level and nature of inquiries that were actually made and then the judge rules upon the objective question of whether there was sufficient evidence to support the prosecution (see also para 13.31).

7.27    It has been suggested that there are a number of steps that an ordinarily prudent and cautious prosecutor would undertake; specifically he or she would:

- take reasonable steps to ascertain the true state of the case;
- consider the matter on the basis of admissible evidence only; and
- in all but plain cases, obtain legal advice as to whether a prosecution is justified and act upon that advice.[45]

7.28    Thus it is possible that a lack of reasonable and probable cause can be established from a failure to follow obvious lines of inquiry, if doing so would have negated a viable case against the claimant.[46] However, it is a question of degree. A prosecutor is not required to test every

---

43    *Gibbs v Rea* [1998] AC 786, PC.

44    See *Glinski v McIver* [1962] AC 726; *Abbott v Refuge Assurance Co* [1962] 1 QB 432.

45    See *Abbott v Refuge Assurance Co* [1962] 1 QB 432.

46    For a recent example in a malicious process case see *Keegan v Chief Constable of Merseyside Police* [2003] 1 WLR 2187.

possible relevant fact before taking action: 'His duty is not to ascertain whether there is a defence but whether there is a reasonable and
probable cause for the prosecution'.[47] If the prosecutor was mistaken
about a matter of fact which, if true, would have given sufficient basis
for the prosecution, the issue is whether the mistake was a reasonable one to make.[48] The significance of taking legal advice has been
considered under the discussion of the subjective element above.
The fact that the claimant may have been convicted at trial is not treated
as decisive of this issue against him or her, if the conviction is later
overturned on appeal.[49] If the Court of Appeal when overturning a
conviction expresses a view about the lack of evidence in support of the
prosecution, it is unclear to what extent the claimant can rely upon
this opinion in a subsequent civil action.[50]

7.29    If a claimant establishes a lack of reasonable and probable cause by
the objective route, rather than by showing that officers did not honestly
believe in the case put forward, it may well be difficult to show the
further necessary ingredient of malice, unless there is clear evidence
of an improper purpose, as discussed below.

## The police acted maliciously

7.30    In order to prove that the police acted maliciously, it must be shown that
their motive, or their main motive, was something other than the
desire to bring the claimant to justice.[51] In circumstances where
the claimant establishes that officers could not have believed he
was guilty because they had concocted the account of his alleged
criminality (usually in an attempt to mask their own misconduct),
there will be no difficulty in establishing malice. For example, in
*Thompson v Commissioner of Police for the Metropolis*[52] police falsely
alleged that the claimant had bitten an officer's finger and assaulted
others in order to cover up their own brutality towards her as she was
manhandled into a cell at the police station.[53] Additionally, malice

---

47    *Herniman v Smith* [1938] AC 305, HL, per Lord Atkin at 319.
48    *Hicks v Faulkner* (1878) 8 QBD 167.
49    See, eg, *Herniman v Smith* [1938] AC 305, HL.
50    Although no question of issue estoppel arises as the two parties are not the
      same, one would expect considerable weight to be attached to the Court of
      Appeal's view.
51    *Stevens v Midland Counties Railway* (1854) 10 Exch 352.
52    [1997] 2 All ER 762.
53    *Commissioner of Police of the Metropolis v Gerald* (1998) 10 June, CA, unreported,
      is another similar example.

should be established in the sorts of circumstances discussed above, where officers have some general belief in the guilt of the claimant, but dishonestly and improperly procure or create a substantial part of the prosecution case. A desire to concoct evidence and/or to procure a conviction at any cost, affords evidence of malice.[54]

7.31    If the police are partly motivated by a desire to bring someone to justice, but also partly by an improper motive, the question is: which was the dominant purpose? If the improper motive was dominant, the claim can still succeed. Examples of improper motives, other than masking officers' own misconduct, would be punishing a claimant for an earlier complaint or civil action or for rudeness to officers.

7.32    Although lack of reasonable and probable cause can never be inferred from malice (see above), a lack of reasonable and probable cause can provide evidence of malice.[55] However, the extent to which this is possible depends upon the particular circumstances. If it has been shown that officers did not honestly believe in the charges brought, this will afford strong evidence of malice,[56] for the reasons already discussed. However, establishing a lack of reasonable and probable cause by showing that, objectively viewed, there was an insufficient basis for the prosecution, does not generally provide evidence of malice as this state of affairs is not inconsistent with the prosecutor acting for the proper motive of seeking justice; he or she may simply have been careless.[57] This is well illustrated by the decision in *Thacker v Crown Prosecution Service*,[58] where an allegedly weak prosecution was ultimately discontinued. The Court of Appeal said that even if it could be shown that on the objective test there was a lack of reasonable and probable cause for the prosecution and that representatives of the CPS were remiss in not appreciating this earlier, there was no evidence that they acted in bad faith.[59] In the malicious process case of *Keegan v Chief Constable of Merseyside Police*[60] the claimant sought to overcome

---

54  See *Clerk & Lindsell on Torts* (18th edn, Sweet & Maxwell, 2000) para 16-37 and the authorities cited therein.

55  *Brown v Hawkes* [1891] 2 QB 718, 722.

56  See *Haddrick v Heslop* (1848) 12 QB 267; *Brown v Hawkes* [1891] 2 QB 718, 722 and *Tempest v Snowdon* [1952] 1 All ER 1.

57  *Meering v Grahame White Aviation* (1919) 122 LT 44; *Gibbs v Rea* [1998] AC 786, PC.

58  (1997) *Times* 29 December, CA.

59  In such circumstances an action in negligence would also be problematic, because of the difficulty of showing the existence of a duty of care, as discussed at para 8.56).

60  [2003] 1 WLR 2187.

this difficulty in relation to officers who sought a search warrant on the basis of slender evidence, by arguing from analogy with caselaw concerning the tort of misfeasance in a public office, that 'malice' now bore an expanded meaning and included circumstances where officers acted with reckless indifference to the legality of their conduct (see para 7.34). The Court of Appeal rejected this argument, reaffirming that malice required proof of an improper purpose. They held there was no evidence of malice on the facts as officers had obtained and executed the search warrant because they were genuinely seeking to recover stolen monies, a perfectly proper purpose (despite the lack of reasonable and probable cause for the warrant).

7.33    Whether there is some evidence of malice so that a jury could properly conclude that this element of the tort was proved, is a matter for the judge to decide. Whether or not, on that evidence, the prosecutor's motive was indeed malicious is a question of fact for the jury to decide.[61]

## European Convention on Human Rights

7.34    Convention rights do not appear to expand the circumstances in which a claimant can succeed in an action for malicious prosecution. ECHR article 5(5) provides that everyone who has been detained in contravention of article 5 shall have an enforceable right to compensation. However, a period of detention is regarded as lawful for these purposes if carried out pursuant to a court order, made within the court's jurisdiction, even if that order was subsequently quashed on appeal.[62] Accordingly, where a conviction is quashed on appeal after the appellant has spent time in custody, any available remedies will normally arise in relation to an action for malicious prosecution or misfeasance in a public office, rather than under the Convention. The possibility of claiming compensation from the Home Office in such circumstances is looked at separately (in chapter 7).

---

61   *Hicks v Faulkner* (1878) 8 QBD 167; *Brown v Hawkes* [1891] 2 QB 718; *Dallison v Caffrey* [1965] QB 348. The respective roles of judge and jury are considered in more detail at paras 13.31–13.34 and 13.39–13.40.
62   *Benham v UK* (1996) 22 EHRR 293.

# Malicious process

7.35 Malicious process is a civil wrong, separate from malicious prosecution, which entails instituting a legal process short of prosecution without reasonable and probable cause and with malice.[63] The two most common examples are applications for arrest warrants and search warrants.[64]

7.36 In relation to such applications there are four ingredients of the tort that the claimant must establish,[65] namely:

- a successful application for the warrant was made;
- there was a lack of reasonable and probable cause for making the application;
- it was made maliciously; and
- there was resultant damage.

7.37 Proving a lack of reasonable and probable cause and proving malice have been described in detail under the preceding section on malicious prosecution. In relation to proceedings that the claimant has no right to attend, such as applications for warrants, it need not be shown that they terminated in his or her favour.[66] Damage for these purposes is not as strictly confined as under the tort of malicious prosecution and encompasses all forms of recognised damage.[67]

7.38 If the ingredients of a malicious process claim are proved, the claimant will overcome the difficulty that otherwise arises because of the Constables Protection Act 1750 in suing in relation to arrests or searches undertaken in obedience to a warrant (see paras 6.76–6.78 and 9.15 ). If the claimant cannot prove a lack of reasonable and probable cause and/or malice, in some circumstances an action in negligence may lie if the warrant was obtained on the basis of inaccurate information.[68]

---

63 *Roy v Prior* [1970] 2 All ER 729, HL; *Gibbs v Rea* [1998] AC 786, PC.

64 For other instances of malicious process see Clayton and Tomlinson *Civil Actions Against the Police* (3rd edn, Thomson Sweet & Maxwell, 2004) paras 8-083–8-089.

65 *Keegan v Chief Constable of Merseyside Police* [2003] 1 WLR 2187.

66 However, if the form of process under challenge involves the attendance of both parties, such as a complaint of breach of the peace, then in the claimant's favour termination must be shown.

67 See the discussion of permitted heads of tortious damage in relation to misfeasance in a public office and in relation to negligence at paras 7.45 and 8.85 respectively.

68 *Hough v Chief Constable of the Staffordshire Constabulary* [2001] EWCA Civ 39, though see the discussion of this case at para 8.66.

# Misfeasance in a public office

## Definition

7.39　The tort of misfeasance in a public office was originally developed during the eighteenth and nineteenth centuries for the benefit of electors who were wilfully denied the right to vote by a returning officer. It was little used for some considerable time afterwards. More recently the value of this tort has been recognised as a broader remedy for abuse of administrative power. Over the last ten years it has come to be increasingly deployed in claims against the police. The rationale of the tort is that executive or administrative power 'may be exercised only for the public good' and not for ulterior or improper purposes.[69] However, the fact that an official acts in excess of his or her powers does not always give rise to a monetary remedy. The elements of the tort of misfeasance in a public office were clarified by the House of Lords in *Three Rivers DC v Bank of England (No 3)*[70] as follows:

- the conduct must be that of a public officer, exercising power in that capacity;
- the officer must either intend to injure the claimant by his or her acts or knowingly/recklessly act beyond his or her powers;
- and thereby cause damage to the claimant;
- in circumstances where he or she knew the act would probably cause damage of this kind.

7.40　These elements are considered in more detail in turn below. Misconduct in a public office can also amount to a criminal offence.[71]

## A public officer

7.41　A police officer who abuses his position will certainly fulfil the first element of the tort. A civilian employed by a police authority is also likely to be a public officer for these purposes, as the comparable offence of misconduct in a public office applies to every person who is appointed to discharge a public duty and is paid to do so.[72] A decision made by an employee of the Crown Prosecution Service in relation to

69　*Jones v Swansea City Council* [1990] 1 WLR 54, 85F.
70　[2003] 2 AC 1, HL.
71　In *Att-Gen's Reference No 3 of 2003* (2004) 2 Cr App R 23 the Court of Appeal considered the ingredients of the criminal offence; they are similar, but not identical to the elements of the tort of misfeasance.
72　*R v Bowden* [1995] 4 All ER 505.

an actual or potential prosecution can also ground a claim in misfeasance (if the other elements of the tort are satisfied).[73]

## The officer's act

7.42 In the *Three Rivers* case the House of Lords emphasised that both limbs of the tort require the claimant to prove bad faith on the part of the relevant officer. Accident, mistake or carelessness is insufficient.[74] The first way of committing the tort, where the officer intends to injure the claimant by his or her acts, is often referred to as 'targeted malice'. The essence is the abuse of power for a specific improper or ulterior motive. The second way of committing the tort involves the relevant officer acting in excess of his or her powers. An example of the difference between the two ways that the tort can be committed could arise from an instance where a police officer misused information he or she gained from police records by leaking it to the claimant's employer, thereby leading to the loss of his or her job. Assuming there was no legitimate reason for the disclosure (see para 10.17 onwards), the conduct could come within the first limb of the tort if the officer acted out of spite and in the hope that it would lead to a dismissal, because the claimant had previously complained about that officer. The conduct could fall within the second limb of the tort if the officer had not acted out of spite but, knowing there were force procedures prohibiting such disclosures, he or she had decided to proceed anyway because he or she thought the procedures were too restrictive.

7.43 In the *Three Rivers* case the House of Lords decided that in order to establish liability under the second limb, the officer must either exceed his or her powers knowingly or be reckless about this occurring, in the subjective sense that the officer actually appreciated the risk that he or she was going beyond his or her powers but proceeded indifferent to this risk. A failure to appreciate such a risk, even if it was obvious, would not suffice for misfeasance. In *Three Rivers* Lord Hutton said that the 'act' in question may be an omission to act, provided it is the product of a deliberate decision not to act as opposed to mere inadvertence or oversight.[75]

---

73 *Elguzouli-Daf v Commissioner of Police of the Metropolis* [1995] 1 All ER 833, CA.
74 See to similar effect: *Thomas v Chief Constable of Cleveland Police* [2001] EWCA Civ 1552.
75 See also *Toumia v Evans* (1999) *Times* 1 April, CA.

7.44    Misfeasance is a tort of personal bad faith and ultimately a claimant must establish bad faith on the part of a particular officer; but it is not always necessary to identify the officer(s) at the outset, if it is sufficiently clear from the conduct pleaded by the claimant that bad faith on the part of individual officers was involved.[76]

*Damage*

7.45    To succeed in establishing liability, the claimant must usually show that he or she suffered a recognisable head of 'damage' in consequence of the public officer's wrongful actions. Unlike the position in relation to the intentional torts of false imprisonment, assault and battery, it is insufficient to rely on the claimant's inconvenience or distress where 'damage' has to be shown. 'Damage' in this context covers financial loss, loss of liberty[77] and death or personal injury.[78] The latter includes both physical injury and psychiatric trauma provided a recognised medical condition is established. Loss of reputation will probably suffice as well.[79] However, where the misfeasance involves an interference with the claimant's constitutional rights it is unnecessary to prove damage.[80] Constitutional rights are those which are of such importance that the right in question cannot be abrogated by the state, save by a specific legislative provision.[81] Examples of constitutional rights are the right to vote and the right of access to justice.[82] The extent to which abuses of power by police officers could involve infringement of the claimant's constitutional rights is currently uncertain. The more serious the abuse, the stronger the chance would be of showing such an infringement.

---

76  *Chagos Islanders v Att-Gen* [2003] EWHC 2222.

77  See *W v Home Office* [1997] Imm AR 302, CA and the speech of Lord Clyde in *Darker v Chief Constable of the West Midlands Police* [2001] AC 435 HL.

78  *Akenzua v Secretary of State for the Home Department* [2003] 1 All ER 35.

79  See Clayton and Tomlinson *Civil Actions Against the Police* (3rd edn, Thomson Sweet & Maxwell, 2004) para 11-024.

80  *Watkins v Secretary of State for the Home Department* [2004] EWCA Civ 966 where the claimant's legally privileged correspondence was opened by prison officers in breach of his constitutional right to unimpeded access to his solicitor.

81  *R v Lord Chancellor ex p Witham* [1998] QB 575.

82  See the discussion in *Watkins v Secretary of State for the Home Department* [2004] EWCA Civ 966.

*The officer's state of mind in relation to the damage*

7.46 The House of Lords' decision in the *Three Rivers* case established that it was sufficient if the relevant officer was aware of the probability of damage being caused by his or her actions; it was unnecessary to show that he or she regarded this as a certainty. The same case also decided it was sufficient if the officer was reckless as to the probability of damage resulting from his or her actions (provided the recklessness was of the subjective type where the officer actually foresaw the risk, as discussed in para 7.43 above). An issue remained as to the extent to which the relevant officer was required to appreciate the risk of damage to the particular victim. This was specifically considered by the Court of Appeal in *Akenzua v Secretary of State for the Home Department*.[83] The claim was brought by relatives of a woman murdered by a violent criminal who had entered the United Kingdom illegally but (it was alleged) had been permitted to remain in breach of usual procedures and in deliberate disregard of the risks he posed, because of his role as a paid police informant. The defendants sought to strike out the claim on the basis that even if the relevant officers were aware of the murderer's violent tendencies, they were not aware that he posed a threat to the particular woman he killed. The Court of Appeal rejected the suggestion that misfeasance in a public office involved a proximity requirement similar to that applied in the tort of negligence (see the discussion of negligence claims at para 8.51). For liability in misfeasance to be established it was sufficient if the relevant officer contemplated harm to one or more victims who were unknown unless or until the expected harm eventuated.

## Chief officer's liability

7.47 It is sometimes suggested on behalf of defendants that the act of alleged misfeasance is, by its nature, beyond anything contemplated by the officer's position and as such outside the scope of the chief officer's liability for the actions of officers of the force. However the usual principles of vicarious liability apply (see para 11.107 onwards). Accordingly, the chief officer of the relevant force will generally be held legally responsible for acts committed in the officer's capacity as a constable, albeit that he or she has exceeded the powers of that office.[84]

---

83 *Watkins v Secretary of State for the Home Department* [2004] EWCA Civ 966.
84 See *Marsh v Chief Constable of Lancashire Constabulary* [2003] EWCA Civ 284 and *Weir v Chief Constable of Merseyside Police* [2003] ICR 708.

## Misfeasance in police cases

7.48 Many instances of police misconduct will fall within the more established torts, such as false imprisonment in relation to a wrongful arrest. In those instances a claim in misfeasance is usually superfluous. However, the tort of misfeasance may be of considerable assistance to claimants in circumstances where misconduct does not relate to arrest, detention or assault. Criminal prosecutions are dealt with separately below. Recent examples of the breadth of misfeasance claims in civil actions against the police include:

- an officer's misuse of information obtained via the police national computer concerning the claimant's convictions: *Elliot v Chief Constable of Wiltshire;*[85]
- an officer's deliberate failure to investigate a complaint of crime and forging of related documentation: *Kuddus v Chief Constable of Leicestershire Constabulary;*[86]
- wrongful identification of the claimants as distributors of stolen imported vehicles, publicised by officers to customers of the business: *Cruickshank Ltd v Chief Constable of Kent Constabulary;*[87]
- misuse of a known violent criminal as a paid police informant: *Akenzua v Secretary of State for the Home Department.*[88]

7.49 Additionally, in *Thomas v Secretary of State for the Home Department*[89] the court accepted that the tort would be made out if prison officers deliberately abused their powers by racially discriminating against and abusing inmates or encouraging other prisoners to so abuse them (albeit this was not established on the evidence in that case). However, despite the wide scope of circumstances that could lead to a successful claim, it is important to bear in mind, as mentioned above, that claims in misfeasance require bad faith to be established and that carelessness, however gross, will never suffice. The Court of Appeal has recently warned against the routine inclusion of allegations of mis-

---

85 (1996) *Times* 5 December, ChD. The court accepted on a strike-out application that the claim was arguable.

86 [2001] 3 All ER 193. Liability was conceded and the case was contested on the issue of damages.

87 [2002] EWCA Civ 1840. The court accepted on a strike-out application that the claim was arguable.

88 [2002] EWCA Civ 1840.

89 (2000) 31 July, QBD, unreported.

feasance in police actions where there is no clear evidence to support a contention of dishonest abuse of power.[90]

## Misfeasance and malicious prosecution

7.50 A vital question in relation to the tort of misfeasance is its inter-relationship with the tort of malicious prosecution in circumstances where a claimant wishes to sue in respect of a failed prosecution brought against him or her. A successful claim in malicious prosecution requires proof that the criminal proceedings against the claimant lacked reasonable and probable cause (see para 7.19 onwards). But a prosecution supported by sufficient evidence to amount to reasonable and probable cause may nonetheless be tainted by false evidence. A relatively common allegation made by claimants is that officers have dishonestly 'improved' the state of the prosecution case against them, by, for example, falsely claiming that admissions were made. In instances where there was a substantial amount of other evidence implicating the claimant, a malicious prosecution action is unlikely to succeed (see para 7.23). The House of Lords considered the viability of a claim in misfeasance in such circumstances in *Darker v Chief Constable of West Midlands Police*,[91] where the defendant sought to strike out a claim in misfeasance concerning allegations that officers fabricated evidence and misused informants. The defendant relied upon the principle of witness immunity (that is, that a person cannot be subjected to a civil claim in relation to evidence he or she gives in court proceedings). Malicious prosecution, unlike misfeasance, is an expressly recognised exception to this principle. Previously, in *Silcott v Commissioner of Police of the Metropolis*,[92] the Court of Appeal had struck out a misfeasance claim brought by Winston Silcott concerning admissions allegedly fabricated by police officers in support of his prosecution for the murder of PC Blakelock. The Court of Appeal said that the principle of witness immunity extended to the preparation of evidence for trial, including the creation of false evidence to be used at trial, so the claim in misfeasance could not proceed (although in that instance the evidence which was said to have been fabricated was sufficiently fundamental to the prosecution case for the civil action to proceed as a malicious prosecution claim). In *Darker* the House of

---

90 *Masters v Chief Constable of Sussex* [2002] EWCA Civ 1482.
91 [2002] EWCA Civ 1482.
92 (1996) 8 Admin LR 633.

Lords rejected the Court of Appeal's approach. They held that witness immunity did not extend to the deliberate fabrication of evidence by police officers. They drew a distinction between officers' conduct that was part of the investigation process, which fell outside the immunity, and action undertaken in an officer's capacity as a witness, which came within the immunity. As the House of Lords observed, the officers never intended their dishonest creation of evidence to form part of the account they gave as witnesses at the criminal trial; on the contrary, they intended to conceal it. Thus in consequence of the *Darker* decision, officers' fabrication of admissions, planting of false evidence and dishonest manipulation of potential witnesses would all fall outside the immunity. In contrast, a complaint that did not concern earlier investigative action, but was simply to the effect that the officer gave a false account of his dealings with the claimant in his evidence at the criminal trial, would be caught by the witness immunity so as to preclude an action in misfeasance.

7.51      If the claimant's case in misfeasance avoids the application of the witness immunity principle, the question remains as to whether as a matter of policy the courts should permit the civil claim despite there having been reasonable and probable cause for the prosecution. In *Darker* both Lords Cooke and Hutton said in terms that this should not bar a claim in misfeasance. Lord Hope appears to have been of a similar view. The other two speeches did not consider this issue. Thus the balance of current authority suggests that a misfeasance claim can proceed in such circumstances.[93] However, practitioners should note that, unlike in malicious prosecution claims, where time runs from the date when the criminal proceedings terminated in the claimant's favour, the normal six-year limitation period runs from the date of misconduct relied upon (see paras 11.69–11.71). Further, if the misfeasance action succeeds, outstanding questions remain as to the level of compensatory damages (as opposed to exemplary damages) that would be considered appropriate for a claimant having to face tainted prosecution evidence in circumstances where a prosecution was in any event justified.

---

93  Contrary to earlier observations made in *McDonagh v Commissioner of Police of the Metropolis* (1989) *Times* 28 December, QBD.

# Negligence and related actions

8.1    This chapter looks at the main causes of action that are likely to arise out of careless or incompetent policing, that falls short of deliberate misconduct. The chapter initially deals with the common law tort of negligence. The criteria needed to establish a successful claim are discussed, with particular focus upon the difficult issue of whether a duty of care exists. The next section analyses the claims that may arise out of a person's death, with particular emphasis upon the opportunities for bereaved relatives to make a claim under the Fatal Accidents Act 1976. Consideration is then given to the limited circumstances where a claim for breach of statutory duty will arise out of a failure to comply with a legislative provision. Specific rules relating to the assessment of damages in negligence and under the Fatal Accidents Act are dealt with in this chapter; more general principles relating to the award of compensation are addressed in chapter 14.

# Negligence

8.2    An action in negligence may be appropriate where it cannot be established that officers acted in bad faith towards the injured party. A successful claim involves showing that the alleged wrongdoer acted carelessly, that is, below the standard of how a reasonable person in the equivalent position would have behaved. However, not all instances of carelessness can found a claim. Liability will only arise if the alleged wrongdoer owed a duty of care to the person who suffered damage. Whether a duty of care is owed will depend upon the relationship of the two parties to each other, the nature of the alleged carelessness and the consequences that flowed from it. The concept of a duty of care is used by the courts as a flexible control mechanism to prevent far-reaching liabilities arising from careless acts. Instances of careless conduct are far more frequent than deliberate abuses of power and the need to establish a duty of care before liability can result enables the courts to limit the reach of claims for such carelessness. Accordingly, much of the caselaw on whether duties of care exist in particular situations is driven by policy considerations and by an attempt to strike a balance between the desire to provide a remedy for those who have suffered injury as against the desire to protect defendants, particularly public bodies, from a multiplicity of claims. Such policy considerations have been influential in the decisions that have considered the extent to which police officers owe duties of care to those damaged by their behaviour. This section will look at the factors that tend to influence whether a duty of care is imposed and the extent to which police officers have been held to be subject to such duties. Assessing whether a duty of care is owed is frequently complex and is an issue that has generated much caselaw.

8.3     The need to show a duty of care is not the only means by which the courts control the ambit of liability for careless acts. In order to succeed in a claim for negligence a claimant must show that:

- the alleged wrong doer owed a duty of care to him or her individually, or to a class of persons to which he or she belongs, to take reasonable steps to prevent the harm suffered; and
- the duty was breached as the alleged wrongdoer failed to act with reasonable care in the circumstances; and
- the breach of duty caused him or her damage of a type recoverable in the law of negligence; and
- that kind of damage was the reasonably foreseeable result of the conduct complained of.

These elements are considered in turn below, with particular focus upon the often difficult question of whether a duty of care is owed in the circumstances.

## The duty of care

8.4     A police officer owes the same duties of care as are owed by ordinary members of the public when he or she is acting in that capacity. Thus, for example, a police officer driving a vehicle owes the same duty of care as that owed by all road users to other motorists and pedestrians and can be liable if an accident results from his or her carelessness.[1] However, the circumstances in which the driving occurred, for example if the officer was in pursuit of an offender, may be relevant to the question of whether the duty was in fact breached (discussed at para 8.80). Similarly if a police officer carelessly damages the claimant's property – for example by dropping a Ming vase while conducting a search of a premises – a duty of care should readily be imposed, just as it usually is when a person directly damages the property of another.[2] These instances are to be contrasted with situations where the alleged negligence relates to the way that officers have performed specific policing

---

1   *Gaynor v Allen* [1959] 2 QB 403. The duty extends even to a criminal who is being pursued: *Marshall v Osmond* [1983] QB 1034, CA.
2   As discussed below, in so far as *Kinsella v Chief Constable of Nottinghamshire* (1999) *Times* 24 August, QBD is to the contrary, it is suggested that it is wrongly decided.

functions and it is said that the claimant has been injured as a result of deficient performance of those functions, for example where a crime is investigated poorly or a public order situation handled incompetently. In these sorts of circumstances the courts have generally been much more reluctant to impose duties of care on police officers.

8.5    In determining whether a duty of care exists in any particular situation, the first question to ask will be whether caselaw has already determined the issue on parallel facts, whether in the claimant's favour or not. However, if the situation is a novel one and/or past caselaw is distinguishable, the courts will usually apply the test identified in *Caparo Industries plc v Dickman*[3] to determine whether a duty of care exists. This entails asking:

- Was the type of harm suffered by the claimant reasonably foreseeable?
- Was the relationship between the parties sufficiently proximate?
- Is it fair, just and reasonable to impose a duty of care in the circumstances?

8.6    A duty of care will only be imposed if all three questions are answered affirmatively. The courts have recognised that there is a significant degree of overlap and inter-relationship between the three questions.[4] For example, the closer the relationship of proximity between the parties, the more likely it will be that the courts will conclude that it is fair, just and reasonable to impose a duty of care. The concepts themselves are relatively imprecise, allowing for maximum judicial flexibility. For example in the *Caparo* case Lord Oliver said of the concept of proximity:

> 'Proximity' is, no doubt, a convenient expression so long as it is realised that it is no more than a label which embraces not a definable concept but merely a description of circumstances from which, pragmatically, the courts conclude that a duty of care exists.[5]

8.7    A further factor that the courts will bear in mind when determining whether a duty of care exists, is that the *Caparo* approach is intended to be applied to novel situations incrementally, that is, by analogy with situations where duties of care have already been established, rather

---

3  [1990] 2 AC 605, HL.
4  See, eg, *Cowan v Chief Constable for Avon and Somerset Constabulary* [2000] 1 All ER 504 at [26]–[27].
5  [1990] 2 AC 605 at 633. The impressionistic nature of the concepts has also been emphasised in subsequent caselaw, see eg *Farah v British Airways* (2000) *Times* 26 January, CA.

than by a major extension of the situations in which such a duty will arise.[6] Each of the elements of the *Caparo* test are discussed in turn and then the factors that will influence the imposition of a duty of care are summarised. This is followed by an analysis of the effect of the European Convention on Human Rights on this area of law, and then particular areas of policing activity are considered. Many of the cases concerning duties of care arose out of applications by the defendant to strike out the claim on the grounds that a duty of care could not arise; in those circumstances the courts were involved in deciding whether a duty of care was arguable, rather than whether it was proven .

### Reasonable foresight

8.8    The claimant has to show that it was reasonably foreseeable that the want of care in question could cause damage of the type sustained to him or her or to a class of people to which he or she belonged. The test is an objective one and is judged by reference to the facts the wrongdoer knew or ought to have known at the time.[7] In *Attorney-General v Hartwell*[8] the Privy Council emphasised that the degree of likelihood of the damage occurring that was required to satisfy this test was not to be found at a fixed point on the scale of probability; it depended upon the circumstances and in particular upon the seriousness of the possible adverse consequences of the carelessness. Accordingly, the more serious the potential consequences, the less probable that eventuality will need to be to satisfy the reasonable foresight test. The Privy Council also suggested in *Hartwell* that a greater degree of foresight may be required in cases where the complaint is that the failings of the defendant (or those for whom he or she is legally responsible) allowed a third party to inflict damage on the claimant, in contrast to where the former's actions directly caused the claimant harm.[9] By way

---

6  The authorities on the incremental approach are reviewed in *Watson v British Boxing Board of Control Ltd* [2000] 1 QB 1134, CA (where, unusually, the court was prepared to develop a duty of care in hitherto unique circumstances to hold the Board liable to the boxer Michael Watson for failing to discharge a duty to take all reasonable steps to ensure he received appropriate medical treatment when he was injured during a fight).

7  See, eg, *Leach v Chief Constable of Gloucestershire* [1999] 1 WLR 1421, CA.

8  [2004] 1 WLR 1273, PC and discussed further at para 8.14.

9  Caselaw on negligent omissions is discussed in more detail below – see paras 8.23–8.27.

of example, in the well-known case of *Dorset Yacht Co Ltd v Home Office*[10] the House of Lords thought that the risk of the borstal boys escaping and causing damage to neighbouring property if not adequately supervised was obvious, so that their supervisors were under a duty of care to take reasonable steps to prevent this.

8.9     The House of Lords' decision in the *Dorset Yacht* case also illustrates another aspect of the foreseeability test. The claimant's yacht was moored in the locality and was damaged by the borstal boys who escaped. He was within a class of persons to whom damage was reasonably foreseeable, that is, those with property situated close to the site of the escape. Had the boys been on the run for several days and then damaged property some distance from the scene of their escape the foresight test may not have been satisfied.[11]

8.10    Although foresight of the type of damage suffered is required, a claimant may recover for psychiatric injury even if this was not specifically foreseeable, provided that physical injury to him or her was foreseeable.[12] Thus, for example if a defendant loses control of his or her car and it hurtles towards the claimant who just escapes physical injury, he or she can recover for psychiatric injury sustained as a result of the trauma in which he or she was placed.

8.11    In *McNern v Commissioner of Police for the Metropolis*[13] the Court of Appeal held that the claimant could not recover in negligence for psychiatric injury sustained as a result of his arrest, as officers had no basis on the information known to them at the time to appreciate the risk of this occuring. It was suggested that had the police known that the claimant had particular psychological vulnerabilities, they could have come under a duty of care in relation to the way they carried out the arrest. However, as being arrested is an inherently stressful process, if there was a sufficient basis upon which to make the arrest,[14] it may be difficult to establish liability even if there was knowledge of vulnerability, unless the arrest was carried out in a particularly insensitive way. The argument would obviously be stronger if the arrest was for a particularly serious offence and/or one carrying a particular moral stigma (whereas in *McNern* the arrest was for vehicle theft).

---

10  [1970] AC 1004, HL.
11  Similarly, the geographical relationship impacted on the proximity question.
12  *Page v Smith* [1996] AC 155, HL.
13  (2000) 18 April, CA, unreported.
14  So that no claim in false imprisonment arose, see chapter 6.

*Proximity*

8.12 The elasticity of this concept has already been emphasised (see para 8.6). However, in general it focuses upon the quality of the connection between the claimant and the alleged wrongdoer. Factors to be considered include: did the defendant's actions directly cause harm to the claimant;[15] were the parties physically close to each other at the material time; were the parties known to each other and was there was any pre-existing relationship linking the two of them (for example an employment relationship).

8.13 The mere fact that one party exercises a statutory power over another does not establish the requisite degree of proximity.[16] Similarly, the mere fact that a police officer comes into contact with a member of the public when carrying out his or her policing duties is insufficient to establish proximity, whether the contact is made between the police and a victim of crime,[17] or the police and a suspect.[18] Circumstances need to be identified that indicate a particular relationship between the parties and/or that the alleged wrongdoer assumed a specific responsibility towards the claimant.[19] For example, in relation to victims of crime, arguable relationships of proximity were said to arise in *Osman v Ferguson*[20] and in *Brooks v Commissioner of Police of the Metropolis*.[21] In the former of these cases the police had failed to arrest and charge a teacher against whom a number of very serious complaints had been made by a former pupil with whom the teacher had become obsessed. Eventually the teacher shot and injured the pupil and killed his father. The frequency, severity and specific nature of the complaints made to the police was sufficient to establish an arguable relationship of proximity. However, the claim failed on the basis that it was not fair, just and

---

15 Discussed in more detail in relation to factors influencing the imposition of a duty of care – see paras 8.26–8.27.

16 See, eg, *W v Home Office* [1997] Imm AR 302, CA (in relation to immigration officers' powers of detention).

17 See, eg, *Alexandrou v Oxford* [1993] 4 All ER 328, CA where there was insufficient proximity between officers and the claimant who had a burglar alarm that directly alerted the local police station when there was a break-in.

18 See, eg, *Heagren v Chief Constable of Norfolk* (1997) 8 July, CA, unreported, where there was insufficient proximity between the claimant and the officers who carried out his arrest.

19 Assumption of responsibility is specifically discussed below – see paras 8.29–8.30.

20 [1993] 4 All ER 344, CA.

21 [2002] EWCA Civ 407.

reasonable to impose a duty of care.[22] In the later case the Court of Appeal held that it was arguable that the police owed a duty of care to Duwayne Brooks, the friend who witnessed the murder of Stephen Lawrence, as the officers involved knew he also had been a victim of the assault by racist thugs, knew he was a key witness to the assault on Stephen and he had spent many hours in the company of police officers giving his account of events.[23] As the decision in *Brooks* illustrates, the presence or absence of sufficient proximity will be related to the particular duty of care alleged. The Court of Appeal in that case held that it was arguable that the police owed the claimant a duty of care in his capacity as a witness and as a victim, to take reasonable care in the way they carried out their investigation. However, they rejected an argument that a duty of care also arose in relation to the provision of appropriate training to those officers; training was a general issue in which all members of the public had an interest and so its provision (or lack of) did not give rise to a relationship of proximity with the claimant.[24]

8.14    In *Attorney-General v Hartwell*[25] the Privy Council was influenced by the gravity of the risks involved in the conduct at issue in determining that the proximity test was satisfied (as they also had been in assessing reasonable foresight, as discussed at para 8.8 above). In that case an officer had deserted his post and in a fit of jealousy shot at his ex-partner in a bar without warning, seriously injuring the claimant. The officer was on probation at the time and the sole officer in charge of a station on Jost Van Dyke Island. He had access at the station to a revolver and ammunition, which he took with him to the bar. The Privy Council concluded that the police authorities were negligent in letting him have unsupervised access to the gun and ammunition and rejected the submission that there was insufficient proximity since the claimant was simply a member of the public who happened to be in the bar at the time of the attack and who had no connection to the officer who used the gun or to the police authorities. The Privy Council said that where an article as dangerous as a gun is entrusted to another, the class of persons to whom a duty of care is owed is wide (and the standard of care required was also high). Given the inherent risks

---

22 The subsequent decision of the European Court of Human Rights in *Osman v United Kingdom* (1998) 29 EHRR 245 is discussed when the influence of the European Convention is considered below – see paras 8.40–8.44.

23 At the time of writing the House of Lords' decision in *Commissioner of Police of the Metropolis v Brooks* is awaited.

24 Following the decision in *Cowan v Chief Constable for Avon and Somerset Constabulary* [2000] 1 All ER 504, CA.

25 [2004] 1 WLR 1273, PC.

involved if the gun was misused the duty was owed to the public at large. The wide reach of the duty was proportionate to the gravity of the risks involved.[26]

8.15 Factors that will influence whether a duty of care is owed in a particular case are further identified and discussed after the courts' approach to when it is fair, just and reasonable to impose a duty of care has been summarised at para 8.22 onwards, below.

### Fair, just and reasonable to impose a duty of care

8.16 An assessment of whether it is fair, just and reasonable to impose a duty of care depends not only on the particular circumstances (including considerations such as the severity of the harm suffered), but also on weighing in the balance the likely benefit and detriment to the public interest of holding that a duty of care would arise in similar cases.[27]

8.17 The starting point for a consideration of whether it is fair, just and reasonable to impose a duty of care in relation to policing functions is the House of Lords' decision in *Hill v Chief Constable of West Yorkshire*.[28] The claim was brought by the mother of the last victim of the 'Yorkshire Ripper' on the basis that officers had been negligent in failing to apprehend him at an earlier stage of the investigation into other attacks he had committed. As well as holding that there was insufficient proximity between the victim and the police in the circumstances, the House of Lords held that it would not be fair, just and reasonable to impose a duty of care in the circumstances. The main reasons given for these conclusions were that the class of people at risk – that is, the female public in general – was too wide for a special relationship to arise and that the imposition of such a duty would: cause a diversion of resources from investigating crime to defending claims; inhibit officers' fearless discharge of their duties as they would tend to act in a detrimentally defensive frame of mind; require the court to make judgment in policy areas more suitable for evaluation by the police and would not appreciably reinforce policing standards.

---

26  The Privy Council rejected a submission that the police authorities could be vicariously liable for the act of shooting the claimant, as at this point the armed officer was on a frolic of his own. (Compare the circumstances in *Bernard v Att-Gen of Jamaica* [2004] UK PC 47, discussed at para 11.116.) The actionable negligence in *Hartwell* lay in the authorities enabling that (junior) officer to access and make use of the weapon.

27  *Barrett v Enfield BC* [2001] 2 AC 550, HL.

28  [1989] AC 53, HL.

8.18      The House of Lords' reasoning in *Hill* has been quoted and applied
in many subsequent cases.[29] However, some subsequent authorities
have thrown into question the factors identified as important to the decision in *Hill*. It has been observed that the diversion of resources to
defending claims is simply the commonplace consequence of litigation
generally.[30] Further, in a number of cases the courts have robustly
rejected the suggestion that the imposition of a duty of care cannot
contribute to the raising of standards and will lead to an inhibited
performance of the tasks in question by police officers or other
professionals.[31]

8.19      There is a helpful review of the authorities concerning when it is fair,
just and reasonable to impose a duty of care in policing cases in the
decision of the Court of Appeal in *Brooks v Commissioner of Police for the
Metropolis*.[32] The court concluded that the policy considerations identified in *Hill* remained substantially valid, but that they must be weighed
against other relevant public policy considerations in each instance
and that it could not be said that the police enjoyed an immunity from
suit in respect of their investigation of crime. It was emphasised that
the public policy consideration that has the first claim on the law is that
wrongs should be remedied and that very potent considerations were
required to override that policy.[33] It remains to be seen whether the
House of Lords will follow this approach when they determine the
further appeal in the *Brooks* case (their decision is awaited at the time
of writing). As the Court of Appeal's decision confirms, the trend over
recent years has been towards a more flexible interpretation of *Hill*
than was employed in the years immediately following that decision.

---

29   By way of example only: *Alexandrou v Oxford* [1993] 4 All ER 328, CA; *Ancell
v McDermott* [1993] 4 All ER 355, CA; *Cowan v Chief Constable for Avon and
Somerset Constabulary* [2000] 1 All ER 504, CA.

30   *Waters v Commissioner of Police for the Metropolis* [2000] 4 All ER 934, HL at
940h and 946f.

31   See, eg, the authorities on this point referred to in *JD v East Berkshire
Community Health* [2004] QB 558, CA at [36], [37], [51], [52], particularly in
relation to social workers. Also see the comments of Lords Cooke and
Hutton in *Darker v Chief Constable of West Midlands* [2001] 1 AC 435, HL in
rejecting comparable contentions regarding police officers when considering
the inter-relationship between the principle of witness immunity and a claim
in misfeasance (discussed in more detail at para 7.50). Similarly in *Arthur JS
Hall & Co v Simons* [2000] 3 All ER 673 a majority of the House of Lords
rejected suggestions that the imposition of a duty of care inhibited the
conduct of advocacy.

32   [2002] EWCA Civ 407.

33   [2002] EWCA Civ 407 at [73].

An example of where it was held that it was arguably fair, just and reasonable to impose a duty of care is *Swinney v Chief Constable of Northumbria*[34] in relation to officers' failure to keep secret the identity of the claimant who had passed information to the police about a third party's criminal activities in return for a promise of anonymity. The Court of Appeal was particularly influenced by the fact that there was a clear public interest in encouraging people to give information to the police without fear of reprisals from the subjects of that information.

8.20    The reasoning of the divided Court of Appeal in *Leach v Chief Constable of Gloucestershire*[35] provides a good illustration of the kind of factors likely to influence the courts. The claimant in that case had been asked by the police to act as an 'appropriate adult' during their interviews of Fred West.[36] She suffered psychiatric trauma as a result of listening to the horrific details of murder and abuse disclosed during those interviews. She claimed that the police were negligent in failing to offer her counselling after the interviews, in asking her to attend as an appropriate adult without warning her as to what was involved in the offences under investigation and in wrongly advising her that she would not be required to testify at the subsequent trial. A majority of the Court of Appeal, Pill LJ dissenting, held that the negligence claim should be struck out as unarguable other than the complaint that she was not given timely counselling (which had been provided to the officers involved). Brooke LJ emphasised that if a duty was owed it would be owed to a wide class of persons, that is, all relatives and professionals in the social welfare area who might act as appropriate adults in distressing cases; that the suggested duty of care conflicted with police priorities during the interview which was to carry out as effective an interview of the suspect as possible without worrying about the sensibilities of those present; and that it was vital to the proper discharge of an appropriate adult's functions that they were entirely independent from the police. Pill LJ, on the other hand, stressed that the police had asked for the claimant's participation (which she had then provided on a voluntary basis) and thereby placed her in an inherently stressful situation and that there was a public interest in encouraging suitable volunteers to act as appropriate adults.

---

34    [1996] 3 All ER 449, CA (though the claim was ultimately unsuccessful at trial: *Swinney v Chief Constable of Northumbria (No 2)* (1999) 11 Admin LR 811).

35    [1999] 1 WLR 1421.

36    An appropriate adult was required as the police suspected West was mentally disordered. The claimant was known to them through her voluntary work on a local homeless project.

8.21    In determining whether it is fair, just and reasonable to impose a duty of care in any particular situation, courts sometimes refer to and appear to be influenced by the public perception, or at least their perception of the public perception. For example in *White v Chief Constable of South Yorkshire*[37] the House of Lords allowed an appeal from the Court of Appeal's decision that the Chief Officer of police owed duties of care to officers who suffered psychiatric injury while on duty during the Hillsborough tragedy, since it would offend the general public if officers were able to recover damages when no duty of care was owed to many of the bereaved relatives.[38] Similarly, in *McFarlane v Tayside Health Board*[39] the House of Lords referred to the views of the general public in determining whether and to what extent a duty of care could be owed to parents in relation to medical negligence that led to an unwanted pregnancy and the birth of a healthy (as opposed to a disabled) child. The danger of this approach, however, is that the court's perception of the public's views may be no more than speculation and/or may be unduly influenced by the court's own opinions. In *Costello v Chief Constable of Northumbria*[40] the Court of Appeal held that a duty of care was owed by a more senior officer who failed to come to the aid of the claimant (a police constable) when she was attacked by a violent prisoner. The Court observed that the law should accord with common sense and that the public would be greatly disturbed if no duty of care arose in the circumstances. Although that may be so, it is arguable the public would be equally disturbed, if made aware of the many circumstances in which duties of care have been denied to claimants harmed through police carelessness.

*Factors influencing the imposition of a duty of care*

8.22    Since there is such a degree of overlap between the three elements of the *Caparo*[40a] criteria, particularly in relation to proximity and whether it is fair, just and reasonable to impose a duty of care, it is helpful to identify factors that are likely to guide the courts' overall conclusion on whether a duty of care exists in the circumstances in these issues. The key factors are listed below with a discussion of examples drawn from the case-law.

37  [1999] 2 AC 455, HL.
38  *Alcock v Chief Constable of South Yorkshire* [1992] 1 AC 310, HL.
39  [2000] 2 AC 59, HL.
40  [1999] 1 All ER 550.
40a  *Caparo Industries plc v Dickman* [1990] 2 AC 605, HL.

## Act or omission

8.23   A duty of care will much more readily be imposed when the complaint is that the claimant has been damaged by a positive act of the
defendant, rather than where the harm has been caused by the officer's
failure to act in a particular way to prevent damages occuring. In general the law is reluctant to impose a duty of care in respect of pure
omissions.[41] Hence a person is generally under no legal obligation to
come to the assistance of another and may, for example, watch someone drown without incurring any legal liability for failing to assist.
This principle underpinned the Court of Appeal's conclusion that the
fire brigade owed no duty of care to an owner or occupier merely by
attending their premises to fight a fire and that liability would only
result if the fire officers actually caused damage or by their actions
enhanced the risk of that happening.[42] A substantial number of the
cases in which the courts have held that a duty of care was not owed by
police officers concerned omissions to act (although this factor is not
always expressly acknowledged as influential in the court's reasoning); see, for example, *Hill v Chief Constable of West Yorkshire*[43] (where
the complaint was that police should have done more to catch the
'Yorkshire Ripper'); *Alexandrou v Oxford*[44] (where the complaint was that
police had failed to respond reasonably to an alarm call); or *Ancell v
McDermott*[45] (where the complaint was that officers had done nothing
about a dangerous spillage of oil on the road). On the other hand, for
example, in *Rigby v Chief Constable of Northamptonshire*[46] liability in
negligence was established where police had fired a CS gas canister into
a building in an effort to force an armed intruder to give himself up.
The building caught fire as a result of this positive act and substantial
damage was sustained.

8.24   Correctly categorising the complaint as involving an act or an
omission is therefore very important. In one sense it can be argued that
a negligence complaint is always about an omission, in the sense that
the defendant (or those he or she is legally responsible for) is being
criticised for failing to act in a certain way. However, a speeding driver

---

41   For a review of the underlying principles see *Smith v Littlewoods* [1987] AC
241, HL.

42   *Capital Counties v Hampshire CC* [1997] 2 All ER 865, CA.

43   [1989] AC 53, HL.

44   [1993] 4 All ER 328, CA.

45   [1993] 4 All ER 355, CA.

46   [1985] 2 All ER 985, CA.

who crashes into another vehicle is responsible for the dangerous act of going too fast, not simply for the omission of failing to put on his or her brakes more promptly. The crux is whether the acts of the defendant created the dangerous situation in the first place. This was central to the Privy Council's reasoning in *Attorney-General v Hartwell*. The facts have been summarised at para 8.14. The court categorised the case as one of an act, rather than an omission; although there was a complaint of lack of supervision, the police authorities had embarked on an inherently dangerous course of conduct by providing the renegade officer with the gun and ammunition in the first place. The court said this distinguished the circumstances from a *Hill* type omissions situation.

8.25    An omission to act will not normally found the basis of a duty of care in negligence unless the alleged wrongdoer created the dangerous situation in the first place and/or exacerbated it. However, there are circumstances where the nature of the relationship between the parties imposes particular responsibilities towards the claimant, so that a broader failure to take reasonable steps to protect him or her may lead to a successful negligence claim. The clearest example of this in the policing context is the duty owed by a custodian towards his or her prisoners. Because the fact of detention inhibits the ability of the prisoner to take care for his or her own safety, the law imposes on the custodian a duty of care that can include culpability for failing adequately to protect the detainee's personal safety.[47]

## Acts of third parties involved

8.26    The courts will much more readily impose a duty of care where the harm in question stems from the direct act of the defendant, as opposed to the intentional act of a third party. This approach is closely linked to the courts' attitude towards omissions; if the damage to the claimant was directly inflicted by a third party, the complaint against the defendant will usually be that he or she or the officers under his or her control failed to act to take steps to prevent this from happening. An example of the distinction is provided by the following two cases. In *L v Reading BC*[48] police officers misrepresented to social services the strength of the evidence against a father accused by the mother of abusing their child. In consequence the family was involved in

---

47    This is discussed below, where the duties owed by a custodian are considered in more detail – see paras 8.57–8.63.

48    [2001] 1 WLR 1575, CA.

protracted proceedings brought by the local authority on the basis of these allegations. The allegations were ultimately shown to be false. The Court of Appeal held that it was arguable that officers owed a duty of care to the claimants (the father and the child) at the time when they took it upon themselves to misrepresent the contents of police interviews to social services.[49] In *Cowan v Chief Constable for Avon and Somerset*[50] police officers called to the scene failed to prevent the claimant from being illegally evicted by his landlord as they were unaware that the latter's conduct in physically evicting the claimant without a possession order amounted to an offence under the Protection from Eviction Act 1977, as they were not familiar with this legislation. The Court of Appeal said that the officers owed no duty of care to the claimant since a failure to act to prevent damage being inflicted by a third party would only be actionable in negligence if the parties were in a special relationship with each other. The sheer fact that officers had attended the scene did not establish such a relationship so as to impose a duty upon the officers to prevent the eviction.[51]

8.27     In summary, liability for the failure to prevent the deliberate acts of a third party is exceptional and is only likely to be imposed where the courts consider that the parties were in a special relationship to each other.[52]

## Degree of risk involved in the activity

8.28     The importance of this factor was identified and discussed by the Privy Council in *Attorney-General v Hartwell,* as has been considered earlier at paras 8.8 and 8.14.

## Assumption of responsibility

8.29     In some cases the concept of assumption of responsibility has been used to determine whether there was sufficient proximity between the parties and whether it is fair, just and reasonable to impose a duty of care. The phrase does not connote a deliberate and conscious

---

49   This case is also discussed in relation to the concept of assumption of responsibility – see para 8.29.

50   [2000] 1 All ER 504, CA.

51   Though Sir Christopher Slade expressly left open the question of whether a duty to warn the landlord that he was committing an offence would have arisen had the officers been aware of the relevant law.

52   See also *Costello v Chief Constable of Northumbria* [1999] 1 All ER 550, CA; *K v Secretary of State for the Home Department* [2002] EWCA Civ 775.

acceptance of responsibility by the alleged wrongdoer. The issue is whether, objectively viewed, the law regards the circumstances as one where such a responsibility is deemed to arise.[53] However, if the circumstances do involve an express assurance or promise given by the alleged wrongdoer, the argument in favour of liability is strengthened. For example, in *Swinney v Chief Constable of Northumbria*,[54] where the Court of Appeal held that it was arguable that a duty of care arose to protect the identity of an informer, officers had specifically reassured the claimant that her identify would not be revealed. In the majority of situations where no equivalent express representation has been made, the court will analyse all the circumstances to see if the defendant's conduct is such that he or she should be taken to have accepted a particular responsibility toward the claimant. Typically this conclusion will be drawn if the defendant has voluntarily undertaken a particular course in relation to the claimant. For example in *L v Reading BC* (see para 8.26), the Court of Appeal held that no duty of care could arise at the stage when officers arrested and interviewed the father – this was simply the carrying out of normal policing duties. On the other hand it was arguable that a duty of care did arise when they elected to pass on (inaccurate) information to the local social services as officers had taken it upon themselves to do this. Similarly, in *Welsh v Chief Constable of Merseyside Police*[55] it was held that when the Crown Prosecution Service agreed to certain offences being taken into consideration when the claimant was before the Crown Court, they assumed a responsibility to relay that information to the magistrates' court who had been dealing with those offences. Accordingly, an arguable duty of care arose in relation to their failure to do so, which led to the claimant's re-arrest and detention.

8.30      An assumption of responsibility will not be inferred simply from officers attending upon the claimant in the course of their duties.[56] Similarly, in *N v Agrawal*[57] the Court of Appeal held that in carrying out an examination of a rape victim, the forensic medical examiner did not assume a responsibility for her psychiatric welfare and that any

---

53  See *Phelps v Hillingdon LBC* [2001] AC 619, HL.

54  [1996] 3 All ER 449, CA.

55  [1993] 1 All ER 693, QBD and discussed in *Elgouzouli Daf v Commissioner of Police of the Metropolis* [1995] 1 All ER 833, CA.

56  See, eg, *Cowan v Chief Constable for Avon and Somerset Constabulary* [2000] 1 All ER 504.

57  (1999) 20 May, CA, unreported.

duty owed was limited to taking care not to make the claimant's condition any worse.

## The type of damage caused

8.31 The courts will more readily impose liability where the claimant has suffered personal injury or damage to property as a result of the alleged carelessness, than where the harm suffered is economic loss.[58] A detailed consideration of the caselaw on duties of care in respect of economic loss is beyond the scope of this work and many of the authorities relate to commercial activities. However, in summary the position is that a duty to avoid causing economic loss is confined to circumstances where the parties are in a special relationship, in the sense that the defendant has assumed a responsibility to protect the claimant's economic welfare. Whether such a special relationship arises is to be determined by reference to the criteria identified in *Hedley Byrne & Co v Heller Partners Ltd*,[59] which applies to cases involving the provision of services as well as to allegations that the defendant gave incorrect advice to the claimant.[60]

## Conflicting interests

8.32 The courts will be reluctant to impose a duty of care where the duty owed to the claimant would potentially conflict with the proper discharge of the defendants' responsibilities. This concern is seen most clearly in the line of cases that have held that social workers do not owe a duty of care to the suspected abusers when investigating allegations that children have been abused. Recently the Court of Appeal has held that a duty of care can be owed to the child itself as here, in contrast to the position with the parents, there is no conflict between that duty and the proper discharge of the social worker's functions, both of which are aimed at protecting the child's welfare.[61] A perception that the alleged duty of care would conflict with the

---

58 See, eg, *Caparo Industries plc v Dickman* [1990] 2 AC 605, HL.

59 [1964] AC 465, HL.

60 For a detailed analysis of liability for the negligent provision of services leading to economic loss see *White v Jones* [1995] 2 AC 207, HL.

61 *JD v East Berkshire Community Health* [2004] QB 558, where the earlier authorities on this issue are reviewed. Similar considerations informed the decision as to whether social workers owed a duty of care in relation to information provided to potential adoptive parents: *A v Essex CC* [2004] 1 FLR 749.

proper discharge of the relevant responsibilities has also been identified as a factor against the imposition of such a duty in a number of
cases involving policing and/or prosecutions.[62]

## Involvement of discretion or policy

8.33    A number of cases suggest that the courts are much more willing to
impose a duty of care where the complaint relates to a simple error in
carrying out a particular task, rather than to a discretionary decision,
potentially involving policy and/or resources issues. The courts tend to
regard themselves as ill-equipped to judge the latter. This distinction
was emphasised by the Court of Appeal in *Kent v Griffiths*[63] where it was
held that the ambulance service owed a duty of care to respond
reasonably after accepting a 999 call to attend the claimant who was
suffering an asthma attack. This distinction may also account in part
for the Court of Appeal's willingness to impose a duty of care in *Clarke
v Crew*[64] where officers failed to endorse correctly the date of arrest on
a committal warrant before the claimant was transferred into the care
of the prison authorities and this led to him spending additional time
in custody beyond his correct release date.[65] However, in cases
concerning the exercise of local authority functions, some judges have
suggested that drawing a distinction between operational and policy
functions is an inadequate way of resolving the duty of care issue.[66]

## Availability of alternative remedies

8.34    In *Brooks v Commissioner of Police for the Metropolis*[67] the Court of Appeal
decided that it was not fair, just and reasonable to impose a duty of
care upon officers in relation to the way they investigated the case as

---

62    For example, *N v Agrawal* (1999) 20 May, CA, unreported, in relation to an
      alleged duty of care owed by a forensic medical examiner to a rape victim;
      *Elgouzouli Daf v Commissioner of Police of the Metropolis* [1995] 1 All ER 833,
      CA in relation to an alleged duty of care owed by the CPS to a suspect; and *L
      v Reading BC* [2001] 1 WLR 1575, CA in relation to an alleged duty of care
      owed to the suspect by officers investigating allegations of abuse.

63    [2001] QB 36, CA.

64    (1999) 149 NLJ 899.

65    Although the responsibilities of the officers as custodians was also
      influential.

66    For example, Lords Hoffman and Nicholls in *Stovin v Wise* [1996] AC 923,
      HL. Though Lords Slynn and Clyde thought the distinction had some validity
      in *Phelps v Hillingdon LBC* [2001] AC 619, HL.

67    [2002] EWCA Civ 407. The House of Lords' decision on the further appeal in
      this case is awaited at the time of writing.

Duwayne Brooks was in any event able to bring a case against them under the Race Relations Act 1976. Similarly in *W v Home Office*[68] the availability of judicial review as a remedy to challenge unlawful detention by immigration officers was emphasised when it was held that no private law duty of care was owed to the detainee in respect of decisions to detain. A number of policing cases where duties of care have been rejected have referred to the possibility of action in misfeasance if bad faith were to be established.[69] However, it is hard to see why a duty of care should not arise if other factors point towards that conclusion, simply by dint of the fact that an alternative form of action (which might or might not succeed) was also available. Plainly this did not deter the courts in a number of the cases cited earlier where duties of care were acknowledged. It is submitted that this factor should carry less weight than the others identified in this text.[70]

### Exercise of a statutory power

8.35   In *Stovin v Wise*[71] the House of Lords held that where the complaint concerned the failure to exercise a statutory power to act in a particular way, liability in negligence could only result if it was shown that it was irrational not to exercise the power in the way the claimant favoured and that there were exceptional grounds for holding that the policy of the statute required compensation to be paid to a person who suffered loss because the power was not so exercised.[72] However, subsequent authorities have qualified the apparent breadth of this proposition. In *Barrett v Enfield LBC*[73] the House of Lords emphasised that it was undesirable for public law concepts of irrationality to be imported into private law tort actions and that the alleged negligence in *Stovin* purely related to an omission to act (failing to remove a bank that restricted visibility at a dangerous junction). They held that acts undertaken within the ambit of a statutory discretion could result in liability in negligence (subject to satisfaction of the usual criteria) unless they

68   [1997] Imm AR 302.

69   For example, *Elgouzouli Daf v Commissioner of Police of the Metropolis* [1995] 1 All ER 833, CA.

70   The Court of Appeal has recently held, in relation to detention authorised by immigration officers, that the potential availability of judicial review does not of itself preclude a claim for false imprisonment and/or under the HRA 1998 relying on a breach of article 5(1) ECHR: *ID v Home Office* [2005] EWCA Civ 38.

71   [1996] AC 923, HL.

72   See also *X v Bedfordshire* [1995] 2 AC 633, HL.

73   [2001] 2 AC 550, HL.

involved policy consideration over which parliament could not have intended that the courts would substitute their own views.[74]

8.36    However, it is clear from these authorities that the statutory framework within which the relevant act or omission took place will be highly relevant to an assessment of whether a duty of care in tort arises; for example a duty of care will not be imposed where that would be inconsistent with the exercise of functions under the statutory provisions. Further, if the statute compels a certain course to be taken, plainly the defendant cannot be negligent for taking that course.

8.37    Although this body of caselaw has not been considered in detail in relating to negligence claims involving policing, the issue could arise, for example in relation to a complaint of negligence that was inter-linked to the discharge of officer's statutory responsibilities for detainees under Police and Criminal Evidence Act 1984 Part IV.

## A breach of ECHR articles 2, 3, and/or 8

8.38    The circumstances in which a breach of these articles may arise in relation to the careless discharge of policing functions is discussed below at paras 8.42–8.49. For present purposes it is relevant to note that where the same circumstances would give rise to a freestanding claim under the Human Rights Act 1998, the courts may also be more willing to find that a duty of care existed. After all, it is difficult for a defendant to argue that it is not fair, just and reasonable to impose a duty of care in a situation where a positive obligation on him or her arises under the Convention. This was recognised by the Court of Appeal in *JD v East Berkshire Community Health*.[75]

## The influence of the European Convention on Human Rights

8.39    Two issues arise for consideration:

- to what extent does the fair trial guarantee contained in ECHR article 6(1) restrict the power of domestic courts to strike out claims in negligence on the basis that the alleged duty of care is unarguable; and
- in what circumstances do ECHR articles 2, 3 and/or 8 impose duties on the police that could be used as an alternative basis for a claim and/or to augment a claim in negligence?

These issues are dealt with in turn.

74  See also *Phelps v Hillingdon LBC* [2001] AC 619, HL to similar effect.
75  [2004] QB 558.

*The effect of article 6*

8.40    Some confusion has arisen on this issue as a result of the decision of the European Court of Human Rights in *Osman v United Kingdom*.[76] The case arose out of the Court of Appeal's decision in *Osman v Ferguson* (discussed above at para 8.13), where a negligence claim had been struck out on the basis that, applying the decision in *Hill v Chief Constable of West Yorkshire*, it was not fair, just and reasonable to impose a duty of care. The Strasbourg Court upheld the claim on the basis that having asserted his claim in negligence, the claimant had a right to seek an adjudication of it on its merits, and the application of an effective immunity for the police against negligence claims arising out of their investigations had therefore breached his rights guaranteed by article 6(1) (since the right to a fair trial implicitly includes the right of access to the courts). This decision was criticised by the House of Lords in *Barrett v Enfield LBC*.[77] Lord Browne-Wilkinson pointed out that the striking-out decision did not involve the application of a blanket immunity (as illustrated by cases such as *Swinney v Chief Constable of Northumbria*[78]), rather it was a fundamental common law principle that a duty of care could only arise where this was fair, just and reasonable in the circumstances. Further, that the decision whether it was fair, just and reasonable to impose a duty of care was a question of law; in cases where it was plain that the argument could not succeed as a matter of law it was a proportionate sanction to strike out that claim at a preliminary stage. In *Z v United Kingdom*[79] the European Court of Human Rights accepted the force of the points made in *Barrett* and accepted that *Osman* had been decided on the basis of a misunderstanding of the domestic law of negligence. Accordingly, it was held that article 6(1) was not infringed where claims in negligence against local authorities were struck out on the basis that no duties of care were owed in law.[80]

8.41    The current situation is therefore that a claimant cannot directly use article 6(1) to bolster his or her claim that a duty of care exists. At most the effect of article 6 has been to make the courts more wary of striking out negligence claims at a preliminary stage, rather than

76  (1998) 29 EHRR 245.
77  [2001] 2 AC 550, HL.
78  [1996] 3 All ER 449, CA.
79  (2002) 34 EHRR 3.
80  This decision was then followed in *TP and KM v United Kingdom* [2001] 2 FLR 549.

permitting arguments on the existence of a duty of care to proceed to trial where the material facts will be determined.[81]

## The impact of articles 2, 3 and 8

8.42    The caselaw suggests that there are three particular circumstances where ECHR articles 2, 3 and/or 8 may have a helpful impact on claims brought by victims or their surviving relatives concerning allegations that officers performed their duties carelessly. These are:

- where the police have failed to protect a victim of crime from a threat posed by a third party;
- where the police have failed properly to investigate a serious attack after it occurred; and
- where inadequate steps are taken to prevent a suicide in custody.[82]

The impact will arise both in terms of potentially permitting a freestanding claim under the Human Rights Act 1998 based on an infringement of the relevant article(s) of the ECHR and in using the caselaw summarised below to inform the content of the common law duty of care in a negligence claim. A freestanding claim can only arise where the events occurred after the Human Rights Act 1998 came into force.[83]

## Failures to protect victims of crime

8.43    Article 2 protects the right to life. Article 3 prohibits torture, inhuman or degrading treatment. Article 8 provides that everyone has

---

81   For example, this was emphasised in *Barrett v Enfield* [2001] 2 AC 550, *HL and W v Essex CC* [2001] 2 AC 592, HL. However, the issue may still be determined on a strike-out application if no additional material information is likely to emerge at trial: *Leach v Chief Constable of Gloucestershire* [1999] 1 WLR 1421, CA. But the appendix to the Resolution of the Committee of Ministers on 8 October 1998 in relation to *Osman v UK* records the UK government as saying 'The government anticipates that the rule established by the *Hill* case will be applied with more circumspection in the future...In addition the judgment has been circulated ...to all Chief Officers of Police. The government notes that it is for the latter officers to decide, in any given case, whether to seek to have such an action struck out on grounds of public policy immunity. The circular letter urges them, in the light of the *Osman* judgment, to exercise considerable caution before applying for a strike-out on these grounds...' (quoted in *Menson v UK* (2003) ECHR 47916/99).

82   Caselaw in relation to the latter of these instances is considered in paras 8.57–8.63 where duties owed by custodians are addressed in detail.

83   See para 10.172.

the right to respect for their private and family life, subject to interferences that can be justified under article 8(2). The right to respect for private life has been interpreted by the European Court of Human Rights to extend to respect for bodily integrity.[84]

8.44    The facts giving rise to the *Osman v Ferguson* and *Osman v United Kingdom* litigation were summarised at para 8.13. The European Court of Human Rights held that article 2 imposed a positive obligation on the police to provide appropriate protection to foreseeable victims. The court identified the duty as arising where it was established that the authorities knew or ought to have known at the time of a real and immediate risk to the life of an identifiable individual from the criminal acts of a third party. The duty would be breached if the authorities failed to take measures within the scope of their powers which, judged reasonably, might have been expected to avoid that risk. The court suggested, without deciding the point, that a similar obligation to safeguard physical integrity would arise in equivalent circumstances under article 8. The court decided that the duty arising from article 2 was not breached on the particular facts as the police had reason to know that the assailant had formed a bizarre attachment to his former pupil, but no specific reason to know that the lives of him or his family were at risk from this individual. In *Edwards v United Kingdom*[85] a breach of article 2 was established where prison authorities had placed a prisoner with a history of psychiatric problems and bizarre behaviour in a normal cell, where he had then gone on to stamp and kick his cellmate to death. The decision emphasised that the danger to the deceased was foreseeable and that persons in custody were in a particularly vulnerable position and reliant upon the proper discharge of their custodian's duties.

8.45    A similar approach was applied in relation to article 3 in *Z v United Kingdom*.[86] The case concerned the failure of social workers to investigate serious abuse and neglect suffered by the claimant children from their parents. It was accepted that the degree of suffering that the children underwent was sufficient to amount to inhuman or degrading treatment within the meaning of article 3. The court found that article 3 had been violated as the authorities knew or ought to have known of the ill-treatment but failed to take reasonable steps to prevent the children from further abuse. The decision was followed in another

---

84  For a more detailed discussion of these articles of the Convention see paras 10.177–10.194 and paras 10.201–10.212.

85  (2000) 35 EHRR 19.

86  (2002) 34 EHRR 2.

case concerning a local authority's failure to prevent abuse and ill-treatment of children, *E v United Kingdom*.[87] The latter case emphasised that a successful claim under article 3 did not require the claimant to prove that reasonable action on the part of the authorities would have prevented the further ill-treatment; it was sufficient if it could be shown that the failure to take reasonable measures could have had a real prospect of altering the outcome or mitigating the harm suffered. It is likely that an equivalent approach would be taken in relation to article 2.

8.46    Accordingly, in circumstances where police officers fail to take reasonable measures to protect an individual from a foreseeable fatal or life-threatening act, a claim under the Human Rights Act 1998 relying on breach of ECHR article 2 should be considered.[88] Equally, if police were or should have been aware that a person was suffering or was at risk of suffering abuse, harassment or other ill-treatment sufficiently severe to come within article 3, a claim based on a breach of this article may well be sustainable. It remains to be seen whether and to what extent the courts will be prepared to accept that an analogous obligation arises in relation to foreseeable threats to bodily integrity by reference to article 8. Plainly the courts may be more wary of imposing a positive obligation if the threat of damage or harm is of a less severe nature.

8.47    As we have seen, in *Osman* the Strasbourg Court characterised the duty as only arising where the foreseeable threat to life arose in relation to an identified individual. Frequently the police may be aware that an individual is a danger to women/children/society in general, but have no idea who the next likely victim will be. As discussed at paras 8.51–8.52 below, this has occasioned a difficulty in establishing liability in common law negligence. The extent to which article 2 may protect unknown victims was considered by the European Court of Human Rights in *Mastromatteo v Italy*.[89] In that case the applicant's son (a passer-by) had been killed by criminals in the course of a bank robbery. The criminals were wanted by the state authorities, having absconded during a period of authorised leave from prison. The applicant claimed that the police were in breach of the positive obligations under article 2 in failing to supervise sufficiently the prison leave and/or in failing to take adequate steps to catch the criminals after they absconded.

---

87    [2002] 1 FLR 348.

88    Note that stricter limitation periods apply under the Human Rights Act 1998 than to claims in negligence – see para 10.230.

89    (2002) ECHR 37703/97.

The court drew attention to the fact that it was not suggested that the authorities had any reason to suppose that the applicant's son, as opposed to other members of the public, was at risk from these individuals and that the claim represented an extension of the principle identified in *Osman*.[90] The Court emphasised that the article 2 obligation should not be interpreted in such a way as to impose an impossible or disproportionate burden on the authorities, bearing in mind the difficulties of policing modern societies, the unpredictable nature of human conduct and the difficult choices that had to be made in relation to priorities and resources. The Court held that on the facts no risk to life was foreseeable. However, the terms in which the decision was couched suggests that where it can be shown that the authorities should have reasonably foreseen a risk to loss of life, liability could arise under article 2 without the need to show that a particular victim was at risk. If this is followed in subsequent cases it will represent a substantial extension of the protection afforded by article 2 and will be of potentially considerable value to those who suffer attack, not because they have any prior link to their assailant, but simply because they happen to be in the wrong place at the wrong time.

8.48    Where the positive obligations under these articles are applicable, the difficulty otherwise presented by a negligence claim based on an omission to prevent another causing damage (discussed at paras 8.23–8.27 above) is avoided.[91]

### Deficient investigations

8.49    Strasbourg caselaw also has implications where the criticism relates to the conduct of an investigation after the attack took place. In *Menson v United Kingdom*[92] the European Court of Human Rights declared the application inadmissible as, on the facts, an adequate investigation had been undertaken. However, the court made some potentially very significant observations about the extent to which article 2 imposed a positive duty on the police to carry out an effective investigation following a fatal or life-threatening attack. The court said that article 2 required that

---

90   In *Bromiley v United Kingdom* (1999) 23 November, unreported, the court had applied *Osman* to reject an article 2 claim where the victim of a known violent offender was not foreseeably at risk of harm.

91   In *Edwards v United Kingdom* (2000) 35 EHRR 19 (see para 8.44 above) the carelessness did not relate solely to an omission; the authorities had taken the positive step of placing a dangerous prisoner in circumstances where he posed a risk to others. The situation was therefore analogous to *Att-Gen v Hartwell* [2004] 1 WLR 1273, discussed above at para 8.24.

92   (2003) ECHR 47916/99.

in such circumstances the investigation should be capable of establishing the cause of the injuries and those responsible for them. That an effective investigation would include taking reasonable steps to secure evidence concerning the incident, including eye witness testimony, forensic and other expert evidence and that any deficiency in the investigation which undermined the ability to establish the cause of the injuries/death and the person responsible, would risk infringing article 2. This duty to conduct an effective investigation applied whether or not officers of the state were involved in the attack upon the applicant. The court also said that this obligation was of particular importance where the attack was a racist one, given the need to reassert continuously society's condemnation of racism and to maintain the confidence of minorities. If this approach is followed it will represent a potentially substantial extension of the circumstances in which victims of serious crime will have a claim against the police (whether or not officers were in a position to prevent the attack from happening) if the subsequent investigation is handled poorly.[93] It remains to be seen whether the courts will find that articles 3 and/or 8 give rise to equivalent obligations to investigate crimes that involve behaviour amounting to torture, inhuman or degrading treatment or other invasions of bodily integrity.

## Instances of careless policing

8.50    The principles that have been identified above are now considered in relation to the main areas of policing where the careless behaviour of officers may give rise to an issue as to whether a duty of care was owed to those who have suffered consequential harm. The areas covered are the extent of the duty owed to:

- victims of crime, both in terms of failing to prevent the commission of crimes and in relation to the investigation of crimes that have been committed;
- suspects in relation to the investigation of crime;
- those held in custody;
- those harmed by dangerous objects held by officers;
- the subjects of data held by the police;
- those to whom the police provide advice;
- police informers;
- those who have property lost or damaged by officers;
- fellow police officers.

93   The current position under domestic law is summarised below – see para 8.54.

## Victims of crime

8.51 As described in paras 8.13 and 8.26–8.27, earlier when factors influencing the imposition of a duty of care were considered, domestic authorities have held that in the absence of a special relationship between the officer(s) and the victim of crime, no duty of care will arise to protect the victim from that crime. This has meant that where a dangerous offender has assaulted a member of the public with whom he or she had no previous connection, the courts have held that no duty of care arose, even where the authorities were involved in releasing the offender into public circulation. This approach is well illustrated by *K v Secretary of State for the Home Department*.[94] A man awaiting deportation was released by immigration officers. He had a history of convictions for sexual assaults. He raped the claimant, with whom he had no previous connection. Plainly, the offender's propensity to attack was foreseeable, but there was no reason for the authorities to suppose that he would attack the claimant, rather than any other woman. The Court of Appeal held that in those circumstances there was no proximity upon which to found a duty of care as there was no special relationship between the claimant and the relevant immigration officers, who could not have had her specifically within their contemplation. The court rejected an argument that the gravity of the harm that was foreseeable in general terms was itself a means of establishing the requisite proximity. A similar approach was also taken in *Palmer v Tees Health Authority*,[95] where a man who had been diagnosed as a psychopath with a dangerous personality disorder was released by the health authority and murdered the claimant's daughter, with whom he had no previous connection.[96]

8.52 Accordingly, if domestic caselaw alone is relied upon (for example where the events pre-date the coming into force of the Human Rights Act 1998), it is unlikely that a duty of care will be established in circumstances where a claimant was harmed by an offender whose relevant propensities were known to the police, but where officers had no reason to contemplate that he or she would be the next victim of that kind of behaviour. On the other hand, it will be possible to establish

---

94 [2002] EWCA Civ 775.

95 (2000) PNLR 87, CA.

96 The position is different if the authorities acted in bad faith and the claim is thus in misfeasance where no equivalent proximity requirement applies, see *Akenzua v Secretary of State for the Home Department* [2003] 1 All ER 35, CA. Discussed at para 7.46.

proximity even on the domestic authorities, where the behaviour of the offender was such as to lead to the conclusion that a particular individual or class of individuals was at risk, as in *Osman v Ferguson*.[97] As discussed above in para 8.47, observations by the European Court of Human Rights when giving judgment in *Mastromatteo v Italy* has opened up the possibility (at least where the harm involved is serious enough to engage article 2) of a broader approach being taken in a Human Rights Act claim, to enable liability to result where the type of offending was foreseeable, albeit the particular victim was not. In addition the approach taken by the Privy Council in *Attorney-General v Hartwell*[98] may be of assistance in this kind of situation; if a duty of care can arise from permitting a junior officer unsupervised access to a gun, because of the considerable dangers for members of the public this entailed, an equivalent argument could be deployed where police are responsible for releasing a highly dangerous offender who attacks a member of the public. (Although this could not apply where the complaint was that the police had simply failed to catch such an offender before he or she attacked the claimant.)

8.53    Domestic caselaw has also decided that the mere fact that police are asked to attend a crime scene by a 999 call or other request for assistance, does not create a special relationship between the victim and the officers so as to create a duty of care to respond to the call or to prevent or detect the crime on arrival.[99] The only recognised duty on the police in such circumstances is to use reasonable care not to exacerbate the situation.[100] In *Kent v Griffiths*[101] the Court of Appeal expressly distinguished those cases from the failure by an ambulance to respond to a 999 call. It was said that once the call had been accepted (as it had been in that case), foreseeable physical injury to a particular person arose and the ambulance service was in the same position as any health care provider – who owes a duty of care to his or her patients. However, if the circumstances are such as to trigger the positive obligations arising under ECHR articles 2, 3 and/or 8 when the police are contacted (as discussed above at paras 8.44–8.48), a freestanding claim under the Human Rights Act 1998 could arise and/or a negligence

---

97 [1993] 4 All ER 344, CA.

98 [2004] 1 WLR 1273, PC. Discussed at paras 8.8, 8.14 and 8.24.

99 *Alexandrou v Oxford* [1993] 4 All ER 328, CA; *Cowan v Chief Constable for Avon and Somerset Constabulary* [2000] 1 All ER 504.

100 See *Cowan v Chief Constable for Avon and Somerset Constabulary*, [2000] 1 All ER 504 at [39]–[40].

101 [2001] QB 36, CA.

claim would be much strengthened. This could arise, for example, if a 999 call reported that a potentially life threatening attack was about to happen and gave sufficient detail, but police failed to attend in time to prevent it due to carelessness.

8.54　　Similarly, domestic cases have held that the police will not owe a duty of care to a victim of crime in terms of the way that they proceed to investigate the offence unless the particular circumstances give rise to a special relationship between the parties.[102] This will not arise simply from the fact of a crime being reported, but could arise from the degree of communication between the police and the victim and the severity of the offence in question.[103] As discussed in para 8.49 above, *Menson v United Kingdom* has potentially opened the door to liability in relation to deficient investigations in a broader range of circumstances.

### Suspects

8.55　　Domestic caselaw indicates that the police will only owe a duty of care to those suspected of committing crime, in relation to the conduct of the investigation, if the circumstances are exceptional and give rise to an inference that officers have assumed a responsibility towards the individual.[104] Accordingly, on the state of current caselaw, a claim in negligence based on a complaint that a claimant has been arrested/prosecuted because police officers misunderstood the available evidence, or failed to assess the available evidence properly or failed to carry out certain lines of investigation, will usually fail as investigating officers will owe no duty of care to those suspected of the crime.[105] Similarly, it has also been held that officers investigating disciplinary offences do not owe a duty of care to the subject of their investigations.[106] Caselaw from Strasbourg does not suggest that reliance on the European Convention would materially alter the position; the articles of the Convention discussed above are focused upon the protection of the rights of victims rather than suspects. Plainly there are underlying policy considerations that are likely to incline the courts more readily to reject the existence of a duty upon officers to use reasonable care towards suspects in the conduct of an investigation. Furthermore, the courts will be alive to the fact that in many instances the interests of the suspect and

---

102　See *Brooks v Commissioner of Police for the Metropolis* [2002] EWCA Civ 407.

103　As stated above, at para 8.13, the decision of the House of Lords is awaited at the time of writing.

104　See the discussion of *L v Reading BC* at para 8.29.

105　See, eg, *Heagren v Chief Constable of Norfolk* (1997) 8 July, CA, unreported.

106　*Calveley v Chief Constable of Merseyside* [1989] AC 1228, HL.

the interests of an effective investigation may stand in direct conflict with each other (a factor discussed at para 8.32).

8.56    A similar approach has been taken in relation to claims that the Crown Prosecution Service (CPS) owed a duty of care to those it prosecuted to assess and deal with the evidence carefully. By way of example, in one of the cases before the Court of Appeal in *Elgouzouli Daf v Commissioner of Police for the Metropolis*[107] the claimant had been charged with handling explosives and had been detained in custody. Forensic swabs taken from his hands showed traces of an explosive residue. The claimant told police in interviews that any such traces were the product of innocent contamination. After the claimant had spent nearly three months in custody the CPS discontinued the case on the basis that innocent contamination could not be excluded. The claimant complained that this had always been apparent and that the CPS were negligent in not appreciating this and/or acting upon it at an earlier stage.[108] For the reasons discussed, the Court of Appeal rejected the existence of a duty of care.

### Persons in custody

8.57    Where one person (A) places him or herself in a relationship with another (B) in which B's physical safety becomes dependent upon the acts and omissions of A, a duty of care is imposed on A to exercise reasonable care for B's safety, as A is taken to have assumed a responsibility for B.[109] The nature and extent of the duty is considered in relation to three situations that the caselaw has looked at in detail:

- where the detainee commits suicide or self-harm while in custody;
- where the detainee is injured by the deliberate act of a fellow prisoner while in custody;
- where the detainee is injured trying to escape from custody.

---

107    [1995] 1 All ER 833, CA.

108    As explained at para 8.29, the CPS can be liable to someone they prosecute in the relatively rare circumstances where they assume a specific responsibility towards him or her as in *Welsh v Chief Constable of Merseyside* [1993] 1 All ER 693, QBD.

109    *Watson v British Board of Boxing* [2000] 1 QB 1134 at [49].

## Suicide or self-harm

8.58    In *Kirkham v Chief Constable of Greater Manchester*[110] the Court of Appeal
held that the police owed a duty to take reasonable care to prevent a
prisoner of unsound mind from killing or mutilating himself. In *Reeves
v Commissioner of Police of the Metropolis*[111] the House of Lords held
that police officers owed the equivalent duty to a prisoner of sound
mind. The duty arose from the complete control which the
police/prison authorities have over a prisoner and the special danger
of persons in custody taking their own lives or inflicting self-harm.
The two key issues that the House of Lords had to decide in *Reeves*
were whether the act of suicide by a person of sound mind broke the
chain of causation from the negligent supervision and whether the
deceased was guilty of contributory negligence in relation to his death.[112]
They held that the chain of causation was not broken as the act of suicide was the very act that the police were under a duty of care to prevent.
They also held that the deceased was 50 per cent liable for his own
death.

8.59    In *Reeves* officers were aware that the deceased was a suicide risk as
he had previously attempted to strangle himself when placed in a cell.
In *Orange v Chief Constable of the West Yorkshire Police*[113] officers were not
aware that the claimant was a suicide risk. He hanged himself from his
belt tied around the horizontal bar of the gate in the cell. It was contended that the police were negligent in permitting him to retain the
belt and/or in the design of the cell gate. The Court of Appeal held
that a duty of care to take reasonable steps to prevent suicide or self-
harm only arose when the custodian knew or ought to have known
that the individual prisoner presented a suicide risk. This in turn gave
rise to a preliminary duty to take reasonable steps to assess the prisoner
for these risks when he was in custody. Provided that assessment was
carried out properly and no particular cause for concern was identified
(as in this case) the duty would not arise. The court rejected a submission that a duty to take reasonable steps to prevent suicide should
arise in relation to all prisoners, given the inherent risks that detainees
will take their lives (which had been referred to in the *Reeves* case).
*Orange* was followed in *Smiley v Home Office*[114] where it was emphasised

---

110    [1990] 3 All ER 246, CA.
111    [2000] 1 AC 360, HL.
112    Causation and contributory negligence are explained below – see paras
        8.82–8.84 and 8.87–8.88.
113    [2002] QB 347, CA.
114    [2004] EWHC 240, 11 February 2004, QBD.

that the scope of inquiries necessary to constitute a reasonable assessment of such risks would depend upon the extent to which the detainee appeared to be vulnerable; the more vulnerable the detainee, the higher the degree of scrutiny that would be expected.

8.60    Cases brought under ECHR article 2 have been decided in a similar way by the Strasbourg authorities,[115] so that a breach of that article will only arise if there was a want of care in relation to the death of a person who presented as a foreseeable suicide risk. It was said that an obligation to take reasonable measures to prevent suicide in relation to all prisoners, whether or not specific risks were known, would place a disproportionate burden on the authorities.

## Assault by fellow prisoners

8.61    The control exercised by the prison authorities over a detainee gives rise to a duty of care to take reasonable steps to prevent an inmate from being attacked by fellow prisoners.[116] What is reasonable in any particular situation will depend upon the extent to which the authorities knew or ought to have known that the victim was at risk of attack and the practicability of measures that could be taken to prevent the same. As many attacks in custody arise in a relatively spontaneous context, liability for the breach of this duty has proved difficult to establish in practice.[117] In principle, the same duty arises on the police to protect detainees from assaults by fellow prisoners. However, given the relatively short period that detainees may be in police custody and the relatively limited space and resources available, breach of the duty may be difficult to establish, save in a case of glaring inactivity or misjudgment.

8.62    Where a prisoner kills or very seriously injures another prisoner in circumstances where the authorities created or contributed to the danger, or failed to take adequate steps to prevent a foreseeable danger, a breach of article 2 may arise as discussed earlier (see para 8.44).

---

115    See *Keenan v United Kingdom* (2001) 33 EHRR 38; *Younger v United Kingdom* (application no 5742/00).
116    *Ellis v Home Office* [1953] 2 QB 135.
117    See, eg, *Egerton v Home Office* [1978] Crim LR 494; *Porterfield v Home Office* (1988) *Times* 9 March, QBD.

## Escape from custody

8.63    In *Sacco v Chief Constable of South Wales*[118] the claimant hit his head and sustained serious injuries after exiting from the back of a moving police van shortly after he had been arrested. The police case, which was accepted at trial, was that this was a deliberate attempt to escape from custody (Sacco's case being that he fell). The Court of Appeal held that no duty of care is owed to an arrested person to take reasonable care to see that he or she is not injured in an attempt to escape from police custody. The reason for this was said to be that escaping from custody is itself a serious crime and the escapee must be taken to have known the dangers involved in choosing to undertake this act.[119] A similar approach was taken by a majority of the Court of Appeal in *Vellino v Chief Constable of the Greater Manchester Police*,[120] where the attempted escape was foreseeable to the officers (as the claimant had a known practice of jumping out of a second floor window when officers came to arrest him). Sedley LJ dissented, holding that there was a duty of care owed by the arresting officers not to afford both a temptation to escape and an opportunity of doing so, where there is a known risk of escape and of consequential harm. As the trial judge had found that officers had deliberately stood by and allowed the claimant to jump, Sedley LJ held that they were a third to blame for his injuries.

### Possession of dangerous objects

8.64    The decision of the Privy Council in *Attorney-General v Hartwell*[120a] has been discussed already in relation to reasonable foresight and proximity and in relation to the situations where liability will be imposed for omissions to act (see paras 8.8, 8.4 and 8.24). It provides a clear example of how the possession of inherently dangerous items can give rise to a duty of care to take reasonable steps to protect those who could be affected by their misuse. The principles identified in *Hartwell* are likely to be equally applicable to other dangerous weapons held by police officers. It remains to be seen whether the same approach would be taken in relation to items that carry a risk of less serious injury.

8.65    Liability in negligence may also arise if an officer causes injury while carrying out his duties through defective use of something with

118    (1998) 15 May, CA, unreported.
119    The court also held that for the same reason the doctrine of ex turpi causa would apply to defeat the claim. This doctrine is discussed at para 8.89.
120    [2002] 1 WLR 218, CA.
120a   [2004] 1 WLR 1273.

the potential for causing harm.[121] For example where a police dog is inadequately trained and/or handled carelessly and bites the claimant.[122]

### Recording data

8.66    In *Clarke v Crew* (see para 8.33) a mistaken failure properly to endorse a committal warrant led to liability in negligence. However, as the claimant was in police custody at the time, awaiting transfer to prison, a significant factor was the particular responsibilities owed by a custodian. In *Hough v Chief Constable of Staffordshire Constabulary*[123] a claim in false imprisonment was rejected where officers arrested the claimant on the basis of an inaccurate entry on the Police National Computer that wrongly led to suspicion arising against him. The false imprisonment claim turned on the state of mind of the officer making the arrest. Simon Brown LJ suggested that the claimant could have sued for negligence on the basis of the careless mistake made by the person inputting the data. However, Simon Brown LJ subsequently observed that had he been aware of the remedies under the data protection legislation at the material time, he would have considered that 'an altogether better basis' than negligence upon which to found a claim.[124] Where there is no existing custodian relationship, it may be difficult to establish sufficient proximity to found a claim for loss caused by inaccurate data in negligence and therefore a claim under the Data Protection Act 1998 may be the more promising.

### Provision of advice

8.67    In *Farah v British Airways*[125] the Court of Appeal accepted that it was arguable that a duty of care was owed by an immigration officer who wrongly advised the airline carrier that the claimant's documents were

---

121   In this instance the chief officer is vicariously liable for the negligence of the officer involved. Whereas in the situations contemplated in para 8.64 the weapon is misused outside of policing duties so that vicarious liability cannot be imposed in relation to the act of using the weapon and negligence can only arise in relation to the way that the weapon was made available to the officer.

122   The relevant authorities concerning police dogs and the circumstances in which assault will be a more appropriate claim are discussed at para 6.87.

123   (2001) *Times* 14 February, CA.

124   *Ogle v Chief Constable of the Thames Valley Police* [2001] EWCA Civ 598, 6 April 2001. Claims under the Data Protection Act 1998 are discussed at para 10.27 onwards.

125   (2000) *Times* 26 January, CA.

not in order. In consequence the carrier refused to take the claimant from Egypt to the United Kingdom and he and his family were deported back to Ethiopia, suffering loss in consequence. The court stressed that it would be relatively rare for a claimant to be able to sue in relation to a statement made to a third party from which the claimant had foreseeably suffered loss. It was accepted that there was sufficient proximity on the facts to make the existence of the duty arguable and the common interest between the parties in getting the decision right was stressed.

8.68    As shown by the authorities discussed earlier in relation to proximity and in relation to factors influencing the existence of a duty of care (see in particular paras 8.13, and 8.29–8.31), it is likely that the courts would be reluctant to impose a duty of care on police officers in respect of advice provided to members of the public, unless the circumstances gave rise to a special relationship and/or the claimant suffered consequential physical injury rather than purely economic harm. Consider, for example, if officers gave inaccurate information on road safety or gave directions that misled the claimant into a hazardous area and injury was sustained in consequence.

## Informants

8.69    The courts have accepted that police officers owe a duty of care in negligence to informants to take reasonable care for the their safety (including, where appropriate, preventing the disclosure of their identify to those who could be minded to take reprisals).[126]

## Property lost or damaged

8.70    If officers damage the claimant's goods through careless handling, a claim in negligence can arise. If the goods were being looked after by the police at the time (for example if they had been seized as part of an investigation), a claim for negligence or for breach of bailment will be available if they were lost or damaged.[127]

8.71    In *Kinsella v Chief Constable of Nottinghamshire*[128] the High Court struck out a claim in negligence based on damage caused to the claimant's property while officers conducted a search of her premises. The claim was struck out on the basis that *Hill* created a general rule that

---

126 The relevant authorities are discussed at paras 10.61–10.62, where claims in both negligence and for breach of confidence are considered.

127 These principles and the relevant caselaw are considered at paras 9.42–9.43.

128 (1999) *Times* 24 August, QBD.

police were not liable for negligence when acting in the course of their duties in investigating or suppressing crime. As the foregoing discussion indicates, this was an oversimplification of the position and one that pays no regard to the fact that the law will usually impose a duty of care in relation to injury or property damage directly caused by the positive actions of the defendant (or those for whom he is legally responsible).[129]

### Claims by fellow officers

8.72    A detailed consideration of such claims is beyond the scope of this book. It is mentioned here for completeness and because a number of the cases concerning claims in negligence by fellow officers contain a general review of the authorities in this area.[130] A police officer is in a stronger position as a claimant than a member of the public if the complaint relates to the conduct of senior officers. In those circumstances the courts will treat the situation as analogous to the well established duties of care that an employer owes to an employee to take reasonable care for his or her health and safety. Accordingly, where senior officers knew or ought to have foreseen that the acts of fellow officers might cause physical or mental harm to the claimant officer (for example, by bullying or other harassment), it was arguable that a duty of care was owed to take reasonable steps to supervise the situation and/or prevent such acts in the future.[131]

8.73    Where the complaint focuses on the conduct of a fellow officer of non-senior rank the position is, or at least should be, more akin to that of a claim brought by a member of the public. It is recognised that in general a police officer owes no duty of care to try and protect a fellow officer from attack, since to impose a duty of care would be to create liability for a pure omission (see paras 8.23–8.25). However, where the circumstances lead to the inference that the officer under criticism had assumed a responsibility towards the claimant officer, a duty of care will arise. Thus in *Costello v Chief Constable of Northumbria* the Court of Appeal held that an inspector who had come to the cells in case help was required but who then stood by while a detainee assaulted the claimant (woman) PC, had assumed a responsibility for her safety. The decision may well be explained by the fact that the

---

129    This is also the view expressed in Clayton and Tomlinson, *Civil Actions Against the Police* (3rd edn, Thomson Sweet & Maxwell, 2004) para 10-63.

130    In particular see *Waters v Commissioner of Police of the Metropolis* [2000] 4 All ER 934, HL and *Costello v Chief Constable of Northumbria* [1999] 1 All ER 550, CA.

131    *Waters v Commissioner of Police of the Metropolis*, [2000] 4 All ER 934, HL.

inspector had admitted in evidence that he had a duty to go to the claimant's assistance but had (falsely) claimed that no assault was taking place. Although it could also be suggested that a duty of care was found in this case rather more readily than in some of the cases involving claimants who were members of the public.[132]

8.74     Where the claim relates to an operational decision, it has been held that a senior officer should not generally be liable to subordinates in negligence for decisions taken in the heat of the moment and where resources may have been stretched.[133] However, liability to a subordinate officer may result where the more senior officer has positively intervened in a way that has caused injury to the subordinate or instructed him or her to act in a particular way that has placed him or her in obvious danger. This is illustrated by *Knightley v Johns*[134] where a police officer took charge of a dangerous traffic situation, negligently failed to close a tunnel and told the claimant police motorcyclist to ride into the tunnel against the flow of the traffic. The officer in charge was held to owe a duty of care to the claimant who suffered injury as a result of carrying out the instruction.

## Primary and secondary victims

8.75     Where the loss claimed is psychiatric harm, the distinction between primary and secondary victims is important. A primary victim is a person who could have foreseeably suffered physical injury as a result of the activity complained of.[135] The usual approach to a duty of care (see para 8.5) applies to a primary victim. However, where the claimant was not a participant in the particular incident and so cannot show that he or she is a primary victim, the courts have developed control mechanisms for limiting the circumstances in which damages can be recovered for psychiatric injury. Thus, for example, a relative or partner who learns after the event that his or her loved one was injured in a fire negligently started by police officers, would be a secondary victim. The scope of liability for psychiatric injury suffered by secondary victims is controlled by requiring the following criteria to be satisfied before a duty of care is owed:

- that the claimant had close ties of love and affection for the person injured or imperilled;

132  See para 8.21 discussing on the courts' reliance upon a stated perception of public opinion.
133  *Hughes v NUM* [1991] 4 All ER 278.
134  [1982] 1 WLR 349, CA.
135  *Page v Smith* [1996] AC 155, HL.

- that he or she was close to the incident in time and space; and
- that he or she directly perceived the incident rather than, for example, hearing about it from a third person.[136]

8.76    The application of this criteria lead to the denial of claims by relatives of those killed by the Hillsborough tragedy who had learnt of the circumstances after the incident or who were present at the stadium but did not satisfy the close ties of love and affection test.[137] The House of Lords subsequently applied the same approach to deny claims by officers who assisted in the aftermath of the incident, stating that the criteria applied to bystanders and to rescuers (unless sufficiently caught up in the events to qualify as a primary victim).[138] Thus, a partner or close relative who saw his or her loved one run over by a police car or shot by an officer or who saw the immediate aftermath of such events could qualify as a secondary victim (if he or she was not a primary victim), whereas a relative who was informed of these events some hours later and suffered trauma in consequence could not. The usual requirements for showing a duty of care and breach of the same then have to be established in addition to meeting the secondary victim criteria.

8.77    There is an exception to the limitation on claims for psychiatric injury by secondary victims where the negligent act of the defendant (or those for whom he or she is responsible) has put the claimant in the position of feeling that he or she is about to be or has been the involuntary cause of another's death or injury and has suffered psychiatric injury from the shock of this (inaccurate) perception. In these circumstances the claimant is treated as a primary victim, although not directly at risk of physical injury from the material events. A broad approach to this principle was taken by the House of Lords in *W v Essex CC*,[139] where the local authority had concealed from foster parents that the child they agreed to foster had a history of sexual abuse. The foster child went on to sexually abuse the children of the family. The House of Lords stressed that the dividing line between primary and secondary victims was a developing area of law and that the claim was arguably within the exception just summarised, as the parents' psychiatric injury had flowed from a feeling that they were responsible for bringing the abuser into a situation where he had injured their children.

136    *Alcock v Chief Constable of South Yorkshire* [1992] 1 AC 310, HL.
137    *Alcock v Chief Constable of South Yorkshire* [1992] 1 AC 310, HL.
138    *White v Chief Constable of South Yorkshire* [1999] 2 AC 455, HL.
139    [2001] 2 AC 592, HL.

## Breach of the duty of care

8.78 This issue can be dealt with much more shortly as the question is dependent on the particular facts of each case. The question is whether the conduct of the defendant (or those he or she is legally responsible for) has fallen below what could reasonably be expected in the circumstances. A variety of factors will influence what was reasonable behaviour in any particular situation, including:

- the likelihood of injury resulting from the conduct;
- the seriousness of the injury that could occur;
- the value to society of the activity that gave rise to the risk;
- the opportunity to assess the circumstances (a person acting in an emergency will be judged less harshly than one who has time available to weigh up the various options);
- the cost and practicability of preventative measures;
- general practice in equivalent situations.[140]

8.79 The conduct in issue will be judged by reference to how a reasonable person of ordinary prudence would have acted in the particular circumstances. Where a person holds a particular post the adequacy of his or her conduct will be judged by reference to what would reasonably be expected of a person in that position. Accordingly the acts of a probationary constable would be judged by a different standard to those of an inspector. The acts will be judged by reference to what was known or ought to have been known of the claimant or any other relevant circumstances at the time.

8.80 Given the nature of policing activities, officers may often be able to show that they were acting in emergency or difficult circumstances where their conduct should not be judged too strictly. For example, where injuries are caused by cars driven by police officers, the urgency of the situation will be taken into account in determining if there was any breach of duty,[141] as will the utility of the conduct in question (such as pursuing the lawful arrest of a suspect).[142] *Attorney-General v Hartwell*[143] is a good example of where the seriousness of the risks involved – that is, death or serious injury from the misuse of a gun – contributed to both the issue of whether a duty of care was

---

140 See, eg, *Tomlinson v Congleton BC* [2004] 1 AC 46, HL and the discussion in John Murphy, *Street on Torts*, (11th edn, Lexis Nexis Butterworths) pp247–254.
141 See, eg, *Scutts v Keyse* [2001] EWCA Civ 715.
142 *Marshall v Osmond* [1983] QB 1034, CA.
143 [2004] 1 WLR 1273, PC.

owed in the circumstances and to whether that duty was breached (the facts are summarised at para 8.14). A further example is provided by *Crooks v Ebanks*[144] where an armed police officer tripped and fell while chasing a robber and dropped the loaded gun he held in his hand, which discharged a bullet into the claimant's head.

8.81    Where the claim relates to injury sustained while in custody, a failure to follow the Code of Practice issued under the Police and Criminal Evidence Act 1984[145] will not render an officer liable to a freestanding civil action for failing to follow the code[146] but could be good evidence of a lack of proper standards being followed and so constitute supporting evidence of a breach of the duty of care. Similarly, failure to follow relevant force manuals, guidelines, training, etc, could be evidence of breach of duty in many instances of alleged negligence by officers, for example where police dogs were handled inappropriately or CS gas used carelessly. Consideration should always be given to asking for disclosure of such documentation before or during the civil claim.[147]

## Causation

8.82    In assessing whether the carelessness of the defendant (or those for whom he or she is responsible) led to the claimant's loss or damage, the courts ask whether 'but for' that negligence the harm would not have occurred. Liability can only result if the question is answered in the negative. Although the test is easy to state, it is not always simple to apply in practice. In some police cases an issue will arise as to whether the officer's negligence should be treated as the operative cause of the claimant's loss or damage or whether an intervening act (known as a *novus actus interveniens*) has broken the chain of causation. While there is no one, comprehensive test for determining this question, the following factors are usually influential:

- whether the subsequent act of the third party was deliberate, careless or pure misadventure. The greater the degree of wrongdoing on the part of the third party, the less likely that the original negligence will be treated as an operative cause of the ultimate injury;

---

144  [1999] 1 WLR 1287, PC (where the negligence claim was remitted for trial).

145  Code C: Code of Practice for the dentention, treatment and questioning of persons by police officers.

146  Police and Criminal Evidence Act 1984 s67(10).

147  See chapters 11 and 12 for pre-action disclosure and disclosure during the course of civil proceedings.

- the extent to which the conduct of the third party should have been foreseen as likely to follow on from the original negligence. The more likely the intervention the less likely it is to break the chain of causation;
- the extent to which the original wrongdoer should be held responsible in law for the acts of the third party (though, as discussed at para 8.26–8.27, this is also likely to influence the question of whether any duty of care on the part of the original wrongdoer should be imposed);
- a subsequent omission to act is much less likely to break the chain of causation, than a positive act.[148]

8.83     An example of a consideration of these factors in the policing context is *Clarke v Crew*.[149] As described at para 8.33, the claimant was detained in prison beyond his proper release date because the police had given inaccurate information on the committal warrant. While he was imprisoned, the claimant queried the release date and an employee working at the prison (wrongly) confirmed that the release date already given was correct. The defendant argued that this confirmation broke the chain of causation from the officers' original error. The Court of Appeal rejected that submission on the basis that the later response was heavily influenced by the original error.

8.84     Conduct of the claimant, rather than that of a third party, can break the chain of causation, but only where it is so wholly unreasonable and/or has such an overwhelming impact that it eclipses the original wrongdoing.[150] The behaviour of the claimant will not break the chain of causation where it constitutes the very thing that the defendant was under a duty to prevent.[151]

## Recoverable loss

8.85     Establishing damage is an essential ingredient of a claim in negligence; if no damage was suffered then the claim will fail even if the police officers have acted in a wholly remiss fashion and all other ingredients of the tort are present. Physical injury, psychiatric injury and financial loss are all recognised forms of damage for this purpose. Distress or

---

148   For a discussion of these factors see *Clerk & Lindsell on Torts* (18th edn, Sweet & Maxwell, 2000) paras 2-36–2-59.

149   (1999) 149 NLJ 899.

150   *Clerk & Lindsell on Torts*, para 2-51.

151   *Reeves v Commissioner of Police for the Metropolis* [2000] 1 AC 360, HL. See para 8.58.

anxiety falling short of psychiatric injury does not amount to damage for these purposes.[152] Detention is a sufficient form of damage.[153] It is unclear whether impairment of reputation would be sufficient.[154]

## Foresight of damage

8.86    As long as some damage, however slight, is caused that is of the kind that was reasonably foreseeable, the claimant can recover for this loss. He or she does not need to show that the full extent of the loss suffered, nor the precise way in which it was caused, was foreseeable.[155] Thus, for example, if it was foreseeable that the claimant would injure him or herself if insufficiently supervised while in custody, the precise means by which he or she then inflicted injury and the extent of those injuries would not need to be foreseeable.[156] This principle includes the concept of what is known as the 'egg-shell skull' rule, that is, if the defendant (or those for whom he or she is responsible) should have foreseen some injury to the claimant in the circumstances, he or she will recover for the full extent of those injuries even if he or she had a peculiar susceptibility that has made the injury worse than would normally be expected in such circumstances.

## Voluntary assumption of risk and contributory negligence

8.87    A claimant is taken to have voluntarily assumed the risk of the conduct he or she alleges as being negligent where the circumstances indicate that he or she consented to the risk of the tort being committed.[157] If this is shown it operates as a complete defence to a claim in negligence. In recent years the most common application of this doctrine has been in the context of claimants who were injured after accepting lifts with drunken drivers.[158] For the doctrine to apply, the defendant must show

---

152    Although it may not preclude a claim under the Human Rights Act 1998 in relation to the same events; see chapter 10.

153    *W v Home Office* [1997] Imm AR 302.

154    See the discussion of 'damage' in relation to misfeasance at para 7.45.

155    *Wagon Mound (No 2)* [1967] 1 AC 617.

156    The position in relation to foreseeability of psychiatric loss is discussed at para 8.10.

157    This doctrine is also known by the Latin maxim, volenti non fit injuria.

158    *Pitts v Hunt* [1990] 3 All ER 334, CA; *Morris v Murray* [1991] 2 QB 6, CA.

that the claimant was well aware of the particular risk that he or she allegedly consented to running.[159]

8.88    Issues of contributory negligence arise much more frequently. This does not operate as a complete defence to a claim in negligence. The effect of the Law Reform (Contributory Negligence) Act 1945 is to reduce the damages otherwise payable to reflect the extent to which the claimant was responsible for causing the damage suffered. This is usually expressed as a percentage; thus if the claimant and the defendant were equally to blame for the accident the claimant would receive 50 per cent of the damages that he or she would otherwise recover. The defendant must show both that the claimant failed to take reasonable care and that this contributed to his or her injury (but need not show that the claimant owed a duty of care).[160] The failure to take reasonable care for him or herself can arise from a deliberate act of the claimant. In *Reeves v Commissioner of Police for the Metropolis*[161] a claimant who committed suicide in custody when of sound mind, was held 50 per cent responsible for his death.

## Ex turpi causa

8.89    This doctrine is based on the rule of policy that the courts will not assist a person who founds his or her claim on an illegal or immoral act. It is discussed in more detail at para 6.116. An example of its application to a claim in negligence is *Vellino v Chief Constable of Greater Manchester*,[162] where the claimant's own illegal act of trying to escape from lawful police custody meant that he was unable to claim damages for the injuries that he suffered during the course of his escape.

## Death

8.90    Civil actions against the police arising out of a death are rare. Although the number of deaths that occur while people are in police custody varies from about 40 to 80 a year, in most of these cases there is no suggestion of any misconduct on the part of the police.[163]

---

159    *Nettleship v Weston* [1971] 3 All ER 581.
160    *Nance v British Columbia Electric Railway Co Ltd* [1951] AC 601, HL.
161    [2000] 1 AC 360, HL.
162    [2002] 1 WLR 218, CA.
163    See annual reports of the Commissioner of the Police for the Metropolis and HM Inspectors of Constabulary .

8.91    Apart from unlawful killing by police officers through, for example, the use of excessive force, there may be other situations, such as some deaths by poisoning by drugs or alcohol or suicide, where the police may have been negligent in the way they cared for the person, and so may be liable in a claim for damages. The other major situation where deaths involving the police often occur is in traffic accidents.

8.92    There are two matters to be considered if a person dies as a result of police misconduct. First, any cause of action that the deceased person would have had if he or she had not died survives the death and his or her estate is able to sue. Second, certain family members can sue for any loss they have suffered as a result of the death.[164]

8.93    It may also be possible to consider an action under the Human Rights Act 1998 for action amounting to a failure to protect the deceased person's right to life (see ECHR article 2) although it is likely that there will be considerable overlap with the causes of action described here (see chapter 10). If the death occurred in police custody there is also very likely to be an inquest prior to any civil action for damages, where much of the evidence concerning the circumstances of the death is likely to be rehearsed (see chapter 16). The view taken by the police of such evidence may well colour any decision to settle a civil claim then brought by relatives. There will also have been an investigation by or under the auspices of the Independent Police Complaints Commission (see chapter 5) and it is likely that there will be an investigating officer's report and other information available as a result of that investigation.

## Survival of cause of action

8.94    Under the Law Reform (Miscellaneous Provisions) Act 1934, the estate of a person whose death has been caused by a tortious act can bring proceedings against the wrongdoer, although the estate can neither claim exemplary damages[165] nor make a claim for defamation. Under the 1934 Act the estate can sue for reasonable funeral expenses. Otherwise, the same principles generally apply to a claim which the deceased may have brought if he or she had not died. Thus, any special damages the person could have claimed, including loss of earnings from the date of the accident to the date of death, and general damages for pain, suffering and loss of amenity suffered by the deceased person before

---

164   See, eg, *Kirkham v Chief Constable of the Greater Manchester Police* [1990] 2 QB 283, CA, where both procedures were pursued.

165   Administration of Justice Act 1982 s4(2), replacing s1(2)(a) of the 1934 Act.

their death.[166] However, a claim is available to the estate for the loss of potential income for the time after the person died.[167]

8.95 Any claim under the 1934 Act is additional to a claim under the Fatal Accidents Act 1976 as described below. In cases involving personal injuries to the deceased person, the limitation period will usually be three years from the date of the death.[168]

## Fatal Accidents Act 1976 – death as a cause of action

8.96 The Fatal Accidents Act 1976 allows dependants to claim for loss they (as opposed to the deceased person) have suffered against anyone who causes death by their wrongful act, neglect or default, provided the person who died could have made a claim if he or she had survived. In other words, the act, neglect or default must constitute a civil wrong: if the police would have had a good defence to the civil wrong, the dependants' claim for damages resulting from the death also fails.

### Who can sue?

8.97 Most members of the family of the dead person can potentially benefit from this cause of action[169] (although there is a more restrictive class for bereavement damages – see para 8.101), including:[170]

- spouse or former spouse;
- parents or grandparents;
- children or grandchildren;
- siblings, uncles and aunts and all their descendants;
- common-law spouse of two years' standing (same sex relationships are therefore excluded);
- anyone treated as a child of the family following a marriage;
- anyone treated as a parent.

### Wrongful act, neglect or default of the police

8.98 It has to be shown that the wrongful act, neglect or default of the police caused the death.[171] The problems involved in this where negligence or

166  Law Reform (Miscellaneous Provisions) Act 1934 s1.
167  Law Reform (Miscellaneous Provisions) Act 1934 s4(2)(a).
168  Limitation Act 1980 s11.
169  However, the action should usually be brought by the executor or administrator of the deceased: Fatal Accidents Act 1976 s2(1) and (2).
170  Fatal Accidents Act 1976 s1(3) (as amended).
171  Fatal Accidents Act 1976 s1(1) (as amended).

default are involved have already been considered (see para 8.2) and the same principles can be applied in cases involving death.

8.99    In some situations, it will be clear that the wrongful act of the police has caused death. Other situations will be less clear. For instance, if a suicide were induced by a wrongful act of the police or if the police failed to prevent a foreseeable suicide, a claim can succeed even though the person who died took his or her own life,[172] although there will be the question of contributory negligence when damages are assessed.[173] But there must be a causative link between the wrongful act and the suicide, such as where the police negligently fail to carry out their responsibilities to a person who is known to be clinically depressed and who subsequently commits suicide. If the police have a good defence to the principal cause of action, for example negligence or assault, the claim for damages arising from the death will also fail.

## Damages

8.100    Damages are awarded under the 1976 Act only for:

- bereavement; and
- the loss of reasonable expectation of financial benefit.[174]

8.101    Damages for bereavement are a fixed amount, currently £10,000 for causes of action accruing on or after 1 April 2002.[175] They are awarded only to the spouse of the deceased or the parents of a deceased child under the age of 18 who never married.

8.102    Damages[176] for loss of reasonable expectation of financial benefit can include such things as loss of a parent's financial support for a child (or vice versa), loss of a son's voluntary gifts during a period of employment,[177] or loss of free services, where a wife who was killed acted as a

---

172    *Reeves v Commissioner of Police for the Metropolis* [2000] 1 AC 360, HL; *Kirkham v Chief Constable of the Greater Manchester Police* [1990] 2 QB 283, CA.

173    In *Reeves,* [2000] 1 AC 360, this was assessed at 50% where the deceased was of sound mind when he committed suicide.

174    Consider the possible wider damages available for an action under the Human Rights Act 1998 for breach of article 2 (see para 10.231).

175    Fatal Accidents Act 1976 s1A, inserted by Administration of Justice Act 1982 s3 as amended by Damages for Bereavement (Variation of Sum) (England and Wales) Order 2002, SI No 644.

176    For further details on the calculation of claims see eg *Clerk & Lindsell on Torts* (18th edn, Sweet & Maxwell, 2000) paras 29-83–29-97.

177    *Hetherington v North-Eastern Railway* (1882) 9 QBD 160.

housewife.[178] Children can claim for the loss of their mother's daily care[179] although not for loss of love and affection. However, if the person who died earned his or her income from a life of crime, the dependants are not allowed to claim for loss of the benefits of crime.[180]

## Breach of statutory duty

8.103   In the majority of instances a breach of a statutory provision does not create a right of action in itself. It might provide evidence of a lack of care, so as to support a claim in negligence, if the other ingredients of that tort were present (as discussed at para 8.81). It might even be some evidence of bad faith – if the breach was deliberate – so as to support a claim in misfeasance (see chapter 7). However, in limited circumstances breach of a provision of an Act of Parliament or of a statutory instrument will of itself ground a claim for breach of statutory duty.

8.104       Such a claim will only arise where the courts construe from the relevant legislation that it was parliament's intention to confer on members of a protected class of which the claimant is a member, a cause of action sounding in damages for a breach of that statutory provision.[181] The best-known examples of such provisions are under the Factories Acts and related legislation concerning employees' safety at work. Thus in establishing whether a claim will lie, the key issue for the court usually revolves around construing the statutory provisions and other relevant materials (such as Hansard reports of parliamentary debates in cases of ambiguity) to establish the intention of the legis-lature. Statutes that are of a regulatory nature or confer a benefit on the public at large will not give rise to such a liability.[182] Consideration will also be given to whether alternative remedies are available in relation to the particular complaint, such as an application for judicial review.[183]

---

178   *Berry v Humm & Co* [1915] 1 KB 627.
179   *Hay v Hughes* [1975] QB 790; *Regan v Williamson* [1976] 1 WLR 305.
180   *Burns v Edman* [1970] 2 QB 541.
181   *X v Bedfordshire CC* [1995] 2 AC 633, HL; *Hague v Deputy Governor of Parkhurst Prison* [1991] 3 All ER 733, HL.
182   See the authorities cited in the preceding footnote and *Olotu v Home Office* [1997] 1 All ER 385.
183   For example, this was a consideration that influenced the majority in *Cullen v Chief Constable of the Royal Ulster Constabulary* [2003] 1 WLR 1763, HL, discussed below.

8.105    It seems that the claimant will also have to show that the nature of the statutory obligation or prohibition is such that a breach of it would be likely to cause recognised harm to a member of the class for whose benefit it is imposed and that he or she suffered such harm in consequence of its breach. This element of the breach of statutory duty cause of action was identified by the House of Lords in *Pickering v Liverpool Daily Post & Echo Newspapers plc*[184] and was approved by the majority of the House of Lords in *Cullen v Chief Constable of the Royal Ulster Constabulary*,[185] with the indication that the categories of harm referred to in *Pickering*, namely personal injury, injury to property or economic loss, should be broad enough to encompass 'any loss or injury of a kind for which the law awards damages' and an example given was substantial inconvenience. In *Cullen* the claimant sued in respect of a breach of a statutory provision relating to legal access for those detained in police custody[186] – although officers had been entitled to deny him access to a solicitor in the circumstances, they had failed to give him reasons for doing so, as the statute required. It was not suggested that he had suffered any harm in consequence. A majority of the House of Lords held that in the circumstances there was no viable claim for breach of statutory duty. A minority of the judicial committee (Lords Bingham and Steyn) held that the statutory provision was of such fundamental importance that a breach of it should be actionable per se without proof of harm.[187]

8.106    Although many aspects of policing are now subject to statutory regulation, claimants have not enjoyed success in arguing claims for breach of statutory duty. In addition to the *Cullen* case discussed above, it has been held that a failure to comply with Police and Criminal Evidence Act 1984 s64, which concerns destruction of fingerprint evidence and samples where a suspect is cleared of an offence, did not give rise to a claim for breach of statutory duty.[188]

184  [1991] 2 AC 370, HL.

185  [2003] 1 WLR 1763.

186  Northern Ireland (Emergency Provisions) Act 1987 s15, which is in the same terms as Police and Criminal Evidence Act 1984 s58.

187  The approach of the minority finds support in *Street on Torts* (11th edn, LexisNexis Butterworths) p496, published before *Cullen* was decided, but referring to older caselaw suggesting that breach of statutory duty can be actionable per se where the subject matter of the statutory obligation is of sufficient importance.

188  *Nathaniel v Commissioner of Police of the Metropolis* (1998) 20 February, QBD, unreported, where the view was expressed that parliament would have expressly so stated had they intended a claim for breach of statutory duty to arise from a failure to comply with the provision.

# Wrongful interference with land and goods

9.1   This chapter deals with trespass to property. Three areas are considered in turn below:

- trespass to land
- seizure of goods
- damage to goods

Claims will most commonly arise out of police searches of claimants' homes and vehicles. The section on seizure of goods includes a consideration of police powers to retain items that were lawfully seized. Compensation is dealt with in chapter 14. Where the primary remedy sought is recovery of property from the police, consideration may also be given to a claim under the Police (Property) Act 1897, discussed in chapter 17.

## Trespass to land

9.2   The right of individuals to be secure in their own homes and free from arbitrary searches is an ancient one that was guaranteed in a series of important constitutional cases in the eighteenth century.[1] Today these rights are principally protected by the law of trespass. Police officers commit trespass if, without permission or lawful authority, they enter or remain on land that the claimant possesses. In determining the extent to which officers are empowered to enter private property to carry out their duties, the courts have carried out a balancing act, on the one hand acknowledging that protection against unlawful searches and seizures is a fundamental human right protected by the common law, but also recognising that there are instances where the power to enter and search without the consent of the owner is necessary for the proper functioning of a democratic society.[2]

### 'Entering or remaining on the land'

9.3   Trespass can be committed by a police officer who merely walks onto land without permission. However, if there is a front garden and the gate is kept unlocked, the law implies that there is permission to walk up the garden path to the house in order to ask for permission to make a more extensive entry on to the land.[3] There is no implied

---

1   *Entick v Carrington* (1765) 19 St Tr 1030; *Wilkes v Wood* (1765) 19 St Tr 1153.
2   For example, *Att-Gen of Jamaica v Williams* [1998] AC 351, PC, at 354–355 and *Hewitson v Chief Constable of Dorset* [2003] EWHC 3296 (Admin), per Rose LJ at [41].
3   *Robson v Hallett* [1967] 2 All ER 407 per Diplock J.

permission to do anything else,[4] for instance to search the garden on the way to the front door. But officers are entitled to assume consent to enter privately owned land to cordon off an area where a crime has been committed, to enable preservation and examination of the scene.[5] If the police are given permission to enter, then they have a licence to be on the land and are not trespassers. The person who gives the police the licence does not necessarily have to be the occupier, so long as it is someone who has the occupier's authority to do so. Once permission has been granted, it can be expressly revoked and if, after a reasonable interval, the police fail to leave, they become trespassers.[6] Officers may not be able to rely on consent to enter land which is not given freely or which is obtained by the provision of misleading information.[7]

9.4    There is no need to show that the police have used force in order to enter or remain on the land, although, if they have done so, it is evidence that they did not have permission and it is likely to affect the amount of damages.

9.5    If the police enter land with lawful authority (rather than merely with the occupier's consent), and then commit a trespass, either to the person or to goods, this may nullify the lawful authority under which they first entered and make them trespassers from the initial moment of entry onwards. This common law doctrine is based on an old line of authority[8] and is known as trespass ab initio. In *Chic Fashions etc Ltd v Jones*[9] Lord Denning described the doctrine as 'obsolete'. However, commentators are divided as to whether it remains applicable.[10] If the doctrine retains any life it seems to be a residual one. If during an otherwise lawful search some items are seized by officers that fall outside the terms of their authority, there will be a case in trespass to goods in relation to those items, but the balance of the search remains lawful.[11]

---

4  *Brunner v Williams* (1977) 73 LGR 266.

5  *DPP v Morrison* [2003] EWHC 683 Admin. In addition Hooper J doubted that in such circumstances the landowner could withhold consent, if he or she did express a view.

6  *Minister of Health v Bellotti* [1944] 1 All ER 238.

7  See the discussion on consent at paras 6.96–6.97.

8  See *Six Carpenters Case* (1610) 8 Co Rep 146a.

9  [1968] 2 QB 299.

10  Compare Clayton & Tomlinson, *Civil Actions Against the Police* (3rd edn, Thomson Sweet & Maxwell, 2004) paras 6-024–6-030 and *Clerk & Lindsell on Torts* (18th edn, Sweet & Maxwell, 2000) para 17-130.

11  *R v Chesterfield JJ ex p Bramley* [2000] 1 All ER 411. See also *Att-Gen of Jamaica v Williams* [1998] AC 351, PC.

9.6    The police can be treated as 'entering' land if they have physical contact with the land, for instance, if a door or window is removed[12] or if a ladder is placed against a wall.[13] In such cases, there is no need to show that they came any further into the home. Additionally, causing a foreign matter to enter the land will be a trespass. This might include a police dog ordered to run on the land.[14]

9.7    As with false imprisonment and assault and battery, a person can sue for trespass to land without showing any actual damage.[15] However, the degree of loss will obviously affect the level of compensation awarded (see paras 14.71–14.76).

## The land possessed

9.8    'Land' has a special meaning. It can include the home and garden; it covers a flat as well as a house, regardless of whether the flat is on the ground floor or the twentieth floor. It also includes anything attached to the land or the structure of the home, such as a door or fitted cupboards. It includes the air-space that is required for the ordinary use of the land.[16]

9.9    The claimant must 'possess' the land. This is certainly the case if he or she owns the freehold or leasehold or is a tenant. The position of licensees, such as a lodger, is less clear. It seems that a licensee can sue for trespass if he or she has a right of exclusive possession, for example, of his or her room (for instance, if he or she is the key holder and has the right to bar other people from the room).[17] There may also be difficulties if the person aggrieved lives with someone else who is the owner, for instance, a parent or partner. In such a case, he or she may be able to sue if he or she has the owner's authority to exclude strangers, but, if feasible, it is preferable to sue in the name of the owner too. It is also possible that a squatter who has actual exclusive possession of land, but no legal estate or other right in it, may sue for trespass,[18] although the limits of such a principle have not been tested. Since the

---

12    *Lavender v Betts* [1942] 2 All ER 72.
13    *Westripp v Baldock* [1938] 2 All ER 779; [1939] 1 All ER 279, CA.
14    *Beckwith v Shordike* (1767) 4 Burr 2092.
15    *Armstrong v Sheppard & Short Ltd* [1959] 2 All ER 651, CA.
16    *Kelsen v Imperial Tobacco Co of Great Britain* [1957] 2 QB 334.
17    *Marcroft Wagons Ltd v Smith* [1951] 2 KB 496 at 501. For a fuller discussion see John Murphy, *Street on Torts* (11th edn, Lexis Nexis Butterworths) pp77–79; Fleming, *Law of Torts* (9th edn, LBC Information Services, 1998) pp49–50.
18    *Graham v Peat* (1801) 1 East 244; *Mason v Clarke* [1955] AC 778, HL and further discussed in *Street on Torts*, p79 and Fleming, p50.

Human Rights Act 1998 came into force a claimant who does not have 'possession' of the land, may nonetheless be able to rely on an infringement of their rights under article 8 of the European Convention on Human Rights (as discussed at paras 9.19–9.20).

## Defences to trespass

9.10 The police have wide powers to enter premises for specific purposes. These include power to enter to carry out an arrest and to conduct a search, either with or without a warrant. It is not possible here to describe all such powers, but reference will be made to those that are most commonly relied upon. To establish lawful authority for their actions, officers must show that their conduct met the prescribed criteria.

9.11 The main statutory powers that enable officers to search premises without a warrant are contained in Police and Criminal Evidence Act 1984 (PACE) ss17, 18 and 32. Section 17 authorises officers to enter premises to execute warrants of arrest; to make arrests for arrestable offences[19] and certain other specified offences; to recapture persons unlawfully at large; and to save life and limb or prevent serious damage to property. Save in the latter instance, the power is only exercisable where the officer has reasonable grounds for believing that the person sought is on the premises. Powers of search conferred by this section are limited to searches for the purpose that the power of entry was conferred.[20] Section 18 permits searches of premises occupied or controlled by a person under arrest for an arrestable offence, if an officer has reasonable grounds for suspecting that there is evidence on the premises relating either to the offence for which the person was arrested or another arrestable offence which is connected with or similar to that offence.[21] The extent of the search is limited to what is reasonably required to discover such evidence.[22] It must be authorised in writing by an officer of at least inspector rank.[23] The power contained in section 32 is not confined to the more serious offences and does not require prior authorisation. Where a person is arrested at a place other than a police station, an officer may search any premises in which the arrested person was when arrested or immediately before arrest, for evidence relating to the offence for which he or she was

---

19  As defined in PACE s24.
20  PACE s17(4).
21  PACE s18(1).
22  PACE s18(3).
23  PACE s18(4).

arrested.[24] Officers entering premises under the section 17 power should inform the occupier of the reason why the entry was required, unless circumstances make it impracticable to do so.[25]

9.12　　All common law powers to enter premises for the purposes listed in section 17 are abolished, save the power to enter to deal with or prevent breaches of the peace.[26] However, common law powers of search remain relevant in relation to searches conducted after arrest, as sections 18 and 32 contain no equivalent provision.[27] Common law powers of search also remain relevant in extradition cases.[28] The common law entitles officers who arrest a person in his or her house or in the grounds of the house, to search the house and seize articles which they reasonably believe to be material evidence in relation to the crime for which they have made the arrest (and if during the course of such a search the officers come across items which show the arrested person to be implicated in some other crime they are entitled to seize those too, provided they act reasonably).[29]

9.13　　The other main source of authority to enter premises is search warrants. These may be granted pursuant to a wide range of statutory powers. The most commonly used power is that contained in PACE s8. This provision enables officers to apply to a magistrate for a warrant to enter premises where a serious arrestable offence is suspected[30] and the officer has reasonable grounds to believe that there is material on the premises likely to be of substantial value to the investigation of the offence (other than items subject to legal privilege or excluded or special procedure material).[31] PACE ss15 and 16 lay down various requirements concerning the granting of the warrant and the execution

---

24　PACE s32(2)(b).

25　*O'Loughlin v Chief Constable of Essex* [1998] 1 WLR 374; the rationale of this decision indicates that equivalent information should be given when other statutory powers of search are exercised if the occupier is present on the premises at the time.

26　PACE s17(5) and (6). For an example of the latter see *McLeod v Commissioner of Police of the Metropolis* [1994] 4 All ER 553, CA.

27　*R (Rottman) v Commissioner of Police of the Metropolis* [2002] 2 All ER 865, HL at [109]–[110] per Lord Rodger; *Cowan v Commissioner of Police of the Metropolis* [2000] 1 All ER 504, CA.

28　*R (Rottman) v Commissioner of Police of the Metropolis* [2002] 2 All ER 865, HL.

29　For a fuller discussion of the ambits of this power see *R (Rottman) v Commissioner of Police of the Metropolis* [2002] 2 All ER 865, HL and *Hewitson v Chief Constable of Dorset* [2003] EWHC 3296 (Admin), and the discussion on the common law powers of seizure at para 9.30.

30　As defined in PACE s116.

31　PACE ss8–14.

of the search. These requirements apply to all searches pursuant to warrants granted under statutory authority.[32] It is important in such cases to check carefully whether there has been compliance with these criteria as in *R v Chief Constable of Lancashire ex p Parker*[33] the Court of Appeal decided that the wording of PACE s15(1) is such that any non-compliance with the requirements of either sections 15 or 16 will render the whole search unlawful. In *Fisher v Chief Constable of Cumbria*[34] the Court of Appeal applied the same approach to a failure to leave a copy of the search warrant at the premises in breach of section 16(7), albeit indicating some disquiet that the effect of a relatively minor breach of the statute provision was to invalidate the legality of the entire search. The same approach was also applied by the Court of Appeal in *R v Chief Constable of Warwickshire ex Fitzpatrick.*[35] Where the legal challenge relates to the magistrate's decision to grant the warrant, rather than the manner of its execution (for example a contention that the prescribed elements of PACE s8 were not fully satisfied), the usual route is to bring proceedings for a judicial review.[36]

9.14    Applications for search warrants and searches of premises are also governed by the provisions of Code B of the Code of Practice issued under PACE.[37] A breach of the Code will not of itself give rise to a legal liability in respect of a search,[38] but such breaches may well constitute an aggravating feature, thereby increasing the amount of damages that are awarded in relation to the search, if liability is established on other grounds.[39]

9.15    Whether a claim for trespass will arise in relation to a search purportedly conducted under the authority of a search warrant will also depend upon the Constables Protection Act 1750 s6. This provision has been discussed in relation to arrest warrants.[40] In essence, a claim will not lie against the police for an entry upon premises if the acts

32    PACE s15(1).

33    [1993] QB 577.

34    (1997) 29 July, unreported.

35    [1998] 1 All ER DC 65, although other aspects of that decision are doubted in *R v Chesterfield JJ ex p Bramley* [2000] 1 All ER 411, DC. A further example is *R v Reading JJ ex p South West Meats Ltd* (1992) 4 Admin LR 401 – see para 9.35.

36    For example, *R (Paul Da Costa & Co) v Thames Magistrates' Court* [2002] STC 267; *R (Miller Gardner Solicitors) v Minshull Street Crown Court* [2002] EWHC 3077 (Admin).

37    'Code of Practice for searches of premises by police officers and the seizure of property found by police officers on person or premises' (2004).

38    PACE s67(10), though see discussion at para 6.101.

39    Aggravated damages are discussed in chapter 14.

40    See para 6.76–6.78.

complained of were 'done in obedience' to the warrant, even if turns out that the warrant was granted on the basis of erroneous information. A recent example of the operation of this rule is provided by *Keegan v Chief Constable of Merseyside*.[41] Officers failed to make proper inquiries, which in turn led to a warrant being issued in respect of premises where the suspect did not in fact reside. However, as officers acted in obedience to the warrant when they entered the premises, the occupiers' action in trespass failed.[42] In contrast, if officers carry out a search that does not accord with the terms of the warrant, for example if they mistakenly enter an address that is not the one specified in the warrant, then the Constables Protection Act 1750 will not provide a defence.[43] Nor will it provide a defence if officers search persons present in the building, when the warrant only empowers a search of premises.[44] If any of the requirements of PACE ss15 and 16 are not complied with, then arguably officers would not be acting pursuant to the warrant, since the authority there granted is for a lawfully conducted search.

9.16       If the police have power to enter in a particular case, they also have power to use reasonable force, if necessary.[45] Obviously, force is not usually necessary if the occupier would have agreed to the police entering his or her home, if given the opportunity. For instance, if a person hears the doorbell ring and as he or she goes to answer it, the door is kicked in and a number of police officers with a search warrant enter, he or she has a good claim for trespass because he or she was not given the opportunity to consent. In *O'Loughlin v Chief Constable of Essex*[46] the Court of Appeal emphasised the 'severe burden' which an officer has to discharge when trying to prove that the use of force was really necessary. In that case the defendant was unable to discharge the burden because officers failed to tell the occupier the real purpose of their visit before permission to enter was refused and force was employed. Where police have valid reason to suspect that the person in the property is armed or otherwise presents a danger to their safety,

---

41   [2003] 1 WLR 2187, CA.

42   As discussed earlier (see para 7.32) there was also insufficient evidence to establish a claim for malicious process.

43   *Hoye v Bush* (1840) 1 Man & G 775.

44   *Chief Constable of Thames Valley v Hepburn* [2002] EWCA Civ 1841, discussed in *DPP v Meaden* [2003] EWHC 3005 (Admin). For further examples of where officers would not be acting in obedience to the warrant and so unable to rely upon the 1750 Act, see *Clerk & Lindsell on Torts* (18th edn, Sweet & Maxwell, 2000) para 17-130.

45   PACE s117. See discussion of this provision in relation to battery at paras 6.103–6.105.

46   [1998] 1 WLR 374 at 383.

then use of force may well be justified in the circumstances. In *DPP v Meaden* the Divisional Court decided that a warrant which empowered officers to search persons present as well as premises, enabled officers to detain those persons in one part of the premises whilst other parts were searched, as this was a legitimate exercise of the statutory power to use reasonable force. The Court distinguished *Chief Constable of Thames Valley Police v Hepburn*, where the Court of Appeal had suggested that a power of detention did not arise from the execution of a search warrant, on the basis that warrant did not extend to searching people. In any event, whether detention during a search can be justified as the use of reasonable force will depend on all the circumstances including the length and nature of the detention and the operational considerations that influenced the decision to detain.

9.17    Mistake is no defence to trespass. The police cannot claim that they are not liable in trespass merely because they intended to enter another person's land and did not intend to interfere with the claimant's rights.[47] If, through negligence, the police unintentionally enter a person's land, this is probably also a trespass.[48]

9.18    On a number of occasions the police have hired video companies to film a search or invited the media to accompany them on a 'raid'. Such people will not be covered by a search warrant and their presence, without consent, on a person's property would be a trespass. In *R v Marylebone Magistrates' Court ex p Amdrell Ltd*[49] the Divisional Court strongly criticised the practices of media representatives accompanying the police on the execution of search warrants.

## European Convention on Human Rights

9.19    Article 8(1) of the Convention provides that 'everyone has the right to respect for his private and family life, his home and his correspondence'. Article 8(2) provides that there shall be no interference with this right except such as is in accordance with the law and is necessary in a democratic society in the interests of 'national security, public safety or the economic well-being of the country, for the prevention of disorder or crime, for the protection of health or morals, or for the protection of the rights and freedoms of others'.

9.20    As the Divisional Court recognised in *R (Cronin) v Sheffield JJ*,[50] any search of premises made without the consent of the occupier

---

47   *Basely v Clarkson* (1681) 3 Lev 37.
48   *League Against Cruel Sports Ltd v Scott* [1986] QB 240.
49   (1998) 31 July, unreported.
50   [2003] 1 WLR 752.

will automatically be an interference with article 8(1). Thus the key question in each instance will be whether the police can show that the search was within the terms of article 8(2). If the search was conducted in accordance with statutory and common law requirements, officers may well be able to establish that it was 'in accordance with the law' and that it pursued a legitimate aim (the prevention of disorder or crime and/or the protection of the rights of others).[51] The more substantial question in most instances is likely to be whether the search was necessary in the sense that it was a proportionate means of pursuing the aim in question.[52] There may be instances where a search would otherwise be lawful under domestic law but where the police will be unable to meet the relatively high threshold test of showing that it was a necessary response in the particular circumstances. An example is provided by *McLeod v United Kingdom*.[53] Officers entered a house in pursuance of their common law power to prevent a breach of the peace. The Court of Appeal (pre-Human Rights Act 1998) found that the search was lawful.[54] However, the European Court of Human Rights decided that there was a violation of article 8 as the officers' entry on the property was disproportionate to their legitimate aim (of preventing a breach of the peace) as they had failed adequately to ascertain the true facts of the situation before making their entry. In evaluating whether a search of premises was a proportionate response to the particular circumstances, courts are also likely to consider factors such as whether the relevant evidence could have been obtained by less intrusive means and whether the relevant legislation and practice afforded adequate and effective safeguards against abuse.[55] The domestic courts have thus far rejected contentions that the process by which magistrates hear and determine applications for search warrants infringes occupiers' article 8 rights.[56]

---

51  Subject to any challenge to the process by which the warrant was granted in search warrant cases – see para 9.13 and note 36.

52  See also para 10.27.

53  (1999) 27 EHRR 493.

54  *McLeod v Commissioner of Police of the Metropolis* [1994] 4 All ER 553, CA.

55  *Funke v France* (1993) 16 EHRR 297.

56  *R (Cronin) v Sheffield JJ* [2003] 1 WLR 752; *Birse v HM Advocate* 2000 SLT 869, although claims are now being pursued to the European Court of Human Rights.

57  See chapter 17.

# Seizure of goods

9.21 If the police unlawfully seize something that belongs to a person, for example, while searching him or her in the street or searching his or her home, that person can claim damages and the recovery of the goods. Technically, the claim may be for 'trespass to goods' or 'conversion'. If the case is straightforward and the person simply wants the goods back and is not concerned about claiming damages, he or she may apply to recover the property in the magistrates' court under the Police (Property) Act 1897 procedure.[57] Article 1 of the First Protocol to the ECHR may also have been infringed where there is a breach of domestic common law, see paras 10.218–10.221.

9.22 There is a considerable overlap between trespass to goods and conversion. In many cases, it may be possible to sue either for one or the other or both. However, in general, a claim in conversion is appropriate in order to assert the right to the physical possession of something and in trespass to goods to assert the right to its physical condition. Conversion should therefore be used if the police have seized and retained something and its return or compensation for its value is required, and trespass to goods should be used if something has been damaged or altered or simply moved. The ingredients of a claim for trespass to goods are dealt with when damage to goods is considered below.

## The act of conversion

9.23 The most common form of conversion in relation to the police occurs when officers take items that they have no lawful authority to seize. However, claims also arise in circumstances where the original seizure of items was lawful, but officers retain them after their authority to do so has been exhausted.[58] Retention of another's goods in circumstances which exclude that other from use and possession of them, coupled with an intention to keep them, amounts to a conversion.[59] To establish a conversion by retention it is not always necessary to show that the return of the goods has been demanded and that the request has been expressly or implicitly refused.[60] However, this is usually the easiest way to establish the criteria for this form of

---

58 Officers' powers of retention are described below.
59 *Kuwait Airways Corp v Iraqi Airways Co (No 3)* [2002] 3 All ER 209, HL.
60 *Kuwait Airways Corp v Iraqi Airways Co (No 3)* [2002] 3 All ER 209; *Martin v Chief Constable of Nottinghamshire* [2003] EWCA 398.

conversion and so it is advisable for such a demand to be made in writing and a negative response received, before a claim is commenced. If goods are lawfully retained by the police at the time, the mere fact that they are transferred temporarily to a third party for safe storage does not amount to a conversion.[61]

9.24    Strict liability applies to any act of conversion. Thus, provided the relevant conduct of the defendant was carried out voluntarily, it does not matter whether he or she intended to interfere with another's goods or whether, for example, the defendant genuinely and reasonably believed that the goods belonged to him or her.[62]

9.25    The claimant's consent to the taking or retention of the relevant items will negate any claim in conversion. However, officers may not be able to rely on permission that is not given freely or which is obtained by the provision of misleading information.[63] Consent cannot be inferred if the claimant does not know of the relevant interference. Where a claimant's vehicle was wheel clamped when it was parked without authority on private land, the Court of Appeal held that consent to the trespass to goods (to the car) could not be inferred simply from the fact that the claimant was trespassing upon the defendant's land at the time; it had to be shown that the car owner was aware of the consequences of parking her car there.[64]

## Who can sue

9.26    To maintain an action in conversion the claimant must show that he or she had actual possession of the goods or the immediate right to possession of the goods at the time when the tort was committed. Although in many instances the claimant will be the owner of the goods, it is unnecessary to establish this.[65] The courts have recently resolved an issue that sometimes arises after the police lawfully seize items they believe to relate to offences, for example suspected stolen

61    *Martin v Chief Constable of Nottinghamshire*, ibid.

62    *Kuwait Airways Corp v Iraqi Airways Co (No 3)* [2002] 3 All ER 209, HL; though the speeches of Lords Nicholls, Hoffmann and Hope suggest that the defendant's degree of culpability will affect the extent of his or her liability for consequential losses.

63    See the discussion on consent at paras 6.96–6.97.

64    *Vine v Waltham Forest LBC* [2000] 4 All ER 169.

65    For a general discussion of the circumstances where a claimant may have possession or a right to possession of the goods without being the owner, see *Clerk & Lindsell on Torts* (18th edn, Sweet & Maxwell, 2000) paras 14-46–14-50; Clayton and Tomlinson, *Civil Actions Against the Police* (3rd edn, Thomson Sweet & Maxwell, 2004) paras 6-055–6-057.

goods or suspected proceeds of crime. If the possessor of the items is ultimately convicted of criminality, the courts will be able to order forfeiture or confiscation in the majority of circumstances.[66] However, if the investigation does not lead to a prosecution or a prosecution is brought unsuccessfully, are the police obliged to return to the previous possessor items that they reasonably believe to be the fruits of criminality? The point arose in *Webb v Chief Constable of Merseyside*[67] in relation to suspected proceeds of drug dealing and in *Costello v Chief Constable of Derbyshire*[68] in relation to a suspected stolen motor vehicle. In both cases the Court of Appeal decided that once their statutory powers of retention were exhausted, the police were obliged to return the items to the individuals that they had been seized from. This was because the claimants were entitled to rely upon their possessory title without reference to the circumstances in which such possession was obtained, whether lawfully or by theft or some other unlawful means. The court said that public policy did not operate to deprive a possessor in such circumstances; a court would only withhold relief if by the nature of the items it would be unlawful to possess them (for example illegal drugs or unlicensed firearms). However, the rights of a possessor in such circumstances are relatively fragile; they may be defeated by anyone who can show a better title to the items, for example, in the case of a car, the owner of the stolen vehicle. Pursuant to the Torts (Interference with Goods) Act 1977 s8, the police can defend a claim in conversion by showing that someone other than the claimant has a superior title to the goods, provided they can point to a specific, identified individual.[69]

## Defences to seizure

9.27    Liability will usually turn on whether statute or common law gave the police lawful authority for their actions in seizing or retaining the goods in question. The police have powers under various statutes to seize a wide range of specific items and types of evidence of particular offences. It is beyond the scope of this book to detail all such powers, however reference will be made to those most commonly employed.

---

66 For example, pursuant to the Powers of Criminal Courts (Sentencing) Act 2000 s143.

67 [2000] QB 427.

68 [2001] 3 All ER 150.

69 *Costello v Chief Constable of Derbyshire* [2001] 3 All ER 150; *Verrechia v Commissioner of Police of the Metropolis* (2001) 15 March, QBD, unreported.

70 PACE s8(2).

9.28    Where search warrants are granted pursuant to PACE s8, officers are empowered to seize and retain anything for which a search has been authorised.[70] The legality of the seizure is therefore likely to depend upon issues equivalent to those discussed above in relation to search warrants and trespass to land, in particular, whether the scope of the seizure was authorised by the terms of the warrant, whether the search and seizure complied with PACE ss15 and 16 and whether the actions complained of were done in obedience to the warrant so that officers are protected by the Constables Protection Act 1750 s6.[71]

9.29    An officer is empowered to seize anything that he or she may search for pursuant to PACE s18.[72] Officers are also given a general power of seizure by PACE s19. The power is exercisable where an officer is lawfully on any premises and he or she has reasonable grounds for believing that the relevant item has been obtained in consequence of the commission of an offence or that it is evidence in relation to an offence and that it is necessary to seize it to prevent it being concealed, lost, damaged, altered or destroyed.[73] This wide power extends to evidence of any crime and is not limited to material that is related to the offence currently under investigation. Thus the police could enter a home on a search warrant for, say, controlled drugs and instead lawfully seize goods which they reasonably suspect to be stolen. The power of seizure does not extend to an item that the officer has reasonable grounds for believing to be subject to legal privilege.[74] The powers of seizure contained in PACE ss18(2) and 19 extend to the seizure of the whole premises where it is physically possible to seize and retain the premises in their totality, for example a caravan, vehicle or tent.[75]

9.30    The common law power of search and seizure where a person is arrested has been described earlier in relation to claims for trespass to land (see para 9.12). There is also a common law power of seizure available to the police in the absence of an arrest, if the criteria laid down by the Court of Appeal in *Ghani v Jones*[76] are satisfied. These are that the police have reasonable grounds for believing: (a) a serious offence has been committed; (b) the article in question is the fruit of

---

71    *R v Bow Street Magistrates' Court ex p McDonald* (1997) 10 June, CA, unreported, suggests that where seizure and retention of items was consequent upon a warrant, but not provided for in the warrant, the actions would not be protected by the 1750 Act.

72    Section 18(2). The scope of s18 is summarised above (see para 9.11).

73    PACE s19(2) and (3).

74    PACE s19(6).

75    *Cowan v Commissioner of Police of the Metropolis* [2000] 1 All ER 504, CA.

76    [1970] QB 693.

the crime, the instrument by which it was committed or material evidence to prove commission of the crime; (c) the person in possession of the item committed the crime, was an accessory to it or his or her refusal to give the item to the officers must be quite unreasonable. The House of Lords has recently confirmed that common law powers of seizure are additional to and are not impliedly repealed by the provisions of PACE.[77] It is unclear whether the common law power of seizure identified in *Ghani v Jones* requires that the officer is lawfully on the premises at the material time.

9.31    Criminal Justice and Police Act (CJPAA) 2001 Part 2[78] reverses the effect of *R v Chesterfield JJ ex p Bramley*.[79] The case was concerned with the situation where officers have to sift through large amounts of material (usually documentary) to establish whether and to what extent it contains items they are empowered to seize. The Divisional Court held that officers were not entitled to remove the material from the premises covered by the warrant in order to carry out this sift and that if they did so and the removed material contained items that fell outside the scope of their powers of seizure, a claim for trespass to goods would succeed. CJPAA 2001 s50 provides that where an officer is lawfully on premises and finds anything which he or she has reasonable grounds to believe may be or may contain something which he or she is authorised to search for and would be subject to a power of seizure, if it is not reasonably practicable for the officer to determine whether what he or she has found is something that he or she is entitled to seize or the extent to which it contains something that he or she is entitled to seize, removal from the premises can occur to enable that determination to be carried out.[80] There is also an equivalent power of removal where the material that can be seized is comprised in something else that there would otherwise be no power to seize and it is not reasonably practicable to separate the two on the premises.[81] Officers are then obliged to carry out an initial examination of the property as soon as is reasonably practicable and to return items that are not within their original power of search or within the power of retention contained in CJPAA 2001 s56, save where it is not reasonably practicable to separate such items from the material they have taken.[82] There are also obligations to return items subject to legal privilege and excluded

---

77    *R (Rottman) v Commissioner of Police of the Metropolis* [2002] 2 All ER 865, HL.

78    In force from 1 April 2003: SI 2003 No 708 art 2(a).

79    [2000] 1 All ER 411, DC.

80    Criminal Justice and Police Act (CJPAA) 2001 s50(1).

81    CJPAA 2001 s50(2).

82    CJPAA 2001 s53(1)–(3).

and special procedure material.[83] The statute contains a specific procedure for challenging the seizure of items under these provisions.[84]

9.32    Once something has been lawfully seized, the police are entitled to retain it for as long as is necessary in all the circumstances.[85] Anything seized for the purposes of a criminal investigation can be retained for use as evidence in a trial or for investigation or forensic examination.[86] However, the police should return the original if a photograph or copy would be sufficient.[87] They can also retain anything in order to establish its lawful owner[88] provided there are reasonable grounds to believe that the goods were obtained as the result of the commission of an offence.[89] However, the police cannot rely upon PACE s22 to justify further retention once the investigation has concluded; if they are unable to trace the true owner of the items, they are obliged to recognise the claimant's possessory title and return the goods to him or her, even if they continue to suspect that they were stolen.[90] The police cannot retain property solely in anticipation of a court making a compensation, forfeiture or restitution order against a person if he or she is later convicted of an offence.[91]

9.33    If the police do seize documents while unlawfully executing a warrant, they have no right to retain them and must return them.[92]

9.34    If something is taken from a person while in police custody or detention, on the ground that it might be used: (a) to cause physical injury to someone; (b) to damage property; (c) to interfere with evidence; or (d) to assist an escape, then it should be returned to him or her on release.[93] If it is not returned, the police can be sued in conversion.

9.35    The case of *R v Reading JJ ex p South West Meats Ltd*[94] neatly illustrates ways in which the police can exceed or abuse their powers

83    CJPAA 2001 ss54–55.
84    CJPAA 2001 ss59–62.
85    PACE s22(1).
86    PACE s22(2)(a).
87    PACE s22(4).
88    PACE s22(2)(b).
89    *Alliance International SA v HM Customs & Excise* (2000) 18 May, QBD, unreported.
90    *Gough v Chief Constable of West Midlands* (2004) *Times* 4 March, applying *Webb v Chief Constable of Merseyside and Costello v Chief Constable of Derbyshire* (discussed above at para 9.26).
91    *Malone v Commissioner of Police of the Metropolis* [1979] 1 All ER 256.
92    *R v Chief Constable of Lancashire ex p Parker* [1993] 2 All ER 56.
93    PACE s22(3).
94    (1992) 4 Admin LR 401, DC.

of search and seizure, even with a warrant, and become liable to pay substantial sums in damages as a result. In this case the police sought a search warrant to search the premises of a company after receiving information from a government agency about possible theft charges. The search warrant was granted by the magistrates' court after an officer swore on oath that, pursuant to PACE s8, the documentation required was relevant evidence, did not consist of or include items subject to legal privilege, and that the purpose of the search might be frustrated or seriously prejudiced unless an officer arriving at the premises could secure immediate entry to them. The warrant was granted, but when it was executed the police did not take part in the search but allowed employees of the government agency to carry it out. A large amount of material was taken away, including information covered by legal privilege. A senior executive of the company sought access to some of the material but this was denied, not by the police, but by the government agency who held the documentation. The court found that:

- There had been no basis for the statement to the magistrates by the police that the purpose of the search might be frustrated without a warrant for immediate entry.
- The police had allowed the government agency to remove and retain documents that only the police had powers to remove and retain under PACE s16.
- Large quantities of documents were removed from the premises which obviously did not fall within the terms of the warrant, contrary to PACE s8(2), including a file whose contents were the subject of legal privilege.
- The delay in allowing the company access to the documents and in returning the documents was far greater than was necessary and in breach of PACE s21.

The court found that the seizure and retention of the documents amounted to trespass and that 'the exercise from start to finish was unlawful'. The officers were not protected by the Constables Protection Act 1750 as they had acted outside the terms of the warrant and the terms of PACE s16.

9.36 In *R v Central Criminal Court ex p AJD Holdings*[95] the court recommended that careful consideration should be given, before applying for a search warrant, to what material it is hoped a search will reveal.

95 (1992) *Times* 24 February.
96 *Blades v Higgs* (1861) 10 CB (NS) 713.

Once the warrant was obtained, the officers carrying out the search should be carefully chosen and properly briefed.

9.37        Issues that may arise under the European Convention of Human Rights in relation to search and seizure of goods are considered at paras 9.19–9.21 above.

## Remedies

9.38     In theory, if the police have wrongfully taken goods out of a person's possession, he or she can lawfully resist the seizure and take them back again and can use reasonable force against anyone who resists.[96] In practice, however, this right is principally relevant as a defence to a criminal charge, such as assault or obstruction, rather than as a 'remedy' which could ever be prudently recommended, as there is almost certain to be legal argument about whether the police were entitled to seize the goods. If it turns out they were acting lawfully, the person might be guilty of a number of criminal offences, including assault and obstructing the police in the course of their duty.

9.39        The legality of seizure should therefore be tested by a court action for damages, or for an order for the return of the property, or both.[97] If the item is not returned, the claimant is entitled to compensation reflecting its value. Whether or not the item is returned, the claimant is entitled to damages for the loss of its use during the period of deprivation and for consequential losses occasioned by its absence.[98]

9.40        If the police lawfully seize items, they must supply a record of everything they have taken within a reasonable time of being asked for such a record.[99] They can be asked for the list at the time the items are taken or at any later time. A person can also ask for access to anything that has been seized, for example, so that he or she can inspect it, or for anything that has been seized to be photographed or copied, provided that this would not prejudice police investigations or any later trial.[100]

9.41        If documents are unlawfully seized, in addition to suing for their return, it is thought that the owner is entitled to receive any copies that have been made,[101] but not to an injunction preventing the use of any information gleaned from them.[102]

97   Torts (Interference with Goods) Act 1977 s3.
98   See paras 14.66–14.67.
99   PACE s21(1), (2).
100  PACE s21(3), (4), (6) and(8); see also *Arias v Commissioner of Police of the Metropolis* (1984) *Times* 1 August for the common law right to require the police to deliver up copies of documents that have been lawfully seized.
101  Byatt, 'Seizure and privilege: the solicitor's Hobson's choice' (1984) 81 LS Gaz 1973.

# Damage to goods

9.42    If the police damage or destroy belongings, for example, while searching a home, there may be a claim for damages. For a claim in trespass to goods, the interference must arise from direct contact.[103] The act of interference must be deliberate, but it is unnecessary to show that the defendant appreciated that he or she was acting wrongfully at the time.[104] If the interference was accidental and non-negligent there is no liability.[105] If the defendant handles or damages the claimant's goods carelessly rather than deliberately, the better view appears to be that the claim should be brought in negligence rather than trespass.[106] If a third party damages goods while they are in the defendant's custody, an action for negligence and/or breach of bailment may lie against the defendant if he or she was at fault in letting this happen.[107]

9.43    Accordingly, if without lawful justification officers smash open a cupboard to access the contents during a search of the claimant's home, the usual cause of action would be trespass to goods. If an officer breaks a vase in the claimant's home by carelessly tripping and falling against it, the usual cause of action would be negligence. If there is any uncertainty as to whether the interference with an item was deliberate or careless it would be advisable to bring the claim in both trespass to goods and negligence. If officers lock a room in the house, depriving the claimant of temporary access to his or her belongings inside, there is no claim in trespass to goods as the alleged wrongdoer made no direct contact with the items. If officers seize the claimant's belongings and then leave them lying around the police station so that they are stolen by someone else, there would be a possible claim for negligence and/or breach of bailment. In *Sutcliffe v Chief Constable of West Yorkshire*[108] a claim for breach of bailment failed in relation to the claimant's car, which was damaged by vandals while in a police compound, since the police had taken all reasonable precautions against such an eventuality.

102    *Frank Truman Export Ltd v Commissioner of Police of the Metropolis* [1977] 3 All ER 431 at 436j.

103    *Hartley v Moxham* (1842) 3 QB 701.

104    *Wilson v Lombank Ltd* [1963] 1 WLR 1294.

105    *National Coal Board v J E Evans & Co (Cardiff)* [1951] 2 KB 861.

106    See para 6.87 in relation to negligent trespass.

107    The main distinction between these two claims is that in relation to breach of bailment, if the item is lost or damaged while in the bailee's possession he or she has to prove that it occurred without his or her fault; whereas in negligence the onus of proving carelessness lies on the claimant.

108    (1995) 19 May, unreported.

9.44    There is some uncertainty as to whether a defendant can be liable for trespass to goods if he or she simply moves an item without causing any damage to it. The prevailing view is that if the touching was done deliberately, for example officers moving items around during a search, liability could be established without showing any loss. However, if the contact with the item was careless rather than intentional, actual damage would probably need to be established for the claim to succeed.[109] Not every occasion of physical contact would lead to a claim. As discussed in relation to claims in battery (see para 6.91), the claimant is assumed to consent to contact arising in the course of ordinary, acceptable behaviour, for example where his or her coat on a peg is moved by someone else to access their own coat.

9.45    To bring a claim in trespass to goods, the claimant must have been in possession of the goods at the time of the interference. Unlike in conversion, a right to possession is generally insufficient.[110]

9.46    If a claim for trespass to goods succeeds, damages can be recovered for the costs of repair or replacement and for loss of use (see para 14.69).

## Defences

9.47    As has already been seen, where the police have a power which can be exercised without consent, they can also use reasonable force if necessary to exercise the power.[111] Thus, if they have power to search a home, they would also have power to break into a locked cabinet in order to search inside it, if this were both necessary and reasonable, given the object of the search. However, this defence could be defeated if, for example, it could be shown that the claimant offered to unlock the cabinet, as the use of force would then be unnecessary (and unreasonable).

109    See *Clerk & Lindsell on Torts* (18th edn, Sweet & Maxwell 2000) para 14-35; Clayton and Tomlinson *Civil Actions Against the Police* (3rd edn, Thomson Sweet & Maxwell 2004) paras 6-062 and 6-068.

110    The exceptions are discussed in *Clerk & Lindsell on Torts*, para 14-136.

111    PACE s117.

# Human rights and discrimination

10.1 This chapter focuses upon three developing areas of law, which are underpinned by fundamental human rights. The section on privacy considers actions for breach of confidence and claims based on an interference with the rights protected by article 8 of the European Convention on Human Rights (ECHR). It also looks at the opportunities provided by the Data Protection Act 1998 and the Freedom of Information Act 2000 in relation to policing issues. The chapter then examines claims that can be brought against the police under the Race Relations Act 1976, the Sex Discrimination Act 1975 and the Disability Discrimination Act 1995, with particular focus on the opportunities for race claims arising out of discriminatory policing since the implementation of the Race Relations (Amendment) Act 2000. The section on the Human Rights Act 1998 considers what is needed to bring a successful claim under the Act and looks at procedure and damages. The articles of the Convention particularly relevant to policing issues are also examined.

## Privacy and the police

### An overview

10.2 The domestic courts have increasingly acknowledged the value of personal autonomy and respect for personal information since the Human Rights Act 1998 came into force. For example in *Campbell v MGN Ltd*[1] Lord Nicholls said in relation to privacy:

> ... it ... lies at the heart of liberty in a modern state. A proper degree of privacy is essential for the well-being and development of an individual.[2]

10.3 The House of Lords have recently confirmed that there is no overarching common law tort of invasion of privacy,[3] indicating that it is a matter for parliament if it wishes to introduce such protection. However, the potential lacuna in protection arising from the absence of a specific tort of privacy interference has been substantially filled by

---

1 [2004] 2 All ER 995, HL.
2 [2004] 2 All ER 995, HL at [12].
3 *Wainwright v Home Office* [2003] 4 All ER 969; see also *Campbell v MGN Ltd* [2004] 2 All ER 995, HL.

the broader judicial interpretation recently given to the action for breach of confidence and by the guarantees afforded by ECHR article 8. The wider approach to breach of confidence claims has been triggered by the Human Rights Act 1998 and ECHR article 8; it is encapsulated in the judgment of Lord Woolf CJ in *A v B*[4] in the following passage:

> Article 8 operates so as to extend the areas in which an action for breach of confidence can provide protection for privacy. It requires a generous approach to the situations in which privacy is to be protected.[5]

10.4   These developments provide an increased opportunity to protect and assert an individual's privacy in the face of action taken by the police and other investigatory authorities, as has been reflected in recent case law. This text will focus on such opportunities in relation to:

- wrongful disclosure of private information by the police to third parties;
- recording, retention, access to information;
- police surveillance;
- police identification of informants.[6]

10.5   Before looking at those areas in detail, the elements of a claim for breach of confidence will be summarised. The essential principles employed by the courts in evaluating an argument based on ECHR article 8 will also be addressed. In relation to infringement of privacy by a public authority such as the police, an article 8 argument could, where appropriate, be used as a ground of challenge in a judicial review application or in a free-standing claim under Human Rights Act 1998 s7. This text will concentrate on breach of confidence and article 8 as providing the main legal sources of protection in this area. However, it should be remembered that particular factual situations may well give rise to additional claims, for example:

- if the police activity was undertaken in bad faith, a claim in misfeasance in a public office may lie; this could occur where damaging information is leaked to others by officers because they have a grudge against the claimant;

---

4   [2002] 2 All ER 545, CA.
5   [2002] 2 All ER 545, CA at [6].
6   Article 8 privacy issues relating to body searches are dealt with at para 6.110 and article 8 issues relating to searches of property are discussed at paras 9.19–9.20.

- if information relating to the claimant is inaccurately recorded and he or she suffers damage as a result, a claim against the police for negligence might lie;[7]
- if use of surveillance devices involves officers gaining unauthorised access to the claimant's property, actions in trespass to land and/or trespass to goods may result.

10.6    In circumstances where the concern relates to the way in which the police have processed information, consideration should also be given to a claim under the Data Protection Act 1998; this is dealt with at para 10.27 onwards concerning recording and retention of information. Because of the inter-relationship between the statutory provisions, the opportunities for accessing information held by the police provided by the Data Protection Act 1998 and the Freedom of Information Act 2000 are also dealt with in the same section.

## Action for breach of confidence

10.7    The circumstances in which a duty of confidence will arise have significantly expanded as a result of the House of Lords' decision in *Attorney General v Guardian Newspapers Ltd (No 2)*[8] and the introduction of the Human Rights Act 1998. Case law pre-dating these developments is largely of historical interest.[9] It is now clearly established that a duty of confidence will arise whenever the party said to be subject to that obligation either knows or ought to know that the other person can reasonably expect his or her privacy to be protected. This approach was first identified in domestic law by Lord Goff in *Attorney-General v Guardian Newspapers (No 2)* and has recently been confirmed in *A v B*[10] by the Court of Appeal and in *Campbell v MGN Ltd* by the House of Lords.[11] As these authorities acknowledge, the situations where a duty

---

7    Although in *Ogle v Chief Constable of Thames Valley* [2001] EWCA Civ 598, Simon Brown LJ indicated that, contrary to his previous suggestion in *Hough v Chief Constable of Staffordshire* (2001) *Times* 14 February, such circumstances would better give rise to a claim under the Data Protection Act 1998, rather than a claim in negligence.

8    [1990] 1 AC 109.

9    For a review of the earlier authorities see, eg, *Clerk & Lindsell on Torts* (18th edn, Sweet & Maxwell, 2000) chapter 27.

10    [2002] 2 All ER 545.

11    [2004] 2 All ER 995; the speeches contain a discussion of the extent to which the concept of privacy now underpins the action for breach of confidence and review earlier case law on this point, such as the judgments of the Court of Appeal in *Douglas v Hello! Ltd* [2001] QB 967.

can arise are extensive: it has been said that in the great majority of situations, if not all situations, where the protection of privacy would be upheld under article 8, the circumstances will also found an action for breach of confidence.[12] The duty of confidence can be expressly created, but more often its existence will have to be inferred from the facts. Whether a duty arises will depend upon all the circumstances of the relationship between the parties and the nature of the material in question.[13] Obviously a duty of confidence will not arise if the claimant has consented to the disclosure of the relevant information.

10.8    If there is an intrusion in a situation where a person can reasonably expect his or her privacy to be respected, then that intrusion will be capable of giving rise to a successful action for breach of confidence unless the intrusion can be justified.[14] As Lord Woolf has said:

> The bugging of someone's home or the use of other surveillance techniques are obvious examples of such an intrusion.[15]

10.9    Three limiting principles upon the action for breach of confidence have been identified.[16] First, the duty of confidence only applies to information that remains confidential; once it has entered the public domain, in the sense that it has become generally accessible, it will not be protected. Thus, for example, in *Elliot v Chief Constable of Wiltshire*[17] it was held that unauthorised disclosure of the claimant's criminal record to a third party was not actionable as a breach of confidence because the convictions had already been announced in open court. This approach was followed by the Divisional Court in *R v Chief Constable of North Wales ex p Thorpe*.[18] However, it is questionable whether the point would be decided in the same way today, given the expanded situations where a duty of confidence arises and the recognition in case law concerning article 8, that in appropriate circumstances protection may extend to material that has a public dimension.[19] The second identified limiting principle is that the duty

12    *A v B* [2002] 2 All ER 545 at [11(vi)].
13    *A v B* at [11(ix)].
14    *A v B* at [11(x)].
15    *A v B* at [11(x)].
16    Lord Goff in *Att-Gen v Guardian Newspapers (No 2)* [1990] 1 AC 109.
17    (1996) *Times* 5 December.
18    [1997] 3 WLR 724, DC and [1999] QB 396, CA, where the breach of confidence argument was not relied upon before the Court of Appeal.
19    See *Peck v United Kingdom* (2003) 36 EHRR 41. Additionally, in *R (Ellis) v Chief Constable of Essex* (2003) FLR 566 information relating to offences was agreed to fall within article 8(1). These authorities are discussed at paras 10.13-10.14.

of confidence will not attach to trivial information; that criterion is unlikely to present a difficulty in police claims. The third, and most significant limiting principle for present purposes, is that the public interest in preserving confidences may be outweighed by some countervailing public interest, which favours disclosure either to appropriate authorities or to the public generally. Consideration of this principle now requires the court to perform an analysis of competing considerations in a very similar, if not identical way, to the exercise undertaken when article 8(2) is in issue.[20] This means that cases decided prior to the coming into force of the Human Rights Act 1998 are of limited assistance in indicating where the outcome of the balancing act should lie. This was recognised in *R (Ellis) v Chief Constable of Essex*[21] in relation to earlier case law concerning police disclosure of information such as *Hellewell v Chief Constable of Derbyshire*.[22] The evaluation undertaken in relation to article 8(2) is discussed at para 10.16.

10.10    It has recently been established that a successful action for breach of confidence can lead to an award of damages for distress/injury to feelings, even if no other damage has been suffered.[23] In appropriate circumstances an injunction will be granted to restrain a proposed breach of confidence[24] or an anticipated repetition of a past breach.

## Article 8

10.11    Article 8(1) ECHR states:

> Everyone has the right to respect for his private and family life, his home and his correspondence.

10.12    Article 8(2) provides:

> There shall be no interference by a public authority with the exercise of this right except such as in accordance with the law and is necessary in a democratic society in the interests of national security, public safety or

---

20    As recognised by the House of Lords in *Campbell v MGN Ltd* [2004] 2 All ER 995, for example, at [19].

21    (2003) FLR 566.

22    [1995] 4 All ER 473.

23    See *Cornelius v De Taranto* (2001) EMLR 329; *Douglas v Hello! Ltd (No 8)* [2004] EMLR 2; and Morland J's award in *Campbell v MGN Limited* [2002] EMLR 30 of £2,500 for distress, plus £1,000 aggravated damages, recently upheld by the House of Lords.

24    For a discussion of the principles the courts should employ in considering whether to grant an interim injunction, particularly in cases involving the media, see *A v B* [2002] 2 All ER 545.

the economic well-being of the country, for the prevention of disorder or crime, for the protection of health or morals or for the protection of the rights and freedoms of others.

10.13    Article 8(1) will encompass traditional forms of covert surveillance such as telephone tapping[25] and the use of listening devices.[26] It has recently been held to cover the random recording of the telephone calls of patients in a high security hospital[27] and the covert taping of suspects in police cells.[28] The Strasbourg authorities have stated that the concept of a private life is a broad term not susceptible to exhaustive definition. They have recognised that elements such as gender identification, name, sexual orientation and sexual life are important elements of the personal sphere protected by article 8. They have also recognised that article 8 protects a right to dignity and personal development and the right to establish and develop relationships with other human beings, including activities of a professional or a personal nature.[29] It has been held that activities in a public context may in certain circumstances fall within the concept of a 'private life' and that in assessing this question, a person's reasonable expectations as to his or her privacy may be a significant, though not necessarily conclusive, factor, as will be the extent to which a systematic or permanent record is made of material apparently in the public domain.[30] A person walking down the street expects to be observed by others, but may not expect his or her movements to become the subject of a permanent data record. Thus, the compilation of data by security services on particular individuals, even without the use of covert surveillance methods, can constitute an interference with their private lives.[31] This aspect of the article 8 protection is well illustrated by *Peck v United Kingdom*. The applicant was recorded on a local authority CCTV system in a public street carrying a large knife shortly after he had cut himself in a suicide attempt. He made no complaint over that initial recording – indeed it had saved his life as the CCTV operator on viewing the scenes alerted the police – but he contended that the subsequent dissemination of the footage to local newspapers and television stations in order to publicise the scheme, infringed his article 8 rights. The European Court of Human Rights decided that

25    See *Malone v United Kingdom* (1984) 7 EHRR 14; *Halford v United Kingdom* (1997) 24 EHRR 523.

26    *Khan v United Kingdom* (2001) 31 EHRR 45.

27    *R v Ashworth Special Hospital Authority ex p N* [2001] HRLR 46.

28    *R v Mason* [2002] 2 Cr App R 38.

29    See, eg, *Peck v United Kingdom* (2003) 36 EHRR 41 at [57].

30    See, eg, *PG and JH v United Kingdom* [2002] Crim LR 308.

31    *Rotaru v Romania* [2000] ECHR 28341/95.

the disclosure of the footage fell within article 8(1); although the applicant was on a public street, he was not there for the purposes of participating in any public event, he was not a public figure and was in a deeply distressed state at the time. His subsequent exposure to hundreds of thousands of viewers and readers of the local media was way beyond his contemplation when he walked into the town centre that night.[32] The applicant's expectations were also central to the European Court of Human Rights' decision in *Perry v United Kingdom*.[33] Police modified the operation of a security camera so as to take photographs of the applicant while he was in the custody suite and then inserted the footage into a montage of film of other persons for the purposes of showing to potential identification witnesses in relation to a robbery. The court held that an interference with the applicant's rights under article 8(1) had occurred as even if he expected to be filmed by security cameras in the custody suite, he would not have expected footage to be used as part of a subsequent identification procedure.[34]

10.14    Article 8(1) will also cover many instances where information relating to offenders is disseminated. In *R (Ellis) v Chief Constable of Essex*[35] police had devised a novel 'offender naming scheme'. This involved displaying posters at busy public locations showing photographs of selected offenders and stating their name, the offence for which they were convicted and the sentence they were serving. It was common ground that this proposal fell within the protection afforded by article 8(1); the extent to which it could be justified by reference to article 8(2) is discussed at para 10.24.

10.15    In *R (Marper) v Chief Constable of South Yorkshire*[36] the House of Lords (disagreeing with the Court of Appeal on this issue) said that the question of whether article 8(1) was engaged should receive a uniform interpretation throughout member states, unaffected by different cultural traditions, so that a perceived cultural unease in the UK over the official collection and retention of information relating to individuals, could not inform the domestic court's assessment of whether article 8(1) was engaged in the circumstances.[37]

32   The court went on to hold that an article 8(2) justification was not made out as the applicant's consent to disclosure had not been sought and there had been no attempt to mask his identity in the disclosed footage.

33   (2004) 39 EHRR 3.

34   The interference was not justified under article 8(2) in that it was not 'in accordance with the law' as domestic procedures requiring identification processes were breached.

35   (2003) FLR 566, DC.

36   [2004] 1 WLR 2196.

37   [2004] 1 WLR 2196 at [32]–[34] and [68].

10.16    If the actions complained of are protected by article 8(1), the court will then consider whether the circumstances fall within article 8(2), so as justify the invasion of privacy. This involves the defendant satisfying the court of three things. First that the interference is in 'accordance with the law'. This largely involves a consideration of whether it was sanctioned under domestic law.[38] Thus, for example, if covert surveillance is undertaken in accordance with the terms of the Regulation of Investigatory Powers Act 2000, discussed below at para 10.55 onwards, this criterion would be satisfied, whereas if it was carried out in contravention of those provisions it would not be in accordance with the law. Second, the court must be satisfied that the intrusion ursued a legitimate aim, that is to say one of those specified in article 8(2). For present purposes the relevant aims are likely to be: 'the interests of national security'; 'public safety'; 'the prevention of disorder or crime' or 'the protection of rights and freedoms of others'. In the vast majority of instances the police would have little difficulty in bringing the activity under challenge within one of those legitimate aims. The third element to be considered is likely to cause more difficulty. The court has to consider whether the interference is 'necessary in a democratic society', that is to say it meets a pressing social need and the particular interference is proportional to the legitimate aim being pursued.[39] This will always depend upon an evaluation of the particular circumstances, as is illustrated by the recent case law discussed below.

## Wrongful disclosure of private information by the police

10.17    The police legitimately record and retain a substantial amount of information relating to individuals who have been under their investigation. In recent years the courts have considered on a number of occasions the circumstances in which it is permissible for officers to disclose such information to third parties. Assuming that there is some genuine and potentially legitimate reason for the proposed disclosure,[40] competing considerations will need to be evaluated and balanced – on the one hand the claimant's entitlement to respect for his

---

38    Intrusions upon private life used to fail this criterion on the basis that the activity was insufficiently regulated by domestic law, see, eg, *Malone v United Kingdom* (1984) 7 EHRR 14; *Halford v United Kingdom* (1997) 24 EHRR 523.

39    *R (Daly) v Secretary of State for the Home Department* [2001] 2 AC 532, HL at 548.

40    As opposed to a plainly unwarranted act of bad faith where a claim in misfeasance may lie – see para 7.42.

or her privacy, and on the other hand an arguable public interest in the dissemination of the information. Circumstances that are likely to give rise to these sorts of assessments will include:

- disclosures intended to warn of a risk posed by paedophiles, or other sexual offenders;
- disclosures to prospective employers under Police Act 1997 s15 in Enhanced Criminal Record Certificates;
- disclosures to deter offending.

These instances will be considered in more detail, after an examination of the circumstances in which a duty of confidence will arise in relation to the police.

## Duties of confidence owed by the police

10.18 A duty of confidence will generally attach to information obtained by the police in the course of investigating crime. This is apparent even from authorities decided before the Human Rights Act 1998 came into force and the protection afforded by ECHR article 8(1) expanded the ambit of the duty of confidence, as discussed above. In *Marcel v Commissioner of Police of the Metropolis*[41] the Court of Appeal recognised that documents legitimately seized and retained by police during an investigation were subject to a duty of confidentiality, owed to the owner of the documents, so that officers were only able to use the documents for public purposes related to the investigation and prosecution of crime. In *Hellewell v Chief Constable of Derbyshire*[42] a duty of confidence was found to be owed to an offender who was the subject of a 'mug shot' that police wished to circulate to local shop owners concerned about shoplifting, since the photograph conveyed the information that the claimant was known to the police. The police are subject to duties of confidentiality owed to suspects in relation to interviews conducted with them[43] and owed to witnesses in relation to statements taken from them,[44] as regards disclosure for purposes other than any contemplated criminal prosecution. The Court of Appeal reviewed the relevant authorities in *Frankson v Home Office*,[45] holding that an

---

41  [1992] 1 All ER 72.
42  [1995] 4 All ER 473.
43  *Bunn v BBC* [1998] 3 All ER 552, ChD; *Woolgar v Chief Constable of Sussex* [1999] 3 All ER 604, CA.
44  See *Preston BC v McGrath* (2000) *Times* 19 May, CA and *Taylor v Serious Fraud Office* [1999] 2 AC 177, HL.
45  [2003] 1 WLR 1952.

obligation of confidentiality attaches to what is said to the police in the course of their investigations and, contrary to submissions made in that case, there is no difference in principle between information given by a suspect interviewed under caution and information given by a potential witness. The court also emphasised that the strength of the obligation of confidence would vary with the particular circumstances of the case. The obligation of confidence ceases, however, if the relevant material comes legitimately into the public domain, for example by being put in evidence in open court during a criminal trial.[46] If a duty of confidence is established, the key question is usually whether the particular disclosure is in the public interest (see para 10.9).

## Disclosures to warn of offending or to deter offenders

10.19   A consideration of the case law relating to the three categories of proposed disclosure identified above (para 10.17) gives a clear indication of how the courts will approach the balancing process between the claimant's interest in avoiding intrusion and the public interest in favour of dissemination. As discussed at para 10.9 above, a similar evaluation process will now occur whether the claim comes before the courts as a breach of confidence action or in reliance on ECHR article 8.

10.20   In *R v Chief Constable of North Wales ex p Thorpe*[47] the Divisional Court and Court of Appeal considered whether the police were entitled to inform the owner of a caravan site where the claimants resided that they were convicted paedophiles. The following principles were identified:

(1) There is a general presumption that information should not be disclosed, such a presumption being based on a recognition of the potentially serious effect on the ability of convicted people to live a normal life, the risk that such disclosure might drive them underground and the risk that it would expose them to violence.

(2) There is a strong public interest in ensuring that the police are able to disclose information about offenders where and to the extent that it is necessary for the prevention or detection of crime or for the protection of young or other vulnerable people. However, disclosure should only occur where a strong pressing need for that action can be shown.

(3) A blanket policy on disclosure should not be adopted; each case should be considered carefully on its own particular facts,

46   See *Bunn v BBC* [1998] 3 All ER 552, ChD.
47   [1997] 3 WLR 724, DC; [1999] QB 396, CA.

assessing the risk posed by the individual offender, the vulnerability of those who may be at risk and the impact of disclosure on the offender. In making such an assessment the police should normally consult other relevant agencies (such as social services and the probation service).

In *ex p Thorpe* the courts ruled that disclosure was permissible given it concerned activities for which the claimants had been convicted and given the severity of risk posed to children who were present on the caravan site.

10.21 These principles were considered and applied in *R v Local authority in the Midlands ex p LM*.[48] The factual circumstances were significantly different to those arising in *ex p Thorpe* in that the proposed disclosure by the police and social services related to alleged sexual offences against children for which the claimant had never been prosecuted and nor had he been the subject of any civil finding of guilt. The claimant owned a bus company which provided transport to local schools and as a result of the disclosure his contract with the local education department was terminated. Dyson J applied the principles identified in *ex p Thorpe* and in addition noted the following factors as relevant. First, the degree of the defendant's own belief that the alleged offences had occurred; second, the degree of the third parties' legitimate interest in obtaining the proposed information; and third, the degree of risk posed if the disclosure was not made. It was decided that the disclosure was unlawful given the unproven nature of the allegations, their age and the substantial effect upon the claimant's business.

10.22 Although these cases pre-dated the coming into force of the Human Rights Act 1998 in October 2000, the courts clearly drew upon the article 8 case law from Strasbourg in formulating their approach. Thus, not surprisingly, the principles and factors identified in them have been applied in more recent cases as well.[49]

10.23 In *X v Chief Constable of West Midlands*[50] the courts were asked to consider for the first time the permissibility of disclosures made in an Enhanced Criminal Record Certificate (ECRC).[51] Police Act 1997 Part V creates a statutory scheme for employers to access criminal records, and, in prescribed situations, other information held by the police

---

48 [2000] 1 FLR 612.
49 See, eg, *R (A) v National Probation Service* [2003] EWHC 2910, QBD.
50 (2004) *Times* 18 August.
51 The courts have yet to consider the principles to be employed in relation to disclosures to prescribed public bodies pursuant to Crime and Disorder Act 1998 s115.

relating to potential employees. Much of the information that police will hold, such as records of convictions or formal cautions, must be disclosed if the circumstances prescribed by the statute are met and no issue of discretion arises. However, ECRCs – which relate to potential employment involving regular care, training or charge of children[52] – may contain broader information, in particular information that chief officers of police consider may be relevant to the purpose for which the certificate is issued.[53] This potentially gives police officers a very broad discretion to include material that may be no more than unproven allegations, but may have a devastating effect on the claimant's employment prospects. In the X case the claimant was a social worker with no criminal convictions; the disclosure in his ECRC related to a sexual offence for which he had been arrested and interviewed by police, but never prosecuted or convicted and where the identity of the perpetrator was in issue. However, the Court of Appeal held that there was no infringement of article 8 in the circumstances. It was said that the question of whether information was relevant and to be included in the certificate was a matter of opinion for the chief constable. The Court of Appeal said that the Administrative Court had erred in finding in the claimant's favour and in determining the issue by reference to the approach in *R v Chief Constable of North Wales ex p Thorpe*.[54] In the circumstances of that case a presumption against disclosure applied, but in relation to ECRCs the chief constable was under a statutory duty to disclose the information if it might be relevant (unless there was a good reason for not making the disclosure). The court acknowledged that the disclosure could be very damaging to X, but held that the disclosure was justified under article 8(2) given the strong public interest in the information being made available to a prospective employer. The Court of Appeal also rejected a secondary argument that had found favour with the court below, namely that the claimant should have been given an opportunity to make representations to the chief constable prior to the disclosure being made. It was held that this would place too onerous a burden on the chief officer.

10.24　　　The features of the 'naming and shaming' scheme considered by the court in *R (Ellis) v Chief Constable of Essex* have already been described (at para 10.14). The Divisional Court decided that it was impossible to come to an overall decision on whether justification for the proposals had been established by reference to article 8(2). The court said

---

52　Police Property Act 1997 s115.

53　Police Property Act 1997, s115(7).

54　[1999] QB 396, CA.

that the strategy could be legitimate but would depend upon the features of each case, for example whether the offender was still in custody at the time and whether a proper risk assessment had been carried out of the likely effects on him or her including any impact upon his or her prospects for rehabilitation, before he or she was included in the scheme. The court was particularly concerned about any offenders with children being used as part of the scheme, as the children could become subject to distressing behaviour, such as taunting, in consequence. Obviously it would be much harder to justify any scheme involving suspected offenders, rather than those convicted and sentenced to terms of imprisonment. In *R (Stanley) v Commissioner of Police of the Metropolis*,[55] the Divisional Court found that the claimants' rights guaranteed by article 8 were not infringed by the distribution of leaflets and other publicity materials that gave their names, photographs and partial addresses. The claimants had previous convictions and had all been made the subject of anti-social behaviour orders. The court held that the orders required publicity to operate, so that publicity designed to inform and reassure the local public, to assist in enforcing the orders and to deter others was legitimate. In contrast, in *Djerdjar v Commissioner of Police of the Metropolis* (Central London County Court, 23 February 2005) the claimant was awarded £7,500 damages for psychiatric injury and distress under the HRA for breach of his article 8 rights to privacy. Police had arranged for publication of a photograph of a suspected thief in local newspapers, but rather than an image of the suspect, officers had erroneously selected a photograph of the claimant, who was an innocent bystander at the scene.

10.25    Unauthorised disclosures by police officers may also give rise to remedies under the Data Protection Act 1998.

### Disclosure in subsequent civil proceedings

10.26    The courts will also balance the interests of maintaining confidentiality against any competing public interest in favour of disclosure, when faced with an application for specific disclosure by a party to subsequent litigation, seeking information that was imparted to the police in circumstances giving rise to an obligation of confidence. In *Frankson v Home Office*[56] the Court of Appeal ruled that police interviews under caution of prison officers suspected of assaulting inmates, should be disclosed in a subsequent civil action for assault and

---

55    [2004] EWHC 2229 (Admin).
56    [2003] 1 WLR 1952.

misfeasance against the prison authorities, as there was a strong in public interest civil actions being tried on the basis of full and complete information.[57]

## Recording, retention and access to information

### Data Protection Act 1998

10.27   The majority of the relevant provisions of the Data Protection Act (DPA) 1998 came into force on 1 March 2000 and were enacted to implement European Council Directive 95/46/EC. Rights conferred by the DPA 1998 concerning access to data and inaccurate data have been amended by the Freedom of Information Act (FOIA) 2000 with effect from 1 January 2005 (see para 10.44 onwards). It is not feasible to give a full summary of the DPA 1998; this text will focus on the provisions that are likely to be material to information recorded by the police. The main issues that tend to arise from the perspective of those who are the subject matter of such information are rights of access to the data held, the opportunity to correct inaccurate data, the protracted retention of data and the unauthorised disclosure of the material. These are considered below, along with the potential remedies available to an aggrieved claimant.

### Data covered by the DPA 1998

10.28   The DPA 1998 regulates the 'processing' of 'personal data' by a 'data controller'. These concepts are all defined in DPA 1998 s1. 'Data' is defined to cover information which is automated or intended for automated processing, or which is part of a relevant filing system[58] or forms part of an accessible record.[59] For the purposes of public authorities to whom the FOIA 2000 applies, the definition of data is substantially extended to cover recorded information held by the authority that does not fall within one of the other categories of 'data'. Accordingly, this expanded definition of data includes loose or isolated papers and

---

57   For litigation seeking disclosure of information gathered in police investigations, see also *R v Secretary of State for the Home Department ex p Hickey (No 2)* [1995] 1 WLR 734, DC and *R (Green) v Police Complaints Authority* [2004] 2 All ER 209, HL.

58   A relevant filing system is one structured by reference to individuals/criteria relating to individuals in such a way that specific information about a particular individual is readily accessible: DPA 1998 s1(1).

59   An accessible record is defined in DPA 1998 s68 and covers certain health, education, social work and housing records.

information that is not filed by reference to individuals. The main bodies involved with policing are covered by the FOIA 2000[60] and so are subject to this expanded definition of data. The expanded definition of 'data' only applies in relation to rights relating to subject access and to inaccurate data[61] (which are discussed at paras 10.39 and 10.42).

10.29 'Personal data' concerns information relating to a living individual who can be identified.[62] This is potentially a very wide concept. However, the Court of Appeal has held that not all information recorded against a person's name or reference is personal data for these purposes. Mere mention of the individual in the data is insufficient; the information must be sufficiently relevant or proximate to the subject, as judged by reference to whether the material was significantly biographical or whether the subject was the focus of attention. The court said that the information must affect the subject's privacy in his or her personal, family, business or professional life to qualify.[63]

10.30 'Processing' is given a wide statutory definition and essentially relates to obtaining, recording, holding, organising, disclosing, transmitting, retrieving or erasing personal data. The 'data controller' is the person who determines the purposes for which and the manner in which any personal data is to be processed. For present purposes the data controller will be the chief officer of the relevant police force.

## The data protection principles

10.31 The data controller is obliged to comply with the data protection principles in relation to all personal data within his or her responsbility,[64] save where a prescribed exemption applies. The data protection principles are contained in DPA 1998 Sch 1. The first principle provides that:

> 1 Personal data shall be processed fairly and lawfully and in particular, shall not be processed unless –
> (a) at least one of the conditions in schedule 2 is met; and
> (b) in the case of sensitive personal data at least one of the conditions in schedule 3 is met.

10.32 Police cases are likely to involve 'sensitive personal data', as this is defined as data consisting of information as to (among other things):

---

60  See Pt V Sch 1 which refers to police authorities, chief officers of police, the British Transport Police and the Ministry of Defence Police.
61  FOIA 2000 s70 inserting section 33A into the DPA 1998.
62  DPA 1998 s1(1).
63  *Durant v Financial Services Authority* [2004] FSR 28.
64  DPA 1998 s4(4).

'the commission or alleged commission by [the subject] of any offence' or 'any proceedings for any offence committed or alleged to have been committed by him, the disposal of such proceedings or the sentence of any court in such proceedings'. Thus most information held by the police would need to satisfy one or more of the criteria prescribed by Schedule 2 and one or more of the criteria prescribed by Schedule 3 to the Act. As regards DPA 1998 Sch 2, the processing by the police is likely to be justified by reference to para 5(a), (b) or (d), which covers processing necessary for the administration of justice; the exercise of any functions conferred on a person by an enactment; and the exercise of any other functions of a public nature exercised in the public interest. The Data Protection (Processing of Sensitive Personal Data) Order 2000[65] made under DPA 1998 Sch 3 para 10 is likely to apply in police cases.[66] The Association of Chief Police officers (ACPO) Code of Practice for Data Protection[67] gives clear and helpful guidance on what amounts to fair and lawful processing of personal information in the policing context.[68] For example, information obtained through trickery or pressure will not satisfy these requirements; nor would information disclosed in breach of civil law obligations.

10.33    Reference should be made to Sch 1 for the full data protection principles. In addition to principle 1 described above, those most likely to be relevant to police activity are:

3    Personal data should be adequate, relevant and not excessive in relation to the purpose or purposes for which they are processed.
4    Personal data shall be accurate and, where necessary, kept up to date.
5    Personal data processed for any purpose or purposes shall not be kept for longer than is necessary for that purpose or those purposes.

10.34    ACPO Code s7 deals with the requirements that data should be adequate, relevant, not excessive and up to date. Examples are given of the possible consequences of failing to follow these principles, such as an arrest undertaken as a result of out of date information left on computerised records, leading to an action for damages under the Act, aside from any common law civil liabilities.

---

65    SI No 417.
66    See in particular Sch paras 1 and 2, which include processing necessary for the prevention or detection of any unlawful act, where it is in the public interest
67    Accessible on the ACPO website: www.acpo.police.uk.
68    ACPO Code s4.

## Unauthorised disclosure of data

Information disclosed by police in breach of a duty of confidence and/or the claimant's article 8 rights (discussed in detail at paras 10.7–10.26 above) will also amount to a breach of the first data protection principle, as the processing would not be 'lawful'. Disclosure that went beyond what was required by the circumstances could amount to 'unfair' and/or 'excessive' processing, and so a breach of the first and/or third data protection principles.

## Retention of data

10.35   Retention of data is a controversial issue in respect of police records, particularly information relating to suspected offences where guilt has not been established. ACPO Code s8 lays down detailed guidance for the 'weeding' of information from police records in relation to convictions, cautions and other formal recognitions of guilt as well as in respect of cases that were discontinued or resulted in acquittals. In the latter instances the basic recommendation is that information should not be retained beyond 42 days, save in cases of sexual offences where prescribed criteria are met.[69] In relation to convictions, the current Code gives various periods for which it is suggested that the data is retained, depending upon the nature of the offence involved. In many instances retention is contemplated for a considerable period, for example for 100 years or until the death of the subject in relation to crimes of violence (which are broadly defined to include offence such as causing actual bodily harm). In some instances, for example where offences are minor and very old, it will be arguable that a rigid application of these suggested periods will result in a wholly disproportionate interference with the claimant's privacy so as to ground a successful article 8 claim, as well as a potential claim under the DPA 1998 (based on a breach of the fifth data protection principle).

10.36   A further linked issue is the extent to which the police should retain criminal intelligence. The ACPO Code suggests that this must be judged on a case by case basis by reference to the nature of the information and whether it is necessary, lawful, proportionate and relevant to the given purpose. Periodic review is also recommended.[70] The guidelines are expressed as no more than recommendations but, given the level of detail set out, a force may have difficulty in persuading a court they were acting lawfully if information is retained

---

69   ACPO Code para 8.4(12)–(14).
70   ACPO Code para 8.5.

beyond the circumstances set out in the guidelines, unless there are compelling reasons to do so. As a result of recommendations made by the Bichard inquiry (arising out of the failures of police intelligence systems in relation to the activities of Ian Huntley), a new code of practice covering issues such as the retention of information concerning convictions and police intelligence is to be prepared.

### Enforcement

10.37    Where a data protection principle is not adhered to and the police are unable to rely on an exemption (see para 10.43), the subject of the data may have a claim for damages.[71] The claimant must show that he or she has suffered 'damage' – which is likely to encompass physical loss, loss of liberty or physical/mental injury. In those circumstances he or she can also recover damages for distress.[72] Thus, for example, if data was not processed lawfully, because it was disclosed in breach of civil law obligations or not processed fairly because it was disclosed in breach of the terms of the ACPO Code and the claimant suffered damage in consequence, a claim under the Act would be available. A similar right of action arises in relation to other contraventions of the Act by the data controller, such as the requirements on access or correction of data discussed below.[73] In proceedings brought for a contravention of the Act it is a defence to show that all such care as was reasonably required to comply with the requirement in question was taken.[74]

10.38        Breaches of the DPA 1998 can also be dealt with by the Information Commissioner under the enforcement procedures contained in DPA 1998 Pt V. Where the Commissioner is satisfied that a data controller has contravened any of the data protection principles, he may serve an enforcement notice specifying the breach and requiring steps to be taken to rectify the situation. Failure to comply with an enforcement notice is a criminal offence, but there are rights of appeal against the issue of an enforcement notice to the Information Tribunal.

---

71   In contrast to the position under the 1984 Act: *Lord Ashcroft v Att-Gen* [2002] EWHC 1122.

72   DPA 1998 s13. Damages for distress alone can only be recovered where personal data is processed for 'special purposes', as defined by DPA 1998 s3, which is unlikely to apply in police cases.

73   DPA 1998 ss13(1) and 15.

74   DPA 1998 s13(3).

## Accessing data

10.39　Rights of access to personal data are dealt with in DPA 1998 s7. An application to supply information relating to data held is made in writing, usually on a prescribed form and with payment of the requisite fee.[75] The data controller may be able to decline to supply information where it involves the identification of third parties[76] or where a relevant exemption (see para 10.43) applies. An application to supply information under the DPA 1998 could provide an alternative route to obtaining documentation held by the police about the applicant, where litigation is under consideration and there are difficulties with obtaining the material by pre-action disclosure. A court may order the data controller to comply with the request if there has been a failure to comply in contravention of the statutory provisions.[77]

10.40　As has been noted earlier, the extended definition of data introduced by the FOIA 2000 applies to the rights of access conferred by DPA 1998 s7. However, qualifications to the access rights apply to some of the information that is only covered by the newer definition. The qualifications apply to 'unstructured personal data', which is defined as information other than that which forms part of or is intended to form part of a set of information structured by reference to individuals or by reference to criteria relating to individuals.[78] Although this is a rather cumbersome concept, the rationale for the distinction is that greater rights of access should apply to information that can be readily accessed by the data controller. Where the recorded information is unstructured personal data the subject access rights conferred by DPA 1998 s7 only apply if the information required is expressly described in the request and the data controller can refuse to provide the information sought where to do so would cost more than the prescribed cost ceiling.[79]

## Preventing processing of data

10.41　Data subjects also have the right to ask the data controller in writing not to process data for a specified purpose where to do so would be likely

---

75　The ACPO standard form is referred to at para 9.2 of the code. Some forces have developed their own standard form. The maximum fee is currently £10.

76　DPA 1998 s7(4)–(6).

77　DPA 1998 s7(9).

78　FOIA 2000 s69 inserting s9A into the DPA 1998.

79　FOIA 2000 s69; DPA 1998 s9A. For the cost ceiling see FOIA 2000 s12 and the Freedom of Information (Appropriate Limit and Fees) Regulations 2004 SI No 3244.

to cause that individual substantial unwarranted damage or distress.[80] Again this right is subject to applicable exemptions and can be enforced by court order where the court is satisfied that the request was justified and has not been complied with.[81]

## Inaccurate data

10.42    A person may also apply to court for an order that the data controller must rectify, block, erase or destroy any personal data relating to him or her and the court may make such an order if satisfied that the data is inaccurate.[82] Such an order can be made even where the data accurately records information provided by a third party, but if the defendant has taken the steps prescribed by DPA 1998 Sch 1 para 7 then the court may instead order that the data is supplemented by a statement of the true facts or – where para 7 has not been complied with – order such steps as it thinks fit for securing compliance with those requirements.[83] The expanded definition of data introduced by the FOIA 2000 (see para 10.28) applies to rights arising in relation to inaccurate data.

## Exemptions

10.43    Part IV of the 1998 Act contains a number of exemptions to the provisions that have been described. The exemption most likely to apply in police cases is contained in section 29. It provides that personal data processed for the purposes of 'the prevention or detection of crime' or for 'the apprehension or prosecution of offenders' is exempt from the first data protection principle (save to the extent of showing that the criteria in Sch 2 and, where appropriate, Sch 3 is satisfied) and from section 7, where the application of those provisions to the data 'would be likely to prejudice' such purposes.[84] Thus, where the exemption is made out an individual could not assert subject access rights or a failure to process data lawfully or fairly. Similarly, personal data is exempt from the non-disclosure provisions where it is disclosed for the purposes of 'the prevention or detection of crime' or for 'the

---

80    DPA 1998 s10(1).
81    DPA 1998 s10(4).
82    DPA 1998 s14(1).
83    DPA 1998 s14(2); the requirements in Sch 1 para 7 relate to taking reasonable steps to ensure the accuracy of the data and to indicating that in the subject's view the data is inaccurate.
84    DPA 1998 s29(1).

apprehension or prosecution of offenders' and the application of those provisions in relation to the disclosure 'would be likely to prejudice' such purposes.[85] The 'non-disclosure provisions' referred to are the first data protection principle (save for compliance with Schs 2 and 3), the second to fifth data protection principles, and DPA 1998 ss10 and 14(1)–(3).[86] Thus, if the section 29 exemption applies, an individual would be unable to take successful court action in relation to an unwarranted disclosure, correction of inaccurate data or wrongly retained data. The scope of the section 29 exemption is therefore very important in police cases. It was narrowly interpreted by the Administrative Court in *R (Lord) v Secretary of State for the Home Department.*[87] In particular the court emphasised that section 29 could not be used to support a blanket policy of non-disclosure; rather the question of whether the exemption applied had to be addressed on a case by case basis and the requisite prejudice to one or more of the stated purposes had to be shown in the particular case. Further, the statutory phrase 'likely to prejudice' connoted a very significant and weighty chance of prejudice to the identified public interests; the degree of risk had to be such that there might very well be prejudice, even if the risk fell short of being more probable than not. This case by case approach to the section 29 exemption is also reflected in para 5.2 of the ACPO Code. Accordingly, section 29 may provide the police with more limited opportunities to exempt themselves from the central provisions of the DPA 1998 than might at first appear to be the case.

## Freedom of Information Act 2000

### Personal data

10.44 The way in which the FOIA 2000 expands the definition of personal data for some purposes under the DPA 1998 has been discussed at para 10.28. Where the information that is sought by an individual is personal data in relation to him or her, the material is exempt from the access requirements of the FOIA 2000.[88] The intention is that access to personal information relating to the applicant is governed by the DPA 1998 rather than the FOIA 2000; the latter is intended to cover information of a more general nature.

---

85    DPA 1998, s29(3) and (4).
86    DPA 1998 s27(3) and (4).
87    [2003] EWHC 2073, 1 September 2003.
88    FOIA 2000, s40.

10.45    Accordingly, the FOIA 2000 also has limited applicability where the information required relates directly to other individuals. Information will be exempt from the rights of access conferred by the FOIA 2000 if it constitutes personal data relating to a person other than the applicant and to disclose it to the applicant would contravene the data protection principles; or where the information would be covered by an exemption provision of the DPA 1998;[89] or where the subject of the information has served notice in writing that disclosure of the information would cause unwarranted distress and damage.[90] The rationale for restricting the circumstances in which an individual may use the FOIA 2000 to obtain information about others is that a balance has to be struck between rights of access and third parties' rights of privacy.

10.46    The data protection principles have already been discussed (see para. 10.31 onwards). The first data protection principle requires that data should be processed lawfully and fairly. An example of unlawful processing in this context would be where the disclosure of information relating to a third party would be an unjustified interference with the rights of that third party guaranteed by ECHR article 8. An example of unfair processing would be where the disclosure of information relating to a third party would cause disproportionate distress to the third party as against any benefit it would confer upon the applicant seeking the information.[91] Thus in both those instances the information would be exempt from a request for access to information made under the FOIA 2000, as to disclose it to the applicant would contravene the data protection principles.

## The right of access to information

10.47    Aside from personal data relating to either the applicant or to third parties, the FOIA 2000 confers broad rights to information. The FOIA 2000 creates a right of access to recorded information held by public authorities covered by the Act.[92] The right of access involves the right to be told whether the information requested is held by the authority

---

89    FOIA 2000 s40.
90    See DPA 1998 s10.
91    Guidance issued by the Information Commissioner suggests that whether the information sought related to the third party's public or private life would be highly material to this issue: see Freedom of Information Act Awareness Guidance No 1 (which can be obtained from www.informationcommissioner.gov.uk).
92    As set out in Sch 1. The extent to which the police are covered is discussed at para 10.28.

and, if the authority does hold it, to be provided with it.[93] However, given the various exemptions contained in the statute and the limited way in which the Act can be enforced, it will remain to be seen how much of an impact it has in practice.

10.48    Information relating to policing that would not be caught by the personal data exemptions from the FOIA 2000 (see paras 10.44-10.46) could include, for example, material concerning:

- force policies, plans and priorities;
- statistical information, for example concerning detection rates, manpower or costings;
- police officers and employees, provided the information related to their public activities;
- organisation of the force;
- individuals no longer alive;
- minutes and accompanying documentation of certain meetings;
- information relating to individuals that did not fall within the relatively narrow definition of personal data determined by the Court of Appeal in *Durant v Financial Services Authority*[93a] (discussed above in relation to the DPA 1998).

10.49    Where the public authority reasonably requires further information before the requested material can be identified and located and seeks this from the applicant, the authority is not obliged to comply with the duty in FOIA 2002 s1 until that further information has been supplied.[94] The request for information must be in writing and describe the information sought.[95] In general, the time for compliance with a request is up to 20 working days.[96] However time will not run during a period when a fees notice is unpaid. The authority is entitled to issue a fees notice and is exempted from disclosing the information sought if it is not paid.[97] The authority is also exempted from disclosing the information requested if the costs of doing so would exceed a

---

93    FOIA 2000 s1.
93a   [2003] EWCA Civ 1746; [2004] FSR 28.
94    FOIA 2000 s1(3).
95    FOIA 2000 s8, which also prescribes the other requirements of an effective request for information.
96    FOIA 2000 s10.
97    FOIA 2000 s9. The levels of fee that may be charged are set out in the Freedom of Information (Appropriate Limit and Fees) Regulations 2004.

prescribed amount.[98] An authority is not obliged to comply with a vexatious or repeated request.[99]

## Exemptions

10.50　Information is exempt from the rights of access if it falls within one of the exemptions set out in FOIA 2000 Pt II. There are two types of exemptions, absolute exemptions and qualified exemptions. In relation to an absolute exemption, it applies to all situations falling within the defined circumstances. An example of an absolute exemption is that relating to personal data, discussed at paras 10.44-10.46. A further pertinent example of an absolute exemption relates to information whose disclosure would give rise to an actionable breach of confidence.[100] On the other hand, where a qualified exemption applies, even if the circumstances defined in the particular exemption are present the exemption will only apply if the harm test is satisfied. This test involves the authority performing a balancing process and determining whether in all the circumstances of the case, the public interest in maintaining the exemption outweighs the public interest in disclosing whether the authority holds that information and/or in disclosing the information itself.[101] The harm test applies to two exemptions that will frequently arise for consideration in relation to the police. The first of these exemptions applies to information held by a police authority for the purposes of a criminal investigation or criminal proceedings conducted by it and to information obtained from a confidential source.[102] The Freedom of Information Manual issued by ACPO indicates that information relating to investigations will only be released in exceptional circumstances, where there is a strong public interest in doing so. The second of these exemptions applies to information where its disclosure would or would be likely to prejudice law enforcement matters or the exercise of functions relating to criminal investigations and prosecutions.[103] Useful examples are given of the application of the harm test to information falling within FOIA 2000 s31 in the 'Freedom of Information Act Awareness Guidance No 3'

---

98　FOIA 2000 s12 and the Freedom of Information (Appropriate Limit and Fees) Regulations 2004.
99　FOIA 2000 s14.
100　FOIA 2000 s41.
101　FOIA 2000 s2.
102　FOIA 2000 s30.
103　FOIA 2000 s31.

issued by the Information Commissioner. It is suggested there that if information was sought regarding relative detection rates for burglaries in certain areas and information was sought about the number of officers who would be guarding visiting dignitaries, in both instances it might be said that there was a risk that criminals could make use of the information in planning their activities. However, the risk presented by the second request appears more specific and stronger than that arising in relation to the first; thus the harm test would be more likely to be satisfied in the second instance. The same guidance also emphasises that there is a presumption of accountability running through the Act and that the public interest in openness and good administration is to be weighed against any specific harm to the public interest identified in a particular case. The ACPO Freedom of Information Manual states that information which might impact on operational effectiveness, reveal police tactics or affect the police's ability to carry out law enforcement or crime protection will not be released.

10.51   If the public authority contends that the duty under FOIA 2000 s1 does not arise or the information sought is exempt, the authority must serve a notice to that effect.[104]

## Enforcement

10.52   Enforcement is dealt with in FOIA 2000 Pt IV. It is important to note that unlike under the DPA 1998; there is no opportunity for an individual to bring a court action for damages for breach of statutory duty if he or she feels that the provisions of the Act have been breached.[105] Enforcement is primarily effected by the Information Commissioner. Anyone who believes that the Act has not been complied with can complain to the Commissioner who will then have to determine this and issue a decision notice.[106] There is an enforcement notice procedure, with rights of appeal to the tribunal, analogous to those set out in the DPA 1998.[107] However, individuals can bring applications for judicial review to challenge decisions made by public authorities in relation to their responsibilities under the FOIA 2000 where any of the usual public law grounds for challenge apply.[108]

---

104   FOIA 2000 s17.
105   FOIA 2000 s56.
106   FOIA 2000 s50. Where the Commissioner decides that the authority is in breach of its duty under s1 he must specify the steps the authority must take to comply with the Act and the time period for doing so: s50(4).
107   FOIA 2000 ss52–61. Enforcement under the DPA 1998 is dealt with at para 10.38.
108   See para 17.70.

*Other retention issues*

10.53   In *R (Marper) v Chief Constable of South Yorkshire*[109] the House of Lords considered whether the retention of fingerprints and DNA samples of unconvicted individuals contravened their ECHR article 8 rights. The challenge arose in relation to the power contained in Criminal Justice and Police Act 2001 s82,[110] which enables the retention of such materials for purposes related to 'the prevention or detection of crime, the investigation of an offence or the conduct of a prosecution'. It was conceded that the taking of fingerprints and DNA samples involved an interference with the rights protected by article 8(1); but the position in relation to the retention of such material was in dispute. The House of Lords held that article 8(1) was not engaged in the circumstances,[111] as a person could only be identified by fingerprint or DNA samples with the use of sophisticated equipment and/or expert techniques and that in any event the stored material said nothing about the physical makeup, characteristics or life of the person from whom they were obtained. Even if article 8(1) was engaged, the modest nature of the interference was justified under article 8(2) as the samples were only kept for limited purposes, not made public, and they did not identify a person to the untutored eye.[112]

## Police surveillance

10.54   As discussed above, covert surveillance techniques are likely to constitute infringements of the rights protected by ECHR article 8(1) and the material thereby obtained is likely to be subject to an obligation of confidence, restricting its use to the purposes of the criminal investigation.

10.55   The use of covert surveillance is governed by the provisions of the Regulation of Investigatory Powers Act (RIPA) 2000 and those of Police Act 1997 Pt III. The former Act repealed the Interception of Communications Act 1985 and was intended to introduce a greater degree of legislative regulation into this area. The bulk of RIPA's provisions came into force on 25 September 2000. A detailed summary of the provisions of this complex legislation is beyond the scope of this text. What follows is a very broad overview, indicating the kind of surveillance that is now covered by statutory regulation.

---

109   [2004] 1 WLR 2196.
110   Amending Police and Criminal Evidence Act 1984 s64.
111   Baroness Hale dissenting on this issue.
112   The claimants in this case have now made an application to the European Court of Human Rights.

10.56    In general, Police Act 1997 Pt III regulates the use of surveillance devices whose installation involves trespass to property, criminal damage or interference with wireless telegraphy. For example, if police planned to make a covert entry onto premises to hide a listening device in the property, the activity would come within these provisions. The statute provides for prior authorisation to be obtained in a prescribed manner from designated senior officers.

10.57    RIPA 2000 Part II provides for a similar structure of prior authorisations to be obtained from designated senior officers in relation to three forms of surveillance: 'directed surveillance', 'intrusive surveillance' and use of 'covert human intelligence sources'. Directed surveillance is defined in section 26(2) as covert surveillance undertaken in relation to a specific investigation, which is likely to result in the obtaining of private information about a person and which does not amount to intrusive surveillance. 'Covert' surveillance is defined as surveillance carried out in a manner calculated to ensure that the subject is unaware that it is or may be taking place.[113] The designated officer should only authorise the proposed surveillance where he or she believes that it is necessary for one or more of a number of specified purposes, including the prevention or detection of crime and that he or she considers it is proportionate to what the officers seek to achieve in carrying it out.[114] Intrusive surveillance is defined as covert surveillance relating to anything taking place on residential premises or in any private vehicle, either by means of a person or a device.[115] The test for granting prior authorisation is stricter than in relation to directed surveillance. The designated officer is more senior and he or she has to believe that the proposed surveillance is necessary on the grounds of (among other things) preventing or detecting serious crime and that the proposed steps are proportionate in the circumstances.[116] A person is a covert human intelligence source if he or she establishes or maintains a personal or other relationship with an individual for the covert purposes of obtaining information or disclosing information obtained by the use of such a relationship.[117] The grant of an authorisation in relation to a proposed covert human intelligence source involves a consideration of the same test as that applied to directed surveillance and also criteria relating to the management

113   RIPA 2000 s26(9).
114   RIPA 2000 s28(3).
115   RIPA 2000 s26(3) and (5).
116   RIPA 2000 s32.
117   RIPA 2000 s26(8).

and supervision of the source.[118] All these forms of surveillance are lawful if carried out in accordance with an authorisation obtained under the provisions of the Act.[119]

10.58    RIPA 2000 Part I deals with interception of telecommunications, that is, telephone tapping. The scheme of the provisions is to create criminal offences and/or civil liabilities in relation to interceptions carried out in circumstances not authorised or permitted by the provisions of this part of the Act.[120]

10.59    RIPA 2000 also creates an Investigatory Powers Tribunal which can deal with complaints made in relation to breaches of the Act and with claims made under Human Rights Act 1998 s7(1) in relation to the use of investigatory powers.[121]

10.60    Police surveillance activity authorised in accordance with RIPA 2000 is likely to be treated as being 'in accordance with the law' for the purposes of ECHR article 8(2) (see para 10.16 above). The Court of Appeal has held that the provisions of RIPA 2000 Part I are article 8 compliant.[122] As described above, the provisions of Part II of the Act require a balancing exercise to be undertaken before surveillance is authorised, weighing the competing interests of the individual's privacy, as against the public interest in effective crime investigation.[123] Accordingly the structure of the Part II provisions is likely to satisfy Convention requirements. As regards individual authorisations, the balancing exercise involved in the grant is likely to make it difficult to challenge particular decisions as failing to satisfy the requirements of ECHR article 8(2), unless the authorising officer has failed to apply his or her mind to the prescribed criteria. Equally, if surveillance is undertaken in breach of the statutory requirements, it would be difficult for the police to establish that the activity was legitimate in a civil law action.

## Police identification of informants

10.61    The courts have accepted that a duty of confidence may be owed to people who provide information to the police in the expectation that their identity will not be revealed to those who are the subject of the

118    RIPA 2000 s29.
119    RIPA 2000 s27.
120    RIPA 2000 s1(1)–(3) indicates when an interception will amount to a criminal offence or a breach of civil law; ss3–5 set out the circumstances in which an interception is lawful.
121    RIPA 2000 ss65–69 and Investigatory Powers Tribunal Rules 2000 SI No 2655.
122    *R v E* (2004) *Times* 27 May.
123    As acknowledged in *R v W* [2003] 1 WLR 2902.

intelligence. In *Swinney v Chief Constable of Northumbria*[124] the Court of Appeal held that it was arguable that such a duty arose in relation to the claimant who had passed information to officers in the belief that it would be used on an anonymous basis.[125] In *Donnelly v Chief Constable of Lincolnshire*[126] it was accepted that officers owed a duty of care in negligence to a participant informer involved in providing information on drug smuggling and the case was not argued on the basis of breach of confidence.[127] The claimants in *X & Y v Chief Constable of Greater Manchester*[128] had received assurances of anonymity from the police when they agreed to supply information relating to a murder, but the Crown Prosecution Service divulged their role and identity to the defendants at the criminal trial. Liability for breach of confidence and negligence was conceded and the hearing involved an assessment of damages. Compensation was awarded to reflect consequential psychiatric trauma, disruption to the claimants' previous life and loss of earnings.

10.62 In summary, in the case of an informant (whether used by police on a casual or a formalised basis) it will probably be relatively straightforward to establish the existence of a duty of confidence and/or a duty of care in negligence, owed by the officers involved. The more difficult issue is likely to be whether the duty was breached in the particular circumstances. This will depend, among other factors, upon the claimant's reasonable expectation, in turn based on any assurances given at the time, the degree of the threat posed to his or her safety and the extent to which disclosure of the material was required in any criminal trial process.

# Discrimination

## Introduction

10.63 This section will focus upon the opportunities for bringing discrimination claims under the Race Relations Act (RRA) 1976, as allegations of racist policing are frequently made by those from minority ethnic communities who have had dealings with the police. The Race Relations

---

124  [1996] 3 All ER 449, CA.
125  At trial the action proceeded in relation to the negligence claim, where no breach was established on the facts: *Swinney v Chief Constable of Northumbria (No 2)* (1999) 11 Admin LR 811, QBD.
126  (2001) 14 September, QBD, unreported.
127  The court found that the duty of care had not been breached on the facts.
128  [2004] EWHC 764, QBD.

(Amendment) Act (RR(A)A) 2000 was enacted to implement recommendations contained in the report arising out of the Stephen Lawrence inquiry[129] and came into force on 2 April 2001. Its material provisions are considered in detail below. In general, it substantially broadened the circumstances in which victims of racially discriminatory policing could bring a claim under the RRA 1976. Further amendments to the race relations legislation were made by the Race Relations Act 1976 (Amendment) Regulations (RRA(A)R) 2003.[130] The Regulations came into force on 19 July 2003. The amendments they introduced have significantly added to the complexity of race discrimination law, since, as explained below, new definitions of discrimination were created by these regulations that only apply to some complaints of race-based treatment. A further hurdle for practitioners to negotiate in this area is the unusual procedural requirements that apply to discrimination claims, particularly in relation to the prescribed time limits for issuing proceedings. These are also described below. Despite the complexity of the current statutory provisions, they can provide potentially powerful remedies for circumstances involving racially discriminatory policing.

10.64    This section will also look more briefly at the possibility of claims against the police for gender discrimination under the Sex Discrimination Act (SDA) 1975 and for discrimination on the grounds of disability under the Disability Discrimination Act (DDA) 1995. A claim under the former might arise, for example, if male officers treated a female victim of crime in an abusive and derogatory way, because of her gender. An action under the DDA 1995 might arise if officers failed to treat seriously a crime reported by a person with hearing and speech impediments and/or failed to take the necessary steps to appreciate the allegations he or she was making. Neither the SDA 1975 nor the DDA 1995 have been amended in a way equivalent to the expansion of the race discrimination legislation brought about by the RR(A)A 2000. As a result, the policing activities covered by the SDA 1975 and the DDA 1995 are much more restricted than those covered by the RRA 1976.

10.65    At present, domestic legislation does not directly afford protection for discrimination on grounds other than race, sex or disability in relation to the way that the police deal with members of the public. Regulations have been introduced prohibiting discrimination on the

---

129    Inquiry by Sir William MacPherson TSO CM 4261-1, Stationery Office.
130    SI No 1626.

grounds of sexual orientation and on the grounds of religion or belief,[131] but they are currently limited to the employment context. On 20 September 2004 the Prime Minister announced that the prohibition on discrimination on the grounds of religion or belief would be extended to the provision of goods, services and facilities. As will be seen from the discussion below concerning the race discrimination legislation, some forms of discriminatory policing can come within the prohibition on discrimination in the provision of goods, facilities or services. The extension of the circumstances in which action can be brought for discrimination on the grounds of religion or belief will be particularly significant for members of those communities who the courts have decided do not constitute 'a racial group' for the purposes of the RRA 1976, most notably Muslims and Rastafarians.[132]

10.66    Where the type of discrimination complained of is not protected by a specific statute, a claim for discrimination could arise nonetheless under the Human Rights Act 1998, based on a breach of European Convention on Human Rights (ECHR) article 14. As discussed below, this affords an opportunity to bring an action concerning discrimination on the part of public authorities, including the police, on a wide variety of grounds, provided the discrimination relates to the enjoyment of rights protected by the Convention.

10.67    If a specific claim for discrimination is not available – for example because of the relatively strict limitation provisions in the statutes prohibiting discrimination – a claimant can nonetheless rely on discriminatory treatment as a feature aggravating the level of damages that he or she should be awarded in a claim based on common law torts. For example, if a claimant was arrested on a groundless basis, he or she could in any event have a claim for false imprisonment, but if race played a part in the decision to arrest, he or she could rely on that in the false imprisonment claim in support of the plea for aggravated and/or exemplary damages.[133] If, in the same example, the claimant could also establish actionable unlawful race discrimination under the provisions of the RRA 1976, he or she could rely on both causes of action, namely the claim in false imprisonment and a claim under the RRA 1976.

---

131 Employment Equality (Sexual Orientation) Regulations 2003 SI No 1661 and Employment Equality (Religion or Belief) Regulations 2003 SI No 1660 respectively.

132 *Crown Suppliers (PSA) Ltd v Dawkins* [1993] ICR 517 and *Mandla v Dowell Lee* [1983] IRLR 209, HL.

133 These kinds of damages are discussed in chapter 14.

# Race Relations Act 1976

## Summary

10.68   In order to succeed in establishing liability under the RRA 1976, a claimant has to show both that the conduct in question amounted to a recognised form of discrimination and that the activity complained of was of a kind prohibited by the Act. The forms of discrimination that the RRA 1976 covers are:

- direct discrimination;
- indirect discrimination;
- victimisation;
- harassment.

10.69   Each of these concepts are discussed in detail below. So far as claims involving discriminatory policing are concerned, the conduct will be of a kind prohibited by the RRA 1976 if it comes within either section 20 or section 19B. The former deals with discrimination in the provision of goods, facilities and services. The latter with discrimination in the exercise of public functions. The parameters of both provisions are analysed below.

## Background

10.70   In response to the Lawrence inquiry (recommendation 1), the Home Secretary produced a Ministerial Priority for the Police Service in 1999/2000, repeated in 2000/01 and 2001/02:

> ...to increase trust and confidence in policing amongst ethnic minority communities.

10.71   There are best value performance indicators that have been devised to reflect and assess this. Important aspects to emerge were as follows:[134]

- Of the 686,100 searches, recorded by the police in 2000/01, 10 per cent were black people, 5 per cent Asian people and 1 per cent 'other' non-white origin.
- Black people are seven times more likely to be stopped and searched than white people.
- Overall, in England and Wales compared with 1999/2000, the number of stop and searches fell by 18 per cent for white

---

134   These figures are contained in 'Race Equality in Public Services', Home Office, November 2002.

people and by 6 per cent for Asian people but rose by 4 per cent for black people.

- The percentage of police staff (officers, special constables and support staff) from minority ethnic backgrounds increased from 3 per cent to 3.1 per cent between April 2000 and March 2001.
- The number of racist incidents recorded by the police rose by 11 per cent in 2000/01.
- There were 25,100 racially aggravated offences recorded by the police in 2000/01 (21,750 in 1999/2000), of which one-third were detected.
- The proportion of police officers from minority ethnic groups increased from 2.2 per cent in 1999/2000 to 2.4 per cent in 2000/01. In 2000/01, 0.9 per cent of police officers were black and 0.8 per cent Asians.

10.72    Racially discriminatory attitudes among police officers continue to give rise to concerns. The Metropolitan Police Authority released figures in the summer of 2004 which showed that the numbers of stops and searches for those of Asian origin had increased by 300 per cent since the new provisions for stop and search in the Anti-Terrorism, Crime and Security Act 2001 came into being.[135] Additionally, the Institute of Race Relations published a report which detailed how hundreds of Muslims had been arrested under terrorism powers before being released without charge and how the special powers granted by parliament to tackle terrorism were being deployed in other spheres, such as routine criminal investigation or in the policing of immigration.[136] Following the broadcast of the BBC documentary 'The Secret Policeman' in late 2003, the Commission for Racial Equality has set up a formal inquiry into policing, which is on-going.[137] The Metropolitan Police Authority also recently ordered an independent inquiry into professional standards and employment matters in the Metropolitan Police Service.[138]

10.73    Concerns involving the prevalence and effect of racially discriminatory attitudes have extended beyond the police to other agencies involved in law enforcement, in particular the Crown Prosecution Service (CPS) and the Prison Service. In July 2001, Sylvia Denman

135   See www.mpa.gov.uk
136   See www.irr.org.uk
137   See www.cre.gov.uk.
138   See www.morrisinquiry.gov.uk

published a report on 'Race Discrimination in the CPS'. At the same time, the Commission for Racial Equality published a report on its investigation into the Croydon branch of the CPS. The DPP accepted the findings of both reports and sent a letter to all staff, acknowledging the need to tackle institutional racism within the service. Recommendations from the reports have been incorporated into the CPS Equality Scheme. The Attorney-General set up an Advisory Group (the Attorney-General's Race Advisory Group) to assist him in overseeing the CPS's implementation of the ten recommendations made by Sylvia Denman.

10.74    Information on the ethnicity of the prison population has been published regularly by the Home Office for many years. On 30 June 2000, there were 12,610 people from minority ethnic groups in prison service establishments – similar to 1999. Minority ethnic groups accounted for 19 per cent of the male prison population (12 per cent black, 3 per cent Asian and 4 per cent other) and 25 per cent of the female prison population (19 per cent black, 1 per cent Asian, and 5 per cent other). These proportions have remained relatively constant in recent years. As a result of concerns about discriminatory treatment of prisoners, the Commission for Racial Equality carried out a formal investigation into the Prison Service which was published in 2003.[139]

## Race Relations (Amendment) Act 2000 – an overview

10.75    One of the recommendations made by the Stephen Lawrence inquiry[140] was:

> That the full force of the Race Relations legislation should apply to all police officers, and that Chief Officers of police should be made vicariously liable for the acts and omissions of their officers relevant to that legislation.[141]

10.76    The government accepted this recommendation and announced that all public services were to be brought within the scope of the RRA 1976. The RR(A)A 2000 came into force on 2 April 2001 and applies to all acts of discrimination from that date. It prohibits discrimination in relation to public functions, by inserting a new section 19B into the RRA 1976, which covers discriminatory behaviour by public authorities that was not previously outlawed by the RRA 1976.

139    See www.cre.gov.uk
140    Inquiry by Sir William MacPherson TSO CM4261–I, Stationery Office.
141    Recommendation 11.

10.77    So far as claims against the police are concerned, the other major change brought about by the RR(A)A 2000 was to render chief officers of police vicariously liable for the discriminatory acts of their officers;[142] prior to that change claims under the RRA 1976 had to be brought against the individual officer(s) responsible for the discrimination.

10.78    The RR(A)A 2000 also placed new statutory duties on public authorities, including the police, to secure equality, including in the field of service delivery.

10.79    These changes are discussed below, where each of these developments is looked at in more detail. However, this section will first focus on the various forms of discrimination that are prohibited by the RRA 1976.

### Forms of discrimination

### Direct discrimination

10.80    Direct discrimination is established when a person is treated less favourably than another is or would be treated in like circumstances on racial grounds.[143]

10.81    Proving direct discrimination is frequently difficult as direct evidence of discrimination is often not available. The House of Lords has accepted[144] that:

> Claims of [race and sex] discrimination present special problems of proof for complainants since those who discriminate on grounds of race or gender do not in general advertise their prejudices.

10.82    The concept of direct discrimination involves establishing two elements, namely:

- less favourable treatment of the claimant as against another person of a different race; and
- that the treatment was on racial grounds.

10.83    The issue of less favourable treatment has to be considered by reference to how the alleged discriminator treated or would have treated someone of a different racial group in the same or relevantly similar circumstances (that is, one must compare like with like).[145] However, it is important to remember that the two issues identified are

142    By inserting s76A into the RRA 1976.

143    RRA s1(1)(a) 1976.

144    *Glasgow City Council v Zafar* [1998] 2 All ER 953.

145    RRA s3(4) 1976.

composite aspects of one overall question; it is not necessary for a claimant to prove that he or she was treated less favourably than another as a threshold test before the question of whether the treatment was on racial grounds is considered.[146] Indeed, as was recognised in *Shamoon*, evidence on the latter issue may well inform the former issue. Thus, while the means of establishing comparative less favourable treatment is discussed below at para 10.87, it is important to note the inter-relationship of the two elements of the statutory definition; in police cases it may frequently be easier to show that the treatment was on racial grounds than it will be to identify the way in which a particular comparator of another race was or would have been treated if that question was asked in isolation. Thus, for example, if a young black man is stopped and searched for no apparent reason and the officer carrying out the search treats him in a surly and dismissive way, there may well be sufficient material from which to infer that the treatment was on the basis of race, and so in turn infer that a young white man would have been treated differently, without specific evidence as to how young white men in comparable situations were treated by the officer.

10.84   Direct discrimination can relate to actions or omissions by the police. It could cover, for example, less favourable treatment of a black person in relation to:

- a failure to respond to a request for help;
- a failure to investigate a crime;
- a failure to offer support to a victim of crime;
- a decision to stop and search a pedestrian or the driver of a vehicle;
- a decision to make an arrest;
- a decision to detain in custody;
- a decision to handcuff or to use other force;
- use of racist language;
- a decision to charge;
- a denial of rights while in police custody.

10.85   'Racial grounds' means any of the following: colour, race, nationality, or ethnic or national origins.[147] 'Racial group' means a group of persons defined by reference to colour, race, nationality or ethnic or national origins, and references to a person's racial group refer to any racial

---

146   *Shamoon v Chief Constable of the Royal Ulster Constabulary* [2003] IRLR 285, HL.
147   RRA 1976 s3(1).

group into which he or she falls.[148] Sikhs are a 'racial group' as are gypsies, Irish travellers and Jews.[149] However, as mentioned above, Muslims and Rastafarians have been held not to fall within the definition of a separate ethnic group,[150] and accordingly victims of discrimination on these grounds are unable to bring an action under the RRA 1976. Frequently a claimant will be unable to tell, particularly at an early stage of proceedings, whether he or she was adversely treated because of his or her colour, race or ethnic origins. For example a young man may have been stopped by the police because he is black (colour) or because of his national origins (Afro-Caribbean). Where there is any doubt, it is advisable to plead the claim in the alternative. As will be seen below when the RRA(A)R 2003 amendments to the RRA 1976 are discussed, in some circumstances it has now become significant to show that the discrimination was on the grounds of race or ethnic or national origins, rather than on the grounds of colour or nationality; which is a further feature for the claimant's advisers to bear in mind in formulating the claim.

10.86    Direct discrimination may be subconscious, rather than intentional and it does not have to be shown that the discriminator acted solely because of racial factors; it is sufficient if they had a 'significant influence' on the conduct in question.[151]

## Comparators

10.87    To establish direct discrimination it is necessary to show that the claimant was treated less favourably than another person of a different race/nationality/colour/ethnic origin. This may be done by specific evidence of how such others have been treated or by establishing on the 'balance of probabilities' how a hypothetical comparator would have been treated.[152] Because of the individualised circumstances inherent in virtually any policing decision (in relation to arrest, stop and search, etc) and the difficulty in finding out about comparable situations, the police frequently argue in race discrimination claims that the

148   RRA 1976 s3(1).
149   *Mandla v Dowell Lee* [1983] IRLR 209, HL; *Commission for Racial Equality v Dutton* [1989] 1 All ER 306; *O'Leary v Allied Domecq Inns* (2000) July, Central London County Court, unreported.
150   *Mandla v Dowell Lee*, [1983] IRLR 209, HL and *Crown Suppliers (PSA) Ltd v Dawkins* [1993] ICR 517 (see para 10.65).
151   *Nagarajan v London Regional Transport* [1999] ICR 877, HL.
152   *Balamoody v UK Central Council for Nursing, Midwifery and Health Visitors* [2002] IRLR 288; *Shamoon v Chief Constable of the Royal Ulster Constabulary* [2003] IRLR 285, HL.

action should fail because the claimant is unable to point to an exactly identical situation where a white person was treated in a different way. However, it is submitted that such a response is over-simplistic and can be met in a number of ways:

- As discussed at para 10.83 above, the issue of less favourable treatment should not be considered in isolation from the question of why the claimant was treated in the manner complained of. If there is strong evidence from which to draw a conclusion of racially discriminatory behaviour, less favourable treatment may be inferred. An instance of this discussed by Lord Scott in *Shamoon v Chief Constable of the Royal Ulster Constabulary* is where the alleged discriminator gives unconvincing denials of a discriminatory intent, coupled with unconvincing assertions of other reasons for the allegedly discriminatory behaviour.[153]

- The treatment of the comparator of a different race can in any event be a matter of inference as to how a hypothetical comparator would be treated; direct evidence of how another was actually treated is not necessary (see the authorities referred to at footnote 152). Of course, if evidence is available of an actual white person being treated differently to a black person in equivalent circumstances it can be very helpful material to support the claim. For example, if a black man and a white man were engaged in a fight in which both were attacking the other and both had sustained only minor visible injuries, there would be some evidence of discrimination if, for no apparent reason, the police arrested the black man and treated the white man as the victim.

- A picture of how the hypothetical comparator would have been treated by the alleged discriminator can be built up from evidence as to how a number of persons of a different race were treated in non-identical, but not wholly dissimilar circumstances.[154] Thus, for example, if a black claimant obtained evidence that the same officer had arrested a number of white men for minor public order offences during the same demonstration but had handcuffed none of them, this could be evidence to support a claim that the handcuffing of the black claimant was discriminatory.

---

153  [2003] IRLR 285 at [116].
154  *Vento v Chief Constable of West Yorkshire* [2001] IRLR 124.

- Statistical information showing an apparent pattern of discriminatory treatment may be relevant even if distilled from non-identical cases, as this may be powerful evidence that the behaviour complained of was undertaken on racial grounds, which in turn may lead to an inference of direct discrimination being drawn.[155] Thus, for example, in a claim for a racially discriminatory stop and search, if statistics showed that the same officer had stopped predominantly black people for searches over the preceding six months, an inference of unlawful discrimination could be drawn (unless the officer had a credible explanation for this apparently striking statistical disparity).[156]

10.88 Until recently, when the treatment complained of was by its very nature specific to a person's race, for example racial abuse, it was said that it was unnecessary to draw a comparison as it was already clear that the less favourable treatment was on racial grounds.[157] However, the House of Lords has now held that, to accord with the statutory wording, it is always necessary to identify a comparator (real or hypothetical) against which the treatment complained of must be judged.[158] However, where the treatment is overtly race based, such as racist abuse, it will usually present no difficulties for a court to infer that a person of a different race would not have been treated in the same way.

### Proving direct discrimination

10.89 The RRA 1976 provides for the use of questionnaires to obtain evidence from the alleged discriminator as to how those of different racial groups have been treated and would have been treated in comparable circumstances.[159] The procedure is to help a person decide whether to institute proceedings and, if he or she does so, to formulate and present the claim in the most effective manner.

---

155 The use of statistical evidence for this purpose was expressly recognised by Lord Scott in *Shamoon v Chief Constable of the Royal Ulster Constabulary* [2003] IRLR 285, HL.

156 The decision in *Okpako v Commissioner of Police of the Metropolis* [2003] Police Law Reports 242 CCLC, sometimes relied upon by the police when statistical information is sought by way of a questionnaire, fails to appreciate that statistical information is relevant in this broader way, and is not only relevant for the purposes of identifying specific comparators.

157 *Sidhu v Aerospace Composite Technology* [2000] IRLR 602.

158 *Pearce v Governing Body of Mayfield Secondary School* [2003] ICR 937.

159 RRA 1976 s65 and Race Relations (Questionnaires and Replies) Order 1977 SI No 842.

10.90   The replies to a questionnaire are admissible in evidence. A questionnaire can be served before proceedings are instituted. If it is served during the period of six months less one day from the act complained of then no permission is required from the court. If a questionnaire is served after proceedings have commenced then permission of the court is required and it must be served within the time specified.[160] There are prescribed forms though they do not have to be used.[161]

10.91   A response to a questionnaire cannot be compelled, however where a defendant omits to reply within a reasonable period or gives replies within that period which are evasive or equivocal, the court may draw any inference that it considers just and equitable in the circumstances, including an inference that the defendant did commit the unlawful act.[162] As a result of recent amendments to the RRA 1976, the period for replying to the questionnaire when allegations of discrimination are made on grounds of race and/or ethnic and/or national origins has now been fixed at eight weeks.[163]

10.92   The questionnaire procedure is potentially useful for obtaining supporting information at an early stage. This might involve general statistical information as to how those of the relevant comparative racial groups have been treated in equivalent circumstances (for example, a racial breakdown of stop and search figures for the relevant area), specific information regarding the alleged discriminator (for example, the racial breakdown of arrests made by the particular officer in question) or material about the particular incident (for example, an explanation as to why the arrest was made). In formulating questions, advisers will want to bear in mind that it will be much easier for the police to justify failing to answer broad questions that do not clearly relate to the matter in issue or which involve a disproportionate amount of work in preparing a response. For example, a request for a racial breakdown of other arrests/stops, etc, made by the alleged discriminator is likely to be more effective if related to a period of months around the incident in question, rather than if it is related to a period of years or simply left open-ended.

---

160   Race Relations (Questionnaires and Replies) Order 1977 reg 4. Note that in *Dattani v Chief Constable of West Mercia Police* (2005) 7 February, the Employment Appeal Tribunal held that evasive, incorrect or nil replies to questions can lead to an inference of discrimination even if the questions were not asked under the statutory procedure.

161   Race Relations (Questionnaires and Replies) Order 1977 reg 3.

162   RRA 1976 s65(2)(b).

163   RRA (A)R 2003 reg 47 amending RRA 1976 s65(2)(b).

10.93    Adverse inferences may not be drawn in relation to claims under RRA 1976 s19B (discussed at para 10.120 onwards) by reason of a failure to reply, or from a particular reply, in circumstances where at the time of doing any relevant acts, the respondent was carrying out public investigator functions or acting as a public prosecutor and he or she reasonably believed that a reply or a different reply would be likely to prejudice any criminal investigation, any decision to institute criminal proceedings or any criminal proceedings or would reveal the reasons behind a decision not to institute, or a decision not to continue criminal proceedings.[164]

10.94    Establishing discrimination usually depends upon the drawing of inferences from all available material, including from any failure to respond to a questionnaire. Where there is an apparent variation in treatment between those of different racial groups the court will look to any explanation put forward by the defendant. If none is put forward or if the explanation is unsatisfactory or inadequate (in the sense that it does not appear to be genuine) it will be legitimate for the court to infer that the discrimination was on racial grounds.[165] Accordingly, wherever a claimant alleges that he or she has been the victim of directly discriminatory treatment by police officers, the quality of their explanation for the conduct complained of is of primary importance.

10.95    It has been emphasised that discrimination cannot be inferred purely from the fact of unreasonable treatment, without any evidence as to how others would be treated by the alleged discriminator.[166] However, it has also been pointed out in the employment context that a court or tribunal should not assume that an employer behaves equally badly to those of other races if he or she does not positively assert this.[167] Moreover, in practice, if there is clear evidence that police officers arrested and abused a black man for no apparent reason (other than his race), a court is unlikely to need direct evidence to infer that the officers do not behave in this way as a matter of course to all members of the public.

### Indirect discrimination

10.96    Indirect discrimination is defined in two ways in the RRA 1976. The first form of indirect discrimination has been in the Act from the outset.

164   RRA 1976 s65(4A) and (4B).
165   *King v Great Britain-China Centre* [1991] IRLR 513, CA; *Zafar v Glasgow City Council* [1998] IRLR 36, HL.
166   *Zafar v Glasgow City Council.*
167   *Anya v University of Oxford* [2001] ICR 847, CA.

Under this definition a claimant has to show[168] :

- the application of a requirement or condition[169] to the claimant's racial group and to those who are not of the same racial group;
- the requirement or condition operated to the claimant's detriment because he or she could not comply with it;
- the proportion of persons of the same racial group as the claimant who can comply with the condition or requirement is considerably smaller than the proportion of persons not of that racial group who can comply with it.

10.97    The essence of indirect discrimination is the application of a rule that in its terms is racially neutral but in practice operates to the substantial disadvantage of those from a particular racial group. It is conceptually distinct from direct discrimination which involves the application of overtly different treatment on the basis of race. For example, if police have a policy of arresting those in a particular area, the policy is ostensibly racially neutral, but if in practice the area is one frequented by Asian youths the operation of the policy could be indirectly discriminatory.

10.98    The defendant may justify indirect discrimination (unlike direct discrimination or victimisation under the RRA 1976). To do so, the defendant needs to prove that the apparently discriminatory rule serves a real need and that it is necessary and appropriate to achieve that aim.[170]

10.99    The main practical points to note in relation to establishing indirect discrimination under this definition are:

(a) It is necessary to identify a 'requirement' or 'condition' that has been applied and that the claimant cannot comply with. The requirement or condition may be express or implicit in the particular circumstances. For example, if the police operated a de facto curfew in a certain area with a high, black residential population, an implicit requirement could be distilled; that in order to avoid arrest you must not be seen out in the 'X' area after 'Y' hours.

(b) In establishing the requisite disparate adverse impact, the selection of the most advantageous racial groups for comparative purposes may be crucial. As discussed in relation to direct

---

168    RRA 1976 s1(1)(b).

169    This concept denotes something that operates as an absolute rule, rather than as simply one of a number of factors influencing a decision: *Perera v Civil Service Commission (No 2)* [1983] IRLR 166.

170    *Hampson v Department of Education and Science* [1989] ICR 179, HL.

discrimination, the claimant may belong to more than one 'racial group'.[171] For example, for the purposes of testing the effect of the requirement or condition referred to in (a), the claimant might classify him or herself as non-white or as Afro-Caribbean.

(c) The RRA 1976 provides that the relevant circumstances of the two racial groups must be the same or not materially different. The two groups who are to be considered are known as the pool.

(d) The scope of the pool is sometimes a matter for debate. Where the requirement prevents access to a positive benefit the size of the pool is usually all those who wish to claim the particular benefit and would qualify for it and all those who wish to claim it and would qualify for it were it not for the requirement or condition. Where the requirement is a negative one such that failure to meet it leads to the imposition of a specific detriment, the pools is usually all those who avoid the detriment because they can meet the condition and those who would avoid the detriment but for the challenged requirement. Again, taking the example canvassed in (a) and (b), the appropriate pool for the requirement or condition concerning the operation of the curfew would probably be all those living in the area covered by the curfew.

(e) In most cases statistical evidence is required to establish the disparate adverse impact, though sometimes tribunals and courts simply accept this if a differential impact is apparent as a matter of common sense. The questionnaire procedure (discussed at para 10.92) is usually one of the best routes for obtaining the relevant statistical evidence.

(f) 'Detriment' has been interpreted fairly broadly by the courts as encompassing anything that might reasonably be perceived as a disadvantage in the circumstances.[172]

(g) The questionnaire procedure may also be useful in finding out the basis of any justification defence the defendant will be seeking to rely upon at a relatively early stage.

(h) It is unnecessary to show any conscious motive or intention to discriminate. However, a lack of such intention may have a significant impact on compensation (see the discussion of quantum at para 10.142).

---

171  RRA 1976 s3(1).
172  *Shamoon v Chief Constable of the Royal Ulster Constabulary* [2003] IRLR 285, HL.

10.100    For events occurring from 19 July 2003, a new broader definition of indirect discrimination may be applicable. This was introduced by the RRA(A)R 2003.[173] The new definition states that:

> A person also discriminates against another if ... he applies to that other, a provision, criteria or practice which he applies or would apply equally to persons not of the same race or ethnic or national origins as that other, but:
>
> a.  which puts or would put persons of the same race or ethnic or national origins as that other at a particular disadvantage when compared with other persons;
> b.  which puts that other at that disadvantage;
> c.  and which he cannot show to be a proportionate means of achieving any legitimate aim.

10.101    The new definition only applies to discrimination covered by the RRA(A)R 2003. This is limited in two ways. First, the Regulations cover discrimination on the grounds of race or ethnic or national origins, but not discrimination on the grounds of colour or nationality.[174] Second, the new definition only applies to claims falling within RRA 1976 s1(1B). Conduct will not come within section 1(1B) simply because it falls within the section 19B prohibition on discrimination in the exercise of public functions (see paras 10.120–10.124). Only certain public functions come within section 1(1B). For police cases the only relevant functions could be those relating to 'any form of social protection' or functions relating to 'any form of social advantage'. These concepts are contained in the EU Directive that the Regulations implement and their interpretation has not as yet been the subject of domestic case law. However, it may be stretching a point to describe policing functions concerning, for example, arrest, detention and prosecution, as the performance of functions relating to a form of social advantage or social protection, particularly if the contemplated claim is on the part of the arrested or prosecuted person. Conduct that comes within RRA 1976 s20 (provision of goods, facilities and services) is covered by section 1(1B) and so the new definition of indirect discrimination will apply to such claims. However, as discussed at paras 10.115–10.119 where RRA 1976 s20 is considered in detail, it will be seen that it relates predominantly to the way that victims of crime, rather than suspects, are treated by the police.

---

173    Inserting s1(1A) into the RRA 1976.
174    This is because the RRA(A)R 2003 were enacted pursuant to EU Directive 2000/43/EC, which only applies to discrimination on grounds of race or ethnic or national origins. The government could not extend the concepts introduced by the RRA(A)R 2003 to discrimination on the grounds of colour or nationality without primary legislation.

10.102    Where it applies, the new definition of indirect racial discrimination makes it easier for claimants to prove their cases, as compared to the old definition. A claimant is not obliged to prove the existence of a rule or condition constituting an absolute bar. This means that practices and policies which disadvantage certain groups can constitute indirect discrimination under the new definition. There is also now no requirement to show that a particular racial group is actually disadvantaged (compared to the other racial group) by the policy or practice in question; it is sufficient to establish that the nature of the policy or practice is such that those of a particular racial group are likely to be disadvantaged by it. Further, the statutory definition makes it clear that the courts should consider the concept of proportionality when assessing whether the policy or practice in question is justified; this entails balancing the discriminatory effects of the measure against the importance of the aim that the defendant seeks to achieve.

## Victimisation

10.103    Victimisation arises where a person is treated less favourably than others are or would be treated in comparable circumstances, by reason of the fact that the person has done a protected act, such as brought proceedings against the discriminator under the RRA 1976 or alleged that another person has committed an act, which would amount to a breach of the Act.[175]

10.104    In the police context it could arise where officers act against someone who has made a police complaint including allegations of race discrimination.

10.105    The comparison to be drawn for the purposes of establishing victimisation should focus on how the alleged discriminator would treat others who had not undertaken the protected act.[176] Accordingly, if the claim is that an officer arrested the claimant because he or she had previously made a police complaint of racism against that officer; the comparison to be drawn is with how the officer would have treated someone who had not made a complaint at all, rather than with how he or she would have treated someone who complained about a non-race related matter.

10.106    It is unnecessary to show that the alleged discriminator had a motive which was consciously connected with the race relations legislation; establishing that the discriminator was consciously or

---

175    RRA 1976 s2.
176    *Chief Constable of West Yorkshire Police v Khan* [2000] IRLR 324.

subconsciously influenced by the fact that the claimant has done a protected act is sufficient.[177]

## Harassment

10.107 The RRA(A)R 2003 also create a new statutory concept of racial harassment. Like the new definition of indirect discrimination discussed at para 10.101 above, it only applies to discrimination on the grounds of race or ethnic or national origins that comes within RRA 1976 s1(1B). Accordingly, it will primarily be of use to those who have dealings with the police in the context of being victims of crime, rather than suspects. It might, for example, apply where officers engaged in racially abusive behaviour towards a person who they felt had made a groundless or trivial report of a crime. Harassment is defined as follows:

> (1) A person subjects another to harassment in any circumstances relevant for the purposes of any provision referred to in section 1(1B) where on grounds of race or ethnic or national origins he engages in unwanted conduct which has the purpose or effect of:
> (a) violating that other person's dignity; or
> (b) creating an intimidating, hostile, degrading, humiliating or offensive environment for him.
>
> (2) Conduct should be regard as having the effect specified in paragraph (a) or (b) of subsection (1) only if, having regard to all the circumstances, including in particular the perception of that other person, it should reasonably be considered as having that effect.[178]

The statutory definition does not require the claimant to show that he or she was treated less favourably than a person of a different race. However, any evidence to that effect will assist in showing that the treatment in question was on the grounds of race rather than for some other reason.

10.108 The conduct in question may either be intended to cause the circumstances set out in RRA 1976 s3A(1)(a) or (b) ('has the purpose of') or, irrespective of intention, has that effect in practice. In many instances conduct complained of will fall within both limbs (a) and (b), although it is conceivable that a 'one off' incident might solely fall under (a). When judging the effect of the conduct complained of, the court has to apply the test contained in RRA 1976 s3A(2), which involves an objective evaluation of the consequences of that behaviour. This is clearly intended to avoid liability resulting from a situation where the

---

177 *Naragajan v London Regional Transport* [1999] IRLR 572, HL.
178 RRA(A) R 2003 reg 5, inserting a new s3A into the RRA 1976.

claimant has been unduly sensitive. However, the statutory wording makes clear that, in making the judgment, the court has to take into account the victim's perception.

10.109 Conduct that could amount to harassment may also be direct discrimination, so that in many instances it would be advisable to plead both.[179]

## Burden of proof

10.110 The RRA(A)R 2003 have also amended the way the burden of proof operates. As with the new definitions of indirect discrimination and harassment (see paras 10.101 and 10.107), this concept only applies in relation to discrimination claims made on the grounds of race or ethnic or national origins which involve conduct coming within RRA 1976 s1(1B).

10.111 RRA 1976 s57ZA(2) provides that:

> Where, on the hearing of the claim the claimant proves facts from which the court could, apart from this section, conclude in the absence of an adequate explanation that the respondent –
>
> (a) Has committed such an act of discrimination or harassment against the claimant, or
> (b) Is by virtue of section 32 or 34 to be treated as having committed such an act of discrimination or harassment against the claimant.
>
> The court shall uphold the claim unless the respondent proves that he did not commit or, as the case may be, is not to be treated as having committed, that act.

10.112 The effect of this provision is that the burden of proof shifts to the defendant in circumstances where the claimant proves facts from which the court could conclude in the absence of an adequate explanation that the defendant had committed an unlawful act of discrimination. The difference brought about by this provision appears to be that where the claimant shows that he or she was treated less favourably than a person of a different racial group was or would have been treated, if the alleged wrongdoer does not supply an adequate explanation for the apparent differential, the court must find direct discrimination proved, whereas previously the court had a choice as to whether to draw such an inference in the circumstances.[180] The courts

---

179 Harassment that is not based on racial grounds could in any event give rise to a claim under the Protection from Harassment Act 1997 – see para 6.120 onwards.

180 See the discussion of *King v Great Britain-China Centre* [1991] IRLR 513, CA at para 10.94.

have given detailed guidance on the way the shifting burden of proof operates on practice[181]

10.113    Unlike the other changes introduced by the RRA(A)R 2003, which only apply to events occurring after the regulations came into force, the change to the burden of proof applies to proceedings begun before 19 July 2003 (the commencement date of the regulations), provided they have not yet been determined.[182]

## Discriminatory conduct prohibited by the Race Relations Act 1976

10.114   As explained above, when the effect of the RRA 1976 was summarised, as well as showing that the conduct in question amounted to a form of prohibited discrimination, the claimant must show that the behaviour in question was of a type outlawed by the legislation. So far as claims against the police are concerned, the applicable provisions are RRA 1976 ss19B and 20. If the conduct does not come within one or other of these provisions, liability will not be established. Section 20 is considered first, as section 19B is a residual section that should only be relied upon if the behaviour in question is not already covered by another provision of the RRA 1976.[183]

### RRA 1976 s20

10.115   RRA 1976 s20 provides that:

> (1) It is unlawful for any person concerned with the provision (for payment or not) of goods, facilities, or services to the public or a section to the public to discriminate against a person who seeks to obtain or use those goods, facilities or services–
>    (a) by refusing or deliberately omitting to provide him with any of them; or
>    (b) by refusing or deliberately omitting to provide him with goods, facilities or services of the like quality, in the like manner and on the like terms as are normal in the first-mentioned person's case and in relation to other members of the public or (where the person so seeking belongs to a section of the public) to other members of that section.

10.116   The key issue is the extent to which policing functions can be described as the provision of goods, facilities or services for these purposes.

---

181   See *Barton v Investec Henderson Crosthwaite Securities Limited* [2003] IRLR 332, EAT and *IGGN Ltd v Wong* [2005] EWCA Civ 142.
182   Reg 2(2).
183   RRA 1976 s19(6).

The section does give some examples of activities that would fall within it and the instances given include: 'the services of any ... public authority'.[184] Thus it is clear that the ambit of the provision extends significantly beyond the acts or omissions of commercial enterprises. It has been recognised that the fact that the conduct in question is done in pursuance of a statutory duty does not preclude it from falling within section 20.[185] In *Farah v Commissioner of Police of the Metropolis*[186] the Court of Appeal held that a police officer's duties involved with giving assistance and/or protection to victims of crime, could amount to the provision of a service for these purposes. The claimant in *Farah*, a Somali refugee, alleged that she had been attacked by white youths with a dog, but that when she called the police for help and protection they attended and arrested her instead of her assailants. The court held that this complaint was capable of falling within section 20.

10.117    The scope of RRA 1976 s20 in police cases was considered for a second time by the Court of Appeal in *Brooks v Commissioner of Police of the Metropolis*.[187] This case concerned a claim brought by Duwayne Brooks, who was present with his friend Stephen Lawrence when the latter was murdered. He complained that police officers had failed to give him proper assistance and support and also that they had failed to investigate the crime adequately. The defendant contended that only the former aspects of this complaint could fall within section 20. The *Farah* case did not deal directly with alleged discrimination by way of inadequate investigation. The Court of Appeal in *Brooks* held that it was inappropriate to draw a 'sharp' distinction between the two types of function, which in many instances would shade into each other. The court held that the investigation of crime could amount to the provision of services to the victim of the offence. The court also held that the claimant did not have to make an express request for police services for the section to apply; the request could be implied from the circumstances, for example if police witnessed a crime but decided not to become involved in the situation.[188]

10.118    Neither the *Farah* nor the *Brooks* cases involved a claim by a suspect, rather than a victim of crime. However, a court would be unlikely to

---

184    RRA 1976 s20(2).
185    See *Savjani v Inland Revenue Commissioners* [1981] QB 458, CA.
186    [1997] 1 All ER 289, CA.
187    [2002] EWCA Civ 407.
188    *Brooks v Commissioner of Police of the Metropolis* was to be considered by the House of Lords only in relation to the claim in negligence (discussed in chapter 8).

regard the actions of arrest, detention or prosecution as the provision of services or facilities to those on the receiving end of them.

10.119    The issue of whether conduct falls within section 19B or section 20 still has a practical importance; as explained earlier the changes introduced by the RRA(A)R in 2003 apply to conduct falling within section 20 but are unlikely to cover many policing functions that fall under section 19B (see paras 10.101, 10.107 and 10.110 above).

## RRA 1976 s19B

10.120    As has been mentioned earlier, the RRA(A)A 2003 inserted a new section 19B into the RRA 1976, making it:

> ... unlawful for a public authority in carrying out any functions of the authority to do any act which constitutes discrimination.

10.121    'Any functions' is a very wide concept. It has the effect of applying the RRA to all policing functions, for example those listed earlier at para 10.84.

10.122    'Public authority' is also a wide concept for this purpose. This means that law enforcement functions are covered whether undertaken by the police, Customs and Excise, local authority officers or tax inspectors. The Prison Service and the CPS are also covered. The Act does not contain a specific definition of 'public authority', but gives examples of what it does and does not include. 'Any person certain of whose functions are functions of a public nature' is a public authority.[189] However, the statute also provides that 'a person is not a public authority by virtue only of subsection (2)(a) if the nature of the act is private'.[190] These provisions introduce a very similar concept of a public authority to that applicable in relation to the Human Rights Act 1998,[191] under which a threefold classification is adopted:

- 'pure' public bodies: where all the functions undertaken by the particular body are public ones for the purposes of RRA 1976 s19B, because of the public nature of the body in question, this includes local authorities, police officers, prison officers, immigration officers and the other law enforcement agencies referred to above;
- 'hybrid' bodies: who are not public bodies by their very nature, but are only public authorities for these purposes when carrying

---

189    RRA 1976 s19B(2)(a); exceptions are set out in s19B(3).
190    RRA 1976 s19B(4).
191    See para 10.172 on claims under the Human Rights Act 1998.

out public functions. For example, Group 4 is a private company but could be acting as a public authority when carrying out security duties involving prisoners or immigration detainees;
- 'pure' private bodies who carry out no public functions.

10.123 Section 19B does not apply to any 'judicial act' (whether done by a court, tribunal or other person) or to 'any act done on the instruction of or on behalf of a person acting in a judicial capacity'.[192]

10.124 Section 19F provides that section 19B does not apply to a decision not to institute criminal proceedings, to any act done for the purpose of enabling such a decision to be made, to a decision not to continue criminal proceedings, to any act done for the purposes of enabling that decision to be made, or to any act done for the purposes of securing that proceedings are not continued. It should be noted that the section 19F exception does not extend to a decision to institute criminal proceedings or to continue them, or to any act done for the purposes of enabling such decisions to be made. Accordingly a claim that a person was prosecuted for racially discriminatory reasons could be brought against the police and/or the CPS or other law enforcement agency, as it would not be caught by this exemption. The scope of this exception relating to a decision not to prosecute or to the discontinuance of a prosecution has yet to be resolved by the courts. Defendants could argue that 'an act done for the purposes of enabling [the] decision to be made' is sufficiently broad to cover the totality of the police investigation that led up to the decision not to prosecute. Such a broad construction of section 19F would be undesirable from a claimant's perspective as it would rule out claims where a decision not to prosecute was in turn the product of deficient policing resulting from racial factors – for example where a claim of racist assault was not properly investigated because officers did not treat the allegation with appropriate seriousness. Statements made in parliament during the passing of the Act support a more restricted construction of this exception: it was said that the exemption should be '... no wider than it needs to be to preserve the role of the criminal courts as the sole forum for determining guilt', so that 'significant but remote' acts such as the initial arrest and the gathering and assessment of the evidence should be subject to section 19B.[193]

192   RRA 1976 s19C(1)(a) and (b).
193   HL Debates, col 180, 14 December 1999; col 589, 11 January 2000.

*Vicarious and secondary liability*

10.125　Prior to the enactment of the RRA(A)A 2003, chief officers of police were not vicariously liable for the discriminatory acts of their officers, as the Court of Appeal had decided that the provision in the Police Act which usually renders the chief officer of police liable for the torts of his or her officers did not apply to the RRA 1976.[194] Suing individual officers was impractical, cumbersome and unlikely to yield any compensation if the defendant had limited assets. However, the RR(A)A 2000 makes chief police officers vicariously liable for their officers' acts.[195] It also makes provision for payment from police funds of any awards made against chief officers of police or for settlement of claims by him or her[196] or for awards made against those under the direction and control of chief officers of police or for settlement of such claims.[197] The new provisions concerning vicarious liability apply to the National Crime Intelligence Service, the National Crime Squad and any other body of constables or cadets.[198] This effectively puts police officers on the same footing as 'employees' for the purposes of the RRA.

10.126　Chief officers can be protected against such claims if they can show that they took reasonable steps to prevent the act of discrimination.[199] This defence could not be raised in a claim brought against the individual officers responsible for the discrimination. Thus, the claimant will need to consider whether to proceed against both individual officers and the chief officer in relation to any race claim and to ask at an early stage whether the chief officer intends to avail him or herself of the RRA 1976 s32 defence. If not, the individual officers need not be pursued further. In practice, chief officers have rarely relied upon this defence so far, but may be more likely to do so if and when they have taken substantial steps to discharge their positive duties under the RRA 1976 (discussed at paras 10.144–10.146).

10.127　If the defence is raised, advisers will need to look at the particular force to see if it has comprehensive guidelines and procedures for eliminating race discrimination. The extent to which complaints relating to race discrimination are adequately dealt with and the effective

---

194　*Farah v Commissioner of Police of the Metropolis* [1997] 1 All ER 289, CA. For a discussion of the general position relating to vicarious liability in actions against the police see para 11.107 onwards.
195　RRA 1976 s76A(3).
196　RRA 1976 s76A(4).
197　RRA 1976 s76A(6).
198　RRA 1976 s76B.
199　RRA 1976 s32(3).

training of officers with regard to race discrimination may also be relevant.

10.128    It is also unlawful to 'knowingly aid a person in committing an unlawful act'.[200] Further, a person who 'knowingly or recklessly makes a false statement to induce another person to believe that an unlawful act which they are assisting is not unlawful' commits not only an unlawful act but also a criminal offence.[201] However, the decision of the House of Lords in *Hallam v Avery*[202] appears to have narrowed the breadth of the concept of 'knowingly aiding' a person in committing discrimination. The House of Lords held that the requirement that the assistance is provided 'knowingly' meant that the secondary party knew that the party from whom his liability is alleged to derive is treating or is about to treat or is contemplating treating the clamant in a discriminatory way. Thus if the defendant does not know that this will occur, or only suspects that it will happen, no liability will arise. In *Hallam* itself it was claimed that police had aided a local authority to discriminate against gypsies as they had advised the council to impose additional conditions on the hire of one of its rooms on the grounds that the event was a 'gypsy wedding'. The claim failed as the requisite knowledge on the part of the police could not be shown.

## Procedure

### Jurisdiction and mode of trial

10.129  Claims under RRA 1976 Pt III (which includes sections 19B and 20, discussed above) may be made the subject of civil proceedings in the like manner to any other claims in tort.[203] Claims of race discrimination may only be brought in a 'designated' county court.[204] The county court has exclusive jurisdiction, so that claims under the RRA 1976 cannot be brought in the High Court.[205]

10.130    In cases where claims are brought under both the RRA 1976 and for false imprisonment and/or malicious prosecution, difficulties may arise in relation to mode of trial. The common law claims will usually entitle the parties to a jury trial.[206] However, in race discrimination

---

200   RRA 1976 s33(1).
201   RRA 1976 s33(4).
202   [2001] 1 WLR 655.
203   RRA 1976 s57(1).
204   RRA 1976 s57.
205   RRA 1976 s57(2).
206   As discussed in chapter 12.

cases the judge must sit with assessors unless the parties consent to the judge sitting without them.[207] The court normally sits with two assessors. The Court of Appeal has confirmed that where assessors sit in claims brought under the RRA 1976, their role extends to assisting the judge with making findings of fact.[208] Accordingly, it is hard to envisage how one trial could take place involving both a jury and assessors because their respective fact-finding roles would overlap with each other.

10.131    Thus in cases that involve both claims under the RRA 1976 and common law torts of false imprisonment and/or malicious prosecution, it seems that the parties will either have to agree to trial by jury or trial with assessors or else the race discrimination claim will have to be severed from the common law claims and be the subject of a separate trial heard with assessors. Advisers would need to consider the relative merits of a trial before a jury against a trial before experienced race relations assessors. If, for example, the allegation is that the acts or omissions by the police were due to a particular racial stereotyping, then advisers may prefer experienced race assessors to a jury. Other examples of where assessors could be preferable from a claimants' prospective would be an indirect discrimination claim where fairly subtle effects of a particular policy or rule had to be assessed or where a court was being asked to consider questions relating to the implementation of the positive duties contained in the RRA 1976 (discussed at paras 10.144–10.146). However, where the claim turns on credibility issues, a jury may be preferable.

10.132    If the RRA 1976 claim was severed with a view to the court holding two separate trials, advisers would need to consider carefully which trial should be heard first. The second trial could well be settled before a full hearing, based on the outcome of the first trial. Practitioners should be aware of the difficulties of getting public funding to extend to two trials, if the claims involved in the second trial were not compromised.

## Time limits

10.133   The primary rule is that claims under the RRA 1976 must be brought within six months less one day from the date of the act complained of.[209] There is a two-month extension where a claim is made to the

---

207   RRA 1976 s67(4).
208   *Ahmed v Governing Body of Oxford University* [2003] 1 WLR 195.
209   RRA 1976 s68(2).

Commission for Racial Equality for assistance within the six-month period.[210] The Commission has the power to extend time by a further month if it cannot reach a decision in the first two months, and often does so.

10.134　　The court has discretion to extend time where it considers that it is just and equitable to do so in all the circumstances of the case.[211] This is a very broad discretion and will include a consideration of factors such as prejudice to the defendant, when the defendant was first notified of a possible claim, the merits of the case, the reasons for the apparent delay, whether the claim concerns facts that in any event form the subject of common law claims that will be pursued and whether part of the RRA 1976 claim is in time.[212]

10.135　　If a claimant shows that the act complained of is in fact a series of related acts constituting 'an act extending over a period', then time runs from the last of those acts.[213] So far, the jurisprudence in relation to 'continuing' acts has been in the employment context. It has been held that a policy, even if an informal rule or practice may constitute a continuing act for the purposes of extending the period of time.[214] In *Hendricks v Commissioner of Police of the Metropolis*[215] the Court of Appeal adopted a broad interpretation of what amounted to an act extending over a period and held that the employment claim involving more than 50 officers and 100 incidents over 11 years in different police stations constituted a continuing act for the purpose of the RRA 1976. The Court of Appeal said that the crucial distinction was between events that were linked by, for example, a discriminatory practice and events that were unconnected or isolated. Thus, for example, if a claimant was harassed by a number of different officers over a several year period, but the harassment all stemmed from a racially prejudiced entry about the claimant on the force's computer or from the fact that the claimant had earlier made a complaint of race discrimination against one of the officers involved, then the act extending over a period test would arguably be met.

10.136　　In any event, acts that are time barred may still form part of the evidence in the case from which inferences of discrimination may be drawn. For example if an officer racially abused the claimant some

---

210　RRA 1976 s68(3).
211　RRA 1976 s68(6).
212　See *Southwark LBC v Afolabi* [2003] IRLR 220 where the Court of Appeal considered the factors in the 'checklist' set out in *British Coal Corp v Keeble* [1997] IRLR 336.
213　RRA 1976 s68(7).
214　*Cast v Croydon College* [1998] IRLR 318, CA.
215　*Hendricks v Commissioner of Police* [2003] IRLR 96.

years ago, a claim in relation to that abuse may be statute barred, but if years later the same officer stops and searches the claimant for no apparent reason, the earlier abuse may be evidence used in support of the contention that the subsequent stop was on racial grounds.

## Quantum

10.137   As far as remedies are concerned, the claim is treated in much the same way as any other claim in tort for breach of statutory duty.[216] Accordingly, a victim of race discrimination may claim compensation for the consequences of the discriminatory act, for example for wrongful detention and/or the stress of a prosecution and/or psychiatric injury. Unlike the position in relation to personal injuries arising out of negligence, the claimant does not have to show that any injury relied upon was the reasonably foreseeable result of the wrongdoing, provided that it was the natural and direct consequence of it.[217] In addition the claimant may claim a declaration that his or her rights have been violated.

10.138    In race discrimination cases, unlike in the majority of other torts, basic damages can include an award for the claimant's injury to feelings.[218] The Scottish Court of Sessions has recently confirmed that injury to feelings awards in goods and services cases should be no lower than those made in employment cases.[219]

10.139    The Court of Appeal has given general guidance on the quantum of awards for injuries to feelings in the employment context.[220] It is likely that the courts will apply this guidance by analogy in discrimination claims against the police. The guidance given was as follows:

 i. The top band should normally be between £15,000 and £25,000. Sums in this range should be awarded in the most serious cases, such as where there has been a lengthy campaign of discriminatory harassment on the grounds of sex or race. Only in the most exceptional case should an award of compensation for injury to feelings exceed £25,000.

 ii. The middle band of between £5,000 and £15,000 should be used for serious cases, which do not merit an award in the highest band.

 iii. Awards of between £500 and £5,000 are appropriate for less serious cases, such as where the act of discrimination is an isolated or a one off occurrence. In general, awards of less than £500 are to be

---

216 RRA 1976 s57(1).
217 *Essa v Laing Ltd* [2004] IRLR 313, CA.
218 RRA 1976 s57(4).
219 *Purves v Joydisk* [2003] IRLR 420.
220 *Vento v Chief Constable of Yorkshire Police (No 2)* [2003] ICR 318.

avoided, as they risk being regarded as so low as not to be a proper recognition of injury to feelings.[221]

10.140 Aggravated damages may also be awarded in circumstances similar to those referred to in *Thompson and Hsu v Commissioner of Police of the Metropolis*.[222] Aggravating features may include the way that the proceedings have been defended.[223] Other compensatory losses, such as for psychiatric injury or for loss of earnings, are calculated on normal tortious compensation principles.

10.141 Exemplary damages can now be awarded under the RRA 1976 as a result of the decision of the House of Lords in *Kuddus v Chief Constable of Leicestershire*.[224]

10.142 No award of damages may be made in respect of a claim of indirect discrimination if the defendant proves that the requirement or condition was not applied with the intention of treating the claimant unfavourably on racial grounds. However, intention in this context does not refer to the defendant's motivation, but to his or her state of mind as may apper to his or her knowledge of the consequences of the act. Thus, if the defendant is aware of the disparate adverse effect that will result from the treatment, it may be inferred that he intended to produce those consequences, even though they were not the purpose of so acting.[225]

10.143 RR(A)A 2000 s5 imposes certain procedural limitations on race discrimination claims arising out of criminal investigations. This applies where the discriminator carries out 'public investigator functions' or 'functions as a public prosecutor'. RRA 1976 s57(4A) provides that a court need not provide any remedy other than damages or a declaration, if to do so will prejudice an on-going criminal investigation.[226] Nevertheless, if the court is satisfied that an alternative remedy would not prejudice a criminal investigation, a decision to institute criminal proceedings or any criminal proceedings, then such an alternative may be imposed.[227]

---

221 *Doshoki v Draeger* [2002] IRLR 340 suggests that the minimum award for race discrimination is now £750.
222 [1997] 2 All ER 762, discussed at para 14.15 onwards.
223 *Zaiwalla & Co v Walia* [2002] IRLR 697.
224 [2001] 3 All ER 193.
225 *JH Walker Limited v Hussain* [1996] ICR 291, EAT.
226 The provision also enables a defendant to obtain an adjournment of the trial if the same test is met.
227 RRA 1976 s57(4A)–(4C).

*Positive duty on public authorities*

10.144  The RR(A)A 2000 gives statutory force to the imperative of tackling institutionalised racism.[228]

## General duty

10.145  The RR(A)A 2000 requires public authorities, in carrying out their functions, to have due regard to the need to eliminate unlawful race discrimination, and to promote equality of opportunity and good race relations.[229] This general duty has the effect of requiring public authorities to consider the implications for racial equality of all their activities. The duty applies to those bodies listed in RR(A)A 2000 Sch 1A. This includes all the main policing bodies. Accordingly, for example, police forces are required to have regard to the matters contained in the general duty when policies are formulated or revised. A breach of the general duty cannot of itself give rise to a civil claim for damages for breach of statutory duty. However, a failure to have regard to the duty could provide evidence of discriminatory attitudes in a particular force. Non-compliance with this duty may also be relevant to the question of whether a chief officer can establish the 'reasonable steps' defence (see para 10.126 in relation to vicarious liability). If the proposed claim seeks to attack a public law decision-making process, for example the introduction of a new policy, by an application for judicial review, a failure to have regard to the general duty could be relied on to support the claim.

## Specific duties

10.146  In addition the Secretary of State has powers to impose specific duties on police forces and oblige them to produce racial equality schemes by 31 May 2002.[230] Non-compliance with these duties is a matter for enforcement by the Commission for Racial Equality by way of compliance notices.[231] However, evidence of non-compliance could be relevant to a claim against the police in a similar way to that discussed above in relation to the general duty. Several police forces currently face the threat of enforcement proceedings by the Commission for failing to produce adequate racial equality schemes.

228  See Stephen Lawrence inquiry report, Sir William MacPherson, TSO CM4261–I, Stationery Office, para 6.34.
229  RRA 1976 s71(1).
230  RRA 1976 s71(2) and Race Relations Act 1976 (Statutory Duties) Order 2001 SI No 3458.
231  RRA 1976 s71E(4).

## Codes of practice

10.147 The Commission for Racial Equality is also empowered to issue codes of practice providing practical guidance that will enable public authorities to understand what they must do to comply with their general and specific duties. A breach of a provision of the code does not of itself give rise to a liability, but may be taken into account in a civil claim if considered by the court to be relevant to any question arising in the proceedings.[232]

## Sex Discrimination Act 1975

10.148 The forms of discrimination prohibited by the Sex Discrimination Act (SDA) 1975 are very similar to those covered by the RRA 1976. Unlawful discrimination may be by way of direct discrimination, if the claimant is treated less favourably than another on the grounds of gender.[233] Discrimination on the grounds of sexual orientation is not covered by the SDA 1975.[234] The original definition of indirect discrimination in the SDA 1975 mirrors the original definition of indirect discrimination in the RRA 1976 discussed at paras 10.96–10.99.[235] Under the SDA 1975 the definition of indirect discrimination has only been amended in relation to activities in the employment sphere and the original definition still applies to police cases. Victimisation is defined in a very similar way under the SDA 1975 to the definition contained in the RRA 1976, discussed at paras 10.103–10.106.[236] There is no specific, statutory tort of sexual harassment equivalent to the statutory tort of racial harassment, discussed at paras 10.107–10.109. However, most instances of sexual harassment would in any event amount to direct discrimination and so be actionable on that basis.

10.149    SDA 1975 s29, concerning the provision of goods, facilities and services, is in the same terms as RRA 1976 s20. Accordingly, the earlier discussion as to the applicability of section 20 to policing functions applies equally to a contemplated claim under the SDA 1975 (see paras 10.115–10.119). However, the range of conduct by police officers covered by the SDA 1975 is substantially narrower than that covered by the RRA 1976 because the SDA 1975 contains no equivalent to

232  RRA 1976 s71C. For Codes issued see www.cre.gov.uk.
233  SDA 1975 s1(1)(a).
234  *Pearce v Governing Body of Mayfield Secondary School* [2003] ICR 937, HL.
235  SDA 1975 s1(1)(b).
236  SDA 1975 s4.

RRA 1976 s19B (discussed at paras 10.120–10.124). Accordingly the SDA 1975 will predominantly apply in relation to discriminatory treatment by police officers towards victims of crime, rather than towards those who are suspects.

10.150    The chief officer of police is vicariously liable for the acts of his or her officers under the SDA 1975 with effect from 19 July 2003.[237] Provisions relating to practice and procedure under the SDA 1975 mirror those in the RRA 1976.

## Disability Discrimination Act 1995

10.151 The definition of disability for the purposes of the Disability Discrimination Act (DDA) 1995 is a complex issue and a detailed consideration of the same is beyond the scope of this work.[238]

10.152    In summary 'disability' is defined by DDA1995 s1, which provides:

> (1) A person has a disability for the purposes of this Act if he has a physical or mental impairment which has a substantial and a long-term adverse effect on his ability to carry out normal day to day activities.

10.153 A disabled person for the purposes of the Act is someone who has a disability.[239] What may amount to a 'mental impairment' is dealt with in Sch 1 to the Act. Physical impairment is not specifically defined. Various conditions are specifically excluded from the definition of mental impairment.[240] 'Normal day to day activities' is not as broad a concept as might first appear; Sch 1 contains an exhaustive list of what are day to day activities for these purposes, including mobility, manual dexterity, speech, hearing and eyesight. The substantial adverse effect must relate to one or more of these activities. The Act also provides that the effect of treatment should be disregarded for the purposes of assessing whether a person has a disability.[241] 'Long term' is defined by the Act as lasting for at least 12 months or likely to last for at least that period.[242] Save in the most obvious of cases, expert evidence establishing that a claimant has a disability as defined by these provisions will be required.

---

237  Sex Discrimination Act 1975 (Amendment Regulations) 2003 SI No 1657.
238  See, eg, Palmer, Gill, Monaghan, Moon and Stacey, *Discrimination Law Handbook*, LAG, 2002, for a more detailed treatment of this issue.
239  DDA 1995 s1(2).
240  See Disability Discrimination (Meaning of Disability) Regulations 1996 SI No 1455.
241  DDA 1995 Sch 1 para 6.
242  DDA 1995 Sch 1 para 2.

10.154    The forms of discrimination outlawed by the DDA 1995 are a little different to those examined in relation to the RRA 1976. There is a similar concept of victimisation.[243] There is no concept of indirect discrimination, as such. The only kind of conduct prohibited by the DDA 1995 that is likely to be relevant to policing cases is that covered by the section dealing with the provision of goods, facilities and services, as there is no equivalent to RRA 1976 s19B prohibiting discrimination by public authorities (see paras 10.120–10.124). Thus, as with the SDA 1975, it is much more likely that victims of crime, rather than suspected offenders, will have the opportunity to bring successful claims under the DDA 1995. The goods, facilities and services provision of the DDA 1995 is section 19. The scope of this section generally equates to the scope of RRA 1976 s20, discussed at paras 10.115–10.119. However, unlike the position under the RRA 1976, the DDA 1995 contains a particular definition of discrimination applicable to conduct falling within the provision of goods, facilities and services section. Thus, DDA 1995 s20(1) states that a provider of goods, facilities or services discriminates against a disabled person if:

(a) for a reason which relates to the disabled person's disability, he treats him less favourably than he treats all the others to whom that reason does not or would not apply; and

(b) he cannot show the treatment in question is justified.

10.155    There are two main differences between this concept of direct discrimination and the definition of direct discrimination in the RRA 1976 (discussed at paras 10.80–10.88). The first is that the claimant has to show that the treatment complained of relates to his or her disability, but does not have to show that he or she was treated less favourably than those in equivalent circumstances who were not so disabled.[244] Thus, in the employment context, a person who is treated adversely because he or she is on protracted sick leave may be so treated by reason of his or her disability, even though other employees would have been similarly disciplined or dismissed if they had been absent for other reasons unconnected with disability. Accordingly, the difficult issues presented by the need to establish how a comparator would have been treated under the RRA 1976 (see paras 10.887–10.88), do not arise in relation to the DDA 1995. The second major difference between direct discrimination under the DDA 1995 and under the

---

243   DDA 1995 s55.

244   The distinction was highlighted by the Court of Appeal in *Clark v Novacold* [1999] IRLR 318.

RRA 1976, is that in the former instance the defendant may justify the alleged discrimination. To establish the justification defence the defendant needs to show that in the opinion of the provider of the relevant service one or more of a number of prescribed conditions are satisfied (for example, that the treatment is necessary so as not to endanger the health and safety of any person) and that it is reasonable in all the circumstances of the case for the service provided to hold that opinion.[245]

10.156   Unlawful discrimination under the DDA 1995 can also be committed where the provider of services fails to comply with a duty to make reasonable adjustments.[246] The duty arises as follows:

> Where a provider of services has a practice, policy or procedure which makes it impossible or unreasonably difficult for disabled persons to make use of the service which he provides, or is prepared to provide, to other members of the public, it is his duty to take such steps as is reasonable in all the circumstances of the case, for him to have to take in order to change that practice, policy or procedure, so that it no longer has that effect.[247]

10.157   Thus these provisions of the DDA 1995 may require the police, for example, to make particular arrangements for the way in which witness statements are taken from disabled victims of crime and/or in relation to the way that they are kept informed as to the progress of the investigation. Since October 2004, DDA 1995 s21(2) has imposed a duty on service providers to adjust physical features – such as access to buildings – that make it impossible or unreasonably difficult for disabled persons to make use of the services provided. Again, a defence of justification can be raised.

10.158   Chief officers of police are vicariously liable for disability discrimination undertaken by their officers with effect from 1 October 2004.[248] Issues relating to practice and procedure under the DDA 1995 are similar to those discussed above in relation to claims brought under the RRA 1976.

245   DDA 1995 s20(3) and (4).

246   DDA 1995 s20(2).

247   DDA 1995 s21(1). There is also a specific duty imposed in relation to the provision of auxiliary aids such as the use of a sign language interpreter: see s21(4).

248   Disability Discrimination Act 1995 (Amendment) Regulations 2003 SI No 1673.

# Human Rights Act 1998

10.159 The European Convention on Human Rights provides at article 14 that:

> The enjoyment of the rights and freedoms set forth in this Convention shall be enjoyed without discrimination on any grounds such as sex, race, colour, language, religion, political or other opinion, national or social origin, association with a minority, property, birth or other status.

A claim for an infringement of article 14 is brought by way of a claim under the Human Rights Act 1998.[249]

10.160 The issues that need to be considered by the courts in assessing whether an infringement of article 14 has been established, are as follows:

- Do the facts fall within the ambit of one or more of the Convention rights?
- If so, was there a difference in treatment in respect of that right between the claimant and those put forward for comparison?
- If so, was the difference in treatment on one or more of the proscribed grounds protected by article 14?
- If so, were the others relied upon for comparison in an analogous situation?
- If so, was the difference in treatment objectively justifiable in the sense that it had a legitimate aim and bore a reasonable relationship of proportionality to that aim?[250]

These points will be discussed in turn.

## Facts within the ambit of a Convention right

10.161 Article 14 does not provide a 'free standing right' to claim for unlawful discrimination. As its wording makes clear, article 14 affords protection against discrimination in the exercise of the other rights protected by the Convention. Thus, a discrimination claim cannot be brought in reliance on article 14 if the conduct in question is

---

249 See paras 10.222–10.230 for an account of the relevant provisions governing the practice and procedure in relation to such claims.

250 *Wandsworth LBC v Michalak* [2003] 1 WLR 617, CA at [20], as amplified in *R (Carson) v Secretary of State for Work and Pensions* [2003] 3 All ER 577, CA at [52] and approved in *R (Marper) v Chief Constable of South Yorkshire* [2004] 1 WLR 2196, HL.

251 *Rasmussen v Denmark* (1995) 7 EHRR 371; *Abdulaziz, Cabales & Balkandali v UK* (1985) 7 EHRR 471.

unrelated to any of the substantive rights protected by the Convention. However, the claimant does not need to show that the conduct amounted to a breach of any of the other rights guaranteed by the Convention. It is sufficient if he or she shows that the treatment complained of falls 'within the ambit' or 'the subject matter' protected by another Convention right.[251] This is a fairly broad concept and the relationship between the conduct complained of and the protection afforded by another article of the Convention may be a loose one.[252] Thus, if discriminatory policing could be shown, a claim under article 14 might arise, for example, as a result of:

- an inadequate investigation into a death in custody – conduct potentially falling within the ambit of article 2;[253]
- a failure to take due care of a suspect in custody – conduct potentially falling within the ambit of article 2;[254]
- strip searching or other actions capable of seriously humiliating the claimant – conduct potentially falling within the ambit of article 3;[255]
- arrest or detention – conduct potentially falling within the ambit of article 5;[256]
- failures to act to prevent foreseeable attacks – conduct potentially falling within articles 2, 3 and/or 8;[257]
- restrictions on prisoners' access to family visits – conduct potentially falling within the ambit of article 8;
- refusal to provide prisoners of a certain religion with prayer facilities – conduct potentially falling within the ambit of article 9.

## A difference in treatment

10.162 This will usually be self-evident, once the relevant evidence has been assembled. The treatment of hypothetical comparators can be relied upon, as discussed in relation to the RRA 1976 above.

---

252  For a more detailed discussion of the case law in this area see Starmer, *European Human Rights Law*, LAG, 2000.
253  The case law on this issue is discussed at para 8.49.
254  The case law on this issue is discussed at para 8.60.
255  Article 3 is discussed in this context at para 6.109.
256  Article 5 is discussed at paras 6.13–6.15.
257  As discussed at paras 8.44–8.47.

## Treatment on a proscribed ground

10.163 Article 14 itself lists a number of grounds upon which discrimination is prohibited by the Convention, namely: sex, race, colour, language, religion, political or other opinion, national or social origin, association with a minority, property and birth. However, this list is not exhaustive as the words 'such as' and 'other status' in article 14 make clear. By way of example, 'other status' has been held to include discrimination on the grounds of sexual orientation,[258] age[259] and poverty.[260] However, the grounds of discrimination covered by article 14 are not unlimited. 'Other status' refers to a ground analogous to those listed in the article and in particular contemplates that discrimination is on the basis of a personal characteristic of the claimant.[261] In *Marper*, claimants whose fingerprints and DNA were retained after the conclusion of a criminal investigation failed in their claim based on article 14 partly on the basis that the retention of this material arose from the historical fact that the material was lawfully taken at the time and not from any personal characteristic of the claimants.

## An analogous situation

10.164 Additionally, it is necessary to show a difference of treatment in comparison to other persons in an analogous or relevantly similar situation. Thus, for example, claims based on article 14 failed where the claimant sought to compare the treatment of married and unmarried couples[262] and where the claimant sought to compare the treatment of juvenile and adult prisoners.[263] A similar concept has been discussed above in relation to direct discrimination under the RRA 1976 (see para 10.87).

## Justification

10.165 Unlike in relation to claims of direct discrimination under the RRA 1976 and the SDA 1975, discrimination claims based on article 14 can be defended by the alleged discriminator showing that the treatment complained of was justifiable in the circumstances. The burden of proof in relation to the four issues discussed above is on the claimant;

---

258  *Dudgeon v UK* (1981) 4 EHRR 149.
259  *Nelson v UK* (1986) 49 DR 170.
260  *Airey v Ireland* (1979–80) 2 EHRR 305.
261  *R (Marper) v Chief Constable of South Yorkshire* [2004] 1 WLR 2196.
262  *Lindsay v UK* (1986) 49 DR 181.
263  *Nelson v UK* (1986) 49 DR 170.

the burden then shifts to the defendant to establish justification. The defendant has to show both that the treatment complained of pursues a legitimate aim and that it is a proportionate response to the aim in question, when balanced against the discriminatory effects involved.[264]

# Claims under the Human Rights Act 1998

10.166   Throughout this book reference is made to possible actions that can be brought for action that is incompatible with the Convention rights set out in Schedule 1 to the Human Rights Act 1998. The most relevant rights themselves are set out in some of these chapters and also below in this section.

10.167      This section provides a brief overview of the Human Rights Act (HRA) 1998 and its main provisions. It then summarises briefly some of the actions involving the police that may include consideration of breaches of Convention rights.

10.168      Some specific procedural points in bringing an action under the HRA 1998 are then described, together with a brief description of the way in which damages in an action under the HRA 1998 are calculated.

## Overview of the HRA 1998

10.169   The effect of the HRA 1998 is that legal remedies are provided where there has been action by public authorities incompatible with Convention rights. The Convention rights are listed in Schedule 1 to the HRA 1998 and those that are most relevant to police misconduct are set out below.

10.170      The HRA 1998 does not give courts the power to strike down primary legislation which is found to be incompatible with Convention rights. Rather, one of the main function of the courts is, so far as it is possible to do so, to read and give effect to both primary and secondary legislation in a way which is compatible with Convention rights.[265] The House of Lords has emphasised that this may mean interpreting a statute in a way which is contrary to the unambiguous intention of Parliament when the statute was passed, so long as such a interpretation does not change a fundamental feature of the legislation.

---

264   *Belgian Linguistics (No 2)* (1968) 1 EHRR 252.
265   HRA 1998 s8

This may mean that the court has to read in words to the statutory provision to make it Convention-compliant or to interpret statutory language restrictively or expansively.[266] Only if it is not possible to interpret primary legislation compliantly with the Convention can the court make a declaration that primary legislation is incompatible with Convention rights.[267] A declaration of incompatibility does not change the law or overturn statute, but Parliament has powers to 'fast-track' new amending legislation to ensure it is Convention compatible.[268]

10.171    A cornerstone of the HRA 1998 is section 6(1) which states that it is unlawful for a public authority to act in a way which is incompatible with a Convention right. However, section 6(1) does not apply where a public authority cannot act otherwise than incompatibly with Convention rights.[269] This will be the case if a statute imposes a duty on a public authority (like the police) to act in a particular way which inevitably breaches Convention rights.

10.172    The HRA 1998 allows a person who is a victim of a breach of Convention rights to bring proceedings against a public authority if it is claimed that the authority has acted in a way which is incompatible with that person's Convention rights.[270] Generally any such acts by a public authority will need to have occurred after the HRA's commencement on 2 October 2000.[271] There is a specific definition of what is a 'public authority' which has generated some significant case law.[272] However, in relation to the police and the other bodies mentioned in this book it is clear that they are covered by the definition. Thus, police forces, police authorities, the Independent Police Complaints Commission (IPCC), the Crown Prosecution Service, coroners, the Criminal Injuries Compensation Authority, the Home Secretary and the civil and criminal courts are all public authorities for the purposes of the HRA 1998.

10.173    A person is a victim for the purposes of the HRA 1998 if he or she would have the right to bring a case in the European Court of Human Rights. The Convention and Strasbourg case law adopt a fairly broad approach to who can claim to be victim. It can include, as well as individuals, non-governmental organisations and companies who have

266    *Mendoza v Ghaidan* [2004] 2 AC 557; [2004] 3 All ER 411.
267    HRA 1998 s4.
268    HRA 1998 s10.
269    HRA 1998 s6(2)
270    HRA 1998 s7.
271    *Re McKerr* [2004] 1 WLR 807.
272    See for example *R (Heather) v Leonard Cheshire Foundation* [2002] 2 All ER 936; *Hampshire County Council v Graham Beer* [2004] 1 WLR 233.

been victims of breaches of the Convention.[273] In Strasbourg, relatives of those who have had Convention rights breached have been found to be victims. If there is a death in custody the relatives will be victims, for example, if there has been a lack of an official effective investigation into the death.

10.174    In relation to any act of a public authority which the court finds is unlawful because incompatible with Convention rights, the court may grant such relief or remedy within its powers as it considers just and appropriate.[274] Thus, for example, a county court will not be able to grant quashing orders or mandatory orders in relation to decisions as these are only available to the High Court through applications for judicial review, but it will be able to make an award of damages.

10.175    The award of damages is one of the remedies that will be available (if the court has the power to award damages in civil proceedings). However, a breach of a Convention right does not automatically lead to an award of damages. Damages for such breaches are dealt with in more depth at para 10.231, but the parameters set out in the HRA 1998 are firstly that the court must be satisfied that an award of damages is necessary to afford just satisfaction to a victim, and secondly that the court must have regard to the principles applied by the European Court of Human Rights (ECtHR)in awarding damages.[275]

## HRA 1998 actions involving the police and other public authorities

10.176   The following includes a brief description of the most common situations in which a breach of a Convention right may occur in the context of police misconduct. Many of the examples are discussed in more depth elsewhere in the book and references are provided where appropriate.

### Article 2

10.177    2   (1) Everyone's right to life shall be protected by law. No-one shall be deprived of his life intentionally save in the execution of a sentence of a court following his conviction of a crime for which this penalty is provided by law.

---

273   See ECHR Art 34 and *Klass v Germany* (1978) 2 EHRR 214.
274   HRA 1998 s8.
275   HRA 1998 s8.

(2) Deprivation of life shall not be regarded as inflicted in contravention of this Article when it results from the use of force which is no more than absolutely necessary:

(a) in defence of any person from unlawful violence;
(b) in order to effect a lawful arrest or to prevent the escape of a person lawfully detained;
(c) in action lawfully taken for the purpose of quelling a riot or insurrection.

10.178 Article 2 contains a positive duty on the state to protect life. It is one of the most important rights under the Convention and the main right – that life shall be protected by law – is not qualified or limited in any way. In relation to the police this manifests itself firstly in a duty to refrain from using lethal force other than in the very limited circumstances in article 2(2) (and only then where the use of such force was 'absolutely necessary').[276] There is also a positive duty to ensure that the criminal law is enforced so as to protect the life of citizens. Thus a failure to provide protection where there is an immediate risk of a threat to life may be incompatible with article 2 (see below).

10.179 Article 2 clearly applies to persons who are in the custody of the police and there is a duty to ensure that the lives of such persons are protected. This extends not only to the police refraining from using life threatening force against those in custody but also to ensuring the welfare of those in custody by, for example, ensuring that adequate medical attention is available and protecting vulnerable prisoners from self-harm and harm from other prisoners (see also para 8.60).

10.180 The case of *Osman v UK*[277] clarified the nature of the duty owed under article 2 to victims of potentially life threatening crime. In that case it was claimed that the police ignored repeated warnings that a pupil was at risk of violence from an ex-teacher who eventually shot the pupil and his father, killing the latter. The ECtHR rejected the government's argument that the police would have to be grossly negligent before there was a breach of article 2 and instead held that article 2 would be breached where the police knew or ought to have known of a real and immediate risk to the life of an identifiable individual from the criminal acts of a third party and not had not taken reasonable measures, within their powers, which might have been expected to have avoided that risk.

---

276   See *McCann v UK* (1995) 21 EHRR 97.
277   *Osman v UK* (1998) 29 EHRR 245.

10.181    An action for breach of article 2 under the HRA 1998 may be considered alongside a claim in negligence or as an addition to the provisions which allow claims to be brought after a person's death (see chapter 8). A free-standing claim under article 2 may be appropriate where the restrictive provisions as to which relatives can sue following death are not applicable. See paragraphs 8.44–8.48 for further discussion.

10.182    The ECtHR and the domestic courts have confirmed that implicit in article 2 is a duty on the state to carry out an effective official investigation where there has been an arguable breach of article 2.[278] The police investigation or the IPCC investigation of the death may form part of the procedures by which the State discharges this duty, as will the coroner's inquest.[279] A discussion of what is necessary to discharge this duty is included in Chapter 16. The recent case of *Menson v UK*[280] included significant comments from the ECtHR in an admissibility decision about the need for the police to carry out an effective investigation of a death, even where state agents were not involved and especially where a person had been the victim of a racist attack: see paragraph 8.49–8.50 for further discussion.

## Article 3

10.183    3   No one shall be subjected to torture or to inhuman or degrading treatment or punishment.

10.184    Article 3 is also an unqualified and unlimited right. In cases against the police will often be relevant where force is used against a person and in relation to the conditions of detention.

10.185    The section at paragraph 6.108–6.110 on assault and battery explains the application of article 3 to some of the situations where force is used by the police and where there is mistreatment in police custody.

10.186    However, not all unlawful use of force will breach this article, and there must be a 'minimum level of severity' before the article is engaged.[281] What constitutes the necessary severity will depend on the circumstances of each case and will take into account the personal attributes of the victim.[282]

---

278   *R (Amin) v Secretary of State for the Home Department* [2004] 1 AC 653; [2003] 4 All ER 1264.

279   *R (Middleton) v HM Coroner for the Western District of Somerset* [2004] 2 AC 182; [2004] 2 All ER 465; *R (Green) v Police Complaints Authority* [2004] 1 WLR 725; [2004] 2 All ER 209.

280   (2003) ECHR 47916/99.

281   See for example, *Tomasi v France* (1993) 15 EHRR 1.

282   *Ireland v UK* (1978) 2 EHRR 25 para 162.

10.187 The terms 'inhuman and degrading treatment' and 'torture' are not synonymous. However, it is not usually necessary to differentiate between them as it is enough for one of the terms to be satisfied for there to be a violation of the article. Compensation may be increased if torture is established.

10.188 'Torture' is deliberate inhuman treatment causing very serious and cruel suffering. Recent examples have emanated from the case law involving Turkey (Palestinian hanging, rape, beatings, use of high pressure hoses); in the *Ireland v UK*[283] case the 'five techniques' were said not to amount to torture. In *Treadaway v Chief Constable of West Midlands*,[284] maltreatment, including placing a plastic bag over a suspects head was held by the High Court to amount to torture. In *Selmouni v France*[285] a large number of blows administered to a suspect were said to amount to torture, and the Court indicated that increasingly high standards could, in effect, upgrade certain practices to the level of torture.

10.189 Inhuman and degrading treatment or punishment can be difficult to define. In *Pretty v UK*[286] the ECtHR confirmed that the case law of the Court was that treatment had to attain a minimum level of severity and involves actual bodily injury or intense physical or mental suffering. The Court went on[287]

> Where treatment humiliates or debases an individual, showing a lack of respect for, or diminishing, his or her human dignity, or arouses feelings of fear, anguish or inferiority capable of breaking an individual's moral and physical resistance, it may be characterised as degrading and also fall within the prohibition of article 3... The suffering which flows from naturally occurring illness, physical or mental, may be covered by article 3, where it is, or risks being, exacerbated by treatment, whether flowing from conditions of detention, expulsion or other measures, for which the authorities can be held responsible...

10.190 Disproportionate force used when effecting an arrest can be degrading treatment.[288] The Court has held that

> ... in respect of a person deprived of his liberty, recourse to physical force which has not been made strictly necessary by his own conduct diminishes human dignity and is in principle an infringement of the right set forth in article 3.[289]

---

283 (1978) 2 EHRR 25.
284 (1994) *Independent* 23 July.
285 (2000) 29 EHRR 403.
286 (2002) EHRR 1.
287 (2002) EHRR 1 at para 52.
288 *Hurtado v Switzerland* (1994) Series A no 280-A.
289 *Ribitsch v Austria* (1996) 21 EHRR 573, and cited in *Keenan v UK* at para 113.

10.191   In general terms, if there has been an assault and battery by the police then a claim that article 3 has also been breached may not add very much to that claim. In contrast, if it is argued that conditions of or treatment in detention have become inhuman or degrading, then article 3 may amount to the main cause of action if the detention is otherwise lawful[290] and there is no claim for assault. The case of *Keenan v UK*[291] is an example where the ECtHR found that additional punishment in segregation for a mentally ill prisoner where there were also inadequate records were kept amounted to a breach of article 3 and compensation was awarded.

10.192   Where the police knew or ought to have known that there has been mistreatment of persons in their custody then the failure to take reasonable steps which had a real prospect of altering the outcome or mitigating the harm suffered may amount to a breach of article 3: see the discussion at para 8.45.

10.193   In addition, effective investigation of possible violations of article 3 are essential. A failure to provide such investigation may itself lead to a finding that article 3 has been breached. In *Assenov v Bulgaria*,[292] the ECtHR said

> ...where an individual raises an arguable claim that he has been seriously ill-treated by the police or other such agents of the State unlawfully and in breach of article 3, that provision, read in conjunction with the State's general duty under article 1 of the Convention to 'secure to everyone within their jurisdiction the rights and freedoms defined in [the] Convention', requires by implication that there should be an effective official investigation. This investigation, as with that under article 2, should be capable of leading to the identification and punishment of those responsible... If this were not the case, the general legal prohibition of torture and inhuman and degrading treatment and punishment, despite its fundamental importance...would be ineffective in practice and it would be possible in some cases for agents of the State to abuse the rights of those within their control with virtual impunity.

As a result of a cursory investigation in this case, the Court found a breach of article 3.

10.194   In relation to alleged claims that there has been a breach of article 3, it may well be the IPCC that provides, in many cases, the main investigation of the claim to satisfy this function. As has been described in chapter 5, some of the most serious complaints are now investi-

290   See more on this in the section on false imprisonment: see chapter 7.
291   (2001) 10 BHRC 319.
292   (1998) 28 EHRR 652, ECtHR.

gated by the IPCC itself or are managed by the IPCC. While this may be sufficient to constitute an effective official investigation of alleged breaches of article 3, the many serious complaints still investigated by the police themselves (albeit some investigations are carried out by difference police forces) may, in some cases, be found not to reach the necessary standards of transparency and accountability required by the Court. In addition, there may also be arguments that the IPCC itself is not sufficiently independent of the police and the government.[293]

## Article 5

10.195     5  (1) Everyone has the right to liberty and security of person. No-one shall be deprived of his liberty save in the following cases and in accordance with a procedure prescribed by law:

(a) the lawful detention of a person after conviction by a competent court;

(b) the lawful arrest or detention of a person for non-compliance with the lawful order of a court or in order to secure the fulfilment of any obligation prescribed by law;

(c) the lawful arrest or detention of a person effected for the purpose of bringing him before the competent legal authority on reasonable suspicion of having committed an offence or when it is reasonably considered necessary to prevent his committing an offence or fleeing after having done so;

(d) the detention of a minor by lawful order for the purpose of educational supervision or his lawful detention for the purpose of bringing him before the competent legal authority;

(e) the lawful detention of persons for the prevention of the spreading of infectious diseases, of persons of unsound mind, alcoholics or drug addicts or vagrants;

(f) the lawful arrest or detention of a person to prevent his effecting an unauthorised entry into the country or of a person against whom action is being taken with a view to deportation or extradition.

---

293   See *Govell v UK* [1999] EHRLR 121 and *Khan v UK* [1999] 8 BHRC 310.

(2) Everyone who is arrested shall be informed promptly, in a language which he understands, of the reasons for his arrest and of any charge against him.

(3) Everyone arrested or detained in accordance with the provisions of paragraph 1(c) of this article shall be brought promptly before a judge or other officer authorised by law to exercise judicial power and shall be entitled to trial within a reasonable time or to release pending trial. Release may be conditioned by guarantees to appear for trial.

(4) Everyone who is deprived of his liberty by arrest or detention shall be entitled to take proceedings by which the lawfulness of his detention shall be decided speedily by a court and his release ordered if the detention is not lawful.

(5) Everyone who has been the victim of arrest or detention in contravention of the provisions of this article shall have an enforceable right to compensation.

10.196  Article 5 sets out firstly the right to liberty and the security of the person, and the limited (and exhaustive) cases in which this can be compromised where prescribed by law, and then sets out a number of procedural protections for those who have been detained. The Strasbourg case law in relation to police powers and detention and article 5 is very closely linked to the domestic law on false imprisonment. This is further discussed in chapter 7. Essentially, if a detention is in breach of article 5, then it will almost invariably amount to false imprisonment. Thus, an action for false imprisonment is not likely to be improved by including a claim for breach of Article 5. Article 5 does not appear to expand the circumstances in which a person can sue for detention pursuant to a court order which usually has to take place in an action for malicious prosecution or misfeasance in public office: see further at para 7.34.

10.197    Article 5(5) provides an enforceable right to compensation for a person who has been deprived of their liberty in contravention of the other provisions of article 5.[294]

## Article 6

10.198    6  (1) In the determination of his civil rights and obligations or of any criminal charge against him, everyone is entitled to a fair and public hearing within a reasonable time by an

---

294  See discussion of article 5(5) and the Home Office ex gratia scheme for compensation for miscarriages of justice at paras 17.31–17.32 below.

independent and impartial tribunal established by law. Judgment shall be pronounced publicly but the press and public may be excluded from all or part of the trial in the interest of morals, public order or national security in a democratic society, where the interests of juveniles or the protection of the private life of the parties so require, or to the extent strictly necessary in the opinion of the court in special circumstances where publicity would prejudice the interests of justice.

(2) Everyone charged with a criminal offence shall be presumed innocent until proved guilty according to law.

(3) Everyone charged with a criminal offence has the following minimum rights:

(a) to be informed promptly, in a language which he understands and in detail, of the nature and cause of the accusation against him;

(b) to have adequate time and facilities for the preparation of his defence;

(c) to defend himself in person or through legal assistance of his own choosing or, if he has not sufficient means to pay for legal assistance, to be given it free when the interests of justice so require;

(d) to examine or have examined witnesses against him and to obtain the attendance and examination of witnesses on his behalf under the same conditions as witnesses against him;

(e) to have the free assistance of an interpreter if he cannot understand or speak the language used in court.

10.199 Article 6 has been invoked in the context of the right to bring proceedings against the police. This may have relevance in the case of negligence where actions against the police, for example in relation to the investigation of crime, have been held not to be permitted for public policy reasons. However, that the effect of article 6 is somewhat limited in this context is discussed in more depth at para 8.40.

10.200 Other contexts in which article 6 might be relevant include police disciplinary proceedings where officers will claim their right to a fair hearing as their employment is. The complainant's article 6 rights are not engaged in the disciplinary process.[295] There was found to be breach

---

295 *R (Melia) v Chief Constable of Merseyside* [2003] EWCH 1121 Admin.

of article 6(2) in *Allenet de Ribemont v France*[296] where police officers stated before trial that a person was the instigator of a crime. For the applicability of the presumption of innocence right enshrined in article 6(2) to the right of compensation for miscarriages of justice see chapter 17.

## Article 8

10.201    8  (1) Everyone has the right to respect for his private and family life, his home and his correspondence.

(2) There shall be no interference by a public authority with the exercise of this right except such as is in accordance with the law and is necessary in a democratic society in the interests of national security, public safety or the economic well-being of the country, for the prevention of disorder or crime, for the protection of health or morals, or for the protection of the rights and freedom of others.

10.202  Article 8 is one of the qualified rights in the Convention. This means that interference with the right as described in paragraph 1 can be justified on one of the grounds set out in paragraph 2.

10.203    The rights protected in article 8(1) are rights to respect for private and family life, home and correspondence, rather than rights to these things in themselves. The right to respect for private life has been given an increasingly wide meaning by the ECtHR. In *Peck v UK*[297] the ECtHR said:

> Private life is a broad term not susceptible to exhaustive definition. The Court has already held that elements such as gender identification, name, sexual orientation and sexual life are important elements of the personal sphere protected by article 8. The article also protects a right to identity and personal development, and the right to establish and develop relationships with other human beings and the outside world and it may include activities of a professional or business nature. There is, therefore, a zone of interaction of a person with others, even in a public context, which may fall within the scope of 'private life'.

10.204  In *Pretty v UK*[298] the Court went on to say that 'the notion of personal autonomy is an important principle underlying the interpretation of [the article 8] guarantees private life.'

---

296  Application No 3/1994/450/529.
297  (2003) 36 EHRR 41 at 57.
298  (2002) EHRR 1 at 61.

*The right to respect for family life*

10.205 This category is concerned most usually with the relationship between members of a family. The ECtHR authorities take a strict approach to any rule of national law that interferes with the relationship between parent and child:

> ... the mutual enjoyment by parent and child of each other's company constitutes a fundamental element of family life and domestic measures hindering such enjoyment amount to an interference with the right protected by article 8[299]

10.206 In the context of this book the most likely application of this category may come if restrictions are placed on parents having access to children in custody. There have been a number of cases which have examined the rights of women and their children in prison which may have some relevance in this context.[300]

*The right to respect for the home*

10.207 The ECtHR has been at pains to emphasise that this category does not give anyone the right to a home as such except in the most extreme cases of need, but it is aimed at providing some protection from unwanted intrusion. The right can extend to the protection of business premises.[301] In the context of this book the category has the most relevance when applied to the exercise of police powers to search premises under warrant or otherwise. In *McLeod v UK*[302] the ECtHR found that the police use of powers to enter a woman's house purportedly to prevent a breach of the peace to enable her husband to collect goods had been exercised in a disproportionate way which could not be justified under article 8 where there was little prospect of any breach of the peace. In *R (Cronin) v Sheffield Justices*[303] the Divisional Court examined the extent to which the procedure for granting search warrants in the magistrates' court was compliant with a person's right to respect for their home. The right to respect for private life can usually be relied upon as well in such circumstances.

---

299   *Johansen v Norway* (1996) 23 EHRR 33 at 52.
300   See, eg, *R v Secretary of State for the Home Department ex p P* [2001] 2 FLR 383. See also the suggested application of article 8 to instances of family separation occasioned by wrongful convictions, discussed at para 17.52.
301   *Niemietz v Germany* (1992) 16 EHRR 97.
302   [1998] 2 FLR 1048. See also the discussions at paras 9.19–9.20.
303   [2003] 1 WLR 752.

## Right to respect for correspondence

10.208 There have been a number of cases where interference with the correspondence of prisoners has been said to be a disproportionate interference with the right to respect for correspondence.[304] Surveillance and monitoring of telephone conversations clearly engages this right (as well as respect for private life).[305]

10.209    As article 8 is a qualified right, then even if a breach of article 8(1) can be established, the court then needs to go on to decide whether the interference can be justified under article 8(2). This involves the defendant satisfying the court of three things. First, the interference must be 'in accordance with law'. This largely concerns a consideration of whether it was sanctioned under domestic law.[306] Secondly, the court must be satisfied that the intrusion pursued a legitimate aim, that is to say one of those specified in Article 8(2). In the context of this book the police are likely to rely on: 'the interests of national security', 'public safety', 'the prevention of disorder or crime' or 'the protection of rights and freedoms of others'. In the vast majority of instances the police would have little difficulty in bringing the activity under challenge within one of those legitimate aims.

10.210    The third element to be considered is likely to cause more difficulty. The court has to consider whether the interference is 'necessary in a democratic society', that is to say it meets a pressing social need and the particular interference is proportional to the legitimate aim being pursued.[307] This will always depend upon an evaluation of the particular circumstances, and will look at, for example, the seriousness of the interference and the effect on the individual, whether there were any alternative measures that could have achieved the same ends, the procedural protections in place and the benefit to the public interest brought about by the interference.

10.211    In *McMichael v UK*[308] the ECtHR confirmed that, while article 8 contains no explicit procedural requirements, 'the decision-making process leading to measures of interference must be fair and such as to afford due respect to the interests safeguarded by article 8'.

---

304   See *R (Szuluk) v Governor of HMP Full Sutton* (2004) *Independent*, November 4.

305   See *Halford v UK* (1997) 24 EHRR 523.

306   See discussion in the context of covert surveillance at para 10.16.

307   *R (Daly) v Secretary of State for the Home Department* [2001] 2 AC 532 at 548; [2001] 3 All ER 433 at 446.

308   (1995) 20 EHRR 205 at para 87.

10.212    The kinds of cases where article 8 may be most relevant include: surveillance of a person and other invasions of privacy;[309] applications for search warrants and their execution;[310] stop and search practices; strip searches in the police station;[311] the taking and retention of DNA samples;[312] publicity aimed at suspects and those convicted.[313] In *Osman v UK*[314] the ECtHR suggested that there was a positive obligation on the police to safeguard physical integrity pursuant to article 8 in much the same way as there was a positive duty to protect life as described above under article 2.

## Article 10

10.213    **10** (1) Everyone has the right to freedom of expression. This right shall include freedom to hold opinions and to receive and impart information and ideas without interference by public authority and regardless of frontiers. This article shall not prevent States from requiring the licensing of broadcasting, television or cinema enterprises.

(2) The exercise of these freedoms, since it carries with it duties and responsibilities, may be subject to such formalities, conditions, restrictions or penalties as are prescribed by law and are necessary in a democratic society, in the interests of national security, territorial integrity or public safety, for the prevention of disorder or crime, for the protection of health or morals, for the protection of the reputation or the rights of others, for preventing the disclosure of information received in confidence, or for maintaining the authority and impartiality of the judiciary.

10.214    Article 10 is another qualified right where the 'headline' right in article 10(1) can be interfered with if the conditions in article 10 (2) are met. It may be of importance in police cases when the police exercise their powers to restrict protest or seek to exercise powers of arrest, for example, for breach of the peace. An example of the application

---

309    *Peck v UK* (2003) 36 EHRR 41: see discussion of cases at 10.13–10.15. In relation to disclosure of information see 10.23–10.24 and 10.60.

310    *R (Cronin) v Sheffield JJ* [2003] 1 WLR 753; and see paras 9.19–9.20

311    *Wainwright v Home Office* [2003] 4 All ER 969; and see paragraph 6.102

312    *R (Marper) v Chief Constable of South Yorkshire Police* [2004] 1 WLR 2196 and see para 10.53.

313    *R (Ellis) v Metropolitan Police Commissioner* [2003] FLR 556.

314    (1998) 29 EHRR 245.

article 10 can be found in *Redmond-Bate v DPP*,[315] a case involving the arrest of a person making an annoying speech in public, where Sedley LJ made wide ranging comments about the nature of the right to freedom of expression. At paragraph 20 he said:

> Free speech includes not only the inoffensive but the irritating, the contentious, the eccentric, the heretical, the unwelcome and the provocative provided it does not tend to provoke violence. Freedom only to speak inoffensively is not worth having. What Speakers' Corner (where the law applies as fully as anywhere else) demonstrates is the tolerance which is both extended by the law to opinion of every kind and expected by the law in the conduct of those who disagree, even strongly, with what they hear. From the condemnation of Socrates to the persecution of modern writers and journalists, our world has seen too many examples of state control of unofficial ideas. A central purpose of the European Convention on Human Rights has been to set close limits to any such assumed power. We in this country continue to owe a debt to the jury which in 1670 refused to convict the Quakers William Penn and William Mead for preaching ideas which offended against state orthodoxy.

10.215  Strasbourg case law has tended to interpret narrowly any restriction on the rights contained in article 10.[316] The issue is whether the restrictions on the right to freedom of expression are necessary for the proper protection of the claimant's rights, and if so whether the restrictions proposed are proportionate. They must be no wider than is necessary to accomplish that objective. Similar principles apply to the qualified rights to freedom of thought and religion in article 9 and to peaceful assembly and freedom of association in article 11.

### Article 14

10.216    **14** The enjoyment of the rights and freedoms set forth in this Convention shall be secured without discrimination on any ground such as sex, race, colour, language, religion, political or other opinion, national or social origin, association with a national minority, property, birth or other status.

10.217  The right not to be subject to discrimination is specifically related to whether other Convention rights are engaged. In *Michalak v Wandsworth LBC*,[317] Brook LJ considered the correct approach to

---

315  (1999) 163 JP 789.
316  *Ezelin v France* (1991) 14 EHRR 362 and *Platform Artze fur das Leben v Austria* (1991) 13 EHRR 204.
317  [2003] 1 WLR 617 at para 20.

article 14. He described a model that the court should follow which included four questions which would usually need to be answered in the affirmative if a case was to succeed. These are set out earlier in this chapter at paras 10.159–10.165 together with a number of examples of the applicability of article 14 in police cases.

## Article 1 of the First Protocol to the Convention

10.218   **Article 1: protection of property**
Every natural or legal person is entitled to the peaceful enjoyment of his possessions. No-one shall be deprived of his possessions except in the public interest and subject to the conditions provided for by law and by the general principles of international law.

The preceding provisions shall not, however, in any way impair the right of a State to enforce such laws as it deems necessary to control the use of property in accordance with the general interest or to secure the payment of taxes or other contributions or penalties.

10.219   The case of *Sporrong and Lonnroth v Sweden*[318] established that this right contains three principles. The first is the right to peaceful enjoyment of possessions. The second, is that deprivation of property can only occur in the public interest and subject to conditions provided by law. The third, is that the State has the right to control property for the general interest or to secure payment of taxes (and the like).

10.220   Thus, the right is hedged around with general exceptions. Although these are to be strictly interpreted, the wide wording gives the State a wide margin of appreciation especially when defining what is in the general interest. So long as a measure controlling property or depriving a person of it has a legitimate aim and is proportionate for the aim pursued then it is likely that a court would find that a 'fair balance' had been reached between the general or public interest and individual rights to property.

10.221   Given the nature of this right it would only be in the most extreme cases of police deprivation of property (for example, following a search and seizure) which would engage this right and in practice if article 1 of Protocol 1 has been breached the police actions are likely to be in breach of domestic law (for example, PACE provisions) as well (see discussion at paragraph 9.21).

---

318   (1982) 5 EHRR 3 para 61.

## Where to bring proceedings under the HRA 1998

10.222　In practice, there are two main ways in which cases are usually brought in relation to Convention rights in the domestic courts. The first is by way of judicial review. As action incompatible with Convention rights is 'unlawful' pursuant to HRA 1998 s6, then this, if proved, would fulfil one of the grounds for judicial review. The procedure for judicial review is described in more depth in chapter 17. Here, it is important to note that a judicial review application must be brought promptly and in any event within three months. Although there is provision to extend this period, this is the time limit that must generally be observed rather than the more lenient 12 months for actions under the HRA 1998 (see below).

10.223　Judicial review is most appropriate in three situations. The first is where there is an ongoing procedure or practice which it is sought to challenge. Thus, the policy of the police to retain all DNA samples obtained from those acquitted of criminal offences was challenged by way of judicial review as unlawful and incompatible with article 8.[319]

10.224　The second is where the aim is to quash a particular decision made by the police as incompatible with Convention rights. Thus, for example, an application to quash a decision to caution a person on the basis that it is incompatible with article 6 could be made by way of judicial review.

10.225　The third is where a definitive declaration as to the law is sought from the High Court. Thus in the case of *Laporte*[320] the exercise of police powers in turning back demonstrators in a coach was challenged and a declaration sought as to whether it was compatible with article 5.

10.226　In all these judicial review cases it is possible to include a claim for damages for the Convention incompatible action in addition to judicial review remedies. Where the action of the public authority would also amount to maladministration then the Court may deal with the damages question after the judicial review action has been decided, and may require the claimant to use complaints and ombudsman procedures if appropriate.[321] However, where damages alone are sought for breach of Convention rights then judicial review cannot be

---

319　*R (Marper) v Chief Constable of South Yorkshire Police* [2004] 1 WLR 2196.

320　*R (Laporte) v Chief Constable of Gloucestershire Police* [2005] 1 All ER 273 but see comments in the judgment by Lord Woolf MR as to whether this was the appropriate route for the claimants to take.

321　*Anufrijeva v Southwark LBC* [2004] 2 WLR 603.

used.[322] In this situation the case can be brought in the county court or the High Court in the way described in chapter 12.[323] Two examples might be: a claim for damages where the conditions in which a person has been detained amount to degrading treatment for the purposes of article 3 (see para 10.191), or where a strip search amounts to a breach of article 8 (see chapter 10).

10.227　　Where a declaration of incompatibility is sought then only, in effect, the High Court and above can make this declaration[324] and the prospect of a declaration of incompatibility is something that will be taken into account when deciding whether a case commenced in the county court should be transferred to the High Court.[325]

10.228　　Section 5 of the HRA 1998 confirms that the Crown is entitled to notice that a declaration of incompatibility is being sought (this can be given at any point during proceedings). The formal notice must be given by the court (and not the parties to the action) and at least 21 days' notice should be given.[326] The relevant practice direction states that consideration of giving notice should usually take place at the case management conference.[327] Further guidance was set out in *Poplar Housing and Regeneration Community Association Ltd v Donoghue*[328] by the Court of Appeal as follows:

> Having considered the submissions which the parties helpfully made, including submissions on behalf of the Department, we suggest that:
>
> (i)　The formal notice which the HRA and the CPR require should always be given by the court. This is because the court will be in the best position to assess whether there is a likelihood of a declaration of incompatibility being made.
>
> (ii)　So as to give the Crown as much notice as possible, whenever a party is seeking a declaration of incompatibility or acknowledges that a declaration of incompatibility may be made, it should give as much informal notice to the Crown as practical of the proceedings and the issues that are involved.

---

322　CPR Pt 54.3(2) and see *Andrews v Reading BC* (2005) Env LR 2; (2004) UKHRR 599 where Collins J confirmed that actions for damages alone under the HRA 1998 should not be brought in the Administrative Court.

323　HRA 1998 s7 states that rules of court can set out the appropriate court or tribunal in which an action can be commenced but no such rules have yet been made.

324　HRA 1998 s4(5).

325　See CPR r30.3(2)(g).

326　CPR Pt 19.4A.

327　CPR Pt 19 PD para 6.2.

328　[2002] QB 48.

(iii) The formal and informal notice to the Crown should be given to a person named in the list published under section 17 of the Crown Proceedings Act 1947.[329]

(iv) At the same time as the party gives notice informally to the Crown, it should send a copy of such notice to the court so that the court is alerted to the fact that it will have to consider whether a formal notice should be given. It should also send a copy of the notice to the other parties.

10.229  Chapter 12 deals with the drafting of particulars of claim in general terms. Where a claim is brought pursuant to the HRA 1998 there are specific practice directions for what should be contained in the statement of case set out at paragraph 15 to the practice direction accompanying CPR Pt 16. These include:

- The fact that the HRA 1998 is relied upon must be stated.
- Precise details of the Convention right alleged to have breached must be stated along with details of the infringement.
- The relief sought.
- If a declaration of incompatibility is sought this should be stated with details of any alleged incompatibility of legislative provisions.
- Details of any decision by a court or tribunal which has made a finding of unlawfulness upon which the claim is based.
- If the claim relates to a judicial act which is said to have infringed a Convention right then details of the court or tribunal concerned should be stated and it should be stated whether damages are sought for the infringement.

10.230  Proceedings under the HRA 1998 should usually be commenced within 'one year beginning with the date on which the act complained of took place' (HRA 1998 s7(5)) although the court has the power to extend this time limit if it considers it equitable having regard to all the circumstances. This time limit is specifically subject to any rule imposing a stricter time limit 'in relation to the procedure in question': see, for example the maximum three-month time limit for judicial review.

329  The list is reproduced as an annex at para 6.6 to the practice direction accompanying CPR Pt 19.

# Damages and the HRA 1998

10.231  Section 8 of the HRA 1998 deals with damages claims under the Act. As described above a court must be satisfied that an award of damages is necessary to afford 'just satisfaction' to a victim, and secondly that the court must have regard to the principles applied by the European Court of Human Rights in awarding damages. The section reads as follows:

8    (1) In relation to any act (or proposed act) of a public authority which the court finds is (or would be) unlawful, it may grant such relief or remedy, or make such order, within its powers as it considers just and appropriate.

(2) But damages may be awarded only by a court which has power to award damages, or to order the payment of compensation, in civil proceedings.

(3) No award of damages is to be made unless, taking account of all the circumstances of the case, including–

(a) any other relief or remedy granted, or order made, in relation to the act in question (by that or any other court), and

(b) the consequences of any decision (of that or any other court) in respect of that act

the court is satisfied that the award is necessary to afford just satisfaction to the person in whose favour it is made.

(4) In determining–

(a) whether to award damages, or

(b) the amount of an award,

the court must take into account the principles applied by the European Court of Human Rights in relation to the award of compensation under Article 41 of the Convention.

10.232  Article 41 of the ECHR is referred to in HRA 1998 s8(4) and it provides:

If the Court [ECtHR] finds that there has been a violation of the Convention or the protocols thereto, and if the internal law of the High Contracting Party concerned allows only partial reparation to be made, the Court shall, if necessary, afford just satisfaction to the injured party.

10.233  In *Kingsley v UK*[330] the Court said:

... it is well established that the principle underlying the provision of just satisfaction ... is that the applicant should as far as possible be put in

330    (2002) 35 EHRR 10.

the position he would have enjoyed had the proceedings complied with the Convention's requirements ... The Court will award monetary compensation under article 41 only where it is satisfied that the loss or damage complained of was actually caused by the violation it has found ... since the State cannot be required to pay damages in respect of losses for which it is not responsible.

10.234   The basis on which the ECtHR awards compensation is described further in chapter 15. Since the HRA 1998 has been in force, judges in this country have commented that it is difficult to elicit more than general principles as to the basis upon which compensation is awarded.[331] However, in *R (Greenfield) v Secretary of State for the Home Department*[332] the House of Lords, in rejecting the view that awards under the HRA 1998 should necessarily be equivalent to domestic tortious awards said:

> The ECtHR routinely describes its awards as equitable, which I take to mean that they are not precisely calculated but are judged by the Court to be fair in the individual case. Judges in England and Wales must also make a similar judgment in the case before them. They are not inflexibly bound by Strasbourg awards in what may be different cases. But they should not aim to be significantly more or less generous than the Court might be expected to be, in a case where it was willing to make an award at all.

10.235   In *Anufrijeva v Southwark LBC*[333] the Court of Appeal further explained the principles to be applied in considering whether the compensation should be is under HRA 1998 s8. These can be summarised as follows:

- The court has a discretion as to whether to make an award (because section 8(1) of the Human Rights Act 1998 says it must be 'just and appropriate' to do so) by contrast to the position in relation to common law claims where there is a right to damage.
- The award must be necessary to achieve 'just satisfaction'; the Court said that this approach is distinct from the approach at common law where a claimant is invariably entitled, so far as money can achieve this, to be restored to the position he would have been in if he had not suffered the injury of which complaint is made.
- The concept of damages being 'necessary to afford just satisfaction' provides a link with the approach to compensation of the European Court of Human Rights under article 41.

---

331   See for example, Stanley Burnton J in *R (KB) v MHRT* [2003] 1 MHLR 28.
332   [2005] UKHL 14.
333   [2004] 2 WLR 603.

- The Court is required to take into account in determining whether damages are payable and the amount of damages payable the different principles applied by the European Court of Human Rights in awarding compensation.
- Exemplary damages are not awarded.

10.236 There are few reported decisions of damages awards under the HRA 1998. In *R(Bernard) v Enfield LBC*,[334] Sullivan J awarded £8,000 to a disabled person left for 20 months in difficult conditions without provision of the specialist accommodation she required. The judge decided that damages should be awarded at the same levels as damages awarded for tortious actions and that it was appropriate to examine the levels of damages the ombudsman would award in similar situations for maladminsitration.

10.237    In *R (KB) v Mental Health Review Tribunal*,[335] Stanley Burnton J awarded amounts between £750 and £4,000 to patients detained under the Mental Health Act 1983 in regards to the lack of a 'speedy determination' of the lawfulness of their detention by a tribunal. The level of the awards depended on the length of delay, the effect on the patient (especially if supported by medical evidence) and the prospects that the patient would have been released from detention earlier if the tribunal had been held in good time. In *Djerdjar v Metropolitan Police Commissioner* (22 February 2005) HHJ Collins at Central London County Court awarded £7,500 to a man whose right to respect for private life under article 8 had been breached by mistaken publication of his photograph in the 'wanted' section of his local newspaper. Of the total, £2,500 related to a specific psychiatric injury.

10.238    In *Greenfield*[336] the House of Lords noted that in most cases damages were not awarded by the ECtHR for breaches of article 6 (right to a fair trial) where it could not be shown that there was a causal connection between the breach and the outcome of the trial, other than for the anxiety and frustration caused by the knowledge that there had been a breach of the article.

334   [2002] EWHC 2282 (Admin); (2002) 5 CCLR 577.
335   [2003] 2 All ER 209.
336   *R (Greenfield) v Secretary of State for the Home Department* [2005] UKHL 14.

CHAPTER 11

# Suing the police:
# pre-action considerations

11.1     Bringing a civil action against the police is a specialist area of law. Lawyers involved in this area need to be fully familiar with the issues of evidence, practice and procedure that are likely to arise. These considerations are described in this and the next two chapters, which between them span pre-action preparation to the conclusion of the civil trial and any appeal. Lawyers should bear in mind that claimants will often have had their confidence in 'authority' badly shaken by their experiences with the police. Accordingly, it is essential that a claimant should not feel that he or she has handed over control of the case to a professional who is remote and unapproachable and who conducts the case in a way that ignores the claimant's ultimate objectives.

11.2     This chapter describes the main strategic and procedural issues that the lawyer and client need to consider before proceedings are issued.

## Change of solicitors

11.3     Claimants have traditionally found it difficult to find solicitors prepared to handle a case against the police or capable of handling it proficiently. Some solicitors feel it is not quite proper to be seen 'attacking' the police, or, especially in small communities, may find it socially embarrassing. However, over the last ten to fifteen years a growing number of firms have developed a speciality in civil actions against the police. These firms tend to be found in the larger urban areas, particularly in London. Names of specialist firms can be obtained from the Law Society and/or from directories on the legal profession.

11.4     The Legal Services Commission (LSC) is currently considering setting up an approved panel of actions against the police specialist solicitors, similar to the panel to be found for those who specialise in, for example, clinical negligence law. The idea is that only these specialists should conduct such cases where they are funded by the LSC. However, such a panel is not envisaged in the immediate future. Currently, only solicitors with a franchise from the LSC in actions against the police work can give preliminary advice and assistance under the Legal Help scheme; but a solicitor with a franchise in any category of law can carry out civil litigation against the police funded by the LSC. (Obtaining public funding is discussed in more detail from para 11.15 onwards.)

11.5     Liberty (the National Council for Civil Liberties) and some law centres also bring cases. However, this is relatively rare. Liberty normally only brings test cases in the hope of establishing new points of law, so the number of cases it handles is small, although it has a pro bono programme. Those law centres that undertake this kind of work (by no means all of them) will usually only act for people living or working in their catchment area.

11.6     Given the limited number of solicitors with the necessary skills and enthusiasm to bring a civil action against the police, it is not unusual for a potential claimant to receive legal advice or services that he or she finds unsatisfactory, and to wish to change solicitors. There is a general principle that a person can dismiss his or her solicitor at any time and appoint another solicitor of his or her choice. However, if the potential claimant is publicly funded the consent of the LSC will need to be obtained to the proposed change. The LSC will have to be convinced that there is a good reason for the proposed transfer and this can be difficult if the original firm proves unco-operative. The new firm will not be paid until public funding has been transferred, although it may be possible to advise the client under the Legal Help scheme pending the transfer.

## Suing after a criminal trial

11.7     Those with a grievance against the police will commonly have been charged with criminal offences themselves. It will usually be wise to wait and see how the criminal trial turns out before making a final decision whether to sue the police, provided limitation periods allow for this (see para 11.65 onwards). The claimant's lawyers will want to see whether new facts emerge at the criminal trial of which the claimant is unaware or about which the claimant has been unforthcoming.

11.8     As described in paras 7.15–7.18 claims for malicious prosecution can only be brought where the criminal case ended in favour of the accused claimant. In other actions an acquittal may, in practice, very much strengthen a civil case. Conversely a conviction may be very damaging to the claimant's credibility and make a civil action difficult to sustain, particularly if the claimant continues to deny the conduct for which he or she was convicted. Additionally, even if the claim succeeds, the damages awarded are likely to be lower if the claimant has a conviction arising out of the same or a related incident as both judges and juries may feel that he or she is less 'deserving' in the circumstances.

11.9     However, there is no general rule that the police cannot be sued for something that arose out of an incident which led to a conviction. A common example is where someone has been arrested for an offence which he or she committed but the police have used an unreasonable degree of force in making the arrest. In those circumstances the arrested person still has a potential claim for assault. This may be the case even though the claimant has been convicted of a crime of violence arising out of the same incident: the conviction does not necessarily mean that the police did not assault the claimant as claimed.[1]

11.10    Similarly, a person who pleads guilty to an offence may still have a claim for false imprisonment if the requirements of the Police and Criminal Evidence Act 1984 have not been complied with during the arrest and subsequent detention (see paras 6.63–6.75). The claim cannot be struck out simply on the ground that the person had indeed committed the offence for which he or she was arrested, since the bare fact of a conviction is not enough to establish that the arrest and detention was necessarily lawful.[2]

11.11    In theory at least, a claimant can seek to show that although he or she was convicted of an offence, he or she did not in fact commit it. If the police plead the conviction in their defence, the claimant can seek to show his or her innocence on a balance of probabilities.[3] Nonetheless, this is generally difficult to do in practice, particularly as the claimant may not have access to all the witnesses and/or other evidence that led to the conviction.

11.12    However, in some circumstances a claimant is unable to dispute the soundness of a conviction in a civil claim. A doctrine called the rule against collateral challenge prevents a claimant from bringing a civil claim where establishing the ingredients of the tort relied upon would necessarily involve disputing the basis of a criminal conviction – unlike the examples given earlier in this section. This could arise, for example, if the claimant alleged that police assaulted him or her to try and obtain a confession, but the confession has already been accepted as valid in the criminal proceedings.[4] The rule against collateral challenge is discussed in detail at para 6.115.

## Suing after accepting a caution

11.13    Clients are sometimes released from a police station after being formally cautioned for the behaviour for which they have been arrested. Accepting a caution usually involves accepting responsibility for the offence that led to the arrest, and therefore may make it difficult to

1    *Simpson v Chief Constable of Yorkshire* (1991) *Times* 7 March.
2    *Hill v Chief Constable of Yorkshire* [1990] 1 All ER 1049, CA.
3    Civil Evidence Act 1968 s11(2)(a).
4    See *Hunter v Chief Constable of West Midlands* [1982] AC 529.

establish subsequently that the arrest was unlawful. However, people sometimes accept cautions at the police station when they have not in fact committed the relevant offence, because they are desperate to leave a hostile environment, or because the police have told them that they will be charged if the caution is not accepted.

11.14     If the potential claimant has a credible explanation for accepting the caution, so that his or her case will not be damaged evidentially by this factor, then there is no rule of law that precludes bringing a civil action relating to the same circumstances as those covered by the caution. In *Abraham v Commissioner of Police of the Metropolis*,[5] the claimant had accepted a formal caution after she admitted a police version of facts which she subsequently said represented a gross exaggeration of the circumstances that led to her arrest. Her arrest had been in respect of disorderly conduct.[6] The defendant had been successful in striking out the claimant's case for false imprisonment as an abuse of process, on the basis that in accepting the caution she had admitted the police's version of the events, which were sufficient to justify the arrest. The Court of Appeal allowed the appeal on the basis that the rule against collateral challenge did not apply in relation to cautions rather than convictions. The Court of Appeal said that the similarities between a formal caution and a conviction were not sufficiently strong to engage that rule. In this case, the court was mindful that on 'the assumed facts,'[7] a lady of previous good character had been brought to the police station under arrest on a false pretext. She had been anxious about her two children from whom she had been separated. Her admission was to an account of events which both she and the police sergeant knew to be false and she had the advice of the duty solicitor.'[8]

# Funding a case

## Public funding

11.15   The LSC funds the majority of civil actions against the police.

---

5   [2001] 1 WLR 1257, CA.
6   Contrary to Public Order Act 1986 s5.
7   The facts had to be assumed in the claimant's favour at this point, as the defendant was seeking to strike out the claim on a preliminary basis.
8   The duty solicitor had told her that accepting a caution would not preclude a future civil claim.

## Legal Help

11.16 The Legal Help and Help at Court scheme can be used to make an application for public funding for full representation (see para 11.20 onwards) and also in relation to police complaints and other ancillary matters that do not result in court actions.[9] Legal Help can also cover taking preliminary instructions on a case and obtaining and assessing police documents and medical notes.

11.17 Only legal providers who have a LSC contract in actions against the police work or who are able to carry out 'tolerance work' under a criminal contract are able to provide this assistance to clients.

11.18 There is a financial eligibility test, which the client needs to satisfy.

11.19 The initial two-hour limit on work carried out under this scheme can be extended by the legal adviser themselves to carry out further work. However, once the upper costs limit has been reached, prior authority is required from the LSC. Disbursements can also be met from this scheme (such as in relation to obtaining medical notes).

## Legal representation

11.20 Save where funding by way of Investigative Help is first appropriate (see para 11.44), the LSC will consider whether to grant funding for full representation to cover the civil action litigation. The Funding Code Criteria issued by the LSC sets out the tests that need to be satisfied before the claim will be accepted as suitable for funding. The Code is augmented by the Funding Code Decision Making Guidance (FCDMG) also issued by the LSC.[10] There is a second part of the Code, 'Funding Code: Procedures', which deals with the mechanisms for obtaining funding. In addition to satisfying the criteria set out in the Funding Code, the applicant must be financially eligible for funding.[11]

11.21 Claims against the police are generally covered by Funding Code s8, 'Claims against Public Authorities'. To obtain funding it is necessary to show both:

- that funding is available for the relevant type of claim; and
- the merits, quantum, costs and other circumstances of the particular claim are such that funding should be granted.

---

9 LSC Manual para 31-004 defines what constitutes 'Legal Help'.
10 Documents issued by the LSC are available from their website at www.legalservices.gov.uk.
11 There is an updated eligibility calculator on the LSC's website.

The applicable tests are considered below. At the time of writing the LSC has recently conducted a consultation process into proposed changes to some aspects of the criteria.[12] On 2 March 2005 the Government announced its conclusions. In most actions against the police cases, applicants for public funding will be expected to pursue a police complaint before they are funded to take civil proceedings. The LSC is to consult further on when such an approach would not be appropriate and on the content of guidance to encourage the use of mediation. The cost benefit test (discussed below from para 11.29) is to be strengthened to reinforce a proportionate relationship between the benefits of the litigation and the likely costs of the same.

## Types of claims covered by section 8 of the Funding Code

11.22   Section 8.1 of the Funding Code provides:

> This section applies to applications for Legal Representation in relation to proceedings or proposed proceedings against public authorities concerned in serious wrong-doing, abuse of position or power or significant breach of human rights, other than cases falling within the scope of section 7 (Judicial Review) or section 10 (Housing).

11.23   The FCDMG emphasises that section 8 is intended to cover cases of serious wrongdoing, abuse of power or significant breaches of human rights. 'Serious wrongdoing' refers either to allegations of deliberately caused harm or to behaviour which 'goes well beyond simple liability for negligence or breach of contract, and which could objectively be considered to be really serious'.[13] As the guidance confirms, many actions against the police will clearly fall within these definitions, in particular cases of malicious prosecution, misfeasance, false imprisonment and assault.[14] Equally a straightforward case of negligence, such as a proposed claim arising out of an accident caused by a police vehicle, would be unlikely to come within section 8.

11.24   If a proposed claim concerns allegations of negligently caused personal injuries or damage to goods, it is unlikely to be funded at all by the LSC if it cannot be brought within Funding Code s8, as funding for 'allegations of negligently caused injury, death or damage to property' (apart from clinical negligence) are otherwise excluded from

---

12   See the LSC Consultation paper 'A New Focus for Civil Legal Aid'.
13   FCDMG para 17.2.1.
14   FCDMG paras 17.2.3 and 17.3.1–17.3.4.

funding.[15] Thus, for example, if the potential claim concerned officers carelessly damaging the proposed claimant's belongings during an otherwise lawful search, it would be difficult to obtain public funding for the litigation.

11.25    However, in some instances a claim for negligence (or for breach of statutory duty) can fall within Funding Code s8. This will be the case if the relevant conduct involves 'serious wrongdoing', which could embrace, for example, behaviour that led to a death in custody or that exposed the claimant to serious risk of injury from a third party. Similarly a claim in negligence may qualify or involving significant breaches of the claimant's human rights.[16]

11.26    A proposed claim may involve two or more allegations, that do not all come within Funding Code s8. For example, a potential claimant may propose to allege that an officer's behaviour was a dishonest abuse of his or her authority and so an act of misfeasance and, in the alternative, that it was a careless discharge of duty. The FCDMG states that a 'mixed claim' can come within section 8 if it contains a significant allegation of serious wrongdoing.[17]

11.27    Aside from negligence actions, claims that do not involve allegations of deliberately caused harm can come within Funding Code s8 if they involve allegations of significant breaches of the proposed claimant's human rights and/or abuse of power on the part of the officers involved. Accordingly, proposed actions against the police involving discrimination, harassment and/or breach of confidence would usually fall within section 8 on this basis.

11.28    As the definition quoted above makes clear, the proposed claim must be against a public authority, for the case to come within section 8. This is determined by reference to the definition of 'public authority' in the Human Rights Act 1998.[18] This provides that a public authority includes a court or tribunal and any person certain whose functions are of a public nature. Accordingly, a claim against individual police officers is a claim against a public authority for these purposes.[19]

---

15  Access to Justice Act 1999 Sch 2. FCDMG para 17.1.5 confirms that this exclusion does not apply if the claim falls within s8 of the Funding Code.

16  This issue is discussed in detail at 8.42–8.49.

17  FCDMG para 17.3.7.

18  Human Rights Act 1998 s6. See para 10.172.

19  The limited circumstances in which a claim would be brought against individual officers instead of or in addition to the chief officer, is discussed at paras 10.125–10.126 and 11.107–11.110.

## Criteria for funding claims within section 8

11.29    The criteria for funding claims under Funding Code s8 are more flexible than the tests contained in the General Funding Code, which
apply to the majority of publicly funded cases.

11.30    Where a claim falls within section 8, the 'general cost benefit' test
applies. This states that a public funding certificate may be refused
unless:

> The likely benefits of the proceedings justify the likely costs, having regard
> to the prospects of success and all other circumstances.

11.31    The effect of this test and the detailed guidance produced by the LSC
in relation to it (discussed below) is that claims within section 8 will
always be refused if prospects of success are poor or unclear, although
if prospects are unclear investigative help may be given (see para
11.44). Most claims against the police will only be funded if prospects
of success are at least 50 per cent. Where prospects of success are in the
borderline category, funding may only be provided if one of the
following three conditions applies:

- the case has significant public interest;[20]
- the case has overwhelming importance to the client;[21]
- the case raises a significant human rights issue.[22]

11.32    For the purposes of the Funding Code 'prospects of success' are
identified by reference to six potential categories:

- Very Good: 80 per cent or more chances of obtaining a
  successful outcome;
- Good: 60-80 per cent;
- Moderate: 50-60 per cent;
- Borderline: where the prospects are not poor, but it is not
  possible to say that they are better than 50 per cent;
- Poor: prospects of success are clearly less than 50 per cent;
- Unclear: the case cannot be put into any of the above categories
  because further research is needed.[23]

---

20   As defined in FCDMG para 5.3 (discussed at para 11.45).
21   FCDMG para 4.10 explains this concept.
22   FCDMG para 6.6 explains this concept.
23   FCDMG para 4.3.

11.33 'Success' for these purposes is defined as 'the likelihood of obtaining a successful outcome in the proceedings assuming the case was determined at trial or other final hearing'.[24] Accordingly, the prospects of the claim settling before trial are ignored for this purpose, even if there is a strong chance of a favourable settlement being obtained. So far as money claims are concerned, a 'successful outcome' means obtaining judgment for the claimant for substantial damages. Where the defendant has made a part 36 payment into court (see chapter 12), the damages awarded must be for a greater amount than that payment to constitute a successful outcome.[25] If the claim is not a money claim then what constitutes a successful outcome will depend upon the particular facts and circumstances of the case.[26]

11.34 For cases coming within Funding Code s5, rigid costs benefit ratios must be satisfied for funding to be granted, if the claim is primarily one for damages. The ratios are as follows:

- if prospects of success are 'very good', likely damages must exceed likely costs;
- if prospects of success are 'good', likely damages must exceed likely costs by a ratio of 2:1;
- if prospects of success are 'moderate', likely damages must excess likely costs by a ratio of 4:1.[27]

Costs for these purposes are the likely gross costs to be incurred on behalf of the client until the case is disposed of.[28] Accordingly, in this context the likelihood of settlement can be taken into account, thereby reducing the estimate of the costs involved in the litigation.

11.35 For cases coming within Funding Code s8, the above cost benefit ratios are highly relevant, but they are applied in a more flexible way. The guidance indicates that in determining whether the likely benefits of the proceedings justify the likely costs (for the purposes of the test for section 8 claims, see para 11.30) the correct approach is as follows:

- If the case is primarily a money claim from the client's point of view, the cost benefit ratios in the General Funding Code should be considered, but as guidelines only. If the claim does not satisfy those ratios, wider issues may be considered.

24  FCDMG para 4.1.1.
25  FCDMG para 4.2.3.
26  FCDMG para 4.2.5.
27  Funding Code para 5.7.3. See para 11.32 for the definitions of 'very good', 'good' and 'moderate'.
28  FCDMG para 4.6.

- If the case is not primarily a money claim, the private client test should be considered. If that test is satisfied, the setion 8 test is met. If that test is not satisfied, it is appropriate to consider wider issues.
- A consideration of wider issues involves an assessment of whether the case is sufficiently worthwhile to justify the expenditure of public funds. This determination should take into account the importance of the issues raised, such as how serious is the alleged wrongdoing and the extent to which the circumstances fall short of the General Funding Code cost benefit criteria.

11.36    It will be apparent from this guidance that the cost benefit ratio is of less importance where the claim is not primarily a money claim from the claimant's point of view. This is judged objectively by reference to the primary remedy that is realistically attainable[29] – it is not enough simply for a client to say that money is not his or her prime concern. A claim that involves both quantifiable and non-quantifiable elements will not be treated as being primarily a money claim unless damages are the 'dominant purpose' of the proceedings.[30] In relation to actions against the police, claimants frequently litigate to establish accountability for abuses of power and to vindicate their own name. Accordingly, it may be possible in many instances to show that the claim is not primarily a money one, so that the private client test applies. For this reason, when seeking funding, advisers should highlight any non-financial benefits that will accrue to their client if the case is won, such as clearing his or her name, obtaining justice, making the police accountable and/or challenging an improper practice or procedure so as to prevent its future repetition. Where medical evidence suggests that successful proceedings will help to alleviate any psychiatric injury suffered by the claimant, this too can be a relevant factor. Whether the claim is primarily about money or not, the application for funding should carefully reflect all heads of damage that could realistically be awarded in the proposed proceedings, including aggravated and exemplary damages (where appropriate), as the level of likely damages will still be relevant to cases that fall to be judged by the private client test.

---

29   FCDMG para 4.5.3.
30   FCDMG para 4.5.4.

11.37    Application of the private client test entails asking whether:

> ... the likely benefits to be gained from the proceedings justify the likely cost, such that a reasonable private paying client would be prepared to litigate, having regard to the prospects of success and all other circumstances.[31]

11.38    The aim of this test is said to be to ensure that there is a level playing field between those who can afford to litigate privately and those who do not have the financial resources to do so.[32] The test must be applied objectively, by reference to what the notional reasonable privately paying client would do – the sheer fact that the particular client feels strongly enough about the issues to litigate is not determinative.[33] Prospects of success and likely costs are still important to the application of this test. In particular the guidance emphasises that:

  i.   if the prospects of success are only a little over 50%, funding should only be granted if benefits to the client will be really substantial, such that the likely costs will be justified;

  ii.  by contrast, if the prospects of success are very high so that recovery of costs is almost certain, then it is recognised that a privately paying client would be prepared to litigate over more modest benefits.[34]

11.39    Funding is unlikely to be granted if the only matter at stake is loss of dignity or reputation, but the guidance acknowledges that privately paying clients may well regard issues of discrimination and/or breaches of their human rights as being of considerable importance.[35]

11.40    Where wider issues fall to be considered (under the approach set out above), it should be noted that the impact on others of successful litigation can be taken into account, even if that impact is not sufficient to bring the case within the 'significant public interest category' (see para 11.45).

## Standard limitations on funding certificates

11.41    Even where public funding is granted, there is likely to be a limit placed on how far the case can be taken before the LSC will want to review the issue of further funding. A common limitation is for public funding to be initially granted only for further evidence to be assembled and a barrister's opinion obtained on merits and quantum.

---

31   FCDMG para 4.8.1.
32   FCDMG para 4.8.3.
33   FCDMG para 4.8.4.
34   FCDMG para 4.8.5.
35   FCDMG paras 4.8.7 and 4.8.8.

The written opinion will be sent to the LSC, who will then decide whether to continue to fund the action. It is therefore vital for counsel to address the criteria discussed above in their advice. Often the LSC will want counsel to give another opinion on the case before extending public funding to cover representation at the trial, as this is usually the most expensive part of the case.

11.42    The fact that the early stages of litigation have been funded by the LSC will not of itself imply that funding will be granted to trial as the assessment of merits, quantum and/or costs may alter as the claim progresses. However, where the LSC discharged a funding certificate on the eve of a trial where there had been no material change in the prospects of success or other relevant factors, the withdrawal of funding at such a late stage was found to constitute a breach of the claimant's right of access to the courts, protected by article 6 of the European Convention on Human Rights.[36]

11.43    As well as giving limitations on the scope of the work that can be carried out, the LSC will also prescribe a limitation on the costs that can be incurred in undertaking that work. Different limitations may be applied for different types of cases, but unless the Commission decides otherwise, the initial costs limitation for obtaining counsel's advice will usually not exceed £2,500. If the claimant subsequently wins the case and the defendant is ordered to pay his or her costs, then the amount of the claimant's solicitor's costs that the defendant is ordered to pay at an assessment hearing can be greater than the LSC costs limitation. However, if costs are not recovered from the other party and the claimant's solicitor is to be paid by the LSC, the costs ordered at the assessment hearing cannot exceed the costs limitation. It is therefore important for legal advisers to ensure that applications to increase the costs limitation are made at the appropriate times.

## Investigative Help

11.44    In most cases work carried out under the Legal Help scheme is sufficient to investigate the merits of a case to prepare an application for full representation funding. However, if the investigative costs are substantial before the merits of the claim can be assessed, funding for Investigative Help should be considered. Investigative Help means legal representation that is limited to investigation of the strength of a proposed claim.[37] It includes the issue and the conduct of

---

36    *R (Allis) v LSC* [2003] ACD 16.
37    Funding Code para 5.6.2.

proceedings only so far as is necessary to obtain disclosure of relevant information or to protect the client's position in relation to any urgent hearing or limitation period.[38] Investigative Help may only be granted if there are reasonable grounds for believing that when the investigative work has been carried out the claim will be strong enough, in terms of prospects of success and cost benefit, to satisfy the relevant criteria for full representation.[39]

## Cases involving a significant wider public interest

11.45 As was indicated above, a case that involves a significant wider public interest may be funded even though the prospects of success are borderline, so that the usual criteria for funding would not be satisfied. Whether a case has a significant wider public interest will depend on the nature of the potential benefits from the litigation and how many people are likely to enjoy those benefits. The more intangible and indirect the benefits, the harder it will be to show that the test is met.[40] Setting a legal precedent or resolving an important issue of law may create a significant wider public interest.[41] The Code sets no limit on the number of people who must benefit before this test is met, but the guidance indicates that as a general rule of thumb it would be unusual to regard the case as having significant wider public interest if fewer than 100 people were likely to benefit from its outcome.[42]

11.46 The LSC has established a Public Interest Advisory Panel to assist it on decision-making in cases that are said to raise public interest issues. The panel includes a member of the LSC as chairman and representatives from consumer organisations, legal representatives and experts in public interest litigation (such as Liberty and Justice). The LSC has a discretion to refer cases to the panel.[43] Reference to the panel can be made in any case but may be particularly important in applications meeting the threshold for referral to the Special Cases Unit (see para 11.53).

---

38  FCDMG para 10.1.4.
39  FCDMG para 10.5.
40  FCDMG para 5.3.1.
41  FCDMG para 5.3.2.
42  FCDMG para 5.3.4.
43  Funding Code: Procedures para C47.

## Applications for judicial review

11.47    There are specific criteria to be satisfied for the funding of judicial review cases. These cases do not come within Funding Code s8 (see paras 11.22–11.28), but have their own tests for the grant of funding, which are set out in Funding Code s7.

11.48    Funding may be granted for Investigative Help (see para 11.44), but this can be refused if there are appeals or other rights of recourse that should be pursued before proceedings are considered.[44]

11.49    Public funding for full representation will be refused unless the proposed respondent has been given a reasonable opportunity to respond to the proposed challenge or to deal with the applicant's complaint, unless it is impracticable in the circumstances.[45]

11.50    Full representation will be refused if the prospects of successfully obtaining the substantive order sought in the proceedings are:

- unclear;
- borderline and the case does not appear to have significant wider public interest or to be of overwhelming importance to the client or to raise significant human rights issues;[46] or
- poor.

Further, full representation will be refused unless the likely benefits of the proceedings justify the likely costs, having regard to the prospects of success and all other circumstances.[47] This test involves similar concepts to those already discussed in relation to the criteria for funding claims under Funding Code s8 (see paras 11.29–11.40). Detailed guidance on the funding of applications for judicial review is set out in part 16 of the FCDMG.

11.51    If a judge has granted permission for a judicial review case to proceed to a full hearing, this indicates that the application for judicial review has some merit. In these circumstances a broader test for continued funding applies. The Code divides cases in which permission has been granted into two categories:

(a) cases where the Commission is satisfied that the claim has a significant wider public interest, is of overwhelming importance to the client or raises significant human rights issues (see para 11.31); and

(b) cases that do not exhibit any features in (a).

---

44    Funding Code para 7.2.3.
45    Funding Code para 7.4.4.
46    The definitions of these concepts in the FCDMG are referred to at para 11.31.
47    Funding Code para 7.4.6.

11.52 Cases which come under (a) must be granted funding unless there is information that was not before the court at the permission stage or that has subsequently come to light, from which it appears unreasonable to provide funding. In cases which come under (b) funding will be refused if the prospects of success are borderline or poor or the likely benefits of the proceedings do not appear to justify the likely costs having regard to the prospects of success and all the circumstances.[48]

## Special Cases Unit

11.53 The LSC has established a Special Cases Unit (SCU) whose responsibilities include dealing with high costs cases and multi-party actions. Solicitors are notified when their cases are referred to the SCU. High costs cases are those where:

- the actual or likely costs of the case exceed £25,000 (this includes counsel's fees, disbursements and any likely uplift or enhancement on profit costs, but excludes VAT); or
- if the case were to proceed to a contested trial or final hearing (or, in the case of appeal proceedings before the Court of Appeal or House of Lords, the conclusion of that appeal stage) the likely costs of the case might exceed £75,000 (again this figures includes counsel's fees, disbursements and any likely uplift or enhancement on profit costs, but excludes VAT).[49]

11.54 Once a case is referred to the SCU, the solicitors involved must prepare a case plan, showing the proposed stages of work on a costed basis.[50] A contract is then entered into with the LSC on the basis of the agreed case plan. The case plan can be amended as the litigation develops. Costs agreed under the plan (after the first £25,000 of work) will be at risk rates, which tend to be relatively low, both for solicitors and counsel. However, both can recover more substantial fees from the defendant if he or she is ultimately ordered to pay the claimant's legal costs. If the costs are paid by the LSC there is, unusually, no detailed assessment of costs by the court and the Commission pays the costs as agreed in the contract. Provided the actual cost is at least 95 per cent of the agreed price, then that price is payable. If the actual cost is between 50–95 per cent of the agreed price, the actual cost plus 5 per cent of the price is payable. If the actual cost is less than 50 per cent of the agreed price, then only the actual cost is payable.

---

48 Funding Code para 7.5.
49 Funding Code: Procedures para C23.
50 There is a template on the LSC's website (www.legalservices.gov.uk) which can be converted into a word document and amended.

*Effect of notices to show cause*

11.55    The full circumstances in which funding certificates can be revoked or discharged is beyond the scope of this work. Where the LSC proposes to revoke or discharge a certificate, a notice to show cause as to why this should not occur is sent by the regional director. Practitioners should note that once the notice is served no further work can be provided under the certificate.[51]

## Alternative sources of funding

11.56    If public funding is refused, the refusal letter from the LSC will briefly explain the reasons. There is a right of appeal against refusal in many cases, although funding does not cover the appeal procedure. If the case has merit and public funding is unavailable, then it may be worthwhile exploring other options, in particular making inquiries as to whether:

- a trade union or other organisation such as Liberty or the Commission for Racial Equality will fund the case;
- the individual can pay for the case with his or her own money;
- there are lawyers prepared to act without charge;
- the case can be funded by way of a conditional fee agreement;
- the case can be funded from before the event insurance.

11.57    There may be other alternatives to litigation that can be pursued, for example a claim under the Criminal Injuries Compensation Scheme or an application to the Home Office for compensation for a wrongful conviction or charge. (Both of these alternatives are discussed in detail in chapter 17.)

*Funding by trade unions and other organisations*

11.58    Some trade unions will pay the legal costs of bringing a case against the police. This is especially likely if the incident arose out of a trade union activity, such as picketing. Other trade unions, whose members are especially likely to be arrested in the course of their work, will also fund cases. For instance, the National Union of Journalists, whose members are sometimes arrested while covering demonstrations, has helped a number of members in cases against the police. Generally,

---

51    Funding Code: Procedures paras C51.2 and C.55.3, in practical terms reversing the effect of *R (Machi) v LSC* [2001] EWCA Civ 2010, [2002] 1 WLR 983.

a client should apply for support through his or her shop steward or branch secretary. If they are unhelpful, he or she should write to the local district office or the general secretary at the union's national headquarters. If a union is unable to help, then consideration should be given to other organisations or individuals who might be interested in helping the case. If there is a lawyer who is able or willing to act without charge or if the claimant is financing the case him or herself it may be possible to get help from a union or other organisation to indemnify the claimant against having to pay the police legal costs if the case is lost.

11.59    The Commission for Racial Equality has power to fund or part fund actions for discrimination against the police that are brought under the Race Relations Act 1976. However, in practice it is very rare for the Commission to fund such a claim.

## Funding by the claimant

11.60    It is difficult to advise a paying client at the start of a case of the likely cost, especially since a high number of cases settle. However, if the case goes to trial, this could be some time after the event by which time substantial costs will have been incurred that could be far beyond the means of an ordinary person.

11.61    It is, of course, important to keep a client informed of costs being incurred on his or her behalf as the case proceeds so that he or she can monitor the situation. The real problem lies with the costs being incurred by the police, which the claimant will probably have to pay if he or she loses the case. Often the claimant may be the only witness on his or her side. But the police will frequently have many witnesses: the arresting officers, their superior officers, the custody officer, officers who saw what happened at the police station. All these witnesses have to be interviewed; statements have to be taken and cross-checked. In many cases it is safe to assume that the police costs will be much higher than the claimant's. This unknown costs risk places a huge burden on any client not in receipt of legal aid.

## Conditional fee agreements

11.62    Conditional fee agreements (CFAs) permit clients to agree with their lawyers that the lawyers will not receive all or part of their fees and/or expenses if the case is lost, but that if it succeeds the lawyers will

52  Courts and Legal Services Act 1990 s58.

receive an uplift in addition to their usual fees.[52] CFAs are now permitted in relation to a wide range of proceedings, including all types of likely claims against the police.[53] The maximum uplift to their fees that lawyers can recover under a CFA is 100 per cent.[54] There are various matters that must be stated in a CFA for it to be effective,[55] including the amount of the agreed success fee (the uplift) and the basis upon which that figure has been calculated. If the claim succeeds, the court can order the unsuccessful party to pay any success fee and insurance payments that the successful party incurred as a result of entering into a CFA.[56] Insurance premiums are usually incurred if a CFA is entered into as the claimant needs to take out insurance to cover the risk that the claim will be lost and he or she will be ordered to pay the defendant's costs. If the claimant is unable to arrange such insurance then he or she would be taking a very considerable financial risk to embark upon litigation by way of a CFA. For straightforward personal injury cases such insurance policies are now commonplace. However, insurers are generally very reluctant to insure against the risk of a claimant losing an action against the police, because the claims tend to be complex, expensive and the prospects of success relatively uncertain. For similar reasons, solicitors are often unwilling to represent claimants in police actions on CFAs.

11.63    It has previously been generally accepted that most claims against the police are unsuitable for conditional fees.[57] However, the LSC has raised the issue of CFAs being used for actions against the police in a recent consultation.[58]

## Before the event insurance

11.64    Sometimes potential claimants will have legal expenses insurance as a part of other insurance policies they hold, for example in relation to their home contents insurance, mortgage policy or car insurance. This form of insurance, if available, will cover the costs of the case from the outset and is known as 'before the event' insurance. In contrast, insurance that is limited to paying the other party's costs if the

53    Courts and Legal Services Act 1990 s58A.
54    Conditional Fees Agreements Order 2000 SI No 823.
55    See Courts and Legal Services Act 1990 s58(3) and (4) and Conditional Fees Agreements Regulations 2000 SI No 692.
56    Access to Justice Act 1999 s20.
57    Institute of Advanced Legal Studies, 'Profiling general civil litigation', June 2002.
58    'A New Focus for Civil Legal Aid'.

claim is lost (discussed at para 11.62 in relation to CFAs) is known as 'after the event' insurance. If a 'before the event' insurer's policy is willing to fund a case against the police then it would usually be a requirement for the solicitor to be a member of the panel of solicitors that the insurance company retains. At the time of writing this book, the writers are unaware of any case where such insurance has been granted to fund an entire case against the police.

# Limitation periods

11.65 Limitation periods should not usually prove to be a problem provided the potential claimant and his or her lawyers act promptly. However, there are different time limits for different types of cases and it is important to be aware of these.

## Negligence claims

11.66 For an action which consists of, or includes, a claim in respect of personal injuries caused by negligence, nuisance or any breach of duty (contractual, statutory or otherwise), the primary limitation period is three years from the date when the cause of action is complete (usually the date of the incident itself).[59] However, the three-year period can run from a subsequent point if the 'date of knowledge' is later. The date of knowledge is the time when the potential claimant first had knowledge:

- that the injury in question was significant;
- that the injury was attributable in whole or in part to the act or omission relied upon; and
- of the identify of the defendant and (if different) the identity of the person responsible for the act or omission relied on.[60]

11.67 An injury is treated as being significant for these purposes if the person in question would reasonably have considered it sufficiently serious to justify instituting proceedings against a defendant who did not dispute liability and who was able to satisfy judgment.[61] Knowledge is judged not only by reference to what the potential claimant actually knew, but also by reference to the information he or she might reasonably be expected

---

59  Limitation Act 1980 s11(4).
60  Limitation Act 1980 s14(1).
61  Limitation Act 1980 s14(2).

to acquire, including with the help of experts,[62] such as solicitors or doctors. If the potential claimant knows of the relevant factual matters necessary to make out a case, it is irrelevant that he or she does not appreciate that as a matter of law a claim exists (for example because he or she has never heard of the tort of negligence). Lack of awareness of the relevant law does not affect the date of knowledge.[63]

11.68    Even if the claimant is outside the three-year period he or she can still apply to the court to allow a claim out of time in cases involving personal injuries and death caused by negligence, nuisance or breach of duty.[64] The court will consider whether it is equitable to allow such a claim to proceed. In determining this issue the court will have regard to:

- the length of and the reasons for the delay;
- the extent to which any relevant evidence has been rendered less cogent by the delay;
- the conduct of the claimant, for example the extent to which he or she sought to obtain expert advice and the nature of any advice received and the extent to which he or she acted promptly once he or she was aware of the need to issue proceedings;
- the conduct of the defendant in so far as that was responsible for any of the delay incurred.[65]

## Intentional torts

11.69    However, the three-year rule does not apply to claims for injuries arising from deliberate assault or from other intentional torts.[66] In these circumstances the applicable limitation period is six years.[67] Thus the six-year period applies to claims in false imprisonment, misfeasance, malicious prosecution, trespass to land and wrongful interference with goods even if the case involves seeking damages for personal injuries. Claims for damages under the Protection from Harassment Act 1997 are excluded from the three-year rule.[68] The six-year period runs from the date when the cause of action exists. Thus, in a case of false imprisonment time runs from the point of detention. In a case of malicious prosecution time does not begin to run until the date when the claimant

---

62    Limitation Act 1980 s14(3).
63    Limitation Act 1980 s14(1).
64    Limitation Act 1980 s33.
65    Limitation Act 1980 s33(3).
66    *Stubbings v Webb* [1993] 1 All ER 322, HL.
67    Limitation Act 1980 s2.

is acquitted or the criminal case is otherwise determined in his or her favour.[69] This is because a favourable termination of the criminal proceedings is an essential ingredient of a successful cause of action for malicious prosecution.[70] However, when the claim is brought in misfeasance the limitation period runs from the point when the misfeasance occurred and damage was suffered (where damage is required to complete the cause of action, as discussed in chapter 7). Accordingly, in a situation where a claimant was acquitted on appeal some years after officers fabricated evidence to support the conviction, the limitation period in relation to a claim in misfeasance would expire some considerable time before an action for malicious prosecution became statute barred.

## Exceptions in the Limitation Act

11.70   The Limitation Act 1980 does contain some exceptions to the rules discussed above. There are two exceptions that may be relevant to claims against the police. Firstly, time does not begin to run against a minor until he or she reaches the age of 18. Thus, if the alleged police misconduct occurred during the claimant's childhood the applicable limitation period would not start to run until he or she attained adulthood.

11.71       Secondly, the running of the appropriate limitation period is delayed where 'any fact relevant to the claimant's right of action has been deliberately concealed from him by the defendant'. In these circumstances the period runs from the time when the claimant discovers the concealment or from the point when he or she could have discovered it by using reasonable diligence.[71] A deliberate breach of duty in circumstances where it is unlikely to be discovered for some time amounts to deliberate concealment for these purposes.[72] Deliberate concealment therefore covers intentional wrongdoing that, by its nature, is unlikely to be discovered for a considerable period of time, if the wrongdoer does nothing to draw it to the claimant's attention.[73] Accordingly, this concept could cover police misconduct that was not readily apparent to

---

68   Limitation Act 1980 s11(1A).
69   *Dunlop v HM Customs & Excise* (1998) *Times* 17 March.
70   See paras 7.15–7.18.
71   Limitation Act 1980 s32(1).
72   Limitation Act 1980 s32(2).
73   *Cave v Robinson* [2002] 2 All ER 641, HL.

the claimant at the time but emerges subsequently, for example if officers pressurised or induced a third party falsely to incriminate the claimant. In this instance the claimant would know from the outset that the testimony incriminating him or her was false, but he or she would not necessarily appreciate that this stemmed from improper police behaviour. The deliberate concealment must relate to a fact that forms part of the 'right of action', as opposed to those which simply strengthen an existing case.[74] Accordingly, it would be difficult for the claimant to obtain an advantage from this statutory provision in a false imprisonment claim, as the cause of action is treated as complete when the detention occurs and any subsequently discovered facts would bolster an existing claim, rather than create a fresh cause of action.[75] In contrast, in a malicious prosecution claim, a lack of reasonable and probable cause for the prosecution and malice on the part of the wrongdoer are intrinsic elements of the cause of action;[76] thus subsequently discovered police misconduct relating to those issues may well amount to facts relevant to the right of action, so that the running of the limitation period is postponed until they came to light.

## Human Rights Act claims

11.72    The limitation period for bringing proceedings against a public authority under the Human Rights Act 1998 is short. Proceedings must be brought before the end of one year beginning with the date on which the act complained of took place.[77] However, there is provision for a longer period if the 'court or tribunal considers it equitable having regard to all the circumstances'.[78] The one-year period is subject to any rule imposing a stricter time limit in relation to the procedure in question.[79] Thus, for example, a judicial review application which relied upon breaches of the Human Rights Act 1998 would be subject to the usual three-month time period applicable to such claims.[80] However, where a person does not bring proceedings against a public authority

---

74    *Johnson v Chief Constable of Surrey* (1992) *Times* 23 November, CA.

75    As is illustrated by the decision in *Johnson v Chief Constable of Surrey*.

76    See para 7.5.

77    Human Rights Act 1998 s7(5)(a).

78    Human Rights Act 1998 s7(5)(b).

79    Human Rights Act 1998 s7(5).

80    See para 17.80.

but merely seeks to rely on his or her rights under the European Convention of Human Rights in relation to legal proceedings brought by others, no limitation period is imposed by the Human Rights Act 1998.[81]

## Discrimination claims

11.73   The time limit for bringing proceedings under the Race Relations Act 1976 is within six months less one day from the date of the act complained of.[82] It is possible to obtain a two-month extension where a claim is made to the Commission for Racial Equality for assistance within the six-month period.[83] The Commission can grant a further month's extension if it is considering the application. The six-month period for bringing a claim does not begin to run until the conclusion of 'an act extending over a period'.[84] The court has a discretion to extend the time limit for bringing discrimination claims where it considers it 'just and equitable to do so'.[85] Similar limitation provisions apply in relation to discrimination on the grounds of sex and disability. These issues are discussed in detail at paras 10.133–10.136.

11.74   There may be instances where the same facts give rise to a number of different limitation periods. For example, if a person is stopped and searched in a manner which gives rise to a potential claim under the Race Relations Act 1976 and is then prosecuted, but the proceedings are not concluded until more than six months after the initial incident, consideration should be given to issuing proceedings in the county court under the Act and then staying these proceedings pending the outcome of the criminal case. The priority for the potential claimant may well be to secure an acquittal on the criminal case and he or she may not wish to aggravate the police or CPS by alerting them to a potential race case. In these circumstances it is open to the adviser to issue proceedings within the initial six-month period, but to delay serving them until the conclusion of the criminal matter.[86]

11.75   A note should be made of the expiry of the limitation period in all cases. This is especially important in cases where there is a criminal trial

---

81   Human Rights Act 1998 s7(1).
82   Race Relations Act (RAA) 1976 s68(2).
83   RRA 1976 s68(3).
84   RRA 1976 s68(7)(b).
85   RRA 1976 s68(6).
86   Subject to compliance with procedural rules relating to service of the claim form: see CPR rr7.5 and 7.6, discussed at paras 12.15–12.16.

to be resolved before a civil action can be considered. Indeed, as a matter of good practice, consideration should be given to opening a civil action file at the first indication that this is a possibility, even if no action is taken until the criminal trial is over.

## Avoiding delay

11.76   When people start off their case they are often fired with enthusiasm and a sense of outrage about what has happened to them. As the case drags on and they begin to realise just how long the whole process is likely to take they begin to wonder if it is all worthwhile. This feeling that the case is never going to end can seem all the worse if it was started with an unrealistic expectation of how soon the case could be concluded, and clients should be warned of the possible delays and the reasons for them at the very start of the case. This is especially important for the growing number of people who have to pay significant contributions to the public funding they receive throughout the case. Any delay can also be used by the police to discredit the claimant. The police may argue that the claimant could not have been badly affected by an incident otherwise he or she would have taken action earlier. Very often barristers instructed by the police will cross-examine claimants as to the reason for delaying in bringing an action.

11.77   Almost all the pressure for a speedy hearing of the case must come from the claimant's side, and almost all the pressure to delay will inevitably come from the defendant. It is also quite usual for defendants in any type of civil action to use the maximum amount of time available in the hope of pressing the claimant to withdraw the case or to accept a very low settlement. Police solicitors are aware that claimants in civil actions against the police can (and do) become disillusioned enough to do this on occasions. However, the position has improved somewhat, from a claimant's perspective, in recent years. The Civil Procedure Rules (CPR) place a duty on both parties to help the court further the overriding objective, which includes ensuring that the case is dealt with expeditiously and fairly.[87] As a result of the procedural reforms introduced by the CPR (discussed in detail in chapter 12) the time scale between issue of proceedings and trial has significantly shortened for the majority of cases. As explained below, this is also in part because of the emphasis now contained in the pre-action protocols upon detailed preparation of the claim before proceedings are issued.

87   CPR r1.3.

# Pre-action protocols

11.78   The purpose of pre-action protocols is to trigger the early exchange of information between the parties, with a view to encouraging prompt settlement of the dispute, where appropriate and, where that cannot be achieved, assisting with the efficient progression of the litigation.[88]

11.79   Attempts to agree a specific pre-action protocol for actions against the police have not proved successful. Currently, most police forces will agree to follow the pre-action protocol that applies to personal injury cases, particularly if there is a personal injury element to the claim. Alternatively, the Practice Direction (PD) Protocols set out the steps that the parties are expected to take prior to the issue of litigation, where there is no applicable protocol. The court will expect substantial compliance with the steps set out in the relevant protocol and/or in the PD.[89] Failure to follow those steps will be taken into account when case management directions are given and can lead to costs sanctions.[90]

11.80   The Pre-Action Protocol for Personal Injury Claims (PI Protocol) includes the following steps:

- The claimant shall send two copies of the letter of claim[91] to the proposed defendant as soon as sufficient information is available to substantiate a realistic claim. The letter should contain a clear summary of the facts on which the claim is based, together with an account of injuries suffered and losses incurred. The letter should seek details of the defendant's insurers (where appropriate). It should contain sufficient information to enable the defendant to commence investigations and put at least a broad valuation on the 'risk'.[92]
- The defendant should acknowledge the letter of claim within 21 days and give details of his or her insurer (where appropriate).[93]
- The defendant/insurers then have a maximum of three months to investigate and reply stating whether liability is denied. If it is denied, reasons should be given.[94]

---

88  PD Protocols para 1.4.
89  PD Protocol para 2.2.
90  PD Protocol paras 2.1, 2.3 and 3.3.
91  Discussed in more detail at para 11.83.
92  PI Protocol paras 3.1–3.5.
93  PI Protocol para 3.6
94  PI Protocol para 3.7.

- If the defendant denies liability he or she should enclose documents with the reply that are material to the issues between the parties and which would be likely to come within the scope of disclosure that would be ordered by the court.[95]
- Where relevant, a schedule of special damages detailing the claimant's financial losses, plus supporting documents, should be sent to the defendant as soon as is practicable.[96]

11.81    The PI Protocol (and the PD) also deal with the instruction of joint experts – this issue has been discussed at paras 2.36–2.37. If it will take some time for the adviser to investigate liability and quantum sufficiently to draft a letter of claim, it is worth sending a letter putting the defendant on notice of the potential claim in the interim, so that relevant documentation is preserved.

11.82    The PD contains comparable pre-action stages to those set out in the PI Protocol. Parties to the dispute are encouraged to follow a reasonable procedure suitable to their particular circumstances and which is intended to avoid litigation.[97] The PD then sets out the steps that this should normally include.[98] They are very similar to those already summarised from the PI Protocol, save that it is suggested that a reasonable time for the defendant's substantive response to the letter of claim may be one month (as opposed to three) and that the letter of claim should draw attention to the court's powers to impose sanctions if the PD is not complied with. The PD also encourages the letter of claim to identify and ask for copies of essential documents that the other party holds. This is good practice, whether or not the PI Protocol is applicable; chapter 2 suggests the kinds of documentation that the claimant's lawyers will want to seek at this stage – see paras 2.47–2.76.

## Letter of claim

11.83    The basic requirements of and time scale for a letter of claim are set out at para 11.80–11.82. The letter of claim is a very important document as it will heavily inform the proposed defendant's perception of the nature, the strength and the value of the claimant's case. It should contain a detailed account of the facts relied upon, the proposed causes of action and the heads of damage sought. It is helpful, where possible, to high-

---

95   PI Protocol para 3.10.
96   PI Protocol para 3.13.
97   PD Protocol para 4.2.
98   PD Protocol paras 4.2–4.10.

light the strengths of the proposed claim and to identify factors relevant to the compensation sought – for example if aggravated and/or exemplary damages are claimed, the letter should explain why. Although the letter does not have the formal status of a pleading, great care should be taken with its contents. If the factual account in the letter is inconsistent with that subsequently given in the particulars of claim or by the claimant at trial, he or she will be cross-examined upon the apparent discrepancies. Appendix B contains a specimen letter of claim.

11.84    Advisers frequently make an offer to settle the proposed action at the same stage as sending the letter of claim, by enclosing a second letter that complies with the requirements of CPR Pt 36.[99]

## Pre-action disclosure

11.85    Although some police forces are quite good at volunteering disclosure prior to proceedings being issued, other forces fail to provide adequate pre-action disclosure, even following a detailed letter of claim requesting specific relevant documents. In those circumstances an application for pre-action disclosure may be appropriate. Applications for disclosure before proceedings have started are permitted under Supreme Court Act 1981 s33 and County Court Act 1984 s52. The court can only make an order for pre-action disclosure where:

- the respondent to the application is likely to be a party to any subsequent proceedings;
- the applicant is also likely to be a party to those proceedings;
- if the proceedings had started, the documents sought would be within the ambit of 'standard disclosure';[100]
- disclosure before proceedings have started is desirable to dispose fairly of the anticipated proceedings, assist the dispute to be resolved without proceedings, or to save costs.[101]

11.86    Although it is necessary to show that the respondent/applicant is likely to be a party to any subsequent proceedings, it is not an additional requirement to establish that the initiation of proceedings is itself likely.[102] Pre-action disclosure may be desirable to dispose fairly of the anticipated proceedings where, for example, the claimant is unable to plead his or her case without the documents sought or where

---

99    See para 12.138 onwards.
100    See para 12.92 for a definition of standard disclosure.
101    CPR r31.16.
102    *Black v Sumitomo Corp* [2003] 3 All ER 631, CA.

he or she is unable to tell if there is sufficient merit to warrant issuing proceedings without the material in question.

11.87    Applications should be made in accordance with CPR Pt 23.[103] The application must be supported by evidence. This would usually be in the form of a witness statement from the claimant's solicitor, addressing each of the criteria summarised above. An order is unlikely to be granted unless voluntary disclosure of the documentation has first been sought and refused.[104]

11.88    However, advisers should be aware that whether the application for pre-action disclosure is successful or not, the courts generally order the applicant to pay the costs of the application. This can have significant ramifications for publicly funded claimants, who are likely to find that any damages they are subsequently awarded will be used to recover costs due to the defendant and to the LSC from the pre-action application. However, if it can be shown that the proposed litigation is a virtual inevitability and that the proposed defendant acted unreasonably in not supplying the documentation voluntarily, the court may be persuaded to award costs in the applicant's favour.

# Publicity

11.89    Complaints and especially civil actions against the police can often be high-profile cases in which the media express a strong interest, whether at a national or a local level. Solicitors need to consider their clients' feelings about publicity and the question should be raised in the first interview. Newspapers will always want photographs of clients to enhance an article and will want to speak to them personally, even if a press release has been put out. If there has been a conspicuous incident or an acquittal in a criminal trial, the media may already have contacted the client before legal advice is sought. However, in many cases, journalists will only really become interested if there is a settlement for a substantial amount of compensation or if the case reaches a full trial. Adverse publicity in itself may persuade the police to offer a generous settlement of the case. Sometimes, however publicity might make them more likely to fight the action.

11.90    If a client's reasons for bringing a case are to clear his or her name or to see the police being held accountable in public for their

---

103    See in particular CPR r23.6 and PD to CPR Pt 23. para 2.

104    In appropriate cases, practitioners will also wish to consider whether the documentation could be obtained by use of the Data Protection Act 1998 or the Freedom of Information Act 2000, as discussed in chapter 10.

misconduct then he or she may be extremely keen on publicity. It is possible to publicise the case at a number of stages – when public funding is granted, when proceedings are commenced, when the result of any police complaint becomes known, when a settlement is accepted or at the end of the trial. All are good opportunities to get the attention of the media. Journalists are bombarded with hundreds of press releases every day, so it is important that it is in an easily accessible format. It may also be important to prepare a press release if the case is lost, in order to put across any positive aspects from the client's point of view, to announce a possible appeal or to act as a counterweight to any statement the police are likely to have made to the press.

11.91    If a claimant does talk to the press before he or she has given evidence at trial, great care should be taken to ensure that nothing is said that could provide the defendant with material for cross-examination, such as inconsistencies or exaggeration in the claimant's account. If the claimant talks to the press at this stage it may very well be advisable to confine the discussion to background and/or very general matters (such as how upsetting the experience was, for example).

11.92    The press release should preferably be sent to a named journalist, usually the home affairs or legal correspondent. It should be faxed and then chased up with a telephone call. Local TV and radio should not be forgotten as quick and accessible ways to get coverage. In a few cases where publicity can be shown to be particularly important, such as in a test case or in achieving a settlement, the time spent on press work may be allowed on the costs assessment.

11.93    As many civil actions against the police are heard before juries, the closer the claim gets to trial, the more caution should be exercised in speaking publicly about the case, so as not to fall foul of the laws of contempt of court and the laws against perverting the course of justice.

11.94    It is equally important to protect clients from unwanted publicity. Some clients, for instance, may find it hugely embarrassing that they have been involved with the police or charged with an offence, even if they have subsequently been acquitted.

# The relationship between a police complaint and a civil action

11.95    Very often when a client first seeks advice, the main thing he or she wants is to see the relevant police officer(s) disciplined and/or criminally prosecuted. In the past, due to the low level of complaints that were upheld, advisers would explain to their clients that there was very little prospect of a formal police complaint succeeding and the officer(s) thereby being disciplined and/or prosecuted. Very often, the only form of accountability that a client could obtain was by bringing a civil action against the police and obtaining damages either by way of a settlement or by a successful finding at trial.

11.96     It is too early to say whether the creation of the Independent Police Complaints Commission (IPCC) will change the success rate of complaints made against the police. Chapter 4 deals in more detail with the new complaints procedure; the vast majority of complaints will still be investigated by the police (as opposed to independent investigators). Even if a complaint is upheld a successful complainant is not entitled to compensation.

11.97     Most experienced practitioners are now advising their clients to make complaints under the new system. As well as the possibility of having the complaint upheld, there are also potential tactical advantages in making a complaint. The procedure for making a complaint is simple and informal (see chapter 4 which deals with this in more detail). At the time of writing, the Government has recently announced plans to require those seeking public funding for civil actions to pursue a police complaint first (see para 11.21).

11.98     As there is now a presumption in favour of disclosure of documents by the IPCC, making a complaint may enable the potential claimant's solicitor to obtain relevant documentation from the complaints investigation at an earlier stage than it would be provided in the civil litigation. The IPCC or the appropriate authority (depending on the type of complaint) must keep the complainant informed of certain decisions and actions if and when they happen throughout the investigation process.[105] The provision of information from the complainant's investigation may enable the claimant's adviser to check for inconsistencies between different versions of events given by police officers. Further, where a complaint is made, the police are under a duty to take steps to obtain and preserve evidence relating to the conduct that is the subject of the complaint as soon as practicable.[106] This means that making a complaint is an invaluable way of ensuring the preservation of evidence. This might involve such things as preserving documentary records, conducting searches, taking photographs and ordering medical examinations of both the complainant and the police officer(s).

11.99     If a complaint is made but the complainant declines to co-operate with the investigation and fails to provide information about the relevant

105  Police Reform Act 2002 s20 and Sch 3.
106  Police Reform Act 2002 Sch 3 para 1.

events, it is likely that the investigation will be dispensed with.[107] Accordingly, if a complaint is initiated, solicitors will usually advise their clients to provide information to the investigation. In many instances the solicitor acting for the complainant will prepare a statement of his or her account of the relevant events, for submission to the investigation, rather than permitting him or her to be interviewed. Provided the statement is carefully drafted, this is likely to minimise the risk of inconsistencies arising between the claimant's account provided for the purposes of the litigation and his or her account given in relation to the complaint. However, one potential drawback of making a complaint from a claimant's perspective is if it leads to a lengthy delay in the progress of the civil action. This issue is discussed at paras 11.101–11.103.

11.100    Advisers should also be aware that the police and the IPCC can now investigate more serious matters even in the absence of a complaint when they are made aware that a civil action is possible (usually through the letter of claim). The procedure for this, and the ramifications for the claimant, are discussed more fully in chapter 4.

## Stay of proceedings

11.101   When a complaints investigation is on-going, defendants to civil actions against the police have tended to seek a stay of the civil proceedings until the complaints process is finally determined. However, if this is likely to lead to a lengthy delay in the progress of the civil claim, then those advising the claimant will wish to consider whether an application for such a stay should be opposed. Complaints investigations can take a considerable amount of time to resolve, often years rather than months, particularly in those cases where the results of the investigation are referred to the CPS to consider whether a criminal prosecution should be brought, before disciplinary charges are considered (as explained in chapter 5). Lengthy delays in the civil litigation may have the effect of demoralising and/or causing undue stress to the claimant. It may lead to him or her being kept out of compensation that is due to him or her for a protracted period. Moreover, the quality of evidence may be adversely affected in the interim as witnesses' powers of recollection diminish and/or they become untraceable.

11.102    The court has a discretion to grant a stay of civil proceedings.[108] A chief officer defendant to a civil action against the police will generally

---

107   See para 4.175 onwards.
108   CPR r3.1(2)(f).

argue that a stay is appropriate because otherwise he or she will have to indicate his or her view on the allegations made in the litigation before decisions are made in the disciplinary context. It is argued that this may in turn lead to successful representations from officers involved in subsequent disciplinary proceedings that their actions have been prejudged, in particular as the chief officer has overall responsibility for discipline in his or her force.[109] It may also be argued that a claimant will be contaminated as a potential witness in disciplinary proceedings if the civil claim progresses and he or she thereby obtains disclosure of material that could affect the content of evidence that he or she might give at the disciplinary hearing.[110]

11.103    However, as has been discussed in chapters 4 and 5, in recent years the vast majority of police complaints have not led to either criminal or disciplinary charges being brought. Thus, while the complaints process is on-going, claimants can argue that any alleged prejudice to potential disciplinary or criminal proceedings asserted by the defendant is, at best, a relatively remote prospect. The general approach of the courts has been to accede to a defendant's application for a stay only where he or she is able to show a real danger of prejudice to either the civil litigation or to the relevant criminal/disciplinary proceedings relied upon, otherwise the claimant is entitled to have his or her claim progressed in the normal way.[111] As the authorities emphasise that the risk of prejudice must be real, rather than notional, before a stay is granted, it is doubtful that a complaints investigation which is unlikely to result in criminal or disciplinary proceedings can give rise to a sufficient risk of prejudice.[112]

11.104    If disciplinary charges have actually been brought in relation to events covered by the civil action, a stay will be more difficult to resist. Nonetheless, a chief officer can minimise the prospect of officers

---

109  As described in chapter 5.

110  In reliance on the views expressed in *R (Green) v Police Complaints Authority* [2004] 1 WLR 725, HL, discussed at para 4.161.

111  *Jefferson Ltd v Bhetcha* [1979] 1 WLR 898, CA; *Surrey Oaklands NHS Trust v Hurley* (1999) 20 May, QBD, unreported; *Secretary of State for Health v Norton Healthcare Limited* [2004] Eu LR 12.

112  Submissions to this effect were accepted by DJ Lightman in refusing the defendant's application for a stay in *Abraham and Reid v Commissioner of Police of the Metropolis* [2004] 18 November. Authorities which defendants have tended to rely upon in support of an application for a stay, in particular *North Yorkshire Police v Rose* (1995) 14 November, EAT, unreported and *North Yorkshire Police v Ashurst* (1996) 19 January, EAT, unreported, are simply decisions made on their particular facts where, in particular, disciplinary proceedings were already on-going and likely to conclude within a reasonable time.

facing disciplinary charges from raising abuse of process or bias type arguments by a careful separation of and delegation of his or her administrative and disciplinary functions.[113]

11.105    In opposing a stay a claimant can also point to his or her right under article 6 of the European Convention on Human Rights to have a determination of civil rights and obligations heard within a 'reasonable time'. Further, part of the overriding objective, which governs the exercise of all discretionary power under the CPR, is for cases to be dealt with expeditiously.[114]

11.106    Even if the defendant does manage to show a real risk of prejudice if a stay is not granted, the court should balance this prospect against any hardship that would be occasioned to the claimant if the stay were granted, to assess where the interests of justice lie overall.[115] Accordingly, a claimant can highlight any prejudice that a stay is likely to cause, whether in terms of increased anxiety and/or adverse effects on potential evidence, as discussed at para 11.101 above.

# Whom to sue

## Vicarious liability

11.107  The principle of vicarious liability (which holds employers jointly liable with employees for their employees' wrongful acts committed in the course of their employment) does not apply at common law to members of a police force because constables are not employees of the police authority (see para 3.9). However the principle has been extended to include the police service by statute.[116] Thus, the chief officer of police is liable for any unlawful conduct committed by police officers, including special constables 'under his direction and control in the performance or purported performance of their functions' in the same manner as an employer is liable in respect of unlawful conduct of its employees in the course of their employment. Accordingly he or she is, in the case of a tort, treated for all purposes as a joint

---

113  As recommended in *R v Chief Constable of Devon and Cornwall ex p Hay* [1996] 2 All ER 711, QBD.

114  CPR r1.2.

115  *Jefferson Ltd v Bhetcha* [1979] 1 WLR 898, CA; *Secretary of State for Health v Norton Healthcare Limited* [2004] Eu LR 12.

116  Police Act 1996 s88(1), as amended by the Police Reform Act 2002 which replaced references to 'torts' with 'unlawful conduct' thus including conduct that is unlawful, eg because it is contrary to the Human Rights Act 1998.

tortfeasor. The chief officer of police can therefore be sued and in practice he or she should normally be sued alone. While it is possible to sue the individual officers either alone or with the chief officer, there is usually no advantage and there will frequently be serious disadvantages. Where individual officers and the chief officer have been sued together, it is common for the chief officer to want to settle out of court but for the individual officers to hold out for a full hearing in court in the hope of clearing their names. This situation only causes greater delay and a greater costs risk.

11.108    A greater sum of damages cannot be won by suing individuals in addition to the chief officer. The only difference is that the damages are apportioned between them. Police authorities have a wide discretion to pay any damages and costs awarded against individual officers in proceedings for unlawful conduct committed by them and in practice usually do so. The power extends to any sum required in connection with the settlement of any claim that has or might have given rise to civil proceedings, and as to any costs incurred and not recovered in any such proceedings.

11.109    If individual officers are not joined as defendants, (but are simply witnesses) this enables the claimant to try and apply for them to be excluded from the courtroom until their evidence is given. Although there is no general rule that witnesses should be kept out of court until they have given their evidence, it is common practice for counsel to make such an application at the trial to avoid a witness's evidence being affected by what he or she may have heard in court. (See para 13.10 which deals with this in more detail.) However, parties to the action have the right to hear all the evidence.

11.110    There is, however, an advantage in suing the chief officer and the individual officers involved if there is a possibility that the chief officer might deny liability on the basis that the officers were not acting in the performance or purported performance of their functions at the relevant time. In such circumstances the case might be lost against the chief officer but still succeed against the individual. In practice, it is possible (subject to limitation periods) to wait and see if the chief officer denies liability on this ground and then to join the individual officer(s) to the action if necessary.

11.111    It is unusual for a chief officer not to take responsibility for the actions of an officer, but in *Makanjuola v Commissioner of Police for the Metropolis* it was held that the Commissioner could not be held liable for an officer who allegedly demanded sexual favours in return for not reporting a suspect's immigration 'irregularities', because the alleged misconduct was so extreme that it could not even purportedly have been done in the performance of a police function.[117]

11.112    However in *Lister v Hesley Hall Ltd*[118] the House of Lords recently reformulated the test to be applied for determining vicarious liability in cases of intentional wrongdoing, particularly when an employee has set out to benefit himself. The case involved whether a children's home was vicariously liable for acts of sexual abuse of children in its care by a warden at the home. The House of Lords held that the overall picture of the abuse carried out and the nature of the warden's employment should be considered, rather than the acts of abuse looked at in isolation. The House of Lords said that the correct test was:

> The question is whether the warden's torts were so closely connected with his employment that it will be fair and just to hold the employers vicariously liable.

11.113   On the particular facts, the defendant was vicariously liable for the acts of abuse as the warden had used and abused his position of employment at the home in order to 'groom' the children and to facilitate his abuse of them. Thus, in assessing whether vicarious liability exists, the correct approach is to concentrate on the relative closeness of the connection between the nature of the job and the particular tort and to ask whether, looking at the matter in the round, it is just and reasonable to hold the employers vicariously liable. In deciding this question a relevant factor to consider is whether the risk to others was created by an employer entrusting duties, tasks and functions to an employee.[119]

11.114    The implications of the *Lister* case for civil actions against the police are potentially far-ranging. The statutory test is that the chief officer can be vicariously liable for unlawful conduct of constables in the performance 'or purported' performance of their functions. If the misconduct is so extreme as to throw doubt on whether the conduct could even be in the purported performance of police functions it will be necessary to ask whether it was so closely connected with police functions that it will be fair and just to hold the chief officer liable. Presumably, if an individual officer is purporting to carry out policing functions then there can be little doubt that his or her chief officer will be vicariously liable for any torts committed by him or her. In other words, if the officer was making the most of an opportunity

117   *Makanjuola v Commissioner of Police of the Metropolis* [1992] 3 All ER 617.
118   [2001] 2 All ER 769.
119   See *Bernard v Att-Gen of Jamaica* [2004] UKPC 47 discussed at para 11.116.

presented to him or her by his office and he or she was taking advantage of the position in which the chief officer had placed him or her, then the chief officer could be liable.

11.115   The potential breadth of the application of the *Lister* principle to actions against the police is illustrated by two recent cases. In *Weir v Bettison (Chief Constable of Merseyside)*[120] the Court of Appeal held that the chief officer was liable for an assault on a member of the public by an off-duty constable. The officer believed that the claimant had interfered with his girlfriend's belongings and manhandled him down a flight of stairs and slapped him hard. The constable told the claimant that he was a police officer and that he was going to take him to the police station. The Court of Appeal held that as the officer had purported to act in his capacity as an officer at the time, vicarious liability was established. The court held that the powers of a police officer are conferred by law, by virtue of the office of constable, so there is no necessity for any authorisation given by a superior officer. Thus in practice the vicarious liability of a chief officer is wider than that of employers.

11.116   In *Bernard v Attorney-General of Jamaica*[121] the Privy Council held that the defendant was vicariously liable for the unlawful shooting of the claimant by a constable of the Jamaica Constabulary Force. The claimant was using a public telephone when the officer intervened saying he was 'police' and demanding to use the phone immediately. The claimant refused to let go of the phone and the officer slapped and shoved the claimant and then shot him in the head with his service revolver. There were some factual uncertainties over the circumstances of the shooting. The Privy Council assumed in the defendant's favour that the constable was not on duty at the time of the shooting and that his indication of needing to use the phone for police business was a pretext to get his own way, rather than due to a genuine police emergency. The Privy Council decided that vicarious liability was nonetheless established as the shooting had arisen from the officer's purported assertion of police authority (to which the claimant refused to yield). In addition the officer had subsequently arrested the claimant for assaulting him in the execution of his duty. Although the arrest was entirely bogus in the circumstances, the arrest for this alleged offence underscored that the constable was purporting to act as a police officer immediately before he shot the claimant.

---

120   [2003] ICR 708
121   [2004] UKPC 47.

The Privy Council also took into account the risk created by the fact that the police authorities routinely permitted constables to take loaded service revolvers home and to carry them while off duty. The latter factor would not have been enough in itself to establish vicarious liability, but it reinforced the court's conclusion in the circumstances.

11.117    The mere fact that a person who is behaving badly happens to be an off-duty officer is insufficient to make a chief officer liable for his or her acts. However, as the authorities discussed above show, if an off-duty police officer seeks to gain some improper advantage in his or her private life when engaged in a confrontation with a member of the public, by purporting to acting as a constable, he or she invokes his or her office and the potential liability of the relevant chief officer.

11.118    In *Racz v Home Office*,[122] which was decided on the pre-*Lister* law, the House of Lords overturned a Court of Appeal decision that the very nature of the tort of misfeasance in a public office was such that in law the Home Office could not be vicariously liable for prison officers who would be necessarily acting outside the scope of their authority or maliciously when the tort was committed. Lord Jauncey said that the nature of the tort was not decisive as to vicarious liability and refused to strike out the part of the claimant's claim that alleged misfeasance in public office. Whether vicarious liability could be established in any particular instance of misfeasance would now depend upon the principles identified in the recent case law discussed above.

## Mutual aid, cross-border aid and collaboration agreements

11.119   The chief officer of any police force in England and Wales may, on the application of any other such chief officer, provide police officers or other assistance for the purpose of enabling the other force to meet any special demand on its resources.[123] If such mutual aid arrangements cannot be made or cannot be made in time the Home Secretary can direct a chief officer to provide such officers or other assistance as he specifies where it appears to him that it is expedient to do so in the interests of public safety or order. While a police officer is provided to another force under a mutual aid arrangement he or

---

122  [1994] 1 All ER 97, HL.
123  Police Act 1996 s24(1). Similar provisions apply to the British Transport Police Force (Police Act 1996 s24(4A)) and to the National Crime Squad (Police Act 1996 s24(5)) and to the National Criminal Intelligence Service (Police Act 1997 s23).

she is treated as being under the direction and control of the receiving chief officer. Accordingly the chief officer of the receiving force is statutorily vicariously liable for the officer's unlawful conduct.[124]

11.120   Analogous arrangements apply for cross-border aid between forces in England and Wales, Scotland and Northern Ireland.[125]

11.121   Mutual aid and cross-border aid must be distinguished from collaboration agreements where chief officers of two or more forces agree that particular functions (for example those performed by underwater search units) can best be carried out by the forces acting jointly.[126] The legislation is silent on the question of whether an officer from one force is under the direction and control of the chief officer in whose area he or she is operating under such an agreement. It may therefore be necessary to establish the question of direction and control as a matter of fact rather than simply assume that the officer is operating under a mutual or cross-border aid arrangement.

11.122   Police officers who are seconded to undertake certain 'relevant services' (sometimes known as 'central services') outside their own force are treated as remaining members of their original police force for certain purposes of the Police Act 1996. However, the Home Secretary is vicariously liable for any unlawful conduct committed by such officers in the performance or purported performance of their functions and in the case of a tort is treated for all purposes as a joint tortfeasor.[127] 'Relevant services' includes such things as duties at police training colleges, forensic science laboratories and staff officers to the Inspectors of Constabulary.

## Cadets

11.123   A police cadet is not a constable or a member of a police force but is treated as being a person undergoing training with a view to becoming a member of a police force. For the purposes of vicarious liability the police authority is treated as the cadet's employer and thus is the body which should be sued, instead of the chief officer.[128]

---

124   Police Act 1996 s24(3).
125   Police Act 1996 s98 as amended.
126   Police Act 1996 s23 as amended.
127   Police Act 1997 s97(9).
128   Police Act 1996 s28 as amended.

## Independent police forces

11.124 Aside from the 43 police forces maintained by police authorities for those areas and the National Crime Squad and the National Criminal Intelligence Service, a number of organisations have powers to maintain bodies of constables. The most important of these so-called 'independent' police forces are the British Transport Police, the Ministry of Defence Police and the Atomic Energy Authority Police (see chapter 3).

11.125 Civil actions concerning officers in other independent police forces, such as harbours or airport police, may usually be brought against the employing body or the individual or both, subject to any local or private Act of Parliament governing the force.[129]

## Special constables

11.126 Special constables are personally liable for their unlawful conduct in the civil courts in the same way as regular members of a police force. A chief officer is liable for the wrongful acts of special constables under his or her control. The main difference between special constables and regular members of a police force in the context of misconduct cases lies in the extent of their geographical jurisdiction. A person who is a special constable and who purports to act as a police officer outside an area in which he or she has jurisdiction is in the same position as an ordinary member of the public. For further information on special constables see paras 3.15–3.18.

## Civilian employees

11.127 There has been a significant move in recent years towards the civilianisation of functions formerly carried out by police officers – see paras 3.21–3.31. Civilian staff carry out a range of duties, including those of control room staff, front desk staff, scene of crimes officers and the handling and transportation of prisoners. Civilian staff employed by police authorities are under the direction and control of the chief officer of police, but the employing police authority nevertheless remains vicariously liable for their wrongful acts. An action may therefore be brought against either the individual or the police authority, although it will usually be preferable to proceed only against the authority.

129 See *Halsbury's Laws*, Vol 36(1) Police, 4th ed, 1999.

## Community safety accreditation schemes

11.128  Chapter 3 explains community safety accreditation schemes which were introduced by the Police Reform Act 2002 to contribute to community safety and security, and (in co-operation with the police) to combat crime, disorder, public nuisance and other forms of anti-social behaviour. In relation to the accredited persons it is the employer who is vicariously liable.[130]

## National Criminal Intelligence Service

11.129  The National Criminal Intelligence Service (NCIS) provides criminal intelligence in the field of serious and organised crime. The Police Act 1997 created the NCIS.

11.130     The head of the NCIS is a Director General who holds the rank of chief constable. Other members of NCIS are either police members of NCIS or members appointed.

11.131     The Director General of NCIS is liable in respect of any unlawful conduct of constables under his or her direction and control in the performance or purported performance of their functions 'in the like manner as a master is liable in respect of any unlawful conduct of his servants in the course of their employment'.[131] (See paras 3.47–3.51. for more information on the NCIS.)

## National Crime Squad

11.132  The function of the National Crime Squad (NCS) is to prevent and detect serious crime which is of relevance to more than one police force in England and Wales. The Police Act 1997 created the NCS.

11.133     The NCS is headed by a Director General who holds the office of constable and the rank of chief constable. Other members of NCS are either police members of NCS or other members appointed to be members of NCS as employees of the NCS Service Authority.

11.134     The Director General of NCS is liable in respect of any unlawful conduct of constables under his direction and control in the performance or purported performance of their functions 'in the like manner as a master is liable in respect of any unlawful conduct of his servants in the course of their employment'.[132]

---

130   Police Reform Act 2002 s42(10).
131   Police Act 1997 s42(1).
132   Police Act 1997 s86.

# CHAPTER 12

# Bringing the action – from issue of proceedings to exchange of witness statements

# Extension of public funding

12.1    Chapter 11 dealt in detail with applying for public funding. Most civil claims against the police are funded by the Legal Services Commission (LSC) under the Access to Justice Act 1999. The initial certificate of public funding granted by the LSC usually has a limitation attached to it, such as: 'limited to obtaining external counsel's opinion or the opinion of an external solicitor with higher court advocacy rights, particularly with regard to merits and quantum'. In these circumstances, the terms of the certificate will need to be extended before proceedings can be issued. This will normally involve the solicitor completing a CLS APP 8 Form, enclosing a positive opinion from counsel, addressing merits, quantum and the prescribed criteria for funding.[1] Practitioners will also need to check that the scope of the certificate includes all the causes of action now contemplated.

# The overriding objective

12.2    It is important for practitioners to be well versed in the rules that govern litigation. The Civil Procedure Rules 1998 (CPR) substantially changed the way civil cases are handled by the courts and also reinforced procedural rules which, although acknowledged in the past, were often not adhered to. Most parts of the CPR are supplemented by practice directions.

12.3    The courts must give effect to the overriding objective when exercising any powers conferred by the CPR.[2] The overriding objective is described as follows:

(1) These rules are a new procedural code with the overriding objective of enabling the court to deal with cases justly.
(2) Dealing with a case justly, includes, so far as it is practicable –
    (a) ensuring that the parties are on an equal footing;
    (b) saving expense;
    (c) dealing with the case in ways which are proportionate–
        (i) to the amount of money involved;
        (ii) to the importance of the case;
        (iii) to the complexity of the issues; and
        (iv) to the financial position of each party;
    (d) ensuring that it is dealt with expeditiously and fairly; and

---

1    The latter is discussed in paras 11.29–11.40.
2    CPR r1.2(a).

(e) allotting to it an appropriate share of the courts resources, whilst taking into account the need to allot resources to other cases.[3]

# Starting a claim

12.4    CPR Pt 7 sets out how to start proceedings. They are commenced by a 'claim form'. This is a single form of originating process for all claims in the High Court and the County Court.

## High Court or County Court?

12.5    If the proceedings include a claim for damages in respect of personal injury, they can only be commenced in the High Court if the financial value of the claim is £50,000 or more.[4] Accordingly, if a claimant in a civil action against the police seeks damages for personal injury, it is mandatory to start proceedings in the county court whenever the overall damages are unlikely to exceed £50,000.

12.6    In cases that do not include a claim for consequential personal injuries, the claimant has a greater freedom to select whether to commence proceedings in the High Court or in the county court. There are often benefits from the claimant's point of view to commencing proceedings in the High Court, in particular because of the generally faster and superior quality of the judicial decision-making and in attaining a potential psychological advantage over the defendant in stressing the seriousness of the matter. However, it is advisable to consider the position carefully before issuing High Court proceedings. The court has power to transfer the case to the county court (and vice versa) if that is considered the more appropriate forum.[5] Factors that will be taken into account in determining whether transfer is appropriate include:

- the financial value of the claim (and the amount in dispute, if different);
- the availability of a specialist judge;
- whether the facts, legal issues, remedies and/or procedure are straightforward or complex;
- the adequacy of the court facilities available.[6]

3   CPR r1.1.
4   High Court and County Court Jurisdiction Order 1991 SI No 724 article 5.
5   County Courts Act 1984 ss40(2), 41(1) and 42(1).
6   CPR r30.3(2).

12.7    As regards the value of the claim, a case with a value of less than £25,000 will generally be heard in the county court, whereas a case with a value of more than £50,000 will usually be heard in the High Court.[7] Where a case has a value of under £50,000 it will usually be transferred to the county court unless it is of a specified kind, including claims for malicious prosecution or false imprisonment and actions against the police.[8] Nonetheless, even these types of cases can still be transferred where the issues appear straightforward and thus county court trial is appropriate.

12.8    Aside from the possibility of transfer, if a case is commenced in the wrong court, there is a power to reduce the costs that would otherwise be awarded by a figure of up to 25 per cent, if the High Court considers that proceedings should have been brought in the county court.[9]

12.9    The High Court also has a power simply to strike out a case if it considers that it should have been brought in the county court.[10] However, such a draconian step would only be exercised in an extreme case.

12.10   In practice, most police cases are commenced in the county court unless there are particularly serious allegations involved and/or quantum is particularly large.

## The claim form

12.11   Proceedings are started when the court issues a claim form at the request of the claimant. It is important to distinguish what the claim form must contain from what the particulars of claim must include. Essentially the claim form contains a brief summary of the claimant's causes of action and the particulars of claim give the details of these.

12.12   There are three possible ways of dealing with the particulars of claim:

   (a) the claimant can include his or her particulars of claim on the claim form itself;
   (b) the claimant may prepare his or her particulars of claim as a separate document and serve them with the claim form;

---

7  High Court and County Court Jurisdiction Order 1991 article 7(5) and PD to CPR Pt 29 para 2.2.
8  PD to Pt 29 para 2.6.
9  Supreme Court Act 1981 s51(8) and (9).
10  County Courts Act 1984 s40(1).

(c) the claimant may prepare his or her particulars of claim as a separate document and serve them within 14 days of the service of the claim form or by the latest time for serving the claim form (if this is a subsequent date).[11]

12.13 If the adviser has been instructed in the case from the outset and has carried out the pre-action considerations referred to in chapters 2 and 11, option (b) will be the most common and preferred option. Option (c) is used where the claim form has to be issued quickly, for example, because otherwise a difficulty with limitation would arise.

12.14 The claim form must contain a concise statement of the nature of the claim and specify the remedy which the claimant seeks. Where the claimant is making a claim for money, it must contain a statement of value in accordance with r16.3; and contain such other matters as may be set out in the practice direction.[12] CPR Pt 22 requires the claim form to be verified by a statement of truth in the following form:

[I believe] [the claimant believes] that the facts stated in the claim form are true.

12.15 A claimant may apply for an order extending the period within which a claim form may be served. The general rule is that the claim form should be served within its initial period of validity (generally, four months).[13] If it is not so served, an application to extend its validity should be made within the same initial period. In those circumstances an extension of time will usually be granted if good reason is shown. However, if no such application has been made during the four-month period, the court can only grant an extension if the requirements of r7.6(3) are met. Thus, where a claimant applies for an order to extend the time for service of the claim form after the end of the period specified by r7.5 or by a previous order extending time, the court can make such an order only if:

- the court has been unable to serve the claim form; or
- the claimant has taken all reasonable steps to serve the claim form but has been unable to do so; and
- in either case, the claimant has acted promptly in making the application.

---

11  CPR r7.4.
12  CPR r16.2.
13  CPR r7.5.

12.16 Most of the cases in relation to extensions of time for serving the claim form have concerned what amounts to taking 'reasonable steps' to effect service.[14]

## The particulars of claim

12.17 Particulars of claim that are not included in the claim form must be verified by a statement of truth in the form that has been set out above. Practitioners need to warn their clients that proceedings for contempt of court can be brought against the maker of a false statement, if it is verified by a statement of truth made without an honest belief in its truth.[15]

12.18 The particulars of claim must include a statement of the facts on which the claimant relies. Save where the claim is a very straightforward one, particulars of claim are usually drafted by counsel. In cases where the facts and/or appropriate causes of action are complex, it may be useful for the claimant to have a conference with counsel before the pleading is prepared or finalised. Aside from specific rules as to what the particulars of claim should contain, it is generally to the claimant's advantage to set out the case in some detail in the pleading, emphasising factors that assist in establishing liability and summarising all elements relevant to the quantum of the damages sought. Such an approach is likely to assist with facilitating an early settlement of the claim in circumstances where the claimant has a strong case. For an example of a Particulars of Claim, see appendix B.

12.19 If the claimant is seeking aggravated damages or exemplary damages, a statement to that effect and the grounds for claiming them must be included. A statement confirming that the claimant is seeking interest should also be included, if that is the case.[16]

12.20 Where the claimant is relying on the evidence of a medical practitioner in support of a claim for personal injuries, that report must be served with the particulars of claim[17] (if it has not already been served with the letter of claim, prior to the issue of proceedings – see para 11.83). In personal injury claims, the particulars of claim must set out

---

14 *Anderton v Clywd CC* [2002] 3 All ER 813, CA; *Goodwin v Swindon* BC [2001] All ER 641, CA. In exceptional circumstances the court will dispense with service of the claim form pursuant to CPR r 6.9. See *Cranfield v Bridgegrove Limited* [2003] EWCA Civ 656.

15 CPR r32.14.

16 CPR r16.4.

17 PD to CPR Pt 16, para 4.3.

the claimant's date of birth and give brief details of the injuries sustained.[18]

12.21　The elements of the various torts for which claims can be made are set out in chapters 6–10. It is important for each of the elements of the torts relied upon to be pleaded in the particulars of claim.

12.22　In actions for assault and battery, the intentional nature of the acts relied upon should be specified if this is not already apparent from the conduct described.

12.23　In actions for false imprisonment, as the burden of proof is on the police to prove that a detention is lawful, strictly speaking, the claimant need only state that he or she has been unlawfully detained. However, in practice, it is usually desirable to set out more fully the nature of the unlawfulness alleged, so that the police are required to address all the relevant allegations in their defence. Also, if the claimant does not include the details in his or her particulars of claim he or she may be cross-examined at trial on the basis that he or she has changed his or her instructions. Further, if the false imprisonment is alleged to stem from an officer's failure to comply with a specific duty – such as giving prescribed information on arrest[19] – this should be specifically pleaded, so that the claimant's case is clear.

12.24　In actions for malicious prosecution, all five elements required to prove malicious prosecution must be specifically pleaded. These are:

- that there was a prosecution which was initiated or continued by the defendant;
- that the prosecution was terminated in the claimant's favour;
- that the prosecution was brought without reasonable or probable cause;
- that the officers acted maliciously; and
- that the prosecution caused the claimant loss or damage.[20]

12.25　In actions for trespass to land, the claimant needs to plead his or her entitlement to possession of the land in question and the acts of the defendant which are alleged to constitute trespass.

12.26　In an action for misfeasance in a public office, all the ingredients which make up the tort will need to be specially pleaded, as set out at para 7.39.

---

18　PD to CPR Pt 16, para 4.1.
19　See Police and Criminal Evidence Act 1984 s28(3), discussed at paras 6.63–6.67.
20　These elements are discussed in detail in chapter 7.

12.27    The claimant must attach to his or her particulars of claim a schedule of any past and future expenses and losses that he or she claims.[21]

12.28    If a claimant wishes to rely on evidence under Civil Evidence Act 1968 s11 of a conviction for an offence, this must be specifically pleaded in the particulars of claim.[22]

## Acknowledgement of service and defence

12.29    CPR Pts 9, 10, and 16 deal with the response a defendant is required to make to the claim form served upon him or her.

12.30    Where the defendant is served with a claim form which states that the particulars of claim are to follow, the defendant must file an acknowledgement of service 14 days after service of the particulars of claim. In any other case, the acknowledgement of service must be filed 14 days after service of the claim form.[23]

12.31    On receipt of an acknowledgement of service, the court notifies the claimant in writing. The acknowledgement of service is a standard form that must be enclosed by the claimant in the documents served upon the defendant. The acknowledgement of service needs to be signed by the defendant or his or her legal representative.

12.32    It is possible for the claimant to apply for judgment without trial (called a default judgment) where a defendant has failed to file an acknowledgement of service or has failed to file a defence.[24] (The grounds for setting aside or varying a default judgment are contained in CPR Pt 13.) Clearly, if there would be grounds to set aside the judgment, then it may not be wise to increase costs and delay matters by applying for a default judgment.

12.33    A defendant who wishes to defend all or part of a claim must file a defence. The general rule is that the period for filing a defence is 14 days after service of the particulars of claim or, if the defendant files an acknowledgement of service under Pt 10, 28 days after service of the particulars of claim.[25] The CPR provide that the defendant and the claimant may agree that the specified period for filing a defence be

21   CPR r6.3.
22   PD to CPR Pt 16 para 8.1. This practice direction also sets out the other matters which must be included in the particulars of claim, if relied on.
23   CPR r10.3.
24   CPR Pt 10.
25   CPR r15.4.

extended by up to 28 days. If agreement is reached for the extension of time, the defendant must notify the court in writing to this effect.[26]

12.34    If the defendant requests an extension of time, the claimant's adviser should consider the justification for doing so. Very often, it will be unreasonable to refuse a short extension of, say, two to three weeks. If agreement is not reached, the defendant can apply to the court for an extension of time. If an extension is to be resisted, it is important for the claimant's solicitors to prepare a chronology for the court showing that the defendant has already had sufficient time to prepare a defence.

12.35    A defence must be verified with a statement of truth. The form of the statement of truth is the same as that required in the particulars of claim:

> [I believe] [the defendant believes] that the facts stated in this defence are true.

12.36    Just as the particulars of claim must contain certain matters to avoid an application being made for them to be struck out, similarly a defence must include certain matters to avoid an application being made by the claimant for judgment. The defence must state which of the allegations in the particulars of claim are denied; which are admitted; and which cannot be admitted or denied and the claimant must prove. If the defendant denies an allegation he must state his or her reasons for doing so and must set out any alternative version of events that he or she intends to put forward.[27]

12.37    Where the claim is for personal injury and the claimant has attached a medical report in respect of his or her injuries, the defendant should state in his or her defence whether he or she agrees, disputes, or neither agrees nor disputes but has no knowledge of the matters contained in the medical report. Where any part of the medical report is disputed, reasons need to be given for doing so. Where the defendant has obtained his or her own medical report on which he or she intends to rely, this needs to be attached to the defence. Similarly, if a schedule of past and future expenses and losses has been served, the defendant needs to set out his or her response in a counter-schedule.[28]

12.38    The defendant must also give details of other matters that he or she seeks to rely upon. For example, if the defendant is taking a point on a limitation period, details must be provided in the defence.[29]

---

26  CPR r15.5.   27   CPR r16.5.
28  PD to CPR Pt 16 para 12.
29  PD to CPR Pt 16 para 13.1.

12.39    In practice, the police are likely to deny anything that can be denied, for example, anything that will need to be proved by the claimant.

12.40    The claimant should be interviewed in person to obtain his or her instructions on the defence and a statement drawn up expressing those instructions.

## Reply

12.41    A claimant is entitled to file and serve a reply to the defence. This must be done when he or she files his or her allocation questionnaire (see para 12.69).[30]

12.42    A reply is not compulsory. A reply should be served if the claimant wishes to respond specifically to any matters raised in the defence. For example, if the police have set out in the defence that they intend to rely on the conviction of the claimant, then, if the claimant intends to deny the conviction or allege that it was erroneous, this must be pleaded and the reply would be the most appropriate time to do this.

12.43    A reply must not contradict or be inconsistent with the particulars of claim and should only be used to allege facts in answer to the defence which were not included in those particulars.

## Further information

12.44    CPR Pt 18 sets out the basis on which an application for further information can be made. Before making an application for an order under Pt 18, the party seeking clarification or information (the first party) should serve on the party from whom it is sought (the second party) a written request for the clarification or information, stating a date by which the response to the request should be served. The date must allow the second party a reasonable time to respond.

12.45    A request should be concise and strictly confined to matters which are reasonably necessary and proportionate to enable the first party to prepare his or her own case or to understand the case he or she has to meet.[31]

12.46    A request may be made by letter if the text of the request is brief and the reply is likely to be brief. Otherwise the request should be made in a separate document.

30  CPR r15.8.
31  PD to CPR Pt 18 para 1.2.

12.47   CPR Pt 18 and the associated practice direction explain the procedure for requesting and providing further information. The response to a request for further information should be verified by a statement of truth. Should the second party refuse to provide further information voluntarily then an application can be made to the court.

## Mediation

12.48   There is currently a pilot scheme for mediation in existence at the Central London County Court. CPR Pt 26 has a practice direction that deals with this pilot scheme.

12.49   The practice direction requires the parties to attend a mediation appointment or to give reasons for objecting to doing so, when mediation is proposed by the court. The court can stay a claim until such an appointment takes place.

12.50   The pilot scheme is based on an automatic referral scheme in Ontario Canada that has been operated successfully for a number of years. At the time of writing, it is intended that the mediation pilot scheme will operate from 1 April 2004 to 31 March 2005. Depending on the results of the pilot scheme, this model may be rolled out to courts around the country.

12.51   The new Practice Direction applies to claims against the police.[32]

12.52   When it serves the allocation questionnaire (see para 12.69), the court may serve a notice of referral to mediation on each party. The parties must serve a reply to the notice within 14 days, in which they must state whether they agree or object to mediation, specify any dates within two months of the date of filing the response in which they would not be able to attend a mediation appointment; and if they do object to mediation, set out their reasons for doing so.

12.53   The mediation gives the parties an opportunity to reach an agreement without a court hearing. All parties meet with a mediator who helps the parties to communicate with each other and to try and reach an agreement to the dispute. The obvious advantages of mediation are the speed within which a case can be resolved as well as the freedom for the parties to reach their own agreed solution. For example, an apology can be forthcoming from a defendant chief officer as one of the terms of a settlement reached via mediation. Sometimes an apology is more important to the claimant than the level of compensation recovered.

32   PD to CPR Pt 26 para 2.

12.54    Parties can decide to use mediation to settle the dispute at any stage in the proceedings. This means that even if the case has not been selected for the pilot mediation scheme, if both parties agree, they can ask the court to use mediation. It is also possible to make alternative arrangements to obtain mediation from one of the organisations offering mediation services, such as CEDR, as long as both sides agree. In this regard, the court should be written to to inform it of this development as it may be necessary to obtain a short stay in the proceedings while mediation is explored.

12.55    Mediation is unlikely to succeed if there is a stark contrast between versions of events given by the claimant and the police. Similarly, if there is a point of law involved which either side wants resolved by a court judgment, then mediation may not be desirable.

12.56    If either party does not want to go ahead with mediation offered by the court, they must state their reasons for objecting using the relevant forms.[33] The case will then be referred to a district judge who will decide whether the mediation should take place or that the case should proceed. A party can be penalised if he or she unreasonably rejects mediation (see paras 12.60–12.61).

12.57    If the claimant is in receipt of public funding then the reasonable costs of mediation can be claimed from the LSC. The cost of mediation in the Central London County Court pilot scheme is £100 per party. The charge of £100 per party must be paid before mediation can take place. Counsel should be instructed to appear on behalf of the claimant at the hearing and the client needs to be present also.

12.58    At the mediation hearing, each party gives a short and brief presentation of how he or she sees the dispute (written case summaries are usually prepared as well). The mediator will then discuss the issues involved with the parties, both individually and together. Once the mediator understands the key issues of the dispute and any areas of agreement, he or she can encourage the parties to think of a possible solution. If an agreement has been reached, the mediator will help the parties to draw up any necessary documents. Once signed, the agreement is binding on both parties.

12.59    If an agreement cannot be reached, then the stay is lifted and the court proceedings continue. Anything said during the mediation is confidential and cannot be used in court, unless both parties agree.

12.60    The Court of Appeal has held in a case where the court at first instance had awarded costs against the successful party, who had earlier refused to go to mediation, that the burden was on an unsuccessful party to show

33   PD to CPR Pt 26 para 4.

why the general rule that the winning party recovers his or her costs should not apply. The Court of Appeal indicated that the fundamental principle was that a departure from the general rule was not justified unless it had been shown that the successful party had acted unreasonably in refusing to agree to mediation.[34]

12.61    The court said that factors relevant to deciding whether a party had acted unreasonably in refusing to agree to mediation would include: the nature of the dispute; the merits of the case; the extent to which other settlement methods had been attempted; whether the costs of mediation would be disproportionately high; whether mediation would involve significant and prejudicial delay; and whether the mediation had a reasonable prospect of success. The Court of Appeal also commented that it was likely that a compulsion to mediate would be regarded by the European Court of Human Rights as an unacceptable constraint on the right of access to the courts and therefore a violation of ECHR article 6.

## Striking out the claim

12.62    The court may strike out all or part of a statement of case if it appears to the court that it discloses no reasonable grounds for bringing or defending the claim and/or that the statement of case is an abuse of the court's process or is otherwise likely to obstruct the just disposal of the proceedings and/or that there has been a failure to comply with a rule, practice direction or court order.[35] Defendants to civil actions against the police tend to apply to strike out the claim if they contend that it is unsustainable in law, even on the facts that the claimant alleges. A common example of this is where the claim is brought in negligence and the defendant alleges that no duty of care exists.[36]

## Summary judgment

12.63    The court may give summary judgment against a claimant or a defendant on the whole of a claim or in relation to a particular issue.

12.64    In order to succeed in an application for summary judgment, the applicant has to show that the other party has no real prospect of

---

34    *Halsey v Milton Keynes General NHS Trust* [2004] EWCA Civ 576; [2004] 4 All ER 920.

35    CPR r3.4.

36    As discussed in chapter 8.

establishing liability or defending the claim or winning on the relevant issue and that there is no other compelling reason why the case or issue should be disposed of at trial.[37] In order to defeat the application for summary judgment, it is sufficient for the respondent to show that he or she has some chance of succeeding at trial on the claim or issue. The courts have held that the inclusion of the word 'real' means that the respondent has to have a case which is better than merely arguable.[38] However, the respondent is not required to show that his or her case will probably succeed a trial. The court at the summary judgment application will consider the merits of the respondent's case only to the extent necessary to determine whether it has sufficient merit to proceed to trial. Although the application notice for a summary judgment will include an identification of the written evidence on which the applicant relies, and why the order is being sought,[39] the application is not a mini trial.[40]

12.65   Most applications for summary judgment are made at the close of pleadings and before witness statements have been exchanged; although an application can also be made after witness statements have been served.

12.66   A claimant may be able to resist an application for summary judgment by showing that resolution of the claim or issue will depend upon findings made at trial in relation to disputes of fact between the parties. Most actions against the police involve the claimant and defendant putting forward starkly different versions of the same incident. Accordingly, issues relating to liability will often be incapable of resolution until the facts have been established and this can only be done when the disputed testimony is heard and evaluated at trial. Many civil actions against the police are heard by a judge sitting with a jury, rather than by a judge alone (as is discussed at para 12.77 onwards). In *Safeways plc v Tate*[41] the Court of Appeal suggested that where a claim involved causes of action that conferred a right to jury trial, a judge was precluded from usurping the role of the jury and entering summary judgment, if this involved assessing any issues of fact. However, the Court of Appeal then reconsidered this point in *Alexander v Arts Council*[42] and concluded that summary judgment could be entered in

---

37   CPR r24.2.
38   *ED&F Man Liquid Products Limited v Patel* [2003] EWCA Civ 472.
39   CPR r24.4.
40   *Swain v Hillman* [2001] All ER 91.
41   [2001] 4 All ER 193, CA.
42   [2001] 1 WLR 840, CA.

a case involving claims that would be heard by a jury, if the judge found that the evidence when taken at its highest was such that a properly directed jury could not find in favour of the party seeking to resist the application. This process does not involve the judge in deciding where the truth lies between rival accounts, but in seeing if the party resisting the application could succeed even if all the disputed facts are assumed in their favour. For example, a judge might decided that even if all points in dispute were found in favour of a claimant, a claim for misfeasance should be struck out because there was insufficient material to support an inference that an officer was acting in bad faith. This approach mirrors the role that a judge has at trial; he or she can withdraw issues from the jury if the factual evidence is incapable of supporting them (see paras 13.31–13.33).

12.67     Advisers will need to consider when it is appropriate to make an application for summary judgment against a defendant. For example, if the detention is clearly unlawful on the basis of a legal point that does not rely on disputed facts and can be established on the version of events given by the defendant, it may be worth making such an application. The application, if well founded, can also put pressure on the police to settle a claim. Advisers should, however, bear in mind the implications should the application for summary judgment be unsuccessful; the claimant will have to pay the defendant's costs as well as his or her own. (For claimants who are publicly funded, this will have an impact on the statutory charge: see chapter 11, which deals with public funding.)

## Directions

12.68   CPR Pt 29 deals with the provisions concerning the courts' management of multi-track cases. Claims against the police will invariably be allocated to the multi-track, as opposed to the small claims track or the fast track.[43] When the court allocates a case to the multi-track, it will give directions for the management of the case and set a timetable for the steps to be taken to prepare for trial. Alternatively, the court will fix a case management conference for the parties to attend, at which directions relating to the management of the case will be made.

12.69     The court will normally send an allocation questionnaire to the parties at the close of the pleadings, which both sides need to complete and return by a stipulated date.[44] The courts usually allocate a claim to a

---

43   CPR r26.6.
44   CPR r26.3.

track once the allocation questionnaires have been received by the court or at the first case management conference.

12.70 If a claim involves false imprisonment or malicious prosecution, thereby usually entitling a claimant to a trial by jury (as discussed at para 12.77 onwards), then an application for a jury trial should be made within 28 days of service of the defence.[45] However, the court has a power to extend the time for making the application.[46] An extension will usually be permitted if the application is made before a case management conference takes place or directions are otherwise given. In such circumstances it would be difficult for a defendant to assert that he or she was prejudiced by the late application. Similarly, if the defendant accepts that jury trial is appropriate, it will be difficult for him or her to resist an application to extend time. On the other hand, if the application is not made until close to the trial date and is opposed, an extension of time is likely to be refused.[47]

12.71 The court will ordinarily fix a case management conference in claims against the police. To avoid a hearing, the parties can agree directions by consent and send them to the court when the allocation questionnaire is filed.

12.72 As well as mode of trial, directions will address matters such as disclosure, exchange of witness statements and expert evidence (all of which are considered in detail below). Directions will also provide, where appropriate, for photographs and/or plans to be admitted in evidence at trial (and for them to be agreed, if possible). Where the court clerk's notes of evidence or a transcript of the evidence given at earlier criminal proceedings is relied upon (see paras 2.77–2.79), a direction is usually made to the effect that the notes or transcript are to be admissible at the trial without the maker being required to give evidence.

12.73 It is important that care is taken when completing the allocation questionnaire. This is particularly the case where the estimate of costs is asked for. The Court of Appeal has given guidance on the application of para 6.6 of the practice direction to CPR Pt 43, which permits the court assessing costs to have regard to any estimate previously filed by the party.[48] Where it becomes clear that the estimate of costs contained in the allocation questionnaire is no longer accurate, it is important to

---

45 CPR r26.11.

46 CPR r3.1(2)(a).

47 Compare *Cooper v Chief Constable of South Yorkshire* [1989] 1 WLR 333 and *Oliver v Calderdale MBC* (1999) *Times* 7 July, CA (both decided under the pre-CPR rules).

48 *Leigh v Michelin Tyre Plc* [2003] EWCA Civ 1766; [2004] 1 WLR 846.

comply with the obligation in para 6.3(2) of the same practice direction, to file an updated estimate of costs at the listing questionnaire stage. If this is not done and there is a substantial difference between the estimated costs and the costs eventually claimed, an explanation will be called for at the costs assessment stage and some of the costs incurred may be disallowed.

12.74    The first case management conference in a claim is likely to be allocated between 30 minutes to an hour. The parties should endeavour to try and agree as many of the necessary directions as possible in advance of the case management conference. The person that attends the case management conference should be someone who is familiar with the case and who has sufficient authority to deal with any issues that are likely to arise.[49]

12.75    A party who fails to keep to the timetable fixed by the court is in real jeopardy of court orders imposing severe sanctions upon him or her, including striking out the whole or part of his or her statement of case and/or costs penalties. There are provisions in the CPR for the variation of a case management timetable.[50]

12.76    Subsequently, the court will send the parties a pre-trial checklist (listing questionnaire) for completion and return by the date specified in the directions given at the case management conference, unless it considers that the claim can proceed to trial without a checklist being completed.[51] Due to the limited number of trial centres that are able to facilitate a trial by jury, often the longest delay in litigation against the police is caused by waiting for the trial date. To avoid this unnecessary delay, it is important for the court to be provided with dates to avoid for counsel, witnesses and experts as soon as possible. The court will endeavour to set a trial timetable and fix a trial date as soon as it has all the information before it.

## Jury trial

12.77    The interplay between claims under the Race Relations Act 1976, which are usually heard by a judge sitting with assessors and common law claims against the police, which entitle a claimant to a jury trial, is discussed at paras 10.130–10.132.

---

49    CPR r29.3.
50    CPR r29.5.
51    CPR r29.6.

12.78 The rules governing entitlement to trial by jury are contained in Supreme Court Act 1981 s69 and County Courts Act 1984 s66 (which are in similar terms). If an application for a jury trial is duly made to the court in a claim in respect of malicious prosecution or false imprisonment (or in respect of libel, slander or fraud) the court 'shall' order trial with a jury, unless the court is of the opinion that the trial 'requires any prolonged examination of documents or accounts or any scientific or local investigation which cannot conveniently be made with a jury'.[52]

12.79 As discussed at para 12.70, an application for a claim to be tried by a jury should be made within 28 days of the service of the defence,[53] but the court has a power to extend this period in appropriate cases.

12.80 Often, an action which involves a claim for either false imprisonment and/or malicious prosecution will also include other torts such as assault, battery, trespass, etc. These other torts do not entitle a claimant to a jury trial. However, once a claimant has a tort entitling him or her to a jury trial then the jury will usually be asked also to consider questions of fact in relation to the other torts.[54]

12.81 Claimants tend to prefer a trial before a judge and jury rather than one with a judge alone. However, it is important that advisers fully explain to them the advantages and disadvantages of a jury trial and a judge-only trial.

12.82 A jury trial will inevitably take longer than a judge-only trial. If funds are limited, then a judge-only trial may be preferable. Additionally, where the claim is one which involves a claimant and/or issues that may be unpopular, it may be desirable to avoid trial by one's peers. In such circumstances the jury may be unduly swayed by prejudicial material. Juries may also sometimes be influenced by negative media reporting of the 'compensation culture', 'police officers only trying to do their job', 'greedy claimants' 'abuse of legal aid' etc. In addition, if the case relies on a close study of documents and inferences to be drawn from them, or it is a case where it is necessary to highlight a departure from usual police practice, it may be desirable to opt for a judge-only trial rather than a jury trial.

12.83 Against this, however, it must be remembered that many claimants who have been acquitted after a jury trial in the Crown Court will have a huge amount of confidence in the ability of their peers to decide upon liability and quantum in a civil action. Further, jurors in urban

---

52 County Courts Act 1984 s66(3) and Supreme Court Act 1981 s69(1).
53 CPR r26.11.
54 Although the judge can choose to determine those issues: *Hutt v Commissioner of Police of the Metropolis* [2003] EWCA Civ 1911.

inner city areas, who may be ethnically diverse and younger, may have had contact with the police and will be able to use their common sense and experiences to assess the credibility of both the claimant's and the defendant's witnesses.

12.84    Where a right to a jury trial applies, either party can take advantage of it. Accordingly, although it is more frequently a claimant that seeks a jury trial, there may be cases where the defendant appreciates that a jury trial is in his or her interests and applies for one, against the claimant's wishes.

12.85    Either party can object to a jury trial on the basis that one or more of the statutory exceptions to trial by jury applies. In those circumstances the court should ask:[55]

- Will the trial involve a prolonged examination of documents or a scientific investigation?
- If so, can it conveniently be made with a jury?
- If not, should it nonetheless exercise its discretion to order trial with a jury?

12.86    Defendant police forces are increasingly trying to argue that cases involving claims for psychiatric injury, with disputed expert evidence and substantial medical records, are too complicated to be heard by a jury. If this is raised by the defendant and the claimant wishes to have the claim heard by a jury, it will be important for the claimant's advisers to convince the court that the material evidence can be properly presented to and understood by a jury.

12.87    Even if the case involves a prolonged examination of documents or a scientific investigation, the right to jury trial is not lost if this can be undertaken conveniently with a jury. It is only if there is 'substantial difficulty' in conducting this exercise with a jury, as compared to with a judge alone, that the exception to the right to a jury trial can be made out.[56] This involves a consideration of the effect of a jury trial on the length of the case and the costs of the litigation, as well as an assessment of a jury's ability to resolve the particular issue(s).[57]

12.88    Even if it can be established that a trial involves the prolonged examination of documents or a scientific investigation, and it cannot conveniently be made with a jury, the court still needs to consider whether it should exercise its discretion to order trial with a jury.

---

55   *Taylor v Anderton* [1995] 1 WLR 447; *Aitken v Preston* [1997] EMLR 415 and *Phillips v Commissioner of Police of the Metropolis* [2003] EWCA Civ 382.
56   *Aitken v Preston,* [1997] EMLR 415.
57   See the authorities cited in note 55 above.

If the case turns on substantial disputes of fact between the parties and/or involves serious wrongdoing, the claimant may be able to persuade the court that the case is nonetheless suitable for jury trial.

12.89 Where the material alleged to make the trial too complicated to be heard by a jury relates to quantum only, rather than liability, then a possible solution is to have a split trial with a jury determining questions of fact relevant to liability and a judge alone assessing damages, if the claimant makes out all or some of the claims.[58] However, where the objection to a jury trial is based on the alleged complexity of medical evidence, the defendant will often persuade the court that the material is relevant to liability as well as to quantum because it impacts on the claimant's credibility.

12.90 The court has a power to order trial by jury even where the action does not include claims in false imprisonment or malicious prosecution (or in libel, slander or fraud).[59] However, this power is rarely exercised in favour of granting a jury trial in practice,[60] even if the action includes claims in assault and/or misfeasance, where it might be said that some issues analogous to the disputes of fact that arise in false imprisonment and/or malicious prosecution cases are present.

# Disclosure

12.91 CPR Pt 31 deals with disclosure of documents. Disclosure is defined as 'stating that a document exists or has existed'.[61] There is no provision under the rules for automatic disclosure. The duty to disclose will arise if and when and to the extent that the court orders disclosure. This will generally be at the first case management hearing or upon an application by a party. (Pre-application disclosure is discussed at paras 11.85–11.88.) The overriding principal is that disclosure should be restricted to what is necessary in the individual case. There is a distinction between disclosure in cases which proceed on the multi-track and those cases which proceed on the fast-track. In multi-track cases the normal direction made by the court is for the parties to give standard disclosure.[62]

---

58   *Conlon v Chief Constable of Northumbria* (2000) 2 March, CA, unreported.
59   Supreme Court Act 1981 s69(3); County Courts Act 1984 s66(2).
60   *H v Ministry of Defence* [1991] 2 WLR 1192, CA.
61   CPR r31.2.
62   CPR r31.5.

12.92    Standard disclosure is defined as encompassing:

(a) documents upon which a party relies;

(b) documents which adversely affect his or her own case or adversely affect another party's case or which support another party's case; and

(c) documents of which disclosure is required by a relevant practice direction.[63]

12.93    A party is required to make a reasonable search for documents referred to under (b) and (c) above.[64] If the claimant is aware of a document that has not been disclosed then consideration should be given to making an application for specific disclosure (see paras 12.102–12.104). ECHR article 6 can be used to reinforce the application, by arguing that the claimant cannot have a fair trial without the particular document(s).

12.94    The rules provide that there is a right to inspect a disclosed document unless it is no longer in the control of the disclosing party, or that party has a right to withhold inspection or it will be disproportionate to the issues in the case to permit inspection.[65] Ordinarily, inspection is carried out by the provision of photocopies of documents on agreement to paying reasonable photocopying costs. However, inspection of original documents should be arranged where there is any issue over their authenticity.

12.95    The procedure for standard disclosure is that each party must make, and serve on every other party, a list of documents using form N265. The list must identify the documents in a convenient order and manner and as concisely as possible. A list should be in chronological date order with the earliest date first and the most recent document last. The list must indicate those documents in respect of which the party claims a right or duty to withhold inspection and those documents that are no longer in the party's control. The list must state what has happened to documents that come within the latter category.

12.96    The list must include a disclosure statement made by the party disclosing the documents. This should indicate the extent of the search that has been made to locate the documents which he or she is required to disclose and certify that he or she understands the duty to disclose documents and that to the best of his or her knowledge he or she has carried out that duty.[66]

---

63  CPR r31.6.
64  CPR r31.7.
65  CPR r31.3.
66  CPR r31.10.

12.97     The parties may agree in writing to disclose documents without making a list and to disclose documents without the disclosing party making a disclosure statement.[67]

12.98     The duty of disclosure continues during the proceedings. This means that if documents to which the duty extends come to a party's notice at any time during the litigation, the party must immediately notify any other party. This is particularly relevant where claims are issued before the IPCC has completed the investigation into a claimant's complaint. Another situation where the on-going duty is relevant is where there is a linked criminal case that has yet to conclude. An additional matter which may be the subject of the continuing duty to disclose is if the claimant or any of his or her witnesses is convicted in relation to a different or separate matter.

12.99     A party may inspect a document mentioned in a statement of case, a witness statement, a witness summary or an affidavit.[68] A party may also apply for an order of inspection of any document mentioned in an expert's report which has not already been disclosed in the proceedings[69] (see para 2.33).

12.100     A party may not rely at trial on any document which he or she fails to disclose or in respect of which he or she fails to permit inspection, unless the court gives permission.[70]

12.101     A party to whom a document has been disclosed may only use the disclosed document for the purposes of the proceedings in which it is disclosed.[71] There are exceptions to this where the documents have been read to or by the court or referred to at the hearing (so long as it was held in public), or where the court gives permission or the party who disclosed the document and the owner of the document agree.[72]

## Specific disclosure

12.102  If a party believes that the disclosure of documents given by the other side is inadequate he or she may make an application for an order for specific disclosure.[73]

---

67   CPR r31.10(A).
68   CPR r31.14(1).
69   CPR r31.14(2).
70   CPR r31.21.
71   CPR r31.22.
72   CPR r31.22.
73   CPR r31.12.

12.103 An application needs to be made to the court in accordance with CPR Pt 23. The application notice must specify the order that the applicant intends to ask the court to make and must be supported by evidence. An order for specific disclosure is an order that a party must do one or more of the following things:

- disclose documents or classes of document specified in the order; or
- carry out a search to the extent stated in the order; or
- disclose any documents located as a result of that search.

12.104 In deciding whether or not make an order for specific disclosure, the court will take into account all the circumstances of the case and, in particular, the overriding objective. If disclosure is objected to on the basis that the documents contain personal information, the court must balance the ECHR article 6(1) right to a fair hearing against the other party's article 8 right to respect for private life.[74] The more relevant the document is to the issues in dispute in the claim; the more likely it is that the court will order disclosure.

12.105 Chapter 2 sets out many of the standard police documents that should be made available on disclosure, if they relate to issues in the case.

## The claimant's documents

12.106 In most cases against the police, the claimant will have few documents to disclose (and most of these are likely to be copies of documents, such as the custody record, received from the police).

12.107 It is important for solicitors to inform their clients as soon as possible of the need to preserve all documents that may be relevant, whether they assist the client's case or not. As disclosure also has to be given of documents created after the action has commenced, no new non-privileged documents should be generated without legal advice.

12.108 Where financial losses are claimed, supporting documents should be disclosed, for example, in relation to loss of earnings documents such as wage slips, employer's letters and benefit details.

12.109 Where there is a claim for personal injuries, medical records will need to be disclosed. The extent to which such records should be disclosed is discussed at paras 2.27–2.31.

---

74 *Nayler v Beard* [2001] EWCA Civ 1201.

## Disclosure from third parties

12.110 The claimant or the defendant can make an application for disclosure against a person who is not a party to the action. The court may make an order for disclosure against the third party only where the documents of which disclosure is sought are likely to support the case of the applicant or adversely affect the case of one of the other parties to the proceedings, and disclosure is necessary in order to dispose fairly of the claim or to save costs.[75]

12.111     An example of where the police were ordered to give third party disclosure occurred in an action by prisoners against the Home Office for alleged assaults by prison officers. The Court of Appeal held that disclosure of prison officers' statements made under caution to the police when they were investigating the assaults should be ordered (see para 10.26). Strict conditions were attached by the court to the extent and manner of the disclosure.[76]

## Documents concerning previous misconduct

12.112 Claimants will be anxious to discover any documents that link the defendant police officers with previous incidents of police misconduct, whether similar in kind, or not. The police, on the other hand, will want to keep as much of this information as possible out of the litigation. Chapter 2 considers some of the means that the claimant's advisers may use to obtain information about officers' previous misconduct (see paras 2.81–2.83). The admissibility of such material as similar fact evidence and/or as relevant to a witnesses' credit is discussed in paras 13.13–13.18. Where evidence of past misconduct is purely admissible in relation to issues of credit, disclosure will not be ordered.[77] Where the material can amount to similar fact evidence, disclosure may be required.[78]

12.113     Any certificates of criminal convictions are admissible under the Civil Evidence Act 1968 s11 and are therefore disclosable.

---

75  CPR r31.17.

76  *Frankson v Secretary of State for the Home Department* [2003] 1 WLR 1952, CA.

77  *Thorpe v Chief Constable of Greater Manchester* [1989] 2 All ER 827, CA.

78  *Steele v Commissioner of Police of the Metropolis* (1993) 18 February, CA, unreported.

## Documents exempt from disclosure

12.114   There are a number of grounds on which the police (or the claimant) may or must refuse to disclose a document which is relevant and material to the determination of issues involved in the civil proceedings. If a privilege or immunity is claimed in respect of a document, then it must still be identified in the list of documents, but it need not actually be produced, unless a court orders that the document is not exempt from production. Those documents for which immunity or privilege is claimed should be listed separately in the list of documents.

### Legal professional privilege

12.115   Legal professional privilege can be claimed for documents where communications are made for the purpose of giving or receiving legal advice. The courts will look at the dominant purpose for which the document was prepared in cases where it appears that there was more than one purpose.[79] Legal professional privilege can be waived expressly or impliedly.

### Public interest immunity

12.116   A party may refuse to disclose documents on the grounds of the harm that would be occasioned to the national or public interest.[80] This principle has become known as public interest immunity. A claim for public interest immunity can only be justified if the public interest in preserving the confidentiality of a document outweighs the public interest in securing justice by determining the action on the basis of all relevant, available documentation.

12.117       There are two kinds of public interest immunity. The first applies to a class of documents, widely or narrowly drawn, so that the immunity attaches to all documents that come within the class, irrespective of their particular contents. The test to be applied in assessing whether a class immunity exists has been said to involve asking whether the withholding of a document because it belongs to a particular class is really 'necessary for the proper functioning of the public service'.[81] The second kind of public interest immunity applies in relation to the contents of a particular document or part of a document, where it contains something that it would prejudice the public interest to disclose.

79   *Waugh v British Railways Board* [1980] AC 521, HL.
80   *Conway v Rimmer* [1968] 1 All ER 874, HL.
81   *Conway v Rimmer* [1968] 1 All ER 874 at 942.

12.118    For many years 'class' public interest immunity was said to attach
to all documents generated during a police complaints investigation,
on the basis that it was necessary for witnesses to be confident that
statements made by them to the investigators would not be disclosed
in civil proceedings.[82] However, in *R v Chief Constable of West Midlands
ex p Wiley*[83] the House of Lords held that a 'class' immunity extending to all the documents generated by the investigation of a complaint
against the police was not justified.

12.119    In *ex p Wiley* the Police Complaints Authority argued that even if all
documents generated by the complaints investigation did not attract
class-based protection, public interest immunity on a class basis was
still appropriate for the reports prepared by the investigating officer.
The House of Lords did not need to decide this issue, but Lord Woolf
expressed reservations as to whether it would be possible to justify a
class claim to immunity as opposed to a claim for contents immunity,
where appropriate, in respect of particular reports. However, the Court
of Appeal subsequently decided that reports of investigating officers
prepared in relation to police complaints did attract class-based public
interest immunity.[84] The reason given was that the investigating
officer needed to be able to comment freely on the view he or she had
formed of the complainant, the officers under investigation and any
witnesses and would feel inhibited from doing so if the report was to
be disclosed. It is questionable whether this reasoning can survive the
new regime for investigating complaints against the police.
As explained in more detail at paras 4.164–4.167, there is now a presumption that documents generated by a complaints investigation
will be disclosed to the complainant during the assessment of the
complaint and such disclosure will, in appropriate cases, include the
investigating officer's report. If these reports will now sometimes be disclosed to complainants by the IPCC, it is hard to see how a class-based
objection to their disclosure can be maintained in civil proceedings; the
rationale previously identified by the courts in support of class immunity can no longer apply. However, contents based public interest
immunity can still be claimed by a defendant by reference to the contents of a particular investigating officer's report.

12.120    Class-based public interest immunity has also been held to cover
communications between the police and the CPS, in so far as the
same was a commentary upon primary material (such as witness

---

82   *Neilson v Laugharne* [1981] QB 736, CA.

83   [1995] 1 AC 274, HL.

84   *Taylor v Anderton* [1995] 1 WLR 447, CA.

statements, forensic reports, etc), rather than the primary material itself.[85] However, it is submitted that this approach is over-restrictive and that a contents-based immunity, dependent upon the nature of the particular document, would be more appropriate.

12.121    Even when documents are part of a class-based immunity, a claimant can argue that the particular circumstances warrant the disclosure of the material and that its importance to the litigation outweighs the public interest in preserving its confidentiality. In *Toombs v Commissioner of Police of the Metropolis*,[86] disclosure of an investigating officer's report was ordered in favour of a claimant police officer who complained he had been wrongfully arrested.

12.122    The police may well claim public interest immunity in relation to documents that relate to sensitive policing operations and/or to police informers. As indicated above, in those circumstances the court will have to weigh up the public interest in withholding the information against its potential value to the party who seeks to make use of it in the litigation.[87]

12.123    In some cases it may be possible to argue that part at least of the material sought should be disclosed or that the document(s) in issue should be provided in a redacted form. As Lord Woolf said in *ex p Wiley*:

> There is usually a spectrum of action which can be taken if the parties are sensible which will mean that any prejudice due to non-disclosure of documents is reduced to a minimum.

## Privilege against self-incrimination

12.124    The heads of claim in a civil action against the police may well, in effect, allege that a criminal offence has been committed. The most common example of this will be assault. People in civil proceedings alleged to have committed a criminal offence are granted, by the common law, a privilege against self-incrimination if there is a reasonable likelihood that they will be charged as a result of disclosing the information. Thus a police officer could refuse to disclose material to the claimant which indicates that a criminal offence has been committed by him or her. However, it is submitted that a chief officer, when sued for actions committed by his or her officers, cannot claim the privilege in relation to documents which incriminate those officers.

---

85    *O'Sullivan v Commissioner of Police of the Metropolis* (1995) *Times* 3 July.

86    (2000) 15 November, QBD, unreported.

87    See eg in relation to informers the approach of the Court of Appeal in *Chief Constable of Greater Manchester v McNally* [2002] 2 Cr App R 617.

12.125    In many civil actions against the police, the CPS will have already considered whether to prefer charges against police officers, as part of the complaints and discipline machinery (see chapters 4 and 5) and, in the vast majority of cases, will have decided not to prosecute. In such cases, it is submitted, a claim of privilege against self-incrimination should not succeed.

## Exchange of witness statements

12.126  In all cases (jury and non-jury) exchange of witness statements is now compulsory. Witness statements contain the factual accounts of the witnesses that the party intends to adduce as evidence at the trial.

12.127    It is important for practitioners to be aware of the difference between a witness statement and a witness summary.[88] A witness summary is a summary of the evidence which would otherwise be included in a witness statement or, where the evidence is not known, a summary of the matters about which the party serving the witness summary proposes to question the witness. A party who is required to serve a witness statement for use at trial but is unable to obtain one – for example because a potential witness is currently untraceable or unco-operative – may apply without notice for permission to serve a witness summary instead. A witness summary must include the name and address of the intended witness. It must also be served in the period in which a witness statement would have had to be served.[89]

12.128    A witness statement should be in the witness's own words and should be restricted to matters of which the witness has personal knowledge.[90] The witness statement should be headed with the title of the proceedings. At the top right hand corner of the first page there should be clearly written the party on whose behalf it is made, the initial and surname of the witness, the number of the statement in relation to that witness, the identifying initials and number of each exhibit referred to and the date when the statement was made.[91] The witness statement should be expressed in the first person and should also state the full name of the witness, his or her place of residence or if he or she is making the statement in his or her professional business,

---

88  CPR r32.4.
89  CPR r32.9.
90  PD to CPR Pt 32 para 18 and *Alex Lawrie Factors Ltd v Morgan* (1999) *Times*, August 18, CA.
91  PD to CPR Pt 32 para 17.

or other occupational capacity, the address at which he or she works, the position he or she holds and the name of his or her firm or employer.

12.129    When drafting witness statements it is important to include all matters that the witness will give evidence upon, as it will be unusual for the court to allow the witness to adduce evidence which is not in his or her statement, unless it relates to an issue that has arisen since the statement was served (for example, as a result of the other party's witness evidence). Further, the claimant and his or her witnesses will usually be cross-examined on the basis that they have just made it up, if they say something at trial that is not in their witness statements.

12.130    By the time witness statements come to be exchanged, the claimant's version of events is likely to have been given already on several occasions of which the defendant is aware. Thus, the claimant's statement in support of a police complaint, the letter of claim, the particulars of claim and any medical reports and records will all need to be carefully examined to ensure that as far as is possible there are no discrepancies between the claimant's account as set out in these documents and the account given in his or her witness statement. Instructions taken on the defence and on the results of the disclosure process should also be included, where relevant.

12.131    It is common for counsel to be instructed to advise upon draft witness statements before they are exchanged. Some solicitors find that this is a good time to have a conference with counsel to review the evidence and to seek advice for the purposes of removing any limitation placed on the certificate of public funding.

12.132    The practice direction to CPR Pt 32 indicates the form that witness statements should take. An exhibit used in conjunction with a witness statement should be verified and identified by the witness and remain separate from the witness statement. Where a witness refers to an exhibit, or exhibits, he or she should say in the statement, 'I refer to (description of exhibits) marked ............'.[92] A witness statement must be verified by a statement of truth as follows: 'I believe that the facts stated in this witness statement are true'.

12.133    If a witness statement or a witness summary is not served in respect of an intended witness within the time specified by the court, the witness may not be called to give evidence unless the court gives permission.[93]

---

92  PD to CPR Pt 32 para 18.
93  CPR r32.10.

12.134    Where a witness is called to give evidence at trial, he or she may be cross-examined on his or her witness statement, whether or not this statement or any part of it was referred to during the witness's evidence in chief.

12.135    The claimant and his or her witnesses need to be advised of the implication of providing a witness statement. Proceedings for contempt of court may be brought against a person if he or she made, or causes to be made, a false statement in a document verified by a statement of truth without an honest belief in its truth.[94]

12.136    The aim of the exchange of witness statements is to effect a fair and speedy trial of the issues and to save costs. It is thought that when all parties 'have their cards on the table' there will be a greater incentive to settle the case. Thus when the witness statements are received from the police they should be carefully studied to see if their contents affect the assessment of the strengths and weaknesses of the case and examined for areas of agreement and lines of potential cross-examination.

## Hearsay notices

12.137   Hearsay is defined as a statement made otherwise than by a person while giving oral evidence in proceedings, which is tendered as evidence of the 'matter stated and references to hearsay include hearsay of whatever degree'.[95] Where a party intends to rely on hearsay evidence at the trial, he or she must serve a hearsay notice no later than the latest date for serving witness statements.[96] The hearsay notice must identify the hearsay evidence, state that the party serving the notice proposes to rely on that hearsay evidence at the trial and give the reason why the witness will not be called.

## Offers to settle and payments into court

12.138   Offers to settle and payments into court made in accordance with the provisions of CPR Pt 36 are called, respectively, Pt 36 offers and Pt 36 payments. There is no prohibition against a party making an offer to

---

94   CPR r32.14.

95   CPR r33.1.

96   Civil Evidence Act 1995 s2(1)(a) and CPR r33.2.

settle in any way he or she chooses, but if the offer made does not comply with the provision of this Pt 36, the consequences specified do not flow unless the court so orders.

12.139    A Pt 36 offer of settlement made by a claimant must be in writing and must contain prescribed information.[97] The offer can relate to the whole or to part of the claim.

12.140    If the defendant wishes to make an offer to settle a money claim, he or she should make a Pt 36 payment. A non-money claim or the non-money aspects of a claim, can be the subject of a defendant's Pt 36 offer.[98] A Pt 36 payment can relate to the whole or to part of a money claim and is made by the defendant filing a notice at court that complies with CPR r36.6(2).[99] Once made, a Pt 36 payment can only be withdrawn or reduced with the permission of the court,[100] for example if new evidence affecting the strength of the claim came to light.

12.141    Part 36 offers and Pt 36 payments can only be made once the proceedings have started and may be made in appeal proceedings.[101] However, where a party makes an offer to settle before proceedings have begun, the court will take that offer into account when making any order as to costs so long as the provisions of r36.10 are complied with. These include that the offer is expressed to be open for at least 21 days after the date on which it was made.

12.142    A Pt 36 offer or a Pt 36 payment can subsequently be increased as the litigation progresses.

12.143    Part 36 offers and Pt 36 payments can be accepted by the other party without seeking the court's permission, if the offer or payment was made not less than 21 days before the trial and written notice of acceptance is given within 21 days of the offer or payment being made.[102] If the offer or payment is made less than 21 days before trial, it can still be accepted without the court's permission if the parties have agreed liability for costs.[103]

12.144    Where a Pt 36 offer or a Pt 36 payment is accepted without needing the permission of the court, the claimant will be entitled to his or her costs of the proceedings up to the date of serving the notice of

---

97    CPR r36.5.
98    CPR rr36.3 and 36.4.
99    The notice is also served on the other party: CPR r36.6(3).
100    CPR r36.6(5).
101    CPR r36.2(4).
102    CPR rr36.11(1) and 36.12(1).
103    CPR rr36.11(2) and 36.12(2).

acceptance.[104] Where the Pt 36 offer of payment relates to part only of the claim and the claimant abandons the balance, he or she will again be entitled to such costs, unless the court orders otherwise. The costs will be on a standard basis, if not agreed.

12.145    Where a claimant rejects the defendant's Pt 36 offer or Pt 36 payment but then fails to do better at trial, the court will order the claimant to pay the defendant's costs from the latest date upon which the payment or offer could have been accepted without needing the permission of the court, unless the court considers it unjust to do so.[105] The effect of such an order will usually mean that any damages awarded to the claimant will be off-set against costs owed to the defendant and/or to the LSC by way of the statutory charge and he or she will be left with no tangible benefit. If a claimant has unwisely rejected a reasonable offer it will usually be difficult to persuade the judge that it would be unjust to make the standard order for costs. However, in one action against the police pre-dating the CPR, where the jury awarded the claimant less than the police had paid into court, the judge held that the defendant should nonetheless pay the claimant's costs, as the officers had been shown to have behaved disgracefully and, as the case was about more than just money, the claimant had been entitled to proceed to trial to obtain vindication from the jury's verdict.[106]

12.146    Where the claimant makes a Pt 36 offer that the defendant rejects, beneficial provisions relating to costs and interest apply if the claimant does better than the Pt 36 offer at trial.[107] Unless the court considers it unjust to do so, it should award interest to the claimant at a rate not exceeding 10 per cent above base rate for some or all of the period starting with the latest date on which the defendant could have accepted the offer without needing the permission of the court and award the claimant costs on an indemnity basis from the same date.

12.147    The fact that a Pt 36 offer or Pt 36 payment has been made cannot be revealed to the trial judge or jury until the question of costs comes to be decided at the end of the case.

## Specific issues in civil actions against the police

12.148  Police solicitors have developed skills in making Pt 36 offers and Pt 36 payments which put pressure on claimants and their advisers to settle

---

104    CPR rr36.13 and 36.14.
105    CPR r36.20.
106    *Wilson & Farbridge v Patterson* (1985) 10 December, HC, unreported.
107    CPR r36.21.

a case before it reaches trial. In many cases the claimant is not interested so much in the financial aspect of the case but in vindicating him or herself in court and making the police accountable for their actions. Very often, then, clients are reluctant to accept a settlement. However, in publicly funded cases such an offer or payment may have ramifications for the continuation of public funding if it is rejected. The offer will need to be reported to the LSC and funding may be withdrawn if a reasonable offer has been refused. Thus, unless an offer or payment is clearly unreasonable, it is usually prudent to obtain counsel's advice upon whether it would constitute a reasonable settlement, before a decision is made to accept or reject it. The difficulty is compounded by the fact that it can be hard to predict the level of damages that a jury will award at trial if the claim succeeds.

12.149    On the other hand, the Pt 36 procedure for making offers can be useful for claimants who want to take the initiative in obtaining a settlement of the claim – for example if there are likely to be funding difficulties in the future or if he or she does not want to go to trial and give evidence. Equally, if it is apparent that the defendant is unlikely to want to settle the claim, a Pt 36 offer pitched at just below what the claimant is likely to recover at trial may lead to an award of enhanced interest and costs at the trial, as discussed at para 12.146.

## Expert evidence

12.150    Examples of expert evidence are reports from medical experts, forensic experts, handwriting experts, accountants and employment consultants. The experts most commonly used in actions against the police are medical experts, as claims for consequential personal injuries are frequently made. However, depending on the facts of the case other experts might be relevant, including experts on restraint techniques, dog handling, firearms, CS gas use and crowd control. The instruction of medical experts is considered in detail in chapter 2, including the issue of when the claimant can instruct his or her own medical expert and when he or she should seek to agree instruction of a joint expert with the defendant.[108]

12.151    The parties are asked in the allocation questionnaire to state whether they will be seeking to adduce expert evidence and if so, the name and other details of the expert whom they wish to use and whether any

---

108    Even where a joint expert is used, the parties may each prepare their own instructions for him or her: CPR r35.8.

progress has been made towards the preparation of reports by single experts or the instruction of a joint expert.[109]

12.152   Expert evidence can only be relied upon at trial with the court's permission. Usually, where expert evidence is appropriate, the court will initially give permission for the evidence to be adduced by way of written report. A direction to this effect is normally considered when directions are given after the filing of the allocation questionnaires. Specific permission is required for a party to call an expert to give oral evidence at trial.[110] This issue is usually considered once the extent of the dispute between the parties' experts has been clarified, as is explained below.

12.153   An expert's report that is relied upon must be disclosed to the other party, whether or not the expert is to give oral evidence. A party may put written questions about an expert's report to an expert instructed by another party.[111] Written questions may be put only once (without the court's permission) and must be put within 28 days of receipt of the expert's report. Where a party sends written questions or questions direct to an expert, a copy of the questions should, at the same time, be sent to the other party's solicitors.[112]

12.154   When permission is given by the court to rely on written expert evidence the court will usually give directions for there to be a discussion between the experts for the opposing parties, in order to narrow the issues, to identify the extent of agreement and disagreement between them and the reasons for any disagreement.[113] The discussions may take place face to face or by any other appropriate means proportionate to the circumstances of the case. The directions will provide for a statement of the areas of agreement and disagreement and the reasons for the latter to be prepared and agreed by the experts. However, the content of the discussions between the experts may not be referred to in court unless the parties expressly agree. Advisers should ensure that experts are fully briefed as to the relevant issues in the case and have all material documentation, before they enter into these discussions.

12.155   Once the experts' statement of areas of agreement and disagreement is available, the court will be able to decide whether oral expert evidence should be given at the trial. In civil actions against the police where there is a jury trial, it is usually very helpful to have the experts give live evidence unless there is no substantial disagreement between them.

109   CPR r35.7.
110   CPR r35.5.
111   CPR r 5.6.
112   PD to CPR Pt 35 para 4.2.
113   CPR r35.12.

# CHAPTER 13

# The civil action: trial, appeals, etc

13.1 Thorough preparation is essential both before and during the trial. The defendant police force is likely to use solicitors and counsel who are widely experienced in this area of litigation. If the decision has been made to defend the case to trial, rather than to offer a settlement, the defence will be conducted vigorously. Claimants are frequently surprised by the force of the defendant's attack on their credibility at trial, so it is important to anticipate and prepare for this. Hearings of civil claims against the police tend to involve many and varied points of law, evidence and tactics; the issues that are likely to arise during the course of the trial are discussed below. Most civil actions against the police are heard by a judge and a jury (see paras 12.77–12.90), so this chapter will also focus on the particular procedural considerations that arise in a civil judge and jury trial.[1]

# Pre-trial preparation

13.2 This section looks at steps that are carried out in the period immediately preceding the trial; for earlier preparatory work see chapters 2, 11 and 12.

## Funding

13.3 In publicly funded cases, it is usually necessary to apply to extend the terms of the claimant's funding certificate to cover trial. This is done after counsel's up-to-date assessment of merits and quantum has been obtained.[2]

## Medical expert evidence

13.4 This should be updated where necessary; for example if the claimant's condition has changed in a way that could affect the expert's earlier prognosis. The expert will need to be furnished with any additional medical records that have come into being in the interim. If the instructed expert is to give oral evidence at the trial and a long period has elapsed since he or she assessed the claimant, a further meeting between the two may be beneficial. A conference with counsel to explore the relevant issues is essential in most cases.

---

1 If the case is heard by a judge alone, the hearing will follow the same course as other civil trials on the multi-track.
2 There is a detailed consideration of the test for obtaining and extending public funding in chapter 11.

## Witnesses

13.5   Witnesses who are to attend trial should be reminded to re-read their statements to refresh their memory before attending court. Counsel may wish to see the witness in conference before he or she gives evidence.[3] If a witness is reluctant to attend court and/or needs permission from an employer to take time off work, a witness summons can be sought.[4] A witness summons should be obtained and served more than seven days before the commencement of the trial, for it to be binding.[5] However, if a witness is really unhappy about attending court, consideration should be given to dispensing with his or her evidence, as it may prove counter-productive to require him or her to attend.

## Briefing counsel and the pre-trial conference

13.6   A full trial brief should be prepared and sent to counsel, in good time before the trial. A pre-trial conference with the claimant is essential and the claimant should be encouraged to re-read his or her witness statement beforehand. At the conference the trial procedure can be explained to the claimant and any outstanding preparation issues resolved. More fundamentally, this will be an opportunity to explore potential weaknesses in the case and to focus on the points that are likely to be raised by the defendant in cross-examination at trial.

## Bundles

13.7   Unless directions provide otherwise, the claimant must file a trial bundle at court not more than seven days and not less than three days before the commencement of the trial.[6] The claimant should seek to agree the contents of the bundle with the defendant.[7] Guidance is given in the practice direction as to the documentation that should be contained in the trial bundle.[8] In an action against the police the bundle is likely to comprise: pleadings; case summary; court orders; exchanged witness statements; any photographs and plans; expert evidence;

---

3   Usually this should be done in the absence of the claimant, to avoid any suggestion of collusion.

4   The procedure is contained in Civil Procedure Rules (CPR) 34.2–34.6.

5   Otherwise the court's permission is required, see CPR 34.3(2) and 34.5(1) and (2).

6   CPR 39.5.

7   Practice Direction to CPR Pt 39 para 3.9.

8   PD to CPR Pt 39 para 3.2.

any transcript/note of the criminal proceedings; and relevant disclosed documentation, such as the custody record, officers' notebook entries, witness statements from the criminal proceedings, documentation generated by a formal complaint and records of conviction. The agreed trial bundle is used by the judge, counsel and – where relevant – the witness giving evidence. The jury is not provided with copies of this bundle, but is usually given a much more limited amount of documentation. There is no specific authority governing what the jury should be given and ultimately the issue is one for the discretion of the trial judge. However, bundles should be prepared by the claimant, following consultation with the defendant. The jury bundles usually comprise documentation that has a visual element or which is otherwise sufficiently complex that the jurors would have difficulty following the evidence without sight of it. Thus the most common materials included in jury bundles are photographs (of the claimant's injuries and/or of the scene of the incident), plans and the custody record. Pleadings and exchanged witness statements are never included in the bundles. Occasionally witness statements from the criminal trial, expert reports or medical records are included, if the jury would have difficulty comprehending the evidence without this documentation.

## The trial: preliminary matters

13.8    Almost inevitably, the trial judge will be asked to rule on certain matters before the jury is empanelled. The most common areas of dispute are set out below.

### Jury bundles

13.9    If the parties have been unable to agree on the contents of the bundles for the jury (see para 13.7, above), the trial judge will have to determine this issue.

### Witnesses

13.10   The respective credibility of the parties' accounts is often central to the success or failure of a civil action. Accordingly, both parties are usually concerned about the prospect of witnesses tailoring their evidence to fit with other testimony already given. Witnesses who are also parties to the action cannot be excluded from the courtroom, but other witnesses can be (save for expert witnesses), albeit in most types of civil cases, witnesses will remain in court throughout the trial. The most commonly adopted solution in actions against the police, is for the police witnesses to be permitted to listen to the claimant's counsel opening the case and to the claimant's evidence, so that they are fully aware of the case against them, and for them then to be excluded from the court room until their evidence has been given. Equally, any witnesses of fact that the claimant proposes to call are usually expected to remain outside court while the claimant and his or her witnesses give evidence, until they are called to testify.

13.11    Issues can arise in relation to proposed witnesses who do not attend for trial, either because they are reluctant to give evidence or because the relevant party has lost track of them and has been unable to notify them of the hearing. If a witness summons has been served, the witness in question will usually attend.[9] However, where a witness does not attend, the party who served his or her evidence may still want to rely upon that statement and may seek permission to read the statement to the jury. If the statement in question contains hearsay evidence, a hearsay notice should have been served at the time when witness statements were exchanged.[10] Application may be made to serve a late notice where this has been overlooked or where the need for one has arisen since the statements were exchanged. In any event the court has power under Civil Procedure Rules (CPR) 32.1(1) and (2) to determine whether the evidence can be given in written form. In so deciding the court will take into account the importance of the evidence; the degree of prejudice occasioned to the other party by the loss of any opportunity to cross-examine the account; and the extent of the efforts made to secure the attendance of the witness at court.[11]

## Questions for the prospective jurors

13.12    This is discussed when empanelment of the jury is considered at para 13.21.

---

9    If he or she does not he or she can potentially be dealt with as being in contempt of court and subject to a penalty of at least a fine, see RSC Ord 52/CCR Ord 34 (preserved by the CPR).

10    See CPR 33.2(1) and (2) and 33.3(aa); and see also para 12.137.

11    For the circumstances in which adverse inferences can be drawn in a civil case from a party's failure to call a witness who might be expected to have material evidence to give, see *Wisniewski v Central Manchester Health Authority* [1987] PIQR P324.

## Admissibility of evidence relating to past conduct

13.13 Issues can arise in relation to the admissibility of proposed evidence of bad character of the claimant or other witnesses. A party may wish to introduce evidence of a witness's previous convictions or other past discreditable conduct. It is important to distinguish between two different situations. The first is where a party seeks to cross-examine a witness called by the other party as to past misconduct, with a view to damaging his or her credibility. In these circumstances, if admissible, the evidence can only be relevant to the witness's credit and cannot be used to found an argument that the earlier act of misconduct makes it more likely that the conduct in issue at the current trial occurred. Further, if the evidence is raised solely for the purposes of damaging credit, the party cross-examining generally cannot adduce evidence relating to the misconduct to rebut whatever answers are given by the witness when cross-examined (see *R v Edwards* discussed in para 13.16). This is the most common way in which evidence of past bad character is used in civil trials. When cross-examining the claimant and his or her witnesses, the defendant will usually seek to refer to any previous convictions they have, with a view to showing they are untrustworthy. In the less likely event that a claimant has material to indicate that an officer has a previous conviction or disciplinary finding, he or she will seek to do likewise.[12] However, in some circumstances a party may wish to lead evidence of a witness's past misconduct – for example by calling others to testify to that behaviour – because it is said to be so related to an issue in the present case as to render the evidence admissible under the doctrine of similar fact evidence. For example, a claimant may want to establish that the officer who fabricated evidence against him or her acted similarly in a previous case. If the evidence is admissible under this principle it can be relied on to establish that it is more likely that the witness behaved in the way alleged in the present case.[13] Admissibility issues in relation to these two kinds of evidence are discussed in turn.

### Convictions and other discreditable conduct affecting credit

13.14 If a criminal conviction is not spent, the only power that the court has to control its admissibility if it is to be adduced as relevant to the witness's credit, is the discretion given to the court by CPR 32.1(2) to

12 Obtaining such material is discussed at paras 2.81–2.83 and 12.112.

13 For an example of the discussion of the two doctrines see *Thomas v Commissioner of Police of the Metropolis* [1997] 1 All ER 747, CA.

exclude evidence that would otherwise be admissible.[14] This discretion is exercised in accordance with the principles laid down in the overriding objective.[15] Thus, reference to a conviction might be excluded if the conviction was trivial, or if its effect would be disproportionately to prejudice the jury against the particular witness. If the conviction is spent[16] the general rule is that the offender is treated as if he or she had never been convicted of the offence.[17] However, a spent conviction can be referred to where the court considers that justice cannot be done except by admitting it in evidence.[18] In claims against the police, defendants usually argue that the spent convictions of a claimant or his or her witness should be admitted in evidence, since credibility is fundamental to the resolution of the issues in the case and the jury should know the full background of the person who is alleging police misconduct. In resisting such applications, claimants may rely on the comparative age of convictions (for example, if they occurred when the individual was a juvenile or much younger person); the extent to which they have any bearing on the conduct in issue in the current proceedings; and the possible risk of them prejudicing the jury. In the leading case on the operation of Rehabilitation of Offenders Act 1974 s7(3),[19] a majority of the Court of Appeal held that the trial judge had not erred in exercising his discretion to admit the claimant's spent convictions for wounding and for criminal damage in an action for false imprisonment, assault and malicious prosecution. The majority held that where previous convictions were relevant to credit, the interests of justice required that evidence of those spent convictions should be admitted; but that in deciding whether to admit such evidence the degree of relevance had to be balanced against the prejudice occasioned by its admission, and the judge had to be satisfied that the parties would not have a fair trial or that a witness's credit could not fairly be assessed if the evidence were to be excluded. As many spent convictions are arguably relevant to credit to at least some degree, this decision makes it difficult in most instances for claimants to resist applications for spent convictions to be admitted in evidence.[20]

14   *Watson v Chief Constable of Cleveland* [2001] EWCA Civ 1547.
15   See CPR 1.1.
16   As determined by reference to the rehabilitation periods set out in Rehabilitation of Offenders Act 1974 s5.
17   Rehabilitation of Offenders Act 1974 s4.
18   Rehabilitation of Offenders Act 1974 s7(3)
19   *Thomas v Commissioner of Police of the Metropolis* [1997] 1 All ER 747, CA.
20   In *Watson v Chief Constable of Cleveland* [2001] EWCA Civ 1547 there is a discussion of the circumstances in which a conviction is relevant to credit.

13.15 In relation to past discreditable conduct falling short of conviction, the principles of admissibility were laid down in *Hobbs v Tinling &* *Co Ltd.*[21] The court should have regard to the degree to which the proposed evidence will affect the credibility of the witness and any disproportionality between the importance of the imputation made and the significance of the witness's evidence. This approach is now also reinforced by the court's power under CPR 32.1 to exclude otherwise admissible evidence.

13.16 In criminal cases where the accused seeks to cross-examine police officer prosecution witnesses about past misconduct, the courts have confined the scope of such cross-examination to misconduct which has already been proven by conviction or disciplinary finding or established by a judgment of the Court of Appeal (Criminal Division) or of a civil court. Unsubstantiated allegations of police misbehaviour may only be raised in cross-examination where the allegations led to the acquittal of a defendant in circumstances which show that the jury must have disbelieved the officer's evidence.[22] There is no direct authority on whether the same limiting principles should be applied in a civil action trial to proposed cross-examination of police officers about their past misconduct, but this was generally assumed to be the case. However, in *O'Brien v Chief Constable of South Wales*[23] the Court of Appeal expressed the opinion that the rule was one of policy specific to criminal trials.[24]

13.17 When convictions are introduced in evidence, the effect is that the person in question is taken to have committed the offence unless the contrary is proved.[25] In practice it is very difficult to prove the contrary, not least because the witness is unlikely to have all the material evidence available; and any attempt to do so is likely further to damage the individual's credibility.[26]

---

21 [1929] 2 KB 1, CA.

22 *R v Edwards* [1991] 2 All ER 266, CA. The principles are further considered in *R v Guney* [1998] 2 Cr App R 242 and *R v Twitchell* [2000] 1 Cr App R 373 and are also discussed in chapter 5 where disciplinary action against police officers is considered.

23 [2003] EWCA Civ 1085.

24 This issue is likely to be revisited when the House of Lords give their decision in *Chief Constable of South Wales v O'Brien*, which is awaited at the time of writing.

25 Civil Evidence Act 1968 s11(2).

26 For the principles relating to proving that the offence was not committed in these circumstances see eg *Cooper v Pitcher* (1999) 18 January, CA, unreported.

## Similar fact evidence

13.18    In recent years the common law test for the admission of similar fact evidence adduced by the prosecution in criminal cases has become increasingly flexible. The leading case is *DPP v P*[27] in which the House of Lords determined that similar fact evidence was admissible if the probative force of the evidence was so great as to make it just to admit the evidence notwithstanding that it was prejudicial to the accused in indicating that he was guilty of committing another crime. Their Lordships stressed that attaining the requisite threshold of probative value was a question of degree which could be achieved by a number of routes; it was no longer necessary to show a striking level of similarity between the earlier conduct and the alleged offence, but similarity was still a means of establishing admissibility. For the purposes of determining whether the admissibility test is satisfied, the similar fact allegations are assumed to be true.[28] This approach has been followed by the Court of Appeal in two civil claims against the police[29] in relation to evidence of officers' past misconduct. By way of example, in *O'Brien* the claimant wanted to adduce evidence from suspects in an other investigation who had been treated in a comparable way by one of the main officers involved in the police investigation against him. In both instances there were similar allegations of fabricated admissions, 'off the record' interviewing, verbal abuse and pressure to incriminate others. The Court of Appeal permitted the material to be introduced as similar fact evidence because there was a strong factual parallel between the allegations in the two cases and because it was considered that the past alleged misbehaviour was so contrary to the proper role of an investigating officer as to make it more likely that the misconduct alleged in the present proceedings occurred.[30] The Court of Appeal said that the test of admissibility was whether the proposed similar fact evidence was relevant in the sense that it was logically probative of an issue in the case and in assessing whether this had been established the approach of *DPP v P* should be followed. Hence, as the law currently stands,[31] in a civil action proposed similar fact evidence may be admissible if there are specific factual parallels with the pleaded allegations in the case, if there is no possibility of collusion between the

27    [1991] 2 AC 447.
28    *R v H* [1995] 2 AC 596, HL.
29    *Steel v Commissioner of Police of the Metropolis* (1993) 10 February, CA, unreported and *O'Brien v Chief Constable of South Wales* [2004] CP Rep 5.
30    [2004] CP Rep 5 at [70] and [80].
31    The decision of the House of Lords in *Chief Constable of South Wales v O'Brien*, which is awaited at the time of writing.

witness concerned in the respective incidents and if the misconduct in question is of a particularly serious nature, thus enabling the conclusion that an officer who was prepared to so transgress the boundaries of accepted propriety on a previous occasion may do so again.[32] If proposed similar fact evidence is admissible under this test then the court nonetheless has a discretion pursuant to CPR 32.1(2) to decide whether to hear the evidence.[33] Thus if the evidence does not appear to be cogent or is likely to add considerably to the length and/or complexity of the trial, it may not be admitted. However, these factors should be balanced against the seriousness of the wrongdoing alleged and any public interest in the evidence being heard. Of course, similar fact evidence is not confined to past misconduct by police officers; a defendant police force may wish to adduce evidence of the claimant's past behaviour if there is a sufficient relationship between that and his or her pleaded conduct.

## Evidence of good character

13.19    Technically, evidence of good character may not be admissible in a civil case to bolster the credibility of a party or other witness.[34] However, in practice this rule is often overlooked and witnesses are permitted to adduce at least brief supporting evidence of their own good character, in particular if the other party to the proceedings calls their credibility into question.[35]

## Other admissibility issues

13.20    Objection is sometimes taken by one party because the other side has adduced evidence late and in breach of directions previously made. On occasions the court is asked to exclude a particular passage in an exchanged witness statement, for example if it introduces prejudicial and irrelevant material or it expresses an opinion (rather than giving a factual account). Disputes can also arise as to the extent to which

---

32  Thus generalised assertions of more routine misconduct such as minor assaults on arrest are unlikely to be admissible as similar fact evidence; see *Thorpe v Chief Constable of Manchester* [1989] 1 WLR 665, CA, as explained by the Court of Appeal in *O'Brien* at [70].

33  *O'Brien* at [71].

34  See, eg, the discussion in *Phipson on Evidence*, 15th ed, Sweet & Maxwell para 19-05.

35  It is less likely that permission would be given to either party to call witnesses solely for the purposes of giving evidence as to the good character of the claimant or one of the police officers involved.

the police can cross-examine the claimant on potentially prejudicial or damaging matters contained in his or her disclosed medical records. Although admissibility issues should be raised at the outset of the trial, depending on the nature of the particular point, the trial judge may sometimes prefer to hear how the case is opened and some of the evidence before making a ruling. Admissibility will be determined by reference to CPR 32.1 and the overriding objective.

# The course of the trial

## Empanelling the jury

13.21   The jurors are selected from a panel by ballot in open court.[36] In a High Court trial there are 12 jurors[37] and there are eight jurors in the County Court.[38] The grounds for challenging jurors are limited. A challenge to the whole jury could only be made in the extremely unlikely event that it could be shown that the officer appointed to summon the jurors was biased or had acted improperly.[39] An individual juror can be challenged for bias. However, in practice this is only likely to arise if the juror is known by one of the parties or their witnesses, since members of the jury cannot be questioned to discover their opinions. Before jurors are sworn in, it is good practice for them to be informed of the names of the parties and their witnesses, so as to avoid a situation where a juror recognises a witness and realises that he or she cannot continue to sit on the case once it is underway. In most civil actions the trial judge will also ask the potential jury members a question along the lines of whether they have any close relatives or close friends who are or were serving police officers or employees of the defendant police force, although the practice varies from court to court. There is no direct authority on the appropriateness of asking this question. The reason for asking it is to exclude from the jury those whose close association with a police officer or police employee would make it difficult for them to bring an independent perspective to the case, in circumstances where the credibility of the rival accounts is central to the outcome of the trial. Arguably, this approach accords with the guarantee of a fair and impartial hearing

---

36   Juries Act 1974 s11.
37   Juries Act 1974 s17
38   County Courts Act 1984 s67.
39   A jury cannot be challenged on the basis of its racial composition: *R v Ford* [1989] 3 WLR 762, CA.

contained in article 6(1) of the European Convention on Human Rights. However, defendants frequently object to such a question being asked on the basis that is it not asked of potential jurors in criminal cases.

## The claimant's opening speech

13.22   In most civil actions the burden of proving contested issues will be shared between the parties, since the police will bear the burden of proving the legality of any arrest and detention and the claimant will have to prove allegations of assault and malicious prosecution. However, even if the burden of proof falls largely on the defendant, it is usual for the claimant to begin if there are damages to be proved. The claimant's case commences by his or her counsel making an opening speech to the jury. In this speech counsel should explain to the jury the difference between a civil and a criminal case; outline the torts (the civil wrongs) that the police are accused of; summarise the parties' rival accounts so that the jury can appreciate the main factual issues in dispute; indicate to the jury the role that they will play in deciding liability and quantum; go through the documents that they have in their bundles and explain the nature of other documents, such as pleadings, that they may hear reference to during the evidence. Legal jargon should be avoided as much as possible. It is a matter of tactical judgment whether and to what extent counsel emphasises factual points in the claimant's favour at this stage. On the one hand it is important to engage the jury's attention; on the other hand it is advisable not to alert the police to lines of attack that they may not yet have anticipated, nor to promise the jury evidential outcomes that may not be delivered.

## The claimant's evidence

13.23   The claimant will be the first witness to give evidence. Evidence in chief is normally given in full orally by all witnesses (unless their evidence has been agreed) as the jury will not have the parties' exchanged witness statements. However, the trial judge can order the witness statements to stand as the evidence in chief and have them read to the jury[40] and some courts adopt this practice. From the claimant's perspective, the reading of his or her witness statement minimises the risk of an account being given in chief that is inconsistent with the exchanged statement, but may mean that impact is lost by the account being read in this way and (apart from any permitted supplementation

---

40  CPR 32.5(2).

of the witness statement), the claimant will have to face cross-examination from an early point in his or her evidence.

13.24     The way in which a claimant responds to cross-examination is frequently vital to the success of the claim. A non-combative demeanour is usually advisable. Claimants should be prepared for detailed cross-examination on all aspects of their accounts. In particular, questions will be asked of any departure in evidence in chief from the account in the exchanged witness statement or in earlier 'on record' accounts such as that given at the criminal trial or for the purposes of a complaint against the police. It is commonplace for defence counsel to cross-examine on inconsistencies between the account given in evidence and that recorded by medical experts or other health care professionals who have had dealings with the claimant. Any apparent divergence between the allegations made and the degree of injury suffered will also be highlighted and counsel for the defendant will be astute to emphasise any apparent exaggeration in the damages claim. As explained at para 13.6, cross-examination should be anticipated on past convictions and on any damaging material in disclosed medical records. All witnesses can be re-examined in relation to matters arising out of cross-examination.

13.25     Once the claimant has given evidence, any supporting witnesses of fact will be called. If their evidence is of importance to the case, they can also expect a sustained challenge to their credibility in cross-examination.

13.26     Although the jury will be asked to consider liability and quantum separately (see paras 13.46–13.47), it is usual for the evidence relating to both to be given at the same time, not least because evidence relating to injuries and other aspects of quantum may have a direct bearing upon credibility.

13.27     As discussed earlier, the claimant may be calling testimony from a medical expert. It is advisable for the expert to be present in court when the expert instructed by the other party gives evidence, so that he or she can comment on that testimony and/or furnish material for counsel to use in cross-examination. For this reason in most trials the parties agree to interpose the expert evidence so that it is heard sequentially, most commonly at the end of the claimant's case or after all the witnesses of fact have testified. It is useful, where possible, for the expert called by the claimant also to hear the claimant's testimony, as he or she may be asked questions based on the account that was given. The experts' evidence will usually affect liability as well as the scale of damages, since in most instances experts will be able to give an opinion on the likely cause of the injury and the extent to which it accords with the claimant's or the defendant's account of events. It is important therefore that all relevant scenarios are explored with the experts when they give their evidence. Any technical terms that are used should be explained to the jury.

## Submission of no case to answer

13.28 At the end of the claimant's evidence the police may submit that there is no case to answer and the claim should be dismissed. This submission is not made in the majority of civil action trials, as most cases include a claim for false imprisonment, where the burden of justifying the detention lies on the police and the evidence they propose to give on that aspect of the case is usually closely interlinked with the other causes of action. However, in a case where the burden of proof lies exclusively on the claimant, for example where malicious prosecution alone is alleged, the submission is sometimes made. If the defendant raises the issue, two preliminary points arise: should the defendant be required to elect to call no evidence if the submission fails and/or what is the proper time for making the submission? In civil cases not involving a jury the Court of Appeal has confirmed that the Civil Procedure Rules have not significantly altered the previous position, so that a defendant should rarely be permitted to make a submission of no case to answer without first being put to his or her election.[41] The two main reasons given for this approach are, first, that it is generally undesirable for the trier of fact to express a view on the facts until all material evidence has been heard and, second, if the submission succeeds, but the claimant overturns that decision on appeal, there will be a need for a re-trial if all material evidence has not been heard.[42] In jury cases the position has always been more flexible; the first stated reason can have no application and the second applies with lesser force, given that in some instances the Court of Appeal will have little choice but to order a re-trial even if all the evidence has been given, to enable a jury to deliver its verdict on the facts. Accordingly, it has been held that in a civil jury trial the court has a discretion whether to require the defendant to elect before the submission of no case to answer is made.[43] The appellate courts have not reconsidered this issue since the CPR came into force, but as they have not significantly affected the practice in non-jury trials, there is no reason to suppose that

41  *Benham Limited v Kythira Investments Ltd* [2003] EWCA Civ 1794 at [32].
42  See *Boyce v Wyatt Engineering* [2001] EWCA Civ 692.
43  *Young v Rank* [1950] 2 All ER 166; *Payne v Harrison* [1961] 2 All ER 873.

they have substantially changed the position in jury trials. In *Payne v Harrison*[44] the Court of Appeal emphasised that in a civil jury trial a judge is not bound to rule upon a submission of no case to answer at the close of the claimant's evidence and may postpone a determination of whether there is a case to go to the jury until after all the evidence has been heard. This approach may commend itself to the court; once the judge has heard all the evidence, a clearer view can be formed of the merits of the submission and the risk reduced of an erroneous decision being made, which ultimately requires a re-trial. From a claimant's perspective, it is likely to be advantageous for any such ruling to be postponed until after the police evidence has been heard, since material may arise in cross-examination of officers that provides support for the claimant's case. In so far as the claimant needs to establish malicious motivation on the part of the officers, the evidence is likely to come predominantly from their testimony, in particular the way they respond to matters put to them in cross-examination. Thus the interests of justice and of affording a fair trial tend to point to the desirability of the ruling being made after all the evidence has been heard.[45]

13.29    If, however, the trial judge is persuaded to make a ruling at the end of the claimant's case in a jury trial, he or she should ask whether on the evidence adduced by the claimant the claim has a real prospect of success.[46] If the evidence fails to meet this threshold the claim will be dismissed; if the ruling is in the claimant's favour the police will normally proceed to call their evidence. In a case where the submission has been made after the defendant has been required to elect not to call evidence, the judge will determine whether there is a sufficient case to go to the jury on the evidence adduced. It is not for the judge to assess whether the claimant has proved his or her case on a balance of probabilities, unless this can be resolved purely by a ruling on the law; in any case involving disputed facts this would be to trespass into the jury's fact finding role (discussed at para 13.31 onwards).

## The defendant's case

13.30    In trials heard in the High Court the defendant has a right to make an opening speech.[47] In the county court the trial judge has a discretion

---

44   [1961] 2 All ER 873.
45   As does the fact that inferences can be drawn from the defendant's failure to give evidence and/or to call certain witnesses: see *Benham Limited v Kythira Investments Ltd* [2003] EWCA Civ 1794 at [25]–[31].
46   *Benham Limited v Kythira Investments Limited*, at [27].
47   Common Law Procedure Act 1854 s18.

whether to permit the defendant's counsel to make both an opening and a closing speech. Opening speeches by defendants in county court trials are in practice relatively rare. This is perhaps surprising as it can be a useful opportunity for the defendant to clarify to the jury the police case, to set the scene for the evidence to be called from the officers and to draw together the strands that have emerged during cross-examination of the claimant's evidence. The defendant's evidence is usually comprised wholly or mainly of police officers; it is relatively rare for significant reliance to be placed on civilian witnesses. In giving their evidence in chief, officers can refresh their memory from any contemporaneous note made of events and are, in that respect, at an advantage over the claimant's witnesses. Officers are likely to be cross-examined about any significant discrepancies between their account and the accounts given by other officers; any discrepancies between their current account and earlier 'on record' accounts that they made; lack of supporting injuries (where relevant) and any failure to employ or adhere to their powers.

## Obtaining a verdict on liability in a civil jury trial

13.31    The key role of the jury in a civil trial is to resolve the main disputed issues of fact – in essence the jurors' job is to decide what actually happened by assessing the relative credibility of the parties' rival accounts. The jury indicates its decision by answering questions provided to it in the affirmative or in the negative. The trial judge then uses these answers to determine whether as a matter of law the claim succeeds or fails. The general approach to be adopted was set out by the Court of Appeal in *Dallison v Caffery*.[48] It is for the judge to rule which issues of fact should go to the jury. The jury does not need to resolve every area of disputed fact; rather it needs to determine those disputes of fact that will enable the judge to rule on the claims. Thus, with the assistance of counsel (as described at para 13.34), the judge must decide which issues the jury should be asked about. It is very well established that for reasons of legal policy the judge and not the jury should decide the objective issues that arise in relation to false imprisonment and malicious prosecution claims, ie, whether there were reasonable grounds to suspect the claimant of the relevant offence and whether there was reasonable and probable cause for the prosecution.[49] Thus, any attempt to ask the jury whether the arresting officer

48    [1964] 2 All ER 610.
49    *Dallison v Caffery*, [1964] 2 All ER 610.

had reasonable grounds to believe that the claimant had committed the offence for which he or she was arrested is a fundamental error of law that will lead to the decision being quashed even where the question had been agreed by counsel.[50] The judge rules upon these objective questions once the jury has resolved any disputed facts that may bear on the issue, for example if there is a dispute over the information that the officer had at the time of the arrest. Aside from false imprisonment and malicious prosecution claims, issues of 'reasonableness' usually involve questions of fact which should be resolved by the jury (after it has been given any appropriate legal guidance by the judge in the summing up). Thus the Court of Appeal expressed the view that the jury rather than the judge should decide whether reasonable force was used in relation to an assault claim.[51] It is submitted that this is correct, albeit the practice varies markedly as to whether the judge or the jury determines whether the force used by the police was reasonable, if the issue arises.[52] *Hutt v Commissioner of Police of the Metropolis*[53] is a good example of where the functions of judge and jury became confused at trial. The action included claims for both false imprisonment and negligence. The judge left the negligence issue to the jury in its entirety with a very broad question. The Court of Appeal held that the judge had erred and that he should either have used his case management powers[54] to deal with the negligence issue himself or he should have put a series of factual questions to the jury and then ruled on the basis of the answers given whether negligence was established as a matter of law.

13.32    Either party may submit to the judge that there is insufficient evidence on a particular issue for it to be left to the jury, as the jury could not properly conclude the point in the other party's favour. For example, this submission may be made by the defendant in relation to a false imprisonment and/or a malicious prosecution claim if there was, objectively viewed, sufficient evidence against the claimant to warrant arrest or prosecution, but the claimant challenges the honesty and propriety of the relevant officer's state of mind.[55] In *Dallison v*

---

50   *Ward v Chief Constable of West Midlands* [1997] *Times* 15 December, CA.

51   *Pollard v Chief Constable of West Yorkshire* [1999] PIQR P219, CA.

52   Compare the views expressed on this point in Clayton & Tomlinson, *Civil Actions Against the Police*, 3rd ed, Thomson Sweet & Maxwell, 2004 para 3-127 and in R Perks, *The Police in the Civil Courts*, Butterworths para 9.21.

53   (2003) *Times* 5 December.

54   See CPR 3.1.

55   For a discussion of the ingredients of the torts of false imprisonment and malicious prosecution see chapters 6 and 7.

*Caffery*[56] Diplock LJ indicated that where there was reasonable and probable cause for an arrest or prosecution the judge should not leave the issue of the honesty of the officer's belief to the jury save in the unlikely event that there was cogent positive evidence that the officer himself did not believe the available material. This dictum is frequently relied upon by defendants. However, it is important to understand what is meant by positive evidence in this context. Given that the evidence in question relates to the officer's state of mind, the claimant will rarely be in a position to lead specific evidence as to the officer's thought process at the time; rather the honesty or otherwise of the officer's belief is a matter of inference to be drawn from all the surrounding evidence. This is well illustrated by the recent decision of the Court of Appeal in *Paul v Chief Constable of Humberside.*[57] The court allowed an appeal from the trial judge's decsion to withdraw the case from the jury and a re-trial was ordered, because the evidence indicated there was material from which the jury could have inferred that the decisions to arrest and prosecute were not based on an honest belief in the case put forward and/or were motivated by an improper consideration (in that case of diverting attention away from any police culpability in relation to the death in custody of one of the claimant's associates).[58]

13.33    A party may also submit that an issue of fact need not go to the jury because even if the other party's case on the facts is believed, their claim/defence is bound to fail. For example, the claimant may submit that even on the officer's account of the events that precipitated the arrest, his or her alleged behaviour did not give sufficient grounds to make a lawful arrest. Equally, a defendant may submit that on the claimant's admitted actions the officer exercised a legitimate power of arrest, irrespective of whether the claimant also behaved in a way that was the subject of disputed evidence.

13.34    The normal procedure is for counsel to prepare draft questions and to try and agree on the wording. The judge is then asked to approve the draft and to rule on any disputed issues. The form of the questions asked should be such that they can always be answered simply 'yes' or 'no'. The questions should incorporate reference to where the burden and standard of proof lies. To avoid the risk of confusion it is

---

56   [1964] 2 All ER 610.
57   [2004] EWCA Civ 308.
58   See also the discussion relating to establishing inferences of bad faith on the part of investigating officers in the analysis of the tort of malicious prosecution at paras 7.22–7.25.

desirable to refer to the parties by name.[59] Questions should be kept clear and concise, multiple sub-clauses should be avoided and no more questions should be asked than are strictly necessary for resolving the issues in dispute.

13.35   In assault cases there should normally be a separate question for each assault. Where the conduct said to amount to the assault is in dispute the question should be along the following lines:

> Has Mr Jackson [the claimant] satisfied you it is more likely than not that Officer Bloggs punched him in the face as he got out of the police van?

If the force that was used is not in dispute, but there is an issue over whether that was reasonable in the circumstances, it is submitted that the jury should be asked in terms to decided this issue, as discussed at para 13.31.

13.36   In the more straightforward false imprisonment cases, where the arresting officer witnessed the events that are said to justify the arrest and the claimant contends that the officer's account of those events is false, resolution of liability is relatively simple. The jury needs to decide who is giving the truthful account and the question is focused accordingly, for example:

> Has the Chief Constable satisfied you it is more likely than not that Mr Jackson [the claimant] kicked Officer Bloggs on the shin before he made the arrest?

13.37   If the arresting officer was not an eye-witness to the alleged offence and the arrest is justified by reference to information supplied by third parties, the jury may need to be asked questions about the material that the officer was aware of when he or she made the arrest and/or whether he or she honestly suspected that the claimant had committed the offence in question (as discussed at para 13.32). Claims in false imprisonment may also be based on an officer's failure to give prescribed information on making the arrest. In those circumstances, if the defendant contends that the information was given on arrest, the jury will be asked a question along the lines of:

> Has the Chief Constable satisfied you it is more likely than not that Officer Bloggs told Mr Jackson [the claimant] that he was under arrest / the grounds of his arrest at the time when the arrest was made?

13.38   Sometimes in false imprisonment cases the jury will also be asked to resolve factual issues relating to the length of the claimant's detention.

---

59  *Igwemma v Chief Constable of Greater Manchester* [2001] 4 All ER 751 provides a cautionary tale in this respect (see para 13.45).

13.39      In the more straightforward malicious prosecution cases, where officers claim to have witnessed the events that are said to justify the prosecution and the claimant contends that their account was false, the position is similar to false imprisonment. The jury needs to decide what actually happened and whether the relevant officers deliberately falsified their account. If the officers did so, the central disputed ingredients of the malicious prosecution claim will be established, namely lack of reasonable and probable cause for the prosecution and malice. Thus the question is normally formulated along the following lines:

> Has Mr Jackson [the claimant] satisfied you it is more likely than not that PC Bloggs fabricated his account of Mr Jackson lunging towards him and kicking him?

13.40   As with a false imprisonment claim, if the prosecution is justified by reference to material supplied to the police by third parties, the question for the jury is likely to relate to the honesty of the relevant officer's belief (if there is sufficient evidence for this issue to go to the jury, as discussed at para 13.32). The appropriate formulation is to ask whether the claimant has proved that the relevant officer(s) did not honestly believe in the charge made or the case that was put forward.[60] If that question is answered in the claimant's favour then it also follows that the prosecution was brought maliciously. In the more unusual instance where a specific, ulterior motive is relied upon by the claimant to found the case that the prosecution was brought maliciously, the jury may need to be asked a specific question about that alleged motivation.

## Closing speeches

13.41   Once the questions for the jury have been resolved and copies of the questions distributed to the jurors, both counsel will make their closing speeches. The defendant's speech is first. Both counsel will try to draw together their best points on the evidence and to meet the points raised by the other party.

## The summing-up

13.42   The judge will outline to the jurors their respective roles, namely that he or she decides the law and they determine the crucial issues of disputed fact. The burden and standard of proof will be explained and any relevant legal directions will be given, for example as to the use the jury can

---

60   *Glinski v McIvor* [1962] AC 726, HL.

make of evidence relating to past bad character (discussed at paras 13.13–13.18). The jurors will be taken through the questions they have to answer and the purpose of the questions will be explained. It is usual for the judge to summarise to the jury the ingredients of the causes of action and to refer to the police's relevant powers, so that the jury can understand the framework in which the questions are asked. However, the extent to which it is necessary or appropriate to do so will be governed by the particular circumstances. In *Ward v Chief Constable of the West Midlands*[61] the Court of Appeal allowed an appeal in relation to a summing up that failed to explain to the jury the legal ingredients of the offence for which the claimant was arrested or the torts relied upon, in a context where the jury had asked for further assistance and the elements of the offence were directly relevant to one of the questions they had to answer. However, in *Sutton v Commissioner of Police of the Metropolis*[62] the Court of Appeal emphasised that jurors should be told as much – and no more – of the law as they need to know in order to be able intelligently to play their part in the trial process; for example if the judge relies on words to which the law has given a particular meaning he or she must also explain that meaning to the jury. The judge should also remind the jury of the salient factual evidence.

## The jury's decision on liability

13.43    In a civil trial there is no fixed time for which the jurors must deliberate before they are given a majority direction. They must be given such time as the court thinks reasonable having regard to the nature and complexity of the case.[63] In practice judges rarely indicate to juries that a majority verdict can be accepted until they have been deliberating for at least two hours. In a High Court case the judge can accept a majority decision of 10:2 or 11:1.[64] In a county court case seven of the jury must agree on the verdict.[65] A decision by a lower majority can only be accepted if both parties agree to this course. This sometimes happens, but many police forces are reluctant to do so.[66] The judge must be

---

61  [1997] *Times* 15 December, CA.

62  (1998) 29 July, CA, unreported.

63  Juries Act 1974 s17(4).

64  Juries Act 1974 s17(1).

65  Juries Act 1974 s17(2)

66  In *Morrison v Chief Constable of West Midlands Police* [2003] EWCA Civ 271, (2003) *Independent* 28 February, Lord Phillips MR queried whether a party's refusal to accept a majority below 7:1 was consistent with the overriding objective laid down by the CPR, given the attendant costs and use of court resources involved in the inevitable re-trial.

careful not to direct the jury in a way that appears to put pressure on them to arrive at a verdict. If the jurors seem to be deadlocked and the judge feels that it may be useful to give them some guidance, the form of words identified by the Court of Appeal (Criminal Division) in *R v Watson*[67] should be used.[68] If the jury remains deadlocked and the parties cannot agree to accept a lower majority, the judge has to discharge the jury and order a re-trial.[69]

13.44    If the jury is able to return answers to the questions it has been asked, the judge will then rule on the claimant's causes of action. As indicated above, in some instances the answers given by the jury will decide whether the claim succeeds, whereas in some circumstances the judge will have to make legal rulings to determine the outcome of the action once he or she has the jury's decision on the material facts (see paras 13.31–13.40).

13.45    *In Igwemma v Chief Constable of Greater Manchester*[70] after the jury's decision had been announced in court, the foreman of the jury indicated that a mistake had been made and the jury was allowed to retire again briefly and then to give a different answer to one of the questions. The mistake had arisen as a result of the jury's confusion over which party was the claimant and which the defendant. The Court of Appeal decided that the trial judge was correct to let the jury alter its verdict, even though it had already been discharged by then. It was emphasised that it was important for the jury's findings to be effectively transmitted to the court, so that if there was some misunderstanding, it should be put right, even if the jury had already returned its verdict and been discharged, if this could be done without causing injustice to either party. Whether or not injustice would result in such circumstances would depend upon factors such as the time that had elapsed since the original answers were returned; whether the jury itself raised the possibility of misunderstanding and whether the jury could have been persuaded to change its view by anything said or done since the original verdicts had been given, in particular if anything had since emerged that the jury would not have heard during the course of the evidence given at the trial.

---

67  (1988) 87 Cr App R 1.
68  *Morrison v Chief Constable of West Midlands Police* [2003] EWCA Civ 271, (2003) *Independent* 28 February.
69  In those circumstances the court should normally order costs in the case: *Camiller v Commissioner of Police of the Metropolis* (1999) *Times* 8 June.
70  [2001] 4 All ER 751.

## Obtaining the jury's decision on quantum

13.46 If the claimant succeeds in whole or in part upon liability he or she will be entitled to damages. In some cases the parties manage to agree a figure at this stage. In the absence of such agreement, the jury will be asked to determine quantum. The directions that the jury should be given by the judge in relation to damages were set out by the Court of Appeal in *Thompson and Hsu v Commissioner of Police of the Metropolis*.[71] These are discussed in detail at paras 14.10–14.37 (and the guidance itself is at Appendix A). The procedure usually adopted is that counsel address the judge in the absence of the jury as to the appropriate brackets of figures that the jury should be given as guidance in relation to the material heads of compensation. Counsel will normally ask the judge to rule upon whether it is an appropriate case for the jury to consider awarding aggravated and/or exemplary damages, if the defendant objects to these heads of damages being put to the jury. Submissions will be made upon any other issues of law on which the judge may need to direct the jury, for example whether it is a case where it is open to the jury to conclude that the claimant's conduct could reduce or wipe out any award of aggravated or exemplary damages that would otherwise be made (see paras 14.22–14.37).

13.47 Counsel will then address the jury on quantum, explaining their respective positions. The defendant's speech is made first. The judge will then sum up to the jurors, explaining to them the heads of damages that they need to consider, the basis upon which they can make an award or decline to make an award under any particular head and indicating to them the guideline figures they should bear in mind. As discussed in more detail in chapter 14, the jury will normally make a separate award of basic damages for each cause of action, such as false imprisonment, assault and malicious prosecution. An award for psychiatric injury is also normally given as a separate figure, although it may stem from two or more causes of action. Separate awards are also made of aggravated and exemplary damages (where appropriate). If a finding of fact is central to the quantum of the claim, but did not need to be resolved at the liability stage, the jury may be asked a specific question on that point, to help guide its assessment of damages. For example, questions might relate to features of the claimant's treatment in custody that are said to aggravate his or her damage, such as alleged denial of medical assistance or delay in permitting access to legal advice.

71 [1997] 2 All ER 762.

## Costs

13.48   The general rule is that the unsuccessful party will be ordered to pay the costs of the successful party.[72] However, the court may make a different order and, in particular, will have regard to: the conduct of the parties; whether a party has succeeded on part only of his or her case; and any payment into court or admissible offer made to settle the claim.[73] Over the last few years courts have become increasingly willing to order that a party who has only succeeded on part of his or her claim will only receive a part of his or her costs. Moreover, the partially successful party may be ordered to pay the other party's costs of the issue on which he or she failed.[74] Such outcomes are frequently expressed in percentage terms, so that, for example, the claimant may recover 70 per cent of his or her costs from the defendant. If a claimant is publicly funded and would not otherwise be able to pay any costs awarded to the defendant, they may be recouped from compensation that he or she has been awarded on the successful part of the claim. For these reasons, coupled with the impact of the Legal Services Commission's statutory charge, a claimant who only succeeds on part of the claim may receive little or no net compensation. However, in *Fleming v Chief Constable of Sussex*[75] the defendant was ordered to pay all the claimant's costs of the trial even though he had succeeded on claims in assault and malicious prosecution but had lost his claim for false imprisonment, as the factual overlap between the causes of action meant that the trial was not prolonged by the unsuccessful claim.

13.49   Offers of settlement made under CPR Pt 36 are considered at paras 12.145–12.146. In brief, if the claimant wins at trial but is awarded less compensation than the defendant's Pt 36 payment, the court will order the claimant to pay any costs incurred by the defendant after the latest date on which the payment could have been accepted without the permission of the court.[76] However, if the claimant recovers more at trial than proposed in his or her own Pt 36 offer, the court will order the defendant to pay interest on compensation at an

---

72   CPR 44.3(2)(a).

73   CPR 44.3(2)(b) and (4). Examples of aspects of the parties' conduct that may be taken into account are set out in CPR 44.3(5).

74   Unreasonable conduct is not a prerequisite to making such an order: *Summit Property Ltd v Pitmans* [2001] EWCA Civ 2020, [2002] CPLR 97.

75   [2004] EWCA Civ 643.

76   CPR 36.20(2). The period for acceptance of the defendant's offer is set out in CPR 36.11.

enhanced rate and award the claimant his or her costs on an indemnity basis from the latest date when the defendant could have accepted the offer without the permission of the court, unless it considers it unjust to do so.[77] Aside from this situation, costs are normally awarded on the standard basis, rather than an indemnity basis.[78] Awards of costs on the indemnity basis are normally reserved for cases where the court wishes to indicate its disapproval of the conduct of the party against whom the order is made.[79]

# Appeals

## Procedure

13.50   Permission to appeal is required from the court making the decision under challenge or from the appeal court.[80] If the application for permission is made to the lower court it can be made orally at the end of the relevant hearing. If the application is made to the appeal court it is made in a written appeal notice, though the application can be renewed at an oral hearing if it is refused on a consideration of the papers.[81] Permission will be granted if the proposed appeal has a real prospect of success or there is some other compelling reason why the appeal should be heard (such as where a point of substantial public interest is raised).[82] An appeal from the outcome of a trial will be heard by the Court of Appeal. However, in relation to county court proceedings, the Court of Appeal only hears appeals in relation to 'final decisions' made in cases allocated to the multi-track.[83] An appeal against a pre-trial decision made in county court proceedings, such as a refusal to give summary judgment or a refusal to permit amendment of the claim, will be heard by the next judge up in the hierarchy: thus if the original decision was made by a district judge, the appeal will be

---

77   CPR 36.21(1) and (4). The period for acceptance of the claimant's offer is set out in CPR 36.12.

78   CPR 44.4 defines the two bases.

79   *Reid Minty v Taylor* [2001] EWCA Civ 1723, [2002] 2 All ER 150, CA.

80   CPR 52.3.

81   CPR 52.3(3) and (4). Time limits for making the application are set out in CPR 52.4.

82   CPR 52.3(6).

83   County Courts Act 1984 s77(1); Access to Justice Act 1999 (Destination of Appeals) Order 2000 SI No 1071. A final decision is one that would finally determine the proceedings before the court, apart from any appeal, whichever way it went.

considered by a circuit judge at the county court; if the original decision was made by a circuit judge the appeal will be to the High Court. Second appeals to the Court of Appeal are only permitted where an important point of principle or practice is raised, see CPRr52.13. Appeals in High Court proceedings are to the Court of Appeal.[84]

## Appeals in jury trials

13.51   In general the appeal court will allow an appeal where the decision of the court below was 'wrong' or was unjust due to a serious procedural or other irregularity.[85] In cases where a judge sits alone, a 'wrong' decision may involve an error of law, an error of fact or relate to the exercise of a discretion (as discussed in more detail at para 13.59). However, in relation to a jury trial the scope for an appeal is more limited. The Court of Appeal will not overturn a jury's decision on the facts unless it is shown to be perverse, or flawed by legal error in the directions given to the jury by the judge. Thus the potential grounds of appeal from the outcome of a civil action jury trial are likely to be confined to one or more of the following.

### Error of law by the judge

13.52   This is largely self-explanatory. The decision may be quashed if the judge has misdirected the jury on the law, given the jury the wrong questions to decide, or failed to direct it on a material matter.[86] Similarly, an appeal will lie if the judge has erred in the questions of law that he or she had to decide. For example in *Balchin v Chief Constable of Hampshire*[87] the trial judge erred when ruling whether the officer had reasonable grounds to arrest the claimant, by making findings of fact that should have been left for the jury to determine. Appeals from the exercise of a judicial discretion are considered in para 13.59 below.

### Wrongly withdrawing issues from the jury

13.53   A clear example is *Paul v Chief Constable of Humberside*[88] where the judge erred in failing to leave questions relating to the honesty of the

---

84  Supreme Court Act 1981 s16(1), apart from Masters' decisions, which are appealed to High Court judges.

85  CPR 52.11(3).

86  See, eg, *Ward v Chief Constable of West Midlands* [1997] *Times* 15 December, CA.

87  [2001] EWCA Civ 538, (2001) *Times* 4 May.

88  [2004] EWCA Civ 308.

officers' beliefs and to the propriety of their motives to the jury in relation to a false imprisonment and malicious prosecution claims. This case is discussed in more detail at paras 7.24 and 13.32.

## Perverse verdict by the jury

13.54    If this arises at all it is likely to arise in one of two ways. A decision may be quashed if a jury has arrived at a conclusion contradicted by the evidence. In *Masters v Chief Constable of Sussex*[89] the Court of Appeal allowed an appeal from a jury's conclusion that the claimant had been assaulted, where his own medical evidence contradicted his case and there was no supporting evidence for his account. They held that in the circumstances the assault claim should have been withdrawn from the jury. The jury's decision will also be quashed if it is perverse in the sense that inconsistent answers have been given to the questions asked. However, the test for establishing perversity is strict; it must be shown that there was a necessary inconsistency, sufficient to vitiate the trial on the ground that the jurors must have based their deliberations on a false approach or otherwise been sufficiently unreliable as to justify a re-trial.[90] It is not perverse for the jury to accept parts of each party's account and to reject others.[91] The House of Lords has emphasised that the Court of Appeal should not find a jury's verdict on liability perverse, unless there was no rational explanation for it.[92]

## Serious procedural irregularity in the course of the trial

13.55    Examples of cases where this could arise have been discussed at para 13.43, such as where undue pressure was put on a deadlocked jury to arrive at a verdict.

## Bias on the part of the judge

13.56    It is not uncommon for claimants to feel that the trial judge has been unduly unsympathetic to their position, whether in terms of interjections during the trial or comments made during the summing up. However, it is very difficult to mount a successful appeal on this basis, where the party would have to prove either actual bias on the part of the trial judge or that his or her conduct was such that the claimant was deprived of a fair trial in breach of the guarantee contained in ECHR

---

89    [2002] EWCA Civ 1482.
90    *Abassy v Commissioner of Police of the Metropolis* [1990] 1 All ER 193.
91    *Purchase v Chief Constable of Thames Valley* [2001] EWCA Civ 682.
92    *Grobbelaar v News Group Newspapers Ltd* [2002] 4 All ER 732.

article 6(1). Comments that caused resentment at the time may appear less significant when reduced to a line or two in a lengthy written transcript. An example of the difficulties of mounting an appeal on this basis is *Sheppard v Secretary of State for the Home Department*.[93]

### New evidence

13.57 Appeals rarely succeed on this ground as the appellant usually needs to show that the evidence could not have been found with reasonable diligence at the time of the original trial and that had it been adduced it would have had an important influence on the result.[94]

13.58    In the situations discussed, a successful ground of appeal is likely to lead to an order for a re-trial, unless the outcome of the case can be resolved without findings of fact being made (for example if the Court of Appeal considers that an issue should have been withdrawn from the jury due to lack of evidence). Where the appeal relates to the jury's decision on compensation, the Court of Appeal may be able to substitute its own conclusion, as it has the power to make an award of damages or to vary an award of damages made by the jury, rather than ordering a re-trial.[95] The Court of Appeal has the power to overturn a jury's award where it considers that the sum was excessive or inadequate, in the sense that a reasonable jury could not have made the award having regard to the guidelines given in *Thompson and Hsu v Commissioner of Police of the Metropolis*[96] and the court can then arrive at its own figure.[97]

## Appeals in judge alone cases

13.59 The scope for appeal in such cases is equivalent to the position in civil cases generally. Judges' conclusions on the law or on the facts can be appealed. However, the Court of Appeal has frequently expressed caution about overturning decisions of fact made by the judge who

---

93  [2002] EWCA Civ 1921, albeit in the context of a judge alone trial.
94  In *Lincoln v Commissioner of Police of the Metropolis* [2001] EWCA Civ 2110 the Court of Appeal held that in the light of new evidence relating to the credibility of the claimant's witness, the interests of justice did require a re-trial.
95  CPR 52.10(3).
96  [1997] 2 All ER 762
97  *Clark v Chief Constable of Cleveland* [2000] CP Rep 22, considering Courts and Legal Services Act 1990 s8.

had the opportunity of hearing and evaluating the witnesses, unless the issue under challenge relates to inferences to be drawn from the primary facts found, rather than the primary facts themselves.[98] Where the complaint relates to the judge's exercise of a discretion, the Court of Appeal will only interfere if the judge erred in law, or misdirected him or herself in some way or reached a conclusion outside of the generous ambit within which reasonable disagreement is possible.[99]

98  The authorities are summarised in *Assicurazioni Generali SpA v Arab Insurance Group (BSC)* [2002] EWCA Civ 1642, [2003] 1 WLR 577 at [6]–[11].

99  See eg *Laine v Chief Constable of Cambridgeshire* (1999) 14 October, unreported, where the appeal related to the judge's discretionary decision to refuse to permit a late amendment to the pleadings.

# CHAPTER 14

# Damages

# Introduction

14.1    Many people bring a civil action against the police as a matter of principle and say that the amount of damages is very much a secondary consideration to disciplining an officer or obtaining an apology. However, if the complaints and discipline system has been unsuccessful in delivering these remedies (see chapters 5 and 6), then a civil action is unlikely to do so. Essentially, an award of damages is the main remedy available in a civil action. It is always an important issue, and the type and level of damages may indicate the court's opinion of the merits of the case and the conduct of the police.

14.2    This chapter begins by introducing the major case in recent years on damages in police cases, *Thompson and Hsu v Commissioner of Police of the Metropolis*,[1] in which guidance was provided by the Court of Appeal on levels and types of damages. The case is used as a benchmark in almost every civil action against the police. The chapter then describes in detail the various types of damages available, referring to the guidance in *Thompson*. It then describes the nature of damages for some of the particular causes of action described earlier in this book.

# Background to Court of Appeal guidelines for police damages

14.3    As will have been seen in chapters 6 and 7, cases involving false imprisonment and malicious prosecution provide for a right to jury trial in the civil courts in most circumstances. The majority of civil actions probably include one of these torts. It is the role of the jury, where there is one, not only to assist the judge to determine liability in a case (see chapter 12) but also, in the absence of agreement between the parties, to determine the level of damages to be awarded to a successful claimant. The traditional approach of the courts was to provide juries with virtually no guidance as to how much might be an appropriate sum to award. For example, in an old case that is no longer good law involving damages for false imprisonment, Purchas LJ in the Court of Appeal said:

> Parliament has seen fit to leave the assessment of damages to the judgment of the jury rather than the judge ... [T]hese are areas where the question of

1 [1998] QB 498; [1997] 2 All ER 762.

damages is so utterly subjective to the individual facts involved that I think it would be wrong to attempt to influence by judicial interference consideration of damages by the jury.[2]

14.4 Such an approach, though, meant there was little consistency in the awards made by juries. Juries were invited not only to consider compensatory damages for the torts committed by the police, but were also asked to consider awards of exemplary damages. Exemplary damages (see para 14.25) constitute an additional amount designed to punish the police for their wrongdoing rather than directly compensate the claimant for his or her loss. When these complicated but largely subjective questions were left to juries with little guidance from the judge, awards could be unfairly small or improbably large.

14.5 It was a number of the improbably large awards which led to the appeals in *Thompson* and in other cases. Prior to this there had already been some developments in statute and case law relating to the award of damages by juries. In 1990 the Court of Appeal was given 'power to order a new trial on the ground that damages awarded by a jury are excessive or inadequate' and to 'substitute for the sum awarded by the jury such sum as appears to the court to be proper'.[3] Then in a series of appeals concerning libel damages awarded by juries, the Court of Appeal became more willing to provide guidance and to interfere with large awards.[4]

14.6 The *Thompson* appeal considered two cases. The first was that of Ms Thompson. She had been lawfully arrested for a driving offence but excessive force was used against her in the police station. She was maliciously prosecuted (but acquitted) for assault against her police officer assailants and taken to court in handcuffs. The jury awarded her £51,500 of which £50,000 constituted exemplary damages. The second case was that of a Mr Hsu. He was arrested at his home when he tried to stop the police entering as they did not have a warrant. He was assaulted during the arrest and detained for 75 minutes at the police station. He was racially abused. The police fabricated a version of events whereby the arrest was justified as Mr Hsu had assaulted an officer. His premises were left unsecured and items went missing, and Mr Hsu suffered post-traumatic stress symptoms for some years. He was awarded £220,000 by a jury of which £200,000 was exemplary damages.

2 *Abassy v Commissioner of Police of the Metropolis* [1990] 1 All ER 193, 204.
3 Courts and Legal Services Act 1990 s8.
4 *John v MGN Ltd* [1997] QB 586 and *Rantzen v Mirror Group Newspapers (1986) Ltd* [1994] QB 670.

14.7    The police appealed these awards. Lord Woolf MR, in opening his judgment, said:

> In a number of recent cases members of the public have been awarded very large sums of exemplary damages by juries against the Commissioner of Police for the Metropolis for unlawful conduct towards them by the police. As a result these two appeals have been brought by the Commissioner. The intention is to clarify the directions which a judge should include in a summing up to assist the jury as to the amount of damages, particularly exemplary damages, which it is appropriate for them to award a plaintiff who is successful in this type of action. As similar appeals are pending any guidance given by us on this subject should influence the outcome of those appeals, in addition to providing guidance for the future.

14.8    The guidance given in 14 numbered paragraphs is reproduced in full in appendix 1. It is referred to at some length in the text below when the various types of damages are considered. The guidance relating specifically to false imprisonment and malicious prosecution is referred to in separate sections on damages for those torts (see paras 14.51 and 14.59). Although the Court of Appeal made it clear that the guidelines set no binding precedent, in practice they have been used in almost all civil actions since the judgment and so provide the 'reasonable degree of predictability' sought by the Court of Appeal. Although the guidelines were designed to assist juries, it is notable that they have also been used by judges hearing cases alone.[5] Practitioners should, of course, remember to make adjustments for inflation.

14.9    Lastly, it should be noted that the Court of Appeal in *Thompson* also indicated that while it was 'highly desirable' that complainants co-operated with complaints investigations, they were not legally obliged to do so. The fact that they did not do so could not be held against them in law so as to reduce the amount payable when assessing the compensation to which they are entitled.

## Basic damages

14.10   Damages to compensate a claimant are usually split into the categories of general and special damages. However, because 'aggravated damages' (see para 14.15) are part of general damages, the

---

5   See, eg, *Russell v Home Office* (2001) *Daily Telegraph* 13 March.

*Thompson* guidance introduced a further categorisation of compensatory damages so as to separate 'basic' damages from 'aggravated' damages.[6]

14.11    Thus, in the terms used by the Court of Appeal, 'basic' damages constitute all those general damages (other than aggravated damages) awarded to compensate for damage suffered by a claimant such as the pain, suffering and loss of amenity following an assault and any injuries caused by it; the harm done to the claimant's reputation by, for example, a malicious prosecution; the loss of liberty because of an unlawful detention; and other consequential damage. Damages for post-traumatic stress disorder and other psychiatric injuries caused by the tortious action of the police can be claimed under this heading. Future loss of earnings (often, for example, caused by physical or psychiatric injuries) can also be claimed.[7]

14.12    The Court of Appeal in *Thompson* stated that the jury should be given assistance in calculating basic damages:

> The jury should be told that the basic damages will depend on the circumstances and the degree of harm suffered by the plaintiff. But they should be provided with an appropriate bracket to use as a starting point.

The 'brackets' mentioned will be based on the levels of damages described in the *Thompson* case (see paras 14.51 and 14.59) in false imprisonment and malicious prosecution cases, and on recognised levels of damages for personal injuries (including physical and psychiatric injuries)[8] The process of deciding on the amounts to be included in the 'brackets' is described further in chapter 13.

14.13    Special damages should be explained to a jury separately. Special damages are designed to make good the past financial loss which can be calculated at the date of trial, such as medical bills, repair bills and

---

6  See guidance (2) in *Thompson v Commissioner of Police of the Metropolis* [1998] QB 498: '(2) As the law stands at present compensatory damages are of two types (a) ordinary damages which we would suggest should be described as basic, and (b) aggravated damages'.

7  For someone who was in work at the time of the torts committed by the police and is consequentially now unable to work, this part of the claim may constitute the largest part of the claim. Practitioners should consult a work such as *Kemp & Kemp: Quantum of Damages* (Sweet & Maxwell, Looseleaf) for the approach to be taken to calculating such loss, which is beyond the scope of this book. Deductions in the calculation may be made through the DSS Compensation Recovery Unit where the claimant has received social security payments as a result of his or her inability to work following an injury caused by the police.

8  See as a starting point 'Judicial Studies Board Guidelines for the Assessment of Damages' (7th ed).

past loss of earnings. In a malicious prosecution case, they can also include travel expenses if, for example, a person has had to attend court on a number of occasions before being acquitted.

14.14   Where a claimant is being compensated for loss of reputation, for instance after malicious prosecution or false imprisonment, damages under this head can be lowered if the plaintiff had little reputation to lose, for example because he or she had previous convictions. However, basic damages should not be reduced even if the claimant's behaviour caused or contributed to the tortious behaviour of the police (for example, by violent behaviour which led to the involvement of the police in an incident), although this might be a factor to take into account when considering aggravated or exemplary damages (see para 14.15).

## Aggravated damages

14.15   Aggravated damages may be payable in addition to general or special damages. They are conventionally seen as an extra element of compensation in recognition that the exceptional motives, conduct or manner of the defendant have aggravated the plaintiff's damage by intangible injury to personality (insult, humiliation, degradation, indignation, outrage, distress, hurt feelings, etc). The Court of Appeal in *Thompson* described their application as follows:

> Such damages can be awarded where there are aggravating features about the case which would result in the plaintiff not receiving sufficient compensation for the injury suffered if the award were restricted to a basic award. Aggravating features can include humiliating circumstances at the time of arrest or any conduct of those responsible for the arrest or the prosecution which shows that they had behaved in a high handed, insulting, malicious or oppressive manner either in relation to the arrest or imprisonment or in conducting the prosecution. Aggravating features can also include the way the litigation and trial are conducted.

14.16   The Law Commission reports that:

> The conduct of the defendant at trial has ... been considered relevant to aggravated damages in cases of malicious prosecution [and] false imprisonment where the persistence by the defendant in damaging allegations about the plaintiff or in attempts to tarnish character can be viewed as analogous to attempts to sully reputation, that is, as a form of defamation.

14.17   The Court of Appeal has held that a persistent denial of liability in the civil action in the face of a judge's indications could justify an aggravated damages award.[9] Other examples of behaviour of the defendant after the incident giving rise to the litigation which might lead to an award of aggravated damages include the clear lack of an apology for the behaviour of the police and the failure to record a complaint or to investigate it properly.

14.18    The fact that the defendant's exceptional behaviour is a precondition to the award of aggravated damages casts doubt on the purely compensatory nature of aggravated damages and suggests that they also contain a punitive element as well. Indeed the Court of Appeal in *Thompson* recognised that 'if aggravated damages are awarded such damages, though compensatory are not intended as a punishment, will in fact contain a penal element as far as the defendant is concerned'. As the Court of Appeal noted, this may have an impact on the availability of exemplary damages.

14.19    The Court of Appeal stated that if aggravated damages are thought appropriate then a separate award should be considered for each tort. If the circumstances were to be serious enough to merit an award of aggravated damages, the Court of Appeal felt that an award should not be less than £1,000 (which now needs to be updated for inflation from the 1997 figure). In a subsequent case, the Court of Appeal confirmed that fear and anxiety falling short of injury, resulting from a police officer's conduct, should be included under the aggravated damages section of the award.[10]

14.20    In *Thompson* the court felt it would be difficult to indicate a precise arithmetical relationship between basic damages and aggravated damages, but 'we would not expect the aggravated damages to be as much as twice the basic damages except perhaps where, on the particular facts, the basic damages are modest'. Thus, for example, a minor assault accompanied by racial abuse might only lead to a small award of basic damages but might justify a proportionately larger award of aggravated damages. The jury should be reminded that the combination of basic damages and aggravated damages should not exceed fair compensation for the injury suffered by the claimant.

14.21    Despite the guidance from the Court of Appeal, given the non-pecuniary and intangible losses that aggravated damages are designed to compensate, coupled with the relevance of the defendant's conduct and the possible inclusion of a punitive element, it is difficult to predict the level of an award. In serious cases, aggravated damages (often together with exemplary damages) can be substantial and sometimes outstrip the purely compensatory element in an award.

9    *Marks v Chief Constable of Greater Manchester* (1992) *Times* 28 January.
10    *Gerald v Commissioner of Police of the Metropolis* (1998) *Times* 26 June.

14.22   Lastly, it should be noted that a claimant's own conduct, behaviour and provocation can be taken into account in calculating aggravated damages. As the Court of Appeal in *Thompson* put it:

> In an appropriate case the jury should also be told that even though the plaintiff succeeds on liability any improper conduct of which they find him guilty can reduce or even eliminate any award of aggravated or exemplary damages if the jury consider that this conduct caused or contributed to the behaviour complained of.[11]

14.23   One example of this might be a claimant who racially abused an officer who later assaulted him during an arrest: the assault would still give rise to an award of basic damages but a court or jury may feel that the claimant's initial conduct meant that aggravated damages should be reduced or eliminated. Of course, there should be some causal connection between the claimant's behaviour and the tortious actions of the police for this to apply.

14.24   Aggravated damages can be awarded for all the torts referred to in this book, although the need for exceptional conduct by the defendant means that it is difficult to envisage circumstances in which they would be appropriately awarded in negligence actions, other than in relation to the manner in which the police have conducted the litigation in defending the claim.

## Exemplary damages

14.25   The availability of exemplary damages is narrower than that of aggravated damages in that they are only generally available where the actions of the police fall into certain categories. However, unlike aggravated damages, they can, in theory, be awarded even where there are no aggravating circumstances[12] and at least in principle can be awarded even where no intangible loss has been suffered.

14.26   Since the landmark case of *Rookes v Barnard*,[13] exemplary damages have only been available in three categories of case, all of which relate to the defendant's conduct. Only one of these categories is usually relevant in police actions and this is described in that case by Lord Reid as 'oppressive, arbitrary or unconstitutional action by servants

---

11   [1998] QB 498, 517.
12   *Isaac v Chief Constable of West Midlands* [2001] EWCA Civ 1405.
13   [1964] AC 1129.

of the government'.[14] The terms 'oppressive, arbitrary or unconstitutional action' should be read disjunctively. Thus, where it was held that in itself a wrongful arrest could be an unconstitutional act by the police, it was not necessary also to show that the arrest was oppressive or arbitrary before exemplary damages were available.

14.27   However, although society might expect police officers to conduct themselves with higher standards than the rest of the public, generally there is no obligation on the court to award exemplary (or aggravated) damages in all cases of tortious acts by the police just because they were committed by a police officer. The court (the judge or the jury if there is one) retains a discretion whether or not to award exemplary damages.

14.28   The 'privatisation' of some police functions raises questions as to whether exemplary damages will be available against the individuals or bodies that exercise these functions given the 'servants of the government' requirement referred to by Lord Reid above. In *AB v South West Water Services Ltd*[15] it was held that employees of a privatised water company could not be described as government servants when the conduct they were engaged in was 'not an exercise of executive power derived from government, central or local'.

14.29   It is submitted that it is wrong in principle for the award of exemplary damages to depend on whether the abuse of power in question has been committed by an individual who happens to be a government servant rather than by an employee of a privatised company, and that functions, such as the care and transportation of prisoners, the handling of 999 calls and forensic examinations by scene of crime officers all involve the exercise of executive power. Indeed, in *Kuddus v Chief Constable of Leicestershire*,[16] Lord Nicholls doubted whether Lord Reid's distinction between abuse of power by government servants and others could be sustained:

> Whatever may have been the position 40 years ago, I am respectfully inclined to doubt the soundness of this distinction today. National and international companies can exercise enormous power. So do some individuals. I am not sure it would be right to draw a hard-and-fast line which would always exclude such companies and persons from the reach of exemplary damages.[17]

14   The other two categories encompass situations where the award of exemplary damages is authorised by statute, and where the wrongful conduct has been calculated to make a profit which may well exceed the compensation payable to the claimant.

15   [1993] QB 507.

16   [2002] 2 AC 122.

17   [2002] 2 AC 122 at [66].

14.30    *Kuddus* considered directly the question as to whether exemplary damages could be awarded in a claim for misfeasance in public office. Until this case, it had been the accepted position that exemplary damages were only available in causes of action where there had been an award of such damages prior to 1964 (the date of the *Rookes v Barnard* case). In *Kuddus* it was accepted that this was an arbitrary approach which should no longer be followed, and that exemplary damages could be available in other common law torts. The House of Lords noted that there remained a question as to whether exemplary damages could be awarded in claims under the Human Rights Act 1998 or discrimination legislation but left the question open for argument in an appropriate case on the point.[18] But Lord Nicholls noted that 'the essence of the conduct constituting the court's discretionary jurisdiction to award exemplary damages is conduct which was an outrageous disregard of the plaintiff's rights'.[19]

14.31    It is noteworthy that in the *Kuddus* case the House of Lords made it clear that if a party had sought to argue that exemplary damages should no longer be available in English law, this was an issue the court would have been prepared to consider.[20] However, the majority of the court seemed inclined to agree with the Law Commission[21] that there remained a place for exemplary damages in English law. Lord Nicholls supported this view in *Kuddus*, commenting that:

> The availability of exemplary damages has played a significant role in buttressing civil liberties, in claims for false imprisonment and wrongful arrest. From time to time cases do arise where awards of compensatory damages are perceived as adequate to achieve a just result between the parties. The nature of the defendant's conduct calls for a further response from the courts. On occasion conscious wrongdoing by a defendant is so outrageous, his disregard of the plaintiff's rights so contumelious, that something more is needed to show that the law will not tolerate such behaviour. Without an award of exemplary damages, justice will not have been done. Exemplary damages, as a remedy of last resort, fill what otherwise would be a regrettable lacuna.

14.32    The present situation, then, is that a trial judge in a civil action against the police is bound by the guidance in the *Thompson* case and also by the Court of Appeal judgment in *Holden v Chief Constable of Lancashire*[22]

18   See Lord Hutton, [2002] 2 AC 122 at [94].
19   [2002] 2 AC 122 at [68] per Lord Nichols.
20   See, eg, Lord Hutton, [2002] 2 AC 122 at [74].
21   *Aggravated, Exemplary and Restitutionary Damages* (Law Com No 247) December 1997.
22   [1987] QB 380.

which held that 'unconstitutional' actions by the police, such as false imprisonment, could in principle and without aggravating features attract exemplary damages, and the question as to their award should be left the jury.

14.33    As is suggested by the above passages, exemplary damages (unlike aggravated damages) are not designed to compensate the claimant for his or her loss. Rather, in the limited circumstances in which they are available, the purpose is to punish the defendant in the action over and above the requirement to compensate and to mark the disapproval of the court of the defendant's acts. However, as reflected in *Gerald v Commissioner of Police of the Metropolis*, the relationship between exemplary and compensatory damages is not an easy one:

> Aggravated damages ... carry with them, as do basic damages, an element of punishment for the defendant. Exemplary damages, on the other hand, are solely intended to punish, or to mark the court's disapproval of, the defendant's exceptionally bad behaviour, and, even then, only to the extent that basic and aggravated damages are inadequate for that purpose. This muddled jurisprudential amalgam of categories of damage, two of which are compensatory, all three of which are capable of punishing and one of which is only punitive or a mark of disapproval, are confusing enough to the lawyer. What juries make of it all, particularly the overlap between aggravated and exemplary damages, must be questionable, even with the best assistance that judges can give them.[23]

14.34    Despite this, the Court of Appeal in *Thompson* has given guidance as to the exceptional nature of exemplary damages and the circumstances in which they could be awarded, which appears to have been sensibly applied by juries in practice. The Court of Appeal held that the jury should be told that:

> ... though it is not normally possible to award damages with the object of punishing the defendant, exceptionally this is possible where there has been conduct, including oppressive or arbitrary behaviour, by police officers which deserves the exceptional remedy of exemplary damages.

14.35    The court went on to list four further factors that should be explained to the jury when consideration is being given to whether to award exemplary damages, all designed to emphasise their exceptional nature.

- First, the jury should bear in mind that if they have awarded aggravated damages these will already have compensated the claimant for the effects of any 'oppressive and insulting

---

23    *Gerald v Commissioner of Police of the Metropolis* (1998) *Times* 26 June.

behaviour' of the police and that these damages will provide 'inevitably, a measure of punishment from the defendant's point of view'.

- Second, a jury must be careful to award exemplary damages only in circumstances where basic and aggravated damages provide an 'inadequate punishment' for the police.
- Third, the jury should be aware that the award of exemplary damages is 'in effect a windfall' for the claimant and that any award will come out of funds used for general policing on behalf of the public (although the court pointed out that this last point would not be relevant if the damages would be payable by insurers for the police).
- Last, the court was anxious to emphasise that the sum awarded by way of exemplary damages 'should be sufficient to mark the jury's disapproval of the oppressive or arbitrary behaviour but should be no more than is required for this purpose'.

14.36    In a subsequent case, *Goswell v Commissioner of Police of the Metropolis*,[24] Simon Brown LJ summed up the guidance thus:

> ... it seems to me that really what the court (generally the jury but now us) is required to do in these cases is to mark its disapproval of the oppressive or arbitrary conduct in question, tempering its outrage, of course, with the thought that the exemplary damage award will constitute a windfall for the plaintiff and a depletion of police funds to the possible disadvantage of the general public.

14.37    As in the case for aggravated damages, the court in *Thompson* noted that any improper conduct by the claimant which caused or contributed to the wrongdoing of the police could reduce or eliminate an award of exemplary damages. The court also gave some very broad guidance on the amounts that should be awarded:

> Where exemplary damages are appropriate they are unlikely to be less than £5,000. Otherwise the case is probably not one which justifies an award of exemplary damages at all. In this class of action the conduct must be particularly deserving of condemnation for an award of as much as £25,000 to be justified and the figure of £50,000 should be regarded as the absolute maximum, involving directly officers of at least the rank of superintendent.

## Vicarious liability in exemplary damages

14.38 A chief officer of police will usually be vicariously liable for the misconduct of his or her officers (see para 11.107), and it is usual, in practice, for the chief constable to pay any exemplary damages awarded. However, when calculating the appropriate exemplary sum, it has been held that the court or jury should take into account the defendant's capacity to pay. If a case was brought against individual officers, it would be their means that were at issue. How should this rule be applied in vicarious liability cases? As the Law Commission said:[25]

> One possibility was that any sum which an employer is liable to pay as exemplary damages could be subject to deduction on account of the employee's lack of means. Another, contrasting, possibility was that the means of the wrongdoing employee are irrelevant to the size of the sum which the employer is vicariously liable to pay.

14.39 In *Thompson* the Court of Appeal resolved the issue as follows:[26]

> In the case of exemplary damages we have taken into account the fact that the action is normally brought against the chief officer of police and the damages are paid out of police funds for what is usually a vicarious liability for the acts of his officers in relation to which he is a joint tortfeasor: see now section 88 of the Police Act 1996. In these circumstances it appears to us wholly inappropriate to take into account the means of the individual officers ...

14.40 This approach, fortified by the previous case of *Holden*,[27] remains binding law on any county court hearing a civil action against the police. In *Kuddus*, the majority of the House did not consider the issue of exemplary damages and vicarious liability, but Lord Scott trenchantly stated that 'vicarious punishment, via an award of exemplary damages, is contrary to principle and should be rejected', thus leaving the point open to be argued in the House of Lords at some point in the future.

14.41 In any event, it appears that credit should be given to a chief officer who has punished a junior officer for wrongdoing when the question of exemplary damages comes to be considered.[28] Where the prospect of disciplinary proceedings is raised at the stage when exemplary

---

25 *Aggravated, Exemplary and Restitutionary Damages* (Law Com No 247) December 1997 para 4.70.
26 [1998] QB 498, 517.
27 [1987] QB 380; and see para 14.32.
28 *Goswell v Commissioner of Police of the Metropolis* (1998) 7 April, CA, unreported.

damages are being considered, the Court of Appeal in *Thompson* said this should only be taken into account where:

> ... there is clear evidence that such proceedings are intended to be taken in the event of liability being established and that there is at least a strong possibility of the proceedings succeeding.

14.42    It is submitted that where an officer has already been convicted of a criminal offence relating to the same subject matter as the civil action, exemplary damages could still, presumably, be recovered from the chief officer of police unless of course it is held that the chief officer is not vicariously liable because the subordinate officer was engaged on a venture of his or her own. (see para 11.111)

# Nominal damages

14.43    Historically, certain legal rights have been considered so important that even a technical breach of them entitles claimants to bring proceedings, without having to prove that they have suffered any 'real' loss. Claims for false imprisonment, assault, trespass to land and to goods are actionable in this way.[29] Nominal damages (ie, damages awarded in the absence of any real loss) are not intended to compensate but rather to demonstrate that an individual's rights were infringed. It is important to note that although nominal damages may be small, exemplary damages, exceptionally, may also be awarded and, if so, may significantly increase the overall award of damages to a claimant.[30]

## Damages for particular causes of action

14.44    This section deals with the heads under which damages can be awarded for the following torts.

- assault and battery
- false imprisonment
- malicious prosecution
- misfeasance in public office
- seizure of goods
- damage to goods
- trespass to land

29    *Williams v Peel River Land Co* [1878] 55 LT 689.
30    But note in *Cumber v Chief Constable of Hampshire* (1995) *Times* 28 January it was held that it had to be rare if not unique for an award of exemplary damages not to be coupled with one of compensatory damages.

14.45 The particular principles applicable to the recovery of damages for negligence, discrimination, breach of statutory duty, breach of the Protection from Harassment Act 1997, breach of confidence and under the Human Rights Act 1998 are dealt with in the chapters that deal with liability for that conduct.[31]

## Damages for assault and battery

14.46 Assault and battery are torts actionable in their own right. It is not necessary to prove that there has been damage before a claim can be brought and the successful claimant will always be entitled to at least nominal damages, even if he or she cannot point to any real loss. All consequences flowing from the unlawful act can lead to compensation including for distress, anxiety, humiliation or other injury to feelings suffered by the claimant. Furthermore, the claimant can recover for the consequences flowing from the assault or battery, whether or not they were the reasonably foreseeable result of the wrongdoer's actions.[32] Accordingly, a significant claim for damages can arise even if the assault has not occasioned serious injury, particularly if it occurred in circumstances that caused substantial fear or humiliation to the victim. On the current state of the case law it is unclear whether these factors should be reflected in the award for basic or the award for aggravated damages, although it is submitted that they are more appropriately considered in an award of aggravated damages.[33]

14.47 Where the assault has resulted in physical or psychiatric injury, the claimant may recover damages for those injuries. The general principles that apply to any case of personal injury apply to cases of assault and battery. Thus, a claim can be made for:

- pain and suffering, both in the past and in the future;
- 'loss of amenity', eg, full or partial loss of a limb or organ;
- loss of enjoyment of life, eg, an amateur footballer who has to give up the game because of the injuries;
- financial loss due to medical expenses, loss of earnings and loss of earning capacity.

---

31  See chapters 8 and 10 respectively.
32  *Wilson v Pringle* [1987] QB 237.
33  Compare this approach in *Gerald v Commissioner of Police of the Metropolis* (1998) *Times* 26 June, CA with the recent case of *Richardson v Howie* [2004] EWCA Civ 1127. The latter did not cite *Gerald* or other police cases.

14.48    It is possible for damages to be assessed both at the conclusion of the case and again at some future date if the claimant's condition may seriously deteriorate or if he or she develops a serious medical condition (for example, epilepsy from head injuries). He or she can, accordingly, apply to receive provisional damages when the court first gives judgment and a further award at some later date.[34]

14.49    Basic damages (see para 14.10) for personal injury cannot be reduced by reason of the claimant's conduct. It was held in *Lane v Holloway*[35] that, on principle, when considering what damages a claimant is entitled to as compensation for physical injury, the fact that the claimant may have behaved badly is irrelevant.

14.50    However, the claimant's conduct may be used to reduce the aggravated damages (see para 14.22). By the same token, a claimant's good conduct or character can be presented to argue for a higher award of aggravated and exemplary damages.

## Damages for false imprisonment

14.51    Damages for false imprisonment are intended to compensate for loss of liberty, discomfort and inconvenience (provided it is substantial),[36] injury to dignity and loss of reputation. This section deals with damages for the usually relatively short periods of time that a person is kept in police custody before release on bail or production before a magistrates' court. For awards made in relation to longer periods of detention (usually in prison) following remand in custody or conviction, see the discussion in chapter 17 on compensation for wrongful convictions.

14.52    In *Murray v Minister of Defence* Lord Griffiths said:

> The law attaches supreme importance to the liberty of the individual and if he suffers a wrongful interference with that liberty it should remain actionable even without proof of special damage.[37]

14.53    Clearly, the crucial factors when assessing damages for false imprisonment will be the length of time for which the claimant was

---

34    See CPR Pt 41.
35    [1968] QB 379.
36    *Bailey v Bullock* [1950] 2 All ER 1167, 1170H – injury to dignity and loss of reputation.
37    [1988] 1 WLR 692, 704.

imprisoned and the damage to his or her reputation.[38] In *Thompson*[39] the Court of Appeal assessed the financial value as follows:

> In a straightforward case of wrongful arrest and false imprisonment, the starting point is likely to be about £500 for the first hour during which the plaintiff has been deprived of his or her liberties. After the first hour, an additional sum is to be awarded, but that sum should be on a reducing scale so as to keep the damages proportionate with those payable in personal injury cases and because the plaintiff is entitled to have higher rate of compensation for the initial shock of being arrested. As a guideline, we consider, for example, that a plaintiff that has been wrongfully kept in custody for 24 hours should for this alone normally be regarded as entitled to an award from about £3,000. Subsequent days, the daily rate will be on a progressively reducing scale.

14.54　The figures need to be increased to take account of inflation. The Court of Appeal emphasised that these were guideline figures only for the jury. Thus they can be increased or reduced to take into account any particular features of the claimant, the nature of the detention or the effect it has on the claimant. Thus, for example, a wrongful detention which begins with an arrest at gun-point in public, might lead to a higher basis for an award than for a person politely but wrongly arrested while voluntarily attending a police station. A person who is no stranger to police cells might be entitled to a lower award than a person detained in a police station for the first time. The shock of detention might, likewise, be greater for a child or a vulnerable adult than for other people. These are factors which may also be taken into account when considering an award of aggravated damages (see para 14.15).

14.55　Other factors might increase the level of damages. Any claim for damage to reputation continues until the police admit the imprisonment was false.[40] It may be possible to claim personal injury damages for substantial emotional shock or post-traumatic stress disorder as a result of the arrest and detention if medical evidence of this can be produced. It will be possible to claim damages for any cash loss, such as loss of earnings as a result of the false imprisonment.[41]

14.56　If the initial arrest and detention was lawful but subsequently becomes unlawful while a person is detained at the police station (see

---

38　*Walter v Alltools* (1944) 61 TLR 39.
39　[1998] QB 498, 515.
40　*Walter v Alltools Ltd* (1944) 171 LT 371, 372 per Lawrence LJ, followed in *Hook v Cunard Steamship Co Ltd* [1953] 1 All ER 1021, 1042H.
41　*Childs v Lewis* (1924) 40 TLR 870; *Hamett v Bond* [1925] AC 689, HL.

chapter 6), then the 'initial shock' of arrest described by the Court of Appeal will not be relevant. If the false imprisonment is 'technical' in nature (for example, there were grounds to detain a person but the PACE rules have not been complied with), then, again, a claimant might expect only to recover limited damages. In *Goswell v Commissioner of Police of the Metropolis*,[42] where the initial arrest and detention were unlawful because the claimant was not provided with the grounds for arrest (contrary to Police and Criminal Evidence Act 1984 s28(3)) but these were provided 20 minutes later at the police station by the custody officer, an award of £100 was made. In this case, the arrest would otherwise have been lawful and the claimant 'cannot realistically have been in doubt as to why he was being arrested'.

14.57      In *Roberts v Chief Constable of Cheshire*[43] the Court of Appeal considered the situation of a claimant who had been lawfully arrested and detained in a police station, but where there had been a delay in carrying out a statutory review of the detention under Police and Criminal Evidence Act 1984 s40. The trial judge had found that 'there was no mala fides, the police were acting in good faith, their error was entirely technical'. The Court of Appeal rejected arguments both that the claimant would have to show that he would have been released as a result of the review before he was entitled to damages, and, in the alternative, that he should only be entitled to nominal damages. While accepting that 'all depends on the circumstance' and that damages might be diminished if the claimant was not conscious of the fact that he was falsely imprisoned, Clarke LJ said:

> A person who was falsely imprisoned but who was unaware of his imprisonment and who suffered no harm would be entitled to only nominal damages. The respondent was not, however in that position here. He was no doubt aware of his imprisonment and, as I see it, he was entitled to be compensated for being unlawfully detained in a police cell for 2 hours 20 minutes when, in the absence of a review, he should have been released.

The court did not disturb the trial judge's award of £500 damages for the false imprisonment but Clarke LJ noted that the sum was 'substantially more than I would have awarded to compensate the respondent for false imprisonment for a period of 2 hours 20 minutes during which he was asleep, especially in circumstances in which if a review had been carried out ... his detention would have been lawful'.

---

42   (1998) 7 April, unreported.
43   [1999] 4 All ER 326.

14.58    In addition to basic damages and special damages, where appropriate aggravated damages and exemplary damages in cases of false imprisonment by the police can be claimed. In practice, these might not be awarded if it appears that the false imprisonment was the result of a 'technical' error or breach in procedures.

## Damages for malicious prosecution

14.59    As discussed in chapter 7, to bring an action for malicious prosecution it must be shown that at least one of three types of loss has been suffered:

- loss of reputation;
- the risk of loss of 'life, limb or liberty';
- financial loss.

14.60    It is not clear whether, having met one of these conditions, *damages* are then limited to these types of loss. The modern approach seems to be that they constitute a hurdle but, once over it, damages are not limited to the three heads and may include such things as the humiliation and indignity of having to face a charge and the distress or anxiety felt while awaiting trial.

14.61    In *Thompson v Commissioner of Police of the Metropolis*,⁴⁴ Lord Woolf MR said:

> In the case of malicious prosecution ... the starting point should be about £2,000 and for prosecution continuing for as long as 2 years, the case being taken to the Crown Court, an award of about £10,000 could be appropriate. If a malicious prosecution results in a conviction which is only set aside on appeal this will justify a larger award to reflect the longer period during which the plaintiff has been in peril and has been caused distressed.

14.62    The 'starting point of £2,000' (set in 1997) now needs to be increased to take into account inflation. The 'starting point' also needs to be increased or reduced to take into account the personal features of the claimant. For example, the figure for a claimant with a long criminal record being prosecuted for an offence may not be the same as a claimant with no previous convictions prosecuted for the same offence. The amount of the basic award will also be affected by factors such as the length of the proceedings; whether the prosecution involved a

44   [1998] QB 498.

trial or was discontinued at an earlier stage; whether the claimant gave evidence at a trial; the number of court hearings he or she had to attend; and the seriousness of the offence charged.

14.63　However, it seems that the claimant's behaviour prior to arrest should not be taken into account when considering the level of basic damages (as opposed to aggravated or exemplary damages – see paras 14.22 and 14.37) for malicious prosecution. This approach is illustrated by *Clark v Chief Constable of Cleveland*[45] where the Court of Appeal increased an award of basic damages from £500 to £2,000 on the ground that the figure should not be reduced to take into account the claimant's aggressive behaviour towards officers immediately prior to the events that they falsified for the prosecution, since the former could not begin to justify the officers' subsequent reprehensible conduct.

14.64　*Clark* also provides an insight into the quantum that the Court of Appeal determined as appropriate for the basic award for a fairly standard malicious prosecution. The court held that if the claimant had been a man of good character a figure of £4,000 – £5,000 would have been appropriate for criminal proceedings in the magistrates' court involving a public order charge,[46] where the claimant was required to attend court on six occasions including trial and the whole proceedings had lasted for just under a year. This figure was then reduced to £2,000 to reflect the claimant's previous convictions.

## Damages for misfeasance in a public office

14.65　As discussed in chapter 7, a successful claim for misfeasance in a public office involves showing that a claimant has suffered 'damage' in the sense of financial loss, detention, physical or psychiatric injury or, possibly, loss of reputation, unless the misfeasance involves an interference with the claimant's constitutional rights.[47] If the claimant establishes that the misconduct led to one or more of those forms of harm he or she can also recover for injury to feelings arising out of the humiliating and/or oppressive manner of the treatment. The latter would be reflected in an award of aggravated damages. As is also considered in chapter 7, the level of damages has yet to be resolved by

---

45　(1999) *Times* 13 May.

46　Public Order Act 1986 s4.

47　*Watkins v Secretary of State for the Home Department* [2004] 4 All ER 1158, where the constitutional right interfered with was unimpeded access to a court for a prisoner. There was no loss to the claimant but the Court of Appeal referred the question of exemplary damages back to the trial judge.

authority in circumstances where the misfeasance relates to the fabrication or other dishonest manipulation of evidence in support of a prosecution. If a claim in malicious prosecution cannot succeed because there is other evidence to support the criminal proceedings so that a lack of reasonable and probable cause cannot be proven, it is doubtful that the claimant would recover basic damages analogous to those awarded for malicious prosecution. However, any conduct involving misfeasance in a public office is likely to lead to a substantial award of aggravated and exemplary damages, because of the degree of wrongdoing necessarily involved in establishing liability.

## Damages for seizure of goods

14.66   If only damages are sought (and not the return of the property), at least the value of the goods at the time they were seized can be expected. However, it can sometimes be difficult to prove the value of items, unless they have an easily ascertainable worth, such as a motor car. If the claimant has not kept receipts relating to the items, efforts should be made to find out their likely purchase price; failing that the claimant will have to provide realistic estimates of value. Whether or not the return of the item seized is sought, damages can be awarded for loss of use during the time it was retained. Depending on the nature of the item, this may have occasioned the claimant financial loss and/or inconvenience. Provided the claimant has acted reasonably, costs of hiring a replacement can be recovered.

14.67   If the action is in trespass to goods, the claimant may be entitled to at least nominal damages,[48] even if he or she cannot show any real loss[49] and, in appropriate cases, there may also be an award of aggravated and exemplary damages.[50] If the action is in conversion, the claim will fail if actual loss cannot be shown.

## Compensation for damage to goods

14.68   If the police damage or destroy belongings, for example while searching a home, there may be a claim for damages. Technically, the claim might be for 'trespass to goods' or 'negligence' (see the discussion in chapter 9).

---

48   See full discussion in chapter 9.
49   *William Leitch & Co v Leydon* [1931] AC 90, 106.
50   *Sears v Lyons* (1818) 2 Stark 317; *Rookes v Barnard* [1964] AC 1129.

14.69    If the police damage goods, their owner is entitled to the cost of repair.[51] If the goods are destroyed or damaged beyond repair, or if it would be uneconomic to repair them, their owner is entitled to the value of their replacement. In addition to damages for repair or replacement, a claim can also be made for the loss of the use of an article; for example, if a television is damaged, compensation for the loss of enjoyment while it was repaired or replaced can be claimed.

14.70    If the claim is for trespass to goods, liability may be established even if no loss or damage in the traditional sense is shown; this is discussed in chapter 9. In such circumstances a claimant may still be able to recover for distress and/or obtain an award of aggravated and/or exemplary damages. However, if the claim was brought as a negligence action the claim would fail if no damage was shown, as explained in chapter 8.

## Damages for trespass to land

14.71   If a claimant's land is damaged by the police he or she is usually entitled to recover only the reduction in the value of the land as a result of the damage and it will be rare that he or she will be able successfully to claim the cost of restoration or rebuilding.[52]

14.72    As with false imprisonment and assault, a person can sue for trespass to land without having to show any damage in the sense of financial or physical loss. The claimant can recover for distress, anxiety and inconvenience caused by the intrusion upon his or her home or other property. The manner and violence the police use to enter the property is relevant to the level of damages,[53] and may justify awards of aggravated or exemplary damages. In *R v Reading JJ ex p South West Meats Ltd*[54] exemplary damages of £22,000 were awarded in addition to compensatory damages of £3,000 for a trespass to land and goods following the unlawful exercise of a search warrant. This was a relatively unusual and serious case of misconduct, and should not be treated as a 'standard'. Special damages are payable to compensate for anything broken or damaged.

14.73    A case which provides a good example of the damages that may be expected for trespass where there have been procedural errors in

---

51   *The Bernina* (1886) 55 LT 781.
52   *Ward v Cannock Chase DC* [1985] 3 All ER 537.
53   *Huxley v Berg* (1815) 1 Stark 98.
54   [1992] Crim LR 672.

executing a warrant is *Fisher v Chief Constable of Cumbria*[55] which involved the search of uninhabited commercial premises. Roch LJ explained the background as follows:

> The act of trespass arose because the police did not leave a copy of the search warrant on the premises. That omission was due to mere forgetfulness. But for that inadvertent omission there would have been no trespass.

14.74    The judge summarised the principles involved thus:

> If a [claimant] proves a trespass to his land, he is entitled to recover nominal damages, even if he has not suffered any actual loss. If the trespass has caused the [claimant] actual damage, he is entitled to receive such an amount as will compensate him for his loss. Where the defendant has made use of the [claimant's] land the [claimant] is entitled to receive by way of damages such a sum as should reasonably be paid for that use.

14.75    Applying these principles Roch LJ said:

> Here the trespass occurred because of mere forgetfulness by [an officer]. That was a mitigating feature ... [T]he search was conducted with reasonable care so as to reveal drugs but not to cause unnecessary damage. That was another mitigating feature. The defendant had offered to pay for the cost of repairing the door into the premises. That was a further mitigating feature. The trespass lasted approximately two hours and had been concluded by the time the plaintiffs arrived at their shop that morning.

> The plaintiffs had to be compensated for this intrusion into their property, carrying with it, as it did the suggestion that they or one of them was somehow linked with illegal dealing in controlled drugs. There was in addition the physical disturbance of their property and the disruption and inconvenience of having to restore the contents of their property to their former order and the need to see that the use of dogs in the search had not compromised the hygiene of their premises.

14.76    Taking the guidelines in *Thompson* into account in relation to other torts, the Court of Appeal found that the proper bracket for general damages for the trespass to the claimants' premises in this case was one starting at £500 with a ceiling of £1,500. This is a useful starting point for claimants in trespass to land cases. Clearly, if a case is more than a wrongful entry case and there is a prolonged and intrusive search of the claimant's home when the claimant is present then the bracket would need to be much higher than this.

---

55    (1997) 29 July, CA, unreported.

# CHAPTER 15

# Taking a case to the European Court of Human Rights

15.1    This chapter describes in outline the procedure to be followed in bringing a case before the European Court of Human Rights (ECtHR) in Strasbourg for alleged breaches of the European Convention on Human Rights ('the Convention'). Of course, since 2 October 2000 it has been possible to bring a case in domestic law under the Human Rights Act (HRA) 1998 for action by public authorities incompatible with rights set out in the Convention. How to bring such a case is described in chapter 10 and there are numerous examples given of potential grounds for bringing such a case in the chapters in this book concerning civil liability. In the vast majority of situations, for alleged breaches of Convention rights after 2 October 2000, it will be necessary to consider an action in domestic law under the HRA 1998 before making an application to the ECtHR.[1] Making an application to the ECtHR will usually only become an option for breaches of Convention rights after October 2000 where an action in the domestic court has come to an end or can no longer be pursued.

15.2    The Convention is an international treaty which provides basic guarantees of a number of fundamental human rights. It is now a part of ordinary English law to the extent that the rights are set out in HRA 1998 Sch 1. However, additionally, and most unusually for an international treaty, it allows individuals as well as states a mechanism to complain about violations.

15.3    The Convention requires the states which ratify it to guarantee the rights it contains to everyone within their jurisdiction, and everyone whose rights are violated 'shall have an effective remedy before a national authority, notwithstanding that the violation has been committed by persons acting in an official capacity'. The HRA 1998 is designed to provide that effective remedy.

15.4    The Convention does not cover the whole field of human rights and notably omits most economic and social rights that might prove politically contentious. The articles of the Convention most applicable to cases involving police conduct are set out at paras 10.117–10.218, together with a brief description of their scope and application in relation to claim under HRA 1998. In general terms, the same principles described there will apply when making an application to the ECtHR.

---

1   For more detailed analysis of the procedure in Strasbourg see Starmer, *European Human Rights Law* LAG, 1999.

## Institutions

15.5    The Convention and its institutions are creatures of the Council of Europe (not the European Union). Complaints about violations of the Convention are dealt with by the ECtHR. Before 1998 the European Commission on Human Rights acted as a filter by deciding whether applications met the admissibility criteria. Now the court deals with this function as well as hearing cases which have been admitted.

15.6    The judges who are members of the court are nominated by member states, must be of high moral character with the relevant legal expertise, and are appointed by the Parliamentary Assembly of the Council of Europe for periods of six years.[2]

15.7    Usually, three judges will decide whether an application is admissible. A chamber of seven judges will usually consider the substantive applications along with the question of remedies and costs. It is possible in exceptional cases to 'appeal' to a grand chamber of 17 judges, which may also hear substantive applications where, for example, there are important matters concerning interpretation of the Convention.[3]

## Making an application

### Who can bring a complaint?

15.8    A complaint can be brought by any 'person, non-governmental organisation or group of individuals'.[4] The nationality of the complainant is irrelevant; it is sufficient for him or her to be within the jurisdiction of a state that has ratified the Convention. There is no age limit: a complaint can be brought by a child. However, the person, organisation or group of individuals must themselves be the victims of a violation,[5] either directly or indirectly. The family of a person who died in the course of a violent arrest, for example, would be indirect victims of a violation. Companies, trade unions, friendly societies and unincorporated associations may all bring complaints provided they have themselves been victims.

2   ECHR articles 21–23.
3   ECHR articles 29–31 and Rules of Court r1, in force from November 2003.
4   ECHR article 34.
5   ECHR article 34.

## Anonymity and confidentiality

15.9    Anonymous complaints, ie, those that do not reveal the identity of the complainant to the Court, will not be accepted. However, if a complainant fears that his or her safety may be jeopardised by making a complaint, a request can be made to the Court for undertakings or other protective measures to be given by the state.

15.10    A complainant can request that his or her name be kept confidential,[6] although it will have to be disclosed to the state.[7] The request should be made in the initial letter of complaint (see para 15.20) and the complainant should thereafter be referred to by initial letters.

## Exhaustion of domestic remedies

15.11    Complaints can only be considered by the court after all effective domestic remedies have been exhausted.[8] This is especially relevant now that the HRA 1998 is in force and violations of the Convention can found an action in domestic law. It will be rare to be able to argue that there is no domestic remedy. Even where counsel has advised that a domestic claim will fail or public funding is not available, there is no guarantee that the court will allow a claim to proceed. In *Menson v UK*[9] the court ruled that claims under article 6 were inadmissible because the applicant had not attempted to bring a claim in negligence (albeit with counsel's advice that it would fail), or for race discrimination (despite unfavourable precedent). The court noted that 'mere doubts about the prospects of success of an action do not in themselves suffice to displace the exhaustion rule'.

15.12    The availability of a domestic remedy will not afford a state a defence unless it can fully rectify the violation. Thus, in prisoner cases, where the parole board, in the past, has only had powers to *recommend* release, this could not fully rectify the violation of article 5. However civil proceedings for damages for physical abuse, assault or mistreatment are generally an adequate remedy for instance for breach of article 3, unless the violation takes the form of an officially approved administrative practice.[10]

---

6   Rules of Court r47.
7   Rules of Court r33.
8   ECHR article 35.
9   (2003) 37 EHRR CD220.
10   DR 20/184.

15.13    Judicial review (see para 17.67) may constitute an effective remedy, but not if the relief is insufficient to meet the violation in all respects.[11] This may well depend on the nature of review adopted by the domestic court: in cases involving human rights the court now applies a higher degree of scrutiny to the decision-making process of public bodies (see para 17.70).

## Time limits

15.14    The complaint must be made within six months from the date on which the final domestic decision was taken.[12] If there is a deemed exhaustion of remedies and thus no 'final effective domestic decision', time runs from the date of the incident constituting the violation.[13] Cases should be brought promptly as the time limit is strictly enforced. However, the time limit is not applicable in the case of a continuing breach such as where domestic legislation constitutes a violation of the Convention.

## Legal aid

15.15    Legal help or public funding is not available in the domestic system for any part of the case (although, of course, it might well be for advice as to whether there has been a breach of the Convention for the purposes of a possible domestic cause of action under the HRA 1998).

15.16    The court can grant its own form of legal aid, but only after it has sent the complaint to the respondent government and that government has replied with written representations on the admissibility of a case (see para 15.24) or the deadline for such representations has passed.[14] At this point, declaration of means forms will be sent to the applicant. If legal aid is granted, it can retrospectively cover the cost of preparing the original application, as well as subsequent work in preparing the case and for representation at any hearing.

15.17    Legal aid is usually subject to a test of financial necessity,[15] but an applicant will qualify if he or she would qualify for English public funding, and may qualify even if he or she would not qualify under the

11 *Agosi v UK* (1986) 9 EHRR 1.
12 ECHR article 35.
13 See Reid, *A Practitioner's Guide to the European Convention on Human Rights* (2nd ed, Sweet and Maxwell, 2004) for more detailed consideration of the time limit.
14 Rules of Court r91.
15 Rules of Court r92(b).

English system. The applicant's means form must be certified by a relevant domestic authority, which is currently the Legal Services Commission.

15.18     The rates of payment, which are calculated on a unit-cost basis, not an hourly rate, are modest in the extreme, even for attending hearings before the court, amounting to little more than token contributions towards the real cost. However, actual out-of-pocket expenses such as travel and accommodation costs can, with prior approval, also be met.

## Contingency fees and costs

15.19  Conditional fee agreements between applicants and their lawyers are common. If a complaint is upheld by the court or if it is struck out as part of a friendly settlement or unilateral decision by the state,[17] it can order the whole or part of the applicant's costs to be met by the respondent government. These should be calculated on a conventional hourly rate basis and presented in the usual form. The court takes a broad brush approach to the level of costs rather than subjecting them to any formal taxation procedure. There is no procedure for costs being awarded against an applicant and the court does not make costs orders in favour of respondent governments.

## Applications

15.20  Complaints about violations of the Convention should be sent to the court in Strasbourg. There is a specific application form to be completed, which can be found on the court's website (www.echr.coe) together with notes for guidance for completing the form. However, if there are concerns about the six-month limitation period, the application can be introduced by letter or fax to stop time running. The complaint can initially be made in the form of a simple letter.[18] A brief description of the facts and complaints is sufficient so long as the substance of the complaint is conveyed.

15.21     On receipt of an initial letter the court will send out an application form (or the form on the website can be used). Although there is no rule to this effect, the practice is to request that the formal application then be submitted within six weeks. This asks for the following information:[19]

17  Rules of Court r43(4).
18  Rules of Court r47.
19  Rules of Court r47.

- the complainant's name, age, sex, address, nationality and occupation;
- the name, occupation and address of any person representing the complainant;
- the name of the government against whom the complaint is made (ie, the United Kingdom);
- the object of the application and the articles of the Convention which it is alleged have been violated;
- a statement of the facts of the case;
- the reasons why the facts of the case amount to a denial of rights under the Convention;
- details of the steps taken to exhaust domestic remedies demonstrating that the six-month time limit has been met;
- supporting documentation.

15.22　The application should contain an explanation of the legal reasoning that supports the applicant's case and should marshal all the arguments the applicant seeks to advance. In practice, the court is often prepared to grant extensions of time beyond the six weeks for good reason and provided the extension is sought in advance.

15.23　　It is not strictly necessary to have a lawyer in order to introduce a complaint, and an application to the court can be made in person. However, once the case has been communicated to the government, unless leave has been obtained from the court, it is necessary to be represented by a qualified lawyer. At oral hearings a person will only exceptionally be permitted to present his or her own case.[20]

## Initial procedure

15.24　On receipt of a complaint it is registered and a provisional file is opened. There will be a wait of at least several months until the case is considered (unless the Chamber or the President decide to give priority to an application – for example, if it involves children or an applicant in poor health).[21] A member of the court will be appointed to act as rapporteur, to report on its admissibility and the procedure to be adopted. An application can be inadmissible if, for example:

---

20  Rules of Court r36.
21  Ruless of Court r41.

- it is manifestly ill-founded[22] (for example, it is unsubstantiated by the material submitted, or no breach of a Convention right has been shown);
- the application is out of time;
- domestic remedies have not been exhausted.

15.25    Applications which are clearly inadmissible or an abuse of process will be referred by the rapporteur to a committee of three judges who, if unanimous, will reject the application with a brief explanation of the reasons. 16,364 applications out of 17,530 were disposed of in this way in 2003.[23]

15.26    If a case is not rejected by the initial committee, it will be examined by the Chamber. If there is an issue to be examined, the Chamber will invite the comments of the government challenged before reaching a decision on admissibility. The government's response is then copied to the complainant for his or her comments and response. The Chamber then gives a final decision on admissibility, usually (but not always) without an oral hearing. Oral hearings usually take place only in novel or complex matters. There is no right of appeal against a finding on admissibility.

15.27    If the complaint is admissible the court will investigate the facts jointly with the complainant and the government. Usually this can be done on the face of the documents with follow up queries, but very occasionally the court carries out a fact-finding mission of its own. The court also invites the parties to consider a 'friendly settlement' of the case. If successful, this will lead to a short report of the settlement (stating for example that the Convention violation is accepted and/or that compensation has been paid), and the court will then formally strike out the case.[24] A unilateral decision by the state, for example to pay compensation and apologise for the actions of state agents while not accepting the breach of Convention rights, should not automatically lead to a case being struck out by the court.[25]

---

22  ECHR article 35.
23  Reid, A Practitioner's Guide to the European Convention on Human Rights (2nd Ed, Sweet & Maxwell, 2004), p11.
24  ECHR article 37.
25  *Tahsin Acar v Turkey* (2004) 38 EHRR 2.

# Procedure before the court

15.28    If the merits of an application are to proceed to consideration by the ECtHR, then often the court will invite observations from the parties on specific points in writing, and in relation to the remedies sought for 'just satisfaction' of the claim.[26] Third party interventions in the form of written submissions dealing with legal issues may be permitted.[27] These can strengthen a case if submitted by a respected lawyer (possibly an academic lawyer) or by an organisation having particular knowledge or expertise in the issues raised by the complaint. For example, Liberty and Justice have made interventions in the kind of cases covered by the subject matter of this book.

15.29    If there is to be a hearing this will take place in Strasbourg before a chamber of the court consisting of seven judges. Parties will rarely receive more than 45 minutes each to make submissions and answer questions from the court. It is unusual for judgments to be given in public, although their release will often be covered by a press release from the court and the judgment will be immediately available on the court's website.

15.30    The judgment will normally cover the award of compensation if this is necessary for the 'just satisfaction' of the claim.[28] Since the HRA 1998 has been in force, judges in this country have commented that it is difficult to elicit more than general principles as to the basis upon which compensation is awarded.[29] In *Kingsley v UK*[30] the court said:

> 40 ... it is well established that the principle underlying the provision of just satisfaction ... is that the applicant should as far as possible be put in the position he would have enjoyed had the proceedings complied with the Convention's requirements ... The Court will award monetary compensation under Art 41 only where it is satisfied that the loss or damage complained of was actually caused by the violation it has found ... since the State cannot be required to pay damages in respect of losses for which it is not responsible.

The court tends to award global sums on an 'equitable' basis with no real explanation as to how the award is made. It is not uncommon for the court not to make an award at all, stating that the finding of a violation is 'just satisfaction' in itself for the applicant.

26   ECHR article 41.
27   ECHR article 36.
28   ECHR article 36.
29   See, eg, Stanley Burnton J in *R (KB) v Mental Health Review Tribunal* [2004] QB 936.
30   (2002) 35 EHRR 10.

15.31   The judgment of the court chamber becomes final after three months unless one of the parties requests referral to the Grand Chamber of 17 judges. Such requests are considered by five members of the Grand Chamber and are very rarely granted.[31]

15.32   Finally, the Committee of Ministers has powers to monitor and supervise the steps taken by a member state to implement the judgment of the court.[32] These have recently been used by the Committee of Ministers to monitor the steps to be taken by the UK government to ensure that deaths in custody are investigated in a way which is compliant with article 2.

15.33   Applicants should be aware that the current procedure does not provide a speedy remedy. Cases that are declared admissible usually take several years to be dealt with by the court.

31   ECHR article 43.
32   ECHR article 46.

# CHAPTER 16

# Inquests

16.1   There will almost invariably be a coroner's inquest where a person has died in police custody or where the police have had contact with a person shortly before his or her death. One main purpose of the inquest is to ascertain the circumstances in which a person died. As described below, there will often be a jury sitting with a coroner, whose role will be to give a verdict on the death with the help of guidance from the coroner. The families and friends of people who have died in controversial circumstances in police custody often use coroners' inquests to establish what happened, and to seek to obtain recommendations for avoiding recurrence in the future.

16.2   Article 2 of the European Convention on Human Rights (the right to protection of life) is almost always engaged in death in custody cases, and the coroner's inquest is a main way by which the state fulfils its obligation to have an effective, official investigation into the circumstances of such a death. This chapter will describe how this role has been developed in recent cases, before summarising the law and practical steps involved in a death in custody inquest.

## The role of the inquest after the Human Rights Act 1998

16.3   In the past, the inquest has been a frustrating and limited forum to obtain meaningful answers to the circumstances surrounding the death of a person in custody. However, to a certain extent the advent of the Human Rights Act 1998 and two recent cases in the House of Lords have transformed the role of inquests.[1]

16.4   Both cases concerned prisoners who had hanged themselves in jail in circumstances where prison officers and health care staff might have done more to prevent the death, but, as will be seen, the principles will apply to all deaths in custody including in the cases where the allegation is that the police directly caused the death by physical force, steps could have been taken to prevent the death, for example, of a suicidal prisoner or a prisoner suffering from the effects of drink, drugs or serious illness.

16.5   The obvious role of the jury in such cases is to pass comment not just on the immediate cause of death but also upon the surrounding circumstances of the death. One main reason for this is to identify what went wrong, and to seek to prevent recurrences in the future.

---

1   *R (Middleton) v West Somerset Coroner* [2004] 2 WLR 800; *R (Sacker) v West Yorkshire Coroner* [2004] 1 WLR 796.

16.6 However, standing in the way of such a sensible approach had been the case of *R v North Humberside Coroner ex p Jamieson*.[2] In that case, the Court of Appeal took a restrictive view of the role of the inquest and the jury in inquests involving deaths in custody. Coroners Act 1986 s11(5)(b) states that one of the questions to be answered by a jury is 'how' a person came by his or her death. The Court of Appeal in *Jamieson* ruled that this meant 'by what means' rather than the more expansive 'in what circumstances'. The only opportunity for a jury to pass comment on such a death was if the coroner could be persuaded to leave, as a contributing factor, a verdict of 'neglect'. But this verdict is so tightly circumscribed that unless a police officer (for example) exercised gross negligence in not preventing a person from harming him or herself, then a coroner could not leave the option to the jury. The upshot was that in many cases members of a jury sat for days listening to a catalogue of errors and failings closely linked to the death, but then were denied the opportunity to draw any conclusions from the evidence they had heard.

16.7 However, the Human Rights Act 1998 offered an opportunity to reopen the argument, which has now been accepted by the House of Lords in the *Middleton* and *Sacker* cases. ECHR article 2 (right to protection of life) requires there to be an effective official investigation into a death involving the state or state agents such as police officers.[3] The House accepted that a coroner and a jury at an inquest would often discharge this requirement. They also found that not only was there a duty to investigate a death, but that the duty extended to drawing conclusions from the investigation as to the accountability of the state and state agents for the death. To this end, the House found that there must be some mechanism for the jury to express its findings on the state's involvement at the end of the hearing. The House of Lords found that:

> The conclusion is inescapable that there are some cases in which the current regime for conducting inquests in England and Wales, as hitherto understood and followed, does not meet the requirements of the Convention.

16.8 The court held that Coroners Act 1986 s11(5)(b) should now be reinterpreted in cases where article 2 was engaged so as to require an investigation into 'by what means and in what circumstances' a person came by his or her death. The result of this small change, the House

---

2 [1995] QB 1.
3 See *R (Amin) v SSHD* [2003] 3 WLR 1169; *Jordan v UK* (2001) 37 EHRR 52.

decided, was to give the jury the opportunity to comment on the facts surrounding the death, as well as the direct cause of death itself.

16.9    The new regime will apply to all cases where the state has an obligation to carry out an effective official investigation under article 2 into a death and will be especially applicable in cases involving deaths in custody where arguably the state – through its systems or employees – could have done more to prevent a person's death. The biggest difference will relate to the role of the jury at the end of the inquest.

16.10    It must be for the coroner, in the exercise of his discretion, to decide how best, in the particular case, to elicit the jury's conclusion on the central issue or issues.[4] The House found that the following methods could be considered:

- narrative form of verdict in which the jury's factual conclusions are briefly summarised;
- inviting the jury's answer to factual questions put by the coroner: where and when the death took place; the cause or causes of such death; the defects in the system which contributed to the death; and any other factors which are relevant to the circumstances of the death.

It will be open to parties appearing or represented at the inquest to make submissions to the coroner on the means of eliciting the jury's factual conclusion.

16.11    The one example of a possible verdict relevant to a suicide in custody case given by the House of Lords was as follows (and has been adopted already in a number of cases):

> The deceased took his own life, in part because the risk of his doing so was not recognised and appropriate precautions were not taken to prevent him doing so.

## General

16.12    Other than the 'how' question discussed above, coroners are directed to ascertain who the deceased was, when and where he or she died, and the details necessary to make out a death certificate.[5]

16.13    Despite the recent House of Lords cases (described above) it is still the case that no verdict can be 'framed in such a way as to appear to

4    *R (Middleton) v West Somerset Coroner* [2004] 2 WLR 800 at [36].
5    Coroners Rules 1984 SI No 552 r36.

determine the question of (a) criminal liability on the part of a named person, or (b) civil liability'.[6] This rule is said to be necessary because a person accused of a crime, or a civil wrong, is provided with certain safeguards when appearing as a defendant at trial, many of which are not provided at an inquest.

16.14    However, the jury at an inquest can still return a range of verdicts (see para 16.45), including lawful killing, unlawful killing or an open verdict, but without naming an individual as being responsible. Sometimes, of course, it will be obvious who is responsible, for example, if a person in custody is unlawfully killed when there is only one officer in a cell with him or her.

16.15    Further, there is nothing to stop the coroner and the jury exploring facts bearing on criminal or civil liability during the inquest itself, provided that the verdict itself is not framed in such a way as to determine liability. Indeed, the duty of the coroner is to conduct a full, fair and fearless investigation.[7]

16.16    In many cases, although the police will not be primarily responsible for a death, they may have contributed to the death by failing to prevent it. Seeking to establish a verdict of 'neglect' in conjunction with other verdicts, like suicide or accidental death, is attractive in cases where the deceased has been in police custody and his or her family feel that the police could or should have done more to prevent their relative committing suicide, or dying as a result of intoxication, illness or injury in the police station. Establishing such 'neglect' used to be the only way of seeking the jury's comments on the circumstances of the death. Now, however, the jury has a wider role on commenting on the contributing factors to the death and the 'neglect' verdict is less crucial.[8]

16.17    Indeed, establishing a contributing verdict of neglect is very difficult. In *Jamieson*,[9] the Court of Appeal laid down guidelines on when the verdict will be appropriate. These can be summarised as follows:

- Although a verdict of 'lack of care' is often sought as a stepping stone to a claim in common law for negligence, the two terms are not connected. 'Lack of care' should be replaced in inquests by the term 'neglect'.
- 'Neglect' in inquests means 'a gross failure by others to provide adequate nourishment or liquid, or provide or procure basic

6  Coroners Rules 1984, r42.
7  *R v North Humberside Coroner ex p Jamieson* [1995] QB 1 at 26.
8  See *R (Middleton) v West Somerset Coroner* [2004] 2 WLR 800.
9  [1995] QB 1.

medical attention or shelter or warmth for someone in a dependent position (because of youth, age, illness or incarceration) who cannot provide it for himself'.

- 'Neglect' can rarely, if ever, be an appropriate verdict on its own, although it will be appropriate in some cases to say that neglect 'contributed to' (usually rather than 'aggravated') death by another cause (say, for instance, drug abuse).

- If it is established that the deceased committed suicide, that must be the verdict. On certain facts it could possibly be correct to hold that neglect contributed to suicide, but not simply on the ground that the deceased was (even carelessly) afforded an opportunity to take his or her own life. There would have to be gross neglect (such as a police officer observing a prisoner about to put a noose round his or her neck, but failing to intervene) before this finding would be appropriate.

- 'Neglect' should never form part of the verdict unless a clear and direct cause or connection is established between the conduct so described and the cause of death.

16.18   Despite this guidance there have been a number of subsequent reported decisions that have adopted a more liberal approach to the availability of the contributing verdict of neglect in cases involving deaths in custody.[10] It may be, however, that the new approach set out in *Middleton*, allowing the jury to comment on the wider circumstances of the death, will make it less likely that 'neglect' verdicts are reached by juries or left to them by coroners.

## Initial considerations

### Public funding

16.19   The police at an inquest where the deceased has died in police custody are likely to be represented by lawyers paid for at the public expense and naturally the deceased's family will also wish to have legal representation. However, until recently, funding was not available at all beyond initial advice, and it remains difficult to obtain adequate funding for representation in many cases.

---

10   *R v Swansea and Gower Coroner ex p Chief Constable of Wales* (1999) 164 JP 191; *R v Coventry Coroner ex p Chief Constable of Staffordshire* (2000) 164 JP 665; *R v Wiltshire Coroner ex p Clegg* (1997) 161 JP 521.

16.20    Recent improvements in the availability of funding for inquests for deaths in custody have been influenced by the requirement for members of the deceased family to be sufficiently involved in the ECHR article 2 official investigation so as to protect their legitimate interests.[11] Deaths in custody have now been brought within the normal scope of Community Legal Service funding and such funding will be granted if there is a significant wider public interest in the client being represented (for example, because of the importance of the issues raised in the inquest) or if the circumstances of the death appear to be such that funded representation is necessary to assist the coroner to investigate the case effectively and establish the facts.[12] In practice, it appears that the Legal Services Commission adopts a test as to whether it might not be an effective investigation without representation and, if this test is passed, funding will be granted.[13] Clearly, it will be helpful (but not essential) if the coroner will support the view that the family members should have funded representation at the inquest.

16.21    The usual financial eligibility rules will normally be applied, but there is discretion to waive these taking into account the assets available to the family and the nature and complexity of the issues raised at the inquest.[14]

16.22    In addition, the organisation Inquest, which monitors inquests and provides advice on deaths in custody and other controversial circumstances, may be able to help. As well as its own case workers, Inquest is in contact with many solicitors and barristers who specialise in representation of families at such inquests.[15]

## First steps[16]

16.23    It is important to be aware of the initial steps that a representative should take on behalf of a deceased's family when an inquest is to be held. Often, the family will have very little information about the death.

---

11  See *R (Amin) v SSHD* [2003] 3 WLR 1169; *Jordan v UK* (2001) 37 EHRR 52; and see Thomas et al, *Inquests*, LAG, 2003 paras 11.7–11.10 for a full description.

12  See Legal Services Commission Guidance on Funding Code para 3C-017 and description of the framework set out in *R (Challender) v Legal Services Commission* [2004] EWHC 925 (Admin).

13  *Challender*, [2004] EWHC 925 (Admin) at [67].

14  Community Legal Service (Financial) Regulations 2000 SI No 516 (as amended), regs 5C and 38(8A) introduced following *R (Khan) v Secretary of State for Health* [2003] 4 All ER 1239, CA.

15  www.inquest.org.uk.

16  For more detail see Thomas et al, *Inquests*, LAG, 2003, ch 10.

They may find it difficult to give instructions simply because they were not present when the death occurred. Inevitably, when someone has died in police custody, there will be rumours about what has happened. However, it is also very likely that the Independent Police Complaints Commission (IPCC) will be involved at a very early stage where there has been a death in custody. The IPCC will decide whether to investigate the death itself, or to manage or supervise an investigation by the police (see chapter 5). Whichever route is chosen, the family of the deceased should expect the IPCC and/or the investigating officer to be in touch at an early stage and to provide as much information as possible about the conduct of any investigation.

16.24    The initial steps for the family can be briefly described as follows:

- Ascertain how the IPCC is handling the case, who is the contact point and what information will be provided to the family. An early meeting with those involved in the investigation will be helpful.
- Ascertain the names of the family members who are providing instructions. It is not uncommon for there to be more than one family faction involved in the case.
- Contact the coroner's officer (usually a seconded police officer) and make sure he or she is aware of the family's interest in the inquest. Often the coroner's officer will already have been in touch with the family. Write also to the coroner formally to record the family's interest.
- Ascertain the date of the post mortem (see para 16.28), although it will often have taken place already, and if the relatives wish to instruct a doctor or a forensic pathologist to attend the post mortem, this should be arranged.
- Request a list of witnesses whom the coroner intends to call. If the relatives have other witnesses that they believe should be called, this information should be submitted to the coroner together with any relevant documentation he or she may not have seen.
- Although there is no right to advance disclosure for the relatives, the police have an agreed protocol on disclosure (see para 16.36) and requests for information in writing to all the relevant parties (including the coroner) should be made. Many coroners are now anxious to ensure that the representatives of the deceased's family have access to as much information as possible before an inquest, but this is not always the case.

## Jurisdiction

16.25 An inquest must be held where a coroner is informed that the body of a person is lying within his or her district and there is reason to suspect that the deceased:

(a) has died a violent or unnatural death; or
(b) has died a death of which the cause is unknown; or
(c) has died in prison (or in a place or circumstances that otherwise require an inquest).[17]

16.26 The jurisdiction referred to is a geographical area, usually comprising a county or part of a county. The coroner's duty arises because of the presence of the body in his or her district, irrespective of where the death occurred.[18] There is no general discretion, outside the above criteria, for a coroner to hold an inquest, for instance if he or she feels it is in the public interest that one should be held.[19] The term 'unnatural death' is to be given its ordinary meaning. Therefore, it has been held that a person who dies of a prolonged asthmatic attack, but whose life may have been saved if an ambulance had arrived in time, has not died an 'unnatural death' which would necessitate an inquest.[20] However, whether this result was correct was doubted in *R (Touche) v Inner London (North District) Coroner*,[21] relating to an inquest concerning alleged failures of clinical staff in hospital. The court found that where there was reason to suspect that 'neglect' in the *Jamieson* sense (see para 16.16) had contributed to a death, then an inquest should be held. Simon Brown LJ went on to consider that all wholly unexpected deaths where there was reason to suspect that the death would not have occurred without some culpable human failure should be categorised as deaths from unnatural causes.

16.27 The term 'prison' in (c) above is not defined, and there is doubt as to whether it would include a police station for the purposes of a coroner's inquest. However, Home Office guidance states that it is

---

17 Coroners Act (CA) 1988 s8(1).
18 CA 1988 s8(1).
17 CA 1988 s8(1).
18 CA 1988 s8(1).
19 *R v Poplar Coroner ex p Thomas* [1993] QB 610.
20 *R v Poplar ex p Thomas*
21 [2001] 3 WLR 148.
20 [2001] 3 WLR 148.
21 [2001] 3 WLR 148.

'desirable for an inquest to be held, with a jury, in all cases of deaths occurring in any form of legal custody, even though the death may have occurred in hospital or elsewhere and even though it may have been due to natural causes'.[22]

## Post mortem examination and toxicology reports

16.28   Coroners have a general power to order a post mortem or a 'special examination'[23] (such as a toxicology report).[24] Anyone who is a 'properly interested person' (this will usually include family members, see para 16.39) is entitled to a copy of the post mortem report,[25] although usually it is not disclosed unless requested. The family may wish to have an independent post mortem, whether or not one has already been held. This is usually arranged by agreement with the coroner. If a coroner refuses to allow an independent post mortem for insufficient reasons, an application for judicial review may be appropriate to challenge the decision.[26]

16.29   Obviously, there will usually be no need to order an independent post mortem if the report of the coroner's pathologist is consistent with the families' views on the cause of death and the report is not likely to be challenged by, for example, the police. Even in controversial deaths there is often no dispute as to how a person died; the real issue is the circumstances surrounding the death (for example, whether the police could have prevented a suicide or used a safer method of restraint).

16.30   If a second post mortem is necessary, it is usually desirable that this should take place as soon as possible after death. While the importance of this varies depending upon the nature of the cause of death (which may, of course, be uncertain), expert medical advice as to the need for an urgent post mortem should be sought at the earliest possible stage.

---

22  Home Office circ 109/1982 as approved in *R v Inner London (North District) Coroner ex p Linnane* [1989] 1 WLR 395.

23  Coroners Act 1988 s20.

24  The jury, when the inquest takes place, has the right to insist on a post mortem if a majority does not believe that the cause of death has been explained satisfactorily: Coroners Act 1988 s21(4).

25  Coroners Rules r57(1).

26  *R v Greater London (Southern District) Coroner ex p Ridley* [1985] 1 WLR 1347.

## Testing for drugs or alcohol

16.31 If the deceased may have been under the influence of drugs or alcohol, a toxicology report will usually be necessary even if there is not to be a second post mortem. To be effective, blood or other samples for a toxicology analysis need to be taken within two to three days of the alcohol or drugs being ingested. The hospital should therefore be requested to take samples immediately and to preserve them, even if it is initially unclear whether a toxicology report will be required.

# Juries

16.32 The coroner must sit with a jury, if, among other situations, it appears to him or her that the death occurred:

- in prison;
- in circumstances the continuation or possible recurrence of which is prejudicial to the health or safety of the public or any section of the public; or
- while the deceased was in police custody, or resulted from an injury inflicted by a police officer in the purported execution of his duty.[27]

16.33 A coroner has a discretion to summon a jury in any other case where it appears 'that there is any reason to do so'. There is no discretion not to summon a jury if it appears to the coroner that one or more of these factors applies. The Police Complaints Authority gave the term 'death in police custody or care' a wide definition and said that it 'covers deaths in hospitals, in court or in the street; deaths in accidents involving on-duty police officers and deaths of people who have voluntarily gone to a police station as witnesses'.[28]

16.34    A coroner's jury consists of between seven and 11 people.[29] The jury is selected in the same way as a Crown Court jury.[30] The family of the deceased has no right to challenge individual members of the jury, but the procedures for summoning the jury are mandatory and if they are not followed then this failure can be challenged by way of judicial review.[31] In practice, the coroner will usually agree that questions can be

27  Coroners Act 1988 s8(3).
28  PCA Annual Report 1994–1995.
29  Coroners Act 1988 s8(2)(a).
30  Coroners' Juries Act 1983.
31  *R v Merseyside Coroner ex p Carr* [1993] 4 All ER 65, DC.

put to the jury before the commencement of the inquest to ensure that members do not have contact with the police or other interested parties whose acts or omissions may be called into question.

## Disclosure of documents

16.35    It used to be the case that representatives of a deceased's family would attend a death in police custody inquest without disclosure of most of the documents held by the coroner. The majority of the documentation is usually provided by the police. This often led to feelings that there had been a cover up and considerable injustice as it would soon become clear at the inquest that the police legal representatives at the inquest had access to all the material.

16.36    The legal position is that documentation provided by the police to the coroner remains the property of the police and that the coroner is not able to order its disclosure without the consent of the police.[32] In practice, the police would often refuse to provide this consent. The injustice of this position was recognised by the Macpherson report which recommended that there should be advance disclosure as of right of documentation to those recognised by the coroner as properly interested parties.[33] Subsequently, the Home Office produced guidance to police forces in 1999 (updated in 2002).[34] This states:

> 4 ... disclosure of information held by the authorities in advance of the hearing should help to provide reassurance to the family of the deceased and other interested persons that a full and open police investigation has been conducted, and that they and their legal representatives will not be disadvantaged at the inquest. Advance disclosure may also remove a source of friction between interested persons and facilitate concentration on the facts surrounding the death. Experience has shown that pre-hearing disclosure in cases relating to deaths in police custody has been useful in allaying suspicions that matters are being deliberately concealed by the police which might otherwise have distracted attention from the real issues and made it more difficult for inquests to achieve the purpose required in law.
>
> 5. Chief Officers are advised, therefore, that there should continue to be as great a degree of openness as possible, and that disclosure of documentary

32    *Peach v Commissioner of Police of the Metropolis* [1986] 2 All ER 129, CA. The principle has been criticised in a number of cases, eg, *R (Bentley) v Avon Coroner* (2002) 166 JP 297.

33    Sir William McPherson of Cluny, *The Stephen Lawrence Inquiry*, Cm 4262-1, TSO 1999, recommendation 43.

34    Home Office circ 31/2002, *Deaths in Custody: Guidance to the police on pre-inquest disclosure.*

material to interested persons before the inquest hearing should be normal practice to all cases of deaths of a member of the public [during or following contact with the police which the police are required to report to the Home Office] ... In all cases Chief Officers will want to consider whether there are compelling reasons why certain documents, or parts of documents, may not be disclosed. But there should always be a strong presumption in favour of openness.

16.37 The kind of material which the police will consider not disclosing for 'compelling reasons' will include material where there is a risk of contamination of forthcoming criminal or disciplinary proceedings, material where disclosure would be distressing to the deceased's family, and material containing sensitive information about third parties.[35] Now that disclosure of the investigating officer's reports at the end of the complaints process is to be commonplace (see chapter 5) there will be far fewer reasons for the police to decline to disclose it for the purposes of the inquest (of course, the family of the deceased may have it already).

## Pre-inquest hearing

16.38 The increased likelihood of disclosure to interested persons, and the need to consider whether the inquest is the ECHR article 2 investigation (and if so, how the jury's conclusions will be obtained) has meant an increase in pre-inquest hearings. These are clearly useful for clarifying the main issue the coroner is considering covering, making submissions about witnesses to be called and documents to be disclosed, and discovering which of the interested parties are intending to be represented.

## The right to examine witnesses

16.39 The following, among others, are entitled to examine any witness at the inquest, either in person or through a barrister or solicitor:

- a parent, child, spouse or personal representative of the deceased;
- the beneficiary under an insurance policy issued on the life of the deceased;
- anyone whose act or omission may have caused or contributed to the death (or his or her agent or servant);

---

35 Guidance para 11. For more detailed discussion see Thomas et al, *Inquests*, LAG, 2003, paras 15.39–15.49.

- a chief officer of police;
- any other person who, in the opinion of the coroner, is a properly interested person.[36]

16.40    Thus, relatives other than those listed above (who are not a personal representative of the deceased) are not specifically included. A more distant relative or an unmarried partner of the deceased would have to qualify under the final catch-all category which is subject to approval by the coroner.[37] The catch-all category would also apply to pressure groups, trade unions and other agencies (such as the IPCC) who sought to be represented at the inquest and to ask questions. The involvement of such groups and organisations is clearly important where wider issues of policy are raised by the circumstances of the death, and/or where the deceased had no relatives to represent his or her interests at the inquest.

16.41    Even if a 'properly interested person' is given the right to examine witnesses, it is important to bear in mind that the nature of the proceedings are, in some respects, unlike a civil action court, where two parties argue out their case against one another. Coroners and their juries are charged with inquiring into deaths and in theory there are no 'parties' to the case. The proceedings have been described as 'a hybrid procedure, not purely inquisitorial or purely adversarial'.[38] So, although there is a right to examine witnesses and to be represented by a lawyer, this does not confer the right to present a case, call witnesses or to make oral submissions on the facts to the jury or to the coroner.[39]

## Witnesses

16.42    The coroner must examine, on oath, anyone who wishes to give relevant evidence and everyone 'having knowledge of the facts whom he thinks it expedient to examine'.[40] Clearly, this discretion must be exercised in a way which does not mean that relevant evidence is excluded. In cases where ECHR article 2 is engaged it will also be necessary for the coroner to ensure that there is an effective

---

36  Coroners Rules 1984 r20.
37  See *R v Greater London (South District) Coroner ex p Driscoll* (1995) 159 JP 45 where the Court of Appeal applied a wide interpretation to the words 'properly interested'.
38  *R (Middleton) v West Somerset Coroner* [2004] 2 WLR 800 at [26].
39  Coroners Rules 1984 r40.
40  Coroners Act 1988 s11(2).

investigation of the death.[41] If it appears that a coroner is not to call evidence that it is thought to be relevant then submissions should be made to the coroner on this issue. The decision of the coroner in relation to evidence to be called is susceptible to an application for judicial review.[42]

16.43 Witnesses are usually examined first by the coroner, then by anyone else entitled to examine witnesses and lastly by their own lawyer, if they are represented.[43] It is usual for a relative to be called to give evidence about the deceased early in the inquest, often to give the jury an idea of the kind of person the deceased was when alive. The post mortem evidence is also often dealt with early in the inquest.

## Verdict[44]

16.44 At the end of the inquest, the coroner will hear submissions in the absence of the jury as to what verdicts should be left to the jury. It will be a breach of natural justice if the coroner refuses to allow counsel's submissions as to what verdicts ought or ought not, as a matter of law, to be left to the jury 'unless it was merely a colourable attempt to persuade the jury of a certain version of the facts'.[45]

16.45 In cases where ECHR article 2 is engaged the coroner will also ask for submissions as to how to elicit the jury's factual conclusions on factors which may have contributed to the death and other relevant circumstances (see para 16.10).[46] The coroner then must sum up to the jury on the facts and the law[47] to enable the jury to complete a document, known as an inquisition, which records who the deceased was, and how, when and where he or she died and the other factual conclusions which have been reached. The part that records 'how' the person died is known as the verdict. If there is evidence upon which a jury, properly directed on the law, could return a specific verdict, then it is the duty of the coroner to leave such a verdict to the jury.[48] However, it is sufficient if the coroner leaves those verdicts which realistically

41 See *R (Middleton) v West Somerset Coroner* [2004] 2 WLR 800.

42 *R v West Yorkshire (Eastern District) Coroner ex p Clements* (1994) 158 JP 17.

43 Coroners Rules r21.

44 See in more depth Thomas et al, *Inquests*, LAG, 2003, ch 17; *Jervis on the Office and Duties of Coroners*, 12th ed, Sweet & Maxwell, 2002 ch 13.

45 *R v East Berkshire Coroner ex p Buckley* (1992) *Times* 1 December.

46 *R (Middleton) v West Somerset Coroner* [2004] 2 WLR 800 at [36].

47 Coroners Rules 1984 r41.

48 *R v Inner London (North District) Coroner ex p Koto* (1993) 157 JP 857.

reflect the thrust of the evidence.[49] Coroners Rules 1984 Sch 4[50] suggests the following forms of verdict (although these are not legally binding):

(a) Where the cause of death is one to which Note 2 applies, it is suggested that one of the following forms be adopted:
C.D. [a person unknown] died from natural causes.
C.D. died from the industrial disease of
C.D. died from dependence on drugs/non-dependent abuse of drugs.
C.D. died from want of attention at birth.
(In any of the above cases, but in no other, it is suggested that the following words may, where appropriate, be added:
'and the cause of death was aggravated by lack of care/self-neglect'.)

(b) In any other case except murder, manslaughter, infanticide or stillbirth, it is suggested that one of the following forms be adopted:
C.D. killed himself [whilst the balance of his mind was disturbed].
C.D. died as a result of an attempted/self-induced abortion.
C.D. died as a result of an accident/misadventure.
C.D. died in the ......... disaster.
Execution of sentence of death:
C.D. was killed lawfully.
Open verdict, namely, the evidence did not fully or further disclose the means whereby the cause of death arose.

(c) In the case of murder, manslaughter or infanticide it is suggested that the following form be adopted:
C.D. was killed unlawfully.

16.46　In the case of unlawful killing, it is uncertain whether it is sufficient for a jury to return such a verdict on the basis that the conduct of a group of police officers 'in aggregate' led to the death. In *R v West London Coroner's Court ex p Gray*[51] the court held that the death has to be attributable to a particular officer (but, of course, on no account can this officer be named in the verdict as this may appear to be determining a question of civil or criminal liability). However, in *R v Inner London (North District) Coroner ex p Koto*[52] it was held that, even though it would be impossible to attribute the death to acts of any single prison officer, an unlawful killing verdict was possible because there was no reason why the ordinary principles of joint enterprise should not apply to an inquest as they did in a criminal trial.

---

49　*R v Inner London (South District) Coroner ex p Douglas-Williams* [1989] 1 All ER 344.
50　Notes to Form 22.
51　[1987] 2 WLR 1020.
52　(1993) 157 JP 857.

16.47    The standard of proof for a verdict of unlawful killing is beyond reasonable doubt. The same standard of proof is also required in cases of suicide, but in relation to other verdicts, apart from an open verdict, proof on the balance of probabilities will suffice.[53] In deciding whether to withdraw a verdict from the jury on the basis that no reasonable jury could hold that the necessary standard of proof could be established, the coroner must not just look at the medical evidence but must take account of all the other evidence (such as eye-witness statements) as well.[54]

16.48    In relation to the enhanced role of juries following the *Middleton* and *Sacker* cases,[55] there is nothing in the judgments which indicates whether there will need to be a threshold to be crossed before the jury is invited to return a narrative verdict on the death or before questions can be put to the jury about a particular issue. It is possible that a coroner will simply invite the jurors to consider all the circumstances and reach their own conclusion. However, it is likely that coroners will at least want to be convinced that '[m]easures may well have been taken ... which arguably would have prevented the death'[56] before inviting the jury to consider whether this is in fact the case.

## Rule 43 recommendations

16.49    The power is reserved to the coroner to make a report to the responsible authority where he or she believes that action should be taken to prevent the recurrence of fatalities similar to that in respect of which the inquest is being held.[57] In the case of the police this will usually be the chief constable and/or the Home Secretary. The rules provide that the fact that a report will be sent should be announced in court by the coroner. However, often coroners will decline to reveal the substance of the report even to the interested parties. That practice is likely to change, following the *Middleton* case where the importance of the role

---

53   (1993) 157 JP 857.
54   (1993) 157 JP 857.
55   *R (Middleton) v West Somerset Coroner* [2004] 2 WLR 800; *R (Sacker) v West Yorkshire Coroner* [2004] 1 WLR 796.
56   See the Court of Appeal judgment in *Sacker* [2003] 2 All ER 278.
57   Coroners Rules 1984 r43.

of such reports in complying with human rights obligations was stressed. The House of Lords found that:[58]

> In the ordinary way, the procedural obligation under article 2 will be most effectively discharged if the coroner announces publicly not only his intention to report any matter but also the substance of the report, neutrally expressed, which he intends to make.

16.50    There is nothing to compel the responsible authority to respond to the coroner or to carry out any recommendations made.

## Challenging the decision of the inquest[59]

16.51    Following the inquest, if the family is dissatisfied with the verdict, consideration should be given to a possible challenge in the High Court. There are two main ways of doing this and, although they may be pursued together if appropriate, an application for judicial review is the most commonly used. In both situations, the court will have a discretion not to order a new inquest if the defects of the original inquest were minor or if there has been a significant passage of time which may be detrimental to the memories of important witnesses.[60]

### Coroners Act 1988 order and the attorney-general's fiat

16.52    The first is a statutory remedy provided by Coroners Act 1988 s13. The High Court can quash an inquisition of an inquest and order a new inquest to be held where this is in the interests of justice due to 'fraud, rejection of evidence, irregularity of proceedings, insufficiency of enquiry, the discovery of new facts or evidence or otherwise'.[61] The fiat of the Attorney-General and leave of the court are necessary in these proceedings.

---

58    *R (Middleton) v West Somerset Coroner* [2004] 2 WLR 800 at [38].
59    See, in more depth, Thomas et al, n11 above, ch 20.
60    *R v Inner London (South District) Coroner ex p Douglas-Williams* [1999] 1 All ER 344.
61    Coroners Act 1988 s13(1) and (2).

## Judicial review

16.53 The second is by way of judicial review (see in general para 17.67). Examples of the possible decisions that may be reviewable include the refusal to summon a jury,[62] misdirections as to the burden of proof,[63] failure to conduct the inquest in a human rights compatible manner[64] and refusal to release documents.[65] Other examples have already appeared in the text of this section to illustrate points of law.[66]

16.54 Applications for public funding can be made for both these remedies.

62 *R v Inner London (North District) Coroner ex p Linnane* [1989] 2 All ER 254.
63 *R v Inner London (South District) Coroner ex p Douglas-Williams* [1999] 1 All ER 344.
64 *R (Sacker) v West Yorkshire Coroner* [2004] 1 WLR 796.
65 *R v Hammersmith Coroner ex p Peach* [1980] 2 WLR 496.
66 And see further list of examples in Thomas et al, *Inquests*, LAG, 2003, para 20.48.

# Other remedies

# Compensation for wrongful convictions

17.1 People who are acquitted at trial after spending time remanded in custody and those who have their convictions quashed on appeal after having served all or part of the sentence imposed, understandably feel a strong sense of grievance. However, compensation does not follow as of right in these circumstances. The possibility of an action in malicious prosecution has already been discussed.[1] In addition there are two routes for obtaining compensation from the Home Office for those who have been wrongfully charged or convicted. The first arises under Criminal Justice Act 1988 s133 and the second under what is usually referred to as the ex gratia scheme. These will be looked at in turn below. There appears to be a growing awareness among practitioners of the possibility of obtaining compensation for clients by these means. In 1989–1990 the Home Office paid out £285,000 in total in compensation to applicants. By 1993–1994 the figure was £1,506,000.[2] In more recent years the figures have been: 1999–2000: £5,647,000; 2000–2001: £8,051,000; and 2001–2002: £6,172,000.[3] Statistics indicating the number of applications made are only available for the more recent period. Between March 2001 and February 2003 the Secretary of State for the Home Department authorised payments to be made in 76 cases.[4] As at 5 November 2003 there were 58 applicants awaiting the determination of their eligibility under the two schemes.[5] These figures suggest that while the number of applications has increased significantly over the last decade, there may still be a considerable number of instances where these routes to compensation are being overlooked. This text will look at the criteria that applicants must satisfy for an award to be made; the basis upon which awards are assessed; and the practicalities of making an effective application.

## Eligibility: Criminal Justice Act 1988 s133

17.2 The statutory scheme for providing compensation in respect of wrongful convictions is based on article 14(6) of the International Covenant on Civil and Political Rights (ICCPR). It provides that:

---

1 See chapter 7.
2 HC Written Answers, 9 March 1995.
3 HC Written Answers, 6 February 2003.
4 HC Written Answers, 6 February 2003.
5 HC Written Answers, 5 November 2003.

Where a person has by a final decision been convicted of a criminal offence and when subsequently his conviction has been reversed, or he has been pardoned on the ground that a new or newly discovered fact shows conclusively that there has been a miscarriage of justice, the person who has suffered punishment as result of such conviction shall be compensated according to law, unless it is proved that the non-disclosure of the unknown fact in time is wholly or partly attributable to him.

17.3    The relevant parts of the domestic statute provide:

(1) Subject to subsection (2) below, when a person has been convicted of a criminal offence and when subsequently his conviction has been reversed or he has been pardoned on the ground that a new or newly discovered fact shows beyond reasonable doubt that there has been a miscarriage of justice, the Secretary of State shall pay compensation for the miscarriage of justice to the person who has suffered punishment as a result of such conviction or, if he is dead, to his personal representatives, unless the non-disclosure of the unknown fact was wholly or party attributable to the person convicted.

(2) No payment of compensation under this section shall be made unless an application for such compensation has been made to the Secretary of State.

(3) The question whether there is a right to compensation under this section shall be determined by the Secretary of State ...

(5) In this section 'reversed' shall be construed as referring to a conviction having been quashed –
   (a) on an appeal out of time; or
   (b) on a reference –
      (i) under the Criminal Appeal Act 1995; or
      (ii) under section 263 of the Criminal Procedure (Scotland) Act 1975.
   (c) on an appeal under section 7 of the Terrorism Act 2000.

(6) For the purposes of this section a person suffers punishment as a result of a conviction when sentence is passed on him for the offence of which he was convicted.

Thus it will be seen that the statutory scheme very closely mirrors the wording of ICCPR article 14(6), except that 'conclusively' is replaced by 'beyond reasonable doubt', a more familiar domestic concept. The wording of ICCPR article 14(6) is also very closely followed in article 3 of Protocol 7 to the European Convention on Human Rights (ECHR). However, the United Kingdom has neither signed nor ratified Protocol 7 and so this does not provide applicants with a free-standing alternative route to obtaining compensation.

17.4 In order to qualify for compensation under section 133 an applicant needs to show:

- the qualifying person was convicted of a criminal offence, which was subsequently reversed following an out-of-time appeal or was the subject of a pardon;
- this was on the grounds of new or newly discovered facts;
- these facts show beyond reasonable doubt that there had been a miscarriage of justice;
- the person suffered punishment as a result of the conviction;
- the earlier non-disclosure of the unknown fact was not wholly or partly attributable to the person convicted.

If all the elements are established, the Secretary of State for the Home Department is under a mandatory duty to pay compensation.[6] These elements are now considered in turn.

## A conviction reversed on appeal or subject to a pardon

17.5 A successful application under section 133 can only be made if the person in question was convicted of a criminal offence. Prosecution for a serious offence with a lengthy remand in custody followed by an acquittal at trial cannot result in compensation under the statutory scheme (though these circumstances may qualify under the ex gratia scheme discussed below). Further, the definition of the conviction being reversed[7] excludes appeals brought within the usual time limits. However, those circumstances may come within the ex gratia scheme if the other prescribed criteria are satisfied. The most common situation that will fall within the definition of 'reversed' is where a conviction has been quashed as a result of a referral of a case back to the Court of Appeal by the Criminal Cases Review Commission.[8] The concept of a conviction being 'quashed' does not include the situation where the Court of Appeal allows an appeal against conviction but substitutes a conviction for a lesser offence, since this is not treated as a quashing of the conviction for the purposes of Criminal Appeal Act 1995 s3.[9] Accordingly, if the Court of Appeal determined that a person was wrongly convicted of murder, but should have been convicted of a lesser offence such as manslaughter, eligibility under the

---

6 Criminal Justice Act 1988 s133(2).
7 Criminal Justice Act 1988 s133(5).
8 Under Criminal Appeal Act 1995 ss9–12.
9 *R (Christofides) v Secretary of State for the Home Department* [2002] 1 WLR 2769.

statutory scheme could not be established, even if the applicant had served the sentence for the more serious offence in the interim. (Again, consideration could be given to an application under the ex gratia scheme in those circumstances.)

## New or newly discovered facts

17.6   A new or newly discovered fact is to be contrasted with a new legal ruling made on previously existing facts. Thus, where a conviction is quashed out of time because of a change in the law or a subsequently appreciated error in the trial judge's summing up, there is no new or newly discovered fact and the circumstances fall outside the statutory scheme.[10] This is illustrated by the facts of the two cases involved in the *Bateman and Howse* litigation. In one case the claimant's conviction had been quashed as a result of the trial judge's error in admitting certain evidence in written form (when the witness was unavailable). In the other case the claimant had been convicted under the Greenham Common Byelaws and her conviction was quashed after the byelaws were declared ultra vires. Neither of these circumstances amounted to a new or newly discovered fact. A distinction has also been emphasised between newly discovered evidence and newly discovered facts; the former in itself is insuff-icient and must lead to new factual conclusions for the statutory provision to be satisfied.[11] The most common situations that come within this provision are where material is discovered after conviction indicating that evidence adduced by the prosecution at the trial was unreliable and/or fabricated, for example where 'confessions' to police officers are undermined by subsequent scientific testing. The new factual information may be a new expert's conclusion, even if it arises on material that was available at the original trial. The criterion could also be satisfied in circumstances where a conviction was quashed as a result of the court receiving evidence from new witnesses unavailable at the trial or as a result of evidence being put before the court that undermined the integrity or reliability of witness evidence upon which the prosecution was based. The new evidence could relate to the accused – for example if new expert evidence established to the Court of Appeal's satisfaction that he or she was so suggestible or vulnerable that an alleged confession to police may have been unreliable.

10   *R v Secretary of State for the Home Department ex p Bateman and Howse* (1994) 7 Admin LR 175; *Re McFarland* [2004] 1 WLR 1289, HL.

11   *R v Secretary of State for the Home Department ex p Garner* [1999] 11 Admin LR 595, as discussed in *R (on the application of Murphy) v Secretary of State for the Home Department* [2005] EWHC 140 (Admin).

17.7    The statutory reference to a 'new or newly discovered fact' is to a fact that is new or newly discovered after the exhaustion of the ordinary appellate process: *R (on the application of Murphy) v Secretary of State for the Home Department.* Thus, a fact discovered between conviction and an original, unsuccessful 'in time' appeal, would not qualify. As is evident from the statutory wording, the new or newly discovered fact(s) relied upon must have led to the conviction being quashed. It is not sufficient that the new or newly discovered fact makes some contribution to the quashing of the conviction. It must be the principal, if not the only, reason for the quashing of the conviction: *R (Murphy) v Secretary of State for the Home Department.* If the applicant was responsible for the fact failing to come to light at an earlier stage, the statutory criteria will not be satisfied.

### Shows beyond reasonable doubt there was a miscarriage of justice

17.8    The meaning of this element of the statutory test has so far caused the most difficulty. It is not immediately clear from the statutory wording what constitutes a miscarriage of justice for these purposes: is it sufficient that a conviction has been quashed, as the Court of Appeal has thereby recognised that the applicant was wrongly convicted; should the circumstances be limited to where it has been positively proved that the accused was innocent of the crime charged; or is the correct position somewhere between the two? The point is of practical importance as when the Court of Appeal quashes a conviction it is relatively rare for it to make a specific pronouncement of innocence. The court is under a statutory duty to quash a conviction if it concludes it is 'unsafe'.[12] In cases where the Court of Appeal receives fresh evidence, the test it applies is to ask whether the new evidence might reasonably have affected the decision of the jury to convict; if it might have done, then the conviction must be treated as unsafe.[13] Accordingly, in the vast majority of cases the Court of Appeal feels no need to reach a conclusion as to whether the accused was positively innocent of the crime and will not do so, irrespective of whether the evidence points in that direction. The circumstances where applicants can showthat their convictions were quashed on the basis of a new fact indicating beyond reasonable doubt that they were innocent, are therefore strictly limited and the scope of the statutory provision will be substantially confined if it is construed in this narrow way. In practice over recent years, the Home Office appears to have adopted a

12   Criminal Appeal Act 1968 s2, as amended.
13   *R v Pendleton* [2002] 1 WLR 72, HL.

middle ground approach, accepting that com-pensation is due in a significant number of cases where innocence as such was not pronounced by the Court of Appeal (because it did not need to be), but where it was clear that the evidence that led to the conviction had been very substantially undermined. It remains to be seen what practice the Home Office will now adopt in the light of the recent important decision by the House of Lords in *R (Mullen) v Secretary of State for the Home Department*.[14]

17.9    Mr Mullen was convicted by a jury of conspiracy to cause explosions and sentenced to a substantial term of imprisonment. After he had been in prison for nearly ten years the Court of Appeal quashed his conviction on an appeal out of time on the basis that it was an abuse of process as he had been deported from Zimbabwe to stand trial in the United Kingdom by British police and intelligence operatives in a way which flouted domestic and international law.[15] It was not alleged as part of the successful appeal that he was innocent of the offence of which he was convicted or that, apart from the abuse of process relating to his unlawful deportation, the trial was in any way flawed. The Secretary of State for the Home Department refused to pay compensation under the statutory scheme on the basis that the quashing of the conviction had not established that Mr Mullen had suffered a miscarriage of justice and he argued before the courts that the statutory phrase was confined to circumstances where a person was shown to be innocent of the crime charged. Mr Mullen's lawyers argued that 'a miscarriage of justice' included all circumstances where a conviction was quashed and particular reliance was placed on the effect of the presumption of innocence. Mr Mullen failed in his application to judicially review the decision before the Divisional Court, but succeeded before the Court of Appeal.[16]

17.10   The House of Lords allowed the Secretary of State's appeal, agreeing unanimously that Mr Mullen did not qualify under the statutory scheme. However, the different reasoning of the members of the Appellate Committee has left the law on this crucial issue in a state of considerable uncertainty. The Law Lords were agreed that, despite their differing perceptions of the meaning of 'miscarriage of justice', Mr Mullen's circumstances did not fall within it, since they all accepted it did not extend to circumstances where, although there had been an abuse of executive power in bringing the accused to the United

14   [2004] 2 WLR 1140.
15   *R v Mullen* [2000] QB 520.
16   *R (Mullen) v Secretary of State for the Home Department* [2002] 1 WLR 1857, DC; [2003] QB 993, CA.

Kingdom, Mr Mullen was unable to show any defect in his trial or in the investigation leading up to it. Thus, it is now plain that a Criminal Justice Act 1988 s133 application cannot succeed if the conviction was not quashed as a result of a failure of the investigation or trial process. This limitation in itself would rule out relatively few cases.

17.11　　　The House of Lords was divided over the actual meaning of a 'miscarriage of justice'. Lord Steyn, with whom Lord Rodger agreed, considered that it only extended to 'clear cases of miscarriage of justice, in the sense that there would be acknowledgement that the person concerned was clearly innocent'.[17] On the other hand Lord Bingham, with whom Lord Walker agreed, considered, without expressing a concluded view, that this was too narrow an approach, and that the phrase could cover those cases where someone should not have been convicted.[18] Lord Scott did not find it necessary to decide between these competing views, since the appeal could in any event be disposed of on the specific basis that there was no failure of the investigation or trial process in Mr Mullen's case.[19]

17.12　　　As it is likely that the courts will have to decide between these differing views in the future, it is worth summarising the basis of them. All members of the Appellate Committee who expressed a view on the issue accepted that the meaning of a 'miscarriage of justice' in Criminal Justice Act 1988 s133 was governed by the intended meaning in ICCPR article 14(6), since this was the basis of the obligation to provide compensation. Lord Steyn emphasised that the phrase was an autonomous Convention concept that must be construed in accordance with internationally accepted principles, rather than by reference to domestic case law; he considered that the Court of Appeal had erred in having regard to the ordinary use of the phrase domestically.He considered that the wording of the obligation to compensate, which excluded payment if there was no new or newly discovered fact or if a miscarriage of justice was only shown to be possible or probable, indicated that the provision should be construed narrowly. He also put store on the views expressed in an Explanatory Report accompanying Protocol 7 to the ECHR when it was published, indicating that compensation should be confined to cases where the person concerned was clearly innocent.[20] He considered that his

17　[2004] 2 WLR 1140 at [56] and [69].
18　[2004] 2 WLR 1140 at [4], [9] and [70].
19　[2004] 2 WLR 1140 at [66].
20　Para 25 of the Explanatory Report to the 7th Protocol prepared by the 21 member Steering Committee for Human Rights appointed by the Council of Europe.

interpretation was workable as sometimes the Court of Appeal did make it clear that it considered a defendant to be innocent[21] and on other occasions this could be inferred.[22] It is suggested that the latter observation is over-optimistic: as discussed above, in the vast majority of cases the Court of Appeal goes no further than it has to in quashing a conviction and does not seek to determine whether the defendant committed the offence. Lord Bingham, on the other hand, thought that the expression 'miscarriage of justice' was apt to describe a case where a defendant should not have been convicted and pointed out other instances where the phrase had been used in that way. He was not persuaded that the contents of the Explanatory Report to Protocol 7 were significant, as the references in the report were not consistent and many more states are parties to the ICCPR than to the ECHR and they could not be bound by a later commentary on a different instrument.[23]

17.13    Mr Mullen's lawyers had relied on the presumption of innocence contained in ICCPR article 14(2) and ECHR article 6(2); they submitted that the presumption extended to the denial of compensation for a quashed conviction on the basis that the applicant was or might be guilty of the relevant offence. The Lords agreed that the presumption did not apply in the circumstances. Lord Steyn considered that the case law relied on under ECHR article 6(2) was of no assistance as it concerned particular domestic compensation schemes operated in Austria and Norway and did not address the inter-relationship between ECHR article 6(2) and article 3 of the Seventh Protocol to that Convention.[24] Lord Bingham highlighted that the case law from the European Court of Human Rights distinguished between circumstances where there had been no acquittal on the merits of the accusation, where the state is permitted to give effect subsequently to its suspicions of the defendant's guilt and cases where there had been an acquittal based on an evaluation of the merits of the evidence, where the state is not permitted to voice such suspicions.[25] As Mr Mullen had not been acquitted on the merits of the accusation, the case law decided under the ECHR did not assist him. Obviously, Lord Bingham's approach leaves open the possibility that where a wrongful

21   For example, *R v Fergus* (1994) 98 Cr App R 313.

22   Lord Steyn's reasoning appears at [35]–[57].

23   Lord Bingham's reasoning is at [9] and [10].

24   The following in particular were considered: *Sekanina v Austria* (1993) 17 EHRR 221; *Rushiti v Austria* (2001) 33 EHRR 56, *Weixelbraun v Austria* (2003) 36 EHRR 45 and *Hammern v Norway* (2003) 11 February, ECtHR.

25   *Leutscher v Netherlands* (1996) 24 EHRR 181 and the authorities referred to in the preceding footnote.

conviction was quashed on the basis of the merits of the evidence, the accused could use the case law decided under ECHR article 6(2) to argue for a broad meaning of the concept of a 'miscarriage of justice'.

17.14  In finding it unnecessary to join with one side or the other, Lord Scott commented that in many situations the debate would be academic as the applicant would qualify for compensation in any event under the ex gratia scheme. As we shall see, this is likely to be the case where a conviction is quashed on the basis of state wrongdoing, for example that the police or other investigating authorities fabricated or suppressed material evidence. However, where a conviction is quashed on the basis that new information has undermined civilian evidence given at the trial, success under the ex gratia scheme will be unlikely. Further, as set out below, the ex gratia scheme only covers circumstances where the applicant has spent time in custody. Accordingly, it is suggested that the correct construction of the statutory phrase 'miscarriage of justice' remains a live and important issue.

### Accused suffered punishment

17.15  As indicated by the statutory wording, the convicted person must have 'suffered punishment', that is to say had a sentence passed on him or her.[26] In order to qualify for compensation it is therefore unnecessary to show that the applicant spent time in custody. A conviction for an offence causing a moral stigma or a conviction that causes a person to lose his or her job, may still occasion significant loss and damage, even though there has been no loss of liberty. Similarly, loss may be sustained where the penalty imposed was a substantial fine.

### The court's role

17.16  If an applicant is dissatisfied with a decision that he or she fails to qualify under the statutory scheme, he or she may challenge the determination by an application for judicial review, as illustrated by the case law summarised above. Whether the elements of the statutory test were satisfied on the evidence available to the Secretary of State is a question of law, so that the Administrative Court will substitute its own view if it disagrees with the former's conclusion. This is in contrast to the much more limited role which the court plays in reviewing the operation of the ex gratia scheme, as set out below.

---

26  Criminal Justice Act 1988 s133(6).

## Eligibility: the ex gratia scheme

17.17   This scheme of compensation is based on a written parliamentary answer given by Mr Roy Jenkins, the then Home Secretary on 29 July 1976.[27] This statement was elaborated on in a written answer to the House of Commons by the then Home Secretary, Mr Douglas Hurd, on 29 November 1985[28] and was adopted by the subsequent Labour Government.[29] Douglas Hurd's statement referred in part to circumstances that have since been covered by Criminal Justice Act 1988 s133. The courts have recently confirmed that this part of the statement has therefore been superseded by the legislation and it is not possible to argue for compensation on the basis that part of the wording used in the Statement went slightly wider than its legislative replacement.[30] It is the second part of Douglas Hurd's statement that sets out the basis under which the scheme now known as the ex gratia scheme is operated. He said:

> I remain prepared to pay compensation to people who do not fall within the terms of the preceding paragraph but who have spent a period in custody following a wrongful conviction or charge, where I am satisfied that it has resulted from serious default on the part of a member of a police force or of some other public authority.
>
> There may be exceptional circumstances that justify compensation in cases outside these categories. In particular, facts may emerge at trial, or on appeal within time, that completely exonerate the accused person. I am prepared, in principle, to pay compensation to people who have spent a period in custody or have been imprisoned in cases such as this. I will not, however, be prepared to pay compensation simply because at the trial or an appeal the prosecution was unable to sustain the burden of proof beyond a reasonable doubt in relation to the specific charge that was brought.

17.18   Thus, broadly, there are two routes to establishing compensation under the ex gratia scheme. Either the applicant may show that the wrongful conviction or charge resulted from serious default on the part of the police or other public authority, or he or she may show that there are exceptional circumstances that warrant the payment of compensation – commonly, although not necessarily, because he or she has been completely exonerated of involvement in the relevant offence.

27   HC Debates, cols 328–330, 29 July 1976.
28   HC Debates, cols 691–692, 29 November 1985.
29   By Mr Jack Straw, the then Home Secretary, on 17 June 1997.
30   *Re McFarland* [2004] 1 WLR 1289, HL.

17.19    Before those two routes are considered in detail some preliminary points are highlighted. The claim can result from a wrongful conviction or charge. In this respect the ex gratia scheme is wider than the statutory scheme, which only applies to convictions. Under the ex gratia scheme compensation can be paid to someone who has been acquitted on the merits at trial or where proceedings were dropped at or before trial. Further, and as noted when the statutory scheme was analysed (at para 17.5), the ex gratia scheme can apply to convictions quashed as a result of appeals brought within time, during the normal course of the criminal law process. On the other hand, the ex gratia scheme is more restrictive in requiring that the applicant must have spent time in custody as a result of the wrongful charge or conviction.

### The serious default limb

17.20    The courts have emphasised that in accordance with the wording of the Home Secretary's statement, the wrongful charge/conviction must have resulted from the serious default in question (or from the exceptional circumstances if the second limb is relied upon). Thus, the applicant cannot rely upon allegedly unjust conduct which did not lead to the wrongful charge/conviction, such as the failure of the Court of Appeal in earlier appeals to recognise that the conviction was unsafe,[31] or a grossly excessive sentence.[32] Accordingly, the conduct that can be relied on will usually pre-date the conviction, particularly under the serious default limb, although this is not always so, for example if the police suppressed evidence tending to show the applicant's innocence which came to light after he or she was convicted.[33]

17.21    The kinds of misconduct that would most commonly ground a successful claim under this limb would be fabrication or deliberate suppression of evidence and/or serious breaches of the Police and Criminal Evidence Act 1984.

17.22    A practical issue that commonly arises is the extent to which and the means by which an applicant can prove to the Secretary of State's satisfaction that the misconduct relied upon occurred. The approach of the Secretary of State has been to focus primarily on the decision of the court that quashed the conviction. If the court found serious misconduct the Home Secretary will accept this conclusion without the

---

31   *R (Christofides) v Secretary of State for the Home Department* [2002] 1 WLR 2769.

32   *R (Daghir) v Secretary of State for the Home Department* [2004] ACD 33.

33   The example given in *Daghir*, at [46].

need for additional evidence. However, in many instances a suspicion of police or prosecutorial misconduct will not be resolved when the conviction is quashed. In these circumstances the Home Secretary's stance has been that as he is unable to embark upon a full investigation of his own, serious default is unlikely to be established, unless the evidence presented by the applicant is particularly compelling. This has been accepted as a legitimate approach for him to adopt, provided the Home Secretary takes into account any representations and material that the applicant submits on the issue.[34] A further issue can arise where the court quashing the conviction has expressed a view on the conduct relied upon, but has not characterised it in serious terms. In those circumstances the applicant may seek to argue that the court was mistaken and that a more serious view of the misconduct should be taken under the ex gratia scheme. However, the House of Lords has accepted that the Home Secretary should be guided predominantly by the decision of the court. 'It would not generally be open to him to treat as minor what the court had treated as serious, or vice versa. He had to take his cue from the court.'[35] This is illustrated by the House of Lords' decision in the *McFarland case*. The claimant's conviction had followed from a private meeting between counsel and the magistrate, initiated by the latter at which he gave an indication as to the course he was minded to take on sentencing if the charge was contested. The indication involved a more severe sentence than the magistrate was in fact empowered to pass and led to a plea of guilty, which the accused subsequently sought to retract. The House of Lords plainly thought that the behaviour of the magistrate was seriously remiss, but accepted that as the court which quashed the conviction had barely criticised it at all, the Home Secretary was entitled to take his cue from that decision and find that serious default had not been established to his satisfaction.

17.23    It is unclear whether circumstances falling short of deliberate abuse of power will come within the concept of 'serious default'. It is submitted that the wording is sufficiently wide to cover instances where public officials have been substantially remiss, even if not deliberately so, particularly if the conduct amounts to gross negligence and/or a clear flouting of prescribed procedures. The issue could arise, for example, where officers have carried out a woefully inadequate investigation and a wrongful conviction results or where the prosecution

---

34  *R (Taylor) v Secretarty of State for the Home Department* [2002] EWHC 2761 (Admin).

35  *Re McFarland* [2004] 1 WLR 1289, HL at [16].

rests on the conclusion of a forensic scientist, who is subsequently thoroughly discredited. In the *McFarland* case (discussed above) the House of Lords clearly thought that it would have been open to the Secretary of State to have found that the magistrate's conduct amounted to 'serious default' had it not been for the attitude of the court that quashed the conviction, although there was no suggestion that he acted in deliberate bad faith.

17.24 In a number of cases applicants have tried to argue that a court (whether presided over by judge or a magistrate) was a public authority for the purposes of the serious default limb of the scheme. This proposition was rejected in a series of earlier cases.[36] More recently it was argued that the developing meaning of a public authority, particularly in relation to the Human Rights Act 1998, should bring about a re-evaluation of this point. However, in the *McFarland* case the House of Lords by a 4:1 majority held that the Home Secretary's statement had to be construed at the time it was made in 1985 and at that time judges and magistrates would not have been regarded as public authorities.[37] Lord Steyn, dissenting, considered that though the phrase was used in a ministerial statement of policy, rather than a legislative provision, the words 'public authority' fell to be interpreted objectively and thus account could be taken of modern developments in the understanding of a public authority and he noted the illogical position that would result if the courts were excluded from this limb of the scheme.[38]

17.25 As we shall see, judicial misconduct may in any event come within the exceptional circumstances limb in limited circumstances. Clear cases of deliberate misconduct by the police or other investigating authorities such as Customs and Excise officers or by the Crown Prosecution Service[39] could all come within this limb.

---

36  *R v Secretary of State for the Home Department ex p Harrison* [1988] 3 All ER 86; *R v Secretary of State for the Home Department ex p Bateman and Howse* (1994) 7 Admin LR 175; *R v Secretary of State for the Home Department ex p Garner* [1999] 11 Admin LR 595 and *R (Conlon) v Secretary of State for the Home Department* (2000) 11 December, QBD (Admin), unreported.

37  [2004] 1 WLR 1289 at [16].

38  [2004] 1 WLR 1289 at [24]–[30].

39  The House of Lords in *Re McFarland* [2004] 1 WLR 1289 indicated that the suggestion to the contrary in *R v Secretary of State for the Home Department ex p Bateman and Howse* (1994) 7 Admin LR 175, was incorrect, see at [13].

*The exceptional circumstances limb*

17.26   As with the serious default limb discussed above, the wrongful charge or conviction must result from the exceptional circumstances relied upon, so that a wait of 30 years between conviction and the quashing of the same could not amount to 'exceptional circumstances' as it was an effect, rather than a cause, of the conviction.[40]

17.27   The example of exceptional circumstances given in the Home Secretary's statement is where the accused person has been completely exonerated. Plainly, this phrase is intended to apply to circumstances where the innocence of the applicant has been established. Outside the statutory scheme (which was enacted to comply with international treaty obligations), the Home Secretary is free to choose who to offer compensation to and since the meaning of the words used is relatively clear, there is no equivalent ambiguity to that arising from the use of the phrase 'miscarriage of justice' in Criminal Justice Act 1988 s133 and no basis for relying on the presumption of innocence to contend that the terms of the ex gratia scheme should be expanded (see the discussion in relation to s133 at paras 17.8–17.14 and 17.33 as well in relation to the ex gratia scheme).

17.28   Although the Home Secretary's statement referred in terms to complete exoneration arising from facts emerging at trial or on appeal in time, it is likely that he would be operating an unlawful fetter on his discretion and/or acting unreasonably if the Home Secretary declined to regard other instances where complete exoneration has been shown as falling within the exceptional circumstances limb.

17.29   The Home Secretary would also unlawfully fetter his discretion, however, if he confined a consideration of exceptional circumstances to those where complete exoneration was shown. This was illustrated, for example, by *ex p Garner*,[41] where the Home Secretary had failed to consider whether judicial misconduct could come within the exceptional circumstances limb. Decisions were quashed and remitted to him for further consideration. However, it is important to emphasise that it is only in rare circumstances that judicial behaviour will lead to compensation under this limb. Judicial error in the course of a summing up or in relation to a decision on admissibility of evidence will not qualify, even if it is a fairly basic error and even if it leads to the conviction being

---

40   *R (Taylor) v Secretary of State for the Home Department* [2002] EWHC 2761 (Admin).
41   [1999] 11 Admin LR 595.

quashed.[42] Eligibility for compensation will only be established if the judge's behaviour warrants the description of 'exceptional'. A good example is provided by the facts of *Tawfick* where the Home Secretary's decision that the judge's behaviour did not amount to exceptional circumstances was quashed with a direction to him to reconsider. The trial judge at the applicant's criminal trial for dishonesty offences (where he appeared unrepresented) had accused him in open court of trying to hoodwink the jury in a way that clearly left them with the impression that he was a liar and a cheat. An example of where the Home Secretary accepted that judicial misconduct fell within the exceptional circumstances limb is the application made by the family of Derek Bentley, where the Home Secretary decided that the cumulative effect of a number of serious errors by the trial judge, which denied the accused a fair trial, constituted exceptional circumstances.[43]

17.30 Internal Home Office guidance quoted by the court in *Daghir* emphasises that for a case to fall within the exceptional circumstances limb on grounds other than complete exoneration, will usually be as a result of a combination of factors that would not have triggered a payment if taken individually, for example default that would not on its own be regarded as sufficiently serious to trigger payment under the first limb coupled with factors which tended to, but which did not completely exonerate the applicant.[44]

## The ECHR and the ex gratia scheme

17.31 Applicants have tried to use the ECHR to reinforce submissions for compensation under the scheme, but hitherto without significant success. In some cases reliance has been placed on article 5(5) which provides that:

> Everyone who has been the victim of arrest/detention in contravention of the provisions of this article shall have an enforceable right to compensation.

17.32 However, article 5(1) permits 'lawful detention of a person after conviction by a competent Court'. It has been held that a subsequent successful appeal does not alter the fact that at the point of conviction

---

42 *R v Secretary of State for the Home Department ex p Garner* [1999] 11 Admin LR 595; *R (Tawfick) v Secretary of State for the Home Department* [2001] ACD 28 and *R (Daghir) v Secretary of State for the Home Department* [2004] ACD 33.

43 As discussed in *R (Tawfick) v Secretary of State for the Home Department* [2001] ACD 28.

44 *R (Daghir) v Secretary of State for the Home Department* [2004] ACD 33 at [14].

the trial court had jurisdiction to sentence the accused and hence impose the detention.[45] Accordingly, imprisonment pursuant to a wrongful conviction will not in the ordinary course of events trigger a right to compensation under article 5(5) and thus this article does not assist an applicant in establishing a liability to compensate him or her under the ex gratia scheme.[46] Alternative arguments have been based on the fair trial guarantee of ECHR article 6. However, the European Court of Human Rights generally considers that there has been a fair trial if the appeal process cures defects from the original trial, even if the successful appeal is a belated one.[47] Furthermore, even if the article 6 fair trial guarantee was infringed, that in itself does not give rise to an enforceable right to compensation in domestic law as articles 13 and 41 (which guarantee an effective remedy and just satisfaction) have not been incorporated into domestic law by the Human Rights Act 1988, so as to oblige the Home Secretary to construe the ex gratia scheme other than in the terms he has set out.[48] The case law also emphasises that an applicant wanting to rely on a Convention argument must raise this first with the Home Secretary before relying upon it in an application to judicially review his decision.[49]

## The court's role in relation to the ex gratia scheme

17.33   As emphasised earlier (see para 17.27), since the terms of the ex gratia scheme go beyond the implementation of the United Kingdom's international treaty obligations, the Secretary of State is free to choose the wording of the scheme. Subject to considerations of fairness, such as giving potential applicants sufficient notice, the Home Secretary could choose to change the wording of the scheme. Equally, it is not open to applicants to argue that the courts should increase the breadth of the scheme on the grounds, for example, of fairness or justice; the parameters of the scheme are for the Home Secretary.

---

45   *Benham v UK* (1996) 22 EHRR 293.

46   *R v Secretary of State for the Home Department ex p Garner* [1999] 11 Admin LR 595 and *R (Christofides) v Secretary of State for the Home Department* [2002] 1 WLR 2769.

47   *Edwards v UK* [1993] 15 EHRR 417; *Findlay v UK* (1997) 24 EHRR 221 and see *R v Secretary of State for the Home Department ex p Garner* [1999] 11 Admin LR 595.

48   *R (Christofides) v Secretary of State for the Home Department* [2002] 1 WLR 2769.

49   *R v Secretary of State for the Home Department ex p Garner* [1999] 11 Admin LR 595 and *R (Christofides) v Secretary of State for the Home Department* [2002] 1 WLR 2769.

17.34    As is apparent from the wording of the parliamentary statement quoted earlier (see para 17.17), the stated test for assessing whether payment will be made is whether the Home Secretary is satisfied that the first or second limb of the scheme is met. This is an issue for his assessment, rather than the court's assessment. However, the courts will review that assessment on the usual public law principles. Hence if the Home Secretary has arrived at a perverse decision or has failed to take into account a relevant consideration, or taken into account an irrelevant consideration or misdirected himself as to the stated terms of the scheme, the courts will be prepared to intervene. It has been held that as a refusal to pay compensation under the ex gratia scheme does not infringe ECHR articles 5(5) or 6, the level of scrutiny that the courts will employ of the Home Secretary's decision will be the normal *Wednesbury* principles, rather than a heightened form of scrutiny, recognised as appropriate where fundamental human rights are involved.[50]

17.35    As a public body, the Home Secretary is under a duty to act fairly and must give a reasonable opportunity for representations to be made, including on material obtained by him that may tell against the thrust of the application.[51] The duty to act fairly may also require the Home Secretary to act consistently as between applicants.[52]

17.36    Applications for judicial review that have challenged the rationality of the Home Secretary's conclusions have been based expressly or implicitly on the proposition that the parliamentary written answer and the adherence to it over successive years has given rise to a legitimate expectation on the part of applicants that their eligibility for compensation will be determined in accordance with its terms.[53] However, in *Re McFarland*[54] Lord Scott suggested that the Secretary

---

50    *R (Taylor) v Secretary of State for the Home Department* [2002] EWHC 2761 (Admin).

51    See, eg, *R v Secretary of State for the Home Department ex p Garner* [1999] 11 Admin LR 595.

52    *R (Christofides) v Secretary of State for the Home Department* [2002] 1 WLR 2769; *R (Mullen) v Secretary of State for the Home Department* [2004] 2 WLR 1140.

53    An expectation of this nature is referred to in *R (Christofides) v Secretary of State for the Home Department* [2002] 1 WLR 2769. In other contexts it has been held that a failure to act in accordance with a settled stated policy may give rise to grounds for judicial review, eg, *R v Commissioner of Police of the Metropolis ex p P* (1995) 160 JP 367 in relation to formal cautioning.

54    [2004] 1 WLR 1289.

of State had a broad freedom to depart from his stated policy, untrammelled by considerations of legitimate expectation. The issue arose directly in the *Mullen* case, where the House of Lords took a more restrictive view of the flexibility available to the Secretary of State. Mr Mullen claimed compensation under the ex gratia scheme on the basis that there had been serious default in relation to the unlawful way in which he had been deported from Zimbabwe to stand trial in the United Kingdom. The Home Secretary accepted that the circumstances fell within the serious default limb of the ex gratia scheme, but indicated that he would not pay compensation as Mr Mullen had been properly convicted of very serious terrorist offences at his trial and that it would be an affront to justice for someone who was rightly convicted to be paid compensation. The House of Lords accepted that the Home Secretary could do this in the particular circumstances. His actions did not defeat a legitimate expectation since even where there is a legitimate expectation of a particular benefit the decision-maker can decline to provide that benefit if the departure would not represent an abuse of power.[55] The House of Lords held that as it was accepted that the conviction was justified on the evidence produced at trial (and that evidence had not been subsequently undermined), it was open to the Home Secretary in the exercise of his discretion to decline to pay compensation. Furthermore, the Home Secretary had not breached the duty to act fairly as he had indicated to Mr Mullen's representatives that he was considering taking this course and had given them an opportunity to make further representations on the issue. Plainly, the circumstances in *Mullen* were striking and unusual and the House of Lords was also influenced by the particular offences involved – ie, serious terrorist crimes. It is less likely that the Secretary of State could claim a freedom to depart from the stated policy in a more conventional case of an unjust conviction, without it being classed as a breach of the applicant's legitimate expectation.

## Making an application

17.37  Applications should be made in writing to the Home Secretary and sent to the Claims Assessment Team, Office for Criminal Justice

---

55   *R v North and East Devon Health Authority ex p Coughlan* [2001] QB 213.

Reform, Trial Policy and Procedure Unit at the Home Office.[56] There is no prescribed form to use. The Home Office indicates that applicants should include their full name, date of birth, place and date of conviction or details of charge and the circumstances in which the conviction was reversed or the charges dropped; and the reason why it is contended that compensation is due. Applications can be made under both the statutory scheme and the ex gratia scheme in the alternative. The application should address the eligibility criteria relied upon. In cases of any complexity it is common to include detailed submissions as to why eligibility should be accepted, drafted by the applicant's solicitor or counsel. If relevant supporting documentation is available, such as the transcript of the Court of Appeal decision quashing the conviction or relevant witness statements or reports from the evidence used in the criminal case, they should be submitted. In any event the Home Office will obtain access to the papers relating to the case. There is no prescribed time limit for making an application.

17.38 The schemes are operated by a group of civil servants known as the Claims Assessment Team. The Team has delegated authority to refuse any application for compensation. Any decision to award compensation starts as a recommendation by a member of the team but the decision is taken by a Home Office minister.[57]

17.39 Once a decision has been made on eligibility a letter will be sent to the applicant or his or her advisers explaining that a payment will be made or, as the case may be, that the criteria are not met. In the latter instance detailed reasons for refusing the application will be given. If the applicant has any further representations to make in the light of that conclusion, additional submissions and/or supporting materials can be submitted. However, if the decision remains a negative one, there is no internal appeal and the only route of challenge is by way of an application for judicial review, as discussed above. If it is accepted that a payment will be made, the next stage for an applicant is to prepare the submission on the amount of compensation that should be awarded.

---

56 Applications can also be emailed to public.enquiries@homeoffice.gsi.gov.uk. For this and further practical guidance see the relevant page on the Home Office website:
www.homeoffice.gov.uk/justice/sentencing/wrongful/index.html.

57 *R (Daghir) v Secretary of State for the Home Department* [2004] ACD 33 at [7]. As the decision is taken in the name of the Home Secretary, he is referred to as the decision-maker throughout this text.

## Assessment of compensation

17.40 Criminal Justice Act 1988 s133(4) provides that if the Home Secretary decides that the applicant is entitled to compensation under the terms of the statute, the amount of such compensation is determined by an assessor appointed by the Home Secretary.[58] The Home Secretary has no role at all in the assessment of compensation under the statutory scheme and the assessor's determination is binding on him. The Home Secretary is not obliged to adopt the same approach to successful applications under the ex gratia scheme, but the then Home Secretary Mr Douglas Hurd indicated an intention to do so in 1985[59] and this has been the accepted practice ever since. The current assessor is Lord Brennan QC for England and Wales. There are separate assessors for Scotland and Northern Ireland.[60]

### Recoverable losses

17.41 The statutory provisions offer surprisingly little guidance as to the basis upon which the assessment of compensation is to be made. The only direct guidance is set out in section 133(4A), which provides:

> In assessing so much of any compensation payable under this section to or in respect of a person as is attributable to suffering, harm to reputation or similar damage, the assessor shall have regard in particular to –
> (a) the seriousness of the offence of which the person was convicted and the severity of the punishment resulting from the conviction;
> (b) the conduct of the investigation and prosecution of the offence; and
> (c) any other convictions of the person and any punishment resulting from them.[61]

17.42 Once an applicant is informed that he or she has been accepted as eligible for compensation under the statutory scheme or the ex gratia scheme, the Home Office sends to the applicant or his or her advisers a document entitled 'Compensation for Miscarriages of Justice: Notes for Successful Applicants' (the Note). This provides some indication of

---

58 Criminal Justice Act 1988 Sch 12 sets out criteria for the appointment of the assessor and contains provisions relating to remuneration, etc.

59 HC Written Answers, cols 691–692, 29 November 1985.

60 Contactable at the Justice Department, Criminal Justice Division, St Andrew's House, Regent Road, Edinburgh EH1 3DG and the Criminal Law Branch, Northern Ireland Office, Massey House, Stoney Road, Belfast BT4 3SX.

61 A deduction in the sum awarded to take account of other offending may be applied to all non-pecuniary losses other than personal injuries: *Independent Assessor v O'Brien, Hickey and Hickey* [2004] EWCA Civ 1035.

the heads of loss for which compensation can be awarded. They are the same whether eligibility is accepted under the statutory scheme or the ex gratia scheme. Both non-pecuniary and pecuniary losses can be claimed.

### Non-pecuniary losses

17.43    Specific aspects of non-pecuniary loss referred to in the Note are:

- loss of liberty;
- damage to character or reputation;
- hardship including mental suffering;
- injury to feelings and inconvenience.[62]

17.44    The Note reinforces Criminal Justice Act 1988 s133(4A)(b) in stating that: 'in considering the circumstances leading to the wrongful charge or conviction the assessor will also have regard, where appropriate, to the extent to which the situation might be attributable to any action, or failure to act, by the police or other public authority'.[63] It is clear that compensation will not include an element analogous to exemplary or punitive damages,[64] ie damages awarded to punish wrongdoing rather than to reflect loss suffered by the applicant.[65] In practice claims frequently include an element for personal injury, in particular if the applicant has suffered psychological trauma as a result of the wrongful conviction and its consequences. Compensation can also encompass factors relating to conditions of imprisonment, such as bullying from other inmates arising from the nature of the offence and/or additional restraints on liberty resulting from the applicant's security classification. Injury to feelings will include family separation, marriage breakdown and other personal circumstances as well as the anguish caused by the knowledge of wrongful conviction. The Note also spells out two factors that the assessor will take into account that may reduce compensation for non-pecuniary loss: first, any other convictions of the applicant and any punishment resulting from them[66] and second, the extent to which the circumstances leading up to the wrongful charge or conviction might have been contributed to by the applicant's

---

62  Note para 5 (set out in *Independent Assessor v O'Brien*).
63  Note para 7.
64  Note para 7.
65  The distinction between aggravated and exemplary damages is explained at para 14.33.
66  As required by Criminal Justice Act 1988 s133(4A).

own conduct.[67]

17.45    In the past, applicants' advisers have identified two inter-linked concerns over the assessment of non-pecuniary losses. First, that the sums awarded have been lower than the equivalent damages that might be expected in a civil claim, particularly in cases involving long periods of imprisonment for serious offences, where the applicant's suffering has been pronounced and protracted. Second, that the award of non-pecuniary loss tends to be made on a relatively broad-brush basis, aside from any sum for personal injuries, which is separately identified. This broad approach may not enable the applicant or his or her advisers to understand the basis of the calculation and/or to determine whether the assessment involved any error of law that could lead to a successful judicial review challenge. The Note states that 'the assessor will apply principles analogous to those governing the assessment of damages for civil wrongs'.[68] In *Independent Assessor v O'Brien, Hickey and Hickey*[69] the Court of Appeal rejected the assessor's argument that this only obliged him to apply civil law principles that were universal to all torts. The issue as to the scope of this obligation arose in the context of determining the extent to which the assessor was obliged to provide a breakdown of his award for non-pecuniary loss and to supply reasons for his assessment. The Court of Appeal held that:

- where the facts permit it and the civil law principles are sufficiently clear and analogous, the assessor should identify the heads of suffering and attempt to evaluate them in monetary terms by reference to the approach used in civil claims;
- where the losses relied on similar to those that would be claimed in tort for false imprisonment and/or malicious prosecution – ie, damages for loss of liberty, for the conditions and effects of imprisonment, for damage to reputation, for the stress of the prosecution process and conviction, and for damage to family life and other personal hardship – the assessment should be by reference to the common law principles applied in those torts;
- the assessor should explain as well as circumstances permit how he has reached his overall award, giving as much of a breakdown as is possible (this being in the interests of fairness, transparency and consistency);

---

67  Note para 7.
68  Note para 5.
69  [2004] EWCA Civ 1035.

- where practicable the assessor should identify as a separate sum the award for 'loss of liberty simpliciter' (ie, for the fact of loss of liberty and its commonplace consequences) and identify significant aggravating features, assessed individually or at least in aggregate.

17.46 The Court of Appeal's judgment emphasised that it was primarily a matter for the assessor to judge whether civil law principles were sufficiently clear and analogous and whether a breakdown of the type described was practical in any particular case. It therefore remains to be seen how much the assessor's approach will alter in practice as a result of this decision. However, the court plainly contemplated that the approach it advocated would be applied in instances where the losses sought were equivalent to those that would feature in a false imprisonment or malicious prosecution tort claim. This should cover the vast majority of successful applications to the Home Office. Accordingly, in those instances it is strongly arguable that the assessor should apply an approach analogous to that identified by the Court of Appeal in *Thompson and Hsu v Commissioner of Police of the Metropolis*[70] and include in the assessment (at least) separate sums for basic damages for loss of liberty; for the stress of the prosecution and conviction process; and for any physical and/or mental injury. Aggravated damages should then be separately identified and in appropriate cases – as the Court of Appeal in *O'Brien* contemplated – themselves broken down. An example might be a breakdown of the aggravated award into a sum for the hurt caused by police misconduct, a sum to reflect conditions of imprisonment peculiar to the applicant, and a sum to reflect specific injury to feelings (for example marriage breakdown or death of loved ones while the applicant was in custody).

17.47 The significance of obtaining a breakdown of the award for non-pecuniary losses is illustrated by the facts of Mr O'Brien's assessment. He had spent over 11 years in prison as a result of a wrongful conviction for murder. The assessor awarded a separate sum for psychiatric damage, a modest sum for 'police misconduct' and then a global figure of £125,000 for the consequences of imprisonment. Mr O'Brien complained that he could not ascertain how much of the £125,000 figure was intended to reflect his protracted loss of liberty, nor whether and to what extent injury to his reputation, damaging conditions of imprisonment and/or injury to feelings had formed a part

70  [1998] QB 498, CA. For a general discussion of this approach see chapter 14.

of this award. He also did not know to what extent aggravated damages had been awarded. The Court of Appeal ordered that the assessment be quashed and remitted to the assessor to provide a reasoned breakdown of the award in accordance with the Court's judgment. Mr O'Brien had wanted to challenge the £125,000 award as being irrationally low, given the length of time he had spent in prison and the other substantial factors of non-pecuniary loss he relied upon. The Administrative Court who heard the original judicial review application decided that the rationality challenge could not be assessed until a greater degree of breakdown had been provided, since it was currently impossible to determine the components of that award. The rationality challenge will be reconsidered when the assessor has provided the reasoned breakdown ordered by the court.

17.48    A difficult issue for applicants who were imprisoned for long periods is the assessment of the appropriate figure for loss of liberty. The assessor tends to stress the importance of keeping non-pecuniary awards proportionate to damages that would be awarded for pain and suffering and loss of amenity in personal injury cases.[71] Many consider the level of personal injury awards to be unduly low and their relatively modest level has a potential knock-on effect for awards for miscarriages of justice. However, it can be emphasised to the assessor that such awards do not include any parallel with a sum for aggravating damages – as will arise with many miscarriage applications. Furthermore, the best guide to the assessment of compensation for loss of liberty is to be found in the awards made in civil claims for this type of loss. Although there are no civil cases that deal with an appropriate sum for imprisonment of several years or more, the best assistance that can be obtained from awards made by the courts, at the time of writing, is as follows:

- *Lunt v Liverpool Justices:*[72] an award of £25,000 for 42 days of imprisonment (including some aggravating features), where no serious offence was involved.
- *R v Governor of Brockhill Prison ex p Evans:*[73] an award of £5,000 for 59 days of detention that came at the end of a lawful sentence of 18 months' imprisonment and involved no loss of reputation, humiliation, shock or injury to feelings.

71    The maximum figure in the Judicial Studies Board Guidelines (7th ed) is £200,000, being the upper bracket for awards for quadriplegia.

72    (1991) 5 March, CA, unreported.

73    [1998] 4 All ER 993, CA, affirmed [2000] 4 All ER 15, HL.

- *R v Secretaary of State for the Home Department ex p B:*[74] £18,000 to an unlawfully imprisoned asylum-seeker detained for two months in prison.
- *Popat v Barnes:*[75] where the claim failed, but the court said that had it succeeded damages would have been awarded in the sum of £50,000 for two years' wrongful detention and £35,000 for 18 months' such detention.

17.49    All the authorities depreciate the abstraction of a daily or monthly rate from one case and its slavish application to another instance of imprisonment. They also emphasise that damages will be calculated on a reducing scale, with the initial period of imprisonment attracting a higher award to reflect the element of shock involved.[76] Nonetheless, the above-mentioned authorities provide some indication of the figures that the assessor should have in mind. Arguably any award for a longer period of imprisonment should bear a reasonable relationship of proportionality to these figures.

17.50    Damages for personal injuries are assessed by reference to the Judicial Studies Board Guidelines (7th edition). The current assessor seems to be relatively sympathetic to the argument that the figures suggested in the guidelines for psychiatric injury do not take sufficient account of situations where the condition has developed over many years, so that a higher award is justified in such circumstances.[77]

17.51    The assessor usually awards interest at 2 per cent per annum on compensation for personal injuries from the date when the relevant conviction was quashed. He does not award interest on other non-pecuniary heads of damage.

17.52    Up until now, as far as the authors are aware, the assessor has declined to include in his award an element for the trauma and anxiety caused to relatives by the applicant's wrongful conviction. This refusal is based on the fact that such damages would not be recoverable in a false imprisonment or malicious prosecution claim at common law. An argument yet to be tested is whether in sufficiently serious circumstances a close relative could ground a claim in the civil

---

74    [1998] INLR 315.

75    [2004] EWHC 741.

76    £3,000 for the first day of imprisonment in a straightforward case was recommended by the Court of Appeal in *Thompson and Hsu v Commissioner of Police of the Metropolis* [1998] QB 498, CA.

77    By parity of reasoning with the approach of the Court of Appeal in *C v Flintshire CC* [2001] 2 FLR 33.

courts by reference to ECHR article 8 (that is, an unwarranted interference with the right to family life). If so, then it could be submitted
to the assessor that he should recognise this head of loss as well.

### Pecuniary losses

17.53  Specific aspects of pecuniary (that is, financial) loss referred to in the
Note are:

- loss of earnings as a result of the charge or conviction;
- loss of future earning capacity;
- additional consequential expenses incurred, for example for
  travelling, by members of the applicant's immediate family.[78]

17.54  However, the assessor will make an award in relation to all properly
evidenced financial losses flowing directly from the wrongful
conviction. Thus, the assessor will award compensation for properly
evidenced losses relating to consequential ill-health, for example the
costs of past or future medical treatment and/or (in cases of appropriately severe injury) costs of caring for the applicant for all or part of
the time. In the latter instance costs may be recovered even if the care
is provided gratuitously by relatives, on the basis of principles
established in relation to personal injury litigation. The assessor has
been known to award a modest sum to reflect care provided to the
applicant's children by other relatives while he or she was in prison.
Other losses associated with the loss of opportunity to work can be
claimed, such as pension losses. Losses could also relate to the
disruption to the running of a business. The assessor will also pay
reasonable costs incurred by the applicant or his or her immediate
family in campaigning against the wrongful charge or conviction.
The assessor will award a sum of money to cover reasonable expenses,
both incurred by the claimant in reversing his or her conviction and in
pursuing the claim for compensation.[79] This will cover, for example,
legal costs and the costs of obtaining appropriate expert reports.
Occasionally, the assessor has agreed to pay costs involved in the applicant or the family moving to a new area to avoid the stigma of the
conviction. Interest is usually paid on financial losses from when they
accrued.

17.55      Successive assessors have adopted a practice of deducting a figure
– usually 25 per cent – from the applicant's award for past loss of earn-

---

78  Note para 5.1.
79  Note para 6.

ings to reflect the fact that during the period of imprisonment he or she did not incur money on the usual, everyday expenses of board, lodging, clothing, etc. The legality of this approach was considered by the Court of Appeal in *Independent Assessor v O'Brien, Hickey and Hickey*.[80] The court held that the deduction was lawful, but relied upon two different bases in reaching this conclusion. Auld LJ held that the deduction should be made as the sums saved by the imprisonment would have been incurred as a necessary incidence of maintaining employment.[81] Longmore LJ did not consider that the sums in question fell within that principle, but decided that an analogy could be drawn with the deduction made for the money the claimant would have spent on him or herself when quantum was assessed in the 'lost years' cases such as *Pickett v British Rail Engineering*[82] (before claims for loss of earnings for the years between pre-accident life expectancy and post-accident diminished life expectancy were precluded by statute). The claimants had argued that neither analogy was apt and that the applicable common law principle was that in assessing quantum the law is not concerned with how the claimant would have spent the money he or she lost as a result of the injury sustained.[83] Although a deduction for saved living expenses is generally permissible, it is open to an applicant in a particular case to argue that in practice imprisonment did not result in a saving of expenditure or resulted in a more modest saving than is normal, for example if mortgage or rental payments on accommodation were maintained during the detention. Further, the applicant can submit that his or her lack of choice over food clothes and living accommodation whilst in prision, should be reflected in the non-pecuniary award.

## Proving loss

17.56 The applicant or his or her advisers should submit a witness statement, usually from the applicant, evidencing in detail each of the heads of loss relied upon. The statement should include a description of the wrongful charge or conviction and the processes undergone to rectify the injustice. The effect upon the applicant should be described in detail, including (where appropriate) the stress of imprisonment and

---

80  [2004] EWCA Civ 1035.
81  *Dews v National Coal Board* [1980] AC 136, HL indicates that a deduction in such circumstances is appropriate.
82  [1979] 1 All ER 774, HL.
83  *Dews v National Coal Board* [1980] AC 136, HL. Permission to appeal to the House of Lords on this issue has been sought.

consequential separation from family, any physical or psychological effects suffered, and damage to reputation. Any police or prosecutorial misconduct relied upon by way of aggravating features and the effect that knowledge of these matters had upon the applicant must be addressed specifically. However, as discussed in relation to the eligibility criteria above, the assessment will be based on misconduct already established by the judgment of the Court of Appeal when the conviction was quashed or by very clear evidence in existence to that effect; the assessor will not undertake a full fact-finding investigation into alleged misconduct that is denied by the authorities involved. The applicant's witness statement must also evidence each head of financial loss claimed.

17.57    Supporting documentation is also required. The nature of that documentation will depend upon what is claimed. For example, if a claim is made for psychiatric injury, the applicant will be expected to submit a medical report on his or her condition prepared by a consultant psychiatrist and accompanied by, where possible, all relevant medical records. Where a claim for future loss of earnings is made as a result of ongoing psychiatric injury, it is important to obtain a clear opinion from the medical expert as to the likely prognosis. If an applicant alleges that he or she suffered particularly badly during imprisonment, it may be useful to submit extracts from his or her prison records. If a claim is made for loss of reputation, it may be helpful to submit copies of articles that appeared in the media (national or local) at the time of the charge or conviction if they were damaging to the applicant. Sometimes a witness statement from a close relative is also useful in describing the extent to which the applicant was adversely affected by the matters complained of. Where loss of earnings is claimed, the assessor will expect to see, where available, documentary evidence supporting the applicant's pre-charge/conviction rate of earnings and/or documentation supporting work that it is said the applicant would have undertaken but for the wrongful charge or conviction, and the anticipated rates of remuneration. The expert instructed to prepare the supporting medical report in relation to any claim for injuries can also assess the likely costs of any future treatment that is proposed. In substantial loss of earnings cases, for example, where pension calculations are involved, the assessor will probably accept that it is reasonable for the applicant to instruct an expert to quantify loss and thus include the costs of this in the ultimate award. Further, where the applicant did not have a clear employment pattern before he or she was imprisoned, a report from an employment consultant may be valuable in indicating the likely earnings that the applicant would have gone on to command had it not been for the wrongful conviction. Employment consultants can also be useful in emphasising how difficult it will be for an applicant to return to work after a lengthy period of imprisonment, thereby assisting the future loss of earnings claim. In loss of earnings cases the applicant must submit details of any state benefits received during the period for which loss of earnings is claimed.[84] All financial losses claimed will need to be quantified, even if in the case of items such as travel costs and campaign costs, this can only be a rough approximation.

17.58   In cases where substantial awards are likely it is quite common for lawyers acting for the applicant to draft detailed submissions, setting out the heads of loss sought, the figures claimed for each item, the reasoning and evidence employed in support of this and any relevant case law. In more straightforward and modest claims a covering letter itemising the heads of loss sought and, where appropriate, the figures claimed may suffice.

## The process of assessment

17.59   Once the applicant has submitted the written material upon which the claim for compensation is based, the Home Office prepares a draft memorandum, which includes a statement of the facts of the case, details of the applicant's antecedents, and reference to any relevant special features of the case and to the applicant's submissions. The applicant or his or her solicitor is sent a draft of this memorandum to comment on and make any suggested amendments before it is supplied to the assessor. In cases where there is a substantial and/or complex claim for loss of earnings, the Home Office instructs its own accountants to prepare a report for the assessor. The applicant is provided with a copy of this document and given an opportunity to comment on it (which may involve reverting to the applicant's own expert first). Sometimes the assessor, through the Home Office, asks for further information on particular points from the applicant before the assessment is made.

17.60   In the vast majority of instances the assessment will be made on the written documentation provided to the assessor. He does have a discretion to hold an oral hearing, but is not obliged to do so in any particular case and thus far has tended to do so only in cases involving particularly novel and/or difficult points. Such meetings are very much the exception, rather than the rule.

---

84   Note para 5.1.

17.61   The assessor provides a written note setting out the basis of the award. Thereafter the assessor will not enter into correspondence about the award. The Home Office will usually only pass further representations to him if they show good grounds for believing that the assessor has failed to take a material point into account or has taken into account erroneous or irrelevant material.[85] In those circumstances the assessor will usually produce a supplementary note in response. There is no appeal process if the applicant is dissatisfied with the assessor's award. The only option is to bring an application for a judicial review of the assessor's award on the basis that he has erred on public law grounds, for example: by failing to apply analogous common law principles (as discussed in paras 17.45–17.46 above); by failing to take into account a relevant consideration; and/or by arriving at an irrationally low award.[86] The position is unsatisfactory from an applicant's perspective, as in a sig-nificant number of instances applicants will feel aggrieved that their award is too low, without being able to identify a specific error of law.

17.62   The assessment process can be protracted and has taken a number of years to complete in some complex cases. The Claims Assessment Team currently state that they aim to make decisions on eligibility within eight months of the application. The current time period for assessment of compensation once all relevant material has been assembled for the assessor is around six to nine months.

17.63   An applicant is not obliged to accept the assessor's award; he or she may decide to pursue a civil action instead for the same heads of loss.[87] For example, where a conviction has been quashed as a result of evidence that admissions relied upon at trial were fabricated or induced by bullying, a civil claim in malicious prosecution and/or misfeasance in a public office may be available.[88] Difficult issues may arise as to the inter-relationship between the Home Office application and a civil claim if the applicant wishes to pursue both, though there is nothing in principle to preclude an applicant from doing this. An applicant may wish to bring a civil action as well for a number of reasons. Exemplary damages cannot be recovered from the Home Office and these may be substantial in a case of serious police or prosecutorial

---

85   Note para 9.

86   A more detailed consideration of general public law grounds of challenge appears at paras 17.70 and 17.73.

87   Note para 9.

88   For a detailed consideration of these torts see chapter 7.

misconduct. Awards made by the assessor to reflect features comparable to basic and aggravated non-pecuniary damages in a civil claim,
have tended to be significantly lower than the equivalent award that
would be made by the courts. As discussed above, the assessor will
not make an award in relation to disputed misconduct and so a civil
action may have to be brought to prove that this occurred and thus to
vindicate the claimant and to establish accountability. On the other
hand, in cases where it is difficult to prove serious misconduct on the
part of state authorities, the applicant may be in a much stronger
position under the statutory compensation scheme than in a civil
action. If a civil action is commenced as well as an application made to
the Home Office, it is clear that the applicant cannot recover twice for
the same heads of loss. The Note states that if civil proceedings are
pursued, the Home Secretary will notify the defendant in those
proceedings of the award made by the assessor in order to avoid double
recovery.[89] However, this does not resolve the crucial question of who
should be the primary compensator – the police (or other defendant to
the civil action) or the Home Office. There are public policy grounds
for submitting that the wrongdoer, ie the tortfeasor in the civil claim,
should bear the primary responsibility to provide compensation and
thus should recompense the Home Office if the latter has already paid
out monies covering the same heads of loss.

17.64    Awards of compensation are confidential, unless the applicant
chooses to waive that confidentiality. Lack of information about other
assessments can present considerable problems for applicants and
their advisers in judging whether they have been awarded a fair and
reasonable amount. It also means that there is no overall check on
the consistency of the awards being made. However, over recent years
applicants' advisers have tended to circulate awards amongst
themselves (with their clients' consent).[90]

## Interim payments

17.65   The assessor has a discretion to make interim payments before the
overall award is finalised. These are then deducted from the overall
award before the final payment is made. In a case of any substance

---

89   Note para 10.
90   A number of previous awards are referred to in the Court of Appeal's
     judgments in *Independent Assessor v O'Brien, Hickey and Hickey* [2004] EWCA
     Civ 1035.

the assessor is usually prepared to make at least one significant interim payment. In cases where applicants have spent a long time in custody, interim awards may be made without the applicant needing to supply a great amount of detail or supporting information, since it is obvious that the overall award will be substantial and a letter summarising the applicant's circumstances and asking for an interim payment may suffice. In other cases the assessor may need to see some proof of loss (such as details of a loss of earnings claim or a medical report evidencing a substantial claim for consequential psychiatric injury) before he will agree to make an interim payment. More than one interim payment can be sought, though the applicant will need to submit additional material to justify a further award after the first has been made. The number of interim payments made and their level is very much within the assessor's discretion. It would be very difficult to mount a legal challenge to such decisions. Decisions on interim payments are usually made within about a month of the application for the payment being received. Advisers should be aware that receipt of a substantial interim payment may affect a client's eligibility for public funding from the Legal Services Commission (LSC) if he or she is also pursuing or contemplating a civil action.

## Funding work on an application to the Home Office

17.66    Work done by lawyers in establishing eligibility under either the statutory or the ex gratia scheme can be done under the Legal Help category of the LSC's funding.[91] If an application for judicial review is brought to challenge a refusal of eligibility, this can be funded by the LSC in the usual way for such litigation.[92] If an applicant has been accepted as eligible, reasonable legal costs and disbursements associated with the application will be paid by the assessor after the applicant has accepted the assessed award. The assessor will not make payments in advance to cover disbursements, such as the costs of expert's fees. However, in practice they are frequently funded out of interim payments received by applicants, unless the expert is prepared to wait for payment until after the assessment has been made.

91  Under an action against the police franchise.
92  See paras 11.47–11.52.

# Judicial review

17.67 Judicial review is the process by which the court supervises the lawfulness of the actions and decisions of inferior courts and tribunals, public bodies and individuals who carry out public duties and functions. In the context of this book it can, therefore, be used to supervise the activities of the Home Secretary, chief officers of police, police authorities, custody officers and even individual police officers in appropriate cases. Judicial review is also available against other bodies, officials and tribunals that have an impact on a person's access to legal remedies for police misconduct. The county courts and magistrates' courts are subject to judicial review, usually in relation to jurisdictional and procedural matters. Judicial review can also be used to review the decisions or refusals to act of the Independent Police Complaints Commission (IPCC), the Criminal Injuries Compensation Authority and coroners.

17.68 Judicial review is not usually considered appropriate by the court where there is another effective remedy, such as an appeal to a tribunal[93] or a statutory complaints procedure – save in circumstances where there is great urgency and interim relief (such as an injunction) is required, or where the case concerns important questions of law which it is clear that the alternative remedy could not cope with. In the context of police misconduct, the police complaints system is the obvious alternative remedy. However, the system is designed to identify whether officers should face criminal or disciplinary proceedings, and is rarely an appropriate forum to deal with disputes as to the extent of powers under, for example, the Police and Criminal Evidence Act 1984.

17.69 If in doubt, both procedures can be invoked in tandem. The court will have the power, if it thinks appropriate, to stay the judicial review application if it thinks that the issue can be dealt with through the complaints procedure.

17.70 The powers of the court are limited. It can usually take action on a decision or a refusal to act only where one of the following applies:

- a decision is illegal in that there was no power for it to be made (ultra vires); [94]

---

93 *R v Chief Constable of Merseyside ex p Calveley* [1986] QB 424, CA.

94 See, eg, *R v Secretary of State for the Home Department ex p Northumbria Police Authority* [1989] QB 26 – unsuccessful application by a police authority for a declaration that the Home Secretary had no general power to issue chief constables with plastic bullets.

- there has been misinterpretation of the meaning of a power or duty and the way it has been applied in a particular case (error of law);[95]
- the decision is so unreasonable as to be perverse (often called *Wednesbury* unreasonableness);[96]
- relevant factors have not been taken into account or irrelevant factors have been taken into account in the decision-making process;
- proceedings have been conducted unfairly (breach of natural justice);

Where Convention rights as listed in the Human Rights Act 1998 are concerned, if an action is incompatible with such a right and therefore unlawful then judical review may be appropriate. Where fundamental rights are concerned the court will also embark on an exercise to decide whether an action of the police is proportionate to the damage done to a person's human rights.[97]

17.71    Where the decision-making process has been shown to be at fault, the court has the power to make one or more of the following orders:[98]

- quash a decision, by a quashing order, with the effect that the person or body has to reconsider the decision (for example, if the IPCC wrongly decides to use its powers to dispense with an investigation);
- order a person or body to carry out its public duty by a mandatory order (for example, compel a chief officer to provide copies of seized documents). This order is sometimes made if there is doubt that the public body will otherwise comply with the findings made by the court;
- order a person not to act in an unlawful way by a prohibiting order (for example, to prevent an inferior court from hearing a case over which it has no jurisdiction);
- grant an injunction (for example, to prevent the continuation of an unlawful road block);

---

95  See, eg, *R v South Western Magistrates' Court ex p Cofie* [1997] 1 WLR 885 – need to specify parts of premises to be searched for warrant to be lawful.

96  After the case of *Associated Provincial Picture Houses Ltd v Wednesbury Corp* [1948] 1 KB 223, CA.

97  *R (Daly) v Secretary of State for the Home Department* [2001] 2 AC 532 and see *R v Chief Constable of Sussex ex p International Trade Ferry Ltd* [1998] 3 WLR 1260.

98  CPR 54.2.

- make a declaration of the rights of the parties (for example, by declaring that a solicitor was wrongly excluded from a police station pursuant to Police and Criminal Evidence Act 1984 s58);
- award damages[99] (but only where a private law civil wrong can be proved as well as the public law grounds for judicial review. This can include damages for action incompatible with Convention rights included in Sch 1 to the Human Rights Act 1998).

17.72 In practice, the courts have been reluctant to interfere where the challenge brought has been to the exercise of wide police powers or duties that are generally or broadly expressed, such as the general duty to enforce the law. The courts are likely to find that it is a matter for the police how they use their resources to fight crime and enforce the law. Notable examples of actions that have been brought (but failed) over the years include:

- An attempt to force the police to enforce the Obscene Publications Act and bring obscene articles before the court. The Court of Appeal refused to interfere in the decisions of the police as to whether to devote resources to this issue.[100]
- An attempt by the Central Electricity Generating Board to force a chief constable to remove demonstrators from the site of a proposed nuclear power station. The demonstrators were peaceful and non-violent throughout. The Court of Appeal decided that although the police had power to enter the site and eject the demonstrators, it was for them to decide how to exercise that power.[101]

17.73 There is a large number of cases where decisions concerning police powers and misconduct have been challenged by judicial review. The following list should give practitioners a flavour of the sort of cases which can be brought.[102]

- whether the Police Complaints Authority had the power to revoke a decision to allow the police to dispense with the investigation of a complaint;[103]

---

99  CPR 54.3 and Supreme Court Act 1981 s31(4).

100  *R v Commissioner of Police of the Metropolis ex p Blackburn (No 3)* [1973] 1 All ER 324, CA.

101  *R v Chief Constable of Devon and Cornwall ex p CEGB* [1981] 3 All ER 826.

102  See also *Judicial Review proceedings: a practitioner's guide* (2nd ed, LAG, 2004) Ch 12 for further examples.

103  *R (Wilkinson) v Police Complaints Authority* [2004] EWHC 678, 19 March 2004.

- whether the refusal to allow a complainant's solicitor to attend a disciplinary hearing was unlawful;[104]
- whether the decision by the police to deny solicitors access to their clients at a magistrates' court before 10am was unlawful;[105]
- the disclosure of documents relating to an investigation by the Police Complaints Authority into a complaint of serious police misconduct (the appellant was not entitled to disclosure of documents);[106]
- whether the detention by police of passengers on a coach en route to an anti-war demonstration and their forced return to London was incompatible with rights under ECHR article 5;[107]
- the limits of the powers under Extradition Act 1989 s8 in relation to a search;[108]
- the execution by the police of search warrants;[109]
- whether it was lawful for the police to issue a blanket direction excluding a solicitor's representative from police stations in the area;[110]
- the approach taken in assessing an award of compensation in respect of sufferings following a miscarriage of justice;[111]
- the police retention of records in relation to an alleged paedophile whose conviction was quashed on appeal;[112]
- a decision whether or not to bring a prosecution against police officers following an unlawful killing verdict in an inquest involving a death in custody;[113]
- a probationary constable has successfully challenged the decision of his chief constable to dismiss him without a disciplinary hearing.[114]

---

104   *R (Melia) v Merseyside Police* [2003] EWHC 1121, 11 April 2003.
105   *R v Chief Constable of South Wales ex p Merrick* [1994] 1 WLR 663.
106   *R (Green) v Police Complaints Authority* [2004] 1 WLR 725.
107   *R (Laporte) v Chief Constable of Gloucestershire* [2004] 2 All ER 874.
108   *R v Commissioner of the Police of the Metropolis ex p Rottman* [2002] 2 WLR 1315.
109   *R v Chief Constable of Lancashire ex p Parker* [1993] QB 577, DC.
110   *R v Chief Constable of Northumbria ex p Thompson* (2002) 1 WLR 1342.
111   *Independent Assessor v O'Brien, Hickey and Hickey* [2004] EWCA Civ 1035.
112   *R v Chief Constable of Greater Manchester ex p Coombs* (2000) LTL 24/78/2000.
113   *R v DPP ex p Manning* [2001] QB 330.
114   *R v Chief Constable of West Midlands ex p Carroll* (1994) 7 Admin LR 45, CA.

## Procedure[115]

17.74　Prior to making an application for permission to claim for judicial review it is usually necessary to write a pre-action protocol letter to the proposed defendant.[116] This sets out the decision it is proposed to challenge, why it is said that the decision is unlawful, what the defendant is required to do to rectify the situation (for example, agree to reconsider the decision made) and what information is sought by the claimant. Increasingly, defendants are willing to agree to reconsider decisions at this early stage if they feel that permission will be granted if the application goes ahead. The application for permission can be brought if the response to the pre-action protocol letter does not provide a solution for the claimant. Public funding to commence proceedings may not be granted until after a pre-action protocol letter has been written and the response (if any) considered.

### Public funding

17.75　There are specific criteria for the funding of judicial review cases in the Funding Code.[117] Judicial review cases are a priority under the Code. As judicial review applications (if they proceed to a full hearing) will often result in a high court judge ruling on the interpretation of statutory provisions or the lawfulness of practices and policies adopted by public bodies (such as the police or the IPCC), there is sometimes scope to argue that there is a significant wider public interest which goes beyond the benefits available to the individual public funding application. The LSC has established a Public Interest Advisory Panel (PIAP) to assist it on decision-making in cases raising public interest issues. The panel includes a member of the LSC as chairman and representatives from consumer organisations, legal representatives and experts in public interest litigation (such as Liberty, Justice etc). If a claimant's case raises potentially significant wider public interest issues then a request to the LSC to refer the case to the PIAP should be considered, especially if the benefits to the claimant are limited or if prospects of success are uncertain.

---

115　Only a very brief description of the procedure is provided here. The relevant rules are to be found in CPR Pt 54 and the accompanying Practice Direction 54. The Legal Action Group publishes a practitioners' guide to judicial review: Jonathan Manning, *Judicial Review Proceedings* (2nd ed). A useful guide is reproduced on the Administrative Court section of the Court Service website, www.courtservice.gov.uk.

116　A precedent is set out in PD54.

117　Considerable guidance is offered in the LSC Manual, Part C – the Funding Code; Decision making Guidance, s16.

## Applying for permission

17.76   Applications for judicial review are dealt with in two stages. First, an application must be made to the court for permission to apply for judicial review;[118] if this has been granted, the application itself is made.

17.77   The initial procedure is relatively simple, requiring only one form which sets out the details of the decision to be challenged, the grounds to be relied upon, and a statement of the facts relied upon. However, counsel is often instructed to settle the grounds for claiming judicial review and sometimes the statement of facts as well. Applications for permission to move for judicial review must be made by claim form – Form N461. The claim form must include or be accompanied by:[119]

- a detailed statement of the claimant's grounds for bringing the claim for judicial review;
- a statement of the facts relied on;
- any application to extend the time limit for filing the claim form;
- any application for directions.

17.78   Where the claimant is seeking to raise any issue under the Human Rights Act (HRA) 1998, or seeks a remedy available under that Act, the claim form must include specific details of the Convention right breached and the remedy sought. Special rules apply if a declaration of incompatibility is sought under HRA 1998 s4[120] (see chapter 10). There are other requirements for the format of the bundle to be filed with the court including relevant statutory material, supporting documentation and a list of essential reading.[121]

17.79   Even if public funding is refused or the claimant would not qualify financially, consideration should still be given to applying for permission on the papers. The cost of lodging the permission application is low – only £30 in 2004. If permission is refused on the papers (see para 17.81) it is unusual for defendants to seek costs, and it seems that they will only be entitled, in other than exceptional cases,[122] to the cost of the preparation of the acknowledgement of service (see para 17.81) in any event, even if the application is pursued to an oral hearing.[123]

---

118   CPR 54.4.
119   CPR PD 54 para 5.6.
120   CPR PD 54 para 5.3 and CPR PD 16 para 15.
121   CPR 54.6(2) and PD 54 para 5.9.
122   *R (Mount Cook Land Ltd) v Westminster CC* [2004] CP Rep 12.
123   *R v Commissioner for Local Administration ex p Leach* [2001] CP Rep 97.

17.80    The application for permission must be brought promptly and, at the very latest, within three months of the date when the grounds for the application first arose,[124] unless the court considers that there are good reasons for extending the time limit[125] (for example, unavoidable delay in applying for public funding)[126]. However, even if a person is within the three-month time limit, the application can still be dismissed if the delay which has ensued would substantially prejudice the other side, any other person or is detrimental to good administration.[127] This might be a factor to consider, for example, in judicial review applications involving the disciplinary process where the officer who is subject to proceedings may object if the application is not made speedily. The claim form must be served on the defendant and other interested parties[128] within seven days of the date of issue.[129]

17.81    The defendant should file an acknowledgement of service within 21 days (or less if the court orders),[130] and this can set out the summary of grounds opposing the grant of permission. The application will generally be considered on the papers first of all.[131] This can take a few weeks and so there is an urgency procedure whereby a request can be made for a judge to consider the papers in a matter of days (or even hours if necessary) and for interim relief if this is required. If a judge then refuses the application on the papers, written reasons are provided.[132] If permission is refused at this stage on the papers, the application can be renewed, as of right, within seven days, using another straightforward form, for an oral hearing of the application for permission.[133] Advisers should take care to ensure that the judge's observations and the summary grounds opposing the claim are fully considered to see if they provide a complete answer to the claim.

17.82    At the permission stage, the court has to determine whether, on the merits, the application is fit for further investigation at a full hearing with both sides present. To this extent, the permission stage acts as a filter to eliminate pointless or hopeless applications. Permission

---

124    CPR 54.5.
125    CPR 3.1(2)(a).
126    *R v Stratford-upon-Avon DC ex p Jackson* [1985] 1 WLR 1319.
127    Supreme Court Act 1981 s31(6).
128    A person directly affected by the claim: CPR 54.1(2)(f).
129    CPR 54.7.
130    CPR 54.8.
131    CPR PD 54 para 8.4.
132    CPR 54.12(2).
133    CPR 54.12(3)(4).

should be granted if an arguable case has been presented, although in practice there is great disparity between the rates of grant of permission between different judges, which suggests that some apply a higher standard of arguability than others.

17.83    There may also be a question as to whether the claimant has standing to make the application, that is, a 'sufficient interest' in the case.[134] Generally speaking, a claimant with a personal interest in the matter will always have standing (for example, the complainant in a judicial review about the IPCC's handling of a complaint; or a member of the family of the deceased in a judicial review about the inquest where there has been a death in custody). However, judges are now more likely to accept that a community organisation or pressure group can qualify under this test. Much will depend on how involved the group is with the subject matter of the particular application.[135]

17.84    The court can give directions when granting permission.[136] This can include expediting the hearing if necessary. The court can also grant a stay of the proceedings or process challenged (such as a magistrates' court hearing or the IPCC complaints process) if, for example, the judicial review application will determine the lawfulness of part of the process or proceedings.[137] Alternatively, the court can exercise its power to grant an interim injunction to achieve the same effect.[138]

## After the grant of permission

17.85    Where permission is granted, this may act as a lever on the defendant to reconsider its position and perhaps to reach a settlement on the issue before the full hearing takes place. If permission is granted, the court will serve the order on the parties,[139] and the claimant should lodge a further fee of £120 (in 2005) with the administrative court office within seven days of service of the judge's decision. If such fee is not lodged, the file may be closed. Unless expedition is ordered, a full hearing of the application will usually take place some months later. In judicial review cases discovery is very unusual (although it is

---

134    Supreme Court Act 1981 s31(3).
135    See, eg, *R v Secretary of State for Foreign and Commonwealth Affairs ex p World Development Movement* [1995] 1 WLR 386.
136    CPR 54.10(1).
137    CPR 54.10(2).
138    CPR 25.1(a).
139    CPR 54.11.

available) and witnesses are almost never called at the full hearing, where argument concentrates on the extent and/or exercise of the legal powers and duties involved, as opposed to the facts of the case.

17.86 A defendant or interested party who wishes to contest the claim (or support it on additional grounds) must, within 35 days of service of the order granting permission, file and serve his or her detailed grounds and written evidence.[140]

17.87 The procedure is fairly straightforward thereafter for the full hearing. The claimant must file a skeleton argument and a trial bundle (which is likely to be the bundle filed for the permission hearing with additional material added to it) 21 working days before the hearing date and the defendant must respond 14 working days before the hearing date.[141] Hearings rarely last more than a day or possibly two before a high court judge, although two judges (a Divisional Court) must hear cases which concern a 'criminal cause or matter'. The judge will usually produce a judgment setting out his or her conclusions as to the application of the law before considering the remedy which should follow. The usual rules for appealing to the Court of Appeal apply.[142]

## Criminal Injuries Compensation Scheme

17.88 The Criminal Injuries Compensation Scheme[143] allows for payments to be made to victims of crimes of violence. A person assaulted by the police is as much the victim of a crime as of a civil wrong. A victim of a police crime of violence is therefore as free as the next person to make a claim.

17.89 A claim for damages in the civil courts is almost always preferable to a claim under the Scheme. Court procedures are designed to allow the evidence to be probed and tested and for all the issues to be thoroughly explored. The procedures under the Scheme do not anticipate that the 'criminal' will participate and deny the crime, yet this has happened in claims alleging police violence. Furthermore, as will be seen below, the level of compensation awarded can be lower than that in the courts.

---

140 CPR 54.14.
141 CPR PD 54 paras 15 and 16.
142 CPR Pt 52.
143 Criminal Injuries Compensation Scheme 2001 (Home Office) (Issue No One 4/01) referred to in this chapter as the 'Scheme'.

17.90    The main advantage of the scheme is that it is cheap and simple. It is usually most appropriate if a person does not qualify for public funding and cannot afford a lawyer or if there is no other means of funding a civil action. The scheme can be used for claims arising out of crimes of violence that result in death. The procedure for such claims is not described in detail here, since claims under the Scheme alleging that police violence resulted in death are rarely if ever made: their complexity makes them suitable for civil claims in the courts.

## The Scheme

17.91    The Scheme is administered by the Criminal Injuries Compensation Authority (CICA).[144] Broadly speaking the Scheme allows financial awards to be made:

- to recognise physical and mental injuries caused by violent crimes;
- in certain circumstances, to compensate for past or future lost earnings or special expenses caused by a violent crime; and
- for the death of a close relative as a result of a violent crime, including, in some cases, compensation for the loss of earnings for the person who was killed.

17.92    The current Scheme applies to all applications received on or after 1 April 2001. For applications made before 1 April 1996, compensation under the scheme was assessed on common law principles and in much the same way that personal injury claims were dealt with in the civil courts at the time. In 1996, the system changed and a tariff of injuries was introduced.[145] The tariff is a list of fixed compensation payments for specific types of injury. The 1996 scheme was changed in 2001 with the new scheme continuing to use a tariff of injuries. Applicants do not need legal advice or representation to apply for compensation. The scheme specifically provides that where an applicant is represented, the cost of the representation will not be met by the CICA.[146]

144    Criminal Injuries Compensation Authority, Tay House, 300 Bath Street, Glasgow, G24 4LN (www.cica.gov.uk).

145    *R v Secretary of State for the Home Department ex p C* (1999) *Independent* 22 February held that the Home Secretary had not acted unlawfully by producing a Scheme, pursuant to the Criminal Injuries Compensation Act 1995, that categorised injuries into bands of seriousness.

146    2001 Scheme, para 19 and *C v Secretary of State for the Home Department* (2003) 22 May, QBD, Mitting J, unreported, which held that a claimant's rights under the ECHR were not breached by the CICA's refusal to pay the claimant's cost of representation to it.

## The main rules of the Scheme

17.93 Compensation can be paid under the Scheme to an applicant who:

- has sustained a criminal injury on or after 1 August 1964 and
- was in Great Britain when injured.

17.94 Criminal injuries include personal injuries directly attributable to a crime of violence. This includes personal injury (including a fatal injury), mental injury and disease. Mental injury or disease may result either directly from the physical injury or (in more limited circumstances) from a sexual offence or may occur without any physical injury.[147]

17.95 The CICA can refuse or reduce an award due to:

- the applicant's failure to inform the police or others of the circumstances of the injury;
- the applicant's failure to co-operate with the police or in attempting to bring the assailant to justice;
- the applicant's failure to give reasonable assistance to the CICA;
- the applicant's conduct, criminal record or character.

17.96 The applicant should also have:

- reported the incident personally to the police as soon as he or she was able to do so; and
- sent the CICA his or her application so that it was received within two years of the date of the incident which caused the injury.

The CICA may still accept the application if the applicant can show good reasons why he or she has not met one or both of the above conditions.

17.97 Once the CICA receives the application and its enquiries show that the applicant is entitled to an award, the CICA assesses the size of any award by using the tariff of injuries.

17.98 The applicant may also get additional compensation if, as a result of a violent crime, he or she has lost earnings or the ability to earn for longer than 28 weeks.[148]

17.99 An applicant may also be eligible for compensation if he or she was a dependant or a close relative of a victim of violent crime who has since died. To be eligible under this provision, a claimant needs to be either:

147  2001 Scheme, para 9.
148  2001 Scheme para 30.

- the partner of the deceased (a person who is living together with the deceased as husband and wife or as a same sex partner in the same household immediately before the date of death and who, unless formally married to him or her, had been so living throughout the two years before that date) or a spouse or former spouse of the deceased who was financially supported by him or her immediately before the date of death; or
- a natural parent of the deceased, or a person who was not the natural parent of the deceased, provided that he or she was accepted by the deceased as a parent of his or her family; or
- a natural child of the deceased, or a person who was not the natural child, provided that he or she was accepted by the deceased as a child of his or her family, or was dependent on him or her.[149]

## How to apply

17.100  Application forms are available from the CICA or can also be filled in online at www.cica.gov.uk. Full information should be included in the application form including a statement, and the police station to which the matter was reported, the crime reference number and full details of the applicant's GP and any hospital where he or she was treated.

17.101  An applicant should be aware that by signing the application form, he or she is giving permission to the CICA to receive all the records, evidence and other information about the applicant and the circumstance of the injury. This includes information about the applicant's medical condition and the evidence that he or she may have given to the police as well as information about the applicant's income, tax and benefits situation (if the claim is being made for loss of earnings or expenses)

## Consideration of applications

17.102  Claims officers in the Claims Assessment Section of the CICA determine claims for compensation in accordance with the Scheme.

17.103  The CICA aims to provide a decision in 90 per cent of cases within 12 months of receiving the application.[150] In most cases, this will be a decision about whether or not the applicant is eligible for an award

---

149  2001 Scheme para 38.
150  Guide to 2001 Compensation Scheme (January 2004), para 33.

plus, as appropriate, the amount of the award. However, cases where there is a criminal trial and cases involving future loss of earnings or future medical expenses, generally take longer than a year to settle. In these cases applicants are able to ask for an interim payment in appropriate cases.

17.104    If an applicant disagrees with a decision of the Claims Assessment Section, he or she is entitled to ask for a more senior officer within the authority to review this. Applicants must complete a review form for this to take place.

17.105    If applicants wish to appeal against the reviewed decision, an appeal is made to the Criminal Injuries Compensation Appeals Panel which is independent of the authority. An appeal form should be used for this. Where an appeal is referred for hearing, the hearing will take place before at least two adjudicators. It is open to the appellant to bring a friend or a legal adviser to assist in presenting his or her case in the appeal hearing, but the cost of representation will not be met by the Authority or the Panel. The adjudicators may, however, direct the Panel to meet reasonable expenses incurred by the appellant and any person who intends to give any evidence at the hearing.[151]

17.106    The procedure at hearings is informal. The adjudicators are not bound by any rules of evidence which may prevent a court from admitting any document or other matter or statement in evidence. The appellant, the claims officer presenting the appeal and the adjudicators may call witnesses to give evidence and may cross-examine them. In practice, it will reflect very poorly on the police if they refuse to attend and it seems that generally they agree to do so. Hearings take place in private.

## Police (Property) Act 1897

17.107 The Police (Property) Act 1897 provides a procedure under which application can be made to the magistrates' court for the return of property that is being held by the police. The main purpose of the Act is to protect the police against civil claims in the event of them 'returning' goods to someone who later turns out not to be the real owner. The procedure will not be appropriate if there is likely to be disagreement about the applicant's right to the goods, as magistrates are not obliged to make an order and, in practice, will probably decline to make a determination if there is a complicated point of law or fact

---

151  2001 Scheme, para 74.

at issue.[152] The procedure may be appropriate, however, in cases where it is felt that a particular police officer is acting unreasonably in refusing to return goods and the priority is to obtain the return of the goods, rather than compensation. An application under this procedure may be used, among other circumstances, where property has been seized and retained by the police under the power contained in the Police and Criminal Evidence Act 1984.[153] Specific statutory provisions permitting police to destroy or otherwise dispose of items seized take precedence over the right to apply for their recovery under the 1897 Act.[154]

## The Court's Powers

17.108    The magistrates have the power to order goods to be delivered to the person who appears to be the owner of the goods or, if the owner cannot be ascertained, to make such order in respect of the property as seems fit.[155] In *Raymond Lyons & Co v Commissioner of Police of the Metropolis*[156] the Divisional Court indicated that magistrates should apply the ordinary popular meaning to the concept of an 'owner'. However, in *R (Carter) v Ipswich Magistrates' Court*[157] the Divisional Court indicated that the Court of Appeal's decision in *Webb v Chief Constable of Merseyside*[158] should apply to a consideration of ownership under the Police (Property) Act 1897.[159] This leaves uncertain the approach that magistrates should take to disputed issues of ownership. In *R (Haley) v Chief Constable of Northumbria*[160] it was argued that it was inappropriate for magistrates to apply the civil law

152    *Raymond Lyons & Co v Commissioner of Police of the Metropolis* [1975] 1 All ER 335, dictum of Lord Widgery at 338 applied in *Hussain v Singh* (1997) 3 November, DC, unreported, and in *R (Haley) v Chief Constable of Northumbria* [2002] EWHC 1942 (Admin).

153    Section 22(5).

154    See, eg, in relation to knives the Knives (Forfeited Property) Regulations 1997 SI No 1907, or in relation to motor vehicles the Police (Retention and Disposal of Vehicles) Regulations 1995 SI No 723.

155    Police (Property) Act 1897 s1(1).

156    [1975] 1 All ER 335.

157    [2002] EWHC 332 (Admin).

158    [2000] 1 All ER 209.

159    *Webb v Chief Constable of Merseyside* [2000] All ER 209, *Costello v Chief Constable of Derbyshire* [2001] 3 All ER 150 and *Gough v Chief Constable of West Midlands* [2004] EWCA Civ 206 are discussed in ch 9 in relation to seizure of goods, see para 9.26 in particular. They concern the circumstances in which police are obliged to return items to suspected thieves or other wrongdoers.

160    [2002] EWHC 1942 (Admin).

concepts identified in *Webb* and *Costello* as this was not in keeping with their obligation to apply an everyday popular meaning to the concept of ownership. The issue was not directly resolved by the Divisional Court's decision. However, it may well be that any claim which would involve issues of this nature is too complex for the Police (Property) Act 1897 procedure and should be framed as a claim in conversion in the civil courts.

17.109    As with claims in conversion, an issue has arisen in Police (Property) Act 1897 applications, as to the extent to which magistrates are entitled to take into account considerations of public policy in determining whether to grant the order sought: if they suspect the complainant acquired the item by unlawful means (but this has not been proved to the criminal standard in relation to an offence), are they obliged to order it to be returned to him or her? In *Chief Constable of West Midlands v White*[161] the Court of Appeal held that the magistrates were entitled to return the proceeds of unlicensed sale of alcohol to the owner. In *R (Carter) v Ipswich Magistrates' Court*[162] the Administrative Court held that as the complainant was the owner of the monies in question (which were linked to the hire of a third party to commit a murder) and the police had no right to retain the money, the magistrates should have ordered its return to him; the power to make such order as seems fit only arises under the second limb of section 1(1), ie, if the owner cannot be ascertained. Accordingly, if ownership of the items is established, the magistrates will have very little opportunity to take public policy considerations into account.

17.110    The advantages of the procedure over a civil claim in the county court or High Court is that it is simple, quick and cheap. The disadvantages are that compensation will not be awarded and the court does not have to make an order. It is, therefore, a suitable procedure if all that is wanted is the return of the goods. If a claimant wants compensation or wants to draw public attention to the manner in which the goods were seized, he or she should sue in the civil courts.

## The property

17.111    The procedure can be used to recover property that 'has come into the possession of the police in connection with their investigation of a suspected offence'.[163] This definition should cover most cases where the

---

161   (1992) 157 JP 222.
162   [2002] EWHC 332 (Admin).
163   Police (Property) Act 1897 s1(1) as amended by Criminal Justice Act 1972 s58 and Police (Property) Act 1997 s4.

police have seized goods, but it may not apply, say, to lost property. It is not necessary that anyone should have been charged or arrested in relation to suspected offence, or even that an offence has been committed.[164] It appears that property can include money.[165] For the jurisdiction to arise, the police must have had the relevant property in their possession at some point.[166] The jurisdiction can extend to the proceeds of sale of an item; for example where the police have sold perishable items and held the cash obtained in lieu.[167]

17.112　　Where a person is convicted of an offence and the court is satisfied that any property lawfully seized from him or her or under his or her possession or control at the time of apprehension, has been used or was intended for use in the commission of the offence, an order can be made depriving the person of his or her rights in the property and providing that it be taken into the possession of the police.[168] If property is then held by the police as a result of such an order being made, an owner of the property has six months in which to apply to the magistrates' court to recover the goods, if he or she can show that he or she did not consent to the offender having possession of the property or did not know and had no reason to suspect that it would be used for a criminal purpose.[169] Thus if, say, a friend borrowed some tools that were later forfeited as being used for a burglary, their owner could apply to get them back if he or she honestly believed that the friend had wanted to use them to put up shelves at home.

## Making an application

17.113　Either the police or anyone who claims the goods can apply. In a straightforward case, the owner will simply be claiming his or her own property, but it may happen that the police apply for an order to allow them to dispose of the goods to someone else. The Act is commonly used, for example, where the police seek to return stolen property but are unsure who is the lawful owner. In such cases, there is no requirement that everyone claiming ownership has to be notified

---

164　*R (Curtis) v Justices of Louth* [1916] 2 IR 616.

165　*Chief Constable of West Midlands v White* (1992) 157 JP 222.

166　*Chief Constable of Nottinghamshire v Parkin* (2000) 24 February, QBD, unreported.

167　See Police (Property) Act 1897 s2(3) and *Hussain v Singh* (1997) 3 November, DC, unreported.

168　Powers of Criminal Courts (Sentencing) Act 2000 s143.

169　Powers of Criminal Courts (Sentencing) Act 2000 s144.

of the application, although in practice either the police or the court would usually attempt to do so.

17.114     If a criminal case has been heard in the magistrates' court, it is usual to deal with any application for an order at the end of the hearing. If there has been a trial at the Crown Court or if there has been no trial at all, applications are dealt with in separate magistrates' court proceedings, usually started by complaint and summons, whereby the court gives notice of the complaint and summonses the police to appear before the magistrates.[170] It will generally be good practice to write to the police first, asking for the return of the property. If the police refuse or fail to return the goods, a letter can be sent to the magistrates' court applying for a summons.[171]

## Effect of an order

17.115 The court can only make an order for the recovery of the property in favour of the person who appears to be the owner of the goods. The making of an order does not immediately give any greater right to the goods than existed before the order. So, if someone else has a better claim to them, he or she can bring civil proceedings against the person in possession of the goods for their recovery. However, he or she must do so within six months of the order being made.[172] After that time, he or she cannot bring a civil claim, and, it seems, the goods become the property of the person who recovered them from the police.[173]

17.116     If the magistrates simply make no order when an application is made (that is, they decline to make an order in favour of the person applying or anyone else), there is nothing to stop the applicant suing the police in the civil courts for the return of the property or for damages for conversion.[174] As no order will have been made by the magistrates, the six-month time limit for commencing the action does not apply.

---

170  Magistrates' Courts Act 1980 s51 (amended by Courts Act 2003 s47(1));
see *R v Uxbridge JJ ex p Commissioner of Police of the Metropolis* [1981] 3 All ER 129, CA.

171  See the suggested precedent at appendix C.

172  Police (Property) Act 1897 s1(2).

173  *Irving v National Provincial Bank* [1962] 2 QB 73.

174  *Rashid v Chief Constable of Northumbria* (1990) 17 December, CA, unreported.

## Disposal of the goods by the police

17.117   The police are generally entitled to dispose of goods after 12 months if no order is made under the Act.[175] It is therefore wise to apply for an order as soon as possible, although there is no time limit as such in the Act. Once the 12 months have expired, the police are entitled to dispose of the goods by sale; though the property may be retained if it can be used for police purposes.[176] If the nature of the property is such that the chief officer of police considers it is not in the public interest for it to be sold or retained (for example, firearms), it can be destroyed or otherwise disposed of.[177] Equivalent powers of sale, retention and destruction apply once items have been retained for six months by the police following the making of an order under Powers of Criminal Courts (Sentencing) Act 2000 s143 (as described at para 17.112).

## Costs

17.118   If the application for an order is started by making a complaint, there is no court fee. The court has a discretion to order legal costs.[178] However, this only empowers the court to make a costs order against the complainant if the claim is dismissed. Thus, magistrates erred in ordering costs against the police when the proceedings they had brought resolved competing claims of ownership between two other parties.[179] If the owner brings a successful claim against the police, the discretion to award costs should be exercised sparingly and only where the police have positively resisted the claim.[180]

---

175   Police (Property) Act 1897 s2(3); Police (Property) Regulations 1997 SI No 1908 reg 4(2). If the goods are perishable or storage involves unreasonable inconvenience or expense, the goods can be sold instead and the proceeds held by the police for a year.

176   Police (Property) Act 1897 s2, as amended by Police (Property) Act 1997 and Police (Property) Regulations 1997 regs 6 and 7.

177   Police (Property) Regulations 1997 reg 8.

178   Magistrates' Courts Act 1980 s64.

179   *R (Chief Constable of Northamptonshire) v Daventry JJ* [2001] EWHC 446 (Admin).

180   *R v Uxbridge JJ ex p Commissioner of Police of the Metropolis* [1981] 3 All ER 129, CA; *Hussain v Singh* (1997) 3 November, DC, unreported; *R v Maidstone Magistrates' Court ex p Knight* (2000) 16 June, unreported.

## Interpleader

17.119 Interpleader proceedings may be used as an alternative to the Police (Property) Act 1897, where money, goods or chattels are claimed by two or more rival claimants.[181] Interpleader is a procedure which allows a holder of property who claims no interest in the same to apply to the court to resolve competing claims of ownership between others.

181   RSC Ord 17; CCR Ord 33; still in force see CPR Schs 1 and 2.

# APPENDICES

# Guidance on levels of damages to be awarded in actions against the police provided by the Court of Appeal in the case of *Thompson v Metropolitan Police Commissioner* [1998] QB 498

While there is no formula which is appropriate for all cases, and the precise form of a summing up is very much a matter within the discretion of the trial judge, it is suggested that in many cases it will be convenient to include in a summing up on the issue of damages additional directions on the following lines. As we mention later in this judgment we think it may often be wise to take the jury's verdict on liability before they receive directions as to quantum.

(1) It should be explained to the jury that if they find in the plaintiff's favour the only remedy which they have power to grant is an award of damages. Save in exceptional situations such damages are only awarded as compensation and are intended to compensate the plaintiff for any injury or damage which he has suffered. They are not intended to punish the defendant.

(2) As the law stands at present compensatory damages are of two types:

    (a) Ordinary damages which we would suggest should be described as basic, and

    (b) aggravated damages.

Aggravated damages can only be awarded where they are claimed by the plaintiff and where there are aggravating features about the defendant's conduct which justify the award of aggravated damages. (We would add that in the rare case where special damages are claimed in respect of some specific pecuniary loss this claim should be explained separately.)

(3) The jury should be told that the basic damages will depend on the circumstances and the degree of harm suffered by the plaintiff. But they should be provided with an appropriate bracket to use as a starting point. The judge will be responsible for determining the 617

bracket, and we envisage that in the ordinary way the judge will have heard submissions on the matter from counsel in the absence of the jury (as suggested by Stuart-Smith LJ in the *Scotland* case). Though this is not what was proposed in the case of a defamation action in *John v MGN Ltd* [1996] 3 WLR 593, submissions by counsel in the absence of the jury are likely to have advantages because of the resemblance between the sum to be awarded in false imprisonment cases and ordinary personal injury cases, and because a greater number of precedents may be cited in this class of case than in a defamation action. We therefore think it would be better for the debate to take place in the absence of the jury.

(4)    In a straightforward case of wrongful arrest and imprisonment or malicious prosecution the jury should be informed of the approximate figure to be taken as the correct starting point for basic damages for the actual loss of liberty or for the wrongful prosecution, and also given an approximate ceiling figure. It should be explained that these are no more than guideline figures based on the judge's experience and on the awards in other cases and the actual figure is one on which they must decide.

(5)    In a straightforward case of wrongful arrest and imprisonment the starting point is likely to be about £500 for the first hour during which the plaintiff has been deprived of his or her liberty. After the first hour an additional sum is to be awarded, but that sum should be on a reducing scale so as to keep the damages proportionate with those payable in personal injury cases and because the plaintiff is entitled to have a higher rate of compensation for the initial shock of being arrested. As a guideline we consider, for example, that a plaintiff who has been wrongly kept in custody for 24 hours should for this alone normally be regarded as entitled to an award of about £3,000. For subsequent days the daily rate will be on a progressively reducing scale. (These figures are lower than those mentioned by the Court of Appeal of Northern Ireland in *Oscar v Chief Constable of the Royal Ulster Constabulary* [1992] NI 290 where a figure of about £600 per hour was thought to be appropriate for the first 12 hours. That case, however only involved unlawful detention for two periods of 30 minutes in respect of which the Court of Appeal of Northern Ireland awarded £300 for the first period and £200 for the second period. On the other hand the approach is substantially more generous than that adopted by this court in the unusual case of *Cumber v Chief Constable of Hampshire Constabulary* (1995) *Times*, 28 January; CA (Civ Div), transcript 95/1995, in which this court awarded £350 global damages where the jury had awarded no compensatory damages and £50 exemplary damages.)

(6)    In the case of malicious prosecution the figure should start at about £2,000 and for prosecution continuing for as long as two years, the case being taken to the Crown Court, an award of about £10,000 could be appropriate. If a malicious prosecution results in a conviction which is only set aside on an appeal this will justify a larger award to

reflect the longer period during which the plaintiff has been in peril and has been caused distress.

(7) The figures which we have identified so far are provided to assist the judge in determining the bracket within which the jury should be invited to place their award. We appreciate, however, that circumstances can vary dramatically from case to case and that these and the subsequent figures which we provide are not intended to be applied in a mechanistic manner.

(8) If the case is one in which aggravated damages are claimed and could be appropriately awarded, the nature of aggravated damages should be explained to the jury. Such damages can be awarded where there are aggravating features about the case which would result in the plaintiff not receiving sufficient compensation for the injury suffered if the award were restricted to a basic award. Aggravating features can include humiliating circumstances at the time of arrest or any conduct of those responsible for the arrest or the prosecution which shows that they had behaved in a high handed, insulting, malicious or oppressive manner either in relation to the arrest or imprisonment or in conducting the prosecution. Aggravating features can also include the way the litigation and trial are conducted. (The aggravating features listed take account of the passages in the speech of Lord Reid in *Broome v Cassell & Co Ltd* [1972] AC 1072 at 1085 and Pearson LJ in *McCarey v Associated Newspapers Ltd* (No 2) [1965] 2 QB 86 at 104.)

(9) The jury should then be told that if they consider the case is one for the award of damages other than basic damages then they should usually make a separate award for each category. (This is contrary to the present practice but in our view will result in greater transparency as to the make up of the award.)

(10) We consider that where it is appropriate to award aggravated damages the figure is unlikely to be less than £1,000. We do not think it is possible to indicate a precise arithmetical relationship between basic damages and aggravated damages because the circumstances will vary from case to case. In the ordinary way, however, we would not expect the aggravated damages to be as much as twice the basic damages except perhaps where, on the particular facts, the basic damages are modest.

(11) It should be strongly emphasised to the jury that the total figure for basic and aggravated damages should not exceed what they consider is fair compensation for the injury which the plaintiff has suffered. It should also be explained that if aggravated damages are awarded such damages, though compensatory are not intended as a punishment, will in fact contain a penal element as far as the defendant is concerned.

(12) Finally the jury should be told in a case where exemplary damages are claimed and the judge considers that there is evidence to support such a claim, that though it is not normally possible to award

damages with the object of punishing the defendant, exceptionally this is possible where there has been conduct, including oppressive or arbitrary behaviour, by police officers which deserves the exceptional remedy of exemplary damages. It should be explained to the jury:

(a)   that if the jury are awarding aggravated damages these damages will have already provided compensation for the injury suffered by the plaintiff as a result of the oppressive and insulting behaviour of the police officer and, inevitably, a measure of punishment from the defendant's point of view;

(b)   that exemplary damages should be awarded if, but only if, they consider that the compensation awarded by way of basic and aggravated damages is in the circumstances an inadequate punishment for the defendants;

(c)   that an award of exemplary damages is in effect a windfall for the plaintiff and, where damages will be payable out of police funds, the sum awarded may not be available to be expended by the police in a way which would benefit the public (this guidance would not be appropriate if the claim were to be met by insurers);

(d)   that the sum awarded by way of exemplary damages should be sufficient to mark the jury's disapproval of the oppressive or arbitrary behaviour but should be no more than is required for this purpose.

(13)   Where exemplary damages are appropriate they are unlikely to be less than £5,000. Otherwise the case is probably not one which justifies an award of exemplary damages at all. In this class of action the conduct must be particularly deserving of condemnation for an award of as much as £25,000 to be justified and the figure of £50,000 should be regarded as the absolute maximum, involving directly officers of at least the rank of superintendent.

(14)   In an appropriate case the jury should also be told that even though the plaintiff succeeds on liability any improper conduct of which they find him guilty can reduce or even eliminate any award of aggravated or exemplary damages if the jury consider that this conduct caused or contributed to the behaviour complained of.

# Letter of Claim

Chief Constable of Wessex Police
Town Hall
Casterbridge

1 April 2005

Re: Our Client: Clym Yeobright
Address: 46 Egdon Heath House, Anglebury Estate, Mistover MV9
NI Number: BG 234578 GB
Date of Birth: 10 May 1985
Custody record no: 634578

## LETTER OF CLAIM

We are instructed by the above named to claim damages in connection with a claim for assault and battery, false imprisonment, and malicious prosecution, arising out of an incident on 9 June 2004 at Egdon Heath House, Anglebury Estate, Mistover MV9

The circumstances of the incident are:–

(a) On 9 June 2004 at about 11pm our client was on a balcony of the sixth floor of Egdon Heath House on the Anglebury Estate, Mistover MV9. He was standing there with his brother and two others when he was grabbed from behind by the right shoulder by an officer of the Defendant's force (thought to be PC Wildeve) who then spun our client around.

(b) As our client turned around the officer struck him on the right side of his jaw. He fell to the ground. Another officer (thought to be PC Nonsuch) then bent his arm behind his back and handcuffed him. The first officer (PC Wildeve) said 'you'll do'.

(c) Our client was lifted by the handcuffs with the officer pressing one arm on our client's right elbow while his left arm and side were pressed against the balcony wall.

(d) The officers then dragged our client by the handcuffs and threw him into the corner of the lift to the building. When our client tried to stand up, the officers kicked his legs so that he fell on his back. The officers continued to kick him in the back a number of times inside the lift as it traveled to the ground floor.

(e) Our client was carried from the lift in a horizontal position, face down, with one officer holding him by the handcuffs and the other by the legs. He was thrown onto the floor of a marked police van number 3771.

(f) While in the van our client tried to get up on the seats but the bigger officer of the two (PC Wildeve) was pushing him down. This officer continuously insulted our client, telling him that he was 'scum'.

(g) The said officers detained our client at Egdon Heath House at about 11pm. He was then taken to Blooms-End police station, arriving at about 11.10pm. He was placed straight in a cell.

(h) He was not informed of the reasons for his arrest at any time during these events, despite repeatedly asking the officers.

(i) After about six hours the same two officers took our client out of the cell. Our client was very frightened and angry. The officers laughed at him and he was charged with being drunk and disorderly. He was released at about 6am on 10 June 2004.

(j) Our client was tried at Casterbridge Magistrates' Court on 7 January 2005 although the Claimant had to attend court on three separate occasions beforehand.

(k) The prosecution was determined on that day in our client's favour when the district judge dismissed the charge against him after hearing oral evidence from our client and police officers.

The reason why we are alleging fault is:

(a) The officers used force used against our client that constituted assault and was unlawful either in every respect or as involving the use of excessive and unreasonable force.

(b) The arrest and detention of our client was not founded upon reasonable suspicion of and/or honest belief in the commission by our client of an arrestable offence, or other lawful authority.

(c) Our client was not informed of the fact and/or the grounds for his arrest, despite it being reasonably practicable to do so at the time of his arrest.

(d) Our client was held in the police custody for an unreasonably long period.

(e) The officers who were involved in our client's arrest fabricated in written statements and/or notebooks an account of events giving rise to the arrest of our client in which they falsely alleged that he was drunk and disorderly, and which led to our client's prosecution. These statements were made by the officers to mask their own wrongdoing in assaulting and wrongly arresting our client.

In light of the above we have advised our client that they have a good case against the Chief Constable of Wessex for damages for the conduct of the officers acting in the purported performance of their police functions under the Chief Constable's direction and control, for assault and battery, false imprisonment and malicious prosecution.

We note that it is for the police to justify both the arrest and the following detention, failing which any claim for false imprisonment will succeed.

Our client suffered acute dizziness at the time of the assault. He had a 4cm laceration to his left cheek and extensive bruising over an area of 6cm x 3cm around the said laceration. Both his upper and lower lips were swollen. There were red marks completely around his neck, bruising on the right shoulder, abrasions over the left superior anterior iliac spine (the bony prominence at the front of the left side of the pelvis), and red marks around both wrists. The injuries took three weeks to resolve fully.

Our client was detained unlawfully for seven hours and had to face the uncertainty of a malicious prosecution for six months before his acquittal.

Our client will also seek aggravated and exemplary damages from you, given the violent, abusive, oppressive and dishonest behaviour of the officers involved in these events.

At this stage of our enquiries we would expect the documents contained in the enclosed schedule to be relevant to this action.

Please treat this letter as a request to maintain and preserve all documentation which may be of relevance to this claim.

Please confirm the identity of the insurers. Please note that the insurers will need to see this letter as soon as possible and it may affect your insurance over if you do not send this to them. A copy of this letter is attached for you to send to your insurers.

We are also instructed to ask you treat this letter as our client's official complaint in this matter pursuant to Pt 2 and Sch 3 of the Police Reform Act 2002. Any communication concerning the complaint should be copied to us.

Finally we expect an acknowledgement of this letter within 21 days by yourselves or your insurers.

Yours faithfully

Eustacia Vye & Co

## SHEDULE OF DOCUMENTS

### General

1. Logs of radio messages to and from the officers.
2. Emergency 999 logs
3. The Incident/Arrest Report notebooks/pocket books of all the officers at the scene
4. Video evidence
5. The original section 9 statements made for the purposes of the criminal trial or otherwise
6. Computer Aided Dispatch print-out
7. Computer Records
8. Plans and maps relating to the criminal investigation
9. Previous convictions/cautions of the proposed claimant
10. Criminal records of the officers concerned
11. Discipline records of the officers concerned
12. Records concerning any upheld complaints against any of the officers concerned

### Detention at police station

13. Custody record

### In relation to assault

14. Any medical records of the proposed claimant at police station
15. Use of Force Reports
16. Photographs of the proposed claimant

### In relation to the prosecution

17. Charge Sheet
18. Prosecution statements
19. Crime/arrest investigation reports
20. Communication with the CPS and CPS summary
21. Transcript of the criminal trial or Clerks notes of evidence

# Particulars of Claim

IN THE BUDMOUTH COUNTY COURT

BETWEEN

CLYM YEOBRIGHT

Claimant

and

CHIEF OFFICER OF WESSEX POLICE

Defendant

## PARTICULARS OF CLAIM

1. The Defendant is and was at all material times the chief officer for the Wessex Police area and the police officers hereinafter referred to were at all material times acting under his direction and control in the purported performance of their police functions within the meaning of the Police Act 1996.

2. On or about 9 June 2004 the Claimant was falsely imprisoned and assaulted by police officers believed to be PC Wildeve and PC Nonsuch.

### PARTICULARS OF ASSAULT AND FALSE IMPRISONMENT

(l) On 9 June 2004 at about 11pm the Claimant was on a balcony of the sixth floor of Egdon Heath House on the Anglebury Estate, Mistover MV9. He was standing there with his brother and two others when he was grabbed from behind by the right shoulder by an officer of the Defendant's force (thought to be PC Wildeve) who then spun the Claimant around.

(m) As the Claimant turned around the officer struck him on the right side of his jaw. He fell to the ground. Another officer (thought to be PC Nonsuch) then bent his arm behind his back and handcuffed him. The first officer (PC Wildeve) said 'you'll do'.

(n) The Claimant was lifted by the handcuffs with the officer pressing one arm on the Claimant's right elbow while his left arm and side were pressed against the balcony wall.

(o) The officers then dragged the Claimant by the handcuffs and threw him into the corner of the lift to the building. When the Claimant tried to stand up, the officers kicked his legs so that he fell on his back. The officers continued to kick him in the back a number of times inside the lift as it traveled to the ground floor.

(p)   The Claimant was carried from the lift in a horizontal position, face down, with one officer holding him by the handcuffs and the other by the legs. He was thrown onto the floor of a marked police van number 3771.

(q)   While in the van the Claimant tried to get up on the seats but the bigger officer (PC Wildeve) of the two was pushing him down. This officer continuously insulted the Claimant, telling him that he was 'scum'.

(r)   The said officers detained the Claimant at Egdon Heath House at about 11pm. He was then taken to Blooms-End police station, arriving at about 11.10pm. He was placed straight in a cell.

(s)   He was not informed of the reasons for his arrest at any time during these events, despite repeatedly asking the officers.

(t)   After about six hours the same two officers took the Claimant out of the cell. The Claimant was very frightened and angry. The officers laughed at him and he was charged with being drunk and disorderly. He was released at about 6am on 10 June 2004.

3.   The force used against the Claimant as described above constituted assault and was unlawful and constituted trespass to the Claimant's person either in every respect or as involving the use of excessive and unreasonable force.

4.   The arrest and detention of the Claimant were unlawful, not being founded upon reasonable suspicion of and/or honest belief in the commission by the Claimant of an arrestable offence, or other lawful authority.

5.   Further or alternatively, the said arrest was unlawful in that the Claimant was not informed of the fact and/or the grounds for his arrest, despite it being reasonably practicable to do so at the time of his arrest.

6.   If , which is denied, the said arrest was lawful, the Claimant was held in the police custody for an unreasonably long period.

7.   As a result the Claimant has suffered pain, personal injury, distress and inconvenience, injury to his feelings, loss of liberty, loss of reputation.

## PARTICULARS

The Claimant was detained for about seven hours after force was used against him by the Defendant's officers. He felt acute distress, humiliation, fear and upset during his arrest and detention.

## PARTICULARS OF INJURY

(a)   The Claimant relies on the report of Dr Angel Clare dated 11 June 2004 annexed hereto

(b)   The Claimant suffered acute dizziness at the time of the assault. He had a 4cm laceration to his left cheek and extensive bruising over an area of 6cm x 3cm around the said laceration. Both his upper and lower lips were swollen. There were red marks completely around his neck, bruising on the right shoulder, abrasion over the left superior anterior iliac spine (the bony prominence at the front of the left side of the pelvis), and red marks around both wrists.

(c) The injuries took three weeks to resolve fully.

8. Further, police officers acting under the direction and control of the Defendant caused the Claimant, without reasonable cause, and maliciously, to be prosecuted for an offence of being drunk and disorderly.

## PARTICULARS OF MALICIOUS PROSECUTION

(a) At a time unknown to the Claimant but prior to his being charged on 9 June 2004, the officers who were involved in his arrest fabricated in written statements and/or notebooks an account of events giving rise to the arrest of the Claimant in which they falsely alleged that they had witnessed the Claimant in the commission of the elements of the offence of being drunk and disorderly.

(b) The said statements were made by the officers to mask their own wrongdoing in assaulting and wrongly arresting the Claimant, to protect themselves from censure for such misconduct and in the knowledge that by reason thereof the Claimant could be wrongly prosecuted for the said offence.

(c) At 6am on 10 June 2004 the said officers maliciously caused the Claimant to be charged with the said offence.

(d) The Claimant was tried at Casterbridge Magistrates' Court on 7 January 2005 although the Claimant had to attend court on three separate occasions beforehand.

(e) The said prosecution was determined on that day in the Claimant's favour when the district judge dismissed the charge against him after hearing oral evidence.

(f) During the course of the trial the said officers repeated on oath the false allegations particularised above.

9. As a result the Claimant has suffered distress and inconvenience, injury to his feelings, loss of reputation, and damage.

## PARTICULARS

The Claimant suffered the distress and anxiety of being charged with an offence which he did not commit and faced a wrongful conviction. He had to attend court on a number of occasions and for a trial in which he was accused of criminal actions.

10. In respect of all the abovementioned matters, the Claimant claims and avers that this is an appropriate case for the award of aggravated damages. The Claimant relies on the facts and matters pleaded above, and the following matters:

(a) the conduct of the Defendant in these proceedings insofar as he fails to apologise to the Claimant for, or seeks to justify the conduct of, his officers.

(b) the conduct of the officers was calculated to and did humiliate the Claimant especially as the assault and arrest took place in a public place

(c) The fact that the police officers insulted the Claimant repeatedly but refused to tell him the reason for his arrest.

11. The Defendant's officers in acting as aforesaid were acting in the purported performance of their police functions. Their actions were arbitrary, oppressive and unconstitutional for which exemplary damages should be awarded. The Claimant relies on the facts and matters above and the additional following matters:

a) This is an appropriate case in which the Court should mark its disapproval or condemnation of the Defendant's officers' actions.

b) The assault on the Claimant was a violent one with numerous blows. The Claimant's life and limb were put at risk by the officers' actions.

c) The assault, false imprisonment and prosecution were, by their very nature, arbitrary, oppressive and unconstitutional and amounted to an arrogant abuse of power, when no offence was being committed by the Claimant.

12. Further, the Claimant claims interest pursuant to Section 69 of the County Courts Act 1984 on the amount found due by the Court at such a rate and for such period as the Court thinks fit.

## AND THE CLAIMANT CLAIMS

(1) Damages in excess of £15,000 but less than £50,000 including aggravated damages and exemplary damages and including damages for personal injury of more than £1,000.

(2) The aforesaid interest pursuant to Section 69 of the County Courts Act 1984.

(3) Costs

DIGGORY VENN

### Statement of truth

I believe that the facts stated in these particulars of claim are true

Signed..................................... (Claimant) Dated..................................

Dated this  1st        day of      October  2005

Eustacia Vye & Co
16 Rainbarrow Road
Mistover

Solicitor for the Claimant  who will accept service
at this address

To the District Judge

And to the Defendant

# Application for summons

The Chief Clerk
The Magistrates' Court
Tendale

1 April 2005

Dear Sir

Ms Mary Tawny
246 Azalea Street, Tendale

We act on behalf of Ms Mary Tawny who wishes to apply under the Police (Property) Act 1897 s1 for the return of two antique silver candlesticks belonging to her and held by the Tendale Constabulary.

The candlesticks were taken from our client's car by PC Lincoln of Tendale Magna police station on 16 June 2004 when she was stopped for an alleged motoring offence. It was alleged at the time that the police were looking for stolen property similar to the property seized but our client has not been charged with any offence in connection with the candlesticks.

We requested the return of the property to our client by letters to the police solicitors dated 1 September and 22 September 2004 but to date the candlesticks have not been returned. We believe the property is still in the possession of PC Lincoln.

We should be grateful if you would treat this letter as an application for the issue and service of a summons against the Chief Constable of the Tendale Constabulary.

Thank you for your help in this matter.

Yours faithfully,

# Useful Websites

## ASSOCIATION OF CHIEF POLICE OFFICERS (ACPO)

**www.acpo.police.uk**
Website with many policy papers adopted by police forces – from firearms to data protection to dog handling.

## COMMISSION FOR RACIAL EQUALITY

**www.cre.gov.uk**
Law, good practice, legal advice and press releases relating to racial equality.

## COURT SERVICE

**www.courtservice.gov.uk**
Contains links to Civil Procedure Rules and practice guides.

## HER MAJESTY'S STATIONERY OFFICE

**www.hmso.gov.uk**
The main provider of documents from Parliament.

## HOME OFFICE

**www.homeoffice.gov.uk**
Contains a large number of policy and research papers about the police and police misconduct.

## INDEPENDENT POLICE COMPLAINTS COMMISSION

**www.ipcc.gov.uk**
Contains guidance, consultation papers, complainants leaflets, research, minutes of the meetings of the Commission, press releases and other useful information.

## INQUEST

**www.inquest.org.uk**

Website for the organisation that assists family members of those who have died in custody and campaigns for reform of inquest law and procedure.

## LEGAL SERVICES COMMISSION

**www.legalservices.gov.uk**

Information, legislation and guidance relating to the legal aid system.

## LIBERTY (NATIONAL COUNCIL FOR CIVIL LIBERTIES)

**www.liberty-human-rights.org.uk**

News, research and information on civil liberties and human rights.

## POLICE FORCES

**www.police.uk**

Provides links to websites for police forces around the country.

# Index